THE PROCESS
OF LEGAL RESEARCH

THE PROCESS OF LEGAL RESEARCH

Sixth Edition

Christina L. Kunz
Professor of Law
William Mitchell College of Law

Deborah A. Schmedemann
Professor of Law
Associate Dean for Skills and Clinics
William Mitchell College of Law

Ann L. Bateson
Director of the Law Library
Associate Dean
Professor of Law
William Mitchell College of Law

Matthew P. Downs
Professor of Law
William Mitchell College of Law

Susan L. Catterall
Leonard, Street, and Deinard, P.A.

ASPEN

PUBLISHERS

1185 Avenue of the Americas, New York, NY 10036
www.aspenpublishers.com

Printed in the United States of America.

ISBN: 0-7355-3666-X

1 2 3 4 5 6 7 8 9 0

Library of Congress Cataloging-in-Publication Data

The process of legal research / Christina L. Kunz ... [et al.].—6th ed.
        p.   cm.
    Includes index.
    ISBN 0-7355-3666-X
    1. Legal research—United States. 2. Information storage and retrieval systems—Law—United States. I. Kunz, Christina L.

KF240.P76 2004
340′.072′073—dc22   2004046356

About Aspen Publishers

Aspen Publishers, headquartered in New York City, is a leading information provider for attorneys, business professionals, and law students. Written by preeminent authorities, our products consist of analytical and practical information covering both U.S. and international topics. We publish in the full range of formats, including updated manuals, books, periodicals, CDs, and online products.

Our proprietary content is complemented by 2,500 legal databases, containing over 11 million documents, available through our Loislaw division. Aspen Publishers also offers a wide range of topical legal and business databases linked to Loislaw's primary material. Our mission is to provide accurate, timely, and authoritative content in easily accessible formats, supported by unmatched customer care.

To order any Aspen Publishers title, go to *www.aspenpublishers.com* or call 1-800-638-8437.

To reinstate your manual update service, call 1-800-638-8437.

For more information on Loislaw products, go to *www.loislaw.com* or call 1-800-364-2512.

For Customer Care issues, e-mail *CustomerCare@aspenpublishers.com*; call 1-800-234-1660; or fax 1-800-901-9075.

Aspen Publishers
A Wolters Kluwer Company

*This book is dedicated to the thousands of students of
William Mitchell College of Law who have worked with and
helped us improve these material during the past twenty-plus years*

and

*to the faculty, administrators, and staff of William Mitchell
College of Law, whose unwavering support for skills
instruction has made this book possible.*

Summary of Contents

CONTENTS

EXHIBITS AND ILLUSTRATIONS

CHAPTER 12   LEGISLATIVE PROCESS MATERIALS

Unit VI   Rules of Procedure and Legal Ethics

Chapter 16   Rules of Procedure

Chapter 17   Rules of Legal Ethics

PREFACE

The first edition of this book was published in 1986, nearly two decades years ago. Since then, legal research has changed little and greatly.

What has changed little is legal authority. Now, as then, the purpose of legal research is to locate pertinent cases, statutes, and rules—the law—governing the client's situation. Now, as then, commentators' discussion of the law is used to lead one to the law and to help one fully understand the law. Now, as then, it is critical for new researchers to learn how the law is made, how different lawmaking bodies interact, how to discern which law is applicable when, how to read the law carefully, and how to integrate the insights of commentators. As with all earlier editions, this book emphasizes these matters. Today, as always, you must master these fundamentals to research competently.

What has changed greatly is the technology of legal research. Legal materials have long been published, of course, in books and microforms (such as microfilm and microfiche). With the development of computers and related technology, legal research has become a multimedia endeavor. The researcher now has a (sometimes bewilderingly) wide range of options for locating a governing statute, for example: books, online subscription services offered by private publishers, Internet websites maintained by the government, and so forth. Indeed, some sources and tools are available only in computer-based media.

Technological change has brought other changes as well. The rate of product development has increased rapidly. Sources published in books tend to change infrequently; computer-based sources are reprogrammed far more easily and, hence, far more often. Furthermore, the corporate structure of legal publishing is in flux, with large, well established companies merging and small, new companies arising.

So, it is an interesting time to be teaching and learning legal research. For us, it has been a challenge to write about a moving target. And we suspect you will find it challenging to adjust your research techniques on a nearly continual basis as publishers change their products.

In writing this book, we chose to take the following approach: As noted above, we have set forth at some length what you need to know about legal authority. Then we have described what we deem the best practices currently employed by lawyers as they research a particular type of legal authority. Some practices have been in use for many years and likely will continue to be best practices. Others are newer and may well evolve as technology and research sources evolve. We have sought to cover the basics as to the various practices; we hope that you will learn and appreciate the analytical processes lawyers employ in legal research. We have not discussed the mechanics and details of the best practices at length; these matters change, and you will be able to learn them easily enough once you master the basics.

A final observation: Excellent researchers are curious, persistent, flexible people. We hope you approach this book with curiosity, persistence, and flexibility. If you do, we believe you will learn a great deal about an important and interesting process.

A Note to Professors: If you have used previous editions of this book, you will notice a number of changes in this edition:

- ☐ far more complete discussion of the analytical steps involved in legal research, from understanding the client's situation to deciding when to quit;
- ☐ more comprehensive discussion of public websites throughout;
- ☐ overall updating, e.g., Search Advisor and KeySearch;
- ☐ deletion of some sources that are now little used, e.g., Federal Rules Service;
- ☐ expanded coverage of "unpublished" cases;
- ☐ substantially rewritten case citators chapter, deciphering Shepard's and KeyCite print-outs, covering a wide range of ways that a case becomes bad law, and not including Shepard's in paper;
- ☐ expanded coverage of LexisNexis Congressional and reduced coverage of CIS paper sources;
- ☐ redesign of the state cases and statutes practice sets, so the issue changes when students move from paper to electronic sources;
- ☐ coverage of *ALWD* as well as *Bluebook* citation rules; and
- ☐ more open format, e.g., more bulleted lists.

We hope these changes work well for you and your students.

Last but not least, we welcome a new author—Susan Catterall, a librarian at Leonard, Street, and Deinard, a major Twin Cities law firm. She has brought an invaluable perspective to this project and spent many hours on the practice sets.

Deborah Schmedemann
Ann Bateson
Matthew Downs
Susan Catterall

St. Paul, Minnesota
May 2004

ACKNOWLEDGMENTS

First and foremost, the authors of this edition—Deborah Schmedemann, Ann Bateson, Matt Downs, and Susan Catterall—would like to recognize the enduring contributions of authors who worked on earlier editions. Professor Christina Kunz began this book over twenty years ago, wrote major portions of the text, devised problem sets, collected illustrations, and managed its production. This edition, like its predecessors, is Chris' brainchild. Professor Peter Erlinder and Professor Clifford Greene, now in practice in Minneapolis, were our co-authors on portions of earlier editions. Former Professor Kevin Millard, now in practice in Colorado, wrote the final draft of a chapter for the first edition of this book.

Our colleague, Professor Ken Kirwin, has coordinated our legal research course ably, energetically, and enthusiastically for many years. He has been an uncommonly faithful and perceptive reader; we thank him for his many insights and suggestions.

We also would like to recognize the work of our research assistants: Stephen Brunn, Molly Gage, Jennifer Henderson, Vickie Loher, Andrew Smith, and Richard Soderberg. They worked hard, long, and diligently on various parts of this book, including Chapter 18 and the practice sets. We would also like to salute the work of our many research assistants on the previous editions. The perspectives and contributions of our research assistants have been invaluable in making this book more useful to our readers.

More so than other publications by law school faculty, this book draws on the talents and hard work of the College's professional librarians: Mary Ann Archer, Elvira Embser-Herbert, Sean Felhofer, Deborah Hackerson, Jane Hopeman, Sonya Huesman, Bill Jack, Ardis Jacobson, Anne Poulter, Jan Stone, and Don Zhou. They tracked down the sources, answered our questions, and offered top-notch suggestions. Jan Stone prepared the index as well; we appreciate her painstaking work.

We are grateful for the expertise of Cal Bonde and Linda Thorstad, who made sense of contorted and detailed revisions and constructed sophisticated exhibits from our mere sketches. Darlene Finch, Linn Averill, and Geneva Turner provided valuable administrative support on this edition.

The College's faculty and administration have shown considerable interest and support for the project. In particular, we want to thank current Dean Harry Haynsworth for his generous support and our colleagues, such as Eric Janus, Neil Hamilton, and Russ Pannier, for their substantive expertise.

This book has been blessed with talented professionals on the publisher's end of the phone. Curt Berkowitz, our editor on this edition, presided over the complex process of assembling this complicated book with great patience and a sharp eye for detail. We want to recognize the work of Tina Cameron in coordinating its manufacture and production. We are grateful for the efforts of the following people who nurtured this book and its predecessors for the past twenty-plus years: Nick Niemeyer and Richard Heuser (formerly at Little, Brown and Company), Carol McGeehan, Elizabeth Kenny, and Melody Davies.

On a larger scale, we would like to thank the community of legal writing and research teachers who have encouraged us and enriched us over the years with their ideas about the pedagogy of legal skills education. The same measure of gratitude and recognition goes to our students, who remain our best source of insights about the process of learning legal research.

We especially thank our spouses, companions, families, and friends for their support and their interest in this project. Every three or four years, they, like us, have been called upon to endure long hours and high stress. We thank them from the bottom of our hearts.

We would also like to acknowledge those publishers who permitted us to reprint copyrighted material in this book:

CHAPTER 1: THE LAY OF THE LAND: THE IMPORTANCE OF LEGAL RESEARCH, LEGAL AUTHORITIES, AND RESEARCH MEDIA

Illustration 1-1: Judicial Case, from Loislaw (electronic source). Reprinted with permission of Aspen Publishers, Inc. & Conway Greene Co.

Illustration 1-2: State Statute, from *New Mexico Statutes Annotated* (paper source). Chapter 50 Employment Law, Article 11, pp. 62-63, 2000 replacement pamphlet. Reprinted with the permission of Matthew Bender & Company, Inc., a member of the LexisNexis Group, and New Mexico Compilation Commission.

Illustration 1-3: Encyclopedia Text, from *American Jurisprudence 2d* (paper source). Vol. 82, Wrongful Discharge, pp. 618-19, 2003. © Thomson West; reprinted with permission.

Illustration 1-4: Periodical Article, from *Georgetown Law Journal* through LexisNexis (electronic source). Vol. 86, issue 3, pp. 783-86, 1998. Reprinted with permission of LexisNexis; reprinted with permission of the publisher, Georgetown Law Journal © 1998.

CHAPTER 2: FROM CURIOSITY TO CLOSURE: EIGHT COGNITIVE TASKS

Illustration 2-3: Overall Table of Contents, from *American Jurisprudence 2d* (paper source). General Index T-Z vol., p. xv, 2003 edition. © Thomson West; reprinted with permission.

Illustration 2-4: Detailed Table of Contents, from *American Jurisprudence 2d* (paper source). Vol. 82, Wrongful Discharge, p. 585, 2003. © Thomson West; reprinted with permission.

Illustration 2-5: Index, from *American Jurisprudence 2d* (paper source). General Index T-Z vol., p. 310, 2004 edition. © Thomson West; reprinted with permission.

Illustration 2-6: Table of Authorities, from *American Jurisprudence 2d* (paper source). General Index, p. 423, 2003 edition. © Thomson West; reprinted with permission.

Illustration 2-7: Citation List, from Search in LexisNexis Periodicals Database (electronic source). Reprinted with the permission of LexisNexis.

CHAPTER 3: ENCYCLOPEDIAS

Illustration 3-1: Encyclopedia Main Volume Text, from *Corpus Juris Secundum* (paper source). Vol. 30, Employer-Employee Relationship, pp. 47-48, 1992. © Thomson West; reprinted with permission.

Illustration 3-2: Encyclopedia Pocket Part, from *Corpus Juris Secundum* (paper source). Vol. 30, Employer-Employee Relationship, p. 2, 2003 pocket part. © Thomson West; reprinted with permission.

CHAPTER 4: TREATISES

Illustration 4-1: Treatise, from *Employment Discrimination* (paper source). Vol. 9, p. 155-37, 2d ed., March 2003. Reprinted with the permission of Matthew Bender & Company, Inc., a member of the LexisNexis Group.

Illustration 4-2: Catalog Entry, from Innovative Interfaces Systems (electronic source). Reprinted with permission of Innovative Interfaces Inc.

CHAPTER 5: LEGAL PERIODICALS

Illustration 5-1: Law Review Article, from *Georgetown Law Journal* (paper source). Vol. 86, issue 3, pp. 789-90, 1998. Reprinted with permission of the publisher, Georgetown Law Journal © 1998.

Illustration 5-2: Expanded Entry for Periodical Article, from *LegalTrac* (electronic source). By Gale Group. Reprinted by permission of the Gale Group.

Illustration 5-3: Shepard's Report for Periodical Article, from LexisNexis (electronic source). Reprinted with the permission of LexisNexis.

CHAPTER 6: A.L.R. ANNOTATIONS

Illustration 6-1: A.L.R. Annotation Case Descriptions (paper source). American Law Reports Annotations 4th, vol. 33, p. 135, 1984. © Thomson West; reprinted with permission.

Illustration 6-2: A.L.R. Annotation Opening Material (paper source). American Law Reports Annotations 4th, vol. 33, pp. 120-23, 1984. © Thomson West; reprinted with permission.

Illustration 6-3: A.L.R. Annotation Pocket Part (paper source). American Law Reports Annotations 4th, vol. 33, p. 32, 2003 pocket part. © Thomson West; reprinted with permission.

CHAPTER 7: RESTATEMENTS

Illustration 7-1: Restatement Rule, Comments, Illustrations, and Reporter's Note, from Restatement (Second) of Contracts (paper source). Main vol. pp. 8-10, 12, 1981. Copyright 1981 by the American Law Institute. Reprinted with permission. All rights reserved.

Illustration 7-2: Restatement Case Summaries, from Restatement of Contracts Appendix (paper source). Appendix vol. 10, p. 70, 1997. Copyright 1997 by the American Law Institute. Reprinted with permission. All rights reserved.

Illustration 7-3: Restatement Recent Case Citations, from *Interim Case Citations to the Restatements of the Law* (paper source). P. 600, July 2002 through August 2003. Copyright 2003 by the American Law Institute. Reprinted with permission. All rights reserved.

CHAPTER 9: REPORTERS, DIGESTS, AND THEIR ALTERNATIVES

Exhibit 9.1: Federal Circuit Map. 2003/Winter Judicial Staff Directory, p. 909, 21st ed. Reprinted with permission of CQ Press, a Division of Congressional Quarterly, Inc.

Illustration 9-1: Judicial Case, from *Pacific Reporter 2d* (paper source). Vol. 48, pp. 507-10, 1988. © Thomson West; reprinted with permission.

Illustration 9-2: Digest Entries, from *New Mexico Digest* (paper source). Vol. 4B, p. 45, 1999. © Thomson West; reprinted with permission.

Illustration 9-3: Topic List, from *New Mexico Digest* (paper source). Vol. 4B, p. xiv, 1999. © Thomson West; reprinted with permission.

Illustration 9-4: Descriptive Word Index, from *New Mexico Digest* (paper source). P. 180, 2002. © Thomson West; reprinted with permission.

Illustration 9-5: Outline of Digest Topic, from *New Mexico Digest* (paper source). Vol. 4B, p. 16, 1999. © Thomson West; reprinted with permission.

Illustration 9-6: Plaintiff Case Name Table, from *New Mexico Digest* (paper source). Vol. 6, p. 316, 2000. © Thomson West; reprinted with permission.

Illustration 9-7: Natural-Language Citation List, from Search in Westlaw Cases Database (electronic source). © Thomson West; reprinted with permission.

Illustration 9-8: Terms-and-Connectors Citation List, from Search in Westlaw Cases Database (electronic source). © Thomson West; reprinted with permission.

Illustration 9-10: Judicial Case, from LexisNexis Cases Database (electronic source). Copyright 1988 LexisNexis, a division of Reed Elsevier, Inc. All rights reserved. No copyright is claimed as to any part of the original work prepared by a government officer or employee as part of that person's official duties. Reprinted with the permission of LexisNexis.

Illustration 9-11: Natural-Language Citation List, from Search in LexisNexis Cases Database (electronic version). Reprinted with the permission of LexisNexis.

Illustration 9-13: Boolean Citation List, from Search in Tenth Circuit Website (electronic source). Screen Shots of Tenth Circuit Search courtesy of Washburn University School of Law.

Illustration 9-14: Judicial Case, from Tenth Circuit Website (electronic source). Screen Shots of Tenth Circuit Results courtesy of Washburn University School of Law.

CHAPTER 10: CASE CITATORS

Illustration 10-1: Shepard's Report for a Case, from LexisNexis (electronic source). Reprinted with the permission of LexisNexis.

Illustration 10-2: KeyCite Report for a Case, from Westlaw (electronic source). © Thomson West; reprinted with permission.

Chapter 10 Practice Set 1st Illustration: First Page of Case in West Reporter, from *Southern Reporter 2d* (paper source). © Thomson West; reprinted with permission.

CHAPTER 11: CODES AND SESSION LAWS

Illustration 11-1: State Constitution, from *New Mexico Statutes Annotated* (paper source). Article 11, sec. 4, p. 3, 1992 replacement pamphlet. Reprinted with the permission of Matthew Bender & Company, Inc., a member of the LexisNexis Group, and New Mexico Compilation Commission.

Illustration 11-2: State Statute, from New Mexico/LexisNexis Website (electronic source). Sections 50-11-1 to 50-11-6, 2003. Reprinted with the permission of

Matthew Bender & Company, Inc., a member of the LexisNexis Group, and New Mexico Compilation Commission.

Illustration 11-4: Provision of Federal Statute and Annotation, from *United States Code Annotated* (paper source). Title 42, §§ 10401 to 12700 vol., pp. 725-27, 1995. © Thomson West; reprinted with permission.

Illustration 11-5: Statutory Pocket Part from *United States Code Annotated* (paper source). Title 42, §§ 10401 to 12700 vol., p. 357, 2003 pocket part. © Thomson West; reprinted with permission.

Illustration 11-6: Table of Amendments and Repeals, from *United States Code Annotated* (paper source). Table 3-Amendments and Repeals, Aug. 2003 [p. 45]. © Thomson West; reprinted with permission.

CHAPTER 12: LEGISLATIVE PROCESS MATERIALS

Exhibit 12.1: How a Bill Becomes Law (LexisNexis Congressional). Reprinted with the permission of LexisNexis.

Illustration 12-3: Hearing Testimony, from *CIS/Microfiche Library* (microfiche source). CIS/Microfiche Library CIS 90: H341-4, 1990. Reprinted with the permission of LexisNexis.

Illustration 12-4: Committee Report, from *United States Code Congressional and Administrative News* (paper source). Vol. 4, pp. 267-68, 1990. © Thomson West; reprinted with permission.

Illustration 12-5: Floor Debate, from *Congressional Record* through LexisNexis Congressional (electronic source). 136 Congressional Record, S9684-S9685, 1990. Reprinted with the permission of LexisNexis.

Illustration 12-6: Presidential Signing Statement, from *United States Code Congressional and Administrative News* (paper source). Vol. 4, p. 601, 1990. © Thomson West; reprinted with permission.

Illustration 12-7: Legislative History References in Statutory Code, from *United States Code Annotated* (paper source). Title 42 §§ 10401-12700 vol., p. 630, 1995. © Thomson West; reprinted with permission.

Illustration 12-8: Bibliography of Compiled Legislative Histories, from *Sources of Compiled Legislative Histories* (paper source). P. B210, 1993 revision. Reprinted with permission of American Association of Law Libraries.

Illustration 12-9: Legislative History Statement, from LexisNexis Congressional (electronic source). 101 CIS Legis. Hist. PL 336. Reprinted with the permission of LexisNexis.

Illustration 12-10: Abstract of Hearing Record, from LexisNexis Congressional (electronic source). 90-H341-4, 1989. Reprinted with the permission of LexisNexis.

Illustration 12-12: Bill Finder, from New Mexico Legislature Website (electronic source). Bill Search Results for SB28, 2003 Regular Session. Permission granted by the New Mexico Legislative Council Service.

Illustration 12-13: Bill Tracking Report, from Westlaw State Net Database (electronic source). Bill Tracking Report for Senate Bill 28, 46th Legislature, First Regular Session, 2003. © State Net and Thomson West; reprinted with permission of State Net and Thomson West.

CHAPTER 13: REGULATIONS

Illustration 13-2: Enabling Statute and Annotation, from *United States Code Service* (paper source). Title 29 Labor §§ 161-205 vol., pp. 30, 31, 68, 1993. Reprinted with the permission of LexisNexis.

Illustration 13-10: KeyCite Report for Agency Regulation, from Westlaw (electronic source). © Thomson West; reprinted with permission.

CHAPTER 14: AGENCY DECISIONS

Illustration 14-2: Agency Decision Descriptions in Annotated Code, from *United States Code Service* (paper source). Title 29 Labor §§ 1-157 vol., p. 580, 1994. Reprinted with the permission of LexisNexis.

Illustration 14-6: Shepard's Report for Agency Decision, from LexisNexis (electronic source). Reprinted with the permission of LexisNexis.

CHAPTER 15: MINI-LIBRARIES

Illustration 15-1: Looseleaf Service Updating Material, from BNA's *Labor Relations Reporter* (paper source). Reproduced with permission from Labor Relations Reporter-Fair Employment Practices Manual, No. 982 (Nov. 24, 2003). Copyright 2003 by The Bureau of National Affairs, Inc. (800-372-1003) http://www.bna.com.

Illustration 15-2: Looseleaf Service General Index, from BNA's *Labor Relations Reporter* (paper source). Reproduced with permission from Labor Relations Reporter-Master Index, p. A 877 (Dec. 2002). Copyright 2002 by The Bureau of National Affairs, Inc. (800-372-1003) http://www.bna.com.

Illustration 15-3: Looseleaf Service Commentary, from BNA's *Labor Relations Reporter* (paper source). Reproduced with permission from Labor Relations Reporter-Labor Relations Expediter, pp. LRX 510:207-510:208 (Oct. 1988). Copyright 1988 by The Bureau of National Affairs, Inc. (800-372-1003) http://www.bna.com.

Illustration 15-4: Looseleaf Service Outline of Case Digest, from BNA's *Labor Relations Reporter* (paper source). Reproduced with permission from Labor Relations Reporter-Master Index, Outline of Classifications, p. C-I 112 (Feb. 14, 2002). Copyright 2002 by The Bureau of National Affairs, Inc. (800-372-1003) http://www.bna.com.

Illustration 15-5: Looseleaf Service Case Digest, from BNA's *Labor Relations Reporter* (paper source). Reproduced with permission from Labor Relations Reporter-Cumulative Digest & Index, 1991-1995, p. 1169. Copyright 1996 by The Bureau of National Affairs, Inc. (800-372-1003) http://www.bna.com.

Illustration 15-6: Electronic Service Overview, from BNA's Labor & Employment Law Library (electronic source). Reproduced with permission from BNA's Labor & Employment Law Library, Decisions of the NLRB, Content Overview, http://laborandemploymentlaw.bna.com. Copyright 2004 by The Bureau of National Affairs, Inc. (800-372-1003) http://www.bna.com.

CHAPTER 16: RULES OF PROCEDURE

Illustration 16-1: Federal Rule of Civil Procedure, from *Federal Civil Judicial Procedure and Rules* Deskbook (paper source). Pp. 88, 89, 91, 2003 Edition. © Thomson West; reprinted with permission.

Illustration 16-3: State Rule of Civil Procedure, from *New Mexico Rules Annotated* (paper source). Vol. 1, pp. 45-46, 2003 edition. Reprinted with the permission of Matthew Bender & Company, Inc., a member of the LexisNexis Group, and New Mexico Compilation Commission.

Illustration 16-4: Deskbook Table of Contents, from *Federal Civil Judicial Procedure and Rules* Deskbook (paper source). P. VIII, 2003 Edition. © Thomson West; reprinted with permission.

Illustration 16-5: Form from Deskbook, from *Federal Civil Judicial Procedure and Rules* Deskbook (paper source). Form 2, p. 280, 2003 Edition. © Thomson West; reprinted with permission.

CHAPTER 17: RULES OF PROFESSIONAL RESPONSIBILITY

Illustration 17-1: State Rule of Professional Conduct and Annotation, from *New Mexico Rules Annotated* (paper source). Vol. 2, pp. 551-53, 2003 edition. Reprinted with the permission of Matthew Bender & Company, Inc., a member of the LexisNexis Group, and New Mexico Compilation Commission.

Illustration 17-2: Treatise Discussion, from *ABA/BNA Lawyers' Manual of Professional Conduct* (paper source). Pp. 31:309-31:310, 2002. Reproduced with permission from ABA/BNA's Lawyer's Manual on Professional Conduct, pp. 31:309-31:310 (June 19, 2003). Copyright 2002 by the American Bar Association/The Bureau of National Affairs, Inc. (800-372-1033) http://www.bna.com.

Illustration 17-3: Advisory Opinion from State Bar Association Committee, from Westlaw Ethics Opinions Database (electronic source). Informal Opinion Number 94-172, p. 1, November 9, 1994. Permission to reprinted granted by Pennsylvania Bar Association Committee on Legal Ethics and Professional Responsibility. © Thomson West; reprinted with permission.

Illustration 17-4: Synopses of Ethics Opinions, from *ABA/BNA Lawyers' Manual of Professional Conduct* (paper source). Ethics Opinions, p. 1101:6001, 2001. Reproduced with permission from ABA/BNA's Lawyer's Manual on Professional Conduct, Ethics Opinions, p. 1001:6001 (May 23, 2001). Copyright 2001 by the American Bar Association/The Bureau of National Affairs, Inc. (800-372-1033) http://www.bna.com.

Illustration 17-5: Ethics Opinions Summaries, from New Mexico State Bar Website (electronic source). Ethics Advisory Opinions originally published by the State Bar of New Mexico. Reprinted with permission.

Illustration 17-6: ABA Model Rule of Professional Conduct and Comments, from *ABA Compendium of Professional Responsibility Rules and Standards* (paper source). Pp. 28-30, 2004. © 2004 by the American Bar Association. All rights reserved. Reprinted by permission of the American Bar Association. Copies of ABA *Model Rules of Professional Conduct, 2004* are available from Service Center, American Bar Association, 750 North Lake Shore Drive, Chicago, IL 60611-4497, 1-800-285-2221.

THE PROCESS
OF LEGAL RESEARCH

OVERVIEW

UNIT I

THE LAY OF THE LAND: THE IMPORTANCE OF LEGAL RESEARCH, LEGAL AUTHORITIES, AND RESEARCH MEDIA

A. THE CANOGA CASE

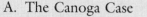

Imagine yourself a lawyer or legal assistant* in a small firm in Taos, New Mexico. Consider the following fictional client problem:

> Your client, Emilia Canoga, began her career as a flutist for a small symphony orchestra in Taos, New Mexico, when she graduated from the Juilliard School five years ago. She has enjoyed her job and performed well. However, she has disagreed from time to time with the orchestra's general manager, especially over personnel issues. One such disagreement led to her termination on January 7, 2003.
>
> Throughout the preceding year, the general manager had been pressuring all smoking members of the orchestra to quit smoking. He argued that smoking is a health risk and that smoking by employees increases the orchestra's health care costs substantially. More particularly, he argued that smoking impairs the wind capacity, and hence performance, of brass and woodwind players. In September 2002, he banned smoking at work. In early December, he issued a memo asking brass and woodwind players to sign either a statement indicating that

---

*This text has several primary audiences: students in law schools, lawyers, students in legal assistant programs, and legal assistants. For ease of discussion, we generally refer to lawyers or law students; we trust that readers who plan to be or are legal assistants will read "legal assistant" where appropriate.

they did not smoke off-duty or a pledge to embark on a no-smoking program.

This memo was met with varying reactions and provoked significant discussion among the orchestra's members. In particular, Ms. Canoga, a smoker who had tried to quit several times, was perturbed by the manager's early efforts and incensed by the December memo. She returned it with a signed note indicating that she intended to sign neither the statement nor the pledge.

The general manager called Ms. Canoga to his office shortly after receiving the note. A heated discussion ensued. Ms. Canoga accused the general manager of overstepping his bounds as an employer and intruding into her personal life. He told her she was fired for insubordination. Ms. Canoga angrily left his office.

Two days later, Ms. Canoga received her paycheck with a note stating that her services were no longer needed by the orchestra. Ms. Canoga sought advice from a senior colleague about how to get her job back. He suggested that she exercise her right to plead her case before the board of directors, as stated in the orchestra's employee handbook. Ms. Canoga received a copy of the handbook when she was hired, and the letter offering her the job refers to it. The handbook reads:

> It is the Orchestra's intent to resolve all employment disagreements amicably. If at any time during your employment or thereafter, you are unable to resolve a disagreement by discussing the issue with management, you may bring the matter to the board. The board will make every effort to listen to both sides and facilitate a just solution.

Ms. Canoga wrote a letter to the board president requesting board consideration of her termination according to the handbook. About a week later, she received a letter stating that the board was aware of her situation, believed management had handled it appropriately, did not intend to revisit the topic, appreciated her contributions to the orchestra, and wished her well in her future endeavors.

Hoping to get her job back or at least some type of compensation and a good reference, Ms. Canoga has sought your assistance.

In asking a lawyer for assistance, Ms. Canoga is seeking not just sympathy, but a resolution of her problem according to the law and within the legal system. The lawyer's role in bringing about that resolution is described well in Rule 1.1 of the Model Rules of Professional Conduct, a widely adopted ethics code for lawyers developed by the American Bar Association: "A lawyer shall provide competent representation to a client. Competent representation requires the legal knowledge, skill, thoroughness and preparation reasonably necessary for the representation."

In Ms. Canoga's case, as in any client representation, a lawyer would employ various skills to solve the problem: listening to Ms. Canoga to determine the facts of her situation and her interests; investigating the facts through other sources; researching the law; analyzing her situation in light of applicable legal rules; identifying and assessing various means of obtaining a resolution, such as negotiating with the orchestra's lawyer, mediating the case, working through a government agency, or pursuing litigation in court; advocating for Ms. Canoga in those processes, in writing and orally; and, at all steps along the way, helping Ms. Canoga determine which actions are to be taken on her behalf.

B.   THE IMPORTANCE OF LEGAL RESEARCH

This text teaches you how lawyers acquire the knowledge of the law necessary for competent client representation—through legal research. As Ms. Canoga's advocate, you could not assess the strengths and weaknesses of her case against the orchestra if you did not know the pertinent law, nor could you negotiate effectively with the orchestra's lawyer or argue her case convincingly before a tribunal without a firm understanding of the law. Similarly, if the orchestra were your client and sought your advice before adopting its no-smoking policy, you could be of service only if you knew the legal constraints on employers in such situations. If you served as an advocate for an employer association before a legislature or administrative agency contemplating new laws on smoking by employees, you would need to be well informed about the current state of the law.

Furthermore, legal research is central to the ethical obligation that accompanies client representation: service to the legal system.[1] As Ms. Canoga's advocate, your efforts would help to ensure the proper functioning of the legal system as a peaceful mode of resolving disputes and contribute to the rational development of the law, should the dispute be adjudicated. As the lawyer advising the orchestra, you would seek to secure the orchestra's compliance with the law. In either setting, you could not fulfill these roles without a firm understanding of the pertinent law.

Thus, it is fitting and not surprising that incompetent legal research can have serious consequences for both the lawyer and the client. In *Smith v. Lewis,*[2] a legal malpractice case, the court approved an award of $100,000 to the client and against a lawyer who had failed to apply principles of law commonly known to well-informed attorneys and to discover principles readily accessible through standard research techniques. Incompetent research may lead to an award of attorney fees to the opposing party;[3] sanctions[4]

---

1. The Preamble to the Model Rules states: "A lawyer, as a member of the legal profession, is a representative of clients, an officer of the legal system and a public citizen having special responsibility for the quality of justice."
2. 530 P.2d 589 (Cal. 1975), *overruled on other grounds, In re Marriage of Brown,* 544 P.2d 561 (Cal. 1976).
3. *See, e.g., Lieber v. ITT Hartford Ins. Center, Inc.,* 15 P.3d 1030 (Utah 2000).
4. *See, e.g., Rodgers v. Lincoln Towing Serv., Inc.,* 771 F.2d 194 (7th Cir. 1985).

against or a stern rebuke[5] of the lawyer; or professional discipline against the lawyer, such as suspension[6] or disbarment. Furthermore, no attorney can afford to tarnish his or her professional reputation by becoming known for poor research.

Legal research is not, of course, the only skill you will learn as a law student and use as a lawyer. It is, however, primarily in law school that lawyers acquire their legal research skills.[7]

As you will soon see, legal research materials are voluminous, complex, and diffuse. Thus, good legal research is neither fast nor easy. It takes careful planning and persistence in execution, an appreciation of the big picture and an eye for detail, a clear focus and openness to inspiration. Regardless of the topic or situation, good legal research has the following attributes:

- ☐ *correct:* leading to the law that governs your client's situation and applied or will apply as of the time of that situation;
- ☐ *comprehensive:* addressing the various issues raised by the client's situation and incorporating an appropriate range of pertinent authorities;
- ☐ *credible:* featuring authority that carries weight because of its nature and quality;
- ☐ *cost-effective:* yielding results that justify the efforts devoted to research, in light of the client's situation and available research options.

These criteria are further developed throughout this text.

As you conduct legal research, you will encounter a wide range of legal materials. Materials used in legal research are not all created equal; rather, the law is a strongly hierarchical field, as discussed in Part C of this chapter. Part D provides an overview of the media in which these materials are published, mainly paper sources and databases available through the Internet.

C.   LEGAL AUTHORITIES

Legal research materials are divided into three categories: primary authority, secondary authority, and finding tools. See Exhibit 1.1. Please note: This text uses the term "authority" to refer to the content of research materials, while "source" refers to the paper or electronic publications in which they are located.

---

5. *See, e.g., Massey v. Prince George's County,* 918 F. Supp. 905 (D. Md. 1996).

6. *See, e.g., Attorney Grievance Comm'n v. Zdravkovich,* 762 A.2d 950 (Md. Ct. App. 2000) (suspension for, inter alia, filing improper petition without consulting statute).

7. In a wide-ranging survey of practicing lawyers, over eighty percent indicated that the general law school curriculum was one of the three most important sources for developing library and computer legal research skills. (This was also so for legal analysis and reasoning.) *See* Bryant G. Garth & Joanne Martin, *Law Schools and the Construction of Competence* Table 8 (1992).

EXHIBIT 1.1	Categories of Legal Research Materials

Primary Authority
   judicial cases
   enacted legislation
   administrative decisions and
     regulations
   rules of procedure and ethics

Secondary Authority (major forms)
   encyclopedias
   treatises
   periodicals
   A.L.R. Annotations
   Restatements

Finding Tools
   library catalogs
   Internet search engines and directories
   periodical indexes
   case digests

---

1. Primary Authority

Primary authority constitutes the law. It is issued by a branch of the government acting in its lawmaking capacity. In basic terms, United States law emanates from three types of government bodies: the judiciary, the legislature, and administrative agencies.

First, the federal and state judiciaries decide cases based on specific disputes that have arisen between two litigants (whether individuals or entities). In doing so, a court not only resolves the dispute for the litigants but also creates precedent. The result, rules, and reasoning in a decided case generally are to be followed in the resolution of future similar disputes within the court's jurisdiction. See Illustration 1-1 (at pages 9–12), a case with significant implications for Ms. Canoga's situation.

Second, legislative bodies at the federal and state levels create constitutions and statutes; legislative bodies at the local level create charters and ordinances. Constitutions and charters create the government and define the rights of citizens vis-à-vis the government. Statutes and ordinances regulate a wide range of behavior by individuals, private entities, and the government. Enacted law typically is written in broad, general terms. It is interpreted according to the legislature's intent; thus the materials created during the legislative process are of some importance. See Illustration 1-2 (at pages 13–14), a statute on employee privacy pertaining to Ms. Canoga's situation.

Third, administrative agencies generate law through two chief mechanisms. Agencies issue decisions, which resemble judicial cases in that they simultaneously resolve specific disputes and operate as precedent for future disputes. Agencies also promulgate regulations, which resemble statutes in that they address a range of behavior and are stated in general terms.

A client's situation may be governed by some combination of judicial, legislative, and administrative agency law. For example, the legislature passes a statute that the courts interpret and apply in specific disputes. In a more complicated example, the legislature creates an agency by statute, that agency promulgates a regulation and then applies it in a series of agency decisions, and the courts review the agency's actions in a series of judicial opinions.

In addition, all three branches create rules governing the functioning of the legal system. Rules governing the operation of a court system are created by the legislature, by the courts, or jointly. The procedural rules promulgated by an agency govern litigation before the agency.

For any particular client's situation, some primary authority is weightier than other primary authority. The weightier primary authority is called "mandatory" or "binding" authority; it emanates from the legislature, courts, or agency with jurisdiction over, or the power to regulate, the client's situation. The less weighty primary authority is called "persuasive" authority; it emanates from a lawmaker without jurisdiction over the client's situation.

For example, as you will see, the Canoga situation is governed by the following forms of primary authority: statutes, judicial cases, regulations, and agency decisions at the federal level; New Mexico cases and a New Mexico statute; and rules governing litigation within the federal or New Mexico state courts (depending on where a suit may be brought). All of these authorities are mandatory because they emanate from the federal or New Mexico governments, which have jurisdiction over the Canoga situation.

2.   Secondary Authority

Secondary authority is defined by what it is not: It is not primary authority. Rather, it is created by lawyers, scholars, nongovernmental bodies, or government officials not acting in a lawmaking capacity. Because most secondary authority comments on the law, it also is called "commentary." All secondary authority describes what the law says, much also explains how the law came to be, and some analyzes and critiques the law. Some secondary authority also states the author's view of what the law should be; on occasion, secondary authority does indeed influence lawmakers.

You will find that some secondary authorities resemble sources you have seen before in other fields, such as encyclopedias, treatises, and periodical articles. Illustration 1-3 (at pages 15–16) is an excerpt from *American Jurisprudence 2d,* a legal encyclopedia; Illustration 1-4 (at pages 17–18) is from a legal periodical article. Other secondary authorities are unique to the law, such as *American Law Reports Annotations* and the Restatements. As you will see, every secondary authority has a particular place in legal research.

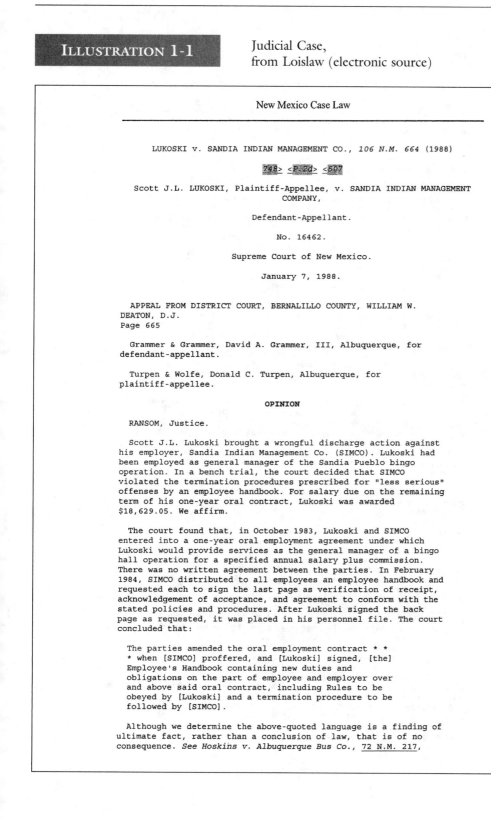

ILLUSTRATION 1-1

Judicial Case,
from Loislaw (electronic source)

New Mexico Case Law

LUKOSKI v. SANDIA INDIAN MANAGEMENT CO., *106 N.M. 664* (1988)

748> <P.2d> <507

Scott J.L. LUKOSKI, Plaintiff-Appellee, v. SANDIA INDIAN MANAGEMENT
COMPANY,

Defendant-Appellant.

No. 16462.

Supreme Court of New Mexico.

January 7, 1988.

APPEAL FROM DISTRICT COURT, BERNALILLO COUNTY, WILLIAM W.
DEATON, D.J.
Page 665

Grammer & Grammer, David A. Grammer, III, Albuquerque, for
defendant-appellant.

Turpen & Wolfe, Donald C. Turpen, Albuquerque, for
plaintiff-appellee.

OPINION

RANSOM, Justice.

Scott J.L. Lukoski brought a wrongful discharge action against
his employer, Sandia Indian Management Co. (SIMCO). Lukoski had
been employed as general manager of the Sandia Pueblo bingo
operation. In a bench trial, the court decided that SIMCO
violated the termination procedures prescribed for "less serious"
offenses by an employee handbook. For salary due on the remaining
term of his one-year oral contract, Lukoski was awarded
$18,629.05. We affirm.

The court found that, in October 1983, Lukoski and SIMCO
entered into a one-year oral employment agreement under which
Lukoski would provide services as the general manager of a bingo
hall operation for a specified annual salary plus commission.
There was no written agreement between the parties. In February
1984, SIMCO distributed to all employees an employee handbook and
requested each to sign the last page as verification of receipt,
acknowledgement of acceptance, and agreement to conform with the
stated policies and procedures. After Lukoski signed the back
page as requested, it was placed in his personnel file. The court
concluded that:

The parties amended the oral employment contract * *
* when [SIMCO] proffered, and [Lukoski] signed, [the]
Employee's Handbook containing new duties and
obligations on the part of employee and employer over
and above said oral contract, including Rules to be
obeyed by [Lukoski] and a termination procedure to be
followed by [SIMCO].

Although we determine the above-quoted language is a finding of
ultimate fact, rather than a conclusion of law, that is of no
consequence. *See Hoskins v. Albuquerque Bus Co.*, 72 N.M. 217,

ILLUSTRATION 1-1   *(continued)*

382 P.2d 700 (1963); *Wiggs v. City of Albuquerque*, 57 N.M. 770,
263 P.2d 963 (1953). SIMCO challenges this finding and for the first
time on appeal raises two other issues. First, it claims that
Lukoski, as general manager, was not the type of employee
intended to be covered by the handbook. Distribution to all
employees with request for signatures constituted evidence to the
contrary, and resolution of any ambiguity regarding management
personnel would have been a specific question of fact. *See*
Shaeffer v. Kelton, 95 N.M. 182, 619 P.2d 1226 (1980). Second,
SIMCO claims that any breach was not material because it neither
went to the substance of the contract nor defeated the object of
the parties. Materiality is likewise a specific question of fact.
See Bisio v. Madenwald (In re Estate of Bisio), 33 Or. App. 325,
576 P.2d 801 (1978). As the contract stood after amendment, it
was not materiality, as argued by SIMCO, but rather severity of
offense that was at issue under the termination procedures. In
any event, by failing to tender requested findings, SIMCO waived
specific
Page 666
findings on these fact issues. SCRA 1986, 1-052(B)(1)(f).

There is substantial evidence supporting the court's findings
of ultimate fact that the termination procedures became an
amendment to Lukoski's contract, and that personality — not the
severe offenses of insubordination or disobedience — was the
cause for termination. He was terminated without warning or
suspension for a cause not so severe as to constitute cause for
immediate termination. His personality and interpersonal dealings
were found by the court to create an atmosphere of fear and
anxiety and bad morale among employees and managers.

Relying only on *Ellis v. El Paso Natural Gas Co.*, 754 F.2d 884
(10th Cir. 1985), the thrust of SIMCO's appeal is that the
language of the employee handbook is "too indefinite to
constitute a contract" and lacks "contractual terms which might
evidence the intent to form a contract." It maintains that the
parties did not conduct themselves as if the employee handbook
was to govern Lukoski or as if they expected it to form the basis
of a contractual relationship. In support of its position, SIMCO
refers to the disciplinary action, suspension, and warning
provisions,[fn1] and argues that the language of the termination
policy is ambiguous and contains no required policy for
termination.

SIMCO's argument, however, overlooks the handbook's
characterization of the disciplinary policy regarding warnings,
suspensions and terminations as "an *established procedure*
regarding suspension of problem employees and termination for
those who cannot conform to Company Policy." (Emphasis added.)
Moreover, the language of the handbook does nothing to alert an
employee against placing reliance on any statement contained
therein or against viewing such discipline and termination policy
as only a unilateral expression of SIMCO's intention that is
subject to revocation or change at any time, in any manner, at
the pleasure of SIMCO. To the contrary, from the language of the
handbook and the conduct of SIMCO in adopting the policy, it
could properly be found that the policy was part of the
employment agreement.

Whether an employee handbook has modified the employment
relationship is a question of fact "to be discerned from the
totality of the parties' statements and actions regarding the
employment relationship." *Wagenseller v. Scottsdale Memorial
Hosp.*, 147 Ariz. 370, 383, 710 P.2d 1025, 1038 (1985) (en banc).

Evidence relevant to this factual decision includes
the language used in the personnel manual as well as

ILLUSTRATION 1-1   *(continued)*

the employer's course of conduct and oral
representations regarding it. We do not mean to imply
that all personnel manual will become part of
employment contracts. Employers are certainly free to
issue no personnel manual at all or to issue a
personnel manual that clearly and conspicuously tells
their employees that the manual is not part of the
employment contract and that their jobs are
terminable

Page 667

at the will of the employer with or without reason.
Such actions * * * instill no reasonable expectations
of job security and do not give employees any reason
to rely on representations in the manual. However, if
an employer does choose to issue a policy statement,
in a manual or otherwise, and, by its language or by
the employer's actions, encourages reliance thereon,
the employer cannot be free to only selectively abide
by it. Having announced a policy, the employer may
not treat it as illusory.

Leikvold v. Valley View Community Hosp., 141 Ariz. 544, 548,
688 P.2d 170, 174 (1984). Here, substantial evidence supports the
finding of the trial court that the employee handbook modified
the employment relationship and created warning and suspension
procedures which were not followed in this case.

Accordingly, based upon the foregoing, the judgment of the
trial court is affirmed.

IT IS SO ORDERED.

SCARBOROUGH, C.J., SOSA, Senior Justice, and WALTERS, J.,
concur.

STOWERS, J., dissents.

[fn1] The referenced handbook provisions state:

OTHER DISCIPLINARY ACTION:

In order to protect the good employees [sic] jobs and Sandia
Indian Bingo, there is an established procedure regarding
suspension of problem employees and termination for those who
can not conform to Company Policy. Suspensions without pay
may be given to employees who violate company policies. There
are violations which are so severe [including insubordination
and disobedience] that immediate termination may be
necessary. . . .

SUSPENSIONS:

Suspension without pay may be given when the incident is not
sufficiently serious to warrant discharge and/or the
particular employee's overall value to the Company [is
considered], if [in] the opinion of the Department Manager
[the employee] warrants another chance. Minimum suspensions
are (3) three days, maximum suspensions are (5) five days. No
employee may be suspended more than once in a year;
thereafter, if the incident would normally warrant suspension
he/she must be discharged.

DISCIPLINARY WARNING:

Disciplinary warning slips will be issued where the offense
is less serious and where corrective action may salvage an
employee. More than one (1) disciplinary warning, whether for

ILLUSTRATION 1-1   *(continued)*

the same offense or not, may subject an employee to
suspension or termination. Warning slips become a permanent
part of an employee's personnel record.

STOWERS, Justice, dissenting.

I respectfully dissent from the majority's holding that SIMCO
did not abide with the termination procedures.

Substantial evidence does support the findings of the trial
court that the employee handbook modified the employment
relationship and that Lukoski was terminated for just cause. The
trial court erred, however, in concluding that SIMCO did not
follow the proper termination procedures. To the contrary, SIMCO
did not breach any of the provisions in the employee handbook
when it discharged Lukoski without a warning and suspension. The
handbook explicitly states that, "there are violations which are
so severe that *immediate termination may be necessary.*" (Emphasis
added).

Overwhelming evidence was presented at trial to show that
Lukowski's violations of company policies were of the type to
fall within the category of "so severe" that a warning and any
suspension procedures were not required. *See State ex rel.*
Goodmans Office Furnishings, Inc. v. Page & Wirtz Constr. Co.,
102 N.M. 22, 24, 690 P.2d 1016, 1018 (1984). Generally, this
evidence indicated that Lukowski had an overall attitude problem
towards his employees, other managers and representatives of the
Sandia Pueblo to the extent that SIMCO was in jeopardy of losing
its bingo contract with the Pueblo; moreover, he was abusive
towards the accountants, argued or fought publicly with
customers, the assistant bingo manager, the construction
supervisor and an admittance clerk; Lukoski also failed to
install proper security measures and verification methods, and
hired unqualified personnel. Further, testimony indicated that on
several occasions, Walker, Lukoski's supervisor, spoke to Lukoski
about this attitude problem, and, in fact, interceded on
Lukoski's behalf when the Sandia Pueblo desired to discharge
Lukoski.

As enumerated in the handbook, Lukoski's violations included,
"fighting on company property, refusal to obey reasonable orders
of a supervisor, discourtesy to customers, and disobeying or
ignoring established written or oral work rules or policies."
These are, and I again quote from the handbook, "violations which
are so severe that *immediate termination* may be necessary."
(Emphasis added.) Therefore, the trial court was in error when it
decided that SIMCO violated the termination procedures prescribed
for "less serious" offenses in the handbook. Lukoski was not
entitled to those termination procedures since his offenses were
not of the "less serious" type. Under the circumstances in this
case, the only process due Lukoski for the seriousness of his
violations was immediate termination. Thus, there was no breach
by SIMCO when it discharged him for just cause.

The judgment of the district court should be reversed and this
case remanded for dismissal.
Page 668

ILLUSTRATION 1-2 State Statute,
from *New Mexico Statutes Annotated* (paper source)

50-10-4. [Safety measures and devices; duty of employer to supply.]

Nothing herein shall be construed to relieve any person, firm or corporation requiring, authorizing or knowingly permitting a person in the employ or subject to the control of such person, firm or corporation, to enter into or remain in a sewer in this state from any duty of taking or supplying proper and reasonable safety measures, practices and devices during the time or times that its said employee or other controlled person shall be in such sewer, to the end that no dangerous concentration of flammable gas or gases, or noxious gas or gases, shall occur; and the requirements of this act [50-10-1 to 50-10-6 NMSA 1978] shall be cumulative of such other duty or duties.

**History: 1953 Comp., § 12-10-4, enacted by
Laws 1959, ch. 175, § 4.**

50-10-5. [Definitions.]

The term "sewer" as used herein shall mean any underground conduit composed of metal, concrete, clay, vitreous or other materials designed for the flowage of water or any waste product or products (including, without being limited to, storm sewers and sanitary sewers), and shall include any and all junction boxes, manholes and gutters and other appurtenances constituting any part of the sewer or of a sewer system.

The term "apparatus to detect the presence of any flammable gas or vapor", as used herein, shall mean any of the standard devices commercially available designed to detect, by the principle of the wheatstone bridge or other recognized technique, the presence in the atmosphere of flammable gas or vapor.

**History: 1953 Comp., § 12-10-5, enacted by
Laws 1959, ch. 175, § 5.**

50-10-6. [Penalties for violation.]

Any person, firm or corporation violating this act [50-10-1 to 50-10-6 NMSA 1978] shall be deemed guilty of a misdemeanor, and upon conviction thereof shall be punished by a fine not less than one hundred dollars ($100) nor more than one thousand dollars ($1,000), or by imprisonment from one day to ten days, or by both such fine and imprisonment, and each day of violation shall constitute a separate offense.

**History: 1953 Comp., § 12-10-6, enacted by
Laws 1959, ch. 175, § 6.**

ARTICLE 11

Employee Privacy

Sec.
50-11-1.   Short title.
50-11-2.   Definitions.
50-11-3.   Employers; unlawful practices.

Sec.
50-11-4.   Remedies.
50-11-5.   Court fees and costs.
50-11-6.   Mitigation of damages.

50-11-1. Short title.

This act [50-11-1 to 50-11-6 NMSA 1978] may be cited as the "Employee Privacy Act".

**History: Laws 1991, ch. 244, § 1.
Am. Jur. 2d, A.L.R. and C.J.S. references. —**
What is "record" within meaning of Privacy Act of

1974 (5 USCS § 552a), 121 A.L.R. Fed. 465.
What is agency subject to Privacy Act Provisions (5 USCA § 552a), 150 A.L.R. Fed. 521.

ILLUSTRATION 1-2   *(continued)*

50-11-2   EMPLOYEE PRIVACY   50-11-6

50-11-2. Definitions.

As used in the Employee Privacy Act [50-11-1 to 50-11-6 NMSA 1978]:

A. "employee" means a person that performs a service for wages or other remuneration under a contract of hire, written or oral, express or implied, and includes a person employed by the state or a political subdivision of the state;

B. "employer" means a person that has one or more employees and includes an agent of an employer and the state or a political subdivision of the state; and

C. "person" means an individual, sole proprietorship, partnership, corporation, association or any other legal entity.

History: Laws 1991, ch. 244, § 2.

50-11-3. Employers; unlawful practices.

A. It is unlawful for an employer to:

(1) refuse to hire or to discharge any individual, or otherwise disadvantage any individual, with respect to compensation, terms, conditions or privileges of employment because the individual is a smoker or nonsmoker, provided that the individual complies with applicable laws or policies regulating smoking on the premises of the employer during working hours; or

(2) require as a condition of employment that any employee or applicant for employment abstain from smoking or using tobacco products during nonworking hours, provided the individual complies with applicable laws or policies regulating smoking on the premises of the employer during working hours.

B. The provisions of Subsection A of this section shall not be deemed to protect any activity that:

(1) materially threatens an employer's legitimate conflict of interest policy reasonably designed to protect the employer's trade secrets, proprietary information or other proprietary interests; or

(2) relates to a bona fide occupational requirement and is reasonably and rationally related to the employment activities and responsibilities of a particular employee or a particular group of employees, rather than to all employees of the employer.

History: Laws 1991, ch. 244, § 3.

50-11-4. Remedies.

Any employee claiming to be aggrieved by any unlawful action of an employer pursuant to Section 3 [50-11-3 NMSA 1978] of the Employee Privacy Act may bring a civil suit for damages in any district court of competent jurisdiction. The employee may be awarded all wages and benefits due up to and including the date of the judgment.

History: Laws 1991, ch. 244, § 4.

50-11-5. Court fees and costs.

In any civil suit arising from the Employee Privacy Act [50-11-1 to 50-11-6 NMSA 1978], the court shall award the prevailing party court costs and reasonable attorneys' fees.

History: Laws 1991, ch. 244, § 5.

50-11-6. Mitigation of damages.

Nothing in the Employee Privacy Act [50-11-1 to 50-11-6 NMSA 1978] shall be construed to relieve a person from the obligation to mitigate damages.

History: Laws 1991, ch. 244, § 6.

63

ILLUSTRATION 1-3

Encyclopedia Text,
from *American Jurisprudence 2d* (paper source)

§ 21
82 AM JUR 2d

ployees does not affect the traditional right of an employer to terminate an at-will employee at any time and for any or no reason.[2]

In determining whether a discharged employee has stated a valid claim for breach of an employment contract based on employer representations, the trier of fact must consider the course of conduct of the parties, including their writings and antecedent negotiations; it is not the employer's subjective intent, nor any single act, phrase, or other expression, but the totality of all these, given the attendant circumstances, the situation of the parties, and the objectives they were striving to attain, which will control.[3]

§ 22 Effect of handbooks and policy manuals, generally

Research References

West's Key Number Digest, Master and Servant ⟝4
What the *Heck*'s going on here? Some unexpected consequences of employee handbook acknowledgments, 34 Idaho L. Rev. 283 (1999)

Absent a disclaimer,[1] in some circumstances, at-will employment can be modified by provisions in an employee manual,[2] if the manual is widely distributed to the employees.[3] Although an employee hired for an indefinite period is presumed to be employed at will, an employee manual, unilaterally published by the employer, may serve as a basis for altering the terms of employment otherwise terminable at will,[4] if the handbook contains language evidencing an intent to create specific discharge procedures and justifications, with an objective manifestation of an assent to contract creating rea-

---

211, 765 P.2d 373 (1988); Pine River State Bank v. Mettille, 333 N.W.2d 622 (Minn. 1983); Morris v. Lutheran Medical Center, 215 Neb. 677, 340 N.W.2d 388 (1983); Weiner v. McGraw-Hill, Inc., 57 N.Y.2d 458, 457 N.Y. S.2d 193, 443 N.E.2d 441, 33 A.L.R.4th 110 (1982); Richardson v. Charles Cole Memorial Hosp., 320 Pa. Super. 106, 466 A.2d 1084 (1983).

[2]White v. Chelsea Industries, Inc., 425 So. 2d 1090 (Ala. 1983); Heideck v. Kent General Hosp., Inc., 446 A.2d 1095 (Del. 1982); Muller v. Stromberg Carlson Corp., 427 So. 2d 266 (Fla. Dist. Ct. App. 2d Dist. 1983); Campbell v. Eli Lilly & Co., 421 N.E.2d 1099 (Ind. 1981); Williams v. Delta Haven, Inc., 416 So. 2d 637 (La. Ct. App. 2d Cir. 1982).

[3]Weiner v. McGraw-Hill, Inc., 57 N.Y.2d 458, 457 N.Y.S.2d 193, 443 N.E.2d 441, 33 A.L.R.4th 110 (1982).

[Section 22]
[1]§ 25.

[2]Almada v. Allstate Ins. Co., 285 F.3d 798 (9th Cir. 2002) (applying Arizona law); Haskins v. Owens-Corning Fiberglas Corp.,

811 F. Supp. 534 (D. Or. 1992) (applying Oregon law); Ex parte Graham, 702 So. 2d 1215 (Ala. 1997); Shoppe v. Gucci America, Inc., 94 Haw. 368, 14 P.3d 1049 (2000); Balmer v. Hawkeye Steel, 604 N.W.2d 639 (Iowa 2000); Samuels v. Tschechtelin, 135 Md. App. 483, 763 A.2d 209, 149 Ed. Law Rep. 784 (2000); O'Brien v. New England Tel. & Tel. Co., 422 Mass. 686, 664 N.E.2d 843 (1996) (parties agree, orally or in writing, that their rights and obligations will include the manual's provisions); Hamersky v. Nicholson Supply Co., 246 Neb. 156, 517 N.W.2d 382 (1994); Dahlberg v. Lutheran Social Services of North Dakota, 2001 ND 73, 625 N.W.2d 241 (N.D. 2001); Burnside v. Simpson Paper Co., 123 Wash. 2d 93, 864 P.2d 937 (1994).

[3]§ 24.

[4]Hardy v. S.F. Phosphates Ltd. Co., 185 F.3d 1076 (10th Cir. 1999) (applying Wyoming law); Gomez v. Martin Marietta Corp., 50 F.3d 1511, 32 Fed. R. Serv. 3d 183 (10th Cir. 1995) (applying Colorado law); Ex parte Graham, 702 So. 2d 1215 (Ala. 1997).

ILLUSTRATION 1-3   *(continued)*

sonable reliance by the employee,[5] or if the handbook contains unequivocal language demonstrating the employer's intent to be bound by the handbook's provisions.[6] In such cases, the provisions in an employee handbook constitute an offer for a unilateral contract; the employees' continuing to work, while under no obligation to do so, constitutes acceptance and sufficient consideration to make the employer's promise binding and enforceable.[7]

◆ **Caution:** An employer's policy statement which lacks the appropriate formalities required by a written employment contract cannot amend the written agreement.[8]

§ 23   —Manuals as not part of employment contract

Research References

West's Key Number Digest, Master and Servant ☞4

As a general rule, where unilateral contracts are not recognized, the courts have held that the issuance of a employee manual setting forth conditions of employment, which may be unilaterally amended or withdrawn by the employer, does not create any mutuality of obligation[1] that is enforceable, or an equitable estoppel[2] that would preclude the employer from terminating an employee's employment except in compliance with the manual.[3] Accordingly, such courts have rejected claims that handbook discharge provisions could

[5]Brown v. City of Niota, Tenn., 214 F.3d 718, 2000 FED App. 180P (6th Cir. 2000) (applying Tennessee law); Fittshur v. Village of Menomonee Falls, 31 F.3d 1401 (7th Cir. 1994) (applying Wisconsin law); Dobbs v. Chevron U.S.A., Inc., 39 F.3d 1064 (10th Cir. 1994) (applying Wyoming law); Palmer v. Arkansas Council on Economic Educ., 344 Ark. 461, 40 S.W.3d 784 (2001); O'Brien v. New England Tel. & Tel. Co., 422 Mass. 686, 664 N.E.2d 843 (1996); Trujillo v. Northern Rio Arriba Elec. Co-op, Inc., 2002 -NMSC-004, 131 N.M. 607, 41 P.3d 333 (2001); Burnside v. Simpson Paper Co., 123 Wash. 2d 93, 864 P.2d 937 (1994).

A contract providing that termination will not occur absent cause will be implied where a handbook contains a detailed list of exclusive grounds for employee discipline or discharge, and a mandatory and specific procedure which the employer agrees to follow prior to any employee's termination. Hollander v. Douglas County, 2000 SD 159, 620 N.W.2d 181 (S.D. 2000).

[6]Schmidt v. Ramsey County, 488 N.W.2d 411 (N.D. Ct. App. 1992); Holland v. FEM Elec. Ass'n, Inc., 2001 SD 143, 637 N.W.2d 717 (S.D. 2001).

[7]Blankenship v. Mingo County Economic Opportunity Com'n, Inc., 187 W. Va. 157, 416 S.E.2d 471 (1992).

As to implied unilateral contracts, generally, see § 8.

[8]Deus v. Allstate Ins. Co., 15 F.3d 506, 40 Fed. R. Evid. Serv. 611, 28 Fed. R. Serv. 3d 11 (5th Cir. 1994) (applying Louisiana law).

[Section 23]

[1]§ 9.

[2]§ 15.

[3]Robinson v. Ada S. McKinley Community Services, Inc., 19 F.3d 359 (7th Cir. 1994) (applying Illinois law); Greely v. Clairol, Inc., 687 F. Supp. 1002 (D. Md. 1988), judgment aff'd, 883 F.2d 68 (4th Cir. 1989) (applying Maryland law); Torosyan v. Boehringer Ingelheim Pharmaceuticals, Inc., 234 Conn. 1, 662 A.2d 89 (1995); Shaw v. S.S. Kresge Co., 167 Ind. App. 1, 328 N.E.2d 775 (3d Dist. 1975); Jackson v. Action for Boston Community Development, Inc., 403 Mass. 8, 525 N.E.2d 411 (1988); Hager v. Union Carbide Corp., 106 A.D.2d 348, 483 N.Y.S.2d 261 (1st Dep't 1984); Williams v. Biscuitville, Inc., 40 N.C. App. 405, 253 S.E.2d 18 (1979); Roy v. Woonsocket Inst. for Sav., 525 A.2d 915 (R.I. 1987).

ILLUSTRATION 1-4

Periodical Article,
from *Georgetown Law Journal* through LexisNexis
(electronic source)

Search - 25 Results - priva! /p smok! /s off-duty or non-working or nonworking   Page 1 of 30

Source: Legal > / . . . / > **Law Reviews, Combined** (i)
Terms: **priva! /p smok! /s off-duty or non-working or nonworking** (Edit Search)

  ☞ Select for FOCUS™ or Delivery
  ☐

*86 Geo. L.J. 783, ***

Copyright (c) 1998 Georgetown Law Journal
Georgetown Law Journal

January, 1998

86 Geo. L.J. 783

LENGTH: 19482 words

NOTE: Blowing Smoke: Do Smokers Have a Right? Limiting the Privacy Rights of Cigarette
Smokers

MICHELE L. TYLER *

* J.D., Georgetown University Law Center, 1998. This note was written in memory of my
grandmother, Mrs. Rita Ann Strote, who quit smoking 20 years ago when she was diagnosed
with emphysema, but who lost her battle with the disease last year. I thank Dean Anita Allen
for her suggestions and guidance on an earlier draft of this note. I also thank Dale Tyler for
his continued support and encouragement.

SUMMARY:
  ... For example, at a Denny's restaurant in California in 1993, nonsmoker Rachelle Rashan
Houston asked Daphnye Luster, a smoker, to extinguish her cigarette. ... The
nonfundamental privacy interests of the smoker are outweighed in the balance against the
interests of children who face increased health risks through exposure to environmental
tobacco smoke. ... Even if some smokers accept that environmental tobacco smoke trapped
within a confined public place is harmful to others, and even if they accept that their second-
hand smoke has health consequences and annoyance costs to those seated next to them in
outdoor stadiums and concerts, they may nevertheless argue that an outright ban on
smoking in the public outdoors unconstitutionally invades their decisional privacy rights. ...
As noted above, public health concerns and the exposure of children to outdoor
environmental tobacco smoke have been offered as justifications for the infringement on the
individual's decisional privacy right to smoke. ... Even if smokers have a privacy right to
smoke in their own homes, anti-smoking advocates argue, their privacy right ends at the
point it invades a nonsmoker's physical and decisional privacy rights not to breathe
environmental tobacco smoke. ...

TEXT:
  [*783] INTRODUCTION

Despite the recent settlement negotiations between the tobacco industry and a group of state
attorneys general, the day-to-day debate between smokers and nonsmokers is anything but
civil. For example, at a Denny's restaurant in California in 1993, nonsmoker Rachelle Rashan
Houston asked Daphnye Luster, a smoker, to extinguish her cigarette. Ms. Luster, who was
seated in the nonsmoking section, complied and shortly thereafter left the restaurant. Later,
Ms. Luster returned with a 12-gauge shotgun and killed Ms. Houston as Ms. Houston was
driving away from the restaurant. [1] This violent example illustrates the growing tension

ILLUSTRATION 1-4   *(continued)*

between smokers and nonsmokers over whether an individual has a "right" to smoke.

Change in the social acceptance of smoking has occurred rapidly, with nonsmokers' passive tolerance of smoking turning within a single lifetime to vocal demands for protection from exposure to tobacco smoke. Not so long ago, smoking was considered an acceptable adult choice; its health effects limited to smoker's cough and yellowed teeth. Smoking was portrayed on television and film as part of a glamorous and sophisticated lifestyle. Lucy and Ricky Ricardo smoked cigarettes they kept in a silver case; [2] Humphrey Bogart, who died of lung cancer, and his co-stars smoked in nearly every scene of Casablanca. [3] Yet the tide of public opinion began to turn after the 1964 Surgeon General's Report, [4] which concluded that smoking increases a person's risk of lung cancer, chronic bronchitis, and emphysema. [5] Until the recent settlement negotiations, [6] **[*784]** the tobacco industry steadfastly denied the negative effects of smoking, [7] even in the face of numerous studies and reports by the Surgeon General and the Environmental Protection Agency that demonstrated otherwise. [8] Nevertheless, as social attitudes about smoking have changed, nonsmokers have had greater success in passing legislation aimed at controlling smoking. [9] As of 1993, forty-four states had passed restrictions on smoking in public places. [10] Additionally, some states and many localities have enacted even more restrictive smoking laws and ordinances to prohibit smoking in workplaces, restaurants, and stadiums. [11] Moreover, the private sector, which includes businesses, universities, hospitals, and nonprofit organizations, has responded to the growing health concerns of nonsmokers. By the early 1990s, eighty-five percent of private businesses had put some type of smoking policy in place, although the terms of these policies vary greatly. [12]

Yet there are signs of a smoker backlash. As of 1995, twenty-nine states had passed some type of legislation prohibiting employers from requiring employees to abstain from smoking outside the course of employment. [13] Additionally, many of the cities and private businesses attempting to enact restrictive smoking legislation have faced political opposition and negative public relations campaigns funded by the tobacco industry. [14]

[*785] Recently, however, the tobacco company Liggett-Myers acknowledged that tobacco is addictive, causes cancer, and that tobacco companies have consciously marketed cigarettes to young teenagers. [15] In light of such acknowledgment, the tobacco industry and smokers can no longer plausibly deny the addictive effects of cigarette smoking. The industry's denials of the harmful effects of "second-hand" tobacco smoke [16] will likely become suspect even to long-time smokers. Nevertheless, many people will continue to smoke, often asserting a privacy right to do so. [17] This note will address that assertion, analyzing controversial anti-smoking legislation and court decisions with regard to three different meanings of the right to privacy: informational privacy, physical privacy, and decisional privacy. [18]

Because infringements on the smoker's "privacy right to smoke" are often justified on the basis of mitigating the harm caused to nonsmokers, Part I will discuss the negative effects of cigarette smoke on nonsmokers, providing background for the change in public attitudes toward smoking. Part II will discuss how recent anti-smoking approaches in the workplace, the home, and public places impact individual privacy rights; it will conclude that smoking is not an activity that should be protected by an individual's privacy rights. Finally, Part III will argue that a conscious effort to shift the civility norms [19] **[*786]** regarding smoking presents an alternative suggestion for protecting the health of nonsmokers while avoiding the backlash a prohibition on smoking might bring.

I. EFFECTS OF TOBACCO SMOKE ON NONSMOKERS

The health effects of tobacco smoke on nonsmokers are well documented and are frequently offered as the justification for impinging upon a smoker's privacy. [20] The debate between smokers and nonsmokers is fueled by the harmful effects of environmental tobacco smoke,

3. Finding Tools

As you would no doubt guess, you will need assistance in locating pertinent primary and secondary authority. Finding tools help you to do so. They do not constitute authority of any sort, however, because they do not themselves assert legal propositions or do so authoritatively.

Some finding tools cover a wide range or set of sources. For example, a library catalog covers many of the sources owned by or accessible in a particular library; Internet search engines and directories index World Wide Web sites. Other finding tools are narrower, covering a particular type of authority. For example, periodical indexes are used to locate periodical articles, and digests are used to locate cases.

Many authorities operate as finding tools for other authorities. For example, a court may cite to a statute, or a treatise author may list cases from which he or she has drawn the legal rule under discussion.

Incidentally, people, including colleagues, professors, and reference librarians, can sometimes be helpful "finding tools."

D. RESEARCH MEDIA

Until relatively recently, legal materials were all published in paper, and legal research took place in a library. Researchers worked with books and occasionally microforms (reels or cards containing tiny photographs of printed pages, read through a microform reader).

Computer-assisted legal research debuted in the mid-1970s and has evolved through several phases since then. Initially, two commercial online services—now known as LexisNexis and Westlaw—dominated; they remain the dominant commercial online services for legal research today. (Online services store information on a server at a remote location; the user gains access to the information through a computer and a network connection.) During the 1990s, CD-ROM products became fairly popular, especially for certain sources, such as a specific state's primary authority and periodical indexes. (A CD-ROM (compact disk—read only memory) is a disk on which information is stored in pits, and it is read via a computer.) In recent years, CD-ROMs have faded in importance, and the Internet has come to play a central role in legal research.

The Internet is a vast, unregulated, international network that connects thousands of computer networks. For research purposes, you will be most concerned with the World Wide Web. You will navigate the Web by use of a web browser, such as Netscape Navigator or Microsoft Internet Explorer. You may locate a pertinent website on the Web by four different methods:

- ☐ You may go directly to a known website by typing in its URL (uniform resource locator), that is, its Web address, for example, www.washlaw.edu.

☐ You may go to a website that serves as a portal to other websites, that is, it collects and organizes URLs for websites, especially government websites, and provides links to those sites. An early service in law and still a very well-regarded academic website is the Legal Information Institute, provided by Cornell University's law school and located at www.law.cornell.edu. Another example is www.washlaw.edu of Washburn University School of Law.

☐ You may use a search engine by typing in words pertinent to websites you hope to locate. Many legal researchers use general-purpose search engines such as Google, Teoma, Alltheweb, and Dogpile. LawCrawler is a search engine covering only legal materials websites.

☐ You may use an online subject directory, such as Findlaw, or a paper directory, such as *The Legal List: Research on the Internet.*

Through the Web, you will gain access to many websites containing legal materials. The online legal research industry is changing rapidly. Your prime objective is to locate a credible site; other important factors are coverage and cost. As of the writing of this text in mid-2003, most of the online services fit into one of the following categories:

☐ Government sites: Increasingly, federal and state governments are providing their legal materials to the public through free websites, such as www.gpoaccess.gov, the federal Government Printing Office's website.

☐ Commercial sites: Various commercial publishers make legal materials available through the Internet for a fee, either by subscription or on a per-use basis. The two most prominent are, as mentioned above, LexisNexis and Westlaw. A newer and increasingly credible service is Loislaw. All are provided by companies that also publish print legal materials: LexisNexis, West Group, and Aspen Publishing, respectively.

☐ Academic sites: Although academic websites primarily serve as portals to other websites, some also provide selected documents as well. For example, the University of Pennsylvania's Biddle Law Library provides the archives of the Restatements, which are very influential secondary authorities.

☐ Lawyer organizations: Recently, bar associations (professional organizations of lawyers) have begun to offer legal materials on the Web. For example, you can locate materials regarding legal ethics at www.abanet.org, the free website of the American Bar Association. Another example is the Casemaker Consortium, available in thirteen states as of mid-2003, which provides federal and state-specific primary materials as a benefit of membership in the state bar association.

☐ Other organizations: Professional, trade, and public interest organizations provide some legal materials in their areas of interest. Some of these materials may be available to subscribers only. These websites generally are not as authoritative as those listed above because they

| EXHIBIT 1.2 | | | | Media Usage of Practicing Lawyers | |

	Print	CD-ROM	Proprietary Online	Fee-based Web	Free Web
state cases	25.50%	13.86%	28.22%	21.29%	11.14%
state statutes	32.59%	10.95%	21.14%	12.69%	22.64%
legal treatises and secondary materials	65.67%	5.67%	14.33%	11.67%	2.67%
legal periodicals	52.38%	0.95%	19.05%	20.32%	7.30%

may have an advocacy orientation and may not be as up to date or accurate as the other types of websites listed above.

The illustrations in this chapter come from both paper and electronic media: the *Lukoski* case from Loislaw (online), the employee privacy statute from a paper code published by Michie (a well-respected legal publisher now owned by LexisNexis), the encyclopedia text from a paper encyclopedia published by West Group (now named Thomson West), and the law review article from LexisNexis (online).

As you develop your legal research skills, you should aim to be ambidextrous—equally adept at paper and electronic research—for three reasons. First, some legal research materials are available in only one medium. Some materials are not yet available in electronic media, and some of those never will be. A fairly recent development in legal publishing is that some very new materials are available only in electronic media. Second, sometimes the medium you would prefer to use will be unavailable—books can be off the shelf, networks can be down—or cost too much for your client to pay. Third, as you will see throughout this text, paper sources work better for some purposes, and electronic sources work better for other purposes.

Practicing lawyers are indeed ambidextrous these days, according to a 2001 American Bar Association survey of lawyers from around the country, representing various firm sizes, practice areas, and years of experience.[8] Asked which format they used most often for researching in various types of materials, the lawyers responded as indicated in Exhibit 1.2. In summary, even as practicing lawyers take advantage of electronic sources, they continue to rely on books for one quarter to one third of their research in primary authorities and for over half of their research in secondary authorities.

---

8. Legal Technology Resource Center, American Bar Association, *2001 Legal Technology Survey Report: Online Research* 75, 76, 70, 67 (2001).

E.   THE APPROACH OF THIS BOOK

To maneuver successfully through the many sources involved in legal research, you must not only know the lay of the land, described above. You also must understand the cognitive tasks involved in legal research, such as how to develop research terms and how to update your initial research results. This is the topic of Chapter 2.

With this ground work set, the text explores the five major categories of research materials, each in its own unit:

- ☐   secondary authorities in Unit II,
- ☐   case law (a type of primary authority) in Unit III,
- ☐   enacted law (a type of primary authority) in Unit IV,
- ☐   administrative materials (a type of primary authority) in Unit V, and
- ☐   rules of procedure and legal ethics (both types of primary authority) in Unit VI.

You may wonder why secondary authorities are discussed before the various forms of primary authority. As you will see, although primary authority ultimately is well more important than secondary authority, you often will start your research in secondary authority and then proceed to one or more categories of primary authority.

Most chapters cover a set of closely related research materials and follow a standard format. They address the following questions:

- ☐   What is the authority?
- ☐   Why would you research in it?
- ☐   How do you research in it?
- ☐   What else should you know?
- ☐   How do you cite it?

Again, please note: This text uses the term "authority" to refer to the content of research materials, while "source" refers to the paper or electronic publications in which they are located. For instance, the legislature enacts a statute as law—primary authority. That statute may appear in several publications, such as a printed code or an online database—primary sources.

Two of the questions stated above merit a paragraph of explanation here. First, as to the *how do you research in it* discussion: Many types of legal authority can be researched multiple ways, in multiple sources. For example, you can research case law through a set of books, through online commercial computer services, or in free websites available through the Web. If we were to describe all ways of conducting legal research, this book would be enormous, and your capacity to fully learn any particular technique would be limited. Thus, we have chosen to describe in each chapter no more than a handful or two of research practices. We think of these practices as best practices because they likely will lead to correct, comprehensive, credible, and cost-effective research in most situations. As you become more expert, and technology and publication patterns evolve, you may develop new best practices, but they probably will build on the practices discussed here. We have synopsized the practices in shaded boxes, each of which presents either steps (signified by arrow bullets ▶) or options (signified by round bullets ●).

Second, as to the *how do you cite it* discussion: Citation is the practice of providing the reader with a precise reference to a source. As you will see, legal citation is complicated and technical—but also manageable if you work through it in a systematic way. This text provides you with starting information on citation and refers you to the two leading manuals on legal citation. *The Bluebook: A Uniform System of Citation*, compiled by upper-level students at four prestigious law schools, was in its seventeenth edition at the time this book was written. *ALWD Citation Manual: A Professional System of Citation*, in its second edition at the time this book was written, is a product of the Association of Legal Writing Directors. Furthermore, some courts have developed their own citation protocols, which you should, of course, follow in appropriate cases.

Most of the chapters present their topics in three forms: a general description, a specific example, and illustrative pages from the sources pertinent to the Canoga case. Please note: This book does not present all legal materials pertinent to the Canoga case, but rather a range of major authorities. In addition, the practice sets at the end of this book present you with fairly straightforward situations to research, using the sources and practices covered in the chapters. Working through the practice sets will not make you an accomplished researcher; no single practice opportunity could do that. The practice sets do, however, give you an occasion to put what you have read into action and to acquaint yourself with the many and varied sources of legal materials.

Finally, Unit VII, a single chapter, presents research journals written by upper-level law students as they researched a typical client situation. These journals demonstrate various ways in which the sources and practices described in this book fit together.

FROM CURIOSITY TO CLOSURE: EIGHT COGNITIVE TASKS

Research is formalized curiosity. It is poking and prying with a purpose.
—Zora Neale Hurston, *Dust Tracks on a Road* (1942)

INTRODUCTION

Competent legal research takes considerable time and intellectual energy. Throughout the process, you will acquire information and make judgments based on what you have learned so far. Thus legal research involves cognition—the process of coming to know something, which includes both awareness and judgment.

This chapter breaks down the research process into four broad phases (A through D above) and eight specific cognitive tasks (1 through 8 above). To a certain extent, the tasks occur in the sequence set forth here. That is, you will:

- ☐ start by considering your client's situation (tasks 1 and 2),
- ☐ proceed to determining which authorities and sources to use (tasks 3 and 4),
- ☐ spend much of your time carefully working with those sources (tasks 5, 6, and 7), and
- ☐ eventually stop researching (task 8).

As you will soon see, legal research is not a totally linear process; midway through, you may well return to an earlier task. For example, if you find little pertinent information in the sources you have selected, you may need to return to task 2 to generate additional research terms and issues or to task 4 to identify additional sources to explore. In addition, your specific research plan will vary somewhat from project to project, reflecting the difficulty of the topic, the knowledge you already have of the pertinent law, the time available, cost considerations, and other factors.

If you accomplish all of the tasks well, your research should meet the criteria stated in Chapter 1:

- ☐ *correct:* leading to the law that governs your client's situation and applied or will apply as of the time of that situation;
- ☐ *comprehensive:* addressing the various issues raised by the client's situation and incorporating an appropriate range of pertinent authorities;
- ☐ *credible:* featuring authority that carries weight because of its nature and quality;
- ☐ *cost-effective:* yielding results that justify the effort, in light of the client's situation and available research options.

As you read through this chapter, you will see simple drawings. For each task, we have developed a symbol, and the text explains the significance of the symbol.

This chapter refers, a number of times, to the Canoga situation presented in Chapter 1 (at pages 3–4) and to the authorities presented in Chapter 1 (at pages 9–18). We encourage you to read or review those materials before proceeding.

A. CLIENT-CENTERED CURIOSITY

Lawyers research the law because clients have problems to be solved, whether disputes to resolve or transactions to plan. Thus you must begin your research with careful consideration of your client's situation. Through this process, you should develop sufficient curiosity to sustain what may be a lengthy research process.

1. Learn and React to Your Client's Situation

On occasion, you will receive a tidy oral or written statement of a client's situation. This is far more common in law school than in real life. Most of the time in practice, you will learn about the client's situation through various sources of information: a conversation with the client, correspondence, documents, a visit to the site, etc.

From these various sources, you must construct a narrative account of the client's situation. Note that the situation involves not only facts but also the client's goals and concerns. As you work on the narrative, you may find one or more of the following activities helpful:

- ☐ Write out a cast of characters, and identify the role each played.
- ☐ Create a timeline of key events.
- ☐ Discern what each of the main characters would say about the situation.
- ☐ Develop a short statement of what your client hopes will happen as a result of your representation of the client.

As you develop the narrative, you likely will realize that you do not know everything you would like to know. If you can get the answer to a question by contacting your client or by some other appropriate means, do so. Fairly often, you will not be able to get answers to all of your questions, because the participants do not remember what you would like to know, because you are not yet in a position to contact the participant who might know, or because you are helping to structure a transaction that will take place in the future. Similarly, you may have conflicting information on some aspect of the situation and no means of resolving the conflict. Be sure to note any unknown or uncertain facts, and proceed in your research on the basis of one or more reasonable assumptions.

Once you have developed the narrative, reflect a bit on your client's situation, as though you were the lawmaker, not your client's lawyer. Ask yourself:

- ☐ What would I think about this situation?
- ☐ What rule would I devise?
- ☐ What would be a fair and just outcome?
- ☐ What are the appealing aspects of my client's position?
- ☐ What are the appealing aspects of the position of my client's opponent or the other participants in the situation?

This process is often described as "weighing the equities" of a case; hence our symbol for this cognitive task is a scale.

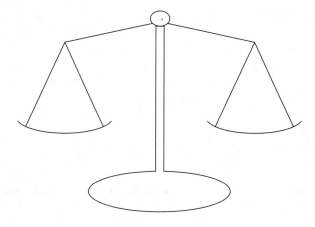

Finally, brainstorm possible solutions that would meet the client's goals, would address the client's concerns, and may be accepted by the client's opponent or other participants in the situation. Once you begin your legal research, you will inevitably focus on the options available through the legal system. But keep in mind that many situations involving legal questions are handled not through formal legal processes but rather through negotiation facilitated or conducted by lawyers.

The statement of the Canoga situation in Chapter 1 (at pages 3–4) is a narrative account of the known facts of her situation as well as her goals and concerns. The appealing aspects of Ms. Canoga's position include her interests in making her own decisions regarding her personal habits, being able to raise an issue of serious concern with management without losing her job, and having the board follow the procedures promised in the handbook. The appealing aspects of the orchestra's position include its interests in securing excellent performances by wind players, controlling health care costs, and preserving managerial prerogative.

2. Develop Research Terms and Research Issues

a. Understanding Legal Language

To develop effective research terms and issues, you must understand how words are used in the law. The core of a primary authority is the rule (or rules) of law it expresses. A rule of law links factual conditions with legal consequences. For example, consider this excerpt from the New Mexico statute presented in Chapter 1 (at pages 13–14):

> It is unlawful for an employer to . . . require as a condition of employment that any employee . . . abstain from smoking or using tobacco products during nonworking hours. . . . Any employee claiming to

be aggrieved by [such an] unlawful action . . . may bring a civil suit for damages. . . . The employee may be awarded all wages and benefits due up to and including the date of the judgment.

This rule refers to the following factual condition: An employer prohibits an employee from smoking during nonworking hours. That factual condition leads to the following legal consequence: The employee may sue the employer for wages and benefits.

Most of the words in this rule are familiar words. Indeed, some words are used just as you would use them in everyday speech, for example, *smoking* and *tobacco products*. Other words carry a legal connotation, for example, *aggrieved, civil suit,* and *judgment*. Still other words have a mixed meaning. For example, an everyday understanding of *employee* is someone who works for another person for pay; the law uses *employee* in a more technical sense to identify people who benefit from certain legal rules.

In some legal rules, one or more words are defined; that definition may or may not accord with its common meaning. For example, the New Mexico legislature defined *employer* to include various legal entities, including the state and its political subdivisions, that have one or more employees. In another statute, *employer* might include only private employers or entities with a specified minimum number of employees.

Most words in a legal rule are quite general, because rules describe classes of situations, not specific situations. For example, the New Mexico statute does not describe a specific employer or employee, particular tobacco products, or a specific means of prohibiting smoking.

Many concepts are expressed not in a word, but in a phrase. Sometimes the words appear in a fixed order; sometimes the words may be inverted with no loss of meaning. As examples, consider the fixed-order phrase *during nonworking hours,* used in the New Mexico statute, and the invertible phrase *employment contract,* which appears in the *Lukoski* case, Illustration 1-1 (at pages 9–12).

Some concepts can be stated in one of several words or phrases with virtually the same meaning, that is, synonyms. The encyclopedia excerpt, Illustration 1-3 (at pages 15–16), refers to *employee manual* and *employee handbook* interchangeably. Similarly, some words and phrases used in legal rules have antonyms. The New Mexico statute excerpted above also has another rule pertinent to *during working hours,* an antonym of *during nonworking hours.*

Many concepts can be expressed in broad or narrow terms. For example, the New Mexico statute employs a very broad term—*unlawful*—to convey that certain employer action is prohibited. The statute also conveys the same idea through a narrower term—*civil suit for damages.*

Finally, some concepts are subsets of other concepts; phrased another way, legal rules have elements. For example, the following are elements of the statute's rule regarding unlawful employer practice: employer, employee, requirement of abstention from smoking, during nonworking hours.

Many legal authorities do more than state legal rules; in so doing, they use non-rule language of various sorts. In describing the facts of a case, a court uses specific factual terms, such as the name of a specific person or company. For example, the *Lukoski* case, Illustration 1-1 (at pages 9–12), refers to Mr. Lukoski, his employer SIMCO, and specific provisions of the SIMCO employee handbook. In critiquing or explaining a rule, a commentary writer may refer to abstract legal concepts and nonlegal ideas. For example, the periodical excerpt, Illustration 1-4 (at pages 17–18), refers to *decisional privacy right* and *environmental tobacco smoke*.

b.   Generating Research Terms

To research effectively in legal sources, you must excel in developing both research terms and research issues. A research term is an expression of a concept you plan to research; a research issue is a combination of terms in question form.

As a first step, think carefully about the following factual dimensions of the client's situation:

(1)   *Who* is involved? The answer may be people or entities, such as a corporation or government body. Focus not on the exact identities of those involved, but on their roles.

(2)   *What* is involved? The answer may be physical items, activities, or intangibles.

(3)   *When* did (or will) the important events occur? Think not only about the precise date and time, but also about the sequence of events.

(4)   *Where* did (or will) the important events occur? Think not only about the precise location, but also about the significance of the location.

(5)   *Why* did (or will) the participants act in this way? Analyze their motives or states of mind.

Many of the factual concepts you identify will appear in some form in the factual conditions of the legal rule or rules governing your problem. Of course, not every factual concept will prove to be a useful research term, but to avoid overlooking something critical, you should include, rather than exclude, too much.

Your answers to two of these questions—*where* and *when*—will contribute to the correctness of your research. Your answer to the *where* question will help you identify the jurisdiction whose law you should research. Your answer to the *when* question will help you identify law that is current as of the time of your client's situation.

You also should think about your problem's legal dimensions. Even before you research the problem, you may have some sense of what it might entail. Many legal rules are based on common notions of what is just and fair, and many legal rules are within common parlance. Hence you should think about the following legal dimensions:

(6)   What is the *legal theory* applicable to this situation? What is the legal basis for penalizing the wrongdoer, benefitting the wronged party, or excusing the wrong?

(7)   What *relief* does the wronged party seek through the legal system?

(8)   What is the *procedural posture* of the case? At what stage of the litigation process is the case at this point?

Many of the legal concepts you identify will appear in the legal consequences of the rule. Although these questions, especially the last, assume that there is litigation, your client's situation may not actually involve litigation, now or ever. Nonetheless, as lawyers research, as a general rule, they imagine what the courts would do with a case involving the client's situation; hence you should look at your problem in this light.

These eight questions—five factual questions, three legal questions—all are important; thus our image for this task is an eight-piece pie. As phrased here, the eight questions probably seem fairly distinct; in practice, you may find them to be less than distinct. Fortunately, it is not important that you properly categorize a particular concept. However, you must think through all eight questions to achieve comprehensive research.

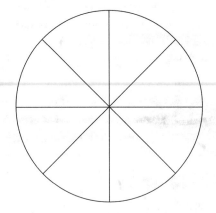

As an example, if you were researching the Canoga problem, you might identify the factual and legal concepts stated below:

(1)   *who:*   musician, flutist, smoker (tried to quit and failed), employee, employer, orchestra, general manager, board of directors

(2)   *what:*   employment, termination, smoking, insubordination, denial of board review, employee manual, no-smoking policy, protest against smoking rules

(3)   *when:*   January 7, 2003; five years after hire; smoking during nonworking hours

(4)   *where:*   Taos, New Mexico; smoking away from the orchestra's premises

(5)   *why:*   protest against policy for privacy reasons, termination for insubordination or refusal to cease smoking

(6)   *legal theory:*   breach of contract, discrimination against
                            smokers, violation of privacy rights
(7)   *relief sought:*   money (damages), return to work (reinstate-
                            ment), cleared work record
(8)   *procedure:*   nothing yet

As a second step, in developing a full set of research terms, work through the following activities: spinning off additional words, analyzing the roots of your words, and analyzing phrases.

For each important concept, you should think of words that are synonyms, antonyms, or broader or narrower terms. Two useful devices for doing so are a hub-and-spokes diagram and a ladder diagram. In the former, the original word appears at the center, with additional words circling it. In the latter, a broad term appears at the top rung and consecutively narrower terms appear below it. Examples appear in Illustration 2-1 (below).

ILLUSTRATION 2-1   Hub and Spokes and Ladder Diagrams

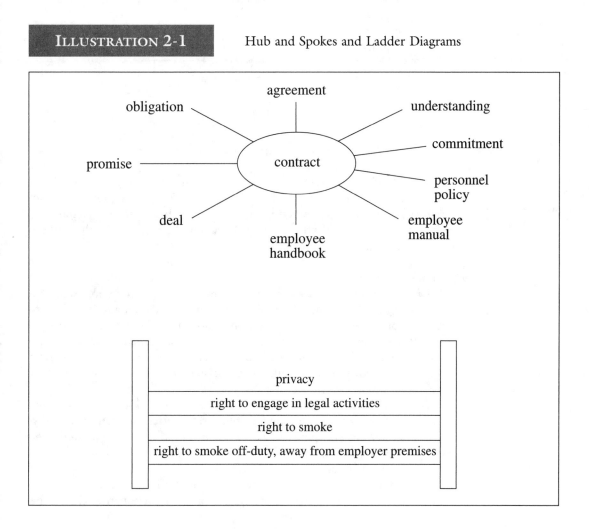

Then consider whether a word has a root that is shared with other potentially pertinent words. For example, the root *employ* appears in several words: *employment, employee, employer;* you probably would want to encompass all of these concepts. Consider also whether a word's root is shared by nonuseful words or, indeed, whether a word has a nonpertinent meaning. For example, the word *employ* is used in many settings unrelated to working for another for pay, as in employing one's energies for a good purpose. You will want to exclude nonpertinent usages to the extent possible.

Finally, consider any phrases you have generated. Be sure you know whether the words always appear in a specific order or whether the order may be inverted.

At the end of this process, you should have a well-developed set of research items. Here are two sets of research terms for the Canoga situation:

Employee	*Discharge*
employ . . .	discharg(e) . . . of / from employment
employer	dismiss "
employee	separat(e) "
employment	terminat(e) "
work, worker	fir(e) . . .
labor, laborer	involuntary
job	
orchestra / musician / flutist	

c.   Using Dictionaries and Thesauri

As you develop research terms, you may want to consult a dictionary or thesaurus for two reasons: First, you should look up your most important research terms in a legal dictionary, to be sure that your understanding is correct and comports with legal usage. Second, dictionaries and thesauri can help you identify additional research terms.

You will find quite an array of legal dictionaries and thesauri, each with strengths and weaknesses. The more comprehensive dictionaries, such as *Black's Law Dictionary,* cover a very wide range of terms and phrases, including some foreign-language phrases; comprehensive dictionaries typically include pronunciations, word derivations, and illustrative references to legal authorities. The more compact dictionaries, such as *Oran's Dictionary of the Law,* contain only the definitions of essential or basic legal terms. Thesauri primarily provide synonyms, antonyms, and associated concepts; some include basic definitions. See Illustration 2-2 (at pages 34–35).

You are most likely to use these sources in book form. Keep in mind that legal words and phrases can be alphabetized letter-by-letter or word-by-word. For instance, the phrase *contract remedy* would appear before *contractor* in word-by-word alphabetizing, but the order would be reversed in letter-by-letter alphabetizing.

You might use a computer-based dictionary if it is expedient to do so. Both LexisNexis and Westlaw have searchable legal dictionaries. Only a few searchable legal dictionaries were available for free via the Web when this book was written; they were not very comprehensive.

Regardless of how you explore these sources, as you discover new potential terms within the definitions, be sure to look them up too.

Also, keep track of where you locate key definitions, in case you need to cite them. It is far better to cite to a primary authority providing a definition than to cite to a dictionary. You may, however, cite to a dictionary for a definition of a term that is undefined in the primary authority in your jurisdiction. For proper form, see Rule 15 of *The Bluebook* and Rule 25 of *ALWD Citation Manual,* as well as the citations in Illustration 2-2 (at pages 34–35).

Researching the Canoga case, we looked up various words. Illustration 2-2 (at pages 34–35) presents pertinent excerpts from various sources. The *contract* definitions focus on an obligation derived from a promise; the thesaurus entry provides numerous synonyms, such as *agreement* and *covenant.* Note that the law formerly used *master* and *servant* to refer to employers and employees. A potentially important term is *employment at will,* which means employment that may be terminated at any time, with or without cause. Yet there also are *retaliatory* and *wrongful discharges,* that is, illegal discharges that violate the law or public policy.

d. Formulating Legal Issues

As you analyze your problem and generate research terms, you probably will note that some concepts seem closely connected. More specifically, certain factual concepts will seem to connect to certain legal concepts. From these connections, you may be able to formulate tentative research issues, that is, questions for which you are seeking legal answers.

For example, in the Canoga situation, breach of contract (a legal theory) probably connects to the employee manual and denial of board review. Here are several possible research issues for the Canoga case with the legal concepts in italics:

☐ Was there a *breach of contract* when the board denied review to a terminated employee though review was promised in the employee handbook?

☐ Was there a *violation of privacy rights* when an orchestra's policy prohibited smoking off-duty and a flutist resisted and was discharged?

☐ Was there unlawful *discrimination against a smoker* when a flutist-smoker who had tried but failed to quit smoking was fired by an orchestra for refusing to agree not to smoke off-duty and off-premises?

ILLUSTRATION 2-2   Dictionaries and Thesauri Excerpts

NOTE: The citations below comport with Rule 15 of *The Bluebook*. Rule 25 of *ALWD Citation Manual* also includes the publisher.

The Plain-Language Law Dictionary 110 (Robert E. Rothenberg & Stephen A. Gilbert eds., 2d ed. 1996).

Contract. An AGREEMENT between two or more people, one PARTY (or parties) agreeing to perform certain acts, the other party (or parties) agreeing to pay for or give other consideration for said performance. The contract places an OBLIGATION on one party to do something and an obligation upon the other party to reward the doer.

Daniel Oran, *Oran's Dictionary of the Law* 114 (3d ed. 2000).

Contract. An agreement that affects or creates legal relationships between two or more persons. To be a *contract,* an agreement must involve: at least one promise, **consideration** (something of value promised or given), persons legally capable of making binding agreements, and a reasonable certainty about the meaning of the terms. A contract is called **bilateral** if both sides makes promises (such as the promise to deliver a book on one side and a promise to pay for it on the other) or **unilateral** if the promises are on one side only. According to the **Uniform Commercial Code,** a contract is the "total legal obligation which results from the parties' agreement," and according to the Restatement of the Law of Contracts, it is "a promise or set of promises for the breach of which the law in some way recognizes a duty." For the many different types of contracts, such as **output, requirements,** etc., see those words.

William C. Burton, *Burton's Legal Thesaurus* 122 (3d ed. 1998).

CONTRACT, *noun,* accord, accordance, agreement, arrangement, articles of agreement, assurance, avouchment, avowal, bargain, binding agreement, bond, charter, collective agreement, commitment, compact, compromise, concordat, *condicio, conductio,* confirmation, *conventio,* covenant, deal, embodied terms, engagement, *entente,* guarantee, instrument evidencing an agreement, ironclad agreement, legal document, mutual agreement, mutual pledge, mutual promise, mutual undertaking, negotiated agreement, obligation, pact, paction, *pactum,* pledge, pledged word, private understanding, promise, ratified agreement, set terms, settlement, stated terms, stipulation, terms for agreement, understanding, undertaking, warranty, written terms

---

Jonathan S. Lynton, *Ballentine's Legal Dictionary and Thesaurus* 211 (1995).

employer [em · *ploy* · er] *n.* A person who hires another to work for her for pay in a relationship that allows her to control the work and direct the manner in which it is done.

ILLUSTRATION 2-2 *(continued)*

The earlier legal term for employer was **master.**
▶ master, contractor, director, boss, chief. *Ant.* employee, servant, agent.

William P. Statsky, *West's Legal Thesaurus/Dictionary: A Resource for the Writer and the Computer Researcher* 273 (1985).

Employee. *n.* A person in the service of another under an express or implied, oral or written contract of hire, in which the employer has the power and the right to control and direct the employee in the material details of how the work is to be performed (the employee acted within the scope of her employment). Servant, salaried worker, agent, wage earner, laborer, jobholder, staff member, hand, apprentice, journeyman, retainer, hireling, lackey, messenger, attendant, subordinate, workman, artisan, mechanic, craftsman, workaholic, breadwinner, helper, aide, henchman, valet, underling, domestic, retainer, white-collar worker, proletarian, hustler, flunky, man Friday, personnel. See also assistant. *Ant.* Employer.

Black's Law Dictionary 545, 475-76 (7th ed. 1999).

employment. 1. The act of employing; the state of being employed. 2. Work for which one has been hired and is being paid by an employer.

. . .

> **employment at will.** Employment that is usu. undertaken without a contract and that may be terminated at any time, by either the employer or the employee, without cause.—Also termed *at-will employment; hiring at will.*

. . .

> "The doctrine of employment at will prescribed that an employee without a contract for a fixed term could be hired or fired for any reason or no reason at all. . . . [The] rule provided that employees categorized as 'at will' had no legal interest in continuing job security. Whereas early American masters had some responsibility to the public as well as to their servants when they turned dependent servants out on the world, under [this] formulation, masters could simply fire employees who had no contracts." Mark A. Rothstein et al., *Employment Law* § 1.4, at 9-10 (1994).

discharge (**dis**-charhrj), *n.* . . . . 7. The firing of an employee.

. . .

> **retaliatory discharge.** A discharge that is made in retaliation for the employee's conduct (such as reporting unlawful activity by the employer to the government) and that clearly violates public policy. • Most states have statutes allowing an employee who is dismissed by retaliatory discharge to recover damages.

. . .

> **wrongful discharge.** A discharge for reasons that are illegal or that violate public policy.

B.   CONTENT AND CONTEXT

As explained in Chapter 1, there are many legal authorities and several research media. After you have developed your research terms and issues, and before you open a book or turn on your computer, you should think carefully about which authorities and media are most likely to be useful, that is, the content and publication context of the authorities you hope to locate.

3.   List and Rank Potential Authorities

Through the first cognitive task, learning and reacting to your client's situation, you should know two important facts: the location of the events and their timing.

From the former, you can deduce potential jurisdictions whose law you should research. Unless you have some specific knowledge of the pertinent law, you should assume that both federal and state law[1] might be involved. You also should assume that statutes, case law, and agency law are involved; if the problem involves litigation, rules of procedure also will be involved.

As to case law, as explained more thoroughly in Chapter 9, most court systems involve trial courts, each with a specific geographic territory; one or more intermediate appeals courts, each with a specific geographic territory (which would be the entire state if there is only one appeals court); and a high court, typically called the "supreme court." Thus, you should discern which geographic judicial districts encompass the location of your client's situation.

Timing is as important as location. In most situations, you will research the state of the law as of today. However, if your client's situation involves a statute, and the statute has changed over time, you will focus on the statutory language in effect as of the date of the events, as explained more thoroughly in Chapter 11.

Although your research and analysis should focus on mandatory primary authority, which is the bull's-eye in your research target, you very likely will research in other authorities as well. Primary authority outside your jurisdiction can be used as persuasive authority; it occupies the middle ring in your research target.

---

1. Local law is not as prevalent.

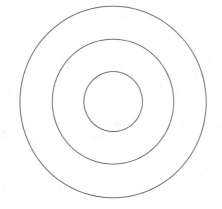

Unless you know a fair amount about the subject already, you most likely will start your research in secondary authority, which occupies the outer ring in your research target. Through secondary authority, you should be able to discern whether federal or state law governs, whether there is a statute involved, whether an agency regulates the situation, etc. You also should acquire an overview of the subject and some references to pertinent primary authorities. As you will see in Unit II, there are many types of secondary authority, each with its distinctive strengths and weaknesses; thus you should think about which type is most likely to be helpful.

For example, in researching the Canoga case, we developed the following list of potential authorities:

- ☐ Bull's-eye authorities:

  Federal law
  - federal statutes
  - U.S. Supreme Court cases
  - Tenth Circuit cases
  - District of New Mexico cases
  - agency regulations and decisions
  - no rules of procedure (no litigation yet)

  New Mexico law
  - New Mexico statutes
  - New Mexico Supreme Court cases
  - New Mexico Court of Appeals cases
  - New Mexico trial court cases, if available
  - agency regulations and decisions
  - no rules of procedure (no litigation yet)

- ☐ Middle-ring authorities: other primary authorities, e.g., cases from other states
- ☐ Outer-ring authorities: an encyclopedia or treatise for general principles, periodical articles for recent legal developments regarding smoking bans by employers and background information on nonlegal aspects of smoking

4.   Assess Available Sources

Any particular authority may well be available in multiple sources, and you may have paper as well as electronic sources to choose from. You should make your choice based on the following important factors:

Scope of coverage: Does the source have as full a range of the authority as you need? For example, as to New Mexico case law, you would hope to find not only New Mexico Supreme Court cases but also important cases from the court of appeals.

Time period—retrospective and recent: Does the source go back far enough to encompass what you need? And does it have very recent material? For example, a source containing cases from 1995 forward very likely is not sufficiently retrospective, and a case law source published in 2000 and not updated thereafter is not by itself recent enough.

Credibility: Is the source sufficiently credible that you could cite it to a court, should the situation develop into litigation? As you will learn in later chapters, for every type of authority, there are well-regarded sources that you can use with confidence, because they have a strong track record and are published by well-regarded companies or organizations. For example, as you will see in Chapter 9, the following are all credible sources of New Mexico case law: an official court website; West case reporters; and LexisNexis, Westlaw, and Loislaw databases.

Ease and efficacy of access: Given limited time and energy, can you reasonably quickly identify both the source and pertinent passages within the source, without needing to work through extraneous passages? For example, a website that posts cases as they are published but does not provide an index or permit searching for key words is not very accessible. By contrast, West's reporter system—a set of paper case reporters accompanied by a sophisticated digest (a well-organized compilation of short descriptions of many cases)—is quite accessible.

Ease and efficacy of reading and retention: Given limited time and energy, can you reasonably quickly peruse what you need to peruse, scan what you need to scan, and obtain a copy of the important passages? In broad terms, paper and electronic sources have different strengths and weaknesses here. Many people find paper sources easier to look at for long periods of time, it is easier to look at an array of paper sources, and it is easier to scan nearby passages in the same paper source. However, it is easier to move from one authority to another in electronic sources that employ links. You may have to look at more than one volume to find up-to-date information in a paper source, whereas many electronic sources cumulate older and more recent information into one document. You will need to photocopy important passages in a paper source, whereas generally you can download or print pertinent passages from an electronic source.

Cost: Given your client's financial resources, how can you accomplish what you need to accomplish at a reasonably low price? Obviously, your bill will depend in large part on how much time you spend, which is a function of the source's ease and efficacy of access, reading, and retention, described above. You also should be aware of the cost of the source itself. Law offices expend considerable money on books themselves, space for books, and maintenance of the collection, although you will not incur these costs if you research in a law school or public library. Beyond the cost of an Internet service provider, the costs of electronic sources vary considerably:

- ☐ An electronic source can be free, most typically if it is a government website.
- ☐ An electronic source may be bought by subscription, e.g., the office pays a monthly fee for access to Loislaw.
- ☐ An electronic source may be purchased on a per-use basis, e.g., a lawyer uses a specialized LexisNexis or Westlaw database not covered by a subscription.

You must understand these cost structures as well as the value of your time as you assess the cost of any source.

Often, you will need to compare two or more available sources for the same authority. You may find it helpful to fill in a chart, with the factors in the left-hand column and the sources in the top row. If there is no perfect source for secondary authority, this may not be a significant concern. However, if there is no perfect source for primary authority, you may well need to use two or more sources, each with different strengths. For example, often you will research case law in paper reporters and then use an electronic service to bring your research up to date.

	Source A	Source B	Source C
coverage			
time			
credibility			
access			
retention and reading			
cost			

C. CONSULTATION AND CREATIVITY

Once you have thoroughly analyzed both your client's situation and the legal authorities and sources to use in your research, you are ready to work with the sources. This entails locating pertinent passages within a source, carefully reading those passages, and following up on those passages.

Sometimes you will find an authority that clearly and precisely addresses your client's situation and provides an indisputable answer. When this happens, lawyers say that the authority is "on all fours."[2] Much more often, you will find an authority that quite clearly but less precisely addresses your client's

---

2. We are not sure of the origins of this phrase. The allusion may be to the four legs of a horse or other animal or to the four sides of a brick.

situation and thus provides guidance but not an indisputable answer. When this happens, lawyers say that the authority is "on point." Thus, most often, legal research is similar to consultation with an expert—the expert provides useful information, but you must still connect that information to your situation. On occasion, you will find little authority on point, and you will have to work with what you do find to, in essence, create a probable rule to govern your client's situation. Then especially, creativity is a very important aspect of legal research.

5.   Use Your Terms and Issues to Locate Pertinent Passages

Success in the task of locating pertinent documents and passages is measured by two criteria, often associated with electronic research but equally applicable to paper research:

☐   *recall,* that is, identification of all pertinent passages within a source, and
☐   *precision,* that is, avoidance of nonpertinent passages.

Hence the image for this task is a double-square diagram: The larger square represents all the passages in the source that might be identified. P stands for pertinent passages, X for nonpertinent passages. The smaller square surrounds the passages actually identified. Note that the research depicted in our diagram captures nearly all of the Ps; that is, it satisfies the recall criterion fairly well. Note also that the research depicted captures quite a few Xs; that is, it is not as successful from a precision standpoint.

Every source you use for legal research, whether a single issue of a legal periodical or a large multifaceted database, has means of access, that is, ways to use your research terms to locate pertinent passages within the source. The first time you work with a source, you should familiarize yourself with its means of access; there are likely to be several. The following discussion describes the most common means of access employed in legal research, with examples drawn from paper encyclopedias and legal periodicals in electronic sources; you will find additional details and variations, source by source, throughout Units II through VI.

The medium and publication pattern of a source relate closely to the means of access it affords. Electronic sources permit you to use search methods typically not available in paper sources, such as searching for key words within the documents in a database. As for publication pattern, consider how a journal is published compared to an encyclopedia: A journal is published periodically, for example, monthly or quarterly, and the contents of an issue are not related to each other. An encyclopedia is published as a set, and there is an overarching organizational scheme. In general, to research in a periodically published source, you will need an external finding tool. In general, when you research in a highly organized source, you will use the source's own index and table of contents.

As you consider the means of access for a source, keep in mind how much you already know about the law pertinent to your client's situation. Some means of access work well when you know fairly little; others are and should be used only when you already are fairly to very knowledgeable about the legal subject.

Options primarily associated with paper sources. Consider the following: You are researching in a legal encyclopedia, in a book, seeking information about the Canoga situation at the beginning of your research process. Two good options are to use a table of contents or an index.

These options have advantages and disadvantages. On one hand, the authors developed both a set of fairly standard terms for the concepts covered in the source and internal finding tools, such as the table of contents and the index, to help you learn and use their terms. Hence, once you discern the authors' terms, you can easily locate and understand pertinent passages. On the other hand, your research will succeed only if you can tap into the authors' vocabulary. The vocabulary can be idiosyncratic to the source, or it can become stale if it does not evolve as concepts and usage evolve. For example, the terms *master* and *servant* have been used for *employer* and *employee;* if a source continues to use this terminology and you do not think of it, you may not locate pertinent passages.

Many sources have overall **tables of contents,** which list the main topics in the order they appear in the source. See Illustration 2-3 (at page 43). The organizing principle probably will be topical; some sources are organized alphabetically. You should skim the list of topics, looking for entries that correspond to or are similar to your research terms. Many sources also have detailed tables of contents, which list the sections within a topic. See Illustration 2-4 (at page 44). You should skim the detailed table of contents for two purposes: to get a sense of the topic's logical structure and to identify the most pertinent sections.

In addition, many legal sources have an **index,** an alphabetical list of covered subjects with references to where each subject is discussed. Highly organized sources, such as encyclopedias, have their own indexes.[3] Legal indexes typically are long and complex, with multiple minor subjects and

3. Some finding tools operate as an index for a set of periodically published sources, such as an index for legal periodicals.

cross-references to other subjects. See Illustration 2-5 (at page 45). Your task is to look for various major and minor subjects that correspond to or are similar to your research terms. Furthermore, some legal indexes, such as an encyclopedia's index, are updated from time to time, so you should take care to use the most current index.

Assume now that you know a bit about the law governing your topic; more precisely, you know of an important primary authority. Many legal sources include **tables of authorities** for specific types of authorities discussed therein, such as cases or statutes. See Illustration 2-6 (at page 46). You can consult such a table, using the name or citation of the known authority as your research term, and learn where the source discusses that authority.

When we researched the Canoga situation, we found the following in the alphabetical list of topics (the table of abbreviations) in the encyclopedia *American Jurisprudence 2d* (Am. Jur. 2d): Contracts, Employment Relationship, Job Discrimination, and Wrongful Discharge. See Illustration 2-3 (at page 43). Skimming the detailed table of contents for the Wrongful Discharge topic, we located a general discussion of employee handbooks in sections 22 through 24. See Illustration 2-4 (at page 44). Am. Jur. 2d also has an extensive index; the Wrongful Discharge listing runs fourteen pages. Illustration 2-5 (at page 45) is one page from that listing. If, when we were researching the Canoga situation, a colleague had alerted us to a federal statute titled the Americans with Disabilities Act, we could look up that statute in an Am. Jur. 2d statutes table. See Illustration 2-6 (at page 46).

Options available in electronic sources. The three options discussed above can be used in some electronic sources as well. For example, you can scan the table of contents of an electronically published encyclopedia. By contrast, the options discussed below are not available in paper sources because the options depend on the technology afforded by computers.

Consider the following: You are researching in legal periodicals by use of an electronic source, seeking information about the Canoga situation, fairly early in your research process. When you research in electronic sources, you can formulate your own search for pertinent passages. This involves keying in sentences, words, or characters; the computer scans the selected database and retrieves documents meeting the requirements of your search.

This process has advantages and disadvantages. On one hand, you can customize a search, using words tailored to your research problem; if those words are distinctive enough, you should obtain excellent results. Because computers process searches quickly, such research can be time-efficient. On the other hand, if the words in your search are very common, the computer may retrieve too many documents to review. Even in a more manageable set of retrieved documents, you may well find nonpertinent documents. For example, if you searched for documents containing *smoke* and *workplace,* an article about health insurance coverage of lung cancer could meet the requirements of the search. Conversely, you may fail to retrieve articles that are pertinent, because they do not use the words you have identified. For example, a pertinent article may refer to *worksite* instead of *workplace.*

In many situations, you can achieve success through skillful use of various search-drafting options. The options are fairly standard across most electronic

ILLUSTRATION 2-3   Overall Table of Contents (Table of Abbreviations), from *American Jurisprudence 2d* (paper source)

TABLE OF ABBREVIATIONS

Summary	Summary Judgment
Sundays	Sundays and Holidays
Support	Support of Persons
Suretyship	Suretyship
Taxation	Taxation
Taxpayers	Taxpayers' Actions
Telecomm	Telecommunications
Tender	Tender
Time	Time
Topicabbrev	Topic
Torts	Torts
Trademark	Trademarks and Tradenames
Treaties	Treaties
Trespass	Trespass
Trial	Trial
Trusts	Trusts
Unemploy	Unemployment Compensation
Unitedsts	United States
Vagrancy	Vagrancy
Vendor	Vendor and Purchaser
Venue	Venue
Veterans	Veterans and Veterans Laws
Veterinar	Veterinarians
War	War
Warehouse	Warehouses
Waste	Waste
Waterco	Waterworks and Water Companies
Waters	Waters
Weapons	Weapons and Firearms
Weights	Weights and Measures
Welfare	Welfare Laws
Wharves	Wharves
Wills	Wills
Witn	Witnesses
Workers	Workers' Compensation
Wrongdisc	Wrongful Discharge
Zoning	Zoning and Planning

| ILLUSTRATION 2-4 | Detailed Table of Contents, from *American Jurisprudence 2d* (paper source) |

ILLUSTRATION 2-5

Index,
from *American Jurisprudence 2d* (paper source)

AMERICAN JURISPRUDENCE 2d

WRONGFUL DISCHARGE—Cont'd
Employment contracts—Cont'd
 ties, **WrongDisc** § 49
 good cause, discharge only for,
  WrongDisc § 46, 47
 grievances, **WrongDisc** § 44
 handbooks and manuals, below
 industry practices, **WrongDisc** § 40
 inference of contractual rights from
  employer representations, **WrongDisc**
  § 21
 intent, **WrongDisc** § 12
 job security, **WrongDisc** § 29
 layoff policies, **WrongDisc** § 39
 modification of implied contracts,
  WrongDisc § 16-20
 mutual assent, below
 oral promises, **WrongDisc** § 29
 pensions and retirement, **WrongDisc**
  § 37
 performance, below
 periodic compensation terms,
  WrongDisc § 31
 permanent employment, **WrongDisc**
  § 29
 probationary period, **WrongDisc** § 33
 progressive discipline, **WrongDisc** § 43
 promises, **WrongDisc** § 29
 promissory estoppel, **WrongDisc** § 15
 raises, **WrongDisc** § 34
 reliance, below
 representations of employers,
  WrongDisc § 21-52
 seniority, **WrongDisc** § 39
 steady employment, **WrongDisc** § 29
 stock options, below
 successor employers, **WrongDisc** § 20
 time, **WrongDisc** § 13
 undistributed manuals, **WrongDisc** § 24
 unilateral contract theory, **WrongDisc**
  § 8
 unilateral modification, **WrongDisc** § 17
Endangerment. Health and safety, endangering, below
Environmental protection
 illegal acts, refusal to commit,
  WrongDisc § 114
 preemption by federal law, **WrongDisc**
  § 201
Equitable relief
 generally, **WrongDisc** § 229-232
 injunctions, **WrongDisc** § 232
 offer of reinstatement as limiting
  liability, **WrongDisc** § 231
 reinstatement, **WrongDisc** § 230, 231
 specific performance, **WrongDisc** § 229
Ethics
 professional ethics, refusal to violate,
  WrongDisc § 117
 public policy exception to at will
  employment, **WrongDisc** § 64
Evidence
 burden of proof, **WrongDisc** § 224
 consideration, **WrongDisc** § 11
 lost earnings, proof of entitlement to,
  WrongDisc § 242
 order of proof, **WrongDisc** § 224

WRONGFUL DISCHARGE—Cont'd
Evidence—Cont'd
 standard of proof, **WrongDisc** § 225
 workers' compensation, **WrongDisc**
  § 96
Exhaustion of remedies, **WrongDisc** § 178
Expenses resulting from discharge, damages
 for, **WrongDisc** § 238
Fair dealing. Good faith and fair dealing, covenants of, below
Fair treatment of employees, **WrongDisc**
 § 30
Falsification
 publicity placing employee in false light,
  action for, **WrongDisc** § 167
 refusal to falsify records, discharge for,
  WrongDisc § 109
Federal courts
 diversity jurisdiction, **WrongDisc** § 212
 pendent jurisdiction, **WrongDisc** § 213,
  214
 removal of actions from state court,
  WrongDisc § 215
Fellow employee, marriage to, **WrongDisc**
 § 141
Fiduciary relationship, intentional infliction
 of emotional distress, **WrongDisc** § 149
Fighting on employer's premises,
 WrongDisc § 136
Financial condition
 defenses, **WrongDisc** § 181
 whistleblowing, **WrongDisc** § 131-134
First Amendment, **WrongDisc** § 79, 80
Forfeiture of stock rights, **WrongDisc** § 74
Forgoing other employment opportunities,
 WrongDisc § 49
Former job, giving up, **WrongDisc** § 48
Fraud and deceit
 generally, **WrongDisc** § 171-175
 benefit to employer, **WrongDisc** § 172
 future events, misrepresentation as to,
  WrongDisc § 173
 intent, **WrongDisc** § 172
 permanence of employment, **WrongDisc**
  § 174
Freedom of speech, **WrongDisc** § 79, 80
Future earnings, **WrongDisc** § 235
Future events, misrepresentation as to,
 WrongDisc § 173
Garnishment, **WrongDisc** § 137
Good cause
 defense of good cause, **WrongDisc**
  § 179, 180
 employment contracts, **WrongDisc** § 46,
  47
 standard for evaluating employer
  justification, **WrongDisc** § 180
Good faith and fair dealing, covenants of
 generally, **WrongDisc** § 65-77
 breach of covenant, generally,
  WrongDisc § 71
 compensation, **WrongDisc** § 73-75
 contract actions, **WrongDisc** § 67
 defense of bad faith, **WrongDisc** § 184

WRONGFUL DISCHARGE—Cont'd
Good faith and fair dealing, covenants of
 —Cont'd
 definitions, **WrongDisc** § 70
 employee benefits, **WrongDisc** § 73-75
 handbook rules, violations of,
  WrongDisc § 72
 implied covenants, **WrongDisc** § 67
 length of service, **WrongDisc** § 76
 public policy, **WrongDisc** § 68
 punitive damages, **WrongDisc** § 245
 retaliatory discharge, **WrongDisc** § 77
 scope of duty, **WrongDisc** § 69
 stock rights, forfeiture of, **WrongDisc**
  § 74
 torts, **WrongDisc** § 67
Governing law, **WrongDisc** § 209, 210
Government employees. Public officers and
 employees, below
Grievances, discipline and discharge
 procedures, **WrongDisc** § 44
Handbooks and manuals
 generally, **WrongDisc** § 22-24
 good faith and fair dealing, violations of
  handbook rules, **WrongDisc** § 72
 not part of employment contracts,
  WrongDisc § 23
 undistributed manuals, **WrongDisc** § 24
Health and safety, endangering
 illegal acts, refusal to commit,
  WrongDisc § 112, 113
 preemption by federal law, **WrongDisc**
  § 201
 whistleblowing, **WrongDisc** § 128-130
Health problems, discharge for
 generally, **WrongDisc** § 138
 drug use, **WrongDisc** § 139
Hiring attorney, discharge for, **WrongDisc**
 § 91
Husband and wife, marriage to coworker or
 employee of competitor, **WrongDisc** § 141
Illegal acts, refusal to commit
 generally, **WrongDisc** § 107-116
 antitrust violations, **WrongDisc** § 110,
  111
 endangering health and safety,
  WrongDisc § 112, 113
 environmental protection, **WrongDisc**
  § 114
 health and safety, endangering,
  WrongDisc § 112, 113
 NRC regulations, **WrongDisc** § 113
 Occupational Safety and Health Act
  (OSHA), **WrongDisc** § 113
 perjury, **WrongDisc** § 108
 price fixing, **WrongDisc** § 110, 111
 professional ethics, refusal to violate,
  WrongDisc § 117
 records, falsifying, **WrongDisc** § 109
 safety, endangering, **WrongDisc** § 112,
  113
 sexual advances, refusal of, **WrongDisc**
  § 115
Illegal conduct, discharge for, **WrongDisc**
 § 135

For assistance using this Index, call 1-800-328-4880

ILLUSTRATION 2-6   Table of Authorities,
from *American Jurisprudence 2d* (paper source)

AMERICAN JURISPRUDENCE

SECOND EDITION

POPULAR NAMES TABLE

ABSENCE AS EVIDENCE OF DEATH AND ABSENTEES' PROPERTY ACT
Main Treatment, Death § 554

ACKNOWLEDGEMENT ACT
Main Treatment, Acknowl § 12 et seq.

ACT FOR PROOF OF BUSINESS TRANSACTIONS
Main Treatment, Evid § 1294 et seq.

ACT FOR SIMPLIFICATION OF FIDUCIARY SECURITY TRANSFERS
Main Treatment, Commercial § 93

ACT ON INTERSTATE COMPROMISE
Main Treatment, Inheritnce § 123

ACT ON PATERNITY
Main Treatment, Parent § 13

ACT TO SECURE ATTENDANCE OF WITNESSES FROM WITHOUT STATE IN CRIMINAL PROCEEDINGS
Main Treatment, Witn § 6, 30, 34-49

ADMINISTRATIVE DISPUTE RESOLUTION ACT
Main Treatment, AdminLaw § 395 et seq.; AltDisp § 39

ADMINISTRATIVE PROCEDURE ACTS
Main Treatment, AdminLaw § 15-17, 25

ADMIRALTY JURISDICTION EXTENSION ACT
Main Treatment, Admiralty § 61-63

ADOPTION ACT
Main Treatment, Adoption § 14, 20

ADOPTION ASSISTANCE AND CHILD WELFARE ACT
Main Treatment, Adoption § 34-39

ADOPTION REFORM ACT
Main Treatment, Adoption § 40-42

ADVISORY COMMITTEE ACT
Main Treatment, FOIA § 35

AFRICAN ELEPHANT CONSERVATION ACT
Main Treatment, CustomsDu § 379

AGE DISCRIMINATION IN EMPLOYMENT ACT
Main Treatment, AlterDisp § 15, 48; CivilRights § 226-228; ConstLaw § 770; JobDiscrim § 16, 17, 37, 38; Judges § 15; WrongDisc § 210, 223, 250

AGRICULTURAL ADJUSTMENT AND MARKETING ACTS
Main Treatment, Agric § 31 et seq.; Markets § 18 et seq.

AGRICULTURAL MARKETING AGREEMENT ACT
Main Treatment, Agric § 31; Markets § 22, 27

AID TO FAMILIES WITH DEPENDENT CHILDREN
Main Treatment, Welfare § 6-24

AIRLINE DEREGULATION ACT
Main Treatment, Aviation § 14 et seq.

AIRPORT DEVELOPMENT ACT
Main Treatment, Aviation § 93-95

ALASKA NATIVE REORGANIZATION ACT
Main Treatment, Indians § 4

ALASKA NATIVE TOWNSITE ACT
Main Treatment, Indians § 83

ALASKAN NATIVE CLAIMS SETTLEMENT ACT
Main Treatment, Indians § 108-110

ALIEN TORT CLAIMS ACT
Main Treatment, Aliens § 2583, 2584

ALL POWERS CLAUSE
Main Treatment, Powers § 140, 151

ALL WRITS ACT
Main Treatment, AdminLaw § 554-557; Decljuds § 263; Exec § 29; Inj § 217; Pat § 762; Prohib § 9

AMERICANS WITH DISABILITIES ACT
Main Treatment, JobDiscrim § 18, 19, 30, 37, 38

ANATOMICAL GIFT ACT
Main Treatment, DeadBodies § 20

ANCILLARY ADMINISTRATION OF ESTATES ACT
Main Treatment, Executors § 1169

ANIMAL WELFARE ACT
Main Treatment, Animals § 36-40

ANTI-CAR THEFT ACT
Main Treatment, Autos § 412

ANTI-GAMBLING ACT
Main Treatment, Gambl § 32, 36, 121 et seq.

For assistance using this index, call 1-800-328-4880   **423**

services, although the expression varies from service to service. For simplicity, the examples in this section reflect the protocols of LexisNexis and Westlaw.

When your knowledge of the law is fairly limited or general, you may want to start with a **natural-language search,** which entails keying in a question or statement in ordinary English. In response to a natural-language search, a computer typically retrieves a prespecified number of documents, identified through application of a semantic-statistical algorithm that, among other steps, ranks your words for distinctiveness and assesses the prevalence of your search words in the many documents in the database you selected. For example, a natural-language search for the smoking issue in the Canoga situation might be:

```
Can an employer prohibit an employee from smoking
during non-working hours?
```

The service may provide a thesaurus to help you identify alternatives for the major words in your question. Some services permit you to refine a natural-language search by adding in your own alternative terms, designating a phrase (the program may do this for your common phrases), requiring a specific word, or excluding a specific word. To the extent you use these options, your natural-language search will come to resemble a Boolean search.

Once you have a fairly sound idea of the words that a writer probably would use to discuss the topic you are researching, you may use a **Boolean,**[4] **or terms-and-connectors, search.** Boolean searches can be simple or rather intricate. Exhibit 2.1 lists the major steps in constructing a Boolean search along with LexisNexis and Westlaw protocols for each step.

| EXHIBIT 2.1 | Boolean Search Tasks and Protocols |

Task	LexisNexis Protocol	Westlaw Protocol
Single Term	! and * root expanders	! and * root expanders
Phrase	space between words	" " around words
Multiple Terms for the Same Concept	or	space
Exclusion of Nonpertinent Usage	and not	%
Multiple-Concept Search	/n and pre/n /s /p and	/n and +n /s and + s /p and +p &

4. The name refers to a nineteenth-century mathematician.

One simple option is to enter one **single-word term** such as *smoking*. You thereby ask the computer to retrieve any document containing that term. The word you select may itself be or contain a root word. For example, *smoking* contains the root *smok*, used not only in *smoking*, but also in *smoke*, *smoker* (and its plural and possessives), *smokes*, etc. Some services automatically retrieve standard variations of search words, such as plurals and possessives. To search for variations that the service does not automatically retrieve, you may use root expanders. For example, on both LexisNexis and Westlaw:

smok!   → will retrieve any word starting with *smok*.
smok***   → will retrieve any word starting with *smok* and
                          continuing for up to three letters.
mari*uana → will retrieve *marijuana* and *marihuana*.

Some concepts are stated not with single words, but with **phrases.** You should be very careful in searching for phrases. Some phrases can be inverted or stated in slightly different terms. Furthermore, some phrases might be written with or without hyphens. Finally, you should be sure you are entering the phrase as a phrase, rather than as a set of distinct search words. For example, on Westlaw:

"non-working hours"   → will retrieve *non-working hours* or
                                           non working hours or *nonworking*
                                           hours.

LexisNexis requires two forms—non-working and nonworking—and does not require the quotation marks.

Often, you will want to search for **multiple terms for the same concept** by use of synonyms, antonyms, or broader or narrower terms. Enter the terms, joined by the symbol for the connector *or.* For example, on LexisNexis:

cigarette or tobacco → will retrieve documents containing
                                         cigarette or *tobacco* or both.

See Exhibit 2.2, in which the shaded area represents the retrieved documents.

On occasion, you will be aware that one of your search words has a distinct **nonpertinent usage.** Sometimes you can exclude documents in which the nonpertinent usage appears by asking the computer to reject documents with some other word associated with the nonpertinent usage. You should use such a search only when you are quite certain that documents with the excluded term really are not pertinent. For example, on LexisNexis:

smok! and not → will retrieve documents that both *do* contain
marijuana   variants of *smoke* and do *not* contain *marijuana*.

Again, see Exhibit 2.2.

If several concepts are likely to appear together, you should consider a **multiple-concept search.** Such a search is more focused than a single-concept search and hence more efficient. However, you should take care not to combine so many concepts that you narrow your search too much and inadvertently exclude pertinent documents.

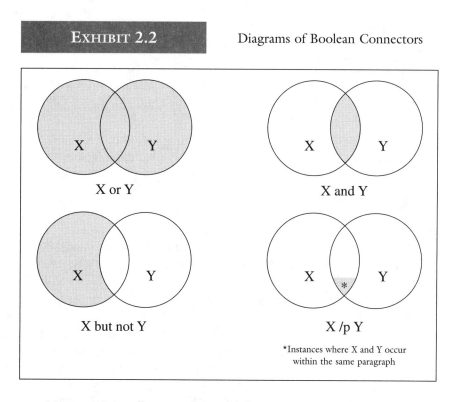

EXHIBIT 2.2   Diagrams of Boolean Connectors

X or Y

X and Y

X but not Y

X /p Y

*Instances where X and Y occur
within the same paragraph

Most services offer several types of connectors for multiple-concept searches. The broadest is the connector signifying *and,* which requires that the joined terms appear in the same document. Often you will prefer a tighter connector, linking concepts in the same sentence, paragraph, or fixed number of words. In the rare instances when you are sure that one concept will precede another, you can use a sequencing connector. As examples, consider the following LexisNexis searches:

`smok! and workplace`	→	Both must appear anywhere in the document.
`smok! /p workplace`	→	Both must appear in the same paragraph.
`smok! /s workplace`	→	Both must appear in the same sentence.
`smok! /20 workplace`	→	Both must appear within twenty words of each other.
`smok! pre/20 workplace`	→	Both must appear within twenty words of each other, *smok!* first.

Again, see Exhibit 2.2. Be sure you understand exactly how each connector works; for example, you should know whether the service counts insignificant words (such as articles or prepositions) when processing a numerical search.

You also should know the service's order of operations, that is, the order in which the computer will process multiple connectors. LexisNexis and Westlaw prioritize the commonly used connectors similarly:

☐ starting with phrases and *or;*
☐ moving through numerical, sentence, paragraph, and *and;*
☐ concluding with *not.*

Some services permit you to create your own order of operations. Placing search words and a connector within parentheses typically places a priority on that operation. For example:

```
discharg!
(terminat!
/3 employ!)
```

→ The computer will search first for variants of *terminat* within three words of variants of *employ,* then search for documents containing variants of *discharg.*

Without the parentheses, the computer would search for variants of *discharg* or *terminat* within three words of a variant of *employ.*

Here is an example of a search involving multiple concepts and connectors that we ran, while researching the Canoga case, in a LexisNexis database of periodical articles:

```
priva! /p
smok! /s
off-duty or
non-working or
nonworking
```

→ The computer will
(1) look first for *off-duty, off duty, non working, non-working,* or *nonworking;*
(2) find one or more of those words in the same sentence as some form of *smok;*
(3) then find that sentence within the same paragraph as some form of *priva.*

The citation list that resulted from that search is excerpted in Illustration 2-7 (at pages 52–53).

Quite often you will need to edit your initial search. The number of pertinent documents to expect from a search varies, from a good handful or two of cases, for example, to one or two statutory sections of rules of procedure. If your search does not yield the number of pertinent documents you expect, first review the protocols for the service you are using and the search you have written; correct any drafting errors. Then consider the following common remedies for common defects:

☐ Too many documents retrieved: Use tighter connectors, e.g., switch from and to /p. Add an additional term. Use less common words for a concept. Limit your search to a component of a document (which, in effect, shrinks the database to a more manageable size). Add a date restriction.

☐ Too few documents retrieved: Use looser connectors, e.g., switch from /p to and. Delete a term. Truncate a term by using root expanders. Use alternative words for a concept; check the thesaurus for ideas.

☐ Too many inapt documents retrieved: Consider excluding a term associated with the inapt documents.

Note that a natural-language search generally will not retrieve the same documents as a Boolean search. In response to a natural-language search, the computer will retrieve the specified number of documents, whether they fit the search very well or only minimally. In response to a Boolean search, the computer will retrieve all documents meeting the requirements, however few or many that will be. Hence, it often is wise to run more than one search.

Once you have a list of documents in response to your search, you will want to sift them as efficiently as possible. A mere citation list generally is not particularly revealing. You can learn more about each document if you view the passages in which the search terms are located. Another option is to view the document page by page with the search terms highlighted; often the first few paragraphs of a document summarize its content.

Sometimes, you will have sufficient knowledge to run a highly tailored search. By adding a date restriction, you may limit the search to documents dating to a specified time period. In addition, you may confine your search to a particular component of a document; this is useful when a document has standard components and your words very likely would appear in a specific part. For example, if when we were researching the Canoga situation, a colleague had referred us to a periodical article written during the 1990s with the words *blowing smoke* in the title, we would enter the following search:

```
title (blowing smoke) and date aft 1989 on LexisNexis
ti("blowing smoke") & da(aft 1989) on Westlaw.
```

In an even more focused search, if you already know the citation of a pertinent authority, you would use the feature that simply pulls up a known document. For example, if you wanted a copy of the article appearing in volume 86 of the *Georgetown Law Journal* starting at page 783, you would type in:

```
86 geo l j 783 in LexisNexis' get-a-document program
86 geolj 783 in Westlaw's find program.
```

Once you identify and obtain a document, you will need to decide how to read and retain it. Typically, your online options will include reading the document on the screen, printing it, downloading it to a disk or other file, e-mailing it to yourself, and reading it in a paper version. There is no single wise choice. If the document is significant, you will want a copy of one sort or another; legal analysis entails very scrupulous attention to the wording of nearly any authority. You should carefully consider the costs associated with each option as well as your personal media preferences.[5]

5. All too often, law students become hooked on expensive online services, such as LexisNexis and Westlaw, during law school when there is no direct out-of-pocket cost to the student. It is quite wonderful to build expertise on these services during law school without having to pay for them—but you should be very mindful of the costs for the service once you are in practice. Excessive and expensive overreliance on LexisNexis and Westlaw by law clerks and new lawyers is a very common complaint of experienced lawyers; the ability to research cost-effectively in paper along with judicious use of online services is highly valued.

ILLUSTRATION 2-7	Citation List, from Search in LexisNexis Periodicals Database (electronic source)

Search - 25 Results - priva! /p smok! /s off-duty or non-working or nonworking   Page 1 of 3

Source: Legal > / . . . / > **US & Canadian Law Reviews, Combined** ⓘ
Terms: **priva! /p smok! /s off-duty or non-working or nonworking** (Edit Search)

☞ Select for FOCUS™ or Delivery

☐   1. Copyright (c) 1997 The American Business Law Association, Inc. American Business Law Journal, Fall, 1997, 35 Am. Bus. L.J. 47, 35039 words, ARTICLE: IT'S MY LIFE - LEAVE ME ALONE: OFF THE-JOB EMPLOYEE ASSOCIATIONAL PRIVACY RIGHTS, TERRY MOREHEAD DWORKIN *
... Rothstein, Refusing to Employ **Smokers:** Good Public Health or ...
... Hansen, Second-Hand **Smoke** Suit, A.B.A. J., ...
... Profits Up in **Smoke?** Bus. & Soc. Rev., ...
... employers discriminated against **off-duty smokers.** Thomas W. Sculco, ...
... Marcia Staimer, Do Workers Have **Private** Lives?, USA Today, ...
... 52; Bill Koenig, **Privacy** at work: A '90s ...

☐   2. Copyright (c) 1995 Boston College Law School Boston College Law Review, September, 1995, 36 B.C. L. Rev 1089, 15750 words, NOTE: A SPARK IN THE BATTLE BETWEEN SMOKERS AND NONSMOKERS: JOHANNESEN V. NEW YORK CITY DEPARTMENT OF HOUSING PRESERVATION & DEVELOPMENT, Kathleen Sablone
... upheld a restriction on **smoking** by employees both on and **off duty** only because it involved the state's ...
... upon firefighters' right to **privacy.** n265 Thus, to the extent that the Fifth ...
... other courts, a **private** employer could probably not ...
... not hiring employees who **smoke** is overly restrictive, and possibly ...

☐   3. Copyright (c) 1992 Case Western Reserve Law Review. Case Western Reserve University, 1992, 42 Case W. Res. 1025, 25421 words, NOTE: Smoking and Parenting: Can They be Adjudged Mutually Exclusive Activities?, VICTORIA L. WENDLING *
... recent intrusions into employees' **private** lives in efforts to ...
... source reports, the limitation of **smoking off-duty** creates a precedent for the **off-duty** regulation of other "bad" ...

☐   4. Copyright (c) 1996 Chicago-Kent College of Law Chicago-Kent Law Review, 1996, 72 Chi.-Kent. L. Rev. 221, 26985 words, THE KENNETH M. PIPER LECTURE: EMPLOYEE PRIVACY, AMERICAN VALUES, AND THE LAW, Matthew W. Finkin *
... but infrequent violations of **privacy** may produce an occasional and ...
... not an applicant was a **smoker.** n108 This is congruent with Westin's ...
... employers the privilege to inquire into **smoking** behavior and to forbid its **off-duty** consumption? A significant ...

☐   5. Copyright (c) 1987 Chicago-Kent College of Law Chicago-Kent Law Review, 1987, 63 Chi.-Kent. L. Rev. 683, 33617 words, ARTICLE: KENNETH M. PIPER LECTURE: DRUG TESTING IN THE WORKPLACE: THE CHALLENGE TO EMPLOYMENT RELATIONS AND EMPLOYMENT LAW, MARK A. ROTHSTEIN *
... state laws restricting **private** sector drug testing ...
... drug testing of certain **private** sector workers. In ...
... tip that the pilot was seen **smoking** marijuana while **off duty.** The pilot brought an action ...

☐   6. Copyright (c) 2000 Center for New York City Law CITYLAW, January / February, 2000, 6 City Law 17, 1745 words, CURRENT DEVELOPMENTS: PUBLIC

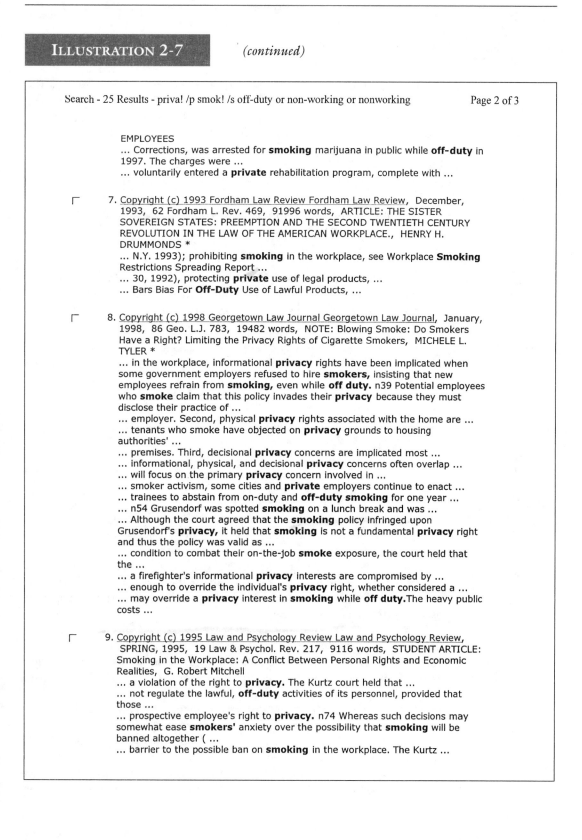

ILLUSTRATION 2-7   *(continued)*

Search - 25 Results - priva! /p smok! /s off-duty or non-working or nonworking   Page 2 of 3

EMPLOYEES
... Corrections, was arrested for **smoking** marijuana in public while **off-duty** in 1997. The charges were ...
... voluntarily entered a **private** rehabilitation program, complete with ...

7. Copyright (c) 1993 Fordham Law Review Fordham Law Review, December, 1993, 62 Fordham L. Rev. 469, 91996 words, ARTICLE: THE SISTER SOVEREIGN STATES: PREEMPTION AND THE SECOND TWENTIETH CENTURY REVOLUTION IN THE LAW OF THE AMERICAN WORKPLACE., HENRY H. DRUMMONDS *
... N.Y. 1993); prohibiting **smoking** in the workplace, see Workplace **Smoking** Restrictions Spreading Report ...
... 30, 1992), protecting **private** use of legal products, ...
... Bars Bias For **Off-Duty** Use of Lawful Products, ...

8. Copyright (c) 1998 Georgetown Law Journal Georgetown Law Journal, January, 1998, 86 Geo. L.J. 783, 19482 words, NOTE: Blowing Smoke: Do Smokers Have a Right? Limiting the Privacy Rights of Cigarette Smokers, MICHELE L. TYLER *
... in the workplace, informational **privacy** rights have been implicated when some government employers refused to hire **smokers,** insisting that new employees refrain from **smoking,** even while **off duty.** n39 Potential employees who **smoke** claim that this policy invades their **privacy** because they must disclose their practice of ...
... employer. Second, physical **privacy** rights associated with the home are ...
... tenants who smoke have objected on **privacy** grounds to housing authorities' ...
... premises. Third, decisional **privacy** concerns are implicated most ...
... informational, physical, and decisional **privacy** concerns often overlap ...
... will focus on the primary **privacy** concern involved in ...
... smoker activism, some cities and **private** employers continue to enact ...
... trainees to abstain from on-duty and **off-duty smoking** for one year ...
... n54 Grusendorf was spotted **smoking** on a lunch break and was ...
... Although the court agreed that the **smoking** policy infringed upon Grusendorf's **privacy,** it held that **smoking** is not a fundamental **privacy** right and thus the policy was valid as ...
... condition to combat their on-the-job **smoke** exposure, the court held that the ...
... a firefighter's informational **privacy** interests are compromised by ...
... enough to override the individual's **privacy** right, whether considered a ...
... may override a **privacy** interest in **smoking** while **off duty.** The heavy public costs ...

9. Copyright (c) 1995 Law and Psychology Review Law and Psychology Review, SPRING, 1995, 19 Law & Psychol. Rev. 217, 9116 words, STUDENT ARTICLE: Smoking in the Workplace: A Conflict Between Personal Rights and Economic Realities, G. Robert Mitchell
... a violation of the right to **privacy.** The Kurtz court held that ...
... not regulate the lawful, **off-duty** activities of its personnel, provided that those ...
... prospective employee's right to **privacy.** n74 Whereas such decisions may somewhat ease **smokers'** anxiety over the possibility that **smoking** will be banned altogether (...
... barrier to the possible ban on **smoking** in the workplace. The Kurtz ...

6.   Study Pertinent Passages

Reading legal authority should be a slow and deliberate process, because nearly every word is significant. Although it generally is useful to skim the passages you have identified to assess whether they are indeed pertinent, you should never rely on a superficial reading of a legal authority. Rather, consider following the SQ3R reading process:

- ☐ *surveying* the source to discern its components and organization,
- ☐ posing *questions* that you think the source may answer,
- ☐ *reading* the source to find the answers,
- ☐ *recording* what you have learned, and
- ☐ *reviewing* by looking over your notes.

The classic formulation of SQ3R uses *reciting* rather than *reviewing;* for difficult and important sources, oral recitation may indeed be helpful. Because this task involves such painstaking work, its symbol is a magnifying glass.

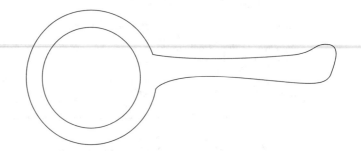

Avoid tempting shortcuts. Many sources include not only the authority itself but also summaries written by the publisher's staff. Focus your attention on the authority itself, not on the summary; rather, use the summary to confirm your understanding. Also read the entire authority, especially primary authority. For example, if you were reading the *Lukoski* case, Illustration 1-1 (at pages 9–12), you would read the footnote and the dissenting opinion as well as the majority opinion.

At the same time, read with your client's situation in mind. Be especially attentive to points that pertain to your client's situation, and sift out those that do not. Focusing too much on truly extraneous points will undermine the cost-effectiveness of your research. For example, you would sift out the cautionary note in the encyclopedia excerpt, Illustration 1-3 (at page 16), because it addresses a situation (a policy statement seeking to amend a written contract) that is not present in the Canoga situation.

As noted above, some legal authority will be on all fours with your client's situation. For example the New Mexico Employee Privacy Act, Illustration 1-2 (at pages 13–14), is on all fours with the Canoga situation. Most legal authorities will be merely on point—both similar to and different than your client's situation. Be sure to notice ways in which an on-point authority diverges from your client's situation. For example, the *Lukoski* case, Illustration 1-1 (at pages 9–12), is on point for the Canoga situation; however, Mr. Lukoski received the handbook well after he started work, whereas Ms. Canoga received her handbook when she was hired.

As you read, be sure to take careful notes and copy, print out, or download significant pertinent passages. The organization of your notes will vary from authority to authority. For example, a set of notes on secondary authority will include what the law is; for some secondary authority, you also will include discussion of policies underlying the law, examples or illustrations that parallel your client's situation, critique of the law, and suggestions for law reform. For primary authorities, you will brief the authority by recording information by category, for example, the facts, procedure, issue, holding (outcome), rule of law, and reasoning in a case (discussed in Chapter 9). Also jot down any ways in which your client's situation and the authority diverge.

In addition, you should record the following information, which will help you to both track your research to date and plan future research:

- ☐ the research terms and means of access you used—both what succeeded and what did not;
- ☐ the means you used to update your research (see task 7 below);
- ☐ the information you need to cite the source properly; and
- ☐ citations from the source you just read to potentially pertinent primary and secondary authority.

Time spent taking meticulous notes is time well spent. If you take meticulous notes, you will avoid backtracking to figure out, for example, whether you used a particular research term in a source or what the date of a source is. Illustration 2-8 (at page 56) is a set of notes on the encyclopedia excerpt, Illustration 1-3 (at pages 15–16).

7.   Research Backwards and Forwards from Major Authorities

Nearly every legal authority you read will be connected to one or more other authorities. For your research to be comprehensive as well as correct, you will need to pursue some of the authorities to which your major authorities are connected. It is useful to think of a timeline, with the date of the authority or source you are reading as the key date. For some major authorities, you must look at authorities written before or after that key date; for others, you may choose whether to do so.

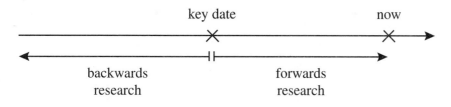

ILLUSTRATION 2-8   Sample Notes on Encyclopedia Excerpt

Am. Jur. 2d—Wrongful Discharge § 22*

Rules

Employee manual may modify employment at will if:

☐   manual is widely distributed
☐   manual contains language evidencing intent to create procedures & justifications w/ objective manifestation of assent creating reasonable reliance by employee
☐   manual contains unequivocal language demonstrating employer's intent to be bound.

Handbook terms are offer for unilateral contract; employee's continuing to work constitutes acceptance & consideration.

Terms & Access

Table of abbreviations → Wrongful Discharge
Table of contents for topic → §§ 22-23

Updating

2003 main volume

Citation Info

82 Am. Jur. 2d *Wrongful Discharge* § 22 (2003).

References

Trujillo v. Northern Rio Arriba Elec. Co-op, Inc., 41 P.3d 333, NMSC 2001
34 Idaho Law Review 283 (1999)
West key number Master and Servant 4
(also persuasive cases)

*These notes cover only section 22; you also would read and takes notes on section 23, which addresses when a handbook is not a contract.

Lawyers tend to use the following terms in discussing this aspect of legal research:

- ☐ The "citing authority" is the authority you are currently reading. Within that authority are references to older authorities.
- ☐ The "cited authority" is the one referred to in the authority you are currently reading.

For example, if you were reading the encyclopedia excerpt in Illustration 1-3 (at pages 15–16), the encyclopedia is the *citing* authority. The cases listed in the encyclopedia's footnotes are the *cited* authorities.

In many situations, you should work backwards in time, especially from a major authority. That is, you should locate and read the most important authorities referred to in the authority at hand. For example, if a case refers to a statute in a pertinent passage, you must read that statute. If an encyclopedia refers to ten cases in support of a pertinent proposition, you probably should read any from your jurisdiction, but you probably can forego reading the cases from other jurisdictions. For example, you would read the *Trujillo* case cited in footnote 5 of the encyclopedia excerpt, Illustration 1-3 (at page 16), because it is a New Mexico case, but you probably would not read the others.

In addition, for your research to be current, you must research forward in time to be sure that a primary authority continues to be good law before you rely on it. For example, if you were reading *Lukoski,* a 1988 case from the New Mexico Supreme Court, in mid-2003, you would need to check that it has not been overruled by a more recent case; we use the term "citing" for this task. If you were reading the Employee Privacy Act in a source published in 2000, you would need to check that the New Mexico legislature has not amended that statute since then. Note that the validity of a primary authority can be affected by an authority of a different sort; for example, a statute may supplant a case, and a case may render a statute unconstitutional. These topics are discussed in detail in Chapter 9 (case law) and Chapter 11 (statutes).

Similarly, you may want to check the influence of a secondary authority that is important to your analysis. For example, if you find a particularly useful point in a periodical article, you may want to determine whether that article has been referred to in any cases since its publication.

Because of the importance of currency in legal research, there are many tools that update sources, including pocket parts, supplementary pamphlets, replacement pages, advance sheets, legislative services, and citators. You will learn about these throughout this text.

On occasion, you will find that a legal authority loses authoritativeness not so much because of subsequent legal developments but because of new knowledge developed outside the law or changes in public policy. For example, advances in medical research regarding the effects of second-hand smoke triggered prohibitions on workplace smoking; a case predating those medical advances would be less authoritative now than it was before those advances.

D. CLOSURE

8. Stop Researching

There is no magic test for when you should stop researching. Different research projects will require different amounts of time, based on your prior knowledge of the subject, the difficulty of the problem, the occasion for the research (you should spend less time for quick advice before a client acts than for an appeal before the highest court), and the client's resources. You may find the following four-step process useful:

(1) Consider quitting when you are seeing the same authorities cited and the same legal rules stated over and over again. Legal research, like many activities, follows the principle of diminishing returns: After a certain point, each additional hour of effort brings fewer and fewer rewards. Hence the symbol for this task is a diminishing-returns graph.

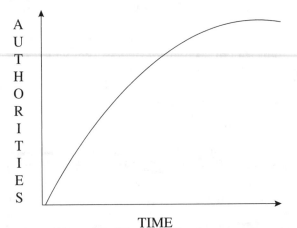

TIME

(2) At the point of diminishing returns, check through your research notes. Make sure that you have properly accomplished the seven tasks above, and look for loose ends. For example, check that you have considered the various types of primary authority (task 3), explored all research issues (task 5), ascertained that the primary authorities are still good law (task 7), etc.

(3) Read a secondary authority that you have not yet read, or re-read one of the better ones you read earlier on. You should be able to say "I've looked into that" as you work through the discussion in that authority.

(4) Start to write out your analysis of the client's situation, or check in with your supervisor or another lawyer in your office. If you get stuck or you find it difficult to answer questions your supervisor poses, you will know that your research is still not complete and which topics need more research.

Finally keep in mind that your research may become stale as time passes. For example, a court may decide an important case, or the legislature may amend the statute. Most lawyers keep their research up to date by reviewing current-awareness publications, such as a weekly newspaper with new cases; by using an electronic e-mail alert service, which sends an e-mail when a specified development occurs; and by repeating the research-forward task (task 7) from time to time or before major events, such as settlement discussions or oral argument.

SUMMARY

As we worked on this book, we asked experts in teaching legal research—legal writing professors and reference librarians—to identify the most common missteps of novice legal researchers. Here are some of their answers, listed under the pertinent cognitive task outlined in this chapter:

(1) **Learn and React to Your Client's Situation**
Getting *too* creative—pursuing issues that are not relevant
Researching too broadly, i.e., including a related but not pertinent topic

(2) **Develop Research Terms and Research Issues**
Relying on irrelevant facts
Failing to look up key words
Formulating a too-narrow research issue
Using the wrong key words or phrases and getting side-tracked

(3) **List and Rank Potential Authorities**
Not having an understanding of how all the sources fit together
Not using a broad source early on and then focusing on the precise issue
Under-relying on secondary authority early in the research process
Jumping too quickly to primary authority, especially cases in electronic form
Over-relying on persuasive primary and secondary authorities
Failing to appreciate the importance of jurisdiction
Unnecessarily searching for secondary authority on matters definitively covered by binding authority

(4) **Assess Available Sources**
Not having enough patience to use different sources
Over-relying on electronic research, more specifically:
☐ turning on the computer too soon
☐ trying to correct a problem by checking via a computer
☐ trying to research on LexisNexis or Westlaw before learning a fair amount about the topic
☐ over-relying on computer services in lieu of paper case digests
☐ over-relying on computer services in lieu of paper annotated statutory codes

(5) **Use Your Terms and Issues to Locate Pertinent Passages**
Not having enough patience to try different search terms
Using only one word for an idea rather than searching under multiple words
Not fully understanding the case digest system
Failing to fully utilize finding tools such as the case synopses in annotated statutes
Failing to write searches well and thinking you can find what you need in ten or even thirty minutes on LexisNexis or Westlaw

(6) **Study Pertinent Passages**
Not stopping to read cases along the way
Failing to recognize a case that is very useful
Failing to fully understand a case, which includes failing to look up key concepts
Failing to grasp the structure of statutory or procedural rules
Not using the current statute

(7) **Research Backwards and Forwards from Major Authorities**
Relying on encyclopedias and other secondary authority rather than using these as a means to locate primary authority
Not finding and reading enough cases
Not following through—copying something that seems to be on point without digging more deeply
Relying on what a case says about a cited authority without reading that cited authority
Failing to update
Not citing cases along the way and failing to properly understand case citators

(8) **Stop Researching**
Deciding you are done when you find anything that appears to be on point, rather than looking at the issue from various angles before stopping
Over-researching and leaving too little time for analysis and writing
Never quitting because you seek a definitive case

By far the most commonly mentioned misstep is looking immediately for pertinent cases by running searches in LexisNexis or Westlaw. One legal writing teacher depicted this approach as looking for a needle in a haystack without knowing what a needle is. You can avoid such an exercise in futility by carefully undertaking all the cognitive tasks described in this chapter in the various sources covered in this book.

SECONDARY AUTHORITIES

UNIT II

PRELIMINARY POINTS

As you learned in Unit I, your ultimate goal is to discern the rule of law governing your client's situation. That rule derives from primary authority, whether cases, statutes, administrative agency materials, or court rules. Yet this text suggests that you start your research in secondary authorities.

There are several reasons for this seemingly circuitous approach. First, secondary authorities comment on the law; they describe, explain, analyze, and, in some cases, critique and suggest changes in rules derived from primary authority. You often will find it easier to grasp the law when you begin with commentary than when you begin with the law itself. Second, secondary authorities provide references to primary authorities, and you can use these references to locate leading primary authorities. Third, compared to primary authorities, secondary authorities are fairly accessible. As you will soon see, it is easier to locate a pertinent portion of a treatise, for example, than it is to locate a pertinent case, especially if you are starting with little background knowledge.

Each type of secondary authority has its strengths and weaknesses. As you research in secondary authorities, evaluate your research by the four criteria for competent research introduced in Chapter 1: correct, comprehensive, credible, and cost-effective. For most research projects, you will want to combine secondary authorities to fully achieve these goals.

Chapters 3 through 7 of this unit each cover one of the major types of secondary authority. The sequence starts with authorities that are analogous to nonlegal sources (such as encyclopedias and treatises) and then moves on to authorities that are unique to the law (such as Restatements of the Law). Chapter 8 covers, in briefer form, several minor secondary authorities and then discusses strategies for secondary-authority research that is correct, comprehensive, credible, and cost-effective.

ENCYCLOPEDIAS

A. WHAT IS AN ENCYCLOPEDIA?

Like nonlegal encyclopedias, legal encyclopedias cover a wide range of topics, present fairly general information, and order the topics alphabetically. Some topics are quite narrow, others very broad. Within each topic, the discussion is organized by subtopics into sections, according to the legal rules and principles involved. In general, the opening sections cover the substantive legal rules, while the closing sections cover procedure and remedies. Each section consists of text as well as fairly extensive footnotes referring to supporting authorities. Encyclopedias are written by authors on the publisher's editorial staff, who generally are not well-known experts.

Two encyclopedias seek to provide broad coverage of American law, including state and federal law. They are *American Jurisprudence* second edition (Am. Jur. 2d) and *Corpus Juris Secundum* (C.J.S.). Both are successors to older encyclopedias, *American Jurisprudence* and *Corpus Juris*, respectively, and both are now published by West. Both cover well over 400 topics and consist of about 150 books in paper form.

Other encyclopedias have narrower scopes. In many states, a state encyclopedia covers all or many legal topics under that state's law. A hint: Some state encyclopedias do not have *encyclopedia* in their titles; they go by such names as *digests* or *jurisprudence*. In some areas of law, such as criminal and international law, specialized encyclopedias exist.

For an example pertinent to the Canoga case, examine Illustration 3-1 (at pages 64–65) from C.J.S.'s discussion of Wrongful Discharge as well as the updating page in Illustration 3-2 (at page 66).

ILLUSTRATION 3-1

Encyclopedia Main Volume Text,
from *Corpus Juris Secundum* (paper source)

---

30 C.J.S.　　　　　　　　　　　　　**EMPLOYER-EMPLOYEE**　§ 25

an employment contract.[86] The theory of an implied covenant of good faith and fair dealing was developed specifically for at-will employment contracts.[87] However, it is also stated that a covenant of good faith is not implied in an employment relationship.[88]

Authority to employ assistants.

Ordinarily, an employee has no implied authority to employ assistants.[89] Such authority may be implied, however, from the nature of the work to be performed, from the general course of conducting the business of the employer by the employee or from the circumstances of the particular case.[90]

c. Parties

A person expressly employed by an individual on behalf of another person, corporation, or other entity becomes the employee of the latter. Whether or not a contract entered into by more than two parties is joint, several, or joint and several is dependent on the intention of the parties.

One who is expressly employed by an individual on behalf of another person, corporation, or other entity becomes the employee of the latter,[91] and a contract of employment made through an employment agency, naming applicant, the employer, and the person authorizing the hiring, does not make the latter, but the one so named, the employer.[92] The addition of the word "trustee" to a writing signed by the employer does not, however, make the latter any the less an employer when the employee does not know whom the employer represents.[93]

Although there may be a more or less complete identity in the stock ownership of two or more corporations, as long as they remain distinct legal entities, an employee of one is not to be regarded as an employee of the others,[94] but where the employee, although employed by one company, is with the knowledge and consent of the others acting for them also, the relation may be regarded as existing as to them.[95]

Where two parties are jointly interested in a business, the presumption is that those employed in such business are the employees of both, although the actual employment and control are by one.[96] Whether or not a contract of employment entered into by more than two parties is joint, several, or joint and several is dependent on the intention of the parties.[97]

§ 25. Personnel Handbooks or Manuals in General

Provisions in a personnel handbook or manual may become part of an employment contract.

Library References

Master and Servant ⊷2, 3(1, 2), 4.

Under some authority, unilaterally promulgated employment handbooks or manuals do not become part of employment contracts [98] unless

---

Ohio—Miller Agency Co. v. Greene, 177 N.E. 534, 39 Ohio App. 503.

85. Fla.—Haiman v. Gundersheimer, 177 So. 199, 130 Fla. 109.

86. U.S.—Gianaculas v. Trans World Airlines, Inc., C.A.9 (Cal.), 761 F.2d 1391.

Ariz.—Wagenseller v. Scottsdale Memorial Hosp., 710 P.2d 1025, 147 Ariz. 370.

Mass.—Kravetz v. Merchants Distributors, Inc., 440 N.E.2d 1278, 387 Mass. 457.

Ohio—Bolling v. Clevepak Corp., 484 N.E.2d 1367, 20 Ohio App.3d 113, 20 O.B.R. 146.

Tenn.—Williams v. Maremont Corp., App., 776 S.W.2d 78.

Rules and regulations

Fair dealing portion of a covenant of good faith and fair dealing between parties to an employment contract is at least the right of an employee to the benefit of rules and regulations adopted for his or her protection.

Cal.—Rulon-Miller v. International Business Machines Corp., 1 Dist., 208 Cal.Rptr. 524, 162 C.A.3d 241.

87. Mass.—McCone v. New England Tel. and Tel. Co., 471 N.E.2d 47, 393 Mass. 231.

88. U.S.—Moore v. McGraw Edison Co., C.A.8 (Minn.), 804 F.2d 1026.

Satterfield v. Lockheed Missiles and Space Co., Inc., D.C.S.C., 617 F.Supp. 1359.

Minn.—Eklund v. Vincent Brass and Aluminum Co., 351 N.W.2d 371, review denied.

89. Pa.—Jacamino v. Harrison Motor Freight Co., 5 A.2d 393, 135 Pa.Super. 356.

90. Emergency

In case of an emergency where employee is unable to perform the work himself, he may employ an assistant.

Pa.—Jacamino v. Harrison Motor Freight Co., 5 A.2d 393, 135 Pa.Super. 356.

91. N.Y.—Byrnes v. Chase Nat. Bank, 232 N.Y.S. 224, 225 A.D. 102, affirmed 168 N.E. 423, 251 N.Y. 551.

92. N.Y.—Schon v. Messer, 194 N.Y.S. 245.

93. N.Y.—Whalen v. Ruegamer, 108 N.Y.S. 38, 123 A.D. 585.

94. Wis.—Bosanich v. Chicago, N.S. & M.R. Co., 181 N.W. 297, 173 Wis. 280.

95. Idaho—Barrow v. B.R. Lewis Lumber Co., 95 P. 682, 14 Idaho 698.

'**96.** Minn.—McMahon v. Davidson, 12 Minn. 357, appeal dismissed 14 S.Ct. 1200, 154 U.S. 566, 19 L.Ed. 52.

97. Or.—Pitts v. Crane, 236 P. 475, 114 Or. 593.

47

ILLUSTRATION 3-1 *(continued)*

§ 25   EMPLOYER-EMPLOYEE 30 C.J.S.

expressly included in them.[99] However, under other authority, provisions of an employer's personnel handbook or manual may become part of an employment contract,[1] and whether an employment manual or handbook creates an employment contract is a question which must be determined on a case by case basis.[2]

The creation of contractual rights by such handbook or manual depends upon whether the elements of a unilateral contract are present;[3] the language of a handbook must constitute an offer definite in form which is communicated to the employee, the offer must be accepted, and consideration must be furnished before a handbook becomes part of an employment contract.[4] An employee's continued service,[5] or the benefit of an orderly, cooperative and loyal work force,[6] may constitute consideration.

An employer is bound by provisions in a handbook or manual where both the employer and employee have obligations thereunder,[7] regardless of whether the manual was actually bargained for,[8] and regardless of whether it modifies an existing employment relationship.[9] A handbook which contains general,[10] or indefinite,[11] language is ordinarily not deemed part of an employment contract.

It has been held that provisions in an employer's handbook or manual may create a term of an employment agreement without any showing of particular reliance by the employee,[12] without any specific words incorporating the manual into the agreement,[13] and notwithstanding that in other respects the employment relationship would be

---

98. U.S.—Spearman v. Delco Remy Div. of General Motors Corp., 717 F.Supp. 1351—Bowser v. McDonald's Corp., S.D.Tex., 714 F.Supp. 839.

Mo.—Johnson v. McDonnell Douglas Corp., 745 S.W.2d 661.

N.C.—Walker v. Westinghouse Elec. Corp., 335 S.E.2d 79, 77 N.C.App. 253, review denied 341 S.E.2d 39, 315 N.C. 597.

Manual alone

An employment manual cannot alone be the basis of an implied contract between employee and employer, where manual is merely a unilateral expression of company policy, it is not bargained for between employer and employee, and is not a reflection of mutual assent between the parties; nonetheless, an employment manual may be one of the relevant circumstances from which an implied contract can be inferred.

U.S.—Rouse v. Peoples Natural Gas Co., D.C.Kan., 605 F.Supp. 230.

99. N.C.—Buffaloe v. United Carolina Bank, 366 S.E.2d 918, 89 N.C.App. 693.

1. U.S.—Thompson v. Kings Entertainment Co., E.D.Va., 674 F.Supp. 1194.

Ariz.—Leikvold v. Valley View Community Hosp., 688 P.2d 170, 141 Ariz. 544.

Minn.—Hoemberg v. Watco Publishers, Inc., App., 343 N.W.2d 676.

Ohio—Brown v. Otto C. Epp Memorial Hosp., 482 N.E.2d 988, 19 Ohio App.3d 25, 19 O.B.R. 90, appeal after remand 535 N.E.2d 325, 41 Ohio App.3d 198.

Tenn.—Hamby v. Genesco, Inc., App., 627 S.W.2d 373.

Wyo.—Leithead v. American Colloid Co., 721 P.2d 1059.

Implied-in-fact contract

U.S.—Marsh v. Digital Equipment Corp., D.Ariz., 675 F.Supp. 1186.

Incorporation

Under Illinois law, personnel policies contained in an employee handbook will be deemed incorporated into employment contract where another document exists which can be construed as an express employment contract and the contract can be construed as subject to "policies" of employer.

U.S.—Enis v. Continental Illinois Nat. Bank and Trust Co. of Chicago, D.C.Ill., 582 F.Supp. 876, affirmed 795 F.2d 39.

2. Ark.—Proctor v. East Cent. Arkansas EOC, 724 S.W.2d 163, 291 Ark. 265.

3. Minn.—Lewis v. Equitable Life Assur. Soc. of the U.S., 389 N.W.2d 876.

4. Ala.—Hoffman–La Roche, Inc. v. Campbell, 512 So.2d 725.

Hawaii—Kinoshita v. Canadian Pacific Airlines, Ltd., 724 P.2d 110, 68 Haw. 594.

Iowa—Fogel v. Trustees of Iowa College, 446 N.W.2d 451.

Minn.—Fitzgerald v. Norwest Corp., App., 382 N.W.2d 290, review denied.

Neb.—Stratton v. Chevrolet Motor Div., General Motors Corp., 428 N.W.2d 910, 229 Neb. 771.

5. U.S.—Vinyard v. King, C.A.Okl., 728 F.2d 428.

Ala.—Hoffman–La Roche, Inc. v. Campbell, 512 So.2d 725.

Colo.—Cronk v. Intermountain Rural Elec. Ass'n, App., 765 P.2d 619, certiorari denied.

Ill.—DeFosse v. Cherry Elec. Products Corp., 510 N.E.2d 141, 109 Ill.Dec. 520, 156 Ill.App.3d 1030.

Iowa—Fogel v. Trustees of Iowa College, 446 N.W.2d 451.

Mass.—Jackson v. Action for Boston Community Development, Inc., 525 N.E.2d 411, 403 Mass. 8.

W.Va.—Cook v. Heck's Inc., 342 S.E.2d 453, 176 W.Va. 368.

6. Wyo.—Leithead v. American Colloid Co., 721 P.2d 1059.

7. U.S.—Pudil v. Smart Buy, Inc., D.C.Ill., 607 F.Supp. 440.

8. U.S.—Pelizza v. Reader's Digest Sales and Services Inc., N.D.Ill., 624 F.Supp. 806.

9. U.S.—Pelizza v. Reader's Digest Sales and Services Inc., N.D.Ill., 624 F.Supp. 806.

10. S.D.—Bauer v. American Freight System, Inc., 422 N.W.2d 435.

General code of conduct

U.S.—Gaiardo v. Ethyl Corp., M.D.Pa., 697 F.Supp. 1377.

11. U.S.—Ellis v. El Paso Natural Gas Co., C.A.N.M., 754 F.2d 884.

Minn.—Hunt v. IBM Mid America Employees Federal Credit Union, 384 N.W.2d 853.

N.M.—Sanchez v. The New Mexican, 738 P.2d 1321, 106 N.M. 76.

12. Ariz.—Loffa v. Intel Corp., App., 738 P.2d 1146, 153 Ariz. 539.

48

ILLUSTRATION 3-2

Encyclopedia Pocket Part,
from *Corpus Juris Secundum* (paper source)

---

§ 10   CORPUS JURIS SECUNDUM

general employer retained ultimate right to control employee's work. Defoor v. Evesque, 694 So. 2d 1302, 119 Ed. Law Rep. 286 (Ala. 1997).

§ 11 Compensation

It has been held, however, that if no financial benefit is obtained by the purported employee from the employer, no plausible employment relationship of any sort can be said to exist; although compensation by the putative employer to the putative employee in exchange for his services is not a sufficient condition, it is an essential condition to existence of an employer-employee relationship.[75.5]

[75.5]O'Connor v. Davis, 126 F.3d 112, 74 Fair Empl. Prac. Cas. (BNA) 1561 (2d Cir. 1997).

B.   INDEPENDENT CONTRACTORS AND THEIR EMPLOYEES

§ 13 In general

Cases
Miami-Dade County v. State Dept. of Labor and Employment Sec., Div. of Unemployment Compensation, 749 So. 2d 574 (Fla. Dist. Ct. App. 3d Dist. 2000).
McKinstry v. Cass County, 228 Neb. 733, 424 N.W.2d 322 (1988).

C.   CONTRACTS OF EMPLOYMENT

§ 22 Form, requisites, and validity in general

A unilateral contract that shortens a federal statutory deadline will not be enforced as such a contract is against public policy and defeats federally protected rights of workers.[56.5]
A provision stating that employment may be terminated upon notice of either party as prescribed constitutes consideration sufficient to support an employment contract.[79.5]

[56.5]U.S.—Scott v. Guardsmark Sec., D.S.C., 874 F.Supp. 117.
[79.5]Mo.—Sanfillippo v. Oehler, App.E.D., 869 S.W.2d 159, reh. and/or transfer den., transfer den.

Cases
Continued employment and compensation was consideration for employment contract which contained nonsolicitation clause. Corson v. Universal Door Systems, Inc., 596 So. 2d 565 (Ala. 1991).
Laverson v. Macon Bibb County Hosp. Authority, 226 Ga. App. 761, 487 S.E.2d 621, 119 Ed. Law Rep. 1220 (1997).
Gross v. Diehl Specialties Intern., Inc., 776 S.W.2d 879 (Mo. Ct. App. E.D. 1989).
Hartbarger v. Frank Paxton Co., 115 N.M. 665, 857 P.2d 776 (1993).
Williams v. Maremont Corp., 776 S.W.2d 78 (Tenn. Ct. App. 1988).

Fremont Homes, Inc. v. Elmer, 974 P.2d 952 (Wyo. 1999).

§ 23 — Contracts for permanent or life employment

Cases
Martin v. Federal Life Ins. Co., 109 Ill. App. 3d 596, 65 Ill. Dec. 143, 440 N.E.2d 998 (1st Dist. 1982).

§ 24 Constitution and operation in general

A written contract of at-will employment trumps an alleged but nonexistent implied contract to the contrary.[65.5]

[65.5]U.S.—Berg v. Norand Corp., 169 F.3d 1140, 9 A.D. Cas. (BNA) 207 (8th Cir. 1999), cert. denied, 120 S. Ct. 174, 9 A.D. Cas. (BNA) 1408 (U.S. 1999).

Cases
Breen v. Norwest Bank Minnesota, N.A., 865 F. Supp. 574 (D. Minn. 1994).
Soucy v. Sullivan & Merritt, 1999 ME 1, 722 A.2d 361 (Me. 1999).
Enyeart v. Shelter Mut. Ins. Co., 693 S.W.2d 120 (Mo. Ct. App. W.D. 1985).
Williams v. Maremont Corp., 776 S.W.2d 78 (Tenn. Ct. App. 1988).

§ 25 Personnel handbooks or manuals in general

The traditional contract requirement that knowledge of an offer is a prerequisite to acceptance will not be followed in the limited context of employee handbook cases.[4.5]
However, handbook representations are enforceable under certain circumstances despite the presence of a disclaimer.[20.5]

[4.5]**Standardized agreement**
Where contract is based upon employee handbook distributed to all employees, the contract is not an individually negotiated agreement, but rather is standardized agreement between employer and a class of employees and thus, it is unnecessary that particular employee seeking to enforce promise made in handbook have knowledge of the promise and this holding produces the salutary result that all employees, those who read handbook and those who did not, are treated alike.
Iowa—Anderson v. Douglas & Lomason Co., 540 N.W.2d 277.
[20.5]Ill.—Perman v. ArcVentures, Inc., 1 Dist., 554 N.E.2d 982, 143 Ill.Dec. 910, 196 Ill.App.3d 758.
Promissory estoppel shown
Employee is entitled to enforce representation in employee handbook, despite disclaimer of contract in handbook, if he can demonstrate that employer should have reasonably expected employee to consider representation as commitment from employer, employee reasonably relied upon representation to his detriment, and injustice can be avoided only by enforcement of representation.

2   2003 Cumulative Supplement

B.   WHY ARE ENCYCLOPEDIAS USEFUL?

For the typical research project, encyclopedias are most useful at the very beginning of the research process. You very likely will find a broad overview of your topic, which can be read fairly easily. Furthermore, you can easily browse within an encyclopedia; that is, you can easily move from subtopic to subtopic or from one topic to related topics. Encyclopedias also operate as finding tools for primary authority. Most encyclopedias are updated annually.

Encyclopedia research has its limitations. If you use Am. Jur. 2d or C.J.S., the text is likely to present general principles but not precisely state the law of your jurisdiction. Similarly, although you may find a reference to a leading primary authority from your jurisdiction in Am. Jur. 2d or C.J.S., neither refers to all pertinent authorities. Because these encyclopedias are not written by well-recognized experts, they are not as credible as some of the other authorities covered in this unit. Thus, they are cited most frequently for general, well-established points.

A state or specialized encyclopedia can be more useful than Am. Jur. 2d or C.J.S. These encyclopedias generally have more credibility, the text generally is more detailed, and there are more extensive references to binding primary authorities.

C.   HOW DO YOU RESEARCH IN ENCYCLOPEDIAS?

You can research encyclopedias in electronic sources; for example, Am. Jur. 2d is available on Westlaw and LexisNexis. However, paper is a more common choice because encyclopedias are well organized with strong internal finding tools and because browsing is desirable. Thus this text focuses on researching in Am. Jur. 2d and C.J.S. in book form.

Encyclopedias in paper:

▶ use the index or topic list (or table of primary authorities)

▶ read the introductory material

▶ consult the topic outline

▶ read the pertinent sections

▶ check the pocket part

There are two primary means of locating pertinent material in an encyclopedia: the index and the topic list. Both Am. Jur. 2d and C.J.S. have multivolume indexes, issued annually and shelved at the end of the set; some entries are updated during the year. Review Illustration 2-5 (at page 45). Encyclopedia indexes are complex and detailed, so you should spend some time looking up alternative terms, pursuing cross-references, and reading through the entries and subentries. Through the index, you should be able to identify one or more pertinent topics and may also identify one or more pertinent sections within a topic.

The second primary means of locating pertinent topics (but not sections within a topic) is through the topic list, which serves as an overall table of contents for the encyclopedia. Review Illustration 2-3 (at page 43). Am. Jur. 2d lists its topics in alphabetical order in the Table of Abbreviations at the front of each index volume. C.J.S. provides the List of Titles in the beginning of each non-index volume as well as the Abbreviations of Titles in the index volumes.

If you begin your research in Am. Jur. 2d or C.J.S. with a citation to a pertinent federal statute, regulation, court rule, or a pertinent uniform act, you can consult either encyclopedia's table of cited laws. These tables appear in their own volumes and list the topics and sections citing the listed authorities. Am. Jur. 2d also has a table listing statutes by their names, the Popular Names Table, located in the final index volume. Review Illustration 2-6 (at page 46). C.J.S. has a Table of Cases volume as well.

Once you have located a potentially useful topic, you should look over the introductory material to the topic. You may find a synopsis of the topic, cross-references to other topics, and references to other secondary authorities. You will find one or more topic outlines. Review Illustration 2-4 (at page 44). Scanning the topic outline(s) is an excellent way to get a big-picture overview of the topic and identify the most pertinent sections to read.

As you read the most pertinent sections, seek first to learn pertinent legal rules, principles, and definitions and then to obtain references to other potentially pertinent authorities. Be sure that you take time to browse through adjacent sections to assure that your research is comprehensive.

Finally, you must seek the most current information in the encyclopedia. Most of the time you will read the material in the main volume and then update that material by checking the pocket part. See Illustration 3-2 (at page 66). A pocket part is a set of pages inserted into a pocket in the back of a bound volume; it is used to bring the bound volume up to date (or typically within no more than one year of the present). The pocket part may provide additional text with supporting authorities or simply additional references.

In addition to pocket parts, Am. Jur. 2d provides the New Topic Service, a looseleaf binder containing topics too new to be located in the appropriate bound volume; it merits a brief check as you complete your research in Am. Jur. 2d. Furthermore, on occasion, when a bound volume becomes very outdated, a new bound volume is issued.

Researching the Canoga case and focusing on the handbook as a contract, as shown in Chapter 2, we used the Am. Jur. 2d Table of Abbreviations and index as well as the topic outline to identify the Wrongful Discharge topic and sections 22 and 23. See Illustrations 2-3, 2-5, and 2-4 respectively (at pages 43–45). We read the text and footnotes of section 22 in the bound volume, found in Illustration 1-3 (at pages 15–16). The bound volume was very new, so there was no pocket part. In broad terms, it appears that an employer and employee may contract, through an employee handbook, for discharge procedures or limitations on the grounds for discharge. The discussion in C.J.S., Illustrations 3-1 and 3-2 (at pages 64–66) is to the same effect.

Focusing on the possibility of protection from discrimination based on disability, we learned from Am. Jur. 2d's Popular Names Table, Illustration 2-6 (at page 46), that the Americans with Disabilities Act is discussed in the Job Discrimination topic. We also learned that the Am. Jur. 2d New Topic Service includes a topic on the Americans with Disabilities Act, which could be of significant interest.

D.   WHAT ELSE?

Conversion Tables: On occasion, a topic is reorganized to better reflect current law. If you know about a pertinent section from the older version and want to locate the corresponding material in a newer version, you should consult a conversion or parallel references table.

Am. Jur. 2d Desk Book: This single volume includes a wide range of miscellaneous information, such as the structure and membership of federal government bodies, statistics on various aspects of life in the United States, selected international legal documents, and financial tables.

E.   HOW DO YOU CITE ENCYCLOPEDIAS?

A proper cite to an encyclopedia includes its title, the volume number, topic name, section number, and year. Here are two examples for the Am. Jur. 2d excerpt in Illustration 1-3 (at pages 15–16).

- ☐   *Bluebook* Rule 15.7(a): 82 Am. Jur. 2d *Wrongful Discharge* § 22 (2003).
- ☐   *ALWD* Rule 26: 82 Am. Jur. 2d *Wrongful Discharge* § 22 (2003).

Here are two additional examples for the C.J.S. main volume and supplement in Illustrations 3-1 and 3-2 (at pages 64–66):

- ☐   *Bluebook* Rule 15.7(a): 30 C.J.S. *Employer-Employee* § 25 (1992 & Supp. 2003).
- ☐   *ALWD* Rule 26: 30 C.J.S. *Employer-Employee* § 25 (1992 & Supp. 2003).

TREATISES

CHAPTER 4

A. WHAT IS A TREATISE?

Put simply, a treatise is an authority that covers one subject at length. The subject may be quite broad (such as contracts or employment law), or it may be quite narrow (such as a single statute protecting disabled workers). Treatises typically are written by private authors, such as law professors and lawyers, although some are written by the staff of a publishing company. A good treatise presents a thorough scholarly discussion of the subject.

Treatises are published initially and still primarily in book form. A treatise may consist of a single volume or multiple volumes, depending on the scope of the subject and the comprehensiveness of the discussion. Treatises are published in paper in hardbound, softbound, or looseleaf forms. A looseleaf treatise consists of separate pages held together by some type of binder.

A treatise typically contains at least three parts:

- [ ] the text itself, with footnotes or endnotes containing supporting references and tangential remarks;
- [ ] means of access, such as one or more tables of contents, an index, and other tables; and
- [ ] miscellaneous features, such as a preface and appendices containing important documents such as statutes.

The text in legal treatises resembles an expository essay. All treatises explain the law, setting out rules, policies, and examples. Some also critique the law and propose legal reforms. A treatise's text typically is organized by chapters and then by sections or paragraphs.

For example, a treatise that is pertinent to the Canoga case is Lex K. Larson's *Employment Discrimination*. A page from that treatise appears as Illustration 4-1 (at page 72).

B.   WHY ARE TREATISES USEFUL?

Most legal treatises provide a fairly comprehensive and scholarly overview of the subject addressed. Because the coverage is typically analytical as well as descriptive, a treatise is often an ideal place to start your research if you know what subject your client's situation involves but still need to learn about the legal framework, major rules, and leading authorities. Furthermore, although treatises are not primary authority, a well-written treatise by a highly respected author is among the most credible secondary authorities. In addition, a good treatise provides abundant references to important primary authorities and other secondary authorities.

Treatises can have drawbacks. Some treatises are updated, but many are not. Some treatises are more credible, better researched, more clearly organized, and more comprehensive than others. Finally, although treatises abound, there still may be a few subjects on which no one has yet written a good treatise.

C.   HOW DO YOU RESEARCH IN TREATISES?

Because you are likely to use a treatise when your knowledge is fairly limited, you should take advantage of the editorial aids and format of a book. Presently, only a fraction of legal treatises are available in electronic media such as LexisNexis, Westlaw, and Loislaw. Hence, this discussion focuses on re-searching in paper.

Treatises in paper:

► locate treatises via a catalog, shelf-browsing or the reserve desk, a recommendation, or a reference in a textbook
► select an appropriate treatise
► consult the index, tables of contents, or table of primary authorities
► read pertinent passages
► check for updates

Locate treatises. To find treatises on your research topic, think first about which legal subject encompasses your research topic. You then may use any of these techniques:

ILLUSTRATION 4-1   Treatise,
                       from *Employment Discrimination* (paper source)

155-37   **PERMITTED PRACTICES; DEFENSES**   § 155.06

that the ADA does not affect pre-existing condition clauses in insurance policies, so long as they are not used as subterfuge to evade the purposes behind the ADA.[7]

In *Anderson v. Gus Mayer Boston Store of Delaware*,[8] the plaintiff was denied *any* coverage under the employer's plan. The employer provided a group insurance plan, and it was clear that the plaintiff's cancer was at least partly responsible for increasing the cost of premiums. The plaintiff was then diagnosed with HIV and AIDS. This further increased the premiums, to the extent that other group members informed the employer that they would withdraw from the group if the premiums could not be reduced. The employer sought a different insurance plan. Not surprisingly, the provider of this plan rejected the plaintiff. The employer switched to this plan without making any effort to secure alternative policies for the plaintiff. The court did not look kindly on the employer's conduct, ruling emphatically that when an employer changes insurance carriers and knowingly excludes an individual because of that individual's disability, and when the employer does so for the purpose of reducing premiums, the ADA is violated. The court emphasized that the violation committed by the employer was the denial of any and all access to coverage to the plaintiff. The insurance defense was ruled inapplicable to this situation, given this complete denial of access.[9]

§ 155.06   Restrictions on Smoking

The ADA provides that nothing in the Act prevents a covered entity from prohibiting or imposing restrictions on smoking in places of employment.[1] This clause curiously appears under the heading "Relationship to Other Laws." The legislative history does not provide any clues about how this came to be or what it means: does it imply that only government-imposed restrictions such as anti-smoking ordinances are referred to? The breadth of the language and the purposes of the ADA militate against any such narrow construction, so that purely employer-imposed workplace smoking rules are no doubt legitimized as well.

---

[7] Senate Report at 29. The Senate Report also suggests that it is permissible for an employer to offer insurance policies that limit coverage for certain procedures or treatments; for example, an annual limit on health coverage benefits. *Id.*

[8] 924 F. Supp. 763, 5 AD Cases 673 (E.D. Tex. 1996).

[9] The court did hold that the employer could attempt to defend its conduct on the basis that providing such alternative coverage would constitute an undue hardship. This and the issue of damages were the only remaining questions of fact, so the court ordered trial on these issues.

[1] 42 U.S.C. § 12201(b).

☐   Look in a library catalog to find out what the library owns or can obtain from other libraries.

☐   Find out the call number range of the subject matter, and browse the shelves containing books with those call numbers. In addition, ask at the library reserve desk to see reserve treatises within that call number range. Exhibit 4.1 lists Library of Congress call numbers for legal topics.

☐   Ask a professor, librarian, lawyer, or colleague who is knowledgeable about the subject for a recommendation.

☐   Look in a textbook for a reference in the footnotes, endnotes, or the bibliography.

Whatever the medium of your library's catalog—most are computer databases—you most likely will be able to search for treatises various ways.

Because a subject search is a broad search, it usually will retrieve a large number of treatises. Of course, you must work within the subject headings used by the cataloger, which usually are based on the Library of Congress system. Be sure to try various research terms and take advantage of the cross-references. If the terms you choose for a subject search are not fruitful, you might try locating a treatise you already know of in the catalog by means of its author or title, and then use the subject headings listed for that treatise to find other treatises. Or you might consult the multivolume set entitled *Library of Congress Subject Headings*; these subject headings are the starting point for the creation of many library catalogs.

Another alternative in an electronic catalog is to employ a key-word search, which permits you to locate all catalog entries containing the words you enter. Especially if your topic has distinctive terms, key-word searching may be a useful place to start, with a subject search as follow-up if you want more choices.

When you use an electronic catalog, pay close attention to the example screens and help screens. Be careful to spell correctly, and consider using both singulars and plurals.

As a novice legal researcher, you may find it difficult to determine what is and what is not a treatise. Do not expect the word *treatise* to appear in the title or the catalog entry. Furthermore, the following categories of books are not treatises useful in your legal research, although they are useful for other purposes:

☐   Manuals for continuing legal education (CLE) courses: CLE manuals tend to have terms such as *institute* or *seminar* in their titles. (CLE manuals are covered in Chapter 8.)

☐   Textbooks: Textbooks tend to have terms such as *cases and materials* or *readings in* in their titles. Textbooks typically present excerpts from legal authorities rather than summarize and comment on the law.

☐   Study aids: Most study aids aimed at law students do summarize the law, but they are not treatises because they follow a different format, such as an outline, and lack footnotes with supporting references. This category includes series such as West's Nutshells, Aspen's Examples and Explanations, and LexisNexis' Understanding [a subject].

EXHIBIT 4.1	Library of Congress Call Numbers

Administrative Law KF 5401-5425

Antitrust KF 1631-1657

Banking KF 966-1032

Bankruptcy KF 1501-1548

Business Associations, generally KF 1355-1480

Children and Law KF 479, 540-550

Civil and Political Rights KF 4741-4786

Civil Procedure KF 8810-9075

Commercial Transactions KF 871-962

Conflict of Laws KF 410-418

Constitutional Law KF 4501-5130

Contracts, quasi-contracts KF 801-1244

Copyright KF 2986-3080

Corporations KF 1384-1480

Criminal Law KF 9201-9763

Criminal Procedure KF 9601-9763

Education Policy and Law KF 4101-4257

Employment Discrimination KF 3464-3470.5

Environmental Law KF 3775-3816

Equity KF 398-400

Evidence

    In civil cases KF 8931-8969

    In criminal cases KF 9660-9678

Federal Courts KF 8700-8807

Immigration Law KF 4801-4836

Insurance Law KF 1146-1238

International Law JX or JZ or KZ

Jurisprudence KF 379-382

Juvenile Criminal Law and Procedure KF 9771-9827

Labor Law KF 3301-3580

Land-Use Planning KF 5691-5710

Legal History KF 350-374

The Legal Profession KF 297-334

Legal Research and Writing KF 240-251

Legislative Process KF 4945-4952

Local Government/Municipal Law KF 5300-5332

Marital Relations and Dissolution KF 501-539

Medical Legislation KF 3821-3832

Mental Health Law KF 480, 3828-3828.5

Oil and Gas KF 1841-1870

Patents and Trademarks KF 3091-3194

Public Safety KF 3941-3977

Real Property KF 560-698

Regulation of Industry, Trade, and Commerce KF 1600-2940

Secured Transactions KF 1046-1062

Securities Regulations KF 1066-1084, KF 1428-1457

Social Legislation KF 3300-3771

Taxation KF 6271-6795

Torts KF 1246-1327

Trial Practice (Civil) KF 8911-8925

Uniform State Laws KF 165

Water Resources KF 5551-5590

Wills and Trusts KF 726-780

On the other hand, one type of book you may use for study purposes can serve you well in your research: the hornbook.[1] A hornbook is a single-volume treatise that explains the basic principles of law in a particular field, provides supporting references, is written by a well-regarded scholar in that field, and is designed for law students. A hornbook can be an excellent place to begin your research on an unfamiliar topic.

1. The term is derived from the name of a child's first book, covered with horn to protect it from soiling.

Select an appropriate treatise. You may find more than one treatise on your research topic. Treatises vary in quality and in usefulness for a particular project. To select an appropriate treatise for your needs, consider the following factors:

Coverage: Pick a treatise with the scope and level of detail you need. If you are not familiar with the subject, you might first examine a single-volume treatise with a broad scope, then read a more detailed discussion in a multivolume treatise.

Currency: In general, you will want to select a treatise that has been published or updated recently. Check the copyright dates of the main volume as well as any pocket parts, pamphlet supplements, or replacement or supplement pages. Because there always is a delay between the completion of the text and its publication, look for any statements about the dates of coverage of the text, generally located in the preface of a bound volume or the cover of a softcover volume. In general, looseleaf treatises are updated more frequently than others.

Credibility: Some treatises are known as the classics in their fields; these treatises are especially credible. To find such a treatise:

- [ ] look for a treatise that has been cited in a textbook or course syllabus,
- [ ] pick a treatise that is kept on reserve,
- [ ] pick a treatise cited by a court, or
- [ ] find a treatise that has been published in multiple editions.

Another approach is to determine whether the author is a true expert, by use of the following strategies:

- [ ] check the author's credentials as noted in the treatise or in a reference book, such as *Who's Who in American Law* or *The AALS Directory of Law Teachers*;
- [ ] check periodical indexes or library catalogs to see if the author has written extensively on the subject; or
- [ ] use a treatise written by the author of a textbook on the subject.

Furthermore, some publishers have good reputations across the board; others have good reputations in certain areas of law. Highly reputable publishers include Aspen; LexisNexis; Matthew Bender; Pratt; RIA; Warren, Gorham & Lamont; and West Group.

Organization: Treatises are organized a variety of ways, including topically, such as by statute or claims and defenses, or chronologically, such as phases of a transaction or litigation. They also vary in the number and quality of the tables of contents, indexes, and tables of authorities. Select a treatise that permits you to locate pertinent passages easily and reliably.

Consult the treatise's index or tables. Once you have located a potentially useful treatise, you most likely will use either its index or table of contents to locate pertinent passages. If you use the index approach, be sure to consult all indexes; a treatise may have both a main index and one or more updates. Similarly, many treatises include both a summary table of contents and a detailed table of contents; start with the summary table of contents, then move to the detailed table of contents.

As another option, if you already know the name of a pertinent case or the name or citation of a statute on point, you could consult a table of primary authorities to learn where the case or statute is discussed in the treatise.

Read pertinent passages. As you read pertinent passages, look for an explanation of the law, a critique of the law (if presented), and references to other potentially pertinent authorities, whether primary or secondary. Take time to browse adjacent passages, such as other sections in the same chapter, and pursue cross-references.

Check for updates. Most multivolume treatises have updates, as do some single-volume treatises. Updates are organized by page, paragraph, or section so as to parallel the material in the main volume. Updates come in several forms:

☐ Pocket parts: These updates are pamphlets that slip into a pocket on an inside cover of a volume. Pocket parts usually are replaced annually. If a pocket part becomes too large, it may be replaced by a softbound supplement.

☐ Supplemental volumes or pamphlets: Some treatises are supplemented by separate hardbound volumes or softcover pamphlets. These supplements usually are shelved next to the volumes they update.

☐ Looseleaf supplements: Treatises published in looseleaf binders may be updated with supplements that are inserted periodically into the looseleaf volumes, typically behind a tab for supplemental pages. These supplements generally are printed on colored paper to distinguish them from the original material.

☐ Looseleaf page replacements: Treatises published in looseleaf binders may be updated with replacement pages that are issued and inserted at regular intervals or on an as-needed basis. A replacement page typically indicates its date of issuance.

Updates usually contain supplementary indexes and tables, which you should be sure to consult.

Some legal treatises are updated through the publication of new editions. If the treatise you are using seems dated, you should check the library catalog or ask a librarian for help.

Researching the Canoga case. In the Canoga case, Illustration 4-2 (at page 78) is an online catalog entry for the Larson treatise. We came to this entry by a subject search, under the main subject heading Discrimination in Employment and subheading Law and Legislation—United States. Note that the entry informs you about the treatise's location and call number, authors, dates of publication, edition(s), and publication format. (The format and information in catalog entries vary from library to library.)

Employment Discrimination, excerpted in Illustration 4-1 (at page 72), is a well-known, multivolume, looseleaf treatise now in its second edition.

The set covers various types of discrimination, including disability discrimination. The second edition dates to 1994, and it was updated in March of 2003 (this text was written in the spring of 2003). The author of the first edition was Arthur Larson, a Duke University professor who was a former Secretary of Labor. As stated on the title page, the author of the second edition is Lex K. Larson, the president of Employment Law, Inc., who also lectures at Duke. The treatise is published by a reputable legal publisher, Matthew Bender, owned by LexisNexis.

The summary table of contents, covering all volumes of the *Employment Discrimination* treatise, directed us to volume 9, which discusses the Americans with Disabilities Act of 1990 (ADA). The detailed table of contents in volume 9 directed us to Chapter 155 Permitted Practices; Defenses under the ADA. Section 155.06 addresses restrictions on smoking.

The excerpt in Illustration 4-1 (at page 72) discusses and refers to a potentially important provision of the federal statute on discrimination against disabled employees, which apparently permits some restrictions on smoking in the workplace. That particular page dates to March 2003.

D. WHAT ELSE?

Additional Techniques for Finding Treatises: The *Index to Legal Periodicals and Books* (covered in more detail in Chapter 5) indexes some treatises. On occasion, periodicals publish bibliographies on certain subjects. A fairly new tool is IndexMaster, a subscription service that currently contains the tables of contents and indexes of over thousands of legal treatises, searchable by key words, authors, or titles.

Treatises in Electronic Media: Increasingly, LexisNexis, Westlaw, and Loislaw are adding treatises, especially treatises that the publisher of the service also publishes in paper. For example, LexisNexis includes the Larson treatise.

E. HOW DO YOU CITE TREATISES?

A citation to a treatise includes the full name(s) of the author(s); the volume number (if the treatise has more than one volume); the main title of the treatise as it appears on the title page (not the cover or spine); the page, section, or paragraph number; the edition (if other than the first); and the year of publication of the main volume or supplement you are using. *ALWD* also includes the publisher. Here are two examples:

- ☐   *Bluebook* Rule 15: 9 Lex K. Larson, *Employment Discrimination* § 155.06 (2d ed. Supp. 2003).
- ☐   *ALWD* Rule 22: Lex K. Larson, *Employment Discrimination* vol. 9, § 155.06 (2d ed., Matthew Bender Supp. 2003).

ILLUSTRATION 4-2   Catalog Entry,
                         from Innovative Interfaces System (electronic source)

William Mitchell College of Law Library   Page 1 of 2

Author	Larson, Lex K
Title	**Employment discrimination / by Lex K. Larson ; practice forms by Lex K. Larson and Jonathan R. Harkavy**
Imprint	New York : M. Bender, 1994-
Call #	KF3464 .L374
Location	Reserve

Location	Reserve
LIB. HAS	1994-
Latest Received:	March 2003 rel. 63

LOCATION	CALL NO.	STATUS
Reserve	KF3464 .L374 v. 1	AVAILABLE
Reserve	KF3464 .L374 v. 2	AVAILABLE
Reserve	KF3464 .L374 v. 3	AVAILABLE
Reserve	KF3464 .L374 v. 4	AVAILABLE
Reserve	KF3464 .L374 v. 5	AVAILABLE
Reserve	KF3464 .L374 v. 6	AVAILABLE
Reserve	KF3464 .L374 v. 7	AVAILABLE
Reserve	KF3464 .L374 v. 8	AVAILABLE
Reserve	KF3464 .L374 v. 9	AVAILABLE
Reserve	KF3464 .L374 v. 10	AVAILABLE

View additional copies or search for a specific volume/copy

Edition	2nd ed
Descript	v. (loose-leaf) : forms ; 26 cm
Note	Earlier ed. by: Arthur Larson
	Includes index
Subject	Sex discrimination in employment -- Law and legislation -- United States
	Discrimination in employment -- Law and legislation -- United States
Alt author	Harkavy, Jonathan R., 1943-
	Larson, Arthur

LEGAL PERIODICALS

A. WHAT IS A LEGAL PERIODICAL?

A legal periodical is a secondary authority that provides commentary on a range of legal topics and is published on a periodic basis, such as quarterly, monthly, or weekly. Most legal periodicals fall into one of four broad categories: law reviews, bar journals, commercial legal journals and newsletters, and legal newspapers.

First, the most prominent type of legal periodical is the law review. Law reviews provide much of the important scholarly work in law; most articles not only describe the current state of the law but also explore underlying policies, critique current legal rules, and advocate law reform. The articles are written by professors, lawyers, lawmakers (most often judges), and law students. Unlike most academic journals, most law reviews are staffed by upper-class students, who select and edit the work; a few are peer-reviewed. Not surprisingly, most law reviews carry the names of their host schools, e.g., the *Georgetown Law Journal*. Many law reviews publish articles on a wide variety of topics; others focus on a specific area, e.g., *Berkeley Journal of Employment & Labor Law*; and a few are interdisciplinary, e.g., *Law and Psychology Review*. There are about 150 general-scope and 250 special-focus law reviews in the United States, and most publish a volume per year in four to eight issues, each containing various types of papers, listed in Exhibit 5.1. For efficiency, this chapter uses *article* to refer to any type of paper.

EXHIBIT 5.1	Types of Periodical Articles
article	a long piece with extensive citations typically written by a professor, lawyer, or lawmaker (typically a judge)
essay	a shorter piece with fewer citations written by a professor, lawyer, or lawmaker
commentary	a short piece responding to a significant lead article by a prominent author
comment note	a long piece written by a student
case comment case note	a shorter piece written by a student that focuses on a specific case
recent developments survey	a set of pieces all on one subject, generally written by a group of faculty and students
symposium	an issue consisting of a collection of articles and student-written pieces all on one subject
book review	a critique of a recently published book

Second, many lawyer organizations, known as "bar associations," publish journals. For example, the American Bar Association, by far the largest national association of lawyers, publishes the *ABA Journal*. The articles in bar journals tend to be more practical than theoretical. Bar journals also report on important legal developments, such as changes in court rules, and cover nonlegal topics of interest to lawyers, such as law firm management. Some ABA sections publish journals that fairly closely resemble academic law reviews and focus on that section's area of law, such as *The Labor Lawyer*, published by the Section of Labor and Employment Law.

Third, for many areas of practice, commercial legal publishers publish journals with articles on emerging legal issues, oriented toward practicing lawyers. In addition, commercial legal newsletters alert readers to new cases, statutes, or rules and also cover recent conferences, studies, and other topics of interest to lawyers in the particular practice area. An example is *Employment Law Weekly*, published by Bureau of National Affairs. Most newsletters are quite short and appear frequently—monthly, weekly, or even daily.

Fourth, commercial legal newspapers typically report new court decisions and other changes in the law, carry legal notices, and present stories about interesting people or significant events in the legal profession. Some legal newspapers are national in scope, e.g., the *National Law Journal*; others cover one city or state, e.g., the *Los Angeles Daily Journal*.

Most well-established legal periodicals are published in paper. Many are available in various electronic sources as well: Westlaw and LexisNexis both have extensive databases containing legal periodicals, although the coverage generally does not extend back to a journal's first volume. Hein-On-Line (a subscription service) provides periodicals from the first issue of each periodical to the last year or two. Obviously, the Web offers a means of quickly publishing and widely distributing articles without the cost and burden of paper publication. To date, there are fairly few well-regarded legal periodicals published only through the Web, although some are available in both paper form and on the school's or publisher's website.

When we researched the Canoga case, we found a note on smokers' rights, written by Michele L. Tyler and published in the *Georgetown Law Journal* in 1998. The opening pages appear as Illustration 1-4 (at pages 17–18), and two additional pages appear as Illustration 5-1 (at pages 82–83).

B.   WHY ARE LEGAL PERIODICAL ARTICLES USEFUL?

When you research in periodicals, you most likely will focus on law reviews. A good law review article provides at least a description and analysis of the law. Most articles cover their subjects in depth; indeed, you may find a lengthy article on a very narrow topic. Many articles also provide valuable background, such as historical information or statistical data. You are likely to find a wealth of references to primary authority, such as cases and statutes; other secondary authorities, such as treatises and other articles; and some nonlegal sources.

Law review articles offer two advantages. First, compared to other secondary authorities, law review articles can be written and published fairly quickly, so they are a good source for discussion of new legal topics. Second, because the special function of law reviews is to present serious, creative legal thought, you may find a critique of present law and proposals for law reform. Although law review articles are merely commentary, a few have, indeed, prompted changes in the law.

Law review articles have disadvantages as well. An article loses currency quickly because the information is current only to the date the article was completed, which may be some time ago, and there is no updating process, as there is with other secondary authorities. In addition, some analysis is idiosyncratic; you need to consider whether it is too unusual to be accepted before you rely on it heavily. Finally, even though law reviews abound, it is possible there will be no article on your research topic.

| ILLUSTRATION 5-1 | Law Review Article, from *Georgetown Law Journal* (paper source) |

A. THE WORKPLACE: INFORMATIONAL PRIVACY RIGHTS

Although neither a constitutional right to smoke, nor a constitutional right to breathe clean air has been recognized,[43] *Shimp v. New Jersey Bell Telephone Co.*[44] is widely cited as recognizing an employer's common law duty to provide a safe work environment. Arguing that employers have such a duty, and taking judicial notice of the dangers of environmental tobacco smoke, the *Shimp* court held that employers must prohibit smoking in work areas.[45] Once employers realized that they could be liable to their nonsmoking employees for violating this common law duty, they began to institute restrictive smoking policies.[46] At the same time, employers were becoming knowledgeable about the health consequences of smoking and the increased costs associated with employing smokers,[47] resulting in an even greater incentive to limit smoking in the workplace. Thus, most of the enacted smoking policies serve the dual purpose of protecting the health of nonsmoking employees and customers and of reducing costs to the employer. States began to take interest as well; as of 1995, eleven states had regulated smoking in private places of employment, others were considering restrictive legislation, and still others had regulated smoking in public employment.[48] Additionally, localities have passed ordinances regulating smoking, though like the state statutes, they vary in the scope of their provisions.[49]

Yet smokers, with the help of the tobacco industry, continue to lobby Congress and state and local legislatures to protect the rights of smokers.[50] By 1995,

---

43. *See* Gasper v. Louisiana Stadium & Exposition Dist., 418 F. Supp. 716 (E.D. La. 1976) (holding that the U.S. Constitution does not guarantee a right to breathe air free of smoke). The class action suit was brought on behalf of all nonsmoking attendees of events in the Louisiana Superdome, a public facility.

44. 368 A.2d 408 (N.J. Super. Ct. Ch. Div. 1976).

45. *See id.* at 416; *see also* Smith v. Western Elec. Co., 643 S.W.2d 10 (Mo. Ct. App. 1982) (holding an employer has a duty to use due care to eliminate harmful conditions, including tobacco smoke); McCarthy v. Department of Soc. & Health Serv., 759 P.2d 351 (Wash. 1988) (holding employer has duty to take "reasonable precautions" to protect employees from environmental tobacco smoke).

46. *See* Sablone, *supra* note 5, at 1090.

47. *See infra* notes 71-77 and accompanying text. The increased cost of employing smokers is not without debate. At least one critic of strict nonsmoking policies argues that smokers' productivity is sacrificed when management denies a smoker the opportunity to smoke at work. *See* Mitchell, *supra* note 1, at 231. Smokers may not want to rely on this argument, however, because it serves as yet another reason why employers should be permitted to refuse to hire smokers altogether. Additionally, employers recognize that by not limiting smoking in the workplace, they are likely to face claims by nonsmoking employees who, years later, develop health problems. *See id.* at 232.

48. *See* Ann H. Zgrodnik, Comment, *Smoking Discrimination: Invading an Individual's Right to Privacy in the Home and Outside the Workplace?*, 21 OHIO N.U. L. REV. 1227, 1238-39 & nn.114-15 (1995). In 1995, the following states had laws regulating smoking in private places of employment: Arizona, Connecticut, Florida, Maine, Minnesota, Montana, Nebraska, New Hampshire, New Jersey, Rhode Island, and Utah. *Id.* at 1239 n.114.

49. *See id.* at 1239. Although the laws vary, most prohibit smoking in certain areas, require signs to be posted indicating whether smoking is permitted, and require that certain areas be set aside as nonsmoking areas. *See* Mark A. Rothstein, *Refusing to Employ Smokers: Good Public Health or Bad Public Policy?*, 62 NOTRE DAME L. REV. 940, 946-47 (1987).

50. *See* Zgrodnik, *supra* note 48, at 1244-45.

ILLUSTRATION 5-1   *(continued)*

790   THE GEORGETOWN LAW JOURNAL   [Vol. 86:783

twenty-nine states had passed some type of smoker-protection legislation prohibiting employers from discriminating against employees or potential employees who smoke while off duty.[51]

Despite smoker activism, some cities and private employers continue to enact restrictive smoking policies. By 1994, an estimated six percent of all companies refused to hire smokers, even individual smokers who do not smoke during work hours.[52] Companies often cite *Grusendorf v. City of Oklahoma City*[53] as support for the constitutionality of this practice. In *Grusendorf*, the Oklahoma City Fire Department required firefighter trainees to abstain from on-duty and off-duty smoking for one year after they were hired.[54] Grusendorf was spotted smoking on a lunch break and was subsequently fired.[55] Although the court agreed that the smoking policy infringed upon Grusendorf's privacy, it held that smoking is not a fundamental privacy right and thus the policy was valid as long as the city could offer a rational basis for it.[56] Because firefighters must be in top physical condition to combat their on-the-job smoke exposure, the court held that the city had passed the rational basis test.[57] Although a firefighter's informational privacy interests are compromised by a requirement that he report legal behavior that he would otherwise keep from his employer, it is not surprising that in the interests of public safety, the city could validly override this individual interest.

More controversial, however, is *City of North Miami v. Kurtz*,[58] in which the Florida Supreme Court upheld the city's anti-smoking regulation that required all prospective city employees to sign an affidavit stating that they had refrained from using tobacco products for the prior year.[59] Because Kurtz admitted that she could not truthfully sign the affidavit, she was told that she would no longer be a candidate for city employment.[60] She then sued, claiming a violation of her federal and state constitutional privacy right to smoke outside the course of

---

51. *See id.*; *see also* Gerhart, *supra* note 13, at 188 & n.50 (quoting BUREAU OF NAT'L AFFAIRS, INDIVIDUAL EMPLOYMENT RIGHTS MANUAL 509:501 (1995)). Although the scope and focus of smoker protection statutes vary, some prohibit employers from refusing to hire smokers or from discriminating against present employees because of their off-duty smoking. *See* Lisa A. Frye, Comment, *"You've Come a Long Way, Smokers": North Carolina Preserves the Employee's Right to Smoke Off the Job in General Statutes Section 95-28.2*, 71 N.C. L. REV. 1963, 1964 (1993).

52. *See* Lewis L. Maltby & Bernard J. Dushman, *Whose Life Is it Anyway—Employer Control of Off-Duty Behavior*, 13 ST. LOUIS U. PUB. L. REV. 645, 645 (1994).

53. 816 F.2d 539 (10th Cir. 1987). *See, e.g.,* Operation Badlaw, Inc. v. Licking County Gen. Health Dist. Bd. of Health, 866 F. Supp. 1059, 1064 (S.D. Ohio 1992) (citing *Grusendorf* for principle that the right to smoke is not a fundamental right); Town of Plymouth v. Civil Serv. Comm'n, 686 N.E.2d 188, 190 n.4 (Mass. 1997) (citing *Grusendorf* and upholding police offficer's termination for smoking while off-duty).

54. *See Grusendorf*, 816 F.2d at 540.

55. *See id.*

56. *See id.* at 541-42.

57. *See id.* at 543.

58. 653 So. 2d 1025 (Fla. 1995).

59. *Id.* at 1026.

60. Kurtz v. City of North Miami, 625 So. 2d 899, 900 (Fla. Dist. Ct. App. 1993).

C.   HOW DO YOU RESEARCH IN LEGAL PERIODICALS?

Research in legal periodicals is quite similar to research in other types of periodicals. The traditional approach, which is the best when you know fairly little about your research topic, is to use a periodicals index to identify pertinent articles and then read the articles in paper or online. When you already have some solid knowledge of your research topic, a good approach is to use a key-word full-text search and then read the articles in a periodicals database. A concluding optional step is to cite a helpful article, that is, to check whether later articles or cases refer to the helpful article.

Traditional periodicals research involving an index:

▶ select a periodicals index

▶ conduct a subject search and possibly also a key-word search in the index

▶ read and assess the identified articles

For many years, the dominant index for legal periodicals was *Index to Legal Periodicals,* first published in 1908 and now known as *Index to Legal Periodicals and Books. Current Law Index* began publication in 1980 and has quickly gained credibility. Although both indexes are available in paper, you most likely will use them in electronic media.

Electronic indexes are preferable because they are very current; cumulate information over time (paper research involves multiple books and pamphlets); provide not only citations but also abstracts (short descriptions) of articles; and afford key-word searching as well as searching by subject, author, and title. *Index to Legal Periodicals and Books*—available through Westlaw, LexisNexis, and WilsonWeb—covers 850 law reviews and journals, yearbooks, institutes, bar association publications, university publications, and government publications as well as 1,400 monographs per year. *Current Law Index* in its electronic version *LegalTrac,* a division of *InfoTrac,* covers 800 major law reviews, legal newspapers, law specialty publications, bar association journals, and international legal journals as well as law-related articles from 1,000 additional business and general-interest sources.

The main advantage of using a periodicals index is the system of subject headings and subheadings, so your goal is to identify a pertinent subject heading and obtain a list of articles on that subject. A good first step is a subject search, in which you enter a term you believe will be a subject heading. If the term you enter in a subject search is not itself and does not lead to a pertinent subject heading, consider running a key-word search; once you find a pertinent article, you can discern the subject heading(s) under which it is listed. See Illustration 5-2 (at page 87). If the list of articles under the pertinent subject heading is lengthy, consider running a key-word search within that list to zero in on the most probably pertinent articles.

For any particular article, you may be able to learn more than the author, title, and citation. If an abstract (brief summary) or full text is available, be sure to check these out. Periodical article titles can be less than revealing; an abstract and the first paragraph or so of text should help you ascertain how pertinent the article is.

On occasion, you may know a bit about a pertinent article and want to find additional information. For example, if you know the author or the title of a potentially pertinent article, you can run an author or title search in an index and obtain information on the article.

Depending on your circumstances, you may have several options for locating and reading articles identified through your index research. You may find a paper copy in a library; many researchers prefer to read articles in paper, in part because the text and corresponding footnotes appear on the same page. Online options may include the index (if text is available); the journal's website; or a commercial source such as Westlaw, LexisNexis, or Hein-On-Line.

If through your research you identify more than one pertinent article, you may well want to look at several but not all of them. Keep the following factors in mind as you select articles to rely upon:

☐ Coverage: Does the article focus on your research topic and cover it thoroughly? Be sure that the article covers your jurisdiction; some articles focus on one state's law.

☐ Currency: Is the journal peer-reviewed? Is the article fairly recent, so that its research and analysis likely are still current?

☐ Credibility: Is the journal peer-reviewed? Is the author reputable, and is the periodical well respected? As you would surmise, student work is viewed as less credible than an article by a professor, for example, and law reviews from well-known and highly ranked law schools tend to be viewed most highly.

☐ Quality of research and analysis: Do the footnotes refer to sufficient authority to support the propositions, and does the analysis make sense?

☐ Persuasiveness: If the article argues for a change in the law, are the arguments logical and convincing?

As you begin to study an article, be sure to first orient yourself: read the synopsis on the first page, if there is one; look over the table of contents or, if there is no table of contents, the headings and subheadings within the article; carefully read the introduction and conclusion. More likely than not, some parts will be more pertinent to your client's situation than others; read those parts carefully and skim the rest. Pay equally close attention to the text and the footnotes; you will want to learn from the author's description of the law but not accept it as true without reading the cited authorities yourself. Finally, take care to differentiate the author's description of existing law, critique of the law, and proposed reforms.

Researching the Canoga case through *LegalTrac*, we found several pertinent subject headings: Privacy, Right of; Smoking; and Workplace Smoking. All included the subheading Laws, Regulations, Etc., which is generally a very useful subheading. We found the Tyler article this way. In addition, a key-word search for `smok* and priva*` identified thirty-five articles, and the Tyler article was sixth on the list. Illustration 5-2 (at page 87) is the expanded *LegalTrac* entry for that article.

The Tyler note covers employer regulation of employee smoking (along with regulation of smoking in other settings), dates to 1998 (five years before this text was written), was written by a student but is in the law review of a well-regarded law school, seems well supported, and reads well. The article is worth reading for research purposes, although it is unlikely that the author's proposals would be highly persuasive to a court because the article is a student note. We focused on the several pages discussing the workplace and only skimmed the discussion of other settings.

Periodicals in full-text key-word searching:

▶ select a service and database
▶ run a key-word search
▶ read and assess the retrieved articles

Both Westlaw and LexisNexis have very substantial full-text legal periodicals databases. Westlaw's database encompasses about 800 periodicals; LexisNexis' database encompasses about 575 periodicals. As noted in Part C of Chapter 2, key-word searching is a good strategy when a source is electronic and follows a periodic (rather than highly organized) publication pattern.

Researching the Canoga case, we searched in LexisNexis' U.S. & Canadian Law Reviews, Combined database. We tried various searches combining the concept of privacy and the facts of smoking and employment; these searches retrieved too many articles to review (many focusing on employer e-mail policies but also touching on smoking policies). We then narrowed our focus to smoking off-duty or during non-working hours and entered this search: `priva! /p smok! /s off-duty or non-working or nonworking`. This search retrieved twenty-five articles; the Tyler note is eighth on the citation list. See Illustration 2-7 (at pages 52–53).

ILLUSTRATION 5-2   Expanded Entry for Periodical Article, from *LegalTrac* (electronic source)

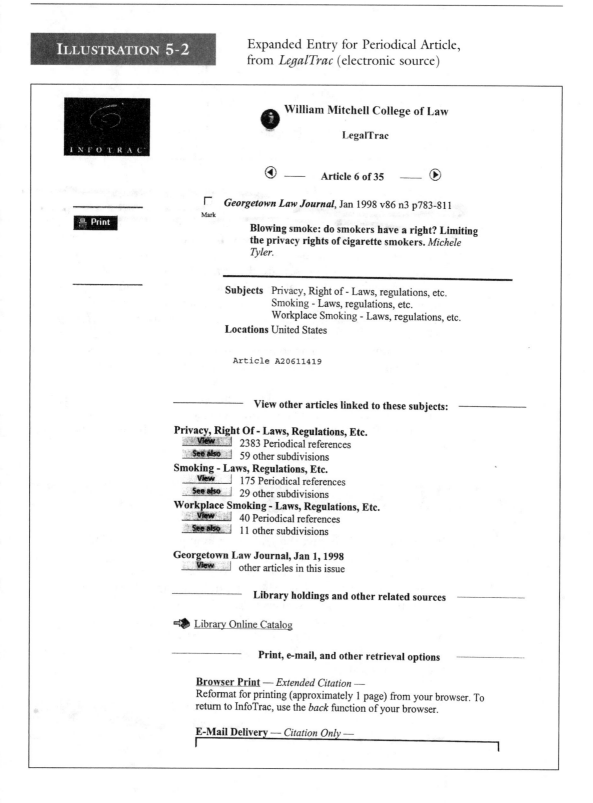

William Mitchell College of Law

LegalTrac

◄ —— Article 6 of 35 —— ►

☐   *Georgetown Law Journal*, Jan 1998 v86 n3 p783-811
Mark

Blowing smoke: do smokers have a right? Limiting the privacy rights of cigarette smokers. *Michele Tyler.*

Subjects   Privacy, Right of - Laws, regulations, etc.
Smoking - Laws, regulations, etc.
Workplace Smoking - Laws, regulations, etc.
Locations United States

Article A20611419

—————   View other articles linked to these subjects: —————

Privacy, Right Of - Laws, Regulations, Etc.
[View]   2383 Periodical references
[See also]   59 other subdivisions
Smoking - Laws, Regulations, Etc.
[View]   175 Periodical references
[See also]   29 other subdivisions
Workplace Smoking - Laws, Regulations, Etc.
[View]   40 Periodical references
[See also]   11 other subdivisions

Georgetown Law Journal, Jan 1, 1998
[View]   other articles in this issue

—————   Library holdings and other related sources   —————

Library Online Catalog

—————   Print, e-mail, and other retrieval options   —————

Browser Print — *Extended Citation* —
Reformat for printing (approximately 1 page) from your browser. To return to InfoTrac, use the *back* function of your browser.

E-Mail Delivery — *Citation Only* —

> **Citating periodical articles:**
>
> ▸ select a periodicals citator
> ▸ cite the article
> ▸ follow up on the citing sources, as appropriate

As in many other disciplines, if you find a particularly important article, you may want to cite it, for two reasons: to learn whether its ideas have been received favorably, not only by other scholars but also by courts, and to locate newer articles on the same topic. As discussed in Chapter 2, Part C, the article you have read is the *cited* article, and the more recent authorities, such as other articles or cases, are the *citing* authorities.

Until quite recently, citing an article was a rather cumbersome process entailing one or more volumes of a paper source, *Shepard's Law Review Citations*; indeed, in legal research, one name for the process of citing is "Shepardizing." Although it is still possible to cite periodical articles in paper, citing in electronic sources is much more efficient. LexisNexis now offers Shepard's in electronic form, and Westlaw has a comparable product in KeyCite.

Researching the Canoga case, we cited the Tyler note through Shepard's on LexisNexis and obtained the report in Illustration 5-3 (at page 89). As of mid-2003, the Tyler note had been cited in eight other articles on a range of topics, but not by any courts.

D.   WHAT ELSE?

Legal Scholarship Network.   A leading example of Web periodicals publication is the Legal Scholarship Network (LSN), which is a division of the Social Science Research Network (SSRN). LSN offers fifty journals, such as Employment and Labor Law Abstracts (in its fourth volume when this text was written in 2003). Subscribers receive, by e-mail, abstracts of new articles as well as working papers, most of which eventually will appear in law reviews or other academic journals. In addition, subscribers may download many articles from the SSRN collection and also search the abstracts by author, title, or key words.

Specialized Indexes.   As extensive as the indexes described in this chapter are, for some advanced research tasks, you may want to consult an index with a more specialized focus, e.g., *Index to Federal Tax Articles, Index to Periodical Articles Related to Law, Index to Foreign Legal Periodicals.*

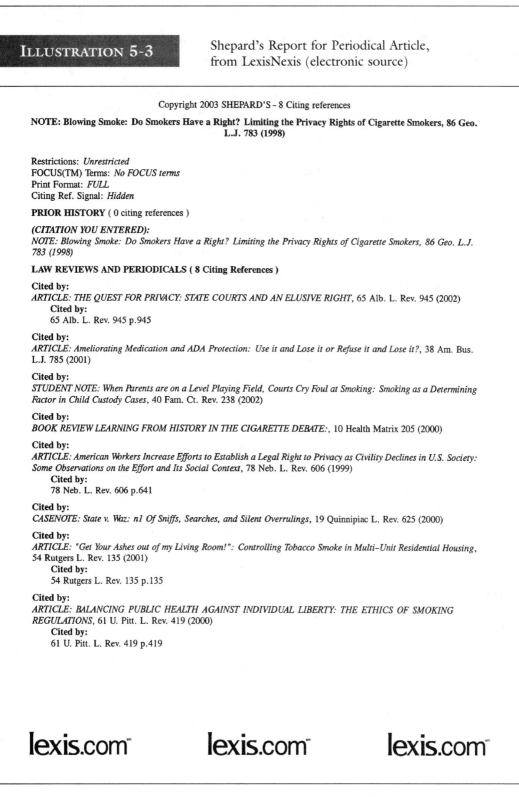

ILLUSTRATION 5-3   Shepard's Report for Periodical Article,
from LexisNexis (electronic source)

Copyright 2003 SHEPARD'S – 8 Citing references

NOTE: Blowing Smoke: Do Smokers Have a Right? Limiting the Privacy Rights of Cigarette Smokers, 86 Geo.
L.J. 783 (1998)

Restrictions: *Unrestricted*
FOCUS(TM) Terms: *No FOCUS terms*
Print Format: *FULL*
Citing Ref. Signal: *Hidden*

PRIOR HISTORY (0 citing references)

(CITATION YOU ENTERED):
NOTE: Blowing Smoke: Do Smokers Have a Right? Limiting the Privacy Rights of Cigarette Smokers, 86 Geo. L.J.
783 (1998)

LAW REVIEWS AND PERIODICALS (8 Citing References)

Cited by:
ARTICLE: THE QUEST FOR PRIVACY: STATE COURTS AND AN ELUSIVE RIGHT, 65 Alb. L. Rev. 945 (2002)
   Cited by:
   65 Alb. L. Rev. 945 p.945

Cited by:
ARTICLE: Ameliorating Medication and ADA Protection: Use it and Lose it or Refuse it and Lose it?, 38 Am. Bus.
L.J. 785 (2001)

Cited by:
STUDENT NOTE: When Parents are on a Level Playing Field, Courts Cry Foul at Smoking: Smoking as a Determining
Factor in Child Custody Cases, 40 Fam. Ct. Rev. 238 (2002)

Cited by:
BOOK REVIEW LEARNING FROM HISTORY IN THE CIGARETTE DEBATE:, 10 Health Matrix 205 (2000)

Cited by:
ARTICLE: American Workers Increase Efforts to Establish a Legal Right to Privacy as Civility Declines in U.S. Society:
Some Observations on the Effort and Its Social Context, 78 Neb. L. Rev. 606 (1999)
   Cited by:
   78 Neb. L. Rev. 606 p.641

Cited by:
CASENOTE: State v. Waz: n1 Of Sniffs, Searches, and Silent Overrulings, 19 Quinnipiac L. Rev. 625 (2000)

Cited by:
ARTICLE: "Get Your Ashes out of my Living Room!": Controlling Tobacco Smoke in Multi–Unit Residential Housing,
54 Rutgers L. Rev. 135 (2001)
   Cited by:
   54 Rutgers L. Rev. 135 p.135

Cited by:
ARTICLE: BALANCING PUBLIC HEALTH AGAINST INDIVIDUAL LIBERTY: THE ETHICS OF SMOKING
REGULATIONS, 61 U. Pitt. L. Rev. 419 (2000)
   Cited by:
   61 U. Pitt. L. Rev. 419 p.419

lexis.com™   lexis.com™   lexis.com™

E.   HOW DO YOU CITE LEGAL PERIODICALS?

A proper cite to an article in a legal periodical includes the author's full name and, as needed, an indication that the author is a student; the title of the article; the volume; the periodical's abbreviation; the first page number; and the date. Here are two examples:

- ☐ *Bluebook* Rule 16: Michele L. Tyler, Note, *Blowing Smoke: Do Smokers Have a Right? Limiting the Privacy Rights of Cigarette Smokers*, 86 Geo. L.J. 783 (1998).
- ☐ *ALWD* Rule 23: Michele L. Tyler, Student Author, *Blowing Smoke: Do Smokers Have a Right? Limiting the Privacy Rights of Cigarette Smokers*, 86 Geo. L.J. 783 (1998).

A.L.R. ANNOTATIONS

A. What Are American Law Reports (A.L.R.) Annotations?
B. Why Is A.L.R. Useful?
C. How Do You Research in A.L.R.?
D. What Else?
E. How Do You Cite A.L.R.?

A. WHAT ARE AMERICAN LAW REPORTS (A.L.R.) ANNOTATIONS?

American Law Reports Annotations (A.L.R.) contain two kinds of material: annotations and cases. An annotation is an article that discusses, in great detail, the various cases on a fairly narrow legal topic. Most annotations focus on issues of some controversy, in which courts in different jurisdictions follow different rules, or on issues that are factually sensitive so that different facts result in different holdings. A typical A.L.R. annotation discusses the law in many jurisdictions within the United States, referring to relevant authority in each of those jurisdictions.

Accompanying the annotation is a case, a court's opinion selected by the publisher as a leading or typical case on the topic—hence the word *Reports* in the title, *reports* being a common term for a compilation of cases. Because other sources of case law are more complete, your primary focus in A.L.R. research will be on the annotation, not the accompanying case.

A.L.R. is published by a commercial publisher, Thomson West. The annotations are written by its staff attorneys or attorneys hired to write particular annotations.

A.L.R. is a large multivolume set, first published in 1919. A.L.R. has been published in multiple series, as listed in Exhibit 6.1. Publication in series is common in the law. After a good number of volumes, the publisher starts a new series and begins the numbering of volumes over, with 1. In general,

EXHIBIT 6.1	A.L.R. Series	

Series	Dates	Topics
A.L.R.1st	1919-1948	state and federal
A.L.R.2d	1948-1965	state and federal
A.L.R.3d	1965-1969	state and federal
A.L.R.3d	1969-1980	state
A.L.R.4th	1980-1991	state
A.L.R.5th	1992 to date	state
A.L.R. Fed.	1969 to date	federal

a new series does not replace an old series. In the case of A.L.R., although most recent annotations cover new topics, some do cover topics covered in earlier annotations and thus supersede those annotations. You are likely to use the more recent series more frequently, so this text focuses on the third, fourth, fifth, and federal series.

Six to ten A.L.R. volumes are issued each year for each current series, and each volume contains approximately ten annotations. Each A.L.R. volume typically covers a wide range of subjects, such as contracts, torts, criminal law, and employment law.

As an example pertinent to the Canoga case, Illustration 6-1 (at page 93) is a page from an annotation on the impact of an employment policy on the employer's right to discharge a stated at-will employee.

B.   WHY IS A.L.R. USEFUL?

An annotation provides a good and fairly current overview of a specific topic. It provides a general description of the topic and then detailed descriptions of the cases on the topic. Because the case descriptions are organized by rule or outcome, you can easily see the different approaches taken by various courts and the importance of key facts. In addition, an annotation provides references to certain other secondary authorities, such as the encyclopedia Am. Jur. 2d. Furthermore, A.L.R. is timely: An annotation may be the first secondary authority published on a new topic, and A.L.R. is kept up to date in various ways.

However, A.L.R. has its limitations. There may be no annotation on your research topic. The topics are quite narrow, so you should turn to A.L.R. only after you have a good sense of the subject encompassing your research topic. Moreover, although the discussion is quite comprehensive, it is more descriptive than analytical or critical. Furthermore, because an annotation

| ILLUSTRATION 6-1 | A.L.R. Annotation Case Descriptions (paper source) |

---

33 ALR4th   EMPLOYMENT AT WILL—RESTRAINTS ON DISCHARGE   § 4[b]
33 ALR4th 120

its discretion in granting the defendant's motion for a new trial.

◆

In Simpson v Western Graphics Corp. (1982) 293 Or 96, 643 P2d 1276, where the parties agreed that the provisions of the employee handbook were contractual terms of the plaintiffs' employment and that therefore the defendant could discharge employees only upon a determination of just cause, the court held that, absent an express provision transferring authority to for making the factual just-cause determination to an outside arbiter, the employer retained the right to make that determination. The court stated that although an employer's statement of employment policy has a degree of contractual effect, its terms are not necessarily to be construed in the same way as those of a negotiated labor contract. The court pointed out that the handbook was a unilateral statement by the employer of self-imposed limitations upon its prerogatives and was furnished to the plaintiff after they were hired and afforded no inference that the plaintiffs accepted or continued in employment in reliance upon its terms. In such a situation, the court said, the meaning intended by the employer is controlling and there was no reason to infer that the employer intended to surrender its power to determine whether facts constituting cause for just termination existed.

[b] Right of discharge held not restricted

Under the particular circumstances in the following cases, it was held that the promulgation of employment policies regarding the procedures and grounds for termination of at-will employees did not operate to restrict an employer's right to freely discharge at-will employees.

Rejecting the contention of the plaintiff, a campus security guard, that the terms of the defendant's personnel manual, in particular, the provisions relating to discharge of employees, adopted by the defendant and issued to its employees upon their appointment became an employment contract binding upon both parties and that thus the defendant's discharge of the plaintiff without first providing written allegations or an opportunity to be heard, as provided for in the personnel manual, was in breach of the contract, the court in Sargent v Illinois Institute of Technology (1979) 78 Ill App 3d 117, 33 Ill Dec 937, 397 NE2d 443, affirmed the dismissal of the plaintiff's action, stating that the personnel manual was not an enforceable contract. Unlike the situation presented in Carter v Kaskaskia Community Action Agency (1974) 24 Ill App3d 1056, 322 NE2d 574, supra § 4[a], where, the court noted, it was found that both the employees and the employer affirmatively adopted the personnel manual and thus accordingly held that the manual became part of the at-will employment contract, in the instant case, the campus police guidelines set forth in the manual were not bargained for, the plaintiff provided no additional consideration to support a predischarge hearing requirement, and the manual was given to the plaintiff at the start of his employment and thus could not be viewed as a contractual modification. Viewed as a whole, the court stated the manual defined the duties and responsibilities of a campus policeman and served as a code for appropriate conduct and that by agreeing to be bound by the guidelines, the plaintiff had merely agreed to properly perform his duties and nothing more.

135

generally is written by a staff lawyer, rather than a recognized scholar, an annotation is not as credible an authority to cite as some other secondary authorities.

C.   HOW DO YOU RESEARCH IN A.L.R.?

There is no single dominant approach for A.L.R. research. The following text describes two standard approaches: researching in books and researching in LexisNexis or Westlaw.

A.L.R. in paper:

- ▶ consult the *ALR Index* (or tables of primary authorities) to identify pertinent annotations
- ▶ read the opening material
- ▶ use the various means of access to identify pertinent passages
- ▶ read the text of the annotation
- ▶ consult the references section
- ▶ update your research

An efficient means of locating a pertinent A.L.R. annotation in paper is to use the *ALR Index,* a multivolume set encompassing the second, third, fourth, fifth, and federal series of A.L.R. The *ALR Index* is updated, so you should check the pocket part as well as the main volume. As an alternative, if you already know of a key primary authority, you can locate an annotation discussing that authority by consulting the tables in the *ALR Index* or the *ALR Federal Tables* volumes.

Once you have located a potentially pertinent annotation, read the opening material to learn the scope of the annotation, to discern whether other annotations might be more helpful, and to obtain an overview of the topic. To locate pertinent passages within an annotation, consult the following means of access: the outline of the annotation; its index; and the list of jurisdictions represented, which permits you to zero in on cases from your jurisdiction. See Illustration 6-2 (at pages 97–99).

As you read the text of the annotation, focus on cases in your jurisdiction, seek to discern patterns in the case law from other jurisdictions, and look for cases with factual parallels to your client's situation. In addition, you may want to read the accompanying case if it is from your jurisdiction or if you discern from its description in the annotation that it could be particularly helpful persuasive precedent.

Next, consult the references section in the opening pages for citations to other secondary authorities. See Illustration 6-2 (at page 96).

The annotations in the third, fourth, fifth, and federal series are updated several ways, and you should explore all three for comprehensive research:

☐ First, check the pocket part for additional text and case descriptions. See Illustration 6-3 (at page 100).

☐ Second, check for a more recent annotation. The pocket part may indicate that the annotation has been superseded, or the Annotation History Table, in the tables volume of the *ALR Index*, may so indicate.

☐ Third, you may bring your research up to the minute by calling the Latest Case Service hot line for cases decided since the last supplement. The telephone number is listed on the front covers of recent pocket parts.

If the annotation you are reading was published some time ago, you may want to check the pocket part earlier in the process, perhaps before you read the text of the annotation. This way, you may learn of a superseding annotation before you invest too much time reading the text. In addition, you may learn of more recent cases; in general, recent cases are more significant than older ones (as discussed in Chapter 9).

Researching the Canoga case, we found in the *ALR Index* the subject heading Discharge from Employment or Office with a subheading At-Will Employee. The annotation excerpted in this chapter was listed there.

The Introduction (§ 1) indicates that the annotation is on point. The outline suggests that courts have used two theories—contract and estoppel—and that outcomes vary. The index points to various potentially pertinent sections, but the table of jurisdictions indicates that no New Mexico cases are covered. See Illustration 6-2 (at pages 97–99).

The annotation in the main volume, published in 1984, summarizes thirty-four cases from twenty-four jurisdictions, identifying facts that lead to one outcome or the other as well as the legal theory of each case. The accompanying case, *Weiner v. McGraw-Hill, Inc.*, 443 N.E.2d 441 (N.Y. 1982), decided by the New York Court of Appeals in 1982, is a leading case that would nonetheless be only persuasive authority for the Canoga case.

We did find additional case descriptions in the pocket part. Indeed, the pocket part runs sixty-five pages, a reflection of the rapid development of this subject over the past two decades. As shown in Illustration 6-3 (at page 100), New Mexico cases now appear, including *Lukoski v. Sandia Indian Management Co.*, the case in Illustration 1-1 (at pages 9–12). There was no indication that the annotation had been superseded. This research project is a good example of a situation in which reviewing the pocket part early on would be wise.

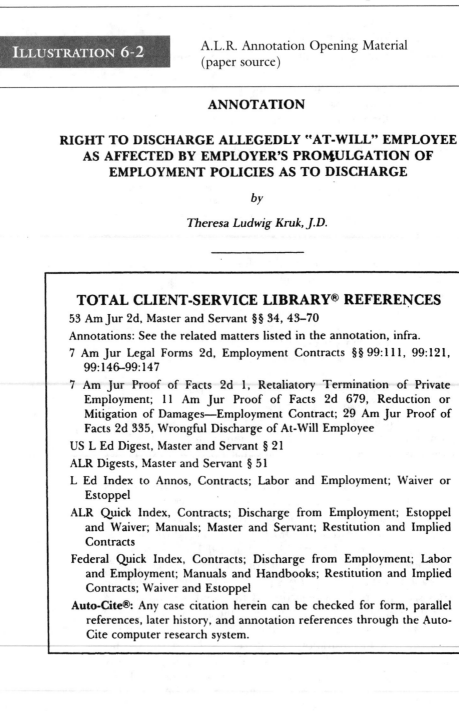

ILLUSTRATION 6-2   A.L.R. Annotation Opening Material
                       (paper source)

ANNOTATION

RIGHT TO DISCHARGE ALLEGEDLY "AT-WILL" EMPLOYEE AS AFFECTED BY EMPLOYER'S PROMULGATION OF EMPLOYMENT POLICIES AS TO DISCHARGE

by

Theresa Ludwig Kruk, J.D.

TOTAL CLIENT-SERVICE LIBRARY® REFERENCES

53 Am Jur 2d, Master and Servant §§ 34, 43–70

Annotations: See the related matters listed in the annotation, infra.

7 Am Jur Legal Forms 2d, Employment Contracts §§ 99:111, 99:121, 99:146–99:147

7 Am Jur Proof of Facts 2d 1, Retaliatory Termination of Private Employment; 11 Am Jur Proof of Facts 2d 679, Reduction or Mitigation of Damages—Employment Contract; 29 Am Jur Proof of Facts 2d 335, Wrongful Discharge of At-Will Employee

US L Ed Digest, Master and Servant § 21

ALR Digests, Master and Servant § 51

L Ed Index to Annos, Contracts; Labor and Employment; Waiver or Estoppel

ALR Quick Index, Contracts; Discharge from Employment; Estoppel and Waiver; Manuals; Master and Servant; Restitution and Implied Contracts

Federal Quick Index, Contracts; Discharge from Employment; Labor and Employment; Manuals and Handbooks; Restitution and Implied Contracts; Waiver and Estoppel

Auto-Cite®: Any case citation herein can be checked for form, parallel references, later history, and annotation references through the Auto-Cite computer research system.

Consult POCKET PART in this volume for later cases

120

ILLUSTRATION 6-2   *(continued)*

INDEX

ILLUSTRATION 6-2   *(continued)*

---

§ 1[a]   EMPLOYMENT AT WILL—RESTRAINTS ON DISCHARGE   33 ALR4th
33 ALR4th 120

Union activities, § 5	Withdrawal of handbook by employer, § 3
Vacation pay loss, § 4[a]	Work force reduction, § 4[a]
Warning slip, § 3	"Writing up" of employee, § 4[b]

TABLE OF JURISDICTIONS REPRESENTED
Consult POCKET PART in this volume for later cases

US: §§ 3, 4[a]	**Mich:** § 4[a]
Ala: § 3	**Minn:** § 4[a]
Cal: § 5	**Mont:** § 4[b]
Del: § 3	**Neb:** § 3
DC: §§ 3, 4[a]	**NY:** §§ 4[a], 5
Fla: § 3	**NC:** § 3
Ill: §§ 4[a], 4[b]	**Or:** §§ 4[a], 4[b]
Ind: §§ 3, 4[a]	**Pa:** § 4[a]
Kan: §§ 3, 4[a]	**SD:** § 4[a]
Ky: § 4[a]	**Tex:** § 3
La: § 3	**Va:** § 3
Me: § 3	**Wis:** § 4[b]

---

§ 1. Introduction

[a] Scope

This annotation[1] collects the state and federal cases that consider whether an employer's promulgation of employment policies regarding the procedures and reasons for termination or discharge of employees[2] affects an employer's right to discharge an at-will employee at any time and for any or no reason.

This annotation includes only those cases in which an at-will employee relies upon the policy statements of his or her employer regarding termination or discharge and contends that his or her discharge was effectuated in a manner or for reasons contrary to the express general policy of the employer,[3] as opposed to personal assurances or representations by the employer, regardless of whether such policy was written or unwritten, and the employer defends against such a charge by asserting the at-will status of the employee.

[b] Related matters

Recovery for discharge from employment in retaliation for filing workers' compensation claim. 32 ALR4th 1221.

Modern status of rule that employer may discharge at-will employee for any reason. 12 ALR4th 544.

---

1. This annotation supersedes § 7 of 12 ALR4th 544.

2. For treatment of cases dealing with an at-will employee's right to severance pay as provided by an employer's general policy on severance, see 53 Am Jur 2d, Master and Servant § 81.

3. For a discussion of cases involving

122

at-will employees who claim to have been hired as "permanent" employees or "for life," see generally 53 Am Jur 2d, Master and Servant §§ 20, 32–34. See also the annotation in 24 ALR3d 1412 entitled "Employer's misrepresentation as to prospect, or duration of, employment as actionable fraud."

ILLUSTRATION 6-2   *(continued)*

33 ALR4th   EMPLOYMENT AT WILL—RESTRAINTS ON DISCHARGE   § 2[a]
33 ALR4th 120

Liability for discharging at-will employee for refusing to participate in, or for disclosing, unlawful or unethical acts of employer or coemployees. 9 ALR4th 329.

Right of corporation to discharge employee who asserts right as stockholder. 84 ALR3d 1107.

Reduction in rank or authority or change of duties as breach of employment contract. 63 ALR3d 539.

Employee's arbitrary dismissal as breach of employment contract terminable at will. 62 ALR3d 271.

Employer's termination of professional athlete's services as constituting breach of employment contract. 57 ALR3d 257.

Nature of alternative employment which employee must accept to minimize damages for wrongful discharge. 44 ALR3d 629.

Employer's misrepresentation as to prospect, or duration of, employment as actionable fraud. 24 ALR3d 1412.

Elements and measure of damages in action by schoolteacher for wrongful discharge. 22 ALR3d 1047.

Liability of federal government officer or employee for causing discharge or separation of subordinate. 5 ALR Fed 961.

§ 2. Background, summary, and comment

[a] Generally

The common-law rule regarding the termination of an at-will employ-ment contract is that if the employment is not for a definite term, and if there is no contractual or statutory restriction on the right of discharge, an employer may lawfully discharge an employee whenever and for whatever cause, without incurring liability for wrongful discharge.[4] Few legal principles have been better settled than the at-will concept, whose roots date back to the 19th century laissez-faire policy of protecting freedom to contract. In recent years, however, there has been a growing trend toward a restricted application of this rule in order to comport with express and implied public policy, as well as statutory concerns. Some jurisdictions have been willing to depart from the traditional contract rule of terminability at will and to impose an implied contractual duty not to discharge an employee for reasons regarded as violative of public policy or to recognize the tortious nature of a discharge violative of public policy, whether such policy is expressly codified or implied.[5]

In keeping with this modern trend of judicial re-evaluation and legislative modification, a number of jurisdictions have held or recognized that under particular circumstances, the right of an employer to freely discharge at-will employees may be contractually restricted as a result of the promulgation of corporate employment policies specifying the proce-

---

4. Although the at-will rule is generally regarded as vesting in the employer absolute discretion to terminate employment, this "right" is actually a rule of contract construction rather than a right grounded in substantive law. Absent an express contractual provision specifying the term of employment, the duration depends upon the intention of the parties as determined from the circumstances of each case. It is still the general rule that an indefinite hiring, under circumstances that do not permit the implication of any fixed period of duration, is presumed to be terminable at the will of either party, with the burden on the party asserting a fixed period. 53 Am Jur 2d, Master and Servant §§ 27, 43.

5. See generally, the annotation in 12 ALR4th 544, for a discussion of the modern status of the at-will rule.

123

ILLUSTRATION 6-3   A.L.R. Annotation Pocket Part
(paper source)

33 ALR4th 120-138   ALR4th

relationship and created warning and suspension procedures which were not followed; termination procedures became amendment to employee's contract and personality, not severe offenses of insubordination or disobedience, caused employee's termination. Handbook characterized disciplinary policy regarding warnings, suspensions, and terminations as established procedure and language of handbook did nothing to alert employee that it was subject to revocation at any time or that employee should not rely on it. Lukoski v Sandia Indiana Management Co. (1988, **NM**) 748 P2d 507, 2 BNA IER Cas 1650. LC ¶ 55496, mod on other gnds 101 NJ 10, 1985 NJ 10, 499 A2d 515.

Personnel manual gives rise to implied contract, for purposes of implied contract exception to employment at will doctrine, if it controls employer-employee relationship and employee can reasonably expect employer to conform to procedures it outlines. Garcia v Middle Rio Grande Conservancy Dist. (1996, **NM**) 918 P2d 7, 11 BNA IER Cas 1328.

Employer may be bound by express statements in its policy manual limiting its otherwise unfettered right to discharge its employees. Disciplined or terminated employee may seek Article 78 review to determine whether employer contravened any of its own rules or regulations in taking that disciplinary action. Hanchard v Facilities Dev. Corp. (1995) 85 **NY2d** 638, 628 NYS2d 4, 651 NE2d 872, 10 BNA IER Cas 1004, 130 CCH LC ¶ 57921.

Employee can rebut presumption of employment at will by establishing that employee was made aware of written policy of limitation on employer's right to discharge at time employment commenced, and in accepting employment, employee relied on termination only for cause limitation. For manual or other written policy to limit employer's right to terminate, it must contain express limitation. Preston v Champion Home Builders, Inc. (1992, 3d Dept) 187 App Div 2d 795, 589 **NYS2d** 940.

To sustain cause of action for breach of employment contract, employee must demonstrate that employment manual contained clear and express limitation that employee would not be terminated or disciplined except for cause, and that employee specifically relied on this language. Charyn v National Westminster Bank, U.S.A. (1994, 2d Dept) 204 App Div 2d 676, 612 **NYS2d** 432.

At-will auditor for brokerage house who alleged he was discharged for reporting illegal money-laundering scheme possessed cause of action for breach of contract, where employment manual contained requirement that em-

ployees report misconduct and also contained reciprocal promise to protect reporters from retaliation. Mulder v Donaldson, Lufkin & Jenrette (1995, 1st Dept) 208 App Div 2d 301, 623 **NYS2d** 560, 10 BNA IER Cas 631.

Discharged employee may recover damages by establishing that employer made employee aware of its express written policy limiting its right of discharge and that employee detrimentally relied on that policy in accepting employment. Mika v. New York State Ass'n for Retarded Children, Inc., 230 A.D.2d 744, 646 **N.Y.S.2d** 168 (2d Dep't 1996).

Under New York law, at-will employee can have cause of action for breach of implied contract against employer where he or she is discharged in absence of circumstances or procedures specified in employer's handbook. Thus, terminated at-will executive of registered securities broker-dealer satisfied all elements of state cause of action for wrongful discharge alleging that employer's manual created implied contract of employment because it assured continued employment as long as employee did not transgress manual's provisions; that employer breached implied contract where it did not fire him for any stated ground contained in manual, but rather for no apparent or stated reason or cause, evidence indicated that no misconduct occurred before firing. Reeves v Continental Equities Corp. (1991, **SD NY**) 767 F Supp 469 (applying NY law).

Presumption that, absent agreement establishing fixed duration, employment relationship is at will does not apply when employer had promulgated policies in personnel manual specifying procedures or grounds for termination; these procedures become part of employment contract and must be followed. Thus, job security policy stated in handbook contractually bound employer and did not amount to nonbinding general statements of policy and supervisory guidelines, where policy set forth very specific and detailed procedure for work force reduction in mandatory and unqualified terms. Further, severance pay provision was explicitly invoked and followed in case of discharged employee asserting cause of action for breach of contract in connection with reduction in force. Handbook's general language of qualification that stated "in the final analysis, specific judgment and discretion will govern," did not negate binding force of handbook's more specific provisions under state law. Mycak v Honeywell, Inc. (1992, **CA2 NY**) 953 F2d 798, 7 BNA IER Cas 117, 120 CCH LC ¶ 56780, (applying NY law).

New York is "employment-at-will" state, and thus, absent express agreement limiting em-

32

For latest cases, call the toll free number appearing on the cover of this supplement.

> **A.L.R. in LexisNexis and Westlaw:**
>
> ▶ select the appropriate database
> ▶ run a key-word search
> ▶ read the annotation (updated automatically)
> ▶ pull in cases via links

Most A.L.R. volumes are available online as well: LexisNexis and Westlaw offer all but the first series. The approach stated above works with some modifications online. For example, on Westlaw, a ci(index) command permits you to browse the index to locate a pertinent annotation. Furthermore, because A.L.R. is periodically published and has no overall topical organization, searching for key words is a sensible approach.

In both LexisNexis and Westlaw, you can use Boolean or natural language searches. The entire A.L.R. database is very large, so unless you can craft a very specific search, you may want to use component restrictions. For example, A.L.R. titles generally are complete and precise; hence a title search may succeed well. So might a date-restricted search.

Once you locate a pertinent annotation, you should read the annotation much as you would read an annotation in a book, although the electronic version is presented somewhat differently. For example, once you identify a pertinent section in the article outline or index, you can link to that section. New material that appears in pocket parts is merged into the original material in the electronic version. Furthermore, you will receive a notice if the annotation has been superseded and can easily link to the new annotation. You can make the transition to case law research in just a moment by linking to the name of a pertinent case described in the annotation. Note, however, that the accompanying case from the book version is not part of the online version.

Researching the Canoga case, we ran the following search in Westlaw: ti(employ! personnel & handbook policy manual). It retrieved forty-five annotations; the annotation excerpted in this chapter was tenth on the list.

D. WHAT ELSE?

Citing A.L.R.s: It is possible to citate (find authorities referring to) A.L.R. annotations in both LexisNexis' Shepard's and Westlaw's KeyCite services. The most likely reason for doing this is to find additional cases and secondary authorities.

Lawyers' Edition Annotations: In addition to those in A.L.R., annotations discussing United States Supreme Court cases on certain major topics appear in a case reporter called *United States Supreme Court Reports Lawyers' Edition*.

A.L.R. Digests: The A.L.R. digests contain synopses of cases covered in A.L.R. and references to annotations and some other secondary authorities. Most people find the *ALR Index* easier to use.

Some Features of the Older Series: The first A.L.R. series has its own index and digest; the same is true of A.L.R.2d. The annotations in the first series are updated by the *A.L.R. Blue Book of Supplemental Decisions*; A.L.R.2d annotations are updated by *A.L.R.2d Later Case Service.*

E.   HOW DO YOU CITE A.L.R.?

A cite to an A.L.R. annotation includes the author's full name (if available), the title of the annotation, the volume and series, beginning page number, and date.[1] Here are two examples:

☐ *Bluebook* Rule 16.5.5: Theresa L. Kruk, Annotation, *Right to Discharge Allegedly "At-Will" Employee as Affected by Employer's Promulgation of Employment Policies as to Discharge,* 33 A.L.R.4th 120 (1984 & Supp. 2002).

☐ *ALWD* Rule 24: Theresa L. Kruk, *Right to Discharge Allegedly "At-Will" Employee as Affected by Employer's Promulgation of Employment Policies as to Discharge,* 33 A.L.R.4th 120 (1984 & Supp. 2002).

---

1. The date to be included is the date of the book; as needed a pocket part date also is included. You may not have this information if you research in electronic media, a glitch yet to be resolved in legal citation manuals.

RESTATEMENTS

A. What Are the Restatements?
B. Why Are Restatements Useful?
C. How Do You Research in Restatements?
D. What Else?
E. How Do You Cite Restatements?

A. WHAT ARE THE RESTATEMENTS?

The Restatements are a distinctly legal form of scholarship; they are the most law-like of the various types of secondary authority. To use the Restatements effectively, you must understand why they came to be, how they are created, how they are formatted, and how courts view them.

During the early twentieth century, two schools of legal scholarship battled: The rationalists believed that the common law—that is, the body of law comprised of decisions of the courts—consisted of immutable principles that could be expressed in an organized manner. The realists believed that the common law reflected the needs of the litigants, the biases of judges, and prevailing social norms. In 1923, the rationalists mobilized to organize the American Law Institute (ALI). The ALI's goal was to promulgate one highly authoritative, rule-like source stating the common law. Because the purpose of the source was not to create law but rather to state what already existed, the source was named the Restatements. The first Restatement, covering the law of contracts, was promulgated in 1932.

The ALI has continued to promulgate Restatements over the past seventy years. See Exhibit 7.1. Note that the Restatements do not cover every legal subject. Note as well that each Restatement carries not only the name of the subject but also a series designation reflecting the date of adoption. The first series Restatements were adopted in 1932-1942, the second series in 1957-1981, and the third in 1986 to the present. Thus, were the ALI to promulgate a Restatement on a new subject, it would be a third series Restatement, even though there has been no first or second series Restatement on that subject.

EXHIBIT 7.1	Restatement Subjects, Series, and Adoption Dates

Subject	Series and Date(s) of Adoption
Agency	first 1933 second 1957
Conflict of Laws	first 1934 second 1969, 1988
Contracts	first 1932 second 1979
Foreign Relations	second 1962, 1964, 1965 third 1986
Judgments	first 1942 second 1980
Law Governing Lawyers	third 1998

Property
  Landlord and Tenant
  Donative Transfers
  Mortgages
  Servitudes
  Wills & Other Donative Transfers
	first 1936, 1940, 1944
	second 1976
	second 1981, 1984, 1987, 1990
	third 1996
	third 1998
	third 1998

Restitution	first 1936
Security	first 1941
Suretyship & Guaranty	third 1995

Torts
 	
  Apportionment of Liability
  Products Liability
	first 1934, 1938, 1939
	second 1963, 1964, 1976, 1977
	third 1999
	third 1997

Trusts Prudent Investor Rule	first 1935 second 1957 third 2001, 2003 third 1990
Unfair Competition	third 1993

As the Restatements have matured, there has been a shift in policy. Early on, the Restatements were to state the rule followed by the majority of courts around the country, even if the minority rule were thought to be wiser. This policy could slow the development of the law, however. Recent Restatements state the minority rule when it is deemed wiser than the majority rule.

Each Restatement is the product of a lengthy and wide-ranging deliberative process, which generally involves the following steps:

☐ preparation of a draft by the reporter, an eminent scholar in the particular field;

☐ review of that draft by a panel of experts;

☐ consideration by the ALI Council—a group of about sixty judges, attorneys, and professors;

☐ consideration by the entire ALI membership (there are 3,000 members);

☐ submission to the public and the legal profession for comment;

☐ approval by the ALI Council and membership.

This process is far more extensive than the process used to create any other type of secondary authority.

Given the purpose of the Restatements and the ALI process, it is not surprising that the Restatements consist not of the expository prose found in other secondary authorities but rather of finely honed sentences, each stating a distinct rule, which appears in bold face[1] in the official books. (The Restatement rules resemble statutes, which also are the product of a lengthy and wide-ranging deliberative process.) To assist the reader, each rule is followed by explanatory material:

☐ comments, which discuss the rule's scope, meaning, and rationale;

☐ illustrations, which are short stories that illustrate the application of the rule and typically reflect influential cases from which the rule was derived; and

☐ for more recent Restatements, reporter's notes, which typically explain the history of the rule and refer to leading cases and secondary authorities.

See Illustration 7-1 (at pages 106–09). The rules and supporting materials on a particular subject are compiled into chapters organized to reflect the logical structure of the subject.

Given the purpose of the Restatements, the ALI process, and the format of the Restatements, it is also not surprising that the Restatements are widely viewed as the most authoritative of the secondary authorities and that courts around the country routinely refer to and indeed even adopt Restatement rules. Note that a court is not obligated to follow the Restatement; a court may reject a Restatement rule, adopt only part of a rule, incorporate one illustration but not another, etc. As of April 1, 2002, the Restatements had been cited by the courts almost 155,000 times.[2]

Researching the employee handbook issue in the Canoga case in the Restatement of Contracts (Second), we found section 2, which defines "promise," a key element of an enforceable contract. See Illustration 7-1 (at pages 106–09).

1. You may hear the term "black-letter law," which means a legal rule that is fundamental and well settled. Although many Restatement rules amount to black-letter law, the term refers not to the bold-face print of the Restatement, but to books printed in Gothic type, which is very bold.

2. 2002 A.L.I. Ann. Rep. 15.

ILLUSTRATION 7-1	Restatement Rule, Comments, Illustrations, and Reporter's Note, from Restatement (Second) of Contracts (paper source)

---

§ 1   CONTRACTS, SECOND   Ch. 1

Wis. L. Rev. 303; Macauley, Contract Law and Contract Research, 20 J. Legal Ed. 452 (1968); Farnsworth, The Past of Promise: An Historical Introduction to Contract, 69 Colum. L. Rev. 576 (1969); Macneil, The Many Futures of Contract, 47 So. Cal. L. Rev. 691 (1974); Macneil, Restatement, Second, of Contracts and Presentation, 60 Va. L. Rev. 589 (1974); Atiyah, Contracts, Promises and the Law of Obligations, 94 L. Q. Rev. 193 (1978); see also Leff, Contract as Thing, 19 Amer. U. L. Rev. 131 (1970).

Comments a and b. For a concise discussion of what constitutes a contract, how it can be created and its relation to tort actions for fraud, see Steinberg v. Chicago Medical School, 69 Ill.2d 320, 371 N.E.2d 634 (1977).

Comment e. Illustration 1 is new.

Comment f. Section 12 of the original Restatement defined unilateral and bilateral contracts. It has not been carried forward because of doubt as to the utility of the distinction, often treated as fundamental, between the two types. As defined in the original Restatement, "unilateral contract" included three quite different types of transaction: (1) the promise which does not contemplate a bargain, such as the promise under seal to make a gift, (2) certain option contracts, such as the option under

seal (see §§ 25, 45), and (3) the bargain completed on one side, such as the loan which is to be repaid. This grouping of unlike transactions was productive of confusion.

Moreover, as to bargains, the distinction tends to suggest, erroneously, that the obligation to repay a loan is somehow different if the actual delivery of the money was preceded by an advance commitment from the obligation resulting from a simultaneous loan and commitment. It also causes confusion in cases where performance is complete on one side except for an incidental or collateral promise, as where an offer to buy goods is accepted by shipment and a warranty is implied. Finally, the effect of the distinction has been to exaggerate the importance of the type of bargain in which one party begins performance without making any commitment, as in the classic classroom case of the promise to pay a reward for climbing a flagpole.

The principal value of the distinction has been the emphasis it has given to the fact that a promise is often binding on the promisor even though the promisee is not bound by any promise. This value is retained in § 25 on option contracts. But the terms unilateral and bilateral are generally avoided in this Restatement.

§ 2.   **Promise; Promisor; Promisee; Beneficiary**

(1) **A promise is a manifestation of intention to act or refrain from acting in a specified way, so made as to justify a promisee in understanding that a commitment has been made.**

(2) **The person manifesting the intention is the promisor.**

ILLUSTRATION 7-1   *(continued)*

Ch. 1   MEANING OF TERMS   § 2

(3) The person to whom the manifestation is addressed is the promisee.

(4) Where performance will benefit a person other than the promisee, that person is a beneficiary.

Comment:

  a. Acts and resulting relations. "Promise" as used in the Restatement of this Subject denotes the act of the promisor. If by virtue of other operative facts there is a legal duty to perform, the promise is a contract; but the word "promise" is not limited to acts having legal effect. Like "contract," however, the word "promise" is commonly and quite properly also used to refer to the complex of human relations which results from the promisor's words or acts of assurance, including the justified expectations of the promisee and any moral or legal duty which arises to make good the assurance by performance. The performance may be specified either in terms describing the action of the promisor or in terms of the result which that action or inaction is to bring about.

  b. Manifestation of intention. Many contract disputes arise because different people attach different meanings to the same words and conduct. The phrase "manifestation of intention" adopts an external or objective standard for interpreting conduct; it means the external expression of intention as distinguished from undisclosed intention. A promisor manifests an intention if he believes or has reason to believe that the promisee will infer that intention from his words or conduct. Rules governing cases where the promisee could reasonably draw more than one inference as to the promisor's intention are stated in connection with the acceptance of offers (see §§ 19 and 20), and the scope of contractual obligations (see §§ 201, 219).

  c. Promise of action by third person; guaranty. Words are often used which in terms promise action or inaction by a third person, or which promise a result obtainable only by such action. Such words are commonly understood as a promise of conduct by the promisor which will be sufficient to bring about the action or inaction or result, or to answer for harm caused by failure. An example is a guaranty that a third person will perform his promise. Such words constitute a promise as here defined only if they justify a promisee in an expectation of some action or inaction on the part of the promisor.

  d. Promise of event beyond human control; warranty. Words which in terms promise that an event not within human control will occur may be interpreted to include a promise to answer for harm caused by the failure of the event to occur. An example is a warranty

See Appendix for Court Citations and Cross References

1 A.L.I.Contracts 2nd—2   9

ILLUSTRATION 7-1   *(continued)*

§ 2   CONTRACTS, SECOND   Ch. 1

of an existing or past fact, such as a warranty that a horse is sound, or that a ship arrived in a foreign port some days previously. Such promises are often made when the parties are ignorant of the actual facts regarding which they bargain, and may be dealt with as if the warrantor could cause the fact to be as he asserted. It is then immaterial that the actual condition of affairs may be irrevocably fixed before the promise is made.

Words of warranty, like other conduct, must be interpreted in the light of the circumstances and the reasonable expectations of the parties. In an insurance contract, a "warranty" by the insured is usually not a promise at all; it may be merely a representation of fact, or, more commonly, the fact warranted is a condition of the insurer's duty to pay (see § 225(3)). In the sale of goods, on the other hand, a similar warranty normally also includes a promise to answer for damages (see Uniform Commercial Code § 2–715).

Illustrations:

1. A, the builder of a house, or the inventor of the material used in part of its construction, says to B, the owner of the house, "I warrant that this house will never burn down." This includes a promise to pay for harm if the house should burn down.

2. A, by a charter-party, undertakes that the "good ship Dove," having sailed from Marseilles a week ago for New York, shall take on a cargo for B on her arrival in New York. The statement of the quality of the ship and the statement of her time of sailing from Marseilles include promises to pay for harm if the statement is untrue.

e. Illusory promises; mere statements of intention. Words of promise which by their terms make performance entirely optional with the "promisor" whatever may happen, or whatever course of conduct in other respects he may pursue, do not constitute a promise. Although such words are often referred to as forming an illusory promise, they do not fall within the present definition of promise. They may not even manifest any intention on the part of the promisor. Even if a present intention is manifested, the reservation of an option to change that intention means that there can be no promisee who is justified in an expectation of performance.

On the other hand, a promise may be made even though no duty of performance can arise unless some event occurs (see §§ 224, 225(1)). Such a conditional promise is no less a promise because there is small likelihood that any duty of performance will arise, as in the case of a promise to insure against fire a thoroughly fireproof building. There

See Appendix for Court Citations and Cross References

10

ILLUSTRATION 7-1 *(continued; page 11 omitted)*

§ 2   CONTRACTS, SECOND   Ch. 1

ise is made; as promise is defined here, the promisee might be the person to whom the manifestation of the promisor's intention is communicated. In many situations, however, a promise is complete and binding before the communication is received (see, for example, §§ 63 and 104(1)). To cover such cases, the promisee is defined here as the addressee. As to agents or purported agents of the addressee, see § 52 Comment *c*.

In the usual situation the promisee also bears other relations to the promisor, and the word promisee is sometimes used to refer to one or more of those relations. Thus, in the simple case of a loan of money, the lender is not only the addressee of the promise but also the person to whom performance is to be rendered, the person who will receive economic benefit, the person who furnished the consideration, and the person to whom the legal duty of the promisor runs. As the word promisee is here defined, none of these relations is essential.

Contractual rights of persons not parties to the contract are the subject of Chapter 14. The promisor and promisee are the "parties" to a promise; a third person who will benefit from performance is a "beneficiary." A beneficiary may or may not have a legal right to performance; like "promisee", the term is neutral with respect to rights and duties. A person who is entitled under the terms of a letter of credit to draw or demand payment is commonly called a beneficiary, but such a person is ordinarily a promisee under the present definition. See Uniform Commercial Code § 5–103.

REPORTER'S NOTE

This Section substitutes the concept of a "manifestation of intention to act . . ." for the phrase used in former § 2(1): "an undertaking . . . that something shall happen. . . ." The older definition did not identify the essential characteristics of an undertaking. See Gardner, An Inquiry Into the Principles of Contracts, 46 Harv. L. Rev. 1, 5 (1932). The present definition of promise is based on 1 Corbin, Contracts § 13 (1963 & Supp. 1980). See also 1 id. § 15; 1 Williston, Contracts § 1A (3d ed. 1957). The definitions of "promisor," "promise" and "beneficiary" are new. Compare Gardner, Massachusetts Annota-

tions, Restatement of Contracts, Chapter 6, at 64 (1935).

Comment a. See Coffman Industries, Inc. v. Gorman-Taber Co., 521 S.W.2d 763 (Mo. Ct. App. 1975); Farnsworth, The Past of Promise: An Historical Introduction to Contract, 69 Colum. L. Rev. 576 (1969).

Comment d. This Comment is based on former § 2(2). Illustrations 1 and 2 are based on Illustrations 2 and 3 to former § 2.

Comment e. See Pappas v. Bever, 219 N.W.2d 720 (Iowa 1974). Illustration 3 is based on Illustration 4 to former § 2.

See Appendix for Court Citations and Cross References

B.   WHY ARE RESTATEMENTS USEFUL?

For the most part, the Restatements are not where you will begin your research. There may not be a Restatement on your research topic. Even if there is a pertinent Restatement, the Restatements are not as easy to read as other secondary authorities. Rather, you are likely to use a Restatement once you already know something about your research topic, in particular for the following purposes:

- ☐ to obtain a succinct and very credible statement of the law on a settled topic;
- ☐ to discern some of the nuances in and policies underlying a rule, through the comments and illustrations; and
- ☐ to obtain a highly credible statement of a favorable rule, when the case law in your jurisdiction disfavors your client and the Restatement rule favors your client.

As you work with the Restatements, keep in mind that they do have limitations. The Restatements are not revised on a regular basis, as you can see from Exhibit 7.1, and the law may have developed away from the rule you have located. A few rules are thought not to restate the law or the desirable rule, but rather to state the views of the primary authors or an awkward compromise of the various views proposed during the deliberations. Furthermore, there is no attempt to capture or explain the variations in approach from courts around the country.

To counter some of these limitations, if you think you will rely to a significant extent on a Restatement rule, you should research how it has been received by the courts. Most important is whether it has been adopted, noted, rejected, or not discussed in the case law of your jurisdiction. If you find no indication of your jurisdiction's view of the rule, you should examine how it has been received by other courts.

C.   HOW DO YOU RESEARCH IN RESTATEMENTS?

Restatements research has, in essence, two phases: research in the Restatements themselves and research in case law referring to the Restatements. The preferable approach to the first phase is to use the single book or multi-volume set of books comprising a Restatement; a somewhat less desirable approach is to research in Westlaw or LexisNexis. The second phase can be handled reasonably well in books but more efficiently in electronic media.

Restatements in paper:

- ▶ select the applicable Restatement and series
- ▶ use the table of contents or index
- ▶ read the rules, comments, illustrations, and reporter's notes

To locate a pertinent Restatement rule, you must first determine which Restatement, e.g., the Restatement of Contracts or the Restatement of Torts, covers your research topic; if you already have done some research in other secondary authorities, this should not be difficult. If the pertinent Restatement has been published in more than one series, you generally should start with the more recent.

To locate pertinent sections, read over the table of contents for the Restatement you chose, and look up your research terms in the index. The locations of the table of contents and the index vary from Restatement to Restatement. Look not just for one pertinent section; for many topics, you will want to read a number of related sections, typically all sections listed under a subject heading or subheading, as shown in the table of contents, as well as any pertinent definitions or overarching principles found at the beginning of the Restatement.

Then read the sections in the main subject volumes—not in the appendix volumes (discussed below). First study the rule itself; then read through the comments, illustrations, and reporter's notes (if available). In reading this material, take care to glean as much as possible, including:

- [ ] the exact language of the rule;
- [ ] comments on the rule that are pertinent to your client's situation;
- [ ] illustrations that factually parallel your client's situation;
- [ ] any discussion of the rule's derivation, e.g., whether it is a majority or minority rule, how it relates to an earlier Restatement;
- [ ] references to other related Restatement sections; and
- [ ] references to leading cases (especially any from your jurisdiction) and secondary authorities.

Researching the employee handbook issue in the Canoga case in the Restatement (Second) of Contracts, we identified several potentially pertinent sections, including the opening sections, which state what a contract is, what a promise is, and how contracts are formed. We focused on the definition of *promise* provided in section 2. See Illustration 7-1 (at pages 106–09). In addition to the succinct definition in the rule itself, we learned that, when the contracting parties differ in their understanding of the language, the proper focus is the promisor's manifestation of intention, rather than any undisclosed intention on the part of the promisor. We also learned that this focus is new to this Restatement and found references to both cases and secondary authorities. And we would follow up on references to sections 19 and 20 regarding acceptance of a contract as well as sections 201 and 219 on the scope of a contractual obligation.

> **Cases referring to the Restatements in paper:**
>
> ► collect all needed publications
> ► browse the case summaries
> ► check for very recent case citations

As noted above, if you plan to rely significantly on a Restatement rule, you should learn how it has been received in your jurisdiction and perhaps in other jurisdictions as well. The appendices to the various Restatements provide case summaries for cases referring to that Restatement, organized first by Restatement series (if there is more than one), then section by section. Each summary contains a brief statement of the facts, the holding, and the court's reasoning as well as the case's citation. See Illustration 7-2 (at page 113). Because the summaries appear in alphabetical order by state, you can fairly easily locate the summaries from your jurisdiction.

The case summaries appear in various publications. You should check for pocket parts to the main volume, separate appendix volumes, pocket parts to the appendix volumes, and supplementary pamphlets. The most recent summaries appear in *Interim Case Citations to the Restatements of the Law,* which covers all the Restatements, and the references to (but not summaries of) very new cases appear in the Table of Citations in *Interim Case Citations.* See Illustration 7-3 (at page 114). Often you will need to collect several publications to cover the entire time period since a Restatement section was adopted.

If the Restatement you are using is not the first on the subject, especially if you have not found a case summary or reference from your jurisdiction, you may want to engage in further retrospective research. If the explanatory material to the current Restatement indicates that it carries over the rule from the earlier Restatement, you could check for cases referring to the earlier Restatement. If the explanatory material to the current Restatement indicates that its rule is new, you may want to research the earlier Restatement. Although the newer version is meant by the ALI to supersede the previous version, some courts may not support the newer version, so you should determine whether your jurisdiction has referred to the earlier version. You would most likely do this retrospective research if reliance on a Restatement section is critical to your analysis.

Researching the Canoga case, in the appendix covering 1991-1996 cases, we found summaries of a New Mexico case referring to section 2. We also found a summary of a Michigan case with similar facts. See Illustration 7-2 (at page 113). There were no pertinent citations in the Table of Citations in *Interim Case Citations.* See Illustration 7-3 (at page 114).

ILLUSTRATION 7-2   Restatement Case Summaries,
                          from Restatement of Contracts Appendix (paper source)

§ 2   **CONTRACTS**   **Ch. 1**

rise to a contract, on a promissory estoppel theory, by virtue of reliance. The court said that bank did not intend, and defendants did not understand, bank's "promise" to be a commitment, because both parties contemplated a written agreement that would govern the construction loan. Rhode Island Hospital Trust National Bank v. Varadian, 419 Mass. 841, 850, 647 N.E.2d 1174, 1179.

Mass.App.1991. Com. (b) cit. in sup. A law firm sued its client to recover a performance premium, alleging that it was part of a fair and reasonable fee. The trial court granted summary judgment for the client, holding that the law firm could not charge the premium. Affirming, this court held, inter alia, that, although the firm had in the past charged clients a premium, their subjective and unexpressed expectations could not refute the expressed manifestations, based on the previous billing pattern and a letter from the firm to the client confirming a time charge fee arrangement, to charge on the basis of time only. Beatty v. NP Corp., 31 Mass.App.Ct. 606, 613, 581 N.E.2d 1311, 1315.

Mich.1993. Subsec. (1) quot. in part in sup. In separate suits, two former employees sued their employers, alleging breach of employment contracts in their "at will" discharges. This court, hearing appeals in both cases after granting leave, reversed the intermediate appellate court's reversal of judgment for the employer in the first case and reversed the intermediate appellate court's reversal of summary judgment for the employer in the second case and remanded, holding, inter alia, that, in the first case, employer assurances of continued employment, an informal policy of discharge only for "good reason," and a handbook promise of fairness were not sufficient to create an agreement for just-cause employment, but, in the second case, although similar assurances and statements to a management employee were not sufficient to create just-cause employment, whether the overall policies of the employer could reasonably have instilled in the employee a legitimate expectation of just-cause employment was a jury issue. Rood v. General Dynamics Corp., 444 Mich. 107, 138, 139, 507 N.W.2d 591, 606.

Mich.1993. Quot. in disc., cit. in ftn., com. (a) quot. in ftn. A bank sued dairy farmers for claim and delivery, seeking to obtain the collateral pledged under a note on which the farmers had defaulted. The farmers counter-

claimed for damages on a promissory estoppel theory, inter alia. The trial court found for the bank on its claim and delivery action, and entered judgment on a jury verdict for the farmers on their promissory estoppel counterclaim. The court of appeals reversed in part, finding insufficient evidence to sustain the promissory estoppel claim. Reversing in part and remanding, this court held that the evidence presented a fact question on whether the bank made a clear and definite promise to extend a loan, ultimately not extended, to the farmers so as to cover the note on which they defaulted, where the evidence indicated that, in reliance on bank officers' statements that the bank would continue to support them, the farmers elected to stay in the dairy business and did not participate in a government dairy buyout program. State Bank of Standish v. Curry, 442 Mich. 76, 85, 500 N.W.2d 104, 108.

Neb.1991. Subsec. (1) quot. in disc. and quot. in case cit. in disc. A purchaser of cable television systems sued the sellers for failing to deliver the promised amount of subscribers specified in the contract. The sellers claimed that the purchaser forfeited any right to damages because it did not comply with the contract notice provisions. The trial court granted the purchaser partial summary judgment on the issue of the sellers' liability for the subscriber shortfall and damages were awarded. Affirming in part, vacating in part, and remanding, this court held, inter alia, that the notice provisions in the contract were promissory rather than conditional and, therefore, the purchaser's noncompliance did not discharge the sellers' liability. The court stated that the absence of any language indicative of a condition precluded a conclusion that the parties clearly intended the notice requirements to constitute a condition to the creation of a contract. Harmon Cable Com. v. Scope Cable Tele., 237 Neb. 871, 468 N.W.2d 350, 359.

N.M.App.1993. Subsec. (1) quot. in diss. op. Terminated employee sued employer for wrongful discharge, alleging that he was fired in retaliation for requesting that occupational health and safety bureau investigate chemical usage and employee health problems at defendant's workplace. The parties entered into settlement agreement approved by the bureau. The trial court entered partial summary judgment for defendant, holding that

See also cases under division, chapter, topic, title and subtitle that include section under examination. For earlier citations see Restatement of the Law, Second, Contracts 2d Appendix Volumes 4–9.

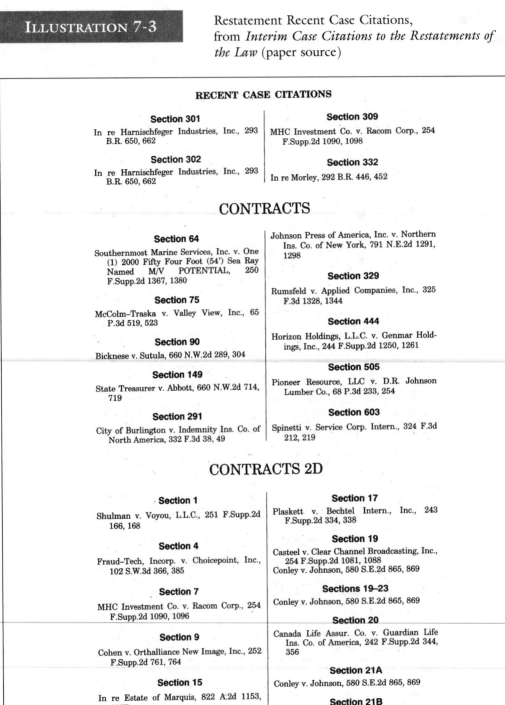

ILLUSTRATION 7-3   Restatement Recent Case Citations, from *Interim Case Citations to the Restatements of the Law* (paper source)

RECENT CASE CITATIONS

Section 301

In re Harnischfeger Industries, Inc., 293 B.R. 650, 662

Section 302

In re Harnischfeger Industries, Inc., 293 B.R. 650, 662

Section 309

MHC Investment Co. v. Racom Corp., 254 F.Supp.2d 1090, 1098

Section 332

In re Morley, 292 B.R. 446, 452

CONTRACTS

Section 64

Southernmost Marine Services, Inc. v. One (1) 2000 Fifty Four Foot (54') Sea Ray Named M/V POTENTIAL, 250 F.Supp.2d 1367, 1380

Section 75

McColm–Traska v. Valley View, Inc., 65 P.3d 519, 523

Section 90

Bicknese v. Sutula, 660 N.W.2d 289, 304

Section 149

State Treasurer v. Abbott, 660 N.W.2d 714, 719

Section 291

City of Burlington v. Indemnity Ins. Co. of North America, 332 F.3d 38, 49

Johnson Press of America, Inc. v. Northern Ins. Co. of New York, 791 N.E.2d 1291, 1298

Section 329

Rumsfeld v. Applied Companies, Inc., 325 F.3d 1328, 1344

Section 444

Horizon Holdings, L.L.C. v. Genmar Holdings, Inc., 244 F.Supp.2d 1250, 1261

Section 505

Pioneer Resource, LLC v. D.R. Johnson Lumber Co., 68 P.3d 233, 254

Section 603

Spinetti v. Service Corp. Intern., 324 F.3d 212, 219

CONTRACTS 2D

Section 1

Shulman v. Voyou, L.L.C., 251 F.Supp.2d 166, 168

Section 4

Fraud–Tech, Incorp. v. Choicepoint, Inc., 102 S.W.3d 366, 385

Section 7

MHC Investment Co. v. Racom Corp., 254 F.Supp.2d 1090, 1096

Section 9

Cohen v. Orthalliance New Image, Inc., 252 F.Supp.2d 761, 764

Section 15

In re Estate of Marquis, 822 A.2d 1153, 1157
Spahr v. Secco, 330 F.3d 1266, 1274

Section 17

Plaskett v. Bechtel Intern., Inc., 243 F.Supp.2d 334, 338

Section 19

Casteel v. Clear Channel Broadcasting, Inc., 254 F.Supp.2d 1081, 1088
Conley v. Johnson, 580 S.E.2d 865, 869

Sections 19–23

Conley v. Johnson, 580 S.E.2d 865, 869

Section 20

Canada Life Assur. Co. v. Guardian Life Ins. Co. of America, 242 F.Supp.2d 344, 356

Section 21A

Conley v. Johnson, 580 S.E.2d 865, 869

Section 21B

Conley v. Johnson, 580 S.E.2d 865, 869

600

> **Restatements in Westlaw and LexisNexis:**
>
> ▶ select one or more appropriate database(s)
> ▶ use one or more means of access: browsing the table of contents, running a Boolean or natural-language search

Both Westlaw and LexisNexis provide the Restatements in various databases. Think carefully as you choose which database to use. A database containing all Restatements is a large and unwieldy database; almost always you will know which Restatement is pertinent and should confine your research accordingly. Using the Westlaw database for a particular Restatement that combines, for each section, the rule, the explanatory material, and the case summaries is a good choice. For similar coverage in LexisNexis, you would search the database containing the Contracts rule sections and a second database containing the Contracts case summaries.

As suggested above, browsing the table of contents to discern which sections are pertinent is a good strategy; you can do this on both Westlaw and LexisNexis. These sources also afford the additional options of Boolean and natural-language searches. Particularly if the database you are searching includes the case summaries and your research topic includes relatively distinctive factual terms, both types of searches can be efficient means of locating not only pertinent sections but also cases. In addition, linking to those pertinent cases is an efficient bridge to case law research.

Researching the Canoga case, we ran the following natural-language search in Westlaw's Restatement of Contracts database: Can the language in an employee handbook be a contractually binding promise? Section 2 was the first section in the citations list, and the highlighted term *employee handbook* in the case summaries made it easy to locate pertinent cases.

D. WHAT ELSE?

Work in Progress. You can follow the development of a pending Restatement through online databases and through the ALI publications, *Annual Reports, Proceedings*, and *The ALI Reporter*. To research the evolution of an existing or past Restatement section, you could visit the University of Pennsylvania's Biddle Law Library, which has ALI archives.

Citing the Restatements. You can citate the Restatements through LexisNexis' Shepard's service. This service may be more up to date than the case summaries and case citations, and you will find not only citing cases but also selected secondary authorities, such as law reviews.

E. HOW DO YOU CITE RESTATEMENTS?

A cite to Restatement material includes the name (including the series) of the Restatement, the section number, and the date of publication (which may differ from the promulgation date). Here are two examples:

☐ *Bluebook* Rule 12.8.5: Restatement (Second) of Contracts § 2 (1981).

☐ *ALWD* Rule 27.1: *Restatement (Second) of Contracts § 2 (1981).*

If you are citing to a comment or illustration, you would so indicate, as follows (with *Bluebook* typeface):

☐ Restatement (Second) of Contracts § 2 cmt. a (1981).

☐ Restatement (Second) of Contracts § 2 cmt. d, illus. 1 (1981).

ADDITIONAL SECONDARY AUTHORITIES AND STRATEGY

A. Additional Secondary Authorities
B. Research Strategy for Secondary Authorities

A. ADDITIONAL SECONDARY AUTHORITIES

In addition to the major secondary sources described in the other chapters in this unit, other categories of secondary sources merit mention.

Practice Materials. After researching and analyzing a client's problem, a lawyer often moves on to various activities designed to solve that problem, such as drafting documents or litigating a case. Some secondary authorities provide practical advice and model forms for such activities. These authorities may also provide an overview of the law behind the advice or form. Examples of such authorities with broad coverage are *American Jurisprudence Trials*, *American Jurisprudence Proof of Facts*, *Shepard's Causes of Action*, *American Jurisprudence Legal Forms*, *American Jurisprudence Pleading and Practice Forms*, and *West's Legal Forms*, some are now in their second or third series. There are numerous subject-specific sources of this type as well, such as form books focused on corporate or tax law. These practice materials are rarely used as authority for the legal propositions they state, but they can provide a helpful bridge between legal analysis and actions to be taken on the client's behalf.

Jury Instructions. At the end of a jury trial, the jury is instructed on the law applicable to the case. Often the instructions are drawn from a set of pattern jury instructions or a jury instruction guide (JIG). JIGs typically are written by private authors (professors or lawyers), a group of judges, a bar association committee, or a combination of these, and they state the law of a specific jurisdiction. Each instruction states the rule in a form paralleling a

Restatement section and typically is supplemented by notes stating the source of the instruction and discussing the pertinent cases and statutes. Thus, JIGs can be useful not only when you are seeking sample instructions in a trial setting but also in nonlitigation settings. Of the authorities discussed in this chapter, JIGs are the most citable; you would cite to a JIG in an appropriate setting, such as a trial brief or an appellate brief discussing how the jury was instructed.

CLE Materials.   Many states require lawyers to take courses to continuously improve their skills. Presenters at continuing legal education (CLE) programs prepare written materials containing outlines, checklists, sample documents, and important cases and statutes. CLE materials can be useful because they address practical aspects of a topic, typically provide significant detail about a specific jurisdiction's law, and may provide the first discussion of new developments. They are rarely cited.

B.   RESEARCH STRATEGY FOR SECONDARY AUTHORITIES

1.   Choosing Among Secondary Authorities

All the secondary authorities covered in this unit serve dual functions as commentary and finding tools for primary authority and other secondary authorities. You do not need to use every authority on every research project. How do you know when to use which authority, so as to produce comprehensive, correct, and credible research and yet avoid costly excessive effort?

Exhibit 8.1 is designed to help you see more clearly the differences among these authorities. Although the characteristics are grouped under the four research goals (comprehensiveness, cost-effectiveness, etc.), many of the characteristics relate to more than one research criteria. For instance, accuracy and lack of bias relate to both correctness and credibility. As you fill in the chart, you may notice some patterns.

A wider scope of coverage usually comes at the expense of detailed coverage. As examples, encyclopedias cover a very full range of legal subjects in general terms, while A.L.R. annotations and legal periodical articles provide detailed coverage of certain specific subjects. The generality of an encyclopedia can be helpful at the outset of a research project when you need big-picture information. A narrow yet pertinent A.L.R. annotation or legal periodical article may be more helpful when you have come to focus on a well-defined research topic.

Some authorities excel at providing a coherent and comprehensive overview of a subject that is fairly static; others excel at providing a shorter analysis of targeted hot topics. For example, new periodical articles and A.L.R. annotations are published frequently, so they are better able to respond quickly to the changes in the law than are encyclopedias and Restatements.

EXHIBIT 8.1		Secondary Authority Factors

	Correctness		Comprehensiveness			
	Accuracy, Lack of Bias	Updating Means & Frequency	Breadth of Topics Covered	Depth of Coverage of Each Topic	Attention to Rules, Facts, & Principles	Description Only, or Critique Too
Encyclopedia						
Treatises						
Periodical Articles						
A.L.R. Annotations						
Restatements						

	Credibility			Cost-Effectiveness			
	Reputation of Author(s), Publisher, or Source	Strength of Supporting References	Clarity, Persua-siveness	Clarity of Organization	Means of Access (Index, Boolean Search, etc.)	Ease of Reading & Retention	Total Cost (Fees & Time)
Encyclopedia							
Treatises							
Periodical Articles							
A.L.R. Annotations							
Restatements							

Authorities written by staff members of publishers tend to differ in nature from those produced other ways. The former tend to be descriptive, the latter analytical and critical. Not coincidentally, the citability of sources varies accordingly. Treatises and periodicals, especially those written by recognized experts, are quite citable, and Restatements, promulgated by a group of experts through a long deliberative process, are highly citable.

Furthermore, you may have more than one of a type of authority, for example, several periodical articles or several A.L.R. annotations from which to choose. If you plow through your list in no particular order, you may find yourself reading more material than you need to; this is not cost-effective research. Instead, you first should rank the authorities by how much promise they show. Give high priority to the authorities with your research terms in their titles and subject descriptions. If you come across more than one citation to an authority, pursue that authority first.

2.   Deciding Whether to Cite Secondary Authorities

As you research, keep in mind which authorities you eventually will be able to cite in the final written product embodying your research. You should cite to primary authority—cases, statutes, administrative materials, rules of procedure—whenever possible. Secondary authorities most often are cited for several purposes:

- ☐ A secondary authority may be cited if primary authority does not support a proposition.
- ☐ A secondary authority can be cited for some general propositions that do not require a citation to primary authority, such as a statement about the number of jurisdictions adopting a certain rule of law.
- ☐ A secondary authority also could be cited for its criticism or policy analysis of an established rule of law.

Moreover, you should not rely on a secondary authority without reading the major primary authority on which it relies. Only by reading the primary authority will you get the full flavor of the law and detect ambiguities, misinterpretations, and perhaps even mistakes made by the commentary author.

CASE LAW

UNIT
III

In the United States legal system, there are many sources of law: cases decided by courts; constitutions and statutes passed by legislatures; regulations and decisions issued by agencies; rules of procedure and practice created by courts and legislatures. Furthermore, law is made at the federal, state, and local levels. This unit is the first of four discussing research in the law itself, that is, primary authority.

This unit focuses on the cases decided by courts and has two chapters:

☐ Chapter 9 explains what cases are and why they are so important in legal research; it then covers various ways of identifying and obtaining pertinent cases.
☐ Chapter 10 covers a critical next step in case law research: what we call "citating"

a case to determine the case's status and to expand your research.

This unit continues to illustrate researching the Canoga case stated at pages 3–4. One of the issues in that case (suggested by the research in secondary authorities presented in Unit II) is whether the orchestra breached its contract with Ms. Canoga when it terminated her employment without following the procedures stated in the handbook. This unit focuses on that issue.

A note about terminology: The term "case" has several meanings for lawyers: a matter handled on behalf of a client, a dispute that is litigated in the courts, and the decision of a court. This book uses the term in all three senses.

REPORTERS, DIGESTS, AND THEIR ALTERNATIVES

CHAPTER

9

A. WHAT IS A CASE?

Courts decide cases for two essential purposes. First, the decision provides a peaceful and principled resolution to a dispute the parties were unable to resolve otherwise. Second, the decision guides participants in future similar situations as they resolve their own disputes or engage in business or other activities. Both purposes are served by the court's written explanation of the case's facts, the outcome, and the reasoning behind the outcome.

1. How Does a Case Come to Be Decided?

Courts are reactive institutions. They resolve disputes brought to them by litigants; they do not render legal opinions on issues unconnected to actual disputes. The lawyers for the litigants bring the facts to the court's attention, frame the issues, and develop the arguments on both sides.

A dispute enters litigation when one party, the plaintiff, sues the other, the defendant. (Complex cases may involve more than two parties.) Many cases are, of course, resolved by the parties themselves. If not, the case is handled initially by a trial court, typically called a "district court." This court provides the forum for presentation of the facts to a jury or judge, determination of the facts in dispute, and application of the law to the facts to yield an initial resolution of the dispute. This resolution may come through trial, at which witnesses testify orally, documents and items are reviewed, and the jury renders a verdict or the court renders judgment. Or the judge may decide the case through motion practice. For example, the judge may dismiss the case early in the proceedings, with little development of the facts, if the plaintiff has sued on a theory without adequate legal support.

A party that loses in whole or in part in the trial court may appeal. The party bringing the appeal is the appellant or petitioner, while the party defending against the appeal is the appellee or respondent. Appellate proceedings differ from trial court proceedings. The appellate court relies on the record of the trial court proceedings along with the written and oral arguments of the lawyers. Cases typically are decided by panels of three or more judges, with the panel drawn from the court's membership, or the case may be heard by the entire court en banc.

Court systems have one or two tiers of appellate courts. In the typical two-tier appellate structure, the judges of the intermediate court, typically called the "court of appeals," review the trial court's handling of the case for reversible errors. The justices of the highest court, typically titled the "supreme court," conduct a secondary review for errors but focus primarily on the development of legal doctrine. Typically, appeal to the intermediate court is as of right, while the supreme court affords discretionary review. In a simpler one-tier structure, the sole appeals court handles both appellate functions and handles all appeals.

2.   How Are Court Systems Structured?

The federal court system is a complex court system with three tiers. The federal trial courts are called "United States District Courts"; each state has one to four district courts, each covering part or all of the state. The intermediate appellate courts are called "United States Courts of Appeals"; there are eleven numbered circuits, each covering several states, and the District of Columbia Circuit. See Exhibit 9.1. The United States Supreme Court hears cases on discretionary review from the courts of appeals. Furthermore, specialized trial and appeals courts exist in such areas as bankruptcy and international trade.

The New Mexico state court system (which probably would handle some aspects of the Canoga case, if it were a real case) is somewhat simpler. The trial courts are called "district courts." The New Mexico Court of Appeals handles appeals from all district courts. The highest court is the New Mexico Supreme Court. New Mexico's system is typical for state courts.

Table T.1 of *The Bluebook* and *ALWD Citation Manual* Appendix 1 list the courts for United States jurisdictions.

3.   What Does a Published Case Look Like?

Many cases are published one way or another so lawyers may research them. For more than a century, West Publishing Company, later called West Group

| EXHIBIT 9.1 | Federal Circuit Map *(2003/Winter Judicial Staff Directory)* |

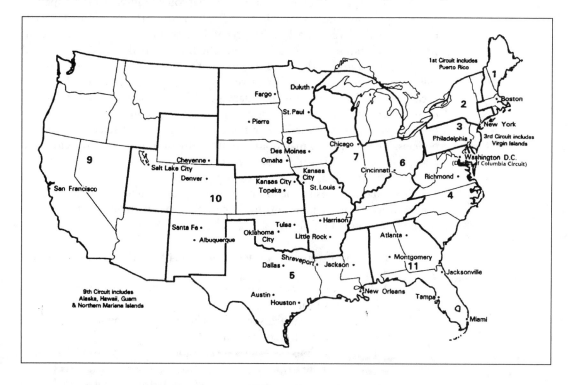

and now Thomson West, has been the dominant publisher of federal and state cases. Most cases published by West follow a fairly standard framework, labeled in the margins of Illustration 9-1 (at pages 127–30), which shows the case of *Lukoski v. Sandia Indian Management Co.*

The opening block includes the names of the parties and their positions in the litigation (item 2), the court deciding the case (item 4), the docket number assigned to the case by the court for administrative purposes (item 3), and the date of decision (item 5). The opening block also may contain a parallel citation (item 1); parallel citations are discussed in Parts C and E of this chapter.

Following the opening block are several brief paragraphs describing the main points in the case. There may be:

☐ a syllabus, written by the court itself or by the court's staff;
☐ a synopsis, a one-paragraph overview of the facts and outcome written by the publisher's staff (item 6); and
☐ headnote paragraphs, each describing a discrete legal point made in the case, written by West editors (item 7).

You should not view this material as legal authority; the opinion itself is the legal authority. The lawyers handling the case appear next (item 8).

Of course, most of the published case is the court's opinion. Each opinion begins with the name of the judge or justice who wrote the opinion (item 9). Note that "judge" refers to a jurist of a trial court or intermediate appellate court; high court jurists are "justices." The text of the opinion (item 10) typically includes a summary of the facts of the case, the course of the litigation, the court's holding, and its reasoning. The holding is the legal outcome of the case; it may be understood in procedural terms, e.g., the lower court's ruling is affirmed, and in substantive terms, e.g., the defendant is liable for breach of contract and must pay damages. The reasoning typically encompasses references to and discussion of pertinent legal authorities, analysis of how the law applies to the facts of the case, and perhaps discussion of public policies. The court also may opine about a situation not squarely before the court; this material is called *obiter dicta* (or *dictum* in the singular) and is not as authoritative as the rest of the opinion.

If the court consists of more than one judge, there is, of course, the potential for disagreement and multiple opinions. In these situations, each opinion is one of the following:

- ☐ The majority opinion garners more than half of the votes and resolves the case.
- ☐ A dissent expresses the view of judge(s) who would have reached a different result in the case.
- ☐ A concurrence expresses the view of judge(s) who favor the majority's result, but for different reasons.
- ☐ A plurality opinion arises when no opinion garners over half of the votes. The opinion garnering the largest number of votes, the plurality opinion, generally is the most influential and resolves the dispute between the parties.

There was a dissent in the *Lukoski* case (item 12).

Lukoski is a case you probably would read if you were researching the Canoga case. In Illustration 9-1 (at pages 127–30), note that *Lukoski* was decided by the New Mexico Supreme Court on January 7, 1988, and bore the docket number 16462. Scott Lukoski, the plaintiff-appellee, sued the Sandia Indian Management Company, the defendant-appellant. Mr. Lukoski, a manager, was terminated for poor interpersonal dealings, yet the employer did not follow the suspension procedures for less serious misconduct that were outlined in its handbook. The case was tried to the judge, who ruled in favor of the employee and awarded him money damages.

The case then proceeded to the New Mexico Supreme Court because contract cases did not go to the court of appeals at that time. The supreme court affirmed. Relying on various state and federal decisions, Justice Ransom, writing for the majority, reasoned that the handbook language about suspensions was enforceable as a contract, and Mr. Lukoski's difficulty in interpersonal dealings should have been handled through the suspension process. Justice Stowers dissented; he would have ruled that the interpersonal problems were so severe as to permit immediate termination under the disciplinary procedures provision of the handbook.

ILLUSTRATION 9-1

Judicial Case,
from *Pacific Reporter 2d* (paper source)

LUKOSKI v. SANDIA INDIAN MANAGEMENT CO.   N.M.   **507**
Cite as 748 P.2d 507 (N.M. 1988)

court's finding of damages, it is our opinion that an "as is" clause provides absolute protection to a seller such as Horizon only when the buyer and seller possess equal knowledge of the property. Here, while Lambert's knowledge of the property was equal to that of Horizon's insofar as most essentials of the contract were concerned, Lambert relied on Horizon for its knowledge of the total acreage in the property, and for such information as would have informed him about the realignment of Golf Course Road. Hence the trial court did not err in finding damages as to the realignment of Golf Course Road despite the "as is" clause. *See Archuleta v. Kopp*, 90 N.M. 273, 562 P.2d 834 (Ct.App.), *cert. dismissed*, 90 N.M. 636, 567 P.2d 485 (1977).

THE ISSUE OF THE ARROYO

[5]   If as to the issue of the realignment of Golf Course Road and the total number of acres conveyed the parties were not in possession of equal knowledge, when the issue of the arroyo is raised, it is clear that Lambert did have knowledge of the property equal to that of Horizon. Indeed, it appears from the testimony of past officers of Horizon that Lambert's knowledge as to the arroyo may in some respects have been superior to that of Horizon. Lambert's principal argument against the terms of paragraph 6 of the contract insofar as it applies to the arroyo is that he talked to Horizon's legal counsel before signing the contract and was told that "natural drainageway" did not refer to the arroyo, but referred to a swale running north and south across the property.

Yet, the court found in its findings of fact that Lambert (1) "read and agreed to all the terms and conditions of the Contract," (2) "had personal knowledge of, and had inspected and investigated" the property before entering into the contract, (3) that George Lambert "is a knowledgeable and sophisticated real estate broker with 20 years of experience" and that he had available to him certain engineering drainage studies dealing with the problems of the arroyo, and (4) "[a]n Arroyo is a natural drainageway." We have no reason to dis-

pute any of these findings since they are all supported by substantial evidence. "[T]he circumstances surrounding the Agreement, the import of that Agreement as a whole, and the undisputed parol evidence of the parties show that [Lambert's] right to acquire [Horizon's] interests was not conditioned upon ..." [an interpretation of "natural drainageway" as a "swale".] *Schaefer v. Hinkle*, 93 N.M. 129, 131, 597 P.2d 314, 316 (1979); *see also Smith v. Price's Creameries*, 98 N.M. 541, 544, 650 P.2d 825, 828 (1982), which likewise involved the issue of a conflict between contractual language and alleged oral assurances modifying the contractual language.

The judgment of the trial court is affirmed.

IT IS SO ORDERED.

WALTERS and RANSOM, JJ., concur.

---

106 N.M. 664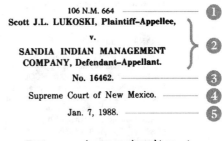

Scott J.L. LUKOSKI, Plaintiff–Appellee,

v.

SANDIA INDIAN MANAGEMENT COMPANY, Defendant–Appellant.

No. 16462.

Supreme Court of New Mexico.

Jan. 7, 1988.

Former general manager brought action against former employer for wrongful discharge. The District Court, Bernalillo County, William W. Deaton, D.J., entered judgment in favor of manager. Employer appealed. The Supreme Court, Ransom, J., held that evidence established that employee handbook amended employment contract and that employer breached contract by failing to comply with warning and suspension procedures.

Notes: 1. parallel citation   4. court
       2. parties   5. date of decision
       3. docket number   6. publisher's synopsis

ILLUSTRATION 9-1   *(continued)*

508 N. M.   748 PACIFIC REPORTER, 2d SERIES

Affirmed.

Stowers, J., dissented and filed opinion.

1. Trial ⚖══392(1)

Defendant waived specific findings of fact on issues on which it failed to tender requested findings. SCRA 1986, Rule 1–052, subd. B(1)(f).

2. Master and Servant ⚖══40(3)

Evidence supported trial court's conclusions that termination procedures in employee handbook amended general manager's employment contract, that handbook created warning and suspension procedures which were not followed, and that personality, rather than insubordination, caused employment termination; handbook characterized disciplinary policy regarding warnings, suspensions, and terminations as established procedure; and handbook did not indicate that it was subject to revocation at any time or that employees should not rely on it.

Grammer & Grammer, David A. Grammer, III, Albuquerque, for defendant-appellant.

Turpen & Wolfe, Donald C. Turpen, Albuquerque, for plaintiff-appellee.

OPINION

RANSOM, Justice.

Scott J.L. Lukoski brought a wrongful discharge action against his employer, Sandia Indian Management Co. (SIMCO). Lukoski had been employed as general manager of the Sandia Pueblo bingo operation. In a bench trial, the court decided that SIMCO violated the termination procedures prescribed for "less serious" offenses by an employee handbook. For salary due on the remaining term of his one-year oral contract, Lukoski was awarded $18,629.05. We affirm.

The court found that, in October 1983, Lukoski and SIMCO entered into a one-year oral employment agreement under which Lukoski would provide services as the general manager of a bingo hall opera-

tion for a specified annual salary plus commission. There was no written agreement between the parties. In February 1984, SIMCO distributed to all employees an employee handbook and requested each to sign the last page as verification of receipt, acknowledgement of acceptance, and agreement to conform with the stated policies and procedures. After Lukoski signed the back page as requested, it was placed in his personnel file. The court concluded that:

> The parties amended the oral employment contract * * * when [SIMCO] proffered, and [Lukoski] signed, [the] Employee's Handbook containing new duties and obligations on the part of employee and employer over and above said oral contract, including Rules to be obeyed by [Lukoski] and a termination procedure to be followed by [SIMCO].

[1] Although we determine the above-quoted language is a finding of ultimate fact, rather than a conclusion of law, that is of no consequence. *See Hoskins v. Albuquerque Bus Co.*, 72 N.M. 217, 382 P.2d 700 (1963); *Wiggs v. City of Albuquerque*, 57 N.M. 770, 263 P.2d 963 (1953). SIMCO challenges this finding and for the first time on appeal raises two other issues. First, it claims that Lukoski, as general manager, was not the type of employee intended to be covered by the handbook. Distribution to all employees with request for signatures constituted evidence to the contrary, and resolution of any ambiguity regarding management personnel would have been a specific question of fact. *See Shaeffer v. Kelton*, 95 N.M. 182, 619 P.2d 1226 (1980). Second, SIMCO claims that any breach was not material because it neither went to the substance of the contract nor defeated the object of the parties. Materiality is likewise a specific question of fact. *See Bisio v. Madenwald (In re Estate of Bisio)*, 33 Or.App. 325, 576 P.2d 801 (1978). As the contract stood after amendment, it was not materiality, as argued by SIMCO, but rather severity of offense that was at issue under the termination procedures. In any event, by failing to tender requested findings, SIMCO waived specific

---

Notes: 7. headnotes
   7a. topic and key number
    8. counsels' names
    9. justice who wrote majority opinion
   10. majority opinion

11. bracketed headnote
    reference

ILLUSTRATION 9-1   *(continued)*

LUKOSKI v. SANDIA INDIAN MANAGEMENT CO.   N. M.   **509**
Cite as 748 P.2d 507 (N.M. 1988)

findings on these fact issues.   SCRA 1986, 1–052(B)(1)(f).

[2] There is substantial evidence supporting the court's findings of ultimate fact that the termination procedures became an amendment to Lukoski's contract, and that personality—not the severe offenses of insubordination or disobedience—was the cause for termination. He was terminated without warning or suspension for a cause not so severe as to constitute cause for immediate termination.   His personality and interpersonal dealings were found by the court to create an atmosphere of fear and anxiety and bad morale among employees and managers.

Relying only on *Ellis v. El Paso Natural Gas Co.*, 754 F.2d 884 (10th Cir.1985), the thrust of SIMCO's appeal is that the language of the employee handbook is "too indefinite to constitute a contract" and lacks "contractual terms which might evidence the intent to form a contract." It maintains that the parties did not conduct themselves as if the employee handbook was to govern Lukoski or as if they expected it to form the basis of a contractual relationship.   In support of its position, SIMCO refers to the disciplinary action, suspension, and warning provisions,[1] and argues that the language of the termination policy is ambiguous and contains no required policy for termination.

SIMCO's argument, however, overlooks the handbook's characterization of the disciplinary policy regarding warnings, suspensions and terminations as "an *estab-*

lished procedure regarding suspension of problem employees and termination for those who cannot conform to Company Policy." (Emphasis added.) Moreover, the language of the handbook does nothing to alert an employee against placing reliance on any statement contained therein or against viewing such discipline and termination policy as only a unilateral expression of SIMCO's intention that is subject to revocation or change at any time, in any manner, at the pleasure of SIMCO. To the contrary, from the language of the handbook and the conduct of SIMCO in adopting the policy, it could properly be found that the policy was part of the employment agreement.

Whether an employee handbook has modified the employment relationship is a question of fact "to be discerned from the totality of the parties' statements and actions regarding the employment relationship." *Wagenseller v. Scottsdale Memorial Hosp.*, 147 Ariz. 370, 383, 710 P.2d 1025, 1038 (1985) (en banc).

Evidence relevant to this factual decision includes the language used in the personnel manual as well as the employer's course of conduct and oral representations regarding it. We do not mean to imply that all personnel manual will become part of employment contracts. Employers are certainly free to issue no personnel manual at all or to issue a personnel manual that clearly and conspicuously tells their employees that the manual is not part of the employment contract and that their jobs are termina-

---

1. The referenced handbook provisions state:
OTHER DISCIPLINARY ACTION:
In order to protect the good employees [sic] jobs and Sandia Indian Bingo, there is an established procedure regarding suspension of problem employees and termination for those who can not conform to Company Policy. Suspensions without pay may be given to employees who violate company policies. There are violations which are so severe [including insubordination and disobedience] that immediate termination may be necessary....
SUSPENSIONS:
Suspension without pay may be given when the incident is not sufficiently serious to warrant discharge and/or the particular employee's overall value to the Company [is con-

sidered], if [in] the opinion of the Department Manager [the employee] warrants another chance. Minimum suspensions are (3) three days, maximum suspensions are (5) five days. No employee may be suspended more than once in a year; thereafter, if the incident would normally warrant suspension he/she must be discharged.
DISCIPLINARY WARNING:
Disciplinary warning slips will be issued where the offense is less serious and where corrective action may salvage an employee. More than one (1) disciplinary warning, whether for the same offense or not, may subject an employee to suspension or termination. Warning slips become a permanent part of an employee's personnel record.

ILLUSTRATION 9-1   *(continued)*

510 N.M.   **748 PACIFIC REPORTER, 2d SERIES**

ble at the will of the employer with or without reason. Such actions * * * instill no reasonable expectations of job security and do not give employees any reason to rely on representations in the manual. However, if an employer does choose to issue a policy statement, in a manual or otherwise, and, by its language or by the employer's actions, encourages reliance thereon, the employer cannot be free to only selectively abide by it. Having announced a policy, the employer may not treat it as illusory. *Leikvold v. Valley View Community Hosp.*, 141 Ariz. 544, 548, 688 P.2d 170, 174 (1984). Here, substantial evidence supports the finding of the trial court that the employee handbook modified the employment relationship and created warning and suspension procedures which were not followed in this case.

Accordingly, based upon the foregoing, the judgment of the trial court is affirmed.

IT IS SO ORDERED.

SCARBOROUGH, C.J., SOSA, Senior Justice, and WALTERS, J., concur.

STOWERS, J., dissents.

STOWERS, Justice, dissenting.

I respectfully dissent from the majority's holding that SIMCO did not abide with the termination procedures.

Substantial evidence does support the findings of the trial court that the employee handbook modified the employment relationship and that Lukoski was terminated for just cause. The trial court erred, however, in concluding that SIMCO did not follow the proper termination procedures. To the contrary, SIMCO did not breach any of the provisions in the employee handbook when it discharged Lukoski without a warning and suspension. The handbook explicitly states that, "there are violations which are so severe that *immediate termination may be necessary.*" (Emphasis added).

Overwhelming evidence was presented at trial to show that Lukoski's violations of company policies were of the type to fall within the category of "so severe" that a

warning and any suspension procedures were not required. *See State ex rel. Goodmans Office Furnishings, Inc. v. Page & Wirtz Constr. Co.*, 102 N.M. 22, 24, 690 P.2d 1016, 1018 (1984). Generally, this evidence indicated that Lukoski had an overall attitude problem towards his employees, other managers and representatives of the Sandia Pueblo to the extent that SIMCO was in jeopardy of losing its bingo contract with the Pueblo; moreover, he was abusive towards the accountants, argued or fought publicly with customers, the assistant bingo manager, the construction supervisor and an admittance clerk; Lukoski also failed to install proper security measures and verification methods, and hired unqualified personnel. Further, testimony indicated that on several occasions, Walker, Lukoski's supervisor, spoke to Lukoski about this attitude problem, and, in fact, interceded on Lukoski's behalf when the Sandia Pueblo desired to discharge Lukoski.

As enumerated in the handbook, Lukoski's violations included, "fighting on company property, refusal to obey reasonable orders of a supervisor, discourtesy to customers, and disobeying or ignoring established written or oral work rules or policies." These are, and I again quote from the handbook, "violations which are so severe that *immediate termination* may be necessary." (Emphasis added.) Therefore, the trial court was in error when it decided that SIMCO violated the termination procedures prescribed for "less serious" offenses in the handbook. Lukoski was not entitled to those termination procedures since his offenses were not of the "less serious" type. Under the circumstances in this case, the only process due Lukoski for the seriousness of his violations was immediate termination. Thus, there was no breach by SIMCO when it discharged him for just cause.

The judgment of the district court should be reversed and this case remanded for dismissal.

Note: 12. dissenting opinion

B. WHY WOULD YOU RESEARCH WHICH CASES?

1. The Common Law, Stare Decisis, and Precedent

In a common law system, as in the United States, case law forms part of the law of the land. The operative principle in a common law system is *stare decisis et non quieta movere*, which means "to adhere to precedent and not to unsettle things which are settled." According to stare decisis, a court should follow previously decided cases, or precedents, on the same subject. Hence, as you research the law applicable to a client's situation, even if you hope and reasonably anticipate that the situation will never come before a court, you should try to deduce how the court would handle the situation.

Stare decisis has several chief advantages. Situations involving similar facts are treated consistently. Outcomes are based on legal principles, rather than the unconstrained biases of judges and juries. Because it generally is possible to predict the outcome of a case by looking to precedents, many cases can be settled. Furthermore, people can conform their conduct to the law by looking to precedents.

Yet overly strict adherence to precedent would produce a static legal rule. Although some areas of law benefit from stability, others do not. When social values change, information improves, or new situations develop, the law must evolve accordingly.

Fortunately, the United States legal system provides for change. A court may distinguish an earlier case by finding factual differences between it and the pending case; then the court may apply a different rule to the pending case. A court may modify the rule of an earlier case. A court may overrule precedent in response to a significant need for change. Finally, the legislature may enact a statute modifying the common law to a greater or lesser degree (as explained in Chapter 11).

In your research, you may find many cases pertaining to your research topic. Not all cases are of equal importance. To focus on the most important cases, you should consider the following factors, all discussed in detail below:

- ☐ You should focus first on whether the case is mandatory or persuasive precedent, given the jurisdiction of your client's situation.
- ☐ Then you must ascertain that the case is what lawyers call "good law"—a case that, indeed, currently states the law of the jurisdiction. In deciding whether a case is good law, you will consider its history and treatment as well as its publication status.
- ☐ Finally, if you have more cases than you can handle well, you should assess several additional factors, such as factual similarity to your client's situation and the quality of the reasoning.

2.   Mandatory versus Persuasive Precedent: Federalism, Jurisdiction, and Level of Court

For a particular client situation, some cases constitute binding or mandatory precedent, while others are merely persuasive. The distinction between mandatory and persuasive precedents is critical: Stare decisis operates as to mandatory precedents only. Persuasive precedents may influence a court, but they do not bind it. The distinction between mandatory and persuasive precedent is based on two main factors: jurisdiction and court level.

a.   Federalism and Jurisdiction

The United States legal system is a federal system, that is, a collection of legal systems. A particular legal topic, or issue, may be governed by federal law, or it may be governed by state law. Or it may be governed by both. A few issues are governed by local (municipal or county) law.

If the legal issue is governed by federal law, then mandatory precedents emanate from federal courts. If the legal issue is governed by state law, then mandatory precedents emanate from the courts of the pertinent state. Decisions from other courts, which lawyers call "sister courts" or "sister jurisdictions," are only persuasive precedent.

The term "jurisdiction" has several common meanings in the law. Often it is used to refer to a legal system of a particular geographic region. In a more technical sense, jurisdiction is the power of a specific court to render and enforce a decision in a particular case. That is, a state court has the power to render and enforce decisions in cases arising under the law of that state and within its geographic region, and a federal court has the power to render and enforce decisions in cases arising under federal law and within its geographic region.

In several situations, a court may apply law that is not its own. For example, in diversity jurisdiction, a federal court has the power to decide cases arising under state law if the case involves citizens of different states and the amount in controversy is high enough. Similarly, under supplemental jurisdiction, a federal court has the power to decide a case arising in part under state law if the case also involves a federal claim. Moreover, Congress has given state and federal courts concurrent jurisdiction over certain claims stated in federal law. Finally, the courts of one state may apply the law of a different state if a multistate contract identifies the second state's law as governing.

In these situations, the mandatory precedents are those decisions from the courts whose law governs. For example, when operating in diversity or supplemental jurisdiction, a federal court will follow the law of the state that governs the claim and will seek to emulate the approach of that state's highest court; the decisions of the federal courts are not as weighty.

Unfortunately, there are few broadly applicable principles to explain the distribution of legal topics among the three levels of government, and jurisdiction can be complex. As you begin to research, you should assume that federal, state, and local law are all potentially applicable, and you should be alert to jurisdictional possibilities. Your research in secondary authorities will provide preliminary guidance, which you should verify in primary authority.

In the Canoga case, the contract issue is a state law question (as is generally true of contract law). New Mexico would be the jurisdiction of the client's situation, and New Mexico state court decisions, such as *Lukoski*, would be mandatory precedent for a court in New Mexico deciding the Canoga case. The *Lukoski* court was itself bound by and cited earlier New Mexico cases—mandatory precedents—in its decision. Note that the *Lukoski* court also cited Oregon, Arizona, and federal cases—persuasive precedents. The federal case, *Ellis v. El Paso Natural Gas Co.*, involved an employee's challenge to his termination under state law; it was heard in federal court under diversity jurisdiction. The federal court in *Ellis* relied on New Mexico Supreme Court cases for guidance on the state law issue.

b.   Level of Court

An additional determinant of mandatory versus persuasive precedent is the level of the court issuing the decision. Stare decisis operates hierarchically. Any particular court is bound by decisions of higher courts within the same court system and must take its own decisions into account. It is not, however, bound by decisions issued by other courts at the same level or by lower courts. Hence, you would rely on a supreme court decision over that of an intermediate appeals court; similarly, you would rely on an intermediate appeals court decision over that of a trial court.

For example, the New Mexico Supreme Court decision in *Lukoski* binds the New Mexico Court of Appeals and the New Mexico trial courts; it also must be taken into account by the New Mexico Supreme Court in future similar cases. A New Mexico Court of Appeals decision binds only the trial courts, not the supreme court. Similarly, a federal Tenth Circuit Court of Appeals decision binds the federal district courts within the Tenth Circuit (including the federal district court in New Mexico), but it does not bind the United States Supreme Court. A Tenth Circuit decision does not bind other federal circuit courts of appeals or district courts within other circuits.

3.   History and Treatment of the Case

Before you rely on a case, you first must determine that it is good law. A case's status is a function primarily of its subsequent history and treatment:

- ☐   Subsequent history consists of later rulings in the same litigation.
- ☐   Treatment consists of decisions rendered in other, later cases that discuss the case at hand.

Subsequent history nearly always affects whether a case is good law; a case's treatment may or may not do so.

a.   Subsequent History

Before you rely on a decision, you must know whether one or both of the parties brought an appeal; whether the decision has indeed been reviewed by a higher court; and, if so, what the outcome was. The higher court may affirm the lower court's decision; reverse the lower court's decision; or take intermediate action, such as modifying or reversing and remanding to the lower court. These later decisions in the same litigation involving the same parties constitute the original decision's subsequent history.

Obviously, your research is not complete until you have identified the subsequent history of any decision you intend to rely on. Then you must carefully read the subsequent decision to discern its impact on your client's situation. The impact will generally be one of the following:

☐   If the subsequent decision adversely affects the outcome and reasoning you are planning to rely on, it is incorrect to rely on the original decision.

☐   If the subsequent decision affirms the material you plan to rely on, the original decision has greater credibility. Ordinarily, you will rely on the higher court's decision.

☐   When the higher court does not expressly rule on a point that is stated by the lower court and that point is not inconsistent with the higher court's ruling, you may rely on the lower court decision.

Furthermore, if you intend to rely on a decision that is very recent and not from the highest court, you should check whether an appeal is pending before a higher court and be prepared to adjust your analysis when the higher court rules.

For example, consider the *Lukoski* case. As already noted, the New Mexico Court of Appeals did not review *Lukoski*. But assume that you had located a court of appeals decision in *Lukoski* that reversed the trial court award in favor of Mr. Lukoski; then the supreme court ruled in favor of Mr. Lukoski. You would rely not on the court of appeals decision, but rather on the supreme court decision.

b.   Treatment

Judges often refer to decisions rendered in earlier similar cases. The court may follow an earlier decision, distinguish it, criticize it, modify it, or even overrule it. For any decided case, there may be several, a dozen, or many more references in later cases. Your research is not complete until you have discerned how later cases have treated each case you intend to rely on. You should focus on courts in the same court system because those courts have the greatest power to undermine the case's validity or enhance its credibility.

You should attend first to adverse treatment. You should be especially concerned with indications that the case has been overruled; it then is no longer good law. You also should be wary of relying on a case that has been modified or criticized significantly or distinguished frequently by courts in your jurisdiction. When you discover such adverse treatment, you must read the citing case carefully. If the case with adverse treatment makes more than one point, you should be sure to note whether the overruling, modification, or criticism in the citing case covers the point on which are you relying. It may be that the case remains good law as to the point you plan to rely on; nonetheless you should use the case with caution.

Adverse treatment from sister jurisdictions is, of course, not nearly as significant. A sister court cannot overrule a case in your jurisdiction. Nor does criticism by one or more sister courts render a case less precedential in its own jurisdiction, although you may want to consider seriously what the basis of the criticism is.

Favorable treatment of a case, by courts in your jurisdiction or sister jurisdictions or both, enhances the case's credibility. If you find many instances of favorable treatment, the case may be what lawyers call a "leading" or "seminal" case, that is, the case that first or most persuasively established a particular legal rule.

For example, as you will see in Chapter 10, the *Lukoski* case has been cited in a dozen New Mexico state court cases; it also has been cited a few times by other courts (the federal Tenth Circuit, the federal district court for New Mexico, California and Washington state courts). It has not been overruled by later New Mexico cases or criticized by any court. Hence *Lukoski* remains good law.

4.   Publication Status

Courts in the United States issue decisions at an astounding rate. For example, the federal courts of appeals issue about 27,000 to 28,000 decisions annually.[1] Some decisions are, of course, more significant than others to the development of the law. For example, when a state's highest court recognizes a tort for the first time or applies a well established contract rule to a new situation, the court resolves what lawyers call an "issue of first impression." Such a decision is more important than a trial court's application of settled law to a common factual situation.

Courts seek to reflect the relative importance of a decision by deciding whether to publish the decision. The highest courts in each court system designate nearly every decision as published, intermediate appellate courts a smaller percentage, and trial courts even fewer. A decision is likely to be published if it establishes a new legal rule, develops or significantly explains an existing rule, criticizes or questions existing law, involves an issue as to

---

1. *Judicial Business of the United States Courts: 2003 Annual Report of the Director* 34 table S-1 (available at www.uscourts.gov/judbus2003).

which there is a conflict in the case law, discusses a little-discussed rule, applies an existing rule to a new factual situation, or concerns an issue of significant public interest, among other factors.[2] About eighty percent of federal appellate decisions are designated as unpublished.[3] In other words, publication status is an indication of the court's own assessment of the importance of the decision.

As contradictory as it may seem, unpublished decisions are, in point of fact, published. This phenomenon has varied over time. Until a few decades ago, a court would provide an unpublished decision only to the parties, not to commercial publishers or government printing operations. Although you could generally obtain a copy of a decision from the clerk of court if you knew about the case, as a practical matter, these unpublished decisions were minimally published and not easily researched.

For several decades, Westlaw and LexisNexis have provided unpublished decisions in their case law databases, although unpublished decisions were not included in paper case reporters. At that point, unpublished decisions became quite researchable. More recently, West has begun to provide some unpublished decisions in paper case reporters, and many courts have posted their decisions—published and unpublished—on their websites. These developments have made unpublished decisions very researchable.

There remains the question of whether unpublished decisions are precedential. Different courts have their own rules on whether unpublished decisions can be cited. Some courts prohibit citing an unpublished decision except in the same litigation, while others permit citation to an unpublished case as persuasive, but not binding, precedent.[4]

As of the writing of this book in summer 2003, this issue was under review as to federal court decisions. In 2000, an Eighth Circuit decision declared unconstitutional that court's rule rendering unpublished cases non-precedential.[5] That decision and the E-Government Act of 2002 requiring all federal decisions, published or unpublished, to be posted on courts' websites,[6] brought significant attention to the issue.[7] In May of 2003, the Advisory Committee on Appellate Rules proposed a rule precluding prohibitions on the citing of unpublished decisions, while also requiring a party citing an unpublished decision not available through a publicly accessible database to provide a copy to opposing counsel and the court.

Thus, as you research in case law, you should learn your jurisdiction's

---

2. Jerome I. Braun, *Eighth Circuit Decision Intensifies Debate over Publication and Citation of Appellate Opinions,* 84 Judicature 90, 91 (2000) (synthesizing appellate rules).

3. Michael Hannon, *A Closer Look at Unpublished Decisions in the United States Courts of Appeals,* 3 J. App. Prac. & Proc. 199, 201 (2001).

4. *See* Charles E. Carpenter, Jr., *The No-Citation Rule for Unpublished Opinions: Do the Ends of Expediency for Overloaded Appellate Courts Justify the Means of Secrecy?,* 50 S.C. L. Rev. 235, 242, 259 (1998).

5. *Anastasoff v. United States,* 223 F.3d 898 (8th Cir.), *vacated as moot and remanded,* 235 F.3d 1054 (8th Cir. 2000).

6. 44 U.S.C.A. § 3501 note (Supp. 2003).

7. *See generally* Melissa H. Weresh, *The Unpublished, Non-Precedential Decision: An Uncomfortable Legality?,* 3 J. App. Prac. & Proc. 175 (2001).

position on this issue and view any unpublished decisions you discover accordingly. While court rules on this issue directly address only the citation of unpublished cases in documents filed in court, you should take guidance from these rules as you analyze your client's situation and provide advice in other contexts, such as settling a dispute or structuring business transactions.

Researching the Canoga case, we discovered two different rules. New Mexico Rule of Appellate Procedure 12-405 calls for informal disposition by order, decision, or memorandum (as distinct from a formal opinion); orders, decisions, and memoranda are not published and may not be cited. The federal Tenth Circuit's Rule 36.3 disfavors but nonetheless permits citation to unpublished decisions when the unpublished decision addresses an important issue not addressed in published decisions, would assist the court, and is provided to the court and the other litigants.

5. Additional Factors

Your research may well yield multiple mandatory precedents that are good law. Then you should consider the following factors as you select cases to emphasize:

- ☐ Similarity: The higher the degree of similarity between the facts and legal issues of your client's situation and those of the case you have located, the better. Your goal is to obtain both factual and legal parallelism, to the extent possible.
- ☐ Clarity: The clearer and more convincing the reasoning of the case you have located, the better. A clear, well-reasoned case is inherently more credible than one with flawed reasoning.
- ☐ Recency: The more recent the case you have located, the better, all else being equal. Age by itself does not render a case bad law, but it may make it less credible than a newer case, because a newer case may more closely reflect current values and perspectives.

For the Canoga case, the *Lukoski* case would be a strong case to rely on. It is about fifteen years old, and the reasoning is fairly straightforward. Furthermore, the facts of *Lukoski* and the Canoga situation are similar, and the issues are nearly identical. Although Mr. Lukoski alleged that his employer should have suspended him, whereas Ms. Canoga would argue that the employer must provide board review, this difference is not substantial.

On some occasions, you may need to rely on persuasive precedent: when there is a dearth of mandatory precedent, the mandatory precedent is outdated, or the mandatory precedent is adverse to your client's interest and you want to seek a change in the law. In selecting from possible persuasive precedents, you should consider the following factors, in addition to those stated above:

☐   which courts or cases are viewed as leaders on the research topic,
☐   how geographically close the sister jurisdiction is to yours,
☐   how closely the law of the sister jurisdiction tracks the law of your
    jurisdiction on related legal topics, and
☐   how closely the policies underlying the precedent mesh with your
    jurisdiction's policies.

Your research in secondary authorities will help you to assess some of these factors.

In the *Lukoski* case, as already noted, the court relied heavily on a persuasive precedent from Arizona, *Wagenseller v. Scottsdale Memorial Hospital*. At that time, *Wagenseller* was a recent case from a nearby state. It involved fairly similar facts and the same legal issues as *Lukoski*. Based on its reasoning, it became a leading case in the developing area of employee's contract rights.

C.   HOW DO YOU RESEARCH CASES?

Given the importance of case law in the United States legal system, it is not surprising that published cases are available in multiple media and from multiple publishers, as follows:

☐   Slip opinion: This is the decision as the court issues it, traditionally
    in paper; sends it to the parties; and maintains it in the files of the
    clerk of court.
☐   Official publications: In most jurisdictions, the court will post the
    decision electronically on a public Internet website. In addition,
    there may be an official reporter, i.e., a set of books containing the
    court's decisions published by or under the auspices of the
    government.
☐   Unofficial publications: Various commercial publishers publish new
    cases very quickly, e.g., in a legal newspaper. Not long thereafter,
    commercial publishers add editorial enhancements designed to assist
    the researcher and publish the case in unofficial reporters, in case law
    databases, or both. In some jurisdictions, a commercially published
    reporter is considered the official reporter.

As noted in Part B above, some unpublished cases are available in court websites and commercial databases; a few also are available in paper. When you research a client's case, you are very unlikely to use all of these sources; however, you likely will use more than one.

While there are many different ways to use these sources, most of the time, you will engage in some combination of five practices. First, quite often, you will have a list of pertinent cases through your research in secondary authorities; it makes sense to start with these cases. However, secondary authorities are unlikely to lead you to all of the case law you need, because the authors were not researching the precise situation presented by your client. The following four additional practices are the most likely to meet the four criteria of excellent legal research—correct, comprehensive, credible, and cost-effective:

- ☐ utilizing West's system of case digests and reporters in paper;
- ☐ running natural-language, terms-and-connectors (Boolean), or key-number searches or using KeySearch in Westlaw's case law databases;
- ☐ using Search Advisor, along with natural-language and terms-and-connectors (Boolean) searching, in LexisNexis' case law databases;
- ☐ searching the court's website.

Each practice has strengths and weaknesses, so you should know which to use when and how to combine the practices. In general, the practices are listed in a start-to-finish sequence, that is, you would start in digests and reporters, progress to Westlaw or LexisNexis research, and conclude with the court's website.

Case law research tools are evolving rapidly, as the major publishers continually expand and re-design their products and as new publishers enter this market. As one example, Loislaw provides case law from all fifty states and the major federal courts; as of summer 2003, its databases and search options were not yet as extensive as those of Westlaw and LexisNexis. Thus, the practices discussed here are by no means exhaustive; however, they do illustrate the major possibilities. You should keep reasonably current with developments in case law research, so that your research is as effective and efficient as current sources permit.

An important note: The discussion in this part covers the bulk of case law research: identifying, locating, obtaining, and reading pertinent cases. The critical step of discerning the subsequent history and treatment of a case is covered in Chapter 10 on case citators.

Cases through West digests and reporters:

- ▶ select an appropriate digest
- ▶ identify a topic and key numbers via the topic list or the Descriptive Word Index
- ▶ assemble the digest volumes and supplements you need
- ▶ skim the outline of the topic in the digest
- ▶ peruse the digest paragraphs under pertinent key numbers
- ▶ use the references in the digest to locate cases in reporters
- ▶ read each case for its rule, outcome, facts, reasoning, and citations
- ▶ cite each case (see Chapter 10)

Paper-based research in West's case law system involves two interlocking sources: digests and reporters, used in that order. A digest is a finding tool that leads you to case law published in a reporter. Because it is difficult to understand digests without an understanding of reporters, the following text provides an overview of reporters before setting out the process of using digests.

Understanding reporters and digests. A case reporter is a book containing the decisions issued during a particular time period by a single court or a set of courts. As already noted, reporters are official or unofficial. Official reporters do not contain the editorial enhancements of unofficial reporters and are not as useful for the researcher.

The National Reporter System published by West beginning in the late 1800s is the most prominent set of reporters. The West system is synopsized in Exhibit 9.2.

EXHIBIT 9.2	West Reporters and Digests

Cases from these courts	*appear in these West reporters*	*and are digested in these West digests.*
Federal Courts		
Supreme Court	*Supreme Court Reporter*	*United States Supreme Court Digest* *Federal Practice Digest* (currently in fourth series) older cases covered by *Modern Federal Practice Digest* and *Federal Digest*
courts of appeals for various circuits	*Federal Reporter* (currently in third series) *Federal Appendix* (unpublished decisions)	*Federal Practice Digest* (currently in fourth series) older cases covered by *Modern Federal Practice Digest* and *Federal Digest* (also separate digests for Fifth and Eleventh Circuits)
district courts	*Federal Supplement* (currently in second series) older cases in *Federal Reporter*	*Federal Practice Digest* (currently in fourth series) older cases covered by *Modern Federal Practice Digest* and *Federal Digest*
State Courts*		
Connecticut Delaware District of Columbia Maine Maryland New Hampshire New Jersey Pennsylvania Rhode Island Vermont	*Atlantic Reporter* (currently in second series)	*Atlantic Digest* state digests (except Delaware) including federal cases from state

*Appendix 1 of *ALWD Citation Manual* indicates, for each state, whether the West reporter is the official reporter.

EXHIBIT 9.2	*(continued)*

Cases from these courts	appear in these West reporters	and are digested in these West digests.
Illinois Indiana Massachusetts New York Ohio	*North Eastern Reporter* (currently in second series) also *New York Supplement* (currently in second series)	state digests, including federal cases from state
Iowa Michigan Minnesota Nebraska North Dakota South Dakota Wisconsin	*North Western Reporter* (currently in second series)	*North Western Digest* state digests (North and South Dakota are merged), including federal cases from state
Alaska Arizona California Colorado Hawaii Idaho Kansas Montana Nevada New Mexico Oklahoma Oregon Utah Washington Wyoming	*Pacific Reporter* (currently in third series) also *California Reporter* (currently in third series)	*Pacific Digest* state digests (except Nevada and Utah), including federal cases from state
Georgia North Carolina South Carolina Virginia West Virginia	*South Eastern Reporter* (currently in second series)	*South Eastern Digest* state digests (Virginia and West Virginia are merged), including federal cases from state
Arkansas Kentucky Missouri Tennessee Texas	*South Western Reporter* (currently in third series)	state digests, including federal cases from state
Alabama Florida Louisiana Mississippi	*Southern Reporter* (currently in second series)	state digests, including federal cases from state

As for federal cases, West currently publishes reporters containing decisions of the federal courts as follows:

- [ ] *Supreme Court Reporter* for decisions of the United States Supreme Court,
- [ ] *Federal Reporter* for decisions of the various courts of appeals, and
- [ ] *Federal Supplement* for decisions of the various district courts.

Although all decisions of the Supreme Court are published, only those decisions of the lower federal courts designated for publication appear in the West reporters listed above. In 2001, West began to publish *Federal Appendix*, containing decisions from the courts of appeals not designated for publication. In addition to the West reporters, there is an official reporter for the Supreme Court, *United States Reports*, but not for the lower federal courts.

As for case law from state courts, West has divided the country into seven regions, drawn from the perspective of a Minnesota publisher in the nineteenth century. Each region contains four to fifteen states, and each is served by one of the regional reporters. Again, see Exhibit 9.2. West's regions are not synonymous with jurisdiction; a case from a sister state within the same West region as your state is no more binding than a case from a sister state outside your state's West region. The regional reporters contain the decisions designated for publication by the various state appellate courts; decisions of lower state courts typically are not published. West also publishes two single-state reporters, for California and New York; these contain some cases not published in the regional reporters. Some states publish official reporters; others in effect rely on the West reporters.

For many reporters, West has published more than one series, for example, F., F.2d, F.3d for the *Federal Reporter*. The first series of a reporter contains the oldest cases, while the second or even third series contains the newest. The volume numbers start again with a new series.

Most volumes of a reporter are hardbound books. However, the most recent decisions appear in advance sheets, which are softcover pamphlets that can be published quickly. Once the hardbound book is prepared, it replaces the advance sheets.

As an example of the West reporter system, consider first the *Lukoski* case, Illustration 9-1 (at pages 127–30), decided by the New Mexico Supreme Court in 1988. *Lukoski* appears in volume 748 of the second series of the *Pacific Reporter* starting at page 507. As a second example, consider the *Ellis* case referred to in *Lukoski*. As a 1985 decision of the federal Tenth Circuit, *Ellis* appears in volume 754 of the second series of the *Federal Reporter* starting at page 884.

Cases are published in case reporters as they arrive at the publisher and clear the editorial process. Thus, case reporters are organized chronologically, not topically. To locate cases on your research topic, you need a digest, that is, a tool for locating pertinent cases within the many volumes of a reporter. A digest presents brief statements of the legal points made in the covered cases, written by the publisher's editorial staff and then fit into a framework of major legal topics and subtopics. See Illustration 9-2 (at page 146). West's digests are the most highly developed and widely used legal digests.

Select an appropriate digest. Your first step in researching in digests and reporters is to select an appropriate digest. There is a rough correlation between West's reporters and its digests, as indicated in Exhibit 9.2. For example, the main federal digest is the *Federal Practice Digest*, which covers the *Supreme Court Reporter*, the *Federal Reporter*, and the *Federal Supplement*. West publishes digests for the Atlantic, North Western, Pacific, and South Eastern regional reporters. It also publishes digests for most states; these digests cover state court decisions published in the regional reporters as well as federal cases arising in or appealed from the state.

West has combined the information in its various federal, regional, and state digests into master—and hence voluminous—digests: *Century Digests*, *Decennial Digests*, and *General Digests*, covering multiple decades, multiyear periods, and years, respectively. You generally will use these master digests only when you already have explored a narrower digest for your jurisdiction and have decided to seek cases from outside your jurisdiction.

Identify a topic and key numbers. Your next step is to identify a pertinent topic and key number. West has divided the law into about 450 main topics. Each topic is divided into subtopics and indeed into sub-subtopics. The subtopics and sub-subtopics are assigned numbers, called "key numbers." This configuration of topics and key numbers is the same across the West system.

One way to find a pertinent topic, but not key numbers, is by scanning the topic list near the front of the digest volumes. See Illustration 9-3 (at page 147). To find not only a pertinent topic but also pertinent key numbers, you would consult the Descriptive Word Index, which appears in its own volumes and typically is updated by pocket parts or pamphlets. See Illustration 9-4 (at page 148). To obtain a thorough list of potentially pertinent topics and key numbers, look up various research terms, read the entries carefully, and check out cross-references.

Assemble a full set. The next step is to assemble the necessary digest volumes and supplements covering your topics and key numbers for the time period you are researching. Many digests consist of more than one bound series. Later series typically contain more recent information than earlier series; some later series incorporate the information from the previous series. Typically, the most recent bound digest is updated by a pocket part inserted into the back of the bound volume. When there is so much new information that the pocket part would be too thick, West issues a pamphlet or prepares one or more bound volumes. Even more recent information appears in pamphlets that cover multiple bound volumes and generally are shelved at the end of a digest set. The most recent information appears in digest pages found within the most recent reporter hardbound volumes and advance sheets. Because recent cases generally are more useful than older cases, and because the newer publications contain fairly few entries, experienced researchers typically follow this sequence:

(1)   the bound volume from the current series,
(2)   its pocket part or pamphlets,

(3)   the supplementary pamphlet for the digest,
(4)   the most recent digest material in recent reporter hardbound volumes and advance sheets, and
(5)   the older series bound volume (if any).

Read the topic outline and headnotes. As you turn to the digest material covering your topic, skim the general and detailed outlines at the outset of your topic. See Illustration 9-5 (at page 149). There may be additional pertinent key numbers you have not yet identified; rarely is there only one pertinent key number for a legal issue. Furthermore, you may find the organization of the topic to be informative.

Then peruse the entries under the pertinent key numbers. The entries are called "digest paragraphs," and they are identical to the headnote paragraphs appearing with the case in the West reporter. Compare Illustrations 9-1 (at page 128) and 9-2 (at page 146). At the end of each digest paragraph is a citation to the case from which it is drawn. The digest paragraphs under a key number are ordered by one or more of the following principles:

☐   hierarchical—federal before state, higher courts before lower courts;
☐   reverse chronological—newer before older;
☐   alphabetical—for example, Iowa before Michigan; and
☐   numerical—for example, First Circuit before Second Circuit.

The court and date appear in bold letters at the beginning of the digest paragraph, so you can quickly prioritize the entries to be read.

On occasion, you may know the name of one or both parties in a pertinent case, but not the citation of the case. Hence you need assistance locating the case in the reporter. Digests contain tables permitting you to look up the plaintiff or defendant by name and discover the case's citation. See Illustration 9-6 (at page 150).

Locate and read the cases in reporters. When you finish with the digest, you will have a list of pertinent cases along with their citations, that is, their locations in the case reporters, and a basic idea of what each case stands for. It is essential, of course, to take the next step—to read the case in full.

As you read the case, take care to use the headnotes properly. Relying only on the headnote is unwise because it will not tell you everything you need to know about the case, it may not reflect an important nuance of the case, and (rarely) it may be erroneous. You can use the headnotes to help you pinpoint the most pertinent portions of the case; the number preceding each headnote in the case reporter is keyed to a small bracketed number West editors insert within the opinion itself. See item 11 in Illustration 9-1 (at page 128). Nonetheless, you should at least skim the apparently less pertinent passages, to be sure you fully understand the legal and factual context of the pertinent passages.

As you read the case, attend to the rule the court used to decide the case and the authorities cited by the court; identify the key facts and outcome; note any factual similarities to or differences from your client's situation; trace the court's reasoning; and take note of what lawyers call the "procedural posture" of the case, that is, the point in the litigation at which the trial court ruled. Also watch for numbers inserted throughout the case; these identify the page breaks in the official reporter, where there is one available before the West reporter is printed.

Finally, take advantage of the case as a finding tool for additional authorities. A case may refer to authorities you have not yet identified. Furthermore, there may be a headnote for the case assigned to a topic and key number you have not yet identified; pursue that topic and key number in the digest, as described above.

The process described thus far is not complete. You still must employ a citator to verify that your case is good law, that is, to ascertain its subsequent history and treatment. Citators are discussed in Chapter 10.

Researching the Canoga case. Because we sought case law in New Mexico on a state law question of contract law, we used the *New Mexico Digest*. Another good option would have been the *Pacific Digest* because New Mexico cases are published in the *Pacific Reporter*.

A quick scan of the topic list suggested that Master and Servant might be a useful topic. See Illustration 9-3 (at page 147). There seemed to be two other potentially useful topics, Employers' Liability and Labor Relations, but neither proved to be pertinent.

We looked up *employee* and *employer* in the Descriptive Word Index and found a cross-reference to the heading Employment Law. There we found, under the subheading Adverse Employment Decisions, Actions Regarding, references to various potentially pertinent key numbers in the Mast & S (Master and Servant) topic. See Illustration 9-4 (at page 148). Note that in the summer of 2003, the Descriptive Word Index consisted of a 2002 hardbound volume, a 2003 pocket part, and a June 2003 pamphlet.

When we researched the Canoga case in summer 2003, we found a single hardbound digest volume, issued in summer 1999, covering New Mexico cases from 1852 forward. To update this main volume, we had to check the 2003 pocket part to that volume, the June 2003 supplementary pamphlet, and digest pages in the most recent hardbound and advance sheet reporters.

The Master and Servant topic begins with nearly fifty subtopics pertaining to the employment relationship, many pertaining to termination, discharge, and discipline. Key number 40(3.1) addresses the weight and sufficiency of the evidence in such a case. See Illustration 9-5 (at page 149). One of the *Lukoski* headnote paragraphs is reprinted along with *Lukoski*'s citation under key number 40(3.1) in the main volume. See Illustration 9-2 (at page 146).

The *Lukoski* case is described in Part A of this chapter. In brief, *Lukoski* recognizes a cause of action for breach of contract when an employer does not follow its employee handbook in discharging an employee.

The *Lukoski* case does lead to additional authority; *Lukoski* refers to cases from New Mexico, other states, and the federal Tenth Circuit. On the other hand, *Lukoski* has only two headnotes: the first regarding a procedural point not pertinent to the Canoga case, the second already revealed by the digest research.

ILLUSTRATION 9-2   Digest Entries,
from *New Mexico Digest* (paper source)

For references to other topics, see Descriptive-Word Index

manual implied that employment would not be terminated except for a good reason and manual strictly controlled employer's and employee's conduct.

> Newberry v. Allied Stores, Inc., 773 P.2d 1231, 108 N.M. 424.

Determination that employee was discharged without a good reason and in violation of implied contract between employer and employee that allowed termination only for cause was not supported by the evidence; evidence showed that employee was discharged for removing merchandise from store in which he worked without filling out the appropriate charge ticket, as was required under company policy.

> Newberry v. Allied Stores, Inc., 773 P.2d 1231, 108 N.M. 424.

Former employee failed to establish that his employer acted in bad faith in the manner and method used to terminate him, as was required for employee to collect punitive damages from employer in his breach of contract action.

> Newberry v. Allied Stores, Inc., 773 P.2d 1231, 108 N.M. 424.

N.M. 1988. Substantial evidence supported finding that employer did not act upon reasonable grounds in terminating employee, where employer's vice-president, before he fired the employee, only reviewed a summary of an investigation into allegations of sexual harassment, illegal conduct, and mismanagement by employee, which failed to differentiate between firsthand knowledge and rumor, which made no attempt to evaluate the credibility of persons interviewed, and which was not intended to stand alone.

> Kestenbaum v. Pennzoil Co., 766 P.2d 280, 108 N.M. 20, certiorari denied 109 S.Ct. 3163, 490 U.S. 1109, 104 L.Ed.2d 1026.

N.M. 1988. Evidence supported trial court's conclusions that termination procedures in employee handbook amended general manager's employment contract, that handbook created warning and suspension procedures which were not followed, and that personality, rather than insubordination, caused employment termination; handbook characterized disciplinary policy regarding warnings, suspensions, and terminations as established procedure; and handbook did not indicate that it was subject to revocation at any time or that employees should not rely on it.

> Lukoski v. Sandia Indian Management Co., 748 P.2d 507, 106 N.M. 664.

N.M. 1984. Evidence supported trial court's finding that former employee did not violate terms of his employment agreement and that he was a good employee thereby warranting conclusion that former employee's employment was terminated by former employer without good cause; therefore, former employee was not bound, as provided in the agreement, by the covenant not to compete contained in the employment agreement and was entitled to 30 days' termination pay.

> Danzer v. Professional Insurors, Inc., 679 P.2d 1276, 101 N.M. 178.

N.M.App. 1995. Presumption that an employee is at-will is rebuttable by an implied contract term that restricts employer's power to discharge.

> Kiedrowski v. Citizens Bank, 893 P.2d 468, 119 N.M. 572, certiorari denied, certiorari denied 890 P.2d 1321, 119 N.M. 389.

N.M.App. 1983. In most instances, claim under judicially created tort action based on employee's discharge which contravenes some clear mandate of public policy will assert serious misconduct; thus, proof should be made by clear and convincing evidence.

> Vigil v. Arzola, 699 P.2d 613, 102 N.M. 682, reversed in part 687 P.2d 1038, 101 N.M. 687.

N.M.App. 1972. In action alleging wrongful discharge from employment in connection with dispute as to duties employee was to perform under contract, finding that employee was employed as a manager, rather than as advisor and supervisor, was supported by substantial evidence.

> Clem v. Bowman Lumber Co., 495 P.2d 1106, 83 N.M. 659.

⬤—40(4). —— **Retaliatory discharge.**

C.A.10 (N.M.) 1994. Employee did not establish that employer retaliated against her for filing written complaint claiming that she had been wrongfully denied promised promotion, based solely on her subjective belief that she did not receive promotions because of filing of complaint; moreover, adverse employment actions which occurred in 1981 and 1984 were not sufficiently close in time to 1978 complaint to support inference of retaliatory motive.

> Candelaria v. EG & G Energy Measurements, Inc., 33 F.3d 1259, rehearing denied.

C.A.10 (N.M.) 1987. Three-part analysis requiring plaintiff to establish prima facie case, requiring employer to show nondiscriminatory reason, and requiring plaintiff to prove discriminatory intent applies in retaliation cases. Age Discrimination in Employment Act of 1967, §§ 2 et seq., 15, 15(a), as amended, 29 U.S.C.A. §§ 621 et seq., 633a, 633a(a); Civil Rights Act of 1964, § 701 et seq., 42 U.S.C.A. § 2000e et seq.

> Lujan v. Walters, 813 F.2d 1051.

District court's conclusion following full trial that employee failed to prove retaliation for filing age discrimination charge was adequate

ILLUSTRATION 9-3   Topic List,
                           from *New Mexico Digest* (paper source)

DIGEST TOPICS

116	Dead Bodies	166	Extradition and	216	Inspection
117	Death		Detainers	217	Insurance
117G	Debt, Action of	167	Factors	218	Insurrection and
117T	Debtor and Creditor	168	False Imprisonment		Sedition
118A	Declaratory	169	False Personation	219	Interest
	Judgment	170	False Pretenses	220	Internal Revenue
119	Dedication	170A	Federal Civil	221	International Law
120	Deeds		Procedure	222	Interpleader
122A	Deposits and	170B	Federal Courts	223	Intoxicating Liquors
	Escrows	171	Fences	224	Joint Adventures
123	Deposits in Court	172	Ferries	225	Joint-Stock
124	Descent and	174	Fines		Companies and
	Distribution	175	Fires		Business Trusts
125	Detectives	176	Fish	226	Joint Tenancy
126	Detinue	177	Fixtures	227	Judges
129	Disorderly Conduct	178	Food	228	Judgment
130	Disorderly House	179	Forcible Entry and	229	Judicial Sales
131	District and		Detainer	230	Jury
	Prosecuting	180	Forfeitures	231	Justices of the Peace
	Attorneys	181	Forgery	232	Kidnapping
132	District of Columbia	183	Franchises	232A	Labor Relations
133	Disturbance of	184	Fraud	233	Landlord and
	Public	185	Frauds, Statute of		Tenant
	Assemblage	186	Fraudulent	234	Larceny
134	Divorce		Conveyances	235	Levees and Flood
135	Domicile	187	Game		Control
135H	Double Jeopardy	188	Gaming	236	Lewdness
136	Dower and Curtesy	189	Garnishment	237	Libel and Slander
137	Drains	190	Gas	238	Licenses
138	Drugs and Narcotics	191	Gifts	239	Liens
141	Easements	192	Good Will	240	Life Estates
142	Ejectment	193	Grand Jury	241	Limitation of Actions
143	Election of	195	Guaranty	242	Lis Pendens
	Remedies	196	Guardian and Ward	245	Logs and Logging
144	Elections	197	Habeas Corpus	246	Lost Instruments
145	Electricity	198	Hawkers and	247	Lotteries
146	Embezzlement		Peddlers	248	Malicious Mischief
148	Eminent Domain	199	Health and	249	Malicious
148A	Employers' Liability		Environment		Prosecution
149	Entry, Writ of	200	Highways	250	Mandamus
150	Equity	201	Holidays	251	Manufactures
151	Escape	202	Homestead	252	Maritime Liens
152	Escheat	203	Homicide	253	Marriage
154	Estates in Property	204	Hospitals	255	Master and Servant ⬅
156	Estoppel	205	Husband and Wife	256	Mayhem
157	Evidence	205H	Implied and	257	Mechanics' Liens
158	Exceptions, Bill of		Constructive	257A	Mental Health
159	Exchange of		Contracts	258A	Military Justice
	Property	206	Improvements	259	Militia
160	Exchanges	207	Incest	260	Mines and Minerals
161	Execution	208	Indemnity	265	Monopolies
162	Executors and	209	Indians	266	Mortgages
	Administrators	210	Indictment and	267	Motions
163	Exemptions		Information	268	Municipal
164	Explosives	211	Infants		Corporations
165	Extortion and	212	Injunction	269	Names
	Threats	213	Innkeepers	270	Navigable Waters

XIV

ILLUSTRATION 9-4

Descriptive Word Index,
from *New Mexico Digest* (paper source)

EMPLOYMENT

10 N M D–180

References are to Digest Topics and Key Numbers

EMPLOYMENT LAW—Cont'd
ACTIONS—Cont'd

Vicarious liability of employer. See subheading VICARIOUS liability of employer, under this heading.

Wrongful acts of employee, **Mast & S** ⟜ 66

Wrongful discharge. See subheading ADVERSE employment decisions, actions regarding, under this heading.

ADDITIONAL work, performance of, **Mast & S** ⟜ 57

ADMISSIONS by employee, **Crim Law** ⟜ 410; **Evid** ⟜ 240-244

ADVERSE employment decisions, actions regarding,
Generally, **Mast & S** ⟜ 34
After-acquired evidence, defense based on, **Mast & S** ⟜ 37
Appeal and error, **Mast & S** ⟜ 45
See also heading APPEAL AND ERROR, generally.
Attorney fees, **Mast & S** ⟜ 46
Burden of proof,
Generally, **Mast & S** ⟜ 40(1)
Damages, **Mast & S** ⟜ 41(6)
Conditions precedent, **Mast & S** ⟜ 36
Costs, **Mast & S** ⟜ 46
Coworker liability, **Mast & S** ⟜ 34.1
Damages,
Generally, **Mast & S** ⟜ 41(.5)-42(3)
Burden of proof, **Mast & S** ⟜ 41(6)
Commencement of suit before expiration of term, **Mast & S** ⟜ 41(3)
Double recovery, prohibition against, **Damag** ⟜ 15
Elements of damage, **Mast & S** ⟜ 41(2)
Evidence, **Mast & S** ⟜ 41(6)
Exemplary damages, **Mast & S** ⟜ 41(5)
Measure in general, **Mast & S** ⟜ 41(1)
Mitigation, **Mast & S** ⟜ 42
Nominal damages, **Mast & S** ⟜ 41(4)
Other employment as ground for reduction,
Generally, **Mast & S** ⟜ 42
Efforts to secure employment, **Mast & S** ⟜ 42(2)
Former employer, working for, **Mast & S** ⟜ 42(3)
Nature of work, **Mast & S** ⟜ 42(2)
Self-employment, **Mast & S** ⟜ 42(3)
Punitive damages, **Mast & S** ⟜ 41(5)
Setoff, **Mast & S** ⟜ 41(1)
Substantial damages, **Mast & S** ⟜ 41(4)
Defenses, **Mast & S** ⟜ 37
Equitable estoppel, **Mast & S** ⟜ 37

EMPLOYMENT LAW—Cont'd
ADVERSE employment decisions, actions regarding,—Cont'd

Evidence,
Generally, **Mast & S** ⟜ 40
Admissibility, **Mast & S** ⟜ 40(2)
After-acquired evidence, defense based on, **Mast & S** ⟜ 37
Burden of proof, **Mast & S** ⟜ 40(1)
Damages, **Mast & S** ⟜ 41(6)
Presumptions, **Mast & S** ⟜ 40(1)
Sufficiency and weight,
Generally, **Mast & S** ⟜ 40(3)
Retaliatory discharge, **Mast & S** ⟜ 40(4)
Exclusive jurisdiction, **Mast & S** ⟜ 36
Exclusive remedy, **Mast & S** ⟜ 35
Exhaustion of remedies, **Mast & S** ⟜ 36
Form of, in general, **Mast & S** ⟜ 35
Instructions, **Mast & S** ⟜ 44
Jury questions, **Mast & S** ⟜ 43
Limitation of actions, **Mast & S** ⟜ 38
See also heading LIMITATION OF ACTIONS, generally.
Nature of, in general, **Mast & S** ⟜ 35
Pleading,
Generally, **Mast & S** ⟜ 39
Variation between proof and pleading, **Mast & S** ⟜ 39(2)
Preemption, **Mast & S** ⟜ 35
Presumptions, **Mast & S** ⟜ 40(1)
Primary jurisdiction, **Mast & S** ⟜ 36
Punitive damages, **Mast & S** ⟜ 41(5)
Setoff of damages, **Mast & S** ⟜ 41(1)
Standing, **Mast & S** ⟜ 34.1
Supervisor liability, **Mast & S** ⟜ 34.1
Time to sue, **Mast & S** ⟜ 38
Variation between proof and pleading, **Mast & S** ⟜ 39(2)

AFTER-ACQUIRED evidence,
Defense in action regarding adverse employment decision, **Mast & S** ⟜ 37

AGE discrimination. See heading EMPLOYMENT DISCRIMINATION, AGE discrimination.

AGENCIES. See heading EMPLOYMENT AGENCIES, generally.

AGENCY
See also heading AGENCY, generally.
Authority to hire or contract with employees for principal,
Generally, **Princ & A** ⟜ 102
Burden of proof, **Princ & A** ⟜ 119(4)
Presumptions, **Princ & A** ⟜ 119(4)

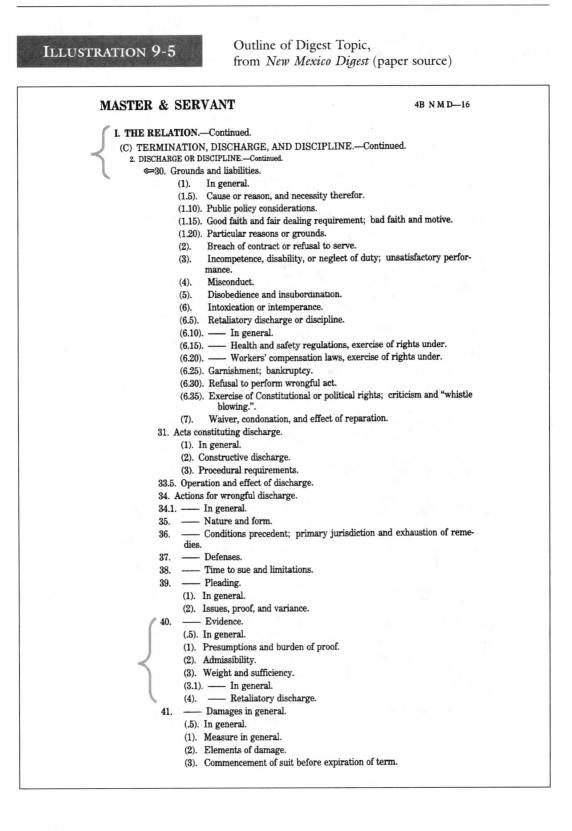

ILLUSTRATION 9-5   Outline of Digest Topic,
from *New Mexico Digest* (paper source)

MASTER & SERVANT   4B N M D—16

I. THE RELATION.—Continued.

(C) TERMINATION, DISCHARGE, AND DISCIPLINE.—Continued.

2. DISCHARGE OR DISCIPLINE.—Continued.

➾30. Grounds and liabilities.

(1).   In general.

(1.5).   Cause or reason, and necessity therefor.

(1.10).   Public policy considerations.

(1.15).   Good faith and fair dealing requirement; bad faith and motive.

(1.20).   Particular reasons or grounds.

(2).   Breach of contract or refusal to serve.

(3).   Incompetence, disability, or neglect of duty; unsatisfactory performance.

(4).   Misconduct.

(5).   Disobedience and insubordination.

(6).   Intoxication or intemperance.

(6.5).   Retaliatory discharge or discipline.

(6.10). —— In general.

(6.15). —— Health and safety regulations, exercise of rights under.

(6.20). —— Workers' compensation laws, exercise of rights under.

(6.25). Garnishment; bankruptcy.

(6.30). Refusal to perform wrongful act.

(6.35). Exercise of Constitutional or political rights; criticism and "whistle blowing.".

(7).   Waiver, condonation, and effect of reparation.

31. Acts constituting discharge.

(1). In general.

(2). Constructive discharge.

(3). Procedural requirements.

33.5. Operation and effect of discharge.

34. Actions for wrongful discharge.

34.1. —— In general.

35. —— Nature and form.

36. —— Conditions precedent; primary jurisdiction and exhaustion of remedies.

37. —— Defenses.

38. —— Time to sue and limitations.

39. —— Pleading.

(1). In general.

(2). Issues, proof, and variance.

40. —— Evidence.

(.5). In general.

(1). Presumptions and burden of proof.

(2). Admissibility.

(3). Weight and sufficiency.

(3.1). —— In general.

(4).   —— Retaliatory discharge.

41. —— Damages in general.

(.5). In general.

(1). Measure in general.

(2). Elements of damage.

(3). Commencement of suit before expiration of term.

ILLUSTRATION 9-6

Plaintiff Case Name Table,
from *New Mexico Digest* (paper source)

LUJAN;

6 N M D—316

See Guidelines for Arrangement at the beginning of this Volume

Lujan; New Mexico Regulation & Licensing Dept. v., NMApp, 979 P2d 744, 127 NM 233, 1999-NMCA-059.—Admin Law 754.1, 763, 796; Mast & S 4; Offic 69.7, 72.10, 72.50, 72.53, 72.54, 72.55(2); 72.63; States 43, 53.

Lujan v. New Mexico State Police Bd., NM, 667 P2d 456, 100 NM 149.—App & E 781(1); Const Law 278.4(5), 318(1); States 53.

Lujan v. Payroll Exp., Inc., NMApp, 837 P2d 451, 114 NM 257, cert den 834 P2d 939, 114 NM 62.—Work Comp 610, 709, 1358, 1573, 1719, 1861, 1949.

Lujan v. Pendaries Properties, Inc., NM, 635 P2d 580, 96 NM 771.—App & E 931(1), 989, 994(3), 996, 1010.1(1); Damag 91(1); Spec Perf 121(9); Ven & Pur 351(1), 351(8).

Lujan; Ramah Navajo Chapter v., CA10 (NM), 112 F3d 1455.—Indians 3(3), 4, 6(2), 7; Statut 188, 190, 219(4).

Lujan v. Reed, NM, 434 P2d 378, 78 NM 556.—App & E 1001(1), 1004(1); Autos 245(24), 245(87), 246(20); Damag 97, 127, 130(3), 135, 208(1); Neglig 213, 506(5), 1694, 1717, 1720; New Tr 76(1); Trial 261, 295(6), 296(12).

Lujan v. Regents of University of California, CA10 (NM), 69 F3d 1511.—Const Law 70.1(2), 70.3(3), 70.3(13); Death 37, 39; Fed Cts 265, 268.1, 269, 424, 427; Lim of Act 1, 95(1), 95(3), 165; Statut 184.

Lujan; Reynolds v., DNM, 785 FSupp 152.—Health & E 25.5(5.5).

Lujan; Reynolds Elec. & Engineering Co. v., NM, 323 P2d 890, 64 NM 43.—Licens 5; Tax 1207.

Lujan; State v., NM, 608 P2d 1114, 94 NM 232, denial of habeas corpus aff Lujan v. Tansy, 2 F3d 1031, cert den 114 SCt 1074, 510 US 1120, 127 LEd2d 392.—Crim Law 338(1), 675, 773(1), 790, 824(3), 1153(1); Homic 45, 309(3), 309(4).

Lujan; State v., NM, 560 P2d 167, 90 NM 103.—Crim Law 982.4(1), 1200, 1202.2, 1203.18; Statut 212.6, 227.

Lujan; State v., NM, 534 P2d 1112, 87 NM 400, cert den Lujan v. New Mexico, 96 SCt 469, 423 US 1025, 46 LEd2d 400.—Const Law 268.2(2); Crim Law 311, 456, 464, 525, 531(1), 532, 1038.3, 1038.4, 1170(1).

Lujan; State v., NM, 441 P2d 497, 79 NM 200.—Crim Law 628(7), 998(6), 998(7), 998(8), 998(11), 1128(1).

Lujan; State v., NM, 412 P2d 405, 76 NM 111.—Crim Law 1038(3), 1201, 1202(1); Statut 158, 161(1), 223.4.

Lujan; State v., NM, 170 P 734, 23 NM 636.—Seduct 34.

Lujan; State v., NMApp, 953 P2d 29, 124 NM 494, 1998-NMCA-032, cert den 953 P2d 1087, 124 NM 589.—Drugs & N 188(4.1), 188(7); Searches 108, 118, 200.

Lujan; State v., NMApp, 815 P2d 642, 112 NM 346, cert den 814 P2d 457, 112 NM 279.—Crim Law 577.8(2), 577.10(1), 577.10(8), 577.10(10), 577.12(1), 577.15(1), 577.16(1), 577.16(8).

Lujan; State v., NMApp, 712 P2d 13, 103 NM 667, cert den 713 P2d 556, 103 NM 740.—Assault 92(1); Crim Law 37.15(2), 351(10); Double J 52; Ind & Inf 144; Infants 13, 20; Judgm 751; Witn 383.

Lujan; State v., NMApp, 659 P2d 905, 99 NM 453, cert den 660 P2d 119, 99 NM 477.—Crim Law 273.1(2), 1119(2); Witn 297(13.1).

Lujan; State v., NMApp, 568 P2d 614, 90 NM 778.—Crim Law 991, 1083, 1202.1, 1203.11, 1203.20.

Lujan; State v., NMApp, 476 P2d 65, 82 NM 95.—Burg 41(3); Crim Law 641.10(2), 810.

Lujan; State v., NMApp, 445 P2d 749, 79 NM 525.—Const Law 250, 270; Crim Law 31, 1042, 1202(1).

Lujan; State ex rel. Rudolph v., NM, 512 P2d 951, 85 NM 378.—Elections 123; Pretrial Proc 552.

Lujan; State ex rel. Stanley v., NM, 93 P2d 1002, 43 NM 348.—Costs 12, 172; Damag 71; Prohib 35.

Lujan; State ex rel. Stanley v., NM, 77 P2d 178, 42 NM 291.—Courts 209(2); Prohib 3(2); Receivers 72.

Lujan v. State of N. M. Health and Social Services Dept., CA10 (NM), 624 F2d 968.—Civil R 378, 389, 411, 422.

Lujan; Streit v., NM, 6 P2d 205, 35 NM 672, appeal dism 52 SCt 405, 285 US 527, 76 LEd 924.—Const Law 42, 121(1), 122; Licens 33, 34; States 167; Tax 1218, 1334, 1345.

Lujan v. Tansy, CA10 (NM), 2 F3d 1031, cert den 114 SCt 1074, 510 US 1120, 127 LEd2d 392.—Crim Law 268(11); Hab Corp 492, 498, 768; Homic 230, 286.1.

Lujan; Transcontinental & Western Air v., NM, 8 P2d 103, 36 NM 64.—Commerce 63, 64.

Lujan v. Triangle Oil Co., NM, 37 P2d 797, 38 NM 543.—Licens 5; Tax 1205, 1294, 1340.

Lujan; U.S. v., CA10 (NM), 9 F3d 890.—Crim Law 1202.5(4), 1202.9, 1202.14, 1203.26(1), 1203.32.

Lujan v. U. S., CA10 (NM), 348 F2d 156, cert den 86 SCt 179, 382 US 889, 15 LEd2d 125.—Crim Law 742(1), 785(4); Drugs & N 116; Poisons 9; Witn 102.

Lujan v. United States, CA10 (NM), 209 F2d 190.—Assault 96(3); Const Law 84; Crim Law 642, 674, 921, 1152(1), 1166.32(1), 1170(1); Ind & Inf 164; Witn 330(1).

Lujan v. United States, CA10 (NM), 204 F2d 171.—Crim Law 951(1), 1069(5), 1081.

Lujan; U.S. v., DNM, 520 FSupp 282.—Bills & N 92(1); Colleges 9.25(2); Lim of Act 56(3).

Lujan v. U. S. Dept. of the Interior, CA10 (NM), 673 F2d 1165, cert den 103 SCt 297, 459 US 969, 74 LEd2d 279, reh den 103 SCt 1238, 459 US 1229, 75 LEd2d 471.—Judgm 634, 713(1), 720, 828.14(6).

Lujan v. Walters, CA10 (NM), 813 F2d 1051.—Civil R 380, 381, 388; Mast & S 40(4).

Lukee Enterprises, Inc. v. New York Life Ins. Co., DNM, 52 FRD 21.—Fed Civ Proc 1414.1; Fed Cts 381, 416.

Lukesh v. Ortega, NM, 623 P2d 564, 95 NM 444.—Work Comp 791.

Lukins v. Traylor, NM, 160 P 349, 22 NM 207.—App & E 356, 633; Hus & W 131(3).

Lukoski v. Sandia Indian Management Co., NM, 748 P2d 507, 106 NM 664.—Mast & S 40(3.1); Trial 392(1).

Lumbermen's Mutual Casualty Co.; Deeg v., CA10 (NM), 279 F2d 491.—Action 50(4); Statut 219, 220.

Lumbermens Mut. Ins. Co. v. Bowman, CA10 (NM), 313 F2d 381.—Courts 406.1(6); Fed Civ Proc 635; Insurance 1634(1), 1638, 1642, 1644, 1894, 1895, 1896, 3147, 3435, 3571, 3578.

Lumbert; Laughlin v., NM, 362 P2d 507, 68 NM 351.—Exemp 3, 4, 110; Garn 58; Home 78, 188, 201; Judgm 720.

Lummus v. Brackin, NM, 281 P2d 928, 59 NM 216.—Adv Poss 29, 36, 60(1), 110(4), 117; Ten in C 15(5), 15(10).

Lumpee; Jasper v., NMApp, 465 P2d 97, 81 NM 214.—App & E 215(1); Emp Liab 120, 132, 249, 266.

Lumpkins v. Lumpkins, NM, 495 P2d 371, 83 NM 591.—Divorce 400(1); Lim of Act 40(1).

Lumpkins; Lumpkins v., NM, 495 P2d 371, 83 NM 591.—Divorce 400(1); Lim of Act 40(1).

Lumpkins v. McPhee, NM, 286 P2d 299, 59 NM 442.—App & E 241, 1010(1); Evid 591, 597; Fraud 58(1); Fraud Conv 61, 102, 273, 282, 290, 299(13).

Luna v. Cerrillos Coal R. Co., NM, 226 P 655, 29 NM 647.—App & E 1096(1), 1187, 1188, 1219; Appear 9(1); Judges 7; States 9.

Luna v. Cerrillos Coal R. Co., NM, 218 P 435, 29 NM 161, hearing den 226 P 655, 29 NM 647.—App & E 1203(1), 1216; Evid 41, 44; Judges 7; States 9.

Luna v. Cerrillos Coal R. Co., NMTerr, 113 P 831, 16 NM 71.—Trial 392(3), 395(3).

Luna; Chapman v., NM, 701 P2d 367, 102 NM 768, cert den 106 SCt 345, 474 US 947, 88 LEd2d 292.—Civil R 296; Const Law 209.

Luna; Chapman v., NM, 678 P2d 687, 101 NM 59, appeal after remand 701 P2d 367, 102 NM 768, cert den 106 SCt 345, 474 US 947, 88 LEd2d 292.—Autos 7, 9; Const Law 70.1(2), 250.5; Mun Corp 122.1(2).

For Later Case History Information, see KeyCite on WESTLAW

Cases in Westlaw:

▶ select an appropriate database
▶ draft and run one or more searches—natural language, terms and connectors, key number, KeySearch—with restrictions, as appropriate
▶ sift the results to identify pertinent cases
▶ read each case
▶ cite each case (see Chapter 10)

In addition to the National Reporter System, West not surprisingly provides a significant electronic source for case law research in Westlaw. Westlaw provides a very wide range of cases and many means of access to those cases.

In some situations, research through Westlaw can have distinct advantages over research in paper:

☐ Westlaw provides more recent cases than paper sources.
☐ Westlaw provides unpublished cases, which may not be available in paper.
☐ You may use specific factual concepts in constructing a Westlaw search that would not be used in a paper source's table of contents or index.
☐ Westlaw's case law databases are automatically cumulated, whereas paper research generally entails working through multiple publications, e.g., a main volume, pocket part, and supplement pamphlet.

On the other hand, Westlaw research does not always work well. In particular, if your research terms are very common words, it will be difficult to draft an effective search. If you do not write your search well, you may believe that you have located all pertinent cases when in fact you have not. For example, if your search focuses on a distinctive fact, you will not retrieve pertinent cases that state the applicable law but do not include the distinctive factual term. Furthermore, Westlaw can be expensive. Pricing structures vary, so you should always be aware of the fees associated with the research you conduct in Westlaw.

Select an appropriate database. Westlaw offers many case law databases, most drawn along jurisdictional lines, others along subject-matter lines. As a general principle, you should start in the narrowest database containing the mandatory precedent for your jurisdiction, then switch to wider or different databases as needed, for example, to find factually parallel cases in other states because you have found no factually similar case in your jurisdiction. As you begin your research, always be sure to check the scope of the database you have chosen.

Draft and run one or more searches. Westlaw offers four main search options for case law research; you may well want to combine two or three

to assure comprehensive results. Search drafting is discussed in detail in Part
C of Chapter 2.

☐ Natural-language searching entails stating an issue, possibly using
   the thesaurus to expand your terms, and obtaining a specified number
   of documents that best fit the search as determined by a semantic-
   statistical algorithm. The cases are presented from best fit to less
   complete fit.

☐ Terms-and-connectors searching, Westlaw's version of Boolean
   searching, entails keying in words, with or without root expanders,
   and connectors, such as *&*, */s*, and */n*, and a space for *or*. The
   computer will retrieve all cases meeting the requirements of the
   search and present them from newest to oldest.

☐ Key-number searching entails entering West's code for a pertinent
   topic and key number as your search term. You may find pertinent
   topics and key numbers in a secondary authority, through your
   research in digests, through a pertinent case you already have located,
   or by browsing the online key-number service. A variation on key-
   number searching is KeyCite Notes, in which you click on that icon
   adjacent to a pertinent headnote you have found. Either way, the
   computer will retrieve cases with headnotes under that key number.

☐ KeySearch entails taking advantage of searches already written by
   West's staff. You select a topic and subtopic, in effect adopting West's
   search for that subtopic; you may add your own search terms as well.
   The computer will present the cases from newest to oldest.

Note that the results will differ from search to search. For example, a
key-number search will retrieve only published cases that have key numbers,
because, for the most part, West has not assigned key numbers to unpublished
cases. Natural-language and terms-and-connectors searches are processed
differently.

For various reasons, you may want to restrict your search. For example,
you would add a date restrictor if you are seeking only recent cases because
you are updating your research in paper sources or updating research done
some time ago. Or you may want to restrict your search to a specific field
(Westlaw's term for components of a document). As an example, if your
research terms are quite common words and you want to, in effect, shrink
the database to a manageable size, you could confine your search to the
synopsis field or the digest field (which contains both the key-number classifications and the headnotes).

On occasion, you will use Westlaw to obtain a known case or to locate
and obtain a nearly known case. If you know the citation of a case, you can
obtain the case through the retrieval function. If you know some information
about a case, for example, the name of one of the parties or the judge or
one of the lawyers, you can run a search in the appropriate database with
that information in the appropriate field.

Sift the results, and read the pertinent cases. However you construct
your search, your next step is to sift through the results to identify pertinent
cases. To identify cases that probably will be pertinent, read the synopsis and
headnotes, read the passages of the case in which your search terms appear,

or both. As you sift your results, if your research yields unpublished cases, consider carefully how precedential they are. Most, if not all, of the cases you select should be published cases.

As you read a pertinent case located and obtained through Westlaw, you should look for the same information detailed above for paper research. And, as with paper research in cases, you must use a citator to verify that your case is still good law. As discussed in Chapter 10, citing through Westlaw is one good option.

Researching the Canoga case. When we researched the Canoga case in the summer of 2003, we ran various searches in Westlaw. We ran several searches in the NM-CS database, which contains cases from the New Mexico Supreme Court and the New Mexico Court of Appeals as well as a limited number of trial court decisions; includes published cases, recent cases not yet in the *Pacific Reporter*, and cases that will not be published; and reaches back to 1852. A somewhat broader database is NM-CS-ALL, which also contains federal court cases that are authoritative in New Mexico, for example, Tenth Circuit cases.

Our natural-language search was: Can an employer discharge an employee without following the procedures in the employee handbook? *Lukoski* was the fourth case on the citation list. For a portion of that citation list with the search terms in context, see Illustration 9-7 (at page 154).

Our initial terms-and-connectors search was employ! /p (discharg! dismiss! terminat!) /p (handbook manual) /p contract. This search yielded thirty-four cases, and *Lukoski* was the twenty-fourth on the list. To see how that citation list first appeared on the screen, see Illustration 9-8 (at page 155). Note the links in the right-hand column to potentially helpful key numbers and A.L.R. annotations. When we edited this search to also include (music! flutist orchestra) & smok!, the computer found no cases. However, when we deleted the parenthetical and continued to search for smok!, the computer found one case, *Mealand v. Eastern New Mexico Medical Center*;[8] in that case, the employer's handbook provided for discipline for unauthorized smoking, but the nurse was fired for reasons unrelated to smoking.

Our key-number search was 255k40, because Master and Servant is the 255th topic and 40 is the key number we identified through the *Lukoski* case. This search yielded eighteen cases, and *Lukoski* was the twelfth.

We also used KeySearch. We picked the topic Employment Law and the subtopic Handbooks and Manuals. The search written by the West staff to cover this subtopic was he(employ! personnel /3 hand-book manual). Note that he signifies a search in headnotes. When we ran this search in NM State Cases with West Headnotes, the computer retrieved twenty-six cases, and *Lukoski* was the nineteenth.

To compare and contrast the results from the four searches described above, all run in the New Mexico state cases database on the same day, see Illustration 9-9 (at page 156), which lists the first ten cases on each citation list.

---

8. 33 P.3d 285 (N.M. Ct. App. 2001).

ILLUSTRATION 9-7

Natural-Language Citation List,
from Search in Westlaw Cases Database (electronic source)

Page 1 of 5

Search Result Citations List - NM-CS - CAN AN EMPLOYER DISCHARGE A...

1.   Sanchez v. The New Mexican, 106 N.M. 76, 738 P.2d 1321, 109 Lab.Cas. P 55,918, 2 IER Cases
      1427 (N.M., Jul 15, 1987) (NO. 16,362)

      discharge had nothing to do with his complaints about the supposed non-payment of gross receipts
      taxes. Therefore we need not decide whether an employee's **discharge** for "blowing the whistle" on
      an **employer** for not making tax payments constitutes the tort of retaliatory **discharge** according to the
      rule established in Vigil. We will continue to define on a case-by-case basis violations of public
      policy in retaliatory **discharge** suits. Here we simply hold that Sanchez's **discharge** was not as a
      matter of law retaliatory, but could have been based, as the jury apparently decided, on grounds which
      authorized his **Employer** to terminate him "at will." II. THE "IMPLIED CONTRACT" ISSUE [3]
      Sanchez asserts that the **employee handbook** constituted an implied contract between him and his HR

2.   Mealand v. Eastern New Mexico Medical Center, 131 N.M. 65, 33 P.3d 285, 2001-NMCA-089
      (N.M.App., Aug 29, 2001) (NO. 20,160)

      Employee Handbook, oral representations, or the conduct of the parties." DISCUSSION
      Plaintiff's Contract Claim {7} On appeal, Plaintiff asserts that ENMMC was mistaken in its
      understanding that she acted without physician authorization; that the **employee handbook** supported
      a reasonable expectation that prior to **discharge, employees** will be given a meaningful opportunity to
      respond to allegations of misconduct; and, that if ENMMC had provided her a meaningful opportunity
      to respond to the charges of misconduct as required by the **handbook,** she would have corrected the
      misunderstanding and her **discharge** would not have occurred. ENMMC argues that whether
      ENMMC afforded Plaintiff an opportunity to demonstrate her innocence is immaterial because
      Plaintiff was an at-will **employee,** who could be terminated for

3. ▶ Hartbarger v. Frank Paxton Co., 115 N.M. 665, 857 P.2d 776, 127 Lab.Cas. P 57,664, 8 IER Cases
      1114 (N.M., Jun 14, 1993) (NO. 19,913)

      employee handbook); Forrester v. Parker, 93 N.M. 781, 782, 606 P.2d 191, 192 (1980) (holding
      that, when terminating non-probationary **employee, employer** is bound by policies established in
      "personnel policy guide" that control the **employer-employee** relationship). We have upheld findings
      that there was no implied contract in cases where the alleged promise by the **employer** was not
      sufficiently explicit. See Shull v. New Mexico Potash Corp., 111 N.M. 132, 135, 802 P.2d 641, 644
      (1990) (affirming summary judgment in favor of **employer** where **employee** had no bargained-for
      expectations and **employee handbook** did nothing to alter at-will relationship); Sanchez v. The New
      Mexican, 106 N.M. 76, 79, 738 P.2d 1321, 1324 (1987) (affirming grant of directed verdict in favor of
      employer where language in **employee**

4.   Lukoski v. Sandia Indian Management Co., 106 N.M. 664, 748 P.2d 507, 2 IER Cases 1650 (N.M.,
      Jan 07, 1988) (NO. 16,462)

      employer for wrongful **discharge.** The District Court, Bernalillo County, William W. Deaton, D.J.,
      entered judgment in favor of manager. **Employer** appealed. The Supreme Court, Ransom, J., held
      that evidence established that **employee handbook** amended employment contract and that **employer**

ILLUSTRATION 9-8   Terms-and-Connectors Citation List,
from Search in Westlaw Cases Database (electronic source)

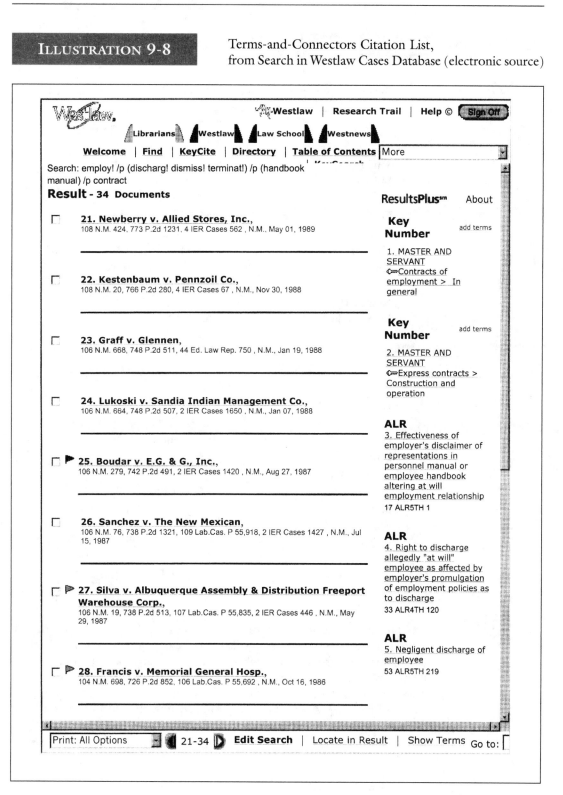

| ILLUSTRATION 9-9 | Comparison of Westlaw Searches in Case Law (first ten citations) |

The cases appearing in three or all four of the lists are checked.

Natural Language	Terms and Connectors
Sanchez	Cockrell (supreme court)
✔ Mealand	Trujillo
Hatbarger	✔ Hudson
Lukoski	✔ Mealand
Paca	Campos de Suenos, Ltd.
✔ Hudson	Handmaker
Shull	Cockrell (court of appeals)
✔ Cates	New Mexico Regulation & Licensing Department
Newberry	✔ Cates
Kiedrowski	Lopez

Key Number	KeySearch
Ettenson	Barreras
Gonzalez	Cockrell (supreme court)
Weidler	Trujillo
Lihosit	✔ Hudson
Kiedrowski	✔ Mealand
Hartbarger	Martinez
Shull	Cockrell (court of appeals)
McGinnes	New Mexico Regulation & Licensing Department
Chavez	✔ Cates
Newberry	Garcia

Finally, before leaving Westlaw, we sought a factually similar case in a sister jurisdiction. We used the MLB-CS database, a multistate database containing cases from various jurisdictions in the area of labor and employment law. Our search was (discharg! dismiss! terminat!) & (smok! /p off-duty); it yielded forty-eight cases. An edited search excluding mari*uana yielded twenty-four documents. Fifth on that list was a South Dakota case, *Wood v. South Dakota Cement Plant*,[9] which involved an assistant kiln operator who was fired for off-duty, off-premises use of tobacco.

9. 588 N.W.2d 227 (S.D. 1999).

Cases in LexisNexis:

▶ select an appropriate database; draft and run natural-language or terms-and-connectors searches

▶ use Search Advisor in an appropriate database

▶ sift the results to identify pertinent cases

▶ read each case

▶ citate each case (see Chapter 10)

LexisNexis provides a wealth of cases along with many means of access to those cases. It offers several advantages over paper research: very recent cases, unpublished cases, use of research terms drawn from the specific facts of your client's situation, and automatic cumulation of new material into existing databases. On the other hand, it is difficult to draft a good search for some research topics, you cannot tell what you have missed, and LexisNexis use can be expensive.

Select an appropriate database; draft and run natural-language or terms-and-connectors searches. LexisNexis offers many case databases. You should start with the narrowest database containing mandatory precedents and switch to wider or different databases as needed. Be sure to check the scope of each database you use.

LexisNexis offers both of the standard search options. Natural-language searching entails stating an issue, adding suggested concepts as you desire, and obtaining a predetermined number of cases, presented from most probably pertinent to least probably pertinent. Terms-and-connectors, or Boolean searching, entails keying in words, with or without root expanders, and connectors; the computer will retrieve all cases meeting the requirements of the search and present them by court level and from newest to oldest. The results may well vary because the two searches operate differently. Search drafting is covered in detail in Part C of Chapter 2.

LexisNexis also permits you to run more focused searches, for example, by adding a date restriction, by searching specific segments (LexisNexis' term for components of a document), by using the retrieval function when you already know the case's citation.

Use Search Advisor in an appropriate database. A fairly new tool, Search Advisor has become the centerpiece of LexisNexis' case law service. It has similarities to Westlaw's key number and KeySearch tools. LexisNexis' staff has devised a system of tiered legal subjects and, in effect, filed cases under pertinent subject headings. Thus, if you can identify a pertinent subject, you can research in a set of presumptively pertinent cases.

You may identify a pertinent subject two ways: You may enter search terms, and the computer will match your terms to a pertinent Search Advisor subject heading. Or you may work through the tiered subject list, first selecting a broad subject, then a major topic within that area, then a minor topic within that major topic. The subject, major topic, and minor topic constitute a Search Advisor path. You then select an appropriate database, depending on your jurisdiction, and search the cases in that database under the subject you have identified. Options include natural-language, terms-and-connectors, date restrictions, and segment searches.

A variation on Search Advisor (that resembles West's KeyCite Notes) is to select a pertinent headnote from a pertinent case. You may obtain cases pertaining to the same Search Advisor path as that headnote by clicking on the retrieval icon for that headnote's path.

Sift the results, and read the pertinent cases. Whatever your search method may be, your next step is to sift through the results. You may peruse a citation list containing a case overview and list of core terms prepared by the LexisNexis staff, as well as see your research terms in context. To further identify cases that probably will be pertinent, peruse the case summary and headnotes. Another option is to look at the passages in which your search terms appear. In addition, attend carefully to whether the case is published or not.

When you obtain a case through LexisNexis, note that it has several editorial enhancements appearing before the text of the opinion:

☐ the case summary (which consists of procedural posture, overview, and outcome);

☐ a list of core terms; and

☐ headnotes (formerly called "core concepts"), which consist of a heading of three linked legal topics and one or two significant senten-ces drawn directly from the decision.

Note that the headnote numbers appear beside that language in the decision (as is done with West headnotes). See Illustration 9-10 (at pages 160–61).

As you read a pertinent case located and obtained through LexisNexis, look for the same information you would seek in a paper reporter. Note that you can discern the pages of the case in other reporters, such as an official reporter and a West reporter, through the brackets containing stars and numbers located throughout the opinion. See Illustration 9-10 (at page 161), in which [*665] refers to the official reporter and [**508] refers to West's *Pacific Reporter 2d*. And be sure to cite the case; as discussed in Chapter 10, using the Shepard's tool on LexisNexis is one good option.

Researching the Canoga case. When we researched the Canoga case in the summer of 2003, we first selected the NM State Cases, Combined database, which reaches back to 1852 and contains decisions of the New Mexico Supreme Court and the New Mexico Court of Appeals. First we ran this natural-language search: Can an employer discharge an employee without following the procedures in the employee handbook? *Lukoski* was the first case on the list. For a portion of that on-screen citation list showing case overviews and core terms, see Illustration 9-11 (at page 162). We also ran a terms-and-connectors search: employ! /p (discharg! or dismiss! or terminat!) /p (handbook or manual) /p contract. This search yielded fifty cases, and *Lukoski* was the twentieth case on the list.

Turning to Search Advisor, we first entered the search "employee handbook"; we were directed to Contract Law > Types of Contracts > Employment Contracts. We also identified Labor & Employment Law > Wrongful Termination > Breach of Contract. In that path in the NM Labor & Employment Law Cases database, we searched for handbook or manual. Note that we deleted terms rendered superfluous by Search Advisor, for example, employ!, contract. Our search yielded thirty-six cases, and *Lukoski* was the eighteenth case on the list.

To compare and contrast the results from the three searches described above, all run in the New Mexico state cases database on the same day, see Illustration 9-12 (at page 163), which lists the first ten cases on each citation list.

Finally, before leaving LexisNexis, we sought a factually similar case in a sister jurisdiction. We ran searches in State Labor & Employment Cases under two Search Advisor subjects: Labor & Employment Law > Wrongful Termination > Breach of Contract and Labor & Employment Law > Wrongful Termination > Public Policy. The search for cases involving musicians yielded no cases, whereas the searches for cases involving smoking yielded quite a few (forty-six under Breach of Contract and sixty-two under Public Policy).

<table>
<tr><td>ILLUSTRATION 9-10</td><td>Judicial Case,
from LexisNexis (electronic source)</td></tr>
</table>

Scott J.L. LUKOSKI, Plaintiff-Appellee, v. SANDIA INDIAN MANAGEMENT
COMPANY, Defendant-Appellant

No. 16462

SUPREME COURT OF NEW MEXICO

106 N.M. 664; 748 P.2d 507; 1988 N.M. LEXIS 17; 2 BNA IER CAS 1650

January 7, 1988

SUBSEQUENT HISTORY:

January 7, 1988, Filed

PRIOR HISTORY:
[***1]

Appeal from the District Court of Bernalillo County,
William W. Deaton, District Judge.

CASE SUMMARY

PROCEDURAL POSTURE: Defendant employer
sought review of the decision from the District Court of
Bernalillo County (New Mexico) which ruled in favor of
plaintiff employee in a wrongful discharge action.

OVERVIEW: The employee brought a wrongful
discharge action against the employer. The trial court
found that the employer had violated the termination
procedures prescribed for "less serious" offenses by an
employee handbook. The employee was awarded the
salary due on the remaining term of his one-year oral
contract. On appeal, the employer claimed the employee,
as general manager, was not the type of employee
intended to be covered by the handbook. The court
affirmed. It found that distribution of the handbook to all
employees with request for signatures refuted the
employer's claims. There was substantial evidence
supporting the trial court's findings of ultimate fact that
the termination procedures became an amendment to the
employee's contract. The employee was terminated
without warning or suspension for a cause not so severe
as to have constituted cause for immediate termination.
Substantial evidence supported the finding of the trial
court that the employee handbook modified the

employment relationship and created warning and
suspension procedures which were not followed.

OUTCOME: The judgment of the trial court was
affirmed.

CORE TERMS: termination, suspension, handbook,
warning, employee handbook, severe,   employment
relationship, personnel manual, bingo, disciplinary,
supervisor,   modified,   manual,   general manager,
discharged, manager, conform,   specific question,
ultimate fact, materiality, customers, abide, procedures
prescribed,   employment   agreement,   employment
contract, oral contract, insubordination, verification,
disobedience, personality

LexisNexis(TM) HEADNOTES - Core Concepts

*Civil Procedure > Jury Trials > Province of Court &
Jury*
Contracts Law > Breach > Causes of Action
[HN1] Materiality is a specific question of fact.

*Labor & Employment Law > Wrongful Termination >
Breach of Contract*
*Civil Procedure > Jury Trials > Province of Court &
Jury*
[HN2] Whether an employee handbook modifies the
employment relationship is a question of fact to be
discerned from the totality of the parties' statements and
actions regarding the employment relationship.

*Labor & Employment Law > Wrongful Termination >
Breach of Contract*
[HN3] If an employer does choose to issue a policy
statement, in a manual or otherwise, and, by its language
or by the employer's actions, encourages reliance

ILLUSTRATION 9-10   *(continued)*

Page 2

106 N.M. 664, *; 748 P.2d 507, **;
1988 N.M. LEXIS 17, ***; 2 BNA IER CAS 1650

thereon, the employer cannot be free to only selectively abide by it. Having announced a policy, the employer may not treat it as illusory.

COUNSEL:

Grammer & Grammer, David A. Grammer, III, Albuquerque, for defendant-appellant.

Turpen & Wolfe, Donald C. Turpen, Albuquerque, for plaintiff-appellee.

JUDGES:

Ransom, Justice. Scarborough, C.J., Sosa, Senior Justice, and Walters, J., concur. Stowers, J., dissents.

OPINIONBY:

RANSOM

OPINION:

[*665] [**508] OPINION

Scott J.L. Lukoski brought a wrongful discharge action against his employer, Sandia Indian Management Co. (SIMCO). Lukoski had been employed as general manager of the Sandia Pueblo bingo operation. In a bench trial, the court decided that SIMCO violated the termination procedures prescribed for "less serious" offenses by an employee handbook. For salary due on the remaining term of his one-year oral contract, Lukoski was awarded $ 18,629.05. We affirm.

The court found that, in October 1983, Lukoski and SIMCO entered into a one-year oral employment agreement under which Lukoski would provide services as the general manager of a bingo hall operation for a specified annual salary plus commission. There was no written agreement between the parties. In February 1984, SIMCO distributed to [***2] all employees an employee handbook and requested each to sign the last page as verification of receipt, acknowledgement of acceptance, and agreement to conform with the stated policies and procedures. After Lukoski signed the back page as requested, it was placed in his personnel file. The court concluded that:

The parties amended the oral employment contract *** when [SIMCO] proffered, and [Lukoski] signed, [the] Employee's Handbook containing new duties and obligations on the part of employee and employer over and above said oral contract, including Rules to be obeyed by [Lukoski] and a termination procedure to be followed by [SIMCO].

Although we determine the abovequoted language is a finding of ultimate fact, rather than a conclusion of law, that is of no consequence. *See Hoskins v. Albuquerque Bus Co.*, 72 N.M. 217, 382 P.2d 700 (1963); *Wiggs v. City of Albuquerque*, 57 N.M. 770, 263 P.2d 963 (1953). SIMCO challenges this finding and for the first time on appeal raises two other issues. First, it claims that Lukoski, as general manager, was not the type of employee intended to be covered by the handbook. [***3] Distribution to all employees with request for signatures constituted evidence to the contrary, and resolution of any ambiguity regarding management personnel would have been a specific question of fact. *See Shaeffer v. Kelton*, 95 N.M. 182, 619 P.2d 1226 (1980). Second, SIMCO claims that any breach was not material because it neither went to the substance of the contract nor defeated the object of the parties. [HN1] Materiality is likewise a specific question of fact. *See Bisio v. Madenwald (In re Estate of Bisio)*, 33 Or.App. 325, 576 P.2d 801 (1978). As the contract stood after amendment, it was not materiality, as argued by SIMCO, but rather severity of offense that was at issue under the termination procedures. In any event, by failing to tender requested findings, SIMCO waived specific [*666] [**509] findings on these fact issues. SCRA 1986, 1-052(B)(1)(f).

There is substantial evidence supporting the court's findings of ultimate fact that the termination procedures became an amendment to Lukoski's contract, and that personality -- not the severe offenses of insubordination or disobedience -- was the cause for termination. [***4] He was terminated without warning or suspension for a cause not so severe as to constitute cause for immediate termination. His personality and interpersonal dealings were found by the court to create an atmosphere of fear and anxiety and bad morale among employees and managers.

Relying only on *Ellis v. El Paso Natural Gas Co.*, 754 F.2d 884 (10th Cir.1985), the thrust of SIMCO's appeal is that the language of the employee handbook is "too indefinite to constitute a contract" and lacks "contractual terms which might evidence the intent to form a contract." It maintains that the parties did not conduct themselves as if the employee handbook was to govern Lukoski or as if they expected it to form the basis of a contractual relationship. In support of its position, SIMCO refers to the disciplinary action, suspension, and warning provisions, n1 and argues that the language of the termination policy is ambiguous and contains no required policy for termination.

n1 The referenced handbook provisions state:

OTHER DISCIPLINARY ACTION:

ILLUSTRATION 9-11	Natural-Language Citation List, from Search in LexisNexis Cases Database (electronic source)

Search - 100 Results - can an employer discharge an employee without f..   Page 1 of 1

● **LexisNexis** · *Total Research System*   Practice Area Pages   Change Client   Options   Feedback   Live Support   Sign Off   He

| Search ▶ | Search Advisor ▶ | Get a Document ▶ | *Shepard's* ® · Check a Citation ▶ | ECLIPSE™   History

View: **Cite** | KWIC | Full | Custom   ◀◀◀ **1-10 of 100** ▶▶▶   **FAST Print**   Print | Download | Fax | Email | Text Only
                                              FOCUS™ | Show Hits

Source: Legal > States Legal - U.S. > New Mexico > Cases > **NM State Cases, Combined** ⓘ
Terms: **can an employer discharge an employee without following the procedures in the employee handbook?** (Edit Search)

☞ Select for FOCUS™ or Delivery

☐   1. Lukoski v. Sandia Indian Management Co., No. 16462, SUPREME COURT OF NEW
            MEXICO, 106 N.M. 664; 748 P.2d 507; 1988 N.M. LEXIS 17; 2 BNA IER CAS 1650,
            January 7, 1988, January 7, 1988, Filed

            OVERVIEW: Where the employee handbook modified the employment relationship and
            created warning and suspension procedures which were not followed, the employer was
            liable to the employee for wrongful termination of employment.

            CORE TERMS: termination, suspension, handbook, warning, employee handbook, severe,
            employment relationship, personnel manual, bingo, disciplinary...

☐ Ⓐ   2. Mealand v. Eastern. N.M. Med. Ctr., Docket No. 20,160, COURT OF APPEALS OF NEW
            MEXICO, 131 N.M. 65; 2001 NMCA 89; 33 P.3d 285; 2001 N.M. App. LEXIS 79; 40 N.M.
            St. B. Bull. 48, August 29, 2001, Filed, Released for Publication October 26, 2001.
            Certiorari Denied, Mealand v. E. N.M. Med. Ctr., 33 P.3d 284, 2001 N.M. LEXIS 346 (N.M.
            Oct. 18, 2001)

            OVERVIEW: Where nurse sued hospital for wrongful termination, there was genuine issue
            of fact as to whether employee handbook supported reasonable expectation that employee
            would be discharged only after being given chance to respond to misconduct charges.

            CORE TERMS: handbook, disclaimer, employee handbook, summary judgment,
            reasonable expectation, terminated, progressive discipline, supervisor, discipline,
            termination...

☐   3. Hartbarger v. Frank Paxton Co., No. 19913, SUPREME COURT OF NEW MEXICO, 115
            N.M. 665; 857 P.2d 776; 1993 N.M. LEXIS 187; 32 N.M. St. B. Bull. 635; 8 BNA IER CAS
            1114; 127 Lab. Cas. (CCH) P57,664, June 14, 1993, Decided, July 14, 1993, Filed,
            Rehearing Denied July 21, 1993.

            OVERVIEW: In an action filed by an employee alleging breach of an implied contract of
            employment, the evidence did not support a finding that employer made an offer or
            promise sufficiently explicit to establish an implied employment contract.

            CORE TERMS: implied contract, termination, at-will, employment relationship, handbook,
            employment contract, mutual assent, yellow, terminable, terminated...

☐ ◆   4. Sanchez v. The New Mexican, No. 16362, SUPREME COURT OF NEW MEXICO, 106 N.M.
            76; 738 P.2d 1321; 1987 N.M. LEXIS 3673; 2 BNA IER CAS 1427; 109 Lab. Cas. (CCH)
            P55,918, July 15, 1987, July 15, 1987, Filed

            OVERVIEW: Dismissal of employee's claim that employer's termination of employee
            breached implied employment contract was proper where evidence supported employer's
            contention that employment handbook lacked terms that evidenced intent to form
            contract.

| ILLUSTRATION 9-12 | Comparison of LexisNexis Searches in Case Law (first ten citations) |

Cases appearing in three of the lists are checked.

Natural Language	Terms and Connectors
Lukoski	Cockrell
Mealand	Trujillo
✔ Hartbarger	Handmaker
Sanchez	Cates
Barreras	✔ Garcia
✔ Garcia	Zamora
Boudar	Wheatley
Newberry	Bourgeous
Hudson	Swinney
Kiedrowski	✔ Hartbarger

Search Advisor

Trujillo
✔ Garcia
Zamora
McDowell
Wheatley
Sanchez
Bourgeous
Swinney
✔ Hartbarger
Economy Rentals

Cases through court websites:

▶ identify an appropriate website

▶ ascertain how to search for pertinent cases, and do so, if possible

▶ or retrieve the case you are seeking

▶ as needed, sift the results to identify pertinent cases

▶ read each case

▶ citate each case (see Chapter 10)

In the abstract, the sequence of steps for case law research in publicly accessible websites is quite similar to that of Westlaw and LexisNexis: find an appropriate website and database, run a search, sift the results, read the pertinent cases, and cite each case (as discussed in Chapter 10). Nonetheless, there are significant differences between the commercial services and public websites:

☐ Although you most likely will find a website for your jurisdiction, it very likely will have cases for the past decade only, if that.

☐ The website may or may not permit searching of the database; if it does, the search options will be limited.

☐ Similarly, the options for displaying the results likely will be limited.

☐ There will be no editorial enhancements of the decisions.

☐ There will be no connected citator (again, see Chapter 10).

☐ On the other hand the decision as posted will be the official version, so it is highly credible.

☐ Research in public websites is inexpensive.

Please note: The statements above describe public website research as of mid-2003, and improvements occur on a regular basis.

As of mid-2003, case law websites varied significantly from jurisdiction to jurisdiction. Every state had a website for appellate decisions (at least the highest court and often also the intermediate appeals court). Most websites reached back to the late 1990s, although a few contained only very recent cases; the latter functioned as a repository of cases not yet available in other sources. At a minimum, you could find a list of cases by docket number or date of decision; about half of the websites also provided key-word searching. As a general rule, as of summer 2003, a lawyer typically used a public website as a source of recent decisions already known to the lawyer. It was not common to use a public website as a main research tool for case law.

When we researched the Canoga case, we first visited the New Mexico Supreme Court's website, supremecourt.nm.org. It had a database with current (2003) decisions of both the supreme court and the court of appeals as well as a limited database of past opinions. At that time, it did not permit key-word searching.

Switching to the Tenth Circuit, we visited two of the three websites listed in Cornell's Legal Information Institute website. At the first, pacer .ca.10.uscourts.gov, we found cases from the past ninety days, the most recent posted the day before our visit, and a key-word searching option; we found no pertinent cases discussing New Mexico law. We then visited kscourts.org/ ca10, a site maintained by the Washburn University School of Law Library, dating to October 1997 and continuing to the present. Our `"employee handbook"` search yielded twenty-five cases, sorted by relevance. We narrowed the search by adding `"New Mexico."` Of the five cases on the list, one was on point, *Baucom v. Amtech Systems Corp.*[10] See Illustration 9-13 (at page 166). The case was designated not to be published and carries a reference to the Tenth Circuit rule disfavoring the citing of unpublished cases. See Illustration 9-14 (at page 167); note that this decision is an electronic version of the slip opinion provided to the parties and maintained at the clerk's office. The third Tenth Circuit site was maintained by Emory University's School of Law and provided decisions from August 1995 to October 1997.

D. WHAT ELSE?

State Versions of Regional Reporters. You may have available to you a state-specific version of a regional reporter, that is, a volume containing only the cases from one of the states covered by a regional reporter, reprinted as they appear in the regional reporter. The advantage of such a reporter is its small size and cost.

Updating of Key Numbers. As the law or legal vocabulary evolves, West occasionally changes topics and key numbers. Generally, you will find a conversion table at the end of the outline of the revised topic.

Specialized Reporters and Looseleaf Services. Specialized reporters contain cases on a single area of law. For example, West publishes *Federal Rules Decisions,* a reporter with cases pertaining only to federal civil or criminal procedure. Furthermore, looseleaf services, discussed in Chapter 15, include cases and digests along with statutes, regulations, and secondary materials in a single area of law.

Lawyers' Edition. Another unofficial case reporter is *United States Supreme Court Reports, Lawyers' Edition,* which encompasses United States Supreme Court cases. The set includes a digest, summaries of the briefs written by the lawyers, and references to secondary sources.

---

10. No. 96-2130 (10th Cir. Dec. 3, 1997) (unpublished decision).

| ILLUSTRATION 9-13 | Boolean Citation List, from Search in Tenth Circuit Website (electronic source) |

Skip to content ⛶ | Search | Case | Docket | Date: Filed / Added | Another Search: Simple / Advanced |

10th Circuit Court of Appeals
Search Opinions

Start new search   Search these results   Search entire Web   *Tip: You can restrict your*
                                                                    search to the title of a document.

Search the results of: "employee handbook" | "new mexico"

[   ]   *Example: title:"New Year's*

[search]   Help Advanced   [Powered by]   *Resolutions"*

Results for: "employee handbook" | "new mexico"   **Document count:** "employee handbook" (25)
                                                        "new mexico" (1629)

---

5 results found, sorted by relevance   score using date   hide summaries   1-5

02-3139 -- Ormsby v. C.O.F. Training Services -- 03/17/2003   47%
... 1063 (10th Cir. 1999) (applying **New Mexico** law to conclude that ... Plaintiff argues   ▊▊▊▊▊▊▊▊
that defendant's **employee handbook** precluded the formation of ...   18 Mar 03
http://www.kscourts.org/ca10/cases/2003/03/02-3139.htm - 8.9KB   Find Similar

---

96-2130 -- Baucom v. Amtech Systems Corp. -- 12/03/1997   45%
... District of **New Mexico** ... In June 1988, Amtech hired Baucom as a manufacturing   ▊▊▊▊▊▊▊▊
manager for its **New Mexico** manufacturing facility. (Appellant's App. at 198-202).   12 Mar 03
Baucom's evaluations from 1989 to 1992 ...   Find Similar
http://www.kscourts.org/ca10/cases/1997/12/96-2130.htm - 28.0KB

99-1095 -- Kerstien v. McGraw-Hill Co. Inc. -- 04/04/2001   30%
... that his discharge constituted a breach of contract based on language in the **employee**   ▊▊▊▊▊▊▊▊
handbook; that the discharge was wrongful based on the doctrine of promissory   12 Mar 03
estoppel ... novo, using the same standard as did the district court. See Scull v. **New**   Find Similar
Mexico , 236 F.3d 588, 595 (10th Cir. 2000). Summary judgment is appropriate ...
http://www.kscourts.org/ca10/cases/2001/04/99-1095.htm - 24.5KB

96-3021 -- Sprague v. Thorn Americas Inc. -- 11/24/1997   25%
... as a secretary in September 1989. (2) I Aplt. App. at 58 (statement of uncontroverted   ▊▊▊▊▊▊▊▊
facts). While attending orientation Sprague was given an **employee handbook**, which she   12 Mar 03
signed on September 7, 1989. By signing the handbook, Sprague acknowledged that her   Find Similar
employment with Thorn was an "at will ...
http://www.kscourts.org/ca10/cases/1997/11/96-3021.htm - 64.2KB

96-3021a -- Sprague v. Thorn Americas Inc. -- 11/24/1997   25%
... as a secretary in September 1989. (2) I Aplt. App. at 58 (statement of uncontroverted   ▊▊▊▊▊▊▊▊

| ILLUSTRATION 9-14 | Judicial Case, from Tenth Circuit Website (electronic source) |

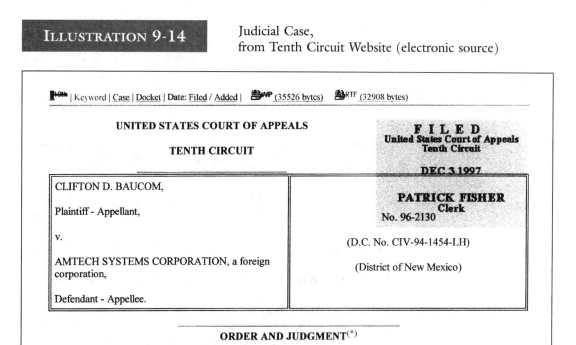

**| Keyword | Case | Docket | Date: Filed / Added | WP (35526 bytes) RTF (32908 bytes)

UNITED STATES COURT OF APPEALS

TENTH CIRCUIT

F I L E D
United States Court of Appeals
Tenth Circuit

DEC 3 1997

PATRICK FISHER
Clerk

CLIFTON D. BAUCOM, Plaintiff - Appellant, v. AMTECH SYSTEMS CORPORATION, a foreign corporation, Defendant - Appellee.	No. 96-2130 (D.C. No. CIV-94-1454-LH) (District of New Mexico)

ORDER AND JUDGMENT[*]

Before **BRISCOE, MCWILLIAMS** and **LUCERO**, Circuit Judges.

Appellant, Clifton Baucom, brought suit against his previous employer, Amtech Systems Corporation ("Amtech"), alleging discrimination in violation of the Age Discrimination in Employment Act ("ADEA"), 29 U.S.C. §§ 621-634, and pendent state law claims of breach of contract, breach of the covenant of good faith and fair dealing, promissory estoppel, and negligent misrepresentation. The district court granted summary judgment in favor of Amtech as to all claims. Baucom now appeals. We exercise jurisdiction under 28 U.S.C. § 1291 and affirm.

We review the district court's ruling on Amtech's summary judgment motion de novo. Cone v. Longmont Hosp. Ass'n, 14 F.3d 526, 527-28 (10th Cir. 1994). We review the record in the light most favorable to Baucom, the party opposing summary judgment. Bolton v. Scrivner, Inc., 36 F.3d 939, 941 (10th Cir. 1994). Summary judgment should be granted "if the pleadings, depositions, answers to interrogatories, and admissions on file, together with the affidavits, if any, show that there is no genuine issue as to any material fact and that the moving party is entitled to a judgment as a matter of law." Fed. R. Civ. P. 56(c).

I

Paper Sources of Very New Cases.   At both the national and state levels, legal newspapers and newsletters provide copies of very recent cases, typically within a week of issuance by the court. For example, *The United States Law Week* publishes decisions of the United States Supreme Court, as well as information on cases pending before the Court and significant cases from other courts, on a weekly basis. Your state may have a similar source.

E.   HOW DO YOU CITE CASES?

Case law citation is in a state of flux. Traditionally, citation format focused on paper resources. As computer-based sources become more prevalent, citation to cases has begun to evolve. Furthermore, some courts have promulgated their own citation rules, in part in response to technological change, in part as a reflection of the preferences of the judges.

Under any citation rule you may be bound by, you will provide the name of the case; a means of locating it; the court and date of decision; and the case's subsequent history and significant adverse treatment, if any. As to each of these items, you will find rather particular rules in both *The Bluebook* and *ALWD Citation Manual,* for example, how to abbreviate party names,[11] how to abbreviate court names, how specifically to state the date of decision, how to order this information. See *Bluebook* Rule 10 and *ALWD* Rule 12.

The major open issue is how to provide information about how to locate a case. For any particular case, one could provide citations to an official reporter, one or more unofficial reporters, various commercial databases, and one or more public websites. Some argue that a better solution is source-neutral citation; knowing a case name, decision number, court, and date should permit a reader to locate a case in various media. This approach is called "medium-neutral citation" or "public-domain citation."

Bluebook Rule 10.3 calls first for citation to the first reporter listed for the jurisdiction in Table 1; in general, this amounts to citing to the West reporter. If the document is written to a state court, you must cite to the court's preferred reporters, which may entail a parallel citation to the official reporter. In other documents, if there is an official public-domain citation, that information must be provided along with the citation to the West reporter; otherwise the citation to the West reporter suffices. If the decision is not available in the sources listed thus far, citation is to another unofficial reporter, a widely used database, a looseleaf service, the slip opinion, an Internet site, or a newspaper, stated in order of preference.

---

11. If the citation appears in a text sentence, the case name is abbreviated less than when the citation appears in its own sentence or clause. The examples here are citations in a citation, not text, sentence.

ALWD Rule 12.4 calls first for compliance with any applicable court rule. Absent a contrary rule, citation is to the West reporter. A parallel citation is required only when a court rule or custom so provide or the parallel citation will be particularly helpful. If the decision is not available in the sources listed this far, citation is to another paper reporter, an online service, a looseleaf service, or any other source containing the case.

If there were no applicable court rule, the *Lukoski* case would be cited as follows:

☐   *Bluebook: Lukoski v. Sandia Indian Mgmt. Co.*, 748 P.2d 507 (N.M. 1988).
☐   *ALWD: Lukoski v. Sandia Indian Mgt. Co.*, 748 P.2d 507 (N.M. 1988).

If a parallel citation to the official state reporter were required, the cite (using the *Bluebook* abbreviation for the title) would be:

☐   *Lukoski v. Sandia Indian Mgmt. Co.*, 106 N.M. 664, 748 P.2d 507 (1988).

A New Mexico Rule of Appellate Procedure calls for inclusion of a public-domain citation for cases decided in 1996 and later along with a citation to the regional reporter, the official reporter, or both. Were there a public domain citation for *Lukoski*, the citation (again using the *Bluebook* abbreviation for the title) would be:

☐   *Lukoski v. Sandia Indian Mgmt. Co.*, 1988-NM-123, 748 P.2d 507 (1988).

The standard citation to a federal case, illustrated with the *Ellis* case referred to in *Lukoski,* is:

☐   *Bluebook: Ellis v. El Paso Natural Gas,* 754 F.2d 884 (10th Cir. 1985).
☐   *ALWD: Ellis v. El Paso Nat. Gas,* 754 F.2d 884 (10th Cir. 1985).

As an example of a citation to an electronic source, consider the Baucom case discovered through the Tenth Circuit website and also published in Westlaw:

☐   *Bluebook: Baucom v. Amtech Sys. Corp.*, No. 96-2130, 1997 WL 748668 (10th Cir. Dec. 3, 1997).
☐   *ALWD: Baucom v. Amtech Sys. Corp.*, 1997 WL 748668 (10th Cir. Dec. 3, 1997).

As appropriate, we recommend a parenthetical indicating that the case is unpublished so that the reader is not misled about its status.

Note that you may have obtained a case from a different source than you are required to cite. Much of the time, you will find the information you need to properly cite the case listed at the beginning of the case. See the information at the beginning of the LexisNexis version of *Lukoski*, Illustration 9-10 (at page 160). Another way to find information about the various sources of a case is to use a case citator, as discussed in Chapter 10.

Furthermore, in most situations you will provide a reference to the specific page on which the material you are relying on appears. This could cause practical difficulties if, for example, you have obtained a case from a database and the case is to be cited to a regional reporter. Again, you may be able to find the information you need, especially if you have obtained the case from a commercial database. For example, the LexisNexis version of *Lukoski*, Illustration 9-10 (at page 161), includes brackets with pagination information from both the official New Mexico reporter and the Pacific Reporter.

F. SUMMARY AND LAST WORDS

Because cases are primary authority, your research will be correct, comprehensive, and credible only if you excel in researching cases. And to research cost-effectively, you must use the various options thoughtfully and strategically.

First, seek cases that are mandatory precedent, good law, published decisions, strong parallels to your client's situation, and well-reasoned discussions of your research topic. Second, in addition to following up on leads from secondary authorities, use a combination of the following four practices:

- ☐ Use case digests to find pertinent cases in paper reporters.
- ☐ Use the various Westlaw tools—natural-language, terms-and-connectors, and key-number searches as well as KeySearch—to find pertinent cases.
- ☐ Use the various LexisNexis tools—natural-language and terms-and-connectors searches as well as Search Advisor—to find pertinent cases.
- ☐ When appropriate, visit public websites for recent cases.

For instance, you may use paper digests and reporters to start, then shift to Westlaw to update your research and find cases with similar facts to your client's situation. You may move from a natural-language search on LexisNexis into Search Advisor or vice versa.

However your research in case law begins, it is not complete until you cite your cases, as discussed in Chapter 10.

CASE CITATORS

A. What Is a Case Citator, and Why Would You Use It?
B. How Do You Use Case Citators?
C. What Else?

A. WHAT IS A CASE CITATOR, AND WHY WOULD YOU USE IT?

A citator is a research tool that is not itself authority of any kind but rather points you to potentially significant authorities. More precisely, it lists authorities that refer to an authority you already have found. Lawyers use the following terms when using citators:

- ☐ The authority you are currently reading is the *cited authority*. You will seek the report for this authority.
- ☐ The authorities that refer to the cited authority are the *citing authorities*. They will be listed in the report for the cited authority.
- ☐ For some years, Shepard's Citators, a paper source, were the most prominent citators. Many lawyers still call research in citators "Shepardizing." We will use the term "citating."

For this chapter, for ease of understanding, we will call the case you already have read and plan to rely on the "case-in-hand."

As you will see, case citators are very sophisticated, reflecting the critical role they play in case law research. You will use a case citator for five reasons, stated in order of importance:

A.   To discern the history of the case-in-hand.   Recall from Chapter 9 that you should rely on a case only if it is good law. You cannot tell whether this is so from reading the case-in-hand itself, because, in general, a case is not removed from case law sources or altered when its validity is undermined by a later decision. Hence you need a tool that alerts you to subsequent decisions affecting the validity of the case-in-hand. These may be later decisions in the same litigation, that is, subsequent history, such as reversal by a higher court. In addition, you may learn about an earlier decision in the litigation that gave rise to the case-in-hand, that is, its prior history. (For further discussion, see Part B3 of Chapter 9.)

B.   To learn of the case-in-hand's treatment in other cases from your jurisdiction.   Whether a case is good law depends not only on its subsequent history but also on its treatment, that is, later decisions in different cases involving different parties but the same topic, in your jurisdiction. Most important are later cases that treat the case-in-hand adversely, in particular by overruling the case-in-hand. Later cases that treat the case-in-hand favorably are also important because they strengthen the credibility of the case-in-hand and are more recent cases on the topic. (For further discussion, again see Part B3 of Chapter 9.)

As you examine the subsequent history and treatment of the case-in-hand, take care to identify the various points made in the case-in-hand and focus on the points that are pertinent to your client's situation. A case that has been reversed or overruled on one point, for example, may still be good law on a different point. For example, *Lukoski* makes two points: a procedural point about waiver of specific findings of fact and a contract law point about the employee handbook. Researching the Canoga case, we focused on the contract point. Had *Lukoski* been overruled on the procedural point, it most likely would have continued to be good law on the contract point. Of course, you must read the cases constituting the case-in-hand's subsequent history and adverse treatment to discern whether the case-in-hand is still good law on the point pertinent to your client's situation.

C.   To expand your research by finding persuasive cases.   Case citators list not only cases from your jurisdiction that refer to the case-in-hand but also cases from sister jurisdictions. Persuasive cases may be very helpful in some situations, e.g., when the legal rule is fairly new and you are seeking a case with more factual similarity to your client's situation than you can find within your jurisdiction.

D.   To expand your research by finding secondary authorities.   Case citators also list some secondary authorities, such as legal periodical articles and A.L.R. annotations, that refer to the case-in-hand. You may find some authorities that are new to you and merit some attention.

E. To learn of the case-in-hand's parallel citation(s). The case-in-hand may be published in several or more sources. Citation rules may require you to provide a citation to a source other than the one you are using. If the source you are using does not provide the citation information for the other source, you can find it in the citator report. (For further discussion, see Part F of Chapter 9.)

B. HOW DO YOU USE CASE CITATORS?

Citing your cases should be an integral part of your research in cases. Once you decide that you may well rely on a case-in-hand if it is good law, you should cite it. Be sure to check at the end of the research process that you have cited all the cases you plan to rely on. In addition, when you come back to your research at a later time, you should update your research by again citing the major cases.

As noted above, for many years, lawyers used paper publications called "Shepard's Citations." Shepard's is now available in LexisNexis, and it is much preferable to the paper version. Westlaw, of course, also has a case citator, KeyCite. You are very likely to use one of these two services; indeed citing is the research function best suited to electronic media.

On both LexisNexis and Westlaw, you can begin the citing function two ways: by typing in the case's citation in the Shepard's or KeyCite box or by clicking into Shepard's or KeyCite when you are reading the case-in-hand online.

The challenging aspect of citing a case is deciphering the report you thus obtain. In the following pages, we have deciphered the Shepard's and KeyCite reports for the *Lukoski* case, found in Illustration 9-1 (at page 127–30). The letters in the margins refer to the five tasks set forth above; the explanation parallels the order in which the information appears in the report. Note that the explanation also covers common Shepard's or KeyCite features that are not present in the *Lukoski* reports.

We used reports printed out in the fall of 2003. The format and details of both Shepard's and KeyCite reports change over time, but the information to decipher stays much the same.

ILLUSTRATION 10-1   Shepard's Report for a Case
                              (electronic source)

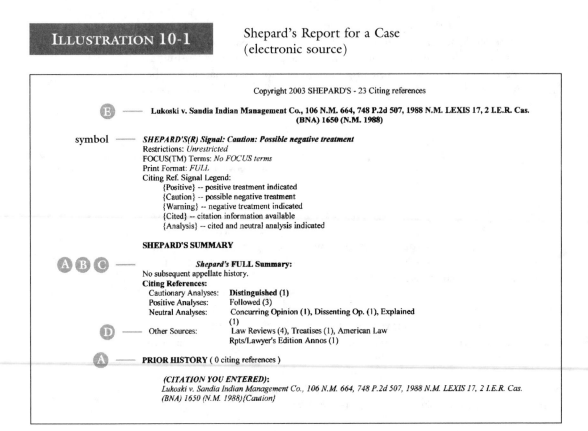

Copyright 2003 SHEPARD'S - 23 Citing references

Ⓔ ———— Lukoski v. Sandia Indian Management Co., 106 N.M. 664, 748 P.2d 507, 1988 N.M. LEXIS 17, 2 I.E.R. Cas.
(BNA) 1650 (N.M. 1988)

symbol ———— *SHEPARD'S(R) Signal: Caution: Possible negative treatment*
Restrictions: *Unrestricted*
FOCUS(TM) Terms: *No FOCUS terms*
Print Format: *FULL*
Citing Ref. Signal Legend:
    {Positive} -- positive treatment indicated
    {Caution} -- possible negative treatment
    {Warning} -- negative treatment indicated
    {Cited} -- citation information available
    {Analysis} -- cited and neutral analysis indicated

SHEPARD'S SUMMARY

Ⓐ Ⓑ Ⓒ ————   *Shepard's* **FULL Summary:**
No subsequent appellate history.
Citing References:
Cautionary Analyses: **Distinguished (1)**
Positive Analyses: Followed (3)
Neutral Analyses: Concurring Opinion (1), Dissenting Op. (1), Explained
                        (1)
Ⓓ ———— Other Sources: Law Reviews (4), Treatises (1), American Law
                        Rpts/Lawyer's Edition Annos (1)

Ⓐ ———— **PRIOR HISTORY** (0 citing references)

(CITATION YOU ENTERED):
Lukoski v. Sandia Indian Management Co., 106 N.M. 664, 748 P.2d 507, 1988 N.M. LEXIS 17, 2 I.E.R. Cas.
(BNA) 1650 (N.M. 1988){Caution}

The Shepard's report begins with the case name and parallel citations (E). *Lukoski* is published in volume 106 of the *New Mexico Reports* starting at page 664 and in volume 748 of the *Pacific Reporter* second series, starting at page 507. It also appears in LexisNexis in a specialized reporter, *Individual Employment Rights Cases.*

Shepard's synopsizes the status of the case-in-hand through five symbols:

☐ Red stop sign: The case has strong negative history or treatment that may be significant, e.g., it has been reversed or overruled.

☐ Yellow triangle: The case has some negative history or treatment that may be significant, e.g., it has been limited or criticized.

☐ Green diamond: The case has positive history or treatment, e.g., it has been affirmed or followed.

☐ Blue circle with the letter A: There is treatment that is neither positive nor negative, e.g., the case has been explained. The A means that the citing case has been analyzed by the Shepard's staff.

☐ Blue circle with the letter I: There is information about citing sources but without analysis, e.g., the citing sources are law reviews.

In Illustration 10-1, the phrase "Caution: Possible negative treatment" appears; this is the equivalent of a yellow triangle. You would see the yellow triangle on the Shepard's screen as well as beside the case itself in a LexisNexis cases database.

The Shepard's summary alerts you to whether the case-in-hand has subsequent or prior history. *Lukoski* has neither, which is not surprising: state trial court decisions are rarely published, the case did not go to the New Mexico Court of Appeals, and the case-in-hand is from the state's highest court.

The Shepard's summary also synopsizes the more detailed report below by, for example, indicating how many citing cases involve cautionary analyses and how many involve positive analyses. Shepard's uses the following case analysis codes, listed from most positive to most negative:

☐ affirmed
☐ followed
☐ explained
☐ distinguished
☐ questioned
☐ criticized
☐ limited
☐ modified
☐ overruled
☐ reversed

The *Lukoski* summary indicates that the case has been referred to in both cases and secondary authorities and flags that one citing case distinguishes *Lukoski*—hence the caution.

ILLUSTRATION 10-1   *(continued)*

CITING DECISIONS (17 citing decisions)

B

NEW MEXICO SUPREME COURT

1. **Cited by:**
   Cockrell v. Bd. of Regents, 2002 NMSC 9, 132 N.M. 156, 45 P.3d 876, 2002 N.M. LEXIS 158, 41 N.M. B. Bull.
   No. 20 19, 41 N.M. B. Bull. 20, 146 Lab. Cas. (CCH) P34521, 7 Wage & Hour Cas. 2d (BNA) 1444
   (2002)*{Positive}*
   132 N.M. 156 p.167, Headnote: P.2d - 2
   45 P.3d 876 p.887, Headnote: P.2d - 2

2. **Followed by:**
   Garcia v. Middle Rio Grande Conservancy Dist., 1996 NMSC 29, 121 N.M. 728, 918 P.2d 7, 1996 N.M. LEXIS
   202, 11 I.E.R. Cas. (BNA) 1328 (N.M. 1996)*{Positive}*
   1996 NMSC 29
   121 N.M. 728 p.732
   918 P.2d 7 p.11

3. **Distinguished by:**
   Hartbarger v. Frank Paxton Co., 115 N.M. 665, 857 P.2d 776, 1993 N.M. LEXIS 187, 32 N.M. B. Bull. 635, 8
   I.E.R. Cas. (BNA) 1114, 127 Lab. Cas. (CCH) P57664 (1993)*{Caution}*
   Distinguished by:
   115 N.M. 665 p.673
   857 P.2d 776 p.784
   Cited by:
   115 N.M. 665 p.669
   857 P.2d 776 p.780

4. **Cited by:**
   Chavez v. Manville Prods. Corp., 108 N.M. 643, 777 P.2d 371, 1989 N.M. LEXIS 241, 4 I.E.R. Cas. (BNA) 833,
   122 Lab. Cas. (CCH) P56927 (N.M. 1989)*{Caution}*
   108 N.M. 643 p.646
   777 P.2d 371 p.374, Headnote: P.2d - 2

5. **Cited by:**
   Paca v. K-Mart Corp., 108 N.M. 479, 775 P.2d 245, 1989 N.M. LEXIS 189, 4 I.E.R. Cas. (BNA) 727 (N.M.
   1989)*{Analysis}*
   108 N.M. 479 p.481
   775 P.2d 245 p.247, Headnote: P.2d - 2

6. **Followed by:**
   Newberry v. Allied Stores, 108 N.M. 424, 773 P.2d 1231, 1989 N.M. LEXIS 139, 4 I.E.R. Cas. (BNA) 562 (N.M.
   1989)*{Positive}*
   108 N.M. 424 p.426
   773 P.2d 1231 p.1233, Headnote: P.2d - 2

7. **Cited by:**
   Kestenbaum v. Pennzoil Co., 108 N.M. 20, 766 P.2d 280, 1988 N.M. LEXIS 326, 4 I.E.R. Cas. (BNA) 67 (N.M.
   1988)*{Caution}*
   108 N.M. 20 p.24
   766 P.2d 280 p.284, Headnote: P.2d - 2

NEW MEXICO COURT OF APPEALS

8. **Cited in Concurring Opinion at:**
   Mealand v. Eastern. N.M. Med. Ctr., 2001 NMCA 89, 131 N.M. 65, 33 P.3d 285, 2001 N.M. App. LEXIS 79, 40
   N.M. B. Bull. No. 48 33, 40 N.M. B. Bull. 48 (2001)*{Analysis}*
   Cited in Concurring Opinion at:
   2001 NMCA 89
   131 N.M. 65 p.76
   33 P.3d 285 p.296
   Cited by:
   131 N.M. 65 p.69
   33 P.3d 285 p.289

In the detailed report, Shepard's presents the citing cases first, ordered by their weightiness, that is, by jurisdiction, court, and reverse chronology. For example, New Mexico Supreme Court cases come first in the *Lukoski* report, then New Mexico Court of Appeals cases (B). For each citing case, Shepard's:

- ☐ indicates in what way the citing case refers to the case-at-hand;
- ☐ provides the name and citation of the citing case;
- ☐ indicates the page of the citing case where the reference to the case-at-hand appears; and
- ☐ for some citing cases, notes for what point the citing case refers to the case-at-hand, by reference to the case-in-hand's headnotes.

For example, *Cockrell* (the first citing case), at page 887 of volume 45 of the *Pacific Reporter* third series, refers to *Lukoski* in a positive manner on the topic of *Lukoski*'s headnote 2; as shown in Illustration 9-1 (at page 128), headnote 2 pertains to the enforcement of the employee handbook's provisions on job security. *Lukoski* received a caution because the *Hartbarger* case distinguishes it, although Shepard's does not indicate the point discussed in *Hartbarger*.

If, as is often the case, you see more citing cases than it is practical to review, you should sift the cases by considering the following factors:

- ☐ the jurisdiction and level of the court;
- ☐ the recency of the case;
- ☐ the headnotes from the case-in-hand involved in the citing case's discussion; and
- ☐ the nature of the discussion, as reflected in the Shepard's case analysis codes.

Thus we would focus on the first three cases in the *Lukoski* report: they are all decisions of the New Mexico Supreme Court within the last decade (as of our research in mid-2003), *Cockrell* discusses the point in *Lukoski*'s headnote 2, and *Hartbarger* distinguishes *Lukoski*. Next we would read, in reverse chronological order, the other cases addressing the point in headnote 2.

In addition to sifting the cases by the information you find on a complete report, you can specify which citing cases you wish to see by jurisdiction, date, headnote, and type of treatment. You also can run a key-word search within the set of citing cases through the focus function.

Once you decide on a citing case to read, you can move directly to the case in LexisNexis through the link in the Shepard's report.

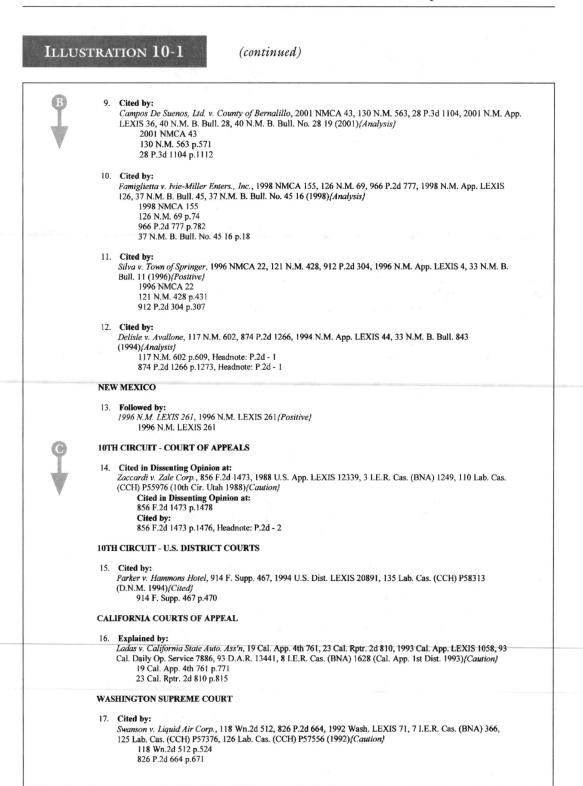

ILLUSTRATION 10-1   *(continued)*

B

9. **Cited by:**
    Campos De Suenos, Ltd. v. County of Bernalillo, 2001 NMCA 43, 130 N.M. 563, 28 P.3d 1104, 2001 N.M. App.
    LEXIS 36, 40 N.M. B. Bull. 28, 40 N.M. B. Bull. No. 28 19 (2001)*{Analysis}*
        2001 NMCA 43
        130 N.M. 563 p.571
        28 P.3d 1104 p.1112

10. **Cited by:**
    Famiglietta v. Ivie-Miller Enters., Inc., 1998 NMCA 155, 126 N.M. 69, 966 P.2d 777, 1998 N.M. App. LEXIS
    126, 37 N.M. B. Bull. 45, 37 N.M. B. Bull. No. 45 16 (1998)*{Analysis}*
        1998 NMCA 155
        126 N.M. 69 p.74
        966 P.2d 777 p.782
        37 N.M. B. Bull. No. 45 16 p.18

11. **Cited by:**
    Silva v. Town of Springer, 1996 NMCA 22, 121 N.M. 428, 912 P.2d 304, 1996 N.M. App. LEXIS 4, 33 N.M. B.
    Bull. 11 (1996)*{Positive}*
        1996 NMCA 22
        121 N.M. 428 p.431
        912 P.2d 304 p.307

12. **Cited by:**
    Delisle v. Avallone, 117 N.M. 602, 874 P.2d 1266, 1994 N.M. App. LEXIS 44, 33 N.M. B. Bull. 843
    (1994)*{Analysis}*
        117 N.M. 602 p.609, Headnote: P.2d - 1
        874 P.2d 1266 p.1273, Headnote: P.2d - 1

NEW MEXICO

13. **Followed by:**
    1996 N.M. LEXIS 261, 1996 N.M. LEXIS 261*{Positive}*
        1996 N.M. LEXIS 261

C

10TH CIRCUIT - COURT OF APPEALS

14. **Cited in Dissenting Opinion at:**
    Zaccardi v. Zale Corp., 856 F.2d 1473, 1988 U.S. App. LEXIS 12339, 3 I.E.R. Cas. (BNA) 1249, 110 Lab. Cas.
    (CCH) P55976 (10th Cir. Utah 1988)*{Caution}*
        Cited in Dissenting Opinion at:
        856 F.2d 1473 p.1478
        Cited by:
        856 F.2d 1473 p.1476, Headnote: P.2d - 2

10TH CIRCUIT - U.S. DISTRICT COURTS

15. **Cited by:**
    Parker v. Hammons Hotel, 914 F. Supp. 467, 1994 U.S. Dist. LEXIS 20891, 135 Lab. Cas. (CCH) P58313
    (D.N.M. 1994)*{Cited}*
        914 F. Supp. 467 p.470

CALIFORNIA COURTS OF APPEAL

16. **Explained by:**
    Ladas v. California State Auto. Ass'n, 19 Cal. App. 4th 761, 23 Cal. Rptr. 2d 810, 1993 Cal. App. LEXIS 1058, 93
    Cal. Daily Op. Service 7886, 93 D.A.R. 13441, 8 I.E.R. Cas. (BNA) 1628 (Cal. App. 1st Dist. 1993)*{Caution}*
        19 Cal. App. 4th 761 p.771
        23 Cal. Rptr. 2d 810 p.815

WASHINGTON SUPREME COURT

17. **Cited by:**
    Swanson v. Liquid Air Corp., 118 Wn.2d 512, 826 P.2d 664, 1992 Wash. LEXIS 71, 7 I.E.R. Cas. (BNA) 366,
    125 Lab. Cas. (CCH) P57376, 126 Lab. Cas. (CCH) P57556 (1992)*{Caution}*
        118 Wn.2d 512 p.524
        826 P.2d 664 p.671

ILLUSTRATION 10-1   *(continued)*

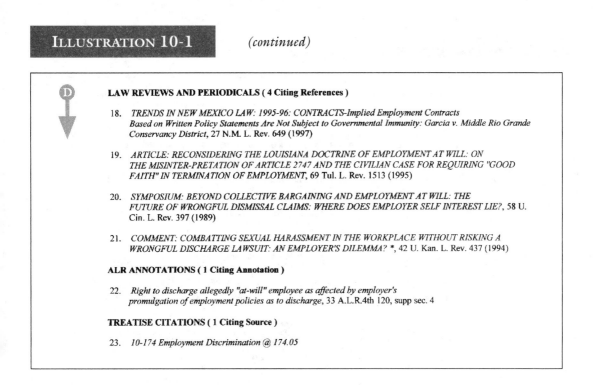

LAW REVIEWS AND PERIODICALS (4 Citing References)

18.   *TRENDS IN NEW MEXICO LAW: 1995-96: CONTRACTS-Implied Employment Contracts
Based on Written Policy Statements Are Not Subject to Governmental Immunity: Garcia v. Middle Rio Grande
Conservancy District,* 27 N.M. L. Rev. 649 (1997)

19.   *ARTICLE: RECONSIDERING THE LOUISIANA DOCTRINE OF EMPLOYMENT AT WILL: ON
THE MISINTER-PRETATION OF ARTICLE 2747 AND THE CIVILIAN CASE FOR REQUIRING "GOOD
FAITH" IN TERMINATION OF EMPLOYMENT,* 69 Tul. L. Rev. 1513 (1995)

20.   *SYMPOSIUM: BEYOND COLLECTIVE BARGAINING AND EMPLOYMENT AT WILL: THE
FUTURE OF WRONGFUL DISMISSAL CLAIMS: WHERE DOES EMPLOYER SELF INTEREST LIE?,* 58 U.
Cin. L. Rev. 397 (1989)

21.   *COMMENT: COMBATTING SEXUAL HARASSMENT IN THE WORKPLACE WITHOUT RISKING A
WRONGFUL DISCHARGE LAWSUIT: AN EMPLOYER'S DILEMMA?* *, 42 U. Kan. L. Rev. 437 (1994)

ALR ANNOTATIONS (1 Citing Annotation)

22.   *Right to discharge allegedly "at-will" employee as affected by employer's
promulgation of employment policies as to discharge,* 33 A.L.R.4th 120, supp sec. 4

TREATISE CITATIONS (1 Citing Source)

23.   *10-174 Employment Discrimination @ 174.05*

Shepard's also lists citing cases from other jurisdictions (C), again ordered
by weightiness. For example, in the *Lukoski* report, the Tenth Circuit case is
the first listed after the New Mexico state court cases, then the case from the
federal district court for New Mexico, then cases from other state courts.
These cases are persuasive, not mandatory.

Finally, Shepard's also directs you to secondary authorities that refer to
the case-in-hand (D). These secondary authorities are not as important as
cases, but you should check for pertinent secondary authorities you have not
already seen. For example, four periodical articles, an A.L.R. annotation, and
a treatise refer to *Lukoski.*

Note that you can restrict a Shepard's report by type of citing document,
e.g., cases only (not secondary authorities).

ILLUSTRATION 10-2   KeyCite Report for a Case
                               (electronic source)

```
    KeyCite                                                     Page    1
                                                  Date of Printing: JUL 15,2003

                                    KEYCITE

 (E) ----  CITATION: Lukoski v. Sandia Indian Management Co., 106 N.M. 664, 748 P.2d 507,
                     2 IER Cases 1650 (N.M., Jan 07, 1988) (NO. 16,462)

                                    History
(A)(B) --- =>    1 Lukoski v. Sandia Indian Management Co., 106 N.M. 664, 748 P.2d 507,
                     2 IER Cases 1650  (N.M. Jan 07, 1988) (NO. 16,462)

                               Citing References
                             Positive Cases (U.S.A.)
                              ****  Examined
(B)(C) --- C     2 Zaccardi v. Zale Corp., 856 F.2d 1473, 1476+ (10th Cir.(Utah) 1988)
                     ""  HN: 1,2 (P.2d)

                              ***  Discussed
         Yel     3 Hartbarger v. Frank Paxton Co., 857 P.2d 776, 780+ (N.M. 1993)  ""
                     HN: 2 (P.2d)
         C       4 Newberry v. Allied Stores, Inc., 773 P.2d 1231, 1233+ (N.M. 1989)  ""
                     HN: 2 (P.2d)
         Yel     5 Ladas v. California State Auto. Assn., 23 Cal.Rptr.2d 810, 816+
                     (Cal.App. 1 Dist. 1993)  ""  HN: 2 (P.2d)

                              **  Cited
         H       6 Cockrell v. Board of Regents of New Mexico State University,
                     45 P.3d 876, 887+ (N.M. 2002)  ""  HN: 2 (P.2d)
         Yel     7 Garcia v. Middle Rio Grande Conservancy Dist., 918 P.2d 7, 11+
                     (N.M. 1996)  ""  HN: 2 (P.2d)
         Yel     8 Chavez v. Manville Products Corp., 777 P.2d 371, 374+ (N.M. 1989)
                     HN: 2 (P.2d)
         C       9 Paca v. K-Mart Corp., 775 P.2d 245, 247 (N.M. 1989)  HN: 2 (P.2d)
         H      10 Kestenbaum v. Pennzoil Co., 766 P.2d 280, 284 (N.M. 1988)
                     HN: 2 (P.2d)
         H      11 Mealand v. Eastern New Mexico Medical Center, 33 P.3d 285, 289+
                     (N.M.App. 2001)  ""  HN: 2 (P.2d)
         H      12 Campos de Suenos, Ltd. v. County of Bernalillo, 28 P.3d 1104, 1112
                     (N.M.App. 2001)  HN: 2 (P.2d)
         H      13 Famiglietta v. Ivie-Miller Enterprises, Inc., 966 P.2d 777, 782
                     (N.M.App. 1998)  HN: 1 (P.2d)
         H      14 Silva v. Town of Springer, 912 P.2d 304, 307 (N.M.App. 1996)
                     HN: 2 (P.2d)
         H      15 DeLisle v. Avallone, 874 P.2d 1266, 1273 (N.M.App. 1994)  HN: 1 (P.2d)
                16 Bayliss v. Contel Federal Systems, Inc., 930 F.2d 32, 32+
                     (10th Cir.(N.M.) 1991) (Table, text in WESTLAW)  ""  HN: 2 (P.2d)
         C      17 Parker v. John Q. Hammons Hotels, Inc., 914 F.Supp. 467, 470
                     (D.N.M. 1994)  HN: 2 (P.2d)

                              *  Mentioned
         Yel    18 Swanson v. Liquid Air Corp., 826 P.2d 664, 671 (Wash. 1992)
                     HN: 2 (P.2d)

                                                              Westlaw.
```

The KeyCite report begins with the case name and parallel citations (E). *Lukoski* is published in volume 106 of the *New Mexico Reports* starting at page 664, as well as in the *Pacific Reporter* second series and a specialized reporter, *Individual Employment Rights Cases.*

Next, the KeyCite report states the history of the case-in-hand (A and B). KeyCite traces three types of history:

- ☐ the direct history of the case-in-hand, including prior and subsequent history;
- ☐ negative indirect history, that is, adverse treatment in later cases; and
- ☐ related references, that is, decisions arising from the litigation that gave rise to the case-in-hand but involve different topics or parties.

Lukoski has neither type of direct history, nor does it have negative indirect history or related references.

KeyCite synopsizes the status of the case-in-hand through four symbols:

- ☐ Red flag: The case is no longer good law for at least one of its points.
- ☐ Yellow flag: The case has some negative indirect history (adverse treatment) but has not been reversed or overruled.
- ☐ Blue H: The case has history that gives rise to neither a red nor a yellow flag.
- ☐ Green C: The case has citing references but no direct or indirect negative history.

There is no flag at the outset of the *Lukoski* report; rather KeyCite used a green C for *Lukoski*. You would see the C on the KeyCite screen as well as beside the case itself in a Westlaw cases database.

The bulk of most KeyCite reports is the list of citing cases, beginning with positive references (B and C). The cases are arrayed from four stars to one star, which usually mean:

   ****   examined, i.e., an extended discussion of the case-in-hand that runs a page or more of text in the citing case;

    ***   discussed, i.e., more than a paragraph but less than a page;

     **   cited, i.e., a paragraph or less; and

      *   mentioned, i.e., only a brief reference to the case-in-hand.

Within a category, the weightiest cases appear first, that is, mandatory precedents before persuasive precedents, higher courts before lower courts, and newer cases before older cases. For each citing case, KeyCite provides as applicable:

- ☐ its name and citation, including the page(s) on which the cited case is discussed;
- ☐ quotation marks signifying that the citing case quotes the case-in-hand;
- ☐ references to the case-in-hand's West headnote(s) pertaining to the point(s) for which the citing case refers to the case-in-hand; and
- ☐ in the left margin, the citing case's—not the case-in-hand's—KeyCite symbol.

ILLUSTRATION 10-2   *(continued)*

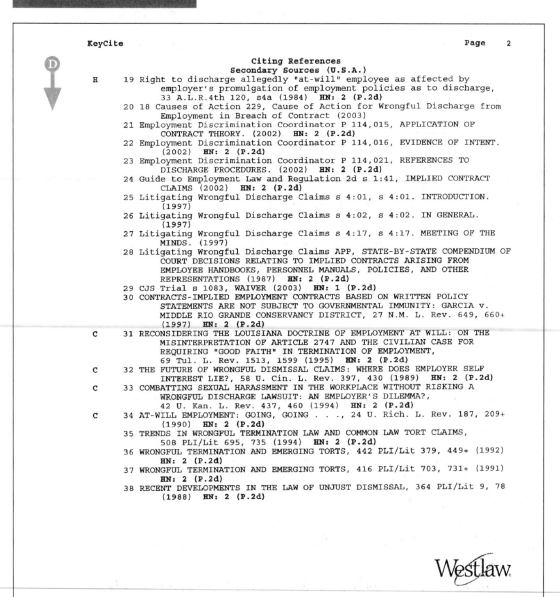

KeyCite   Page   2

                                      Citing References
                                   Secondary Sources (U.S.A.)

H   19 Right to discharge allegedly "at-will" employee as affected by
       employer's promulgation of employment policies as to discharge,
       33 A.L.R.4th 120, s4a (1984) **HN: 2 (P.2d)**
    20 18 Causes of Action 229, Cause of Action for Wrongful Discharge from
       Employment in Breach of Contract (2003)
    21 Employment Discrimination Coordinator P 114,015, APPLICATION OF
       CONTRACT THEORY. (2002) **HN: 2 (P.2d)**
    22 Employment Discrimination Coordinator P 114,016, EVIDENCE OF INTENT.
       (2002) **HN: 2 (P.2d)**
    23 Employment Discrimination Coordinator P 114,021, REFERENCES TO
       DISCHARGE PROCEDURES. (2002) **HN: 2 (P.2d)**
    24 Guide to Employment Law and Regulation 2d s 1:41, IMPLIED CONTRACT
       CLAIMS (2002) **HN: 2 (P.2d)**
    25 Litigating Wrongful Discharge Claims s 4:01, s 4:01. INTRODUCTION.
       (1997)
    26 Litigating Wrongful Discharge Claims s 4:02, s 4:02. IN GENERAL.
       (1997)
    27 Litigating Wrongful Discharge Claims s 4:17, s 4:17. MEETING OF THE
       MINDS. (1997)
    28 Litigating Wrongful Discharge Claims APP, STATE-BY-STATE COMPENDIUM OF
       COURT DECISIONS RELATING TO IMPLIED CONTRACTS ARISING FROM
       EMPLOYEE HANDBOOKS, PERSONNEL MANUALS, POLICIES, AND OTHER
       REPRESENTATIONS (1987) **HN: 2 (P.2d)**
    29 CJS Trial s 1083, WAIVER (2003) **HN: 1 (P.2d)**
    30 CONTRACTS-IMPLIED EMPLOYMENT CONTRACTS BASED ON WRITTEN POLICY
       STATEMENTS ARE NOT SUBJECT TO GOVERNMENTAL IMMUNITY: GARCIA v.
       MIDDLE RIO GRANDE CONSERVANCY DISTRICT, 27 N.M. L. Rev. 649, 660+
       (1997) **HN: 2 (P.2d)**
C   31 RECONSIDERING THE LOUISIANA DOCTRINE OF EMPLOYMENT AT WILL: ON THE
       MISINTERPRETATION OF ARTICLE 2747 AND THE CIVILIAN CASE FOR
       REQUIRING "GOOD FAITH" IN TERMINATION OF EMPLOYMENT,
       69 Tul. L. Rev. 1513, 1599 (1995) **HN: 2 (P.2d)**
C   32 THE FUTURE OF WRONGFUL DISMISSAL CLAIMS: WHERE DOES EMPLOYER SELF
       INTEREST LIE?, 58 U. Cin. L. Rev. 397, 430 (1989) **HN: 2 (P.2d)**
C   33 COMBATTING SEXUAL HARASSMENT IN THE WORKPLACE WITHOUT RISKING A
       WRONGFUL DISCHARGE LAWSUIT: AN EMPLOYER'S DILEMMA?,
       42 U. Kan. L. Rev. 437, 460 (1994) **HN: 2 (P.2d)**
C   34 AT-WILL EMPLOYMENT: GOING, GOING . . ., 24 U. Rich. L. Rev. 187, 209+
       (1990) **HN: 2 (P.2d)**
    35 TRENDS IN WRONGFUL TERMINATION LAW AND COMMON LAW TORT CLAIMS,
       508 PLI/Lit 695, 735 (1994) **HN: 2 (P.2d)**
    36 WRONGFUL TERMINATION AND EMERGING TORTS, 442 PLI/Lit 379, 449+ (1992)
       HN: 2 (P.2d)
    37 WRONGFUL TERMINATION AND EMERGING TORTS, 416 PLI/Lit 703, 731+ (1991)
       HN: 2 (P.2d)
    38 RECENT DEVELOPMENTS IN THE LAW OF UNJUST DISMISSAL, 364 PLI/Lit 9, 78
       (1988) **HN: 2 (P.2d)**

                                                                        Westlaw.

For example, *Hartbarger* (the first citing case receiving three stars), at page 780 of volume 857 of the *Pacific Reporter* second series, quotes *Lukoski* in a positive manner on the topic of *Lukoski*'s headnote 2, which pertains to the Canoga case.

If, as is often the case, you see more citing cases than it is practical to review, you should sift the cases by considering the following factors:

- ☐   the jurisdiction and the level of the court;
- ☐   the recency of the case;
- ☐   the headnotes from the case-in-hand involved in the citing case's discussion;
- ☐   the extent of the discussion, as reflected in the KeyCite stars; and
- ☐   the case's KeyCite symbol.

Thus we would focus on cases 3, 6, and 7 in the *Lukoski* report: they are all decisions of the New Mexico Supreme Court within the last decade, and all discuss or cite the point in *Lukoski*'s headnote 2. Then we would proceed to the other New Mexico cases, based on extent of discussion and date.

In addition to sifting the cases by the information you find on a complete report, you can specify which citing cases you wish to see by jurisdiction, date, headnote, and depth of treatment (number of stars). You also can run a key-word search within the set of citing cases through the locate function.

Once you decide on a citing case to read, you can move directly to the case in Westlaw through the link in the KeyCite report.

Finally, KeyCite also directs you to secondary authorities that refer to the case-in-hand (D). These authorities are not as important as cases, but you should check for pertinent secondary authorities you have not already seen. For example, the KeyCite report for *Lukoski* directs you to an A.L.R. annotation, several treatises, C.J.S., and five periodical articles, among others.

Note that you can restrict a KeyCite report by type of citing document, e.g., you can ask for only citing cases.

The limitations of Shepard's and KeyCite.   It is not uncommon to find somewhat different information for the same case through Shepard's and KeyCite, as you can see by comparing the *Lukoski* reports in Illustration 10-1 (at pages 174, 176, 178–179) and Illustration 10-2 (at pages 180, 182). Although most of the citing authorities will be the same, you often will find that one service includes an authority not included in the other. For example, unlike Shepard's, KeyCite includes the unreported *Bayliss* case (number 16) and various West commentary sources. Furthermore, fairly often, the two services will come to different conclusions about the validity of a case. For example, *Lukoski* drew a caution (yellow triangle) from the Shepard's editors and a green C from the KeyCite editors. Some researchers thus recommend citing the most important cases-in-hand in both services.

In providing information about the validity of a case-in-hand, the two services share an inherent limitation—they present only cases that cite the case-in-hand. Yet a case-in-hand may be undermined other ways, as depicted in Exhibit 10.1. First, a statute, regulation, or rule may overturn or undermine a case, as discussed in Units IV through VI; unless a citing case notes the impact of the law, this situation will not be noted in a case citator.

Second, a case that does not refer to the case-in-hand may undermine the case-in-hand as follows:

☐ Assume that *Alvarez* is an important and old case on your research topic.

☐ Over the years, the court decided several more cases on your topic— *Baker, Carlson, Davis,* and *Edward*—all employing the rule from *Alvarez.*

☐ You find a quite recent case, *Friedman,* that is factually parallel to your client's situation, so *Friedman* becomes your leading case-in-hand.

☐ More recently, the court decides another case on your research topic, *Green,* that changes the law. The opinion explicitly refers to and overrules *Alvarez*—but it does not refer to *Friedman.*

Note that if you cite *Friedman,* you will not learn about *Green* because *Green* does not refer to *Friedman.* One way to guard against such a situation is to use the table-of-authorities function in either LexisNexis or KeyCite. The table-of-authorities function acts as a reverse citator; it cites the cases referred to in your case-in-hand. Thus if *Friedman* refers to *Alvarez,* the table-of-authorities will cite *Alvarez* and flag *Green* as overruling *Alvarez.*

However, if *Friedman* does not refer to *Alvarez,* but rather to one of the more recent cases such as *Davis,* the table-of-authorities program will not flag the overruling of *Alvarez.* To avoid missing this critical information, you must rely not only on citators but also on other research sources. A good up-to-date secondary authority should alert you both to a *Green*-type case and to pertinent statutes, regulations, and rules. So too will thorough research in case law sources, described in Chapter 9, and sources of statutes, regulations, and rules, described in Units IV through VI.

C. WHAT ELSE?

Checking the cites in a paper.   LexisNexis and Westlaw both offer a service that citates the cases cited in a paper you have written, such as an office memo or appellate brief. LexisNexis' service is CheckCite, and Westlaw's is WestCheck.

Alert services.   Westlaw's KeyCite Alert updates you by e-mail when the report on a case you have specified is updated. Although there is no comparable Shepard's service on LexisNexis, you can ask to have a search re-run periodically through Eclipse; if you use the case-in-hand's citation as the search term, you will learn of new citing authorities within the database(s) specified in your Eclipse request.

EXHIBIT 10.1	How a Case Becomes Bad Law

In the examples below, the case-in-hand is *Friedman*.

Type of Invalidity	Research Tools
The case-in-hand is modified, reversed, or otherwise undermined on appeal. Example: The court of appeals decision in *Friedman* is reversed by the supreme court.	• case citators • secondary authorities • case law sources
The case-in-hand is criticized, distinguished, or otherwise undermined in a decision in a different later case. Example: The supreme court overrules *Friedman* in the *Green* case.	• case citators • secondary authorities • case law sources
The case on which the case-in-hand relies is criticized, distinguished, or otherwise undermined in a later case, which does not in doing so refer to the case-in-hand. Example: *Friedman* refers to *Alvarez*. *Green* overrules *Alvarez* but does not refer to *Friedman*.	• table-of-authorities function of case citators • secondary authorities • case law sources
A case on the topic, which is neither the case-in-hand nor a case on which the case-in-hand relies, is criticized, distinguished, or otherwise undermined in a later case. Example: *Friedman* does not refer to *Alvarez* but rather relies on a different case, *Davis*, stating the same point. *Green* overrules *Alvarez*.	• *not* citators • secondary authority • case law sources
A statute, regulation, or rule states a rule contrary to or different from the rule in the case-in-hand. Example: The legislature enacts a statute that overturns the rule in *Friedman*.	• *not* citators (unless a citing case so states) • secondary authority • statutory sources • sources of regulations • rules sources

ENACTED LAW

UNIT

IV

PRELIMINARY POINTS

Thus far, you have learned how to use secondary authorities to locate and understand primary authority, and you have learned how to research one form of primary authority—case law. In this chapter, you will learn to research an additional body of primary authority—enacted law, that is, statutes, constitutions, and related materials.

This unit has two chapters.

☐ Chapter 11 explains what statutes and constitutions are, how they relate to case law, and why they are so important in legal research. It then covers various ways of researching enacted laws and related case law.

☐ Chapter 12 covers methods of researching the legislative process; this research helps you discern what a legislature meant when it enacted a statute, as well as what a legislature is considering enacting for the future.

This unit continues to illustrate the research of the Canoga case stated on pages 3–4. This unit addresses two of the issues in that case, suggested by the research in secondary authorities presented in Unit II: Does a prohibition of smoking off-duty impermissibly intrude on the employee's privacy? Does a prohibition of smoking off-duty impermissibly discriminate against employees who are disabled due to nicotine addiction?

Finally, a note about terminology: This unit uses the following terms:

☐ A *bill* is potential legislation under consideration by a legislature.
☐ A *law* is a bill that has passed, thereby becoming law.
☐ A *statute* is the law on a particular topic that has been created by the legislature through one or more enacted laws and that is in effect on a specific date.

CODES AND SESSION LAWS

A. WHAT ARE CONSTITUTIONS AND STATUTES?

United States law is dominated by enacted law, created at the federal, state, and local levels. Federal and state constitutions and local charters create government structures, defining the powers of the government and the rights of the governed. Federal and state statutes and local ordinances govern a wide range of activities by public and private entities and individuals. Constitutions and statutes have somewhat different roles in the United States legal system, yet they resemble each other and are researched in much the same way.

1. What Is a Constitution?

A constitution is the highest law in a constitutional democratic regime. A constitution states the structure of the government, the inherent powers of the government, and the limits placed on the government's authority with regard to certain matters.

The United States Constitution dates to the late 1700s. In 1781, the Articles of Confederation created the United States of America. However, certain defects soon became apparent in the Articles of Confederation, and a constitutional convention was assembled in Philadelphia in 1787. The major political figures at that time submitted drafts that were debated and revised many times. The Constitution was finally ratified and became effective in 1789. The Bill of Rights, comprised of the first ten amendments to the Constitution, which spell out specific protections afforded the governed, soon followed.

To amend the United States Constitution, a proposed amendment first must pass two-thirds of both houses of Congress or the legislatures of two-thirds of the states; it then must be ratified by three-fourths of the states. In more than 200 years, only twenty-seven amendments (including the Bill of Rights) have been made to the United States Constitution.

The United States Constitution creates our three branches of government. The Constitution creates the Congress, empowers it to enact legislation, and places limits on that power. For example, the First Amendment limits the power of Congress to pass statutes that infringe on the freedoms of speech, the press, and religion. The United States Constitution also creates the federal court system, detailing the process for selecting Supreme Court justices, defining the jurisdiction of the federal courts, and granting Congress the right to establish lower federal courts. Constitutional provisions pertaining to the executive branch detail how presidents are elected, impeached, and succeeded. The Constitution also provides for presidential powers such as the right to veto legislation (subject to congressional override), to negotiate international treaties, and to serve as commander-in-chief of the military.

Under our federalist system, each state also has its separate constitution, which likewise details the structure of the state and local governments, grants them powers to act in certain areas, and protects the rights of persons within the state. Some states have had several constitutions, and state constitutions are amended more frequently than the federal constitution. In the typical process, amendments are initiated by the state legislature or by public initiative and are then approved by public referendum. Typically, the rights protected by a state constitution mirror the rights protected by the federal constitution. However, a state constitution may grant additional rights to its people, so long as those rights do not conflict with the federal constitution. Some state constitutions also govern the conduct of private citizens or entities.

A constitution states broad principles that are intended to stand the test of time, so most provisions have little detail or explanation. A constitution is organized by parts and subparts, such as articles and clauses. In general, amendments are not integrated into the text of the original constitution, but rather appear as separate provisions in the order ratified.

Illustration 11-1 (at page 191) is an excerpt from the New Mexico Constitution. It is a part of New Mexico's bill of rights.

ILLUSTRATION 11-1   State Constitution,
                          from *New Mexico Statutes Annotated* (paper source)

Art. II, § 4   BILL OF RIGHTS   Art. II, § 4

Sec. 4. [Inherent rights.]

All persons are born equally free, and have certain natural, inherent and inalienable rights, among which are the rights of enjoying and defending life and liberty, of acquiring, possessing and protecting property, and of seeking and obtaining safety and happiness.

Rights described in this section are not absolute, but are subject to reasonable regulation. Otero v. Zouhar, 102 N.M. 493, 697 P.2d 493 (Ct. App. 1984), aff'd in part and rev'd in part on other grounds, 102 N.M. 482, 697 P.2d 482 (1985), overruled on other grounds, Grantland v. Lea Regional Hosp., Inc., 110 N.M. 378, 796 P.2d 599 (1990).

Unreasonable interference with others. — This section means that each person may seek his safety and happiness in any way he sees fit so long as he does not unreasonably interfere with the safety and happiness of another. 1966 Op. Att'y Gen. No. 66-15.

Graduated income tax provisions are in no way related to or in conflict with the inherent rights provision in this section. Such income tax provisions do not prevent or deny a person's natural inherent and inalienable rights. 1968 Op. Att'y Gen. No. 68-9.

Economic policy adopted by state. — A state is free to adopt an economic policy that may reasonably be deemed to promote the public welfare and may enforce that policy by appropriate legislation without violation of the due process clause so long as such legislation has a reasonable relation to a proper legislative purpose and is neither arbitrary nor discriminatory. Rocky Mt. Whsle. Co. v. Ponca Whsle. Mercantile Co., 68 N.M. 228, 360 P.2d 643, appeal dismissed, 368 U.S. 31, 82 S. Ct. 145, 7 L. Ed. 2d 90 (1961).

Laws 1937, ch. 44, § 2, Fair Trade Act (49-2-2, 1953 Comp., now repealed), was unconstitutional and void as an arbitrary and unreasonable exercise of the police power without any substantial relation to the public health, safety or general welfare insofar as it concerned persons who were not parties to contracts provided for in Laws 1937, ch. 44, § 1 (49-2-1, 1953 Comp., now repealed). Skaggs Drug Center v. General Elec. Co., 63 N.M. 215, 315 P.2d 967 (1957).

The right of association emanating from the first amendment is not absolute. Its exercise, as is the exercise of express first amendment rights, is subject to some regulation as to time and place. Futrell v. Ahrens, 88 N.M. 284, 540 P.2d 214 (1975).

The right of association has never been held to apply to the right of one individual to associate with another, and certainly it has never been construed as an absolute right of association between a man and woman at any and all places and times. Futrell v. Ahrens, 88 N.M. 284, 540 P.2d 214 (1975).

Constitutional rights of teachers and students. — Neither students nor teachers shed their constitutional rights to freedom of speech or expression at the schoolhouse gate; school officials do not possess absolute authority over their students, and among the activities to which schools are dedicated is personal communication among students, which is an important part of the educational process. Futrell v. Ahrens, 88 N.M. 284, 540 P.2d 214 (1975).

A regulation of the board of regents of the New Mexico state university which prohibited visitation by persons of the opposite sex in residence hall, or dormitory, bedrooms maintained by the regents on the university campus, except when moving into the residence halls and during annual homecoming celebrations, where the regents placed no restrictions on intervisitation between persons of the opposite sex in the lounges or lobbies of the residence halls, the student union building, library or other buildings, or at any other place on or off the campus, and no student was required to live in a residence hall, did not interfere appreciably, if at all, with the intercommunication important to the students of the university, the regulation was reasonable, served legitimate educational purposes and promoted the welfare of the students at the university. Futrell v. Ahrens, 88 N.M. 284, 540 P.2d 214 (1975).

Although personal intercommunication among students at schools, including universities, is an important part of the educational process, it is not the only, or even the most important, part of that process. Futrell v. Ahrens, 88 N.M. 284, 540 P.2d 214 (1975).

Status of resident for divorce purposes. — The New Mexico legislature may constitutionally confer the status of resident for divorce purposes upon those continuously stationed within this state by reason of military assignment. Wilson v. Wilson, 58 N.M. 411, 272 P.2d 319 (1954).

Right to protect property. — The right to protect property being a specifically mentioned right, its presence in this section might provide the basis for additional protection against unreasonable searches and seizures. State v. Sutton, 112 N.M. 449, 816 P.2d 518 (Ct. App. 1991).

Reclamation district contract. — A provision of a reclamation contract allowing a reclamation district to enter into a lawful contract with the United States for the improvement of the district and the increase of its water supply does not violate this section or art. II, § 18. Middle Rio Grande Water Users Ass'n v. Middle Rio Grande Conservancy Dist., 57 N.M. 287, 258 P.2d 391 (1953).

Cause of action as property right. — Cause of action which Indian acquires when tort is committed against him is property which he may acquire or become invested with, particularly if tort is committed outside of reservation by a state citizen who is not an Indian; where Indian is killed as result of such tort, the cause of action survives. Trujillo v. Prince, 42 N.M. 337, 78 P.2d 145 (1938).

Recovery of damages as property right. — A tort victim's interest in full recovery of damages calls for a form of scrutiny somewhere between minimum rationality and strict scrutiny. Therefore, intermediate scrutiny should be applied to determine the constitutionality of the cap on damages in Subsection A(2) of 41-4-19 NMSA 1978 of the Tort Claims Act. Trujillo v. City of Albuquerque, 110 N.M. 621, 798 P.2d 571 (1990).

Ordinance denying right to canvass. — Green River ordinance was held valid despite contention that it deprived photographer who employed solicitors to canvass residential areas of right to acquire and enjoy property. Green v. Town of Gallup, 46 N.M. 71, 120 P.2d 619 (1941).

Comparable provisions. — Idaho Const., art. I, § 1.
Iowa Const., art. I, § 1.
Montana Const., art. II, § 3.
Utah Const., art. I, § 1.

Law reviews. — For survey, "The Statute of Limitations in Medical Malpractice Actions," see 6 N.M. L. Rev. 271 (1976).

Am. Jur. 2d, A.L.R. and C.J.S. references. —

3

2.   What Is a Statute?

Statutes are enacted by the federal Congress or a state legislature in a highly collaborative process involving legislators, the executive branch, and members of the public, who act as lobbyists or as interested individuals. Legislatures are both reactive and proactive institutions. Although interested individuals and groups bring concerns to the legislature, legislators also seek to anticipate or respond to trends and evolving issues they identify. The legislative process is open to all constituencies, so it is inevitably political in the sense that a government body listens to the diverse interests of its constituents and decides how to honor those interests.

Nearly anyone may generate a bill—a new piece of proposed legislation. The bill itself must be introduced by a legislator. In a typical process, the bill then passes through committee hearings, committee deliberations, full-chamber floor debates, and votes in both houses of the legislature before the bill is sent to the executive (governor or president) for approval or veto. Of course, the bill may be amended or may perish at any of these steps.

A law once passed is not written in stone. Should circumstances or public sentiment change, a legislature may return to the statute, to amend it or even repeal it, through the process described above. Obsolete language is deleted, and new language is inserted. This revision generally is accomplished within the organizational framework set by the original statute.

Although the statutory law on a topic may consist of a single brief section, many statutes consist of multiple related sections. An elaborate statute has many of the following provisions:

- ☐ opening provisions—the statute's name, its definitions, and scope;
- ☐ operative provisions—the general rule, any exceptions to the rule, the consequences of violating the rule, and enforcement provisions;
- ☐ closing provisions, e.g., severability (if part of it is invalid, the rest continues to operate), effective date.

In an elaborate statute, the sections and subsections are separately numbered (sometimes with gaps in the numbering sequence to accommodate later additions and to set off separate topics).

Not all statutes fit this description. Compact statutes do not contain all these components. In some statutes, the components are unlabeled or presented in a different order.

Regarding the Canoga case, Illustration 11-2 (at pages 193–95) is New Mexico's Employee Privacy Act, a six-section statute organized with definitions at the outset, the general rule in the third section, and the consequences of a violation in the remaining sections. Illustration 11-3 (at pages 196–97) is a list of the fifty sections of the federal Americans with Disabilities Act, consisting of one short preliminary unit and four topical subchapters (on employment, public services, public accommodations, and miscellaneous topics). Within each subchapter, definitions generally come first, then operative and enforcement provisions.

ILLUSTRATION 11-2   State Statute,
                              from New Mexico/LexisNexis Website (electronic source)

Document 1 of 6

Source:
Statutes/Statutory Chapters in New Mexico Statutes Annotated 1978/CHAPTER 50 EMPLOYMENT
LAW/ARTICLE 11 EMPLOYEE PRIVACY/50-11-1. Short title. (1991)

50-11-1. Short title.

This act [50-11-1 to 50-11-6 NMSA 1978] may be cited as the "Employee Privacy Act".
  History: Laws 1991, ch. 244, § 1.

Document 2 of 6

Source:
Statutes/Statutory Chapters in New Mexico Statutes Annotated 1978/CHAPTER 50 EMPLOYMENT
LAW/ARTICLE 11 EMPLOYEE PRIVACY/50-11-2. Definitions. (1991)

50-11-2. Definitions.

As used in the Employee Privacy Act [50-11-1 to 50-11-6 NMSA 1978]:

A. "employee" means a person that performs a service for wages or other remuneration under a contract of hire, written or oral, express or implied, and includes a person employed by the state or a political subdivision of the state;

B. "employer" means a person that has one or more employees and includes an agent of an employer and the state or a political subdivision of the state; and

C. "person" means an individual, sole proprietorship, partnership, corporation, association or any other legal entity.
  History: Laws 1991, ch. 244, § 2.

Document 3 of 6

Source:
Statutes/Statutory Chapters in New Mexico Statutes Annotated 1978/CHAPTER 50 EMPLOYMENT
LAW/ARTICLE 11 EMPLOYEE PRIVACY/50-11-3. Employers; unlawful practices. (1991)

ILLUSTRATION 11-2   *(continued)*

50-11-3. Employers; unlawful practices.

A. It is unlawful for an employer to:

(1) refuse to hire or to discharge any individual, or otherwise disadvantage any individual, with respect to compensation, terms, conditions or privileges of employment because the individual is a smoker or nonsmoker, provided that the individual complies with applicable laws or policies regulating smoking on the premises of the employer during working hours; or

(2) require as a condition of employment that any employee or applicant for employment abstain from smoking or using tobacco products during nonworking hours, provided the individual complies with applicable laws or policies regulating smoking on the premises of the employer during working hours.

B. The provisions of Subsection A of this section shall not be deemed to protect any activity that:

(1) materially threatens an employer's legitimate conflict of interest policy reasonably designed to protect the employer's trade secrets, proprietary information or other proprietary interests; or

(2) relates to a bona fide occupational requirement and is reasonably and rationally related to the employment activities and responsibilities of a particular employee or a particular group of employees, rather than to all employees of the employer.

History: Laws 1991, ch. 244, § 3.

Document 4 of 6

Source:
Statutes/Statutory Chapters in New Mexico Statutes Annotated 1978/CHAPTER 50 EMPLOYMENT LAW/ARTICLE 11 EMPLOYEE PRIVACY/50-11-4. Remedies. (1991)

50-11-4. Remedies.

Any employee claiming to be aggrieved by any unlawful action of an employer pursuant to Section 3 [50-11-3 NMSA 1978] of the Employee Privacy Act may bring a civil suit for damages in any district court of competent jurisdiction. The employee may be awarded all wages and benefits due up to and including the date of the judgment.

History: Laws 1991, ch. 244, § 4.

Document 5 of 6

Source:

ILLUSTRATION 11-2   *(continued)*

Statutes/Statutory Chapters in New Mexico Statutes Annotated 1978/CHAPTER 50 EMPLOYMENT LAW/ARTICLE 11 EMPLOYEE PRIVACY/50-11-5. Court fees and costs. (1991)

50-11-5. Court fees and costs.

In any civil suit arising from the Employee Privacy Act [50-11-1 to 50-11-6 NMSA 1978], the court shall award the prevailing party court costs and reasonable attorneys' fees.
   History: Laws 1991, ch. 244, § 5.

Document 6 of 6

Source:
Statutes/Statutory Chapters in New Mexico Statutes Annotated 1978/CHAPTER 50 EMPLOYMENT LAW/ARTICLE 11 EMPLOYEE PRIVACY/50-11-6. Mitigation of damages. (1991)

50-11-6. Mitigation of damages.

Nothing in the Employee Privacy Act [50-11-1 to 50-11-6 NMSA 1978] shall be construed to relieve a person from the obligation to mitigate damages.
   History: Laws 1991, ch. 244, § 6.

ILLUSTRATION 11-3   Outline of Federal Statute,
from *United States Code* (paper source)

---

§ 12007   TITLE 42—THE PUBLIC HEALTH AND WELFARE   Page 658

(D) include annual and five-year cost estimates for individual programs under this chapter; and

(E) identify program areas for which funding levels have been changed from the previous year's Plan.[2]

(6) Within one year after October 24, 1992, the Secretary shall submit a revised management plan under this section to Congress. Thereafter, the Secretary shall submit a management plan every three years at the time of submittal of the President's annual budget submission to the Congress.

(c) Report on options

As part of the first report submitted under subsection (a) of this section, the Secretary shall submit to Congress a report analyzing options available to the Secretary under existing law to assist the private sector with the timely commercialization of wind, photovoltaic, solar thermal, biofuels, hydrogen, solar buildings, ocean, geothermal, low-head hydro, and energy storage renewable energy technologies and energy efficiency technologies through emphasis on development and demonstration assistance to specific technologies in the research, development, and demonstration programs of the Department of Energy that are near commercial application.

(Pub. L. 101–218, § 9, Dec. 11, 1989, 103 Stat. 1868; Pub. L. 102–486, title XII, § 1202(c), (d)(5), title XXIII, § 2303(b), Oct. 24, 1992, 106 Stat. 2959, 2960, 3093.)

AMENDMENTS

1992—Subsec. (a). Pub. L. 102–486, § 1202(d)(5), substituted "and projects" for ", projects, and joint ventures".

Subsec. (b)(1). Pub. L. 102–486, § 1202(c)(1), inserted "three-year" before "management plan".

Subsec. (b)(4). Pub. L. 102–486, § 2303(b), inserted before period at end "and the plan developed under section 5905 of this title".

Subsec. (b)(5), (6). Pub. L. 102–486, § 1202(c)(2), added pars. (5) and (6) and struck out former par. (5) which read as follows: "The plan shall accompany the President's annual budget submission to the Congress."

TERMINATION OF REPORTING REQUIREMENTS

For termination, effective May 15, 2000, of provisions of law requiring submittal to Congress of any annual, semiannual, or other regular periodic report listed in House Document No. 103–7 (in which reports required under subsecs. (a) and (b) of this section are listed as the 20th item on page 84 and the 19th item on page 86), see section 3003 of Pub. L. 104–66, as amended, set out as a note under section 1113 of Title 31, Money and Finance.

SECTION REFERRED TO IN OTHER SECTIONS

This section is referred to in section 12003 of this title.

§ 12007. No antitrust immunity or defenses

Nothing in this chapter shall be deemed to convey to any person, partnership, corporation, or other entity immunity from civil or criminal liability under any antitrust law or to create defenses to actions under any antitrust law. As used in this section, "antitrust laws" means those Acts set forth in section 12 of title 15.

(Pub. L. 101–218, § 10, Dec. 11, 1989, 103 Stat. 1869.)

---

[2]So in original. Probably should not be capitalized.

CHAPTER 126—EQUAL OPPORTUNITY FOR INDIVIDUALS WITH DISABILITIES

ILLUSTRATION 11-3   *(continued)*

Sec.
12149.   Regulations.
    (a) In general.
    (b) Standards.
12150.   Interim accessibility requirements.

SUBPART II—PUBLIC TRANSPORTATION BY INTERCITY AND COMMUTER RAIL

12161.   Definitions.
12162.   Intercity and commuter rail actions considered discriminatory.
    (a) Intercity rail transportation.
    (b) Commuter rail transportation.
    (c) Used rail cars.
    (d) Remanufactured rail cars.
    (e) Stations.
12163.   Conformance of accessibility standards.
12164.   Regulations.
12165.   Interim accessibility requirements.
    (a) Stations.
    (b) Rail passenger cars.

SUBCHAPTER III—PUBLIC ACCOMMODATIONS AND SERVICES OPERATED BY PRIVATE ENTITIES

12181.   Definitions.
12182.   Prohibition of discrimination by public accommodations.
    (a) General rule.
    (b) Construction.
12183.   New construction and alterations in public accommodations and commercial facilities.
    (a) Application of term.
    (b) Elevator.
12184.   Prohibition of discrimination in specified public transportation services provided by private entities.
    (a) General rule.
    (b) Construction.
    (c) Historical or antiquated cars.
12185.   Study.
    (a) Purposes.
    (b) Contents.
    (c) Advisory committee.
    (d) Deadline.
    (e) Review.
12186.   Regulations.
    (a) Transportation provisions.
    (b) Other provisions.
    (c) Consistency with ATBCB guidelines.
    (d) Interim accessibility standards.
12187.   Exemptions for private clubs and religious organizations.
12188.   Enforcement.
    (a) In general.
    (b) Enforcement by Attorney General.
12189.   Examinations and courses.

SUBCHAPTER IV—MISCELLANEOUS PROVISIONS

12201.   Construction.
    (a) In general.
    (b) Relationship to other laws.
    (c) Insurance.
    (d) Accommodations and services.
12202.   State immunity.
12203.   Prohibition against retaliation and coercion.
    (a) Retaliation.
    (b) Interference, coercion, or intimidation.
    (c) Remedies and procedures.
12204.   Regulations by Architectural and Transportation Barriers Compliance Board.
    (a) Issuance of guidelines.
    (b) Contents of guidelines.
    (c) Qualified historic properties.
12205.   Attorney's fees.
12206.   Technical assistance.
    (a) Plan for assistance.
    (b) Agency and public assistance.
    (c) Implementation.

Sec.
    (d) Grants and contracts.
    (e) Failure to receive assistance.
12207.   Federal wilderness areas.
    (a) Study.
    (b) Submission of report.
    (c) Specific wilderness access.
12208.   Transvestites.
12209.   Instrumentalities of Congress.
12210.   Illegal use of drugs.
    (a) In general.
    (b) Rules of construction.
    (c) Health and other services.
    (d) "Illegal use of drugs" defined.
12211.   Definitions.
    (a) Homosexuality and bisexuality.
    (b) Certain conditions.
12212.   Alternative means of dispute resolution.
12213.   Severability.

CHAPTER REFERRED TO IN OTHER SECTIONS

This chapter is referred to in sections 290bb–34, 608, 1760, 1786, 3796gg–7, 15007, 15024 of this title; title 2 sections 1302, 1331, 1371, 1434; title 3 sections 402, 421; title 16 sections 410aaa–41, 410aaa–52; title 20 sections 1011, 1140c, 1415, 8507; title 23 section 133; title 25 section 2005; title 26 section 44; title 29 sections 720, 721, 762, 764, 781, 793, 795, 3011; title 49 sections 5302, 5307, 5314, 5323, 5335, 47102.

§ 12101. Findings and purpose

(a) Findings

The Congress finds that—

(1) some 43,000,000 Americans have one or more physical or mental disabilities, and this number is increasing as the population as a whole is growing older;

(2) historically, society has tended to isolate and segregate individuals with disabilities, and, despite some improvements, such forms of discrimination against individuals with disabilities continue to be a serious and pervasive social problem;

(3) discrimination against individuals with disabilities persists in such critical areas as employment, housing, public accommodations, education, transportation, communication, recreation, institutionalization, health services, voting, and access to public services;

(4) unlike individuals who have experienced discrimination on the basis of race, color, sex, national origin, religion, or age, individuals who have experienced discrimination on the basis of disability have often had no legal recourse to redress such discrimination;

(5) individuals with disabilities continually encounter various forms of discrimination, including outright intentional exclusion, the discriminatory effects of architectural, transportation, and communication barriers, overprotective rules and policies, failure to make modifications to existing facilities and practices, exclusionary qualification standards and criteria, segregation, and relegation to lesser services, programs, activities, benefits, jobs, or other opportunities;

(6) census data, national polls, and other studies have documented that people with disabilities, as a group, occupy an inferior status in our society, and are severely disadvantaged socially, vocationally, economically, and educationally;

(7) individuals with disabilities are a discrete and insular minority who have been

3.   How Does Enacted Law Relate to Case Law?

Although cases and statutes are both primary authority, they develop and are analyzed differently. As discussed in Chapter 9, case law develops case by case, each case focusing on the situation that prompted the litigation. Cases serve as binding or persuasive precedent for future disputes involving similar situations. In contrast, enacted laws are enacted by legislators who are seeking to describe and set rules for a broad class of situations that will arise in the future.

Constitutions are the supreme law in a jurisdiction, yet most provisions are framed in vague and general terms. Hence the courts play a very active role in the development of constitutional law. It is up to the courts to discern what spare constitutional language means in myriad particular circumstances. As you research a constitutional issue, you most likely will find yourself grappling with a substantial body of case law.

Statutes bear various relationships to common law. Some statutes codify, clarify, or supplement preexisting common law. Some statutes overturn the common law. Still other statutes create whole new areas of law not covered in the common law. Because the constitution grants the legislative branch broad powers, statutes usually take precedence over common law.

In turn, statutes become the subject of discussion in case law as courts apply statutes to disputes in litigation. Courts have two primary tasks in such cases, one common, the other rare. First, courts interpret the statutory language and use it to resolve the parties' dispute. Second, less commonly, courts assess whether the statute is constitutional; if not, the statute is declared unconstitutional and has no further effect. The number of cases varies greatly from statute to statute, depending on the breadth of the statute's impact, the clarity of its language, and its age. Some statutes have no interpreting cases; some have thousands. Thus, as you research a statute, almost always, you will also research case law interpreting the statute; otherwise, your research will be incomplete.

4.   What Is a Uniform Act?

Uniform acts are proposals for statutes drafted by various organizations that seek to standardize the statutory law of the fifty states. Model acts address topics that may not be of critical concern to all jurisdictions or that likely will not be enacted by a substantial number of jurisdictions. The drafters of both uniform and model acts seek to persuade state legislatures to enact the proposed language. The Uniform Commercial Code is an example of a widely adopted uniform act.

Uniform and model acts come from a variety of organizations:

☐   The National Conference of Commissioners on Uniform State Laws, consisting of attorneys, judges, legislators, and law professors appointed from each state, has approved over a hundred model and uniform acts.

☐ The American Law Institute, which promulgates Restatements of the Law (discussed in Chapter 7), also drafts model codes.

☐ Section committees of the American Bar Association (ABA) and the Council of State Governments promulgate model acts on occasion.

Private individuals, most notably law faculty, occasionally propose model legislation as well.

Complete uniformity is rarely achieved because few acts are enacted by every jurisdiction and because few uniform or model acts are enacted verbatim. Nonetheless, achieving some uniformity in state statutes through these efforts promotes and simplifies interstate activities.

The organization of most uniform or model acts resembles the organization of other statutes. In addition, you may find very helpful explanatory material in the accompanying notes or comments.

B. WHY WOULD YOU RESEARCH CONSTITUTIONS AND STATUTES?

Succinctly stated, you research constitutions and statutes because they are the law. They are mandatory primary authority if validly enacted by the legislature in your jurisdiction and approved or ratified.

Constitutions generally regulate only governmental action. They thus are primarily pertinent in two circumstances: when a party seeks to assess the validity of a law or when a party seeks to challenge action taken by a government official, on constitutional grounds. On rare occasions, nongovernmental action may be regulated by a constitution. Some nongovernmental entities are governed by a constitution when their actions are quasi-governmental or tightly enmeshed in government functions. In addition, some state constitutional provisions are written broadly enough to apply to private actors as well.

Statutes have potentially broad application. Many apply to private actions, some to governmental actions, some to both. The statute itself indicates or implies how broadly it applies.

Often it may be unclear to you initially which law applies: federal, state, local, or a combination. Under our federal system, federal and state governments have separate as well as overlapping rights to enact law within constitutionally prescribed limits. For example, the federal government has authority to govern in areas that preserve its national sovereignty or that have been expressly granted to it by the United States Constitution. State governments have authority to govern matters that are state concerns, have been delegated to them by Congress, or are not expressly assigned to the federal government.

The federal system is hierarchical in that federal law sometimes preempts state law on the same topic. In areas of potential federal authority, Congress can dictate whether its laws preempt state laws or coexist with them. If Congress is silent, the courts must decide whether the federal law impliedly preempts the state law; courts consider the strength of the state interest and the potential for interference with the overall federal regulatory scheme.

If you are uncertain whose law governs a particular topic, begin with research in federal law, then turn to your state and then local law. Often you will learn whose law governs through your research in secondary authorities.

Timing is very important in statutory research. The correct law is the language in effect at the time of your client's situation. Although there are some exceptions, enacted law is prospective, that is, a law governs conduct occurring on or after its effective date. The effective date of a law is the date stated in the law's effective-date provision or, if none, the default date for the jurisdiction. For federal legislation, the default effective date is the date of the president's approval. Once effective, a statute remains in effect unless it is repealed or replaced; is declared unconstitutional; or expires by operation of a provision in the statute so stating, often called a "sunset provision."

As already noted, courts decide cases involving statutes, so you generally will research cases when you research statutes. Stare decisis operates in a statutory context, so a court asked to interpret a particular statute will, of course, first turn to mandatory precedent interpreting that statute. If the court finds no pertinent mandatory precedent, it may seek guidance in some other court's interpretation of a similarly, if not identically, worded statute from another jurisdiction. For example, if a state statute tracks the language of a federal statute and the federal courts have interpreted that language, the state court may well adopt the federal interpretation for its own statute. Similarly, if a state statute derives from a uniform or model act, you can use case law interpreting identical or similar language in other jurisdictions.

As for the Canoga case, the employer, as a private organization, is more likely to be governed by statutes than constitutions. Potentially pertinent provisions appear in a federal statute, the 1990 Americans with Disabilities Act (ADA), outlined in Illustration 11-3 (at pages 196–97). A New Mexico statute on employee privacy, dating to 1991, reproduced in Illustration 11-2 (at pages 193–95), is clearly pertinent.

C.   HOW DO YOU RESEARCH CONSTITUTIONS AND STATUTES?

Enacted laws appear in several forms over time, as follows:

☐ A *slip law* is a copy of the individual law as enacted. The slip law carries the public law number (for federal laws) or chapter number (typically used for state laws), which typically reflects the order in which the laws in a legislative session were passed.

☐ The *session laws* are the slip laws for a session collected and published in order of enactment.

☐ An *official code* is a set of statutes currently in force, organized topically and published by the government or its designated publisher[1] Thus, if a new law amends an existing statute, the old language is displaced by the new language. If a new law covers new ground, it is inserted near other statutes on the same broad subject. Codes have fairly elaborate numerical schemes, for example, the federal code uses title, chapter, and section numbers.

☐ An *unofficial code* is published by a private publisher. It uses the same numbering scheme and should contain the same statutory language (subject to differences in updating and minor editorial features) as the official code.[2] Unlike most official codes, most unofficial codes are annotated, that is, they provide references to judicial cases interpreting the statute, related administrative materials, and secondary authorities discussing the topic of the statute. Unofficial codes are updated more frequently than official codes.

Some states have only one code, published by a commercial publisher on contract with the state. Table T.1 of *The Bluebook* and Appendix I of *ALWD Citation Manual* list the session laws and codes for United States jurisdictions.

Note that a law has more than one number—a session law number and a code number. For example, the New Mexico statute in Illustration 11-2 (at pages 193–95) is the 244th chapter of the laws enacted in 1991 by the New Mexico legislature, as noted after each section. That statute comprises article 11 of chapter 50, which consists of employment statutes; the first section is number 50-11-1.

Slip and session laws and codes have long been and continue to be published in paper. They also are now available electronically through commercial services and public websites. Thus, for any particular statute, you often will have several sources and approaches from which to choose.

Quite often, you will find a reference to a pertinent statute through your research in secondary authorities. Or you may become aware of a statute when you read a pertinent case that discusses it. However, you should not rely solely on such leads; you also should research statutes directly.

This part first discusses two paper sources: annotated codes and session laws. It then discusses the major options available through commercial electronic services and through public websites. Exhibit 11.1 provides an overview of the four statutory practices. To a great extent, these practices operate

---

1. A jurisdiction's code typically contains only public permanent laws, not private laws (which relate to a particular person or specific situation) or temporary laws (such as appropriations for government agencies).

2. Although there rarely is conflict among session laws, official codes, and unofficial codes, there is a hierarchy among them. From time to time, Congress examines specific titles of the official code and re-enacts those titles as positive law; once re-enacted, those titles are the law. Titles that have not been re-enacted as positive law are only prima facie (presumptively correct) evidence of the law, and the session law governs in the event of a conflict. A similar process occurs at the state level.

EXHIBIT 11.1		Overview of Statutory Research Practices	

Practice	Statutory Material	Other Material	Currency and Updating
Annotated Code in Paper	• public permanent laws • current statutory language and limited historical material	• case descriptions • references to administrative materials • references to secondary sources	fairly current via • pocket parts • supplement pamphlets • looseleaf pages • advance legislative service
Session Laws in Paper	• public and private laws • permanent and temporary laws • language passed in specific legislative session	• cross-references and margin notes	• limited to specific session
Commercial Electronic Services	depends on database • annotated codes: same as first row above • unannotated code: same as first row above • session laws: same as second row above	depends on database • annotated code: same as first row above; also links to cases and other authorities • unannotated code: none • session laws: none	very current via • statutory updating features • case law research
Public Websites	depends on database • annotated code: same as first row above • session laws: same as second row above		• probably current

identically for constitutions. This part concludes with a brief discussion of researching local ordinances.

This chapter does not discuss several tools that have important but less central roles in statutory research. Chapter 12 discusses legislative process materials, which are used to establish the legislature's intent in passing a statute or to track pending bills.

Statutes in annotated codes in paper:

▶ select an appropriate annotated code
▶ use the index or statutory outlines or popular names table
▶ locate the statute's current language in the main volume or updating materials or both
▶ study the correct and complete statutory language
▶ review the annotation: case descriptions, references to secondary authorities, and notes

Annotated codes exist at the federal and state levels. While each annotated code is unique, they share various general characteristics. This part focuses on federal statutory codes.

Select an appropriate code. Your first step is to select an annotated code for your jurisdiction. Federal statutes appear in two unofficial codes: *United States Code Annotated* (U.S.C.A.), published by West, and *United States Code Service* (U.S.C.S.), now published by LexisNexis. In addition, the *United States Code* (U.S.C.) is published by the United States government. These three codes contain the same statutory sections and use the same organizational scheme. There are two importance differences:

- [ ] The unofficial codes are published and updated far more frequently than is the official code.
- [ ] The official code, U.S.C., is unannotated; it contains only the statutory text. By contrast, the two unofficial codes, U.S.C.A. and U.S.C.S., are very thoroughly annotated. See Illustration 11-4 (at pages 208–10).

A note about vocabulary: *Annotation* often is used to refer only to the case descriptions. For brevity, this discussion uses *annotation* to refer to the full range of case descriptions, references to other authorities, and explanatory material.

The currency and annotations of annotated, often unofficial codes make them more powerful research tools than the unannotated, often official codes. However, some find it easier to read the statute in an official code without the distraction of the annotation.

Use an index, outlines, or table. To locate a pertinent statute within a code, you generally will choose from three research approaches.

The index approach is probably the most successful in most situations. U.S.C.A. and U.S.C.S. both have a multivolume general index that is issued annually, so it is fairly current. In addition, each of the fifty titles in U.S.C.A. and U.S.C.S. has an individual title index, which usually is located in the last hardbound volume of the title. Because the title indexes are not updated, the general index generally is more current than the individual title indexes.

A second method for finding a pertinent statute within a code is to use the statute's outlines. For many codes (including the federal codes), you will start with a list of titles, then move to a list of chapters within a title, and then to a list of sections within a chapter. Exhibit 11.2 lists the current titles for the federal code. In U.S.C.A. and U.S.C.S., the list of chapters for each title appears at the front of each volume for the title or at the beginning of a new title in mid-volume; the list of sections within a chapter is found at the beginning of each chapter. The outline approach can be more difficult than the index approach if the title topics are very general, as is often true.

If you already know the name of the statute you are seeking, a third approach is to use a popular names table. Some, but not all, statutes have official or popular names for easy identification. U.S.C.A. has a Popular Names Table volume; the U.S.C.S. Tables volumes include a table of popular names, supplemented in a softbound cumulative supplement.

EXHIBIT 11.2	Titles of United States Code

1. General Provisions
2. The Congress
3. The President
4. Flag and Seal, Seat of Government, and the States
5. Government Organization and Employees; and Appendix
6. Domestic Security
7. Agriculture
8. Aliens and Nationality
9. Arbitration
10. Armed Forces; and Appendix
11. Bankruptcy; and Appendix
12. Banks and Banking
13. Census
14. Coast Guard
15. Commerce and Trade
16. Conservation
17. Copyrights
18. Crimes and Criminal Procedure; and Appendix
19. Customs Duties
20. Education
21. Food and Drugs
22. Foreign Relations and Intercourse
23. Highways
24. Hospitals and Asylums
25. Indians
26. Internal Revenue Code; and Appendix

27. Intoxicating Liquors
28. Judiciary and Judicial Procedure; and Appendix
29. Labor
30. Mineral Lands and Mining
31. Money and Finance
32. National Guard
33. Navigation and Navigable Waters
*34. [Navy]
35. Patents
36. Patriotic and National Observances, Ceremonies and Organizations
37. Pay and Allowances of the Uniformed Services
38. Veterans' Benefits; and Appendix
39. Postal Service
40. Public Buildings, Property, and Works; and Appendix
41. Public Contracts
42. The Public Health and Welfare
43. Public Lands
44. Public Printing and Documents
45. Railroads
46. Shipping; and Appendix
47. Telegraphs, Telephones, and Radiotelegraphs
48. Territories and Insular Possessions
49. Transportation
50. War and National Defense; and Appendix

*This title has been eliminated by the enactment of Title 10.

Locate the current language. After you have identified a potentially pertinent statute, your next task is to locate its current language. Much of the time, the current language will be in the main volume. Sometimes the language will be newer than the main volume and thus will appear in updating materials. Most codes are updated in stages:

(1) The initial update generally is an annual pocket part or supplement pamphlet, filed in the back of or after the main hardbound volume to which it pertains. The initial update for a looseleaf code generally consists of supplement pages filed under a supplement tab in the same binder. See Illustration 11-5 (at page 211).

(2) Even newer information appears in one or more supplements that update the entire code and accordingly are shelved at the end of the code; these pamphlets appear as needed and may or may not be cumulative.

(3) The advance legislative service provides the language of newly enacted laws.

U.S.C.A. and U.S.C.S. both use these various supplements.

The first and second updating publications contain material that is similar in kind to that found in the main volume, and they typically are organized as the annotated code itself is, so it is easy to see whether there is any updating material for your statute. New statutory language is presented so that its relationship to the old language is clear. For example, there may be references to the main volume for sections that were not changed, while an amended section will be printed as amended.

Advance legislative service pamphlets contain reprints of new laws; they do not contain annotation material. Because advance legislative service pamphlets typically are not organized so as to parallel the code, but rather by sequence of enacted laws, they typically have two means of access. The table of statutory sections affected by new legislation is useful when you have located a pertinent statute in the code and want to see whether it has changed. See Illustration 11-6 (at page 212). The subject index is most useful when there is no pertinent statute in the code. Because these two means of access serve somewhat different functions, you should use both means of access.

The task of locating the current language and the task of studying the statute tend to overlap. You probably will skim the language you find first, typically in the main volume or perhaps in a pocket part, to ascertain whether it is indeed pertinent. Next you will want to check for newer language and discern how new language fits with older language. Then you will study the statute, as you have assembled it.

Study the correct and complete statutory language. If you are working with a multisection statute, first look over the statute to discern how it is organized. Then read through it as follows:

(1) the statement of purpose or other introductory section,
(2) the definitions and scope,
(3) the general rule and exceptions, and
(4) consequences or enforcement provisions.

As you work on understanding the statute, be sure to determine the law in effect as of the time of your client's situation. Most of the time, the correct language will be the current language as described above, but on occasion, you will need to read old language:

☐ If your client is seeking advice about its future plans, the current language is the correct language.[3]
☐ If your client's events occurred since the most recent enactment's effective date, again, the current language will be the correct language.
☐ If your client's events occurred before the most recent enactment's effective date, old language is the correct language (unless the most recent enactment is retroactive, which is rare).

---

3. You may need to monitor proposed legislation as well. See Chapter 12 for a discussion of bill tracking.

To sort this out, read the material provided in the annotated code about the statute's history. See Illustration 11-4 (at page 209). At the least, you should find a list of laws with enactment dates. Some codes also explain how the language evolved over time. If you need information beyond that provided in the annotated code, you should consult an older code or the appropriate session laws (see below). If your client's events occurred very close to the enactment of a pertinent law, you will need to pinpoint the law's effective date; if the session law does not state a specific date, the default effective date operates.

You may wonder why you should determine what the current language is if an older version is the correct language for your client's situation. Often, new language helps you understand older language or infer what the legislature's concerns are and have been.

Many statutes are self-contained; others refer to and rely on provisions in other statutes. Each time you read a reference to another section of the same statute or a different statute, be sure to note and follow up on these references.

Finally, pay close attention to every word in a statute. Unlike cases, statutes do not contain dicta. You should assume that each word has a purpose and is potentially significant. If you encounter vague, ambiguous, or conflicting language, you may want to locate rules of statutory construction. Some jurisdictions have statutory provisions that set forth rules for analyzing statutory language, or check for a treatise on the topic.[4]

Review the annotation. Once you have studied the statute itself, you should review the annotation, in both the main volume and updating volumes. Again, see Illustrations 11-4 (at page 210) and Illustration 11-5 (at page 211).

Of particular importance are the descriptions of cases interpreting the statute. There may be a few to literally hundreds of case descriptions, depending on how much litigation the statute has spawned. The editors may have created a topical framework for the case descriptions; if so, be sure to review that framework to discern where cases pertinent to your research topic should appear and focus on those portions of the annotation. See Illustration 11-4 (at page 210). As you read the case descriptions, look for cases that will be particularly useful to you, based on legal and factual similarity to your client's situation, court, and date of decision.

Next, review the other annotation material. You may, for example, find references to administrative agency materials or potentially pertinent secondary authorities.

U.S.C.A. and U.S.C.S. both provide abundant annotation material. There are some differences. For example, U.S.C.A. provides references to pertinent West key numbers; U.S.C.S. does not. Because the two competing annotated codes are not identical, you may research in both at times, particularly when the first one you consult has no pertinent case descriptions or does not present the case descriptions in a framework that fits your needs.

---

4. An example is Norman J. Singer, *Statutes and Statutory Construction* (6th ed. 2000).

Researching the Canoga case. We actually located the provision featured here via a reference in a treatise (Illustration 4-1 on page 72). The 2003 U.S.C.A. General Index did not refer to the ADA provision under the Smoking subject heading, and there was no entry for nicotine. Under Disability, we found a reference to Handicapped Persons, which in turn referred to the heading Equal Opportunity for Individuals with Disabilities. There we found a reference to 42 § 12101 et seq., that is, the Americans with Disabilities Act. It would not have been easy to find the ADA by use of title and chapter outlines; title 42 is a very broad title covering the Public Health and Welfare, with over 170 chapters. On the other hand, we could easily find the location of the ADA through the U.S.C.A.'s popular name table. Once we found the ADA, we could peruse the table of contents and skim the statute to locate pertinent sections.

When we researched the Canoga case in the summer of 2003, the main volume of the pertinent title of U.S.C.A. was fairly new—1995. The pocket part came out in 2003, and there was a July 2003 supplement pamphlet as well.

Illustration 11-4 (at pages 208–10) is from U.S.C.A's 1995 volume. It presents § 12201, a provision with some pertinence to the Canoga case; that provision was enacted in July 1990. Section 12201 is only a small portion of the Americans with Disabilities Act (ADA). In general terms, that statute prohibits discrimination against employees based on disability and requires employers to provide reasonable accommodation of disabilities. The statute does not explicitly state whether nicotine addiction is a protected disability. Section 12201 does, however, state that the ADA does not preclude prohibitions or restrictions on smoking in workplaces covered by the ADA. However, this provision does not squarely address the Canoga case, because the prohibition reached beyond the workplace and was imposed not by law but by the employer.

The annotation to § 12201 in U.S.C.A. is fairly short. See Illustration 11-4 (at page 210) and Illustration 11-5 (at page 211). The annotation, including the main volume and the pocket part, includes descriptions of about two dozen cases—none on point, however. The annotation also provides a cross-reference to another federal statute (29 U.S.C. §§ 791, 793, 794); references to various secondary authorities, including the encyclopedia C.J.S. and periodical articles; and key numbers to use in the West digests and on Westlaw. There was no additional information in the supplement pamphlet.

We checked U.S.C.A.'s advance legislative service as well. The table of amendments and repeals showed no changes in the ADA. See Illustration 11-6 (at page 212).

Because we found no pertinent case description in U.S.C.A., we also checked U.S.C.S.'s annotation for § 12201. A case appeared under the heading Smoking Regulations, but it involved smoke-sensitive customers suing McDonald's for not providing a smoke-free restaurant.[5]

---

5. *Staron v. McDonald's Corp.*, 51 F.3d 353 (2d Cir. 1995).

ILLUSTRATION 11-4   Provision of Federal Statute and Annotation,
from *United States Code Annotated* (paper source)

Ch. 126   **MISCELLANEOUS PROVISIONS**   **42 § 12201**

WESTLAW ELECTRONIC RESEARCH

Civil rights cases: 78k[add key number].
See, also, WESTLAW guide following the Explanation pages of this volume.

NOTES OF DECISIONS

Bar examinations   1

---

1. Bar examinations

Evidence was insufficient to support finding that applicant for bar examination suffered from learning disability entitling him to special examination accommodations under ADA; expert on dyslexia testified that applicant did not have learning disability, applicant performed well on reading comprehension test, applicant's grades in college did not improve significantly once he received examination accommodations, and his performance on tests refuted conclusion that he suffered from dysgraphia.   Pazer v. New York State Bd. of Law Examiners, S.D.N.Y.1994, 849 F.Supp. 284.

Applicant for bar examination showed presence of irreparable injury to her ability to be admitted to practice law and secure legal employment as result of alleged ongoing discrimination in violation of Americans with Disabilities Act (ADA)

from refusal of Board of Law Examiners to allow four-day period to take test rather than usual two days in light of applicant's severe visual disability, which supported issuance of preliminary injunction to compel board to provide applicant with her requested testing accommodations.   D'Amico v. New York State Bd. of Law Examiners, W.D.N.Y.1993, 813 F.Supp. 217.

Evidence did not support board of bar examiner's decision to disregard recommendation of applicant's expert who recommended, that because of her learning disability, that she be given additional time to complete both sections of bar examination and board's decision to grant applicant additional time with respect to essay portion only; in addition, board's ultimate decision did not reflect that it was product of orderly and logical deductive process.   Petition of Rubenstein, Del.Supr.1994, 637 A.2d 1131.

SUBCHAPTER IV—MISCELLANEOUS PROVISIONS

§ 12201.   Construction

(a) In general

Except as otherwise provided in this chapter, nothing in this chapter shall be construed to apply a lesser standard than the standards applied under title V of the Rehabilitation Act of 1973 (29 U.S.C. 790 et seq.) or the regulations issued by Federal agencies pursuant to such title.

(b) Relationship to other laws

Nothing in this chapter shall be construed to invalidate or limit the remedies, rights, and procedures of any Federal law or law of any State or political subdivision of any State or jurisdiction that provides greater or equal protection for the rights of individuals with disabilities than are afforded by this chapter.   Nothing in this chapter shall be construed to preclude the prohibition of, or the imposition of restrictions on, smoking in places of employment covered by subchapter I of this chapter, in transportation covered by subchapter II

ILLUSTRATION 11-4   *(continued)*

---

42 § 12201   **OPPORTUNITY FOR THE DISABLED   Ch. 126**

or III of this chapter, or in places of public accommodation covered by subchapter III of this chapter.

(c) Insurance

Subchapters I through III of this chapter and title IV of this Act shall not be construed to prohibit or restrict—

(1) an insurer, hospital or medical service company, health maintenance organization, or any agent, or entity that administers benefit plans, or similar organizations from underwriting risks, classifying risks, or administering such risks that are based on or not inconsistent with State law; or

(2) a person or organization covered by this chapter from establishing, sponsoring, observing or administering the terms of a bona fide benefit plan that are based on underwriting risks, classifying risks, or administering such risks that are based on or not inconsistent with State law; or

(3) a person or organization covered by this chapter from establishing, sponsoring, observing or administering the terms of a bona fide benefit plan that is not subject to State laws that regulate insurance.

Paragraphs (1), (2), and (3) shall not be used as a subterfuge to evade the purposes of subchapter [1] I and III of this chapter.

(d) Accommodations and services

Nothing in this chapter shall be construed to require an individual with a disability to accept an accommodation, aid, service, opportunity, or benefit which such individual chooses not to accept.

(Pub.L. 101–336, Title V, § 501, July 26, 1990, 104 Stat. 369.)

[1] So in original. Probably should be "subchapters".

HISTORICAL AND STATUTORY NOTES

Revision Notes and Legislative Reports
1990 Acts. House Report No. 101–485(Parts I–IV), House Conference Report No. 101–596, and Statement by President, see 1990 U.S. Code Cong. and Adm. News, p. 267.

References in Text
This chapter, referred to in text, was in the original this Act, meaning Pub.L. 101–336, July 26, 1990, 104 Stat. 327, which is classified principally to this chapter. For complete classification of this Act to the Code, see Short Title of 1990 Acts note set out under section 12101 of this title and Tables.

The Rehabilitation Act of 1973, referred to in subsec. (a), is Pub.L. 93–112, Sept. 26, 1973, 87 Stat. 355, as amended. Title V of the Rehabilitation Act of 1973 is classified generally to subchapter V (section 790 et seq.) of chapter 16 of Title 29, Labor. For complete classification of this Act to the Code, see Short Title note set out under section 701 of Title 29 and Tables.

Title IV of this Act, referred to in subsec. (c), means Title IV of Pub.L. 101–336, July 26, 1990, 104 Stat. 366, which enacted section 225 of Title 47, Telegraphs, Telephones, and Radiotelegraphs, and amended sections 152, 221, and 611 of Title 47.

726

ILLUSTRATION 11-4   *(continued)*

Ch. 126   MISCELLANEOUS PROVISIONS   **42 § 12201**
                                                            Note 2
CROSS REFERENCES
Standards same as under this section for determining violation of vocational
  rehabilitation provisions—
Employment of individuals with disabilities, see 29 USCA § 791.
Employment under federal contracts, see 29 USCA § 793.
Nondiscrimination under federal grants and programs, see 29 USCA § 794.

LIBRARY REFERENCES
American Digest System
  Construction and operation of statutes in general; construction with reference to
    other laws, see Statutes ⊕174 et seq., 222 et seq.

Encyclopedias
  Construction and operation of statutes in general; construction with reference to
    other laws, see C.J.S. Statutes §§ 311 et seq., 362 et seq.

Law Reviews
  AIDS-related benefits equation: Costs times needs divided by applicable law.
    Peter D. Blanck, Clifford H. Schoenberg and James P. Tenney, 211 N.Y.L.J.
    1 (Feb. 28, 1994).
  An employer's guide to the Americans with Disabilities Act: From job qualifica-
    tions to reasonable accommodations. Lawrence P. Postol and David D.
    Kadue, 24 J. Marshall L.Rev. 693 (1991).
  Beyond reasonable accommodation: Availability and structure of a cause of action
    for workplace harassment under the Americans with Disabilities Act.
    Frank S. Ravitch, 15 Cardozo L.Rev. 1475 (1994).
  ERISA preemption and its efforts on capping the health benefits of individuals
    with AIDS: a demonstration of why the United States health and insurance
    systems require substantial reform. Comment, 30 Hous.L.Rev. 1347 (1993).
  Of diagnoses and discrimination: Discriminatory nontreatment of infants with
    HIV infection. Mary A. Crossley, 93 Colum.L.Rev. 1581 (1993).
  Uncharted waters: ADA's insurance and employee benefits exemption. David C.
    Feola, 22 Colo.Law. 961 (1993).

WESTLAW ELECTRONIC RESEARCH
Statutes cases: 361k[add key number].
See, also, WESTLAW guide following the Explanation pages of this volume.

NOTES OF DECISIONS

Relationship to other laws
    Generally   1
    Workers' compensation laws   2
___

**1. Relationship to other laws—General-
ly**

  Plaintiffs are free to bring suit under
both state statutes and ADA, to extent
those state statutes are consistent with
accomplishment of federal purpose stated
in ADA. Wood v. County of Alameda,
N.D.Cal.1995, 875 F.Supp. 659.

2. ——— Workers' compensation laws

  Exclusive remedy provision, but not
substantive protections, of California's
Workers' Compensation Act was

preempted by the ADA; Congress did not
intend ADA to defer to such exclusivity
provisions, but rather intended that compliance with federal law not excuse compliance with applicable state statutes
which establish higher standards, and
giving effect to exclusive remedy provision in manner limiting availability of
federal remedies would stand as obstacle
to Congress' purpose in enacting ADA of
providing federal remedy for disability
discrimination. Wood v. County of
Alameda, N.D.Cal.1995, 875 F.Supp. 659.

  Trial court in workers' compensation
proceeding in which employee seeks total
and permanent disability benefits is not
required to consider effects of Americans
with Disabilities Act (ADA) on employ-

ILLUSTRATION 11-5	Statutory Pocket Part, from *United States Code Annotated* (paper source)

residency and internship programs would regard the annotation as a signal of invalidity, and had not proven that his scores were comparable to non-accommodated scores. Doe v. National Bd. of Medical Examiners, C.A.3 (Pa.) 1999, 199 F.3d 146.

Fourth-year medical student who suffered from dyslexia was not entitled to permanent mandatory injunction requiring national medical examination board, which administered examinations which physicians must pass to be licensed, to allow him accommodation of additional time beyond standard eight-hour period in which to complete step two examination, in order to provide a reasonable accommodation for his claimed disability under ADA; student, who passed step one examination without extra time, failed to show that he would suffer irreparable harm, as no showing was made that his impairment would substantially impair a major life activity without accommodation. Biank v. National Bd. of Medical Examiners, N.D.Ill.2000, 130 F.Supp.2d 986.

SUBCHAPTER IV—MISCELLANEOUS PROVISIONS

§ 12201. Construction

LIBRARY REFERENCES

Law Review and Journal Commentaries

Employer health-care plans: Feasibility of disability-based distinctions under ERISA and the Americans With Disabilities Act. Susan Nanovic Flannery, 12 Hofstra Lab.L.J. 211 (1995).

Insurance provisions under the ADA: how will it impact employee benefits? Lawrence Z. Lorber & Kenneth J. Raphael, 39 Fed.B.News 87 (1992).

Paving the path to parity in health insurance coverage for mental illness: New law or merely good intentions? Brian D. Shannon, 68 U.Colo. L.Rev. 63 (1997).

Self-insured group medical plans: A search for protection of benefits. 22 Cap.U.L.Rev. 749 (1993).

Simplifying the Disabilities Act. John P. Furfaro and Maury B. Josephson, 214 N.Y.L.J. 3 (Nov. 3, 1995).

Subterfuge: Do coverage limitations and exclusions in employer-provided health care plans violate the Americans with Disabilities Act? 69 N.Y.U.L.Rev. 850 (Oct./Nov. 1994).

Title I: Protecting the obese worker? 29 Ind.L.Rev. 207 (1995).

Who is "us" and who is "them"—Common threads and the discriminatory cut-off of health care benefits for AIDS under ERISA and the Americans with Disabilities Act. Samuel A. Marcosson, 44 Am.U.L.Rev. 361 (1994).

NOTES OF DECISIONS

Generally ½
Actuarial data 8
Bona fide plans 3
Complete denial of insurance coverage 6
Preexisting conditions clauses 7
Regulations 5
Rehabilitation Act, relationship to other laws 2a
Relationship to other laws
   Rehabilitation Act 2a
   State law 2b
State law, relationship to other laws 2b
Subterfuge generally 4

½. Generally

Decision by administrator of employer's disability plan to classify risks of mental illness, alcoholism, and drug abuse differently from physical disabilities fell within ADA's safe harbor provision for insurance companies, and thus did not constitute discriminatory denial of public accommodations. Weyer v. Twentieth Century Fox Film Corp., C.A.9 (Wash.) 2000, 198 F.3d 1104.

Safe harbor provision of ADA covering insurance industry does not require insurance company to justify its policy coverage or show actuarial data demonstrating that their plan is not a subterfuge after plaintiff makes prima facie allegation of discrimination in disability benefits. Ford v. Schering-Plough Corp., C.A.3 (N.J.) 1998, 145 F.3d 601, certiorari denied 119 S.Ct. 850, 525 U.S. 1093, 142 L.Ed.2d 704.

"Risk classification," for purposes of safe harbor provision of Americans with Disabilities Act (ADA) protecting insurers engaged in underwriting and classifying risks, refers to the identification of risk factors and the groupings of those factors which pose similar risks. Zamora-Quezada v. HealthTexas Medical Group of San Antonio, W.D.Tex.1998, 34 F.Supp.2d 433.

Safe harbor provisions of Americans with Disabilities Act (ADA) permit insurers subject to ADA as public accommodations to base decisions in underwriting, classifying, or administering risks upon either actuarial principles or reasonably anticipated experience. Carparts Distribution Center, Inc. v. Automotive Wholesaler's Ass'n of New England, Inc., D.N.H.1997, 987 F.Supp. 77.

Insurers retain their safe harbor exemption from public accommodation provisions of Americans with Disabilities Act (ADA) so long as their underwriting decisions are in accord with sound actuarial principles, or actual or reasonably anticipated experience. Cloutier v. Prudential Ins. Co. of America, N.D.Cal.1997, 964 F.Supp. 299.

1. Relationship to other laws—Generally

South Carolina did not violate ADA's safe-harbor provision or any other part of ADA in failing to justify its long-term disability plan's separate classification of mental and physical disabilities with actuarial data. Rogers v. Department of Health and Environmental Control, C.A.4 (S.C.) 1999, 174 F.3d 431, 164 A.L.R. Fed. 775.

ILLUSTRATION 11-6   Table of Amendments and Repeals,
                           from *United States Code Annotated* (paper source)

TABLE 3—AMENDMENTS AND REPEALS

U.S.Code and U.S.C.A.		2003–108th Cong.		117 Stat. at Large and 2003 Cong. News
Title	**Sec.**	**P.L.107–**	**Sec.**	**Page**
42 (Cont'd)				
	10401(1)	36	415(1)	830
	10402(a)(2)(C)	36	401(a)	825
			415(2)(A)(i)	830
	10402(a)(2)(F)	36	415(2)(A)(ii)	830
	10402(a)(4)	36	415(2)(B)	830
	10402(a)(5)	36	401(b)	825
	10402(c)	36	401(c)(1)	825
			401(c)(2)	825
	10402(d)	36	401(c)(1)	825
	10402(e)	36	401(c)(1)	825
	10402(f)	36	401(c)(1)	825
	10402(g)	36	401(c)(1)	825
			415(3)	830
	10404(a)	36	402	825
	10404(b)(2)(A)	36	415(4)	830
	10405	36	403	825
	10407(b)	36	404(1)	826
	10407(g)	36	404(2)	826
	10408	36	415(5)	830
	10408(5)	36	405	826
	10409(a)	36	406(a)	827
	10409(b)	36	406(b)	827
	10409(c)	36	406(b)	827
	10409(d)	36	406(b)	827
	10410(a)(2)(K)	36	415(6)(A)	830
	10410(a)(3)	36	415(6)(B)(i)	830
	10410(a)(3)(D)	36	415(6)(B)(ii)	830
	10410(a)(3)(H)	36	415(6)(B)(iii)	830
	10410(g)	36	406(c)	827
	10410(h)	36	407	827
	10412(c)	36	408	827
	10413	36	409	827
	10415	36	410	827
	10416	36	411	827
	10417	36	412	829
	10418(h)	36	413(a)	830
	10418(i)	36	413(b)	830
	10419(f)	36	414	830
	10421	36	415(5)	830
	10601 nt	7	617	102
	13001b(c)(4)(B)(ii)	21	381(a)(1)(A)	667
	13001b(c)(4)(B)(iii)	21	381(a)(1)(B)	667
	13001b(c)(4)(B)(iv)	21	381(a)(1)(C)	667
			381(a)(2)	667
	13001b(c)(4)(B)(v)	21	381(a)(1)(C)	667
	13001b(c)(4)(C)	21	381(a)(1)(C)	667
	13001b(c)(4)(D)	21	381(a)(1)(C)	667
	13001b(e)(1)(B)(ii)	21	381(a)(2)	667
	13001b(e)(2)(A)	21	381(a)(2)	667
	13001b(e)(3)	21	381(a)(2)	667
	13004	21	381(b)	667
	13032(b)(1)	21	508(a)(1)	683
	13032(b)(3)	21	508(a)(4)	683
			508(a)(5)	683
	13032(b)(4)	21	508(a)(4)	683
	13032(c)	21	508(a)(2)	683
	13032(f)(1)(D)	21	508(a)(3)	683

[45]

> **Statutes in session laws in paper:**
>
> ▶ locate the pertinent law via its public law number from the code
>   or via the session laws' subject index
> ▶ study the language of the law

As complete as codes, especially annotated codes, are, you very likely
will research in session laws from time to time as well, for several reasons:

☐ Codes are designed to provide the law of the present, although they
   may provide some historical material as well. If your client's situation
   arose under law preceding that now stated or explained in the code,
   you will research in session laws (or an old code, if still available).
☐ Session laws make it possible to track changes in a statute from year
   to year, which can assist you in discerning the legislature's thinking
   and hence the intended meaning of the statute.
☐ Session laws contain all the laws enacted during a particular legislative
   session, including private laws (which affect a particular person or
   specific situation) and temporary laws that are not codified.

This discussion focuses on the federal session laws; similar sources exist at
the state level.

The official compilation of federal session laws is *United States Statutes
at Large (Statutes at Large)*. *Statutes at Large* is organized by public law
numbers. *Statutes at Large* is also available in a West publication, *United
States Code Congressional and Administrative News*. Illustration 11-7 (at page
214) is an excerpt from *Statutes at Large*, showing a portion of the Americans
with Disabilities Act as passed by Congress in 1990.

Your first task is to locate the pertinent law within the session law volumes.
Annotated codes generally provide, immediately following the text of the
statute, the public law designations for statutes currently in force; some also
provide this information for obsolete language in historical notes. If you do
not have a reference from a code or elsewhere, you may use the subject index
to the sessions laws to locate acts on your topic. Every *Statutes at Large*
volume contains an index that pertains only to the acts contained in that
volume.

Your second task is to study the law, as you would read a statute in a
code. Be sure to examine any editorial enhancements, such as cross-references
to related statutes and margin notes. Take particular note of the effective
date provision, typically located at the end of the law or in major parts of
the law.

When we researched the Canoga case, U.S.C.A. provided easy access to
Statutes at Large (as did U.S.C.S.). The text of § 12201 in U.S.C.A. is
followed by references to the public law—Pub.L. 101-336, Title V, § 501—
and session laws—104 Stat. 369. See Illustration 11-4 (at page 209). Illustration 11-7 (at page 214) shows § 12201 in session law form.

ILLUSTRATION 11-7   Public Law,
                         from *Statutes at Large* (paper source)

PUBLIC LAW 101–336—JULY 26, 1990   **104 STAT. 369**

"(i) within 180 days after the complaint is filed with such State; or
"(ii) within a shorter period as prescribed by the regulations of such State; or
"(B) the Commission determines that such State program is no longer qualified for certification under subsection (f).".
(b) CONFORMING AMENDMENTS.—The Communications Act of 1934 (47 U.S.C. 151 et seq.) is amended—
(1) in section 2(b) (47 U.S.C. 152(b)), by striking "section 224" and inserting "sections 224 and 225"; and
(2) in section 221(b) (47 U.S.C. 221(b)), by striking "section 301" and inserting "sections 225 and 301".

SEC. 402. CLOSED-CAPTIONING OF PUBLIC SERVICE ANNOUNCEMENTS.

Section 711 of the Communications Act of 1934 is amended to read as follows: 47 USC 611.

"SEC. 711. CLOSED-CAPTIONING OF PUBLIC SERVICE ANNOUNCEMENTS.

"Any television public service announcement that is produced or funded in whole or in part by any agency or instrumentality of Federal Government shall include closed captioning of the verbal content of such announcement. A television broadcast station licensee—
"(1) shall not be required to supply closed captioning for any such announcement that fails to include it; and
"(2) shall not be liable for broadcasting any such announcement without transmitting a closed caption unless the licensee intentionally fails to transmit the closed caption that was included with the announcement.".

TITLE V—MISCELLANEOUS PROVISIONS

SEC. 501. CONSTRUCTION.   42 USC 12201.

(a) IN GENERAL.—Except as otherwise provided in this Act, nothing in this Act shall be construed to apply a lesser standard than the standards applied under title V of the Rehabilitation Act of 1973 (29 U.S.C. 790 et seq.) or the regulations issued by Federal agencies pursuant to such title.
(b) RELATIONSHIP TO OTHER LAWS.—Nothing in this Act shall be construed to invalidate or limit the remedies, rights, and procedures of any Federal law or law of any State or political subdivision of any State or jurisdiction that provides greater or equal protection for the rights of individuals with disabilities than are afforded by this Act. Nothing in this Act shall be construed to preclude the prohibition of, or the imposition of restrictions on, smoking in places of employment covered by title I, in transportation covered by title II or III, or in places of public accommodation covered by title III.
(c) INSURANCE.—Titles I through IV of this Act shall not be construed to prohibit or restrict—
(1) an insurer, hospital or medical service company, health maintenance organization, or any agent, or entity that administers benefit plans, or similar organizations from underwriting risks, classifying risks, or administering such risks that are based on or not inconsistent with State law; or
(2) a person or organization covered by this Act from establishing, sponsoring, observing or administering the terms

---

Statutes in commercial electronic services:

▶ select an appropriate service and code database
▶ run one or more searches
▶ obtain and carefully study the current, correct, and complete statutory language
▶ review the annotation for additional information
▶ conduct additional searches, e.g., session laws, very recent cases, citators

---

Paper is a medium well suited to statutes. As discussed above, a statutory code is a well-organized source, accompanied by several helpful means of access—indexes, outlines, and popular name tables. In addition, you often will move back and forth through a statute, reading various sections. Thus, many lawyers research statutes primarily in paper.

On the other hand, commercial services, including Westlaw, LexisNexis, and Loislaw, provide substantial federal and state statute databases. These databases and the search methods they afford have several distinct advantages:

☐ The information is very current, because electronic publication is a quick process, and you may be alerted to very recent changes.

☐ The databases are cumulative; you need not work through several separate publications to be up to date.

☐ It is easier to use specific factual concepts as research terms. Factual research terms may not appear in a paper code's table of contents or index. But they may appear in a case description or elsewhere in the annotation of a pertinent section, and a well-crafted search will retrieve that section.

☐ You may move quite easily from one section of the statute to other sections, cases, and some secondary authorities through links.

It is important, of course, to consider the costs of using a commercial service as well.

In broad strokes, researching in a statutory database parallels researching in paper codes. You will select an appropriate source; use some means of access to identify the pertinent statute and sections; obtain and carefully study the correct and complete language of the statute; and review the annotation for additional information about the statute and other authorities, such as cases and secondary authorities. The following discussion focuses on the steps where paper and electronic media differ. As with the rest of this part, the discussion focuses on federal statutes; research in state statutes is very similar. The discussion covers the three main commercial services—Westlaw, LexisNexis, and Loislaw—together; Exhibit 11.3 summarizes the main features of each.

EXHIBIT 11.3	Commercial Services for Statutory Research		
	Westlaw	*LexisNexis*	*Loislaw*
databases	• generally option of unannotated code or annotated code • subject-specific databases • session laws • table of contents • index • popular names table	• one code (annotated or not) • subject-specific databases • session laws • table of contents	• unannotated code • session laws • table of contents
typical means of access	• key-word search in index • browse table of contents • natural-language search • terms-and-connectors search with or without component restrictions • search popular names table • retrieval function	• search or browse table of contents • natural-language search • terms-and-connectors search with or without component restrictions • retrieval function	• browse table of contents • Boolean search with or without component restrictions • retrieval function
currency and updating options	• KeyCite with status flags • search session laws • search cases database	• Shepard's • search session laws • search cases databases	• GlobalCite to obtain citing cases • search session laws • search cases databases

Select an appropriate code database. The initial decision to make is whether to search in an unannotated or annotated code. An unannotated code is smaller, and generally it is wise to search in the smallest useful database. However, the information provided in an annotation generally proves very useful; for example, the terms in your Boolean search may very well appear not in the statute itself but in a case description. Thus, the better choice overall is an annotated code. Especially if you are researching federal statutes, which are voluminous, you may want to use a subject-specific database if you know the subject of your research topic. As with all electronic research, be sure you know the scope and currency of the database, including the most recent legislative session and law covered in the database.

Run one or more searches. To identify and obtain pertinent sections, you may use various means of access, some paralleling paper research, some available only electronically. The options are many; the following lists the most commonly used, beginning with options you would use if you know fairly little about your research topic and ending with options you would use if you already know of a pertinent statute.

☐   Run a key-word search in the index only (which may be a separate database). This parallels using a paper index.

☐   Run a key-word search in or browse the table of contents (which also may be a separate database). Browsing the table of contents parallels reading the outlines of a paper code.

☐   Run a natural-language search in the entire database.

☐   Run a Boolean search in the entire database.

☐   Or run a Boolean search in certain documents in the database, e.g., the pertinent chapter identified through browsing the table of contents.

☐   Or run a Boolean search in certain components of the documents in the database. For example, if the terms you are using are very common, you may want to confine your search to the title, chapter, and section names.

☐   If you already know the name but not the citation of the statute, run a search in the popular names table or in the material at the beginning of the document. The former parallels use of a paper popular names table.

☐   If you already know the citation of the statute, use the document retrieval function to obtain the statute.

Obtain and study the statutory language. Nearly always, the statutory language you obtain through an electronic service will be the language currently in effect. Indeed this is one of the advantages of electronic media for statutory research. If the service provides a means of checking for very recent legislative activity involving the statute, be sure to do so.

In addition, to be sure you are using the correct language for your client's situation, read the information about the statute's effective date. If it appears that the current language was not in effect at the time of your client's situation, seek the correct language in a session law database.

As you read statutory material in an electronic database, take care to read the complete statute governing your client's situation. Often your search will lead you to a specific section, but you will need to read additional sections of the statute as well. Use the service's means of switching to adjacent documents, and use links to pursue cross-referenced sections.

Review the annotation. If you are researching in an annotated code, then you will obtain not only the statutory language but also the annotation. Peruse this material as you would when researching in a paper annotated code, focusing on the cases that will be particularly useful, based on jurisdiction and court as well as legal and factual similarity to your client's situation.

Conduct additional searches. Before you sign off the commercial service, you may want to conduct one or more additional searches to update and perhaps expand your research. The options include:

☐   Run a search or two in the appropriate session law database, to check for additional legislative activity. If you use the statute's citation as the search term, you will obtain amendments to the statute. If you use your research terms and not the statute's citation, you will obtain pertinent legislation that does not refer to the statute you have just read.

☐ Run a search in an appropriate case law database, using the statute's citation as a search term, perhaps also including additional search terms and employing a date restriction to focus on very recent cases. This search may yield cases that are not covered in the annotation because, e.g., they are very recent.

☐ Cite the statute. Using a citator is not necessary in researching statutes, as it is with cases. Annotated codes and session laws provide much of the information a citator provides and some in more detail, e.g., a case description in an annotated code provides more information than a case listing in a statutory citator. Nonetheless, you may find citing the statute a sound final step. You may find some new citing authorities, such as a case or law review article not covered in the annotation, and you can easily check whether the statute's constitutionality has been decided by a court.

Researching the Canoga case. We chose to research in LexisNexis, which offers U.S.C.S. Because U.S.C.S. is so massive, we chose a subject-specific statutory database, Labor & Employment > Statutes & Legislative Materials > Federal > U.S.C.S. Labor Titles 5, 8, 26, 29, 30, 38, 39 and 42. The terms-and-connectors search disabilit! /p discriminat! /p (smok! or nicotine) yielded sixty documents. Many seemed to pertain to employees of the federal government, so we added and not government. This edited search yielded five documents, including three sections of the Americans with Disabilities Act: § 12201 discussed above; § 12203, which prohibits retaliation; and § 12102, which defines "disability." For the two new sections, the references to smok! and nicotine appeared not in the statutory language, but in the case descriptions. The case discussing § 12203 involved an employee who was allergic to second-hand smoke.[6] The case discussing § 12102 holds that a prisoner with nicotine addiction is not disabled under the Americans with Disabilities Act.[7]

To check for very recent material, we ran a search in the U.S.C.S. Public Laws database with a date restrictor; there were no documents. We also ran a search for the three statutory sections along with the key factual concepts— 42 /5 (12201 or 12203 or 12102) and (smok! or nicotine)— in a database containing labor and employment cases, with a date restriction of the previous six months. This search yielded several cases brought by employees challenging smoking at their workplaces.[8]

---

6. *Muller v. Costello*, 5 A.D. Cas. 779 (N.D.N.Y. 1996). A.D. Cas. refers to a specialized reporter focused on the Americans with Disabilities Act.

7. *Brashear v. Simms*, 138 F. Supp. 2d 693 (D. Md. 2001) (Congress would not have intended to render twenty-five to thirty percent of Americans disabled; nicotine addiction is remediable, albeit not easily).

8. *E.g., Murphy v. Bd. of Educ. of Rochester City Sch. Dist.*, 273 F. Supp. 2d 292 (W.D.N.Y. 2003).

> **Statutes via public websites:**
>
> ► identify an appropriate website
> ► use the means of access afforded by the website
> ► update the results as permitted
> ► study the statute

There is an abundance of statutory material available through public websites. These websites vary quite a bit; as you assess the utility of a website, consider the following factors:

☐ the credibility of the website;
☐ the currency of the information, i.e., the most recent session and law covered;
☐ the means of access the website affords; and
☐ the extent of the information provided beyond the statutory language itself.

Depending on your research project, you also may be concerned with the website's retrospectivity, that is, how far back in time the site reaches, and its breadth of coverage, for example, whether it covers temporary and private laws.

In general, you should focus on websites maintained by the legislature itself or a similarly credible government agency. In these public websites, you can expect to find the current statutes in force, basic search options, and little information beyond the statute itself. Thus, public websites are not yet as useful as the other sources described above. However, these public websites are free.

The specific steps for researching statutes via public websites vary from site to site, but the general outline parallels the steps for researching in annotated codes in paper and researching in commercial electronic services. That is, first you must identify an appropriate website and figure out its scope of coverage. Then you must discern how you can research in the site and employ the most useful means of access. If the website permits updating, do so. Once you have obtained the statutory language and explanatory material, if any, study them carefully.

To show the variability of public legislative websites, we researched the Canoga case in both federal and New Mexico legislative websites. Not surprisingly, the options on the federal side were more plentiful and sophisticated.

At uscode.house.gov, we found federal statutes maintained by the Office of the Law Revision Counsel of the U.S. House of Representatives; this office prepares U.S.C. As of the summer of 2003, the statutes were current to either 2002 or 2001 depending on the title (U.S.C. is updated in installments). Among the features of this sophisticated website are:

☐   a retrieval function;
☐   Boolean searching;
☐   an update signal, if you search by statutory section;
☐   a classification table in which you can learn of new legislation affecting your statute;
☐   a cross-reference section in which you can learn of other statutes referring to your statute; and
☐   limited retrospectivity back to 1988.

We ran a simple Boolean search, `disability AND smoking`; this search yielded a list of twelve statutory sections, including § 12201 (listed seventh). The information provided for § 12201 was the language itself and statutory cross-references, but no case descriptions or references to secondary authorities.

At gpoaccess.gov, maintained by the federal Government Printing Office, we found a website providing the public and private laws for the 104th through the present Congress. In the 108th set, we searched for `disability and employ!`; this search yielded three laws, none on our research topic. We also entered the search `"42 USC 12201"`; this search yielded no documents.

By comparison, the New Mexico Legislature collaborates with a private publisher, Matthew Bender, which is owned by LexisNexis, to provide the current New Mexico statutes through a public website. In the summer of 2003, the website was current through the first regular session of 2003. We could work through the list of chapters and then the list of articles, or we could run a Boolean search. Both approaches brought us to the Employee Privacy Act. The version supplied through this website was unannotated, whereas the commercial publications in paper and supplied electronically through LexisNexis have extensive annotations. Compare Illustration 11-2 (at pages 193–95), which is the website version of the Employee Privacy Act, with Illustration 11-1 (at page 191), which is the commercial paper version of the New Mexico constitutional provision.

Local ordinances:

●   the clerk's office or the government's website
●   websites specializing in ordinances
●   Westlaw or LexisNexis databases

Until recently, the main source for researching the law made by cities or counties, that is, ordinances, was the clerk's office. This continues to be a practical approach. In addition, if the local government has a website, its ordinances may appear there.

Several companies publish ordinances through publicly accessible websites. These include Municipal Code Corporation, Sterling Codifiers, and American Legal Publishing. The Seattle Public Library has collected some ordinances and also provides a portal at spl.org to other website publishers of city and county ordinances. The most extensive collection is offered by Municipal Code, covering over 1,100 codes nationwide. Some of the websites, notably Municipal Code and American Legal Publishing, offer key-word searching and a browsable table of contents. Westlaw and LexisNexis also offer limited ordinance databases.

Researching the Canoga case, we could find ordinances for just over a dozen New Mexico local governments through the sources listed above, but we did not find Taos ordinances. If Ms. Canoga's situation occurred in Albuquerque, that city's Clean Indoor Air Regulations would be of interest. Section 9-5-5-6 provides that an employer must maintain smoke-free common areas, section 9-5-5-8 provides that private residences are not subject to the smoke-free rule, and section 9-5-5-16 prohibits retaliation against an employee for exercising the rights provided in the ordinance. We found this ordinance through American Legal Publishing's website, current to spring 2003.

D.   WHAT ELSE?

More on the Constitution.   The United States Constitution is among the most analyzed legal texts in the world. *The Constitution of the United States of America: Analysis and Interpretation* is prepared by the Library of Congress and provides case summaries, historical information, and extensive commentary. Scholarly commentary includes treatises (such as those by Professors Tribe, Nowak, and Rotunda) and periodicals specializing in constitutional law. Some state annotated codes also include the United States Constitution.

Conversion Tables.   If you know a session law citation or public law number for a statute but not its code citation, or if you have an outdated section number for a statute that has been renumbered, you can consult conversion tables. For example, the federal annotated codes' *Statutes at Large* tables list statutes in chronological order, by public law number, along with corresponding code sections. The federal annotated codes' tables of revised titles show where renumbered sections now appear.

KeyCite Alert.   When you use this Westlaw service, you ask Westlaw to monitor the KeyCite report for a particular statute and notify you when the report changes. LexisNexis' Eclipse service also provides updating information.

Researching Uniform and Model Laws.   You are most likely to research uniform and model acts when your jurisdiction has adopted one and you are seeking information about how it has been interpreted in other jurisdictions. *Uniform Laws Annotated*, published by West and available in paper and online, functions much like an annotated code. For each act, you can discern which states have adopted it and find NCCUSL commentary, West key numbers, references to cases from various jurisdictions, and references to selected secondary sources. The Council of State Governments annually publishes its model acts in a publication entitled *Suggested State Legislation*.

Compilations of State Laws.   Should you seek information about the statutes of multiple states on a subject, you should check whether a compilation exists on that subject. The following compile state statutes on various major subjects: *Subject Compilations of State Laws; National Survey of State Laws;* and *Statutes Compared: A U.S., Canadian, Multinational Research Guide to Statutes by Subject.*

Interstate Compacts.   States may enter into agreements with each other, with the approval of Congress. These compacts appear in *Statutes at Large,* the session laws of the involved states, and *Interstate Compacts & Agencies* (a publication of the Council of State Governments). Two strong websites are csg.org (the Council of State Governments' website) and American Law Sources On-Line at lawsource.com.

Treaties.   Treaties (compacts with other countries that are ratified by Congress) are not codified into the federal code. They appear in various publications, including *Treaties and Other International Act Series, United States Treaties and Other International Agreements,* and *Treaties and International Agreements Online.* Other research options include Westlaw and LexisNexis databases and websites for particular treaties.

E.   HOW DO YOU CITE CONSTITUTIONS AND STATUTES?

The form for citing a constitutional provision is quite spare. Here are two citations to the New Mexico constitutional provision in Illustration 11-1 (at page 191):

    ☐   *Bluebook* Rule 11: N.M. Const. art. II, § 4.
    ☐   *ALWD* Rule 13: N.M. Const. art. II, § 4.

The citation forms for statutes and session laws are more elaborate. Any particular law may be located in several sources, and there is a hierarchy among them for citation purposes. *Bluebook* Rule 12's hierarchy is the current official code, the current unofficial code, official or unofficial session laws, and other sources including electronic databases. *ALWD* Rule 14's hierarchy is the official code, whether print or electronic; the unofficial code, whether print or electronic; the session laws; and the slip law.

The citation forms for these sources include an abbreviation of the publication's name; the numbers needed to permit the reader to locate the exact section(s) of interest; for most forms, a date; and, where helpful, the statute's name. Note that when you cite to a code, the date is the year of the code, not the date of enactment. By contrast, when you cite to session laws, the date is the year of enactment or the date the statute became effective.

The New Mexico Employee Privacy Act in Illustration 11-2 (at pages 193–95) would be cited slightly differently under the two citation manuals, as follows:

- ☐ *Bluebook*: N.M. Stat. Ann. §§ 50-11-1 to -6 (Michie Supp. 2000).
- ☐ *ALWD*: N.M. Stat. Ann. §§ 50-11-1 to -6 (Supp. 2000).

The federal Americans with Disabilities Act provisions found in Illustration 11-3 (at page 197) and Illustration 11-4 (at pages 208–09) would be cited the same under the *Bluebook* and *ALWD* rules, as follows:

- ☐ Citing to U.S.C.: 42 U.S.C. § 12101 (2000).
- ☐ Citing to U.S.C.A.: 42 U.S.C.A. § 12201 (West 1995).

The session law at Illustration 11-7 (at page 214) would be cited slightly differently under the *Bluebook* and *ALWD* rules, as follows:

- ☐ *Bluebook* Rule 12.4: Americans with Disabilities Act of 1990, Pub. L. No. 101-336, § 501, 104 Stat. 327, 369 (codified at 42 U.S.C. § 12101).
- ☐ *ALWD* Rule 14.7: *Americans with Disabilities Act of 1990*, Pub. L. No. 101-336, § 501, 104 Stat. 327, 369 (codified at 42 U.S.C. § 12101).

Note that we have included the title in the last two ADA examples; it could be included in the previous two as well.

The Albuquerque ordinance discussed at the end of Part C would be cited somewhat differently under the two citation manuals, as follows:

- ☐ *Bluebook* Rule 12.8.2: Albuquerque, N.M., Code § 9-5-5-8 (2003).
- ☐ *ALWD* Rule 18: Albuquerque City Code (N.M.) § 9-5-5-8 (2003).

F. SUMMARY AND LAST WORDS

Because enacted laws are primary authority, your research will be correct, comprehensive, and credible only if you excel in researching enacted laws. And to research cost-effectively, you must use the various options thoughtfully and strategically. In addition to following up on leads from other authorities, use a combination of the following practices:

☐ Use an annotated code in paper.
☐ Use session laws in paper.
☐ In a commercial electronic service, explore various databases; employ various means of access, such as browsing the table of contents or running a Boolean search; and take advantage of the updating options.
☐ Visit the legislature's website.

For instance, you may start with an annotated code and update your research in the legislature's website and a commercial cases database.

However you research, be sure to locate and carefully study the constitution, statute, or ordinance that is the correct law for your client's situation. Be sure that you have all the pertinent statutory language and the major cases discussing that language.

LEGISLATIVE PROCESS MATERIALS

A. INTRODUCTION: THE LEGISLATIVE PROCESS

1. Introduction

This chapter covers the legislative process and its relationship to the statutory sources described in Chapter 11. Part A describes the legislative process. The next two parts describe how to research legislative process materials in two rather different situations:

- ☐ Part B identifies the legislative history materials generated during the legislative process; then it explains how to locate those materials and evaluate their usefulness in discerning the legislative intent behind an *enacted law* that governs your client's situation.
- ☐ Part C covers how to track *pending legislation* to learn of its content or its progress; lawyers track pending legislation so they can counsel clients about laws that may affect their future operations and assist clients who want to participate in the legislative process.

This chapter continues to illustrate the research of the Canoga case with a focus on Congress' enactment of the Americans with Disabilities Act (ADA), which is discussed in Chapter 11. If the Act governs Ms. Canoga's situation and she can prove that her smoking is caused by an addiction to nicotine, her employer may be prohibited from discriminating against her due to that addiction. Thus, a key issue is whether nicotine addiction is a "disability" under the ADA.

2. The Legislative Process

The process of enacting a statute is similar at both the federal and state levels. The following discussion focuses on the United States Congress. See Exhibit 12.1 for a diagram of how a bill becomes law. The diagram shows a common path; not all bills follow the same path.

The legislative process typically begins with the introduction of a bill. While anyone can draft a bill, only a member of Congress can introduce a bill. Some bills have multiple sponsors, to reflect broad political support. When a bill is introduced, it is given a number, beginning with "S." for Senate or "H.R." for House of Representatives. Since bill numbering starts over again in each Congress, a complete bill number also includes the number of the Congress in which a bill was introduced. The exact same bill may be introduced in both the House and Senate; the bill then has two bill numbers, and the two bills are companion bills. Different bills on the same subject also may be introduced in either or both chambers.

After a bill is introduced, it may be referred to one or more committees, held at the desk of the chamber, or placed on a legislative calendar for floor action. A bill that is held at the desk may be placed on a calendar at any time.

If a bill is referred to a committee, the committee chair may refer the bill to one or more subcommittees, or the chair may handle the bill at the committee level. A subcommittee, the full committee, or (more rarely) both may hold a hearing on the bill. One or more of the bill's sponsors will appear. Witnesses may include representatives of the Administration and of groups affected by the proposed legislation, as well as experts on the topic. Other interested parties can submit written comments for the hearing record.

After the hearing, or at any time if there is no hearing, the subcommittee or the full committee may meet to consider and mark up the bill. If a subcommittee approves a bill (with or without amendments), it forwards the bill to the full committee. If the full committee approves the bill (with or without amendments), it prepares a committee report, setting forth its analysis and recommendations on the bill and any amendments to it, and reports the bill to its parent body.

Next, the bill goes to the floor of the House or the Senate for debate. Floor managers explain the bill and respond to questions about it. Other members may offer arguments for and against the bill, and amendments may be offered and either passed or defeated.

If the bill passes in one chamber, it becomes known as an "act," and it is sent to the other chamber. The second chamber may pass the bill without change, or it may amend the bill and return it to the first chamber. The first chamber may accept the amendment, or it may amend the amendment and return the bill to the other chamber, or it may insist on its version of the bill and request a conference committee to resolve the differences.

EXHIBIT 12.1	How a Bill Becomes Law (LexisNexis Congressional)

How a Bill Becomes Law.

Step-by-step review of the process by which a bill becomes a law, noting the pitfalls and politics involved. Includes tips relating to online research as well as research in printed or microfiche congressional information resources.

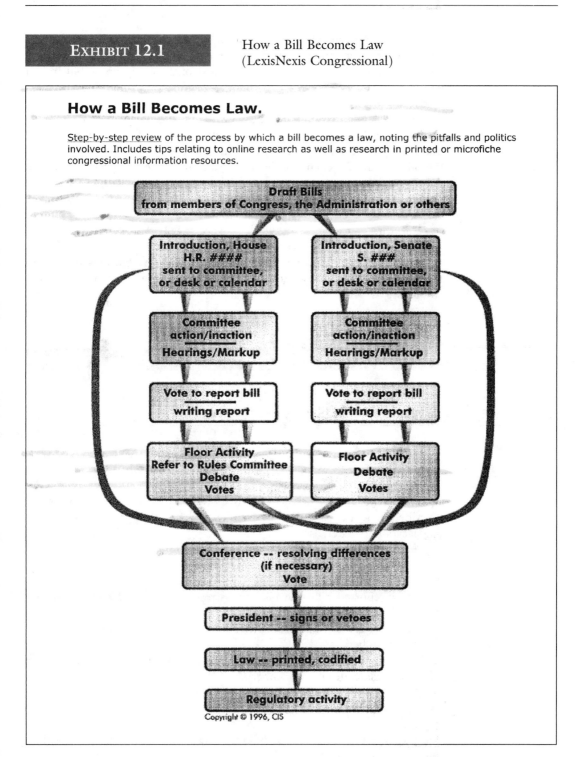

Copyright © 1996, CIS

If the second chamber agrees to a conference committee, leaders of both chambers appoint conferees. If the conferees reach agreement, they prepare a conference committee report with the text of the compromise bill and an explanation. If both chambers vote to accept the compromise bill, it is sent to the President.

The President has ten days, excluding Sundays, in which to sign or veto a bill. If the President signs a bill, the bill becomes effective upon signing, unless a different date is specified in the bill. If the President vetoes a bill, the bill and the President's objections are returned to Congress, where the bill dies unless two-thirds of each chamber vote to override the veto. If the President does not act on a bill within ten days and Congress is still in session, the bill becomes law without the President's signature. If Congress has adjourned, however, the bill dies; this is called a "pocket veto."

Each Congress has two one-year sessions. If a bill does not pass by the end of the Congress in which it was introduced, the bill dies. However, the bill may be re-introduced with a new bill number in a subsequent Congress.

B.   LEGISLATIVE HISTORY

1.   What Are Legislative History Materials?

In the broadest sense, legislative history consists of all the background and events giving rise to the enactment of a law. In a narrower sense, the term "legislative history" refers to the materials considered or created by the legislature at each stage of the legislative process. The legislative process just described generates seven categories of materials, although some legislation may lack some materials.

First, a **bill or act** is printed in various versions:

- □ an introduced bill;
- □ a reported bill—the bill as it is reported out of a committee to a particular chamber;
- □ an engrossed bill—an official copy of a bill as it passed a particular chamber;
- □ an act—the version as it passed one chamber and is printed for consideration in the other; and
- □ an enrolled act—the official version prepared for presentation to the President.

Because each version reflects a different stage in the legislative process, it is important to understand which version you are reading. In addition, sometimes you may need to examine amendments that were proposed but not adopted and that therefore never appeared in any version of the bill. Illustration 12-1 at page 230 is the first page of an introduced bill, and Illustration 12-2 at page 231 is a proposed amendment.

Second, if a **committee or subcommittee** holds a hearing, it may publish a **record of the hearing.** The record may include the witnesses' oral and written statements, committee questions and answers, statements and exhibits submitted by interested parties, and supplemental material added to the hearing record by committee members and staff. See Illustration 12-3 at page 232 for an example of hearing testimony.

Third, a committee may rely on **research reports** prepared by committee staff, consultants, the Library of Congress, or others. These reports, published as **committee prints,** may contain statistics, scientific and social studies, historical data, bibliographies, compilations of statutes, bill comparisons, and other analyses.

Fourth, a communication from the President or an executive agency, such as a message proposing or vetoing legislation, may appear as a **House or Senate document.** Reports of committee activities, the texts of committee-sponsored studies, background information reports, and some other miscellaneous materials also may be issued as House and Senate documents.

Fifth, **committee reports** typically include a description and analysis of the bill, a discussion of its background, the committee's findings and recommendations, the text of the recommended bill, any minority views, and an estimate of the costs of or revenues produced by the bill. See Illustration 12-4 at pages 233–34. Of particular importance are conference committee reports, which contain the text of the compromise bill and an analysis of how the compromise was reached.

Sixth, **floor debates and proceedings** include statements made and actions taken in a chamber of Congress. The *Congressional Record* contains more or less verbatim transcripts of floor debates and reports of proceedings, including remarks by members of Congress, their votes, proposed amendments, conference committee reports, messages from the President, and on occasion the text of the bills under consideration. The *Congressional Record* report is not a completely accurate account of what transpired because members of Congress may revise their remarks and may add extended remarks, that is, comments never made on the floor. See Illustration 12-5 at pages 235–36.

Seventh, **presidential messages** include signing statements and veto messages, as appropriate. See Illustration 12-6 on page 237.

 **ILLUSTRATION 12-1**   Senate Bill,
                              from U.S. Government Printing Office (paper source)

II

101ST CONGRESS
1ST SESSION   **S. 933**

To establish a clear and comprehensive prohibition of discrimination on the basis
of disability.

IN THE SENATE OF THE UNITED STATES

MAY 9 (legislative day, JANUARY 3), 1989

Mr. HARKIN (for himself, Mr. KENNEDY, Mr. DURENBERGER, Mr. SIMON, Mr. JEFFORDS, Mr. CRANSTON, Mr. MCCAIN, Mr. MITCHELL, Mr. CHAFEE, Mr. LEAHY, Mr. STEVENS, Mr. INOUYE, Mr. COHEN, Mr. GORE, Mr. PACK-WOOD, Mr. RIEGLE, Mr. GRAHAM, Mr. PELL, Mr. DODD, Mr. ADAMS, Ms. MIKULSKI, Mr. METZENBAUM, Mr. MATSUNAGA, Mr. WIRTH, Mr. BINGA-MAN, Mr. CONRAD, Mr. BURDICK, Mr. LEVIN, Mr. LIEBERMAN, Mr. MOYNI-HAN, Mr. KERRY, Mr. SARBANES, Mr. BOSCHWITZ, and Mr. HEINZ) intro-duced the following bill; which was read twice and referred to the Committee on Labor and Human Resources

---

A BILL

To establish a clear and comprehensive prohibition of
discrimination on the basis of disability.

1   *Be it enacted by the Senate and House of Representa-*

2   *tives of the United States of America in Congress assembled,*

3   SECTION 1. SHORT TITLE; TABLE OF CONTENTS.

4   (a) SHORT TITLE.—This Act may be cited as the

5   "Americans with Disabilities Act of 1989".

6   (b) TABLE OF CONTENTS.—The table of contents is as

7   follows:

ILLUSTRATION 12-2   Proposed Amendment to a Bill,
                            from THOMAS (electronic source)

```
THIS SEARCH        THIS DOCUMENT        THIS CR ISSUE        GO TO
Next Hit           Forward              Next Document        New CR Search
Prev Hit           Back                 Prev Document        HomePage
Hit List           Best Sections        Daily Digest         Help
                   Contents Display
```

Congressional Record article 5 of 10	*Printer Friendly Display* - 812 bytes. [Help]

ARMSTRONG (AND HATCH) AMENDMENT NO. 722 (Senate - September 07, 1989)

[Page: S10833]

Mr. ARMSTRONG (for himself and Mr. **Hatch**) proposed an amendment to the bill S. 933, supra, as follows:

At the end of the bill, add the following:

Under this act the term `disability' does not include `homosexuality,' `bisexuality,' `transvestism,' `pedophilia,' `transsexualism,' `exhibitionism,' `voyeurism,' `compulsive gambling,' `kleptomania,' or `pyromania,' `gender identity disorders,' current `psychoactive substance use disorders,' current `'psychoactive substance-induced organic mental disorders,' as defined by DSM-III-R which are not the result of medical treatment, or other sexual behavior disorders.'

ILLUSTRATION 12-3   Hearing Testimony,
                          from *CIS/Microfiche Library* (microfiche source)

5

TESTIMONY OF

EVAN J. KEMP, JR., COMMISSIONER

U. S. EQUAL EMPLOYMENT OPPORTUNITY COMMISSION

BEFORE THE HOUSE SUBCOMMITTEES ON SELECT

EDUCATION AND EMPLOYMENT OPPORTUNITIES

SEPTEMBER 13, 1989 AT 10:00 A.M.

I am here today not as a Commissioner of the U.S. Equal Employment
Opportunity Commission, but as a person with a disability. I am
100% for the Americans With Disabilities Act. But there are those
who ask "Does it make economic sense to integrate disabled people
into society?" Other people inquire "How many disabled people are
there really?" While others ask "Does it really matter? Isn't
medical science going to cure most disabling conditions?" Both
disabled people and nondisabled and politician and nonpoliticians
have all asked these questions many times.

To answer these questions and others, I have found it necessary
and helpful to have a philosophical framework to work from. I
would like to share it with you.

The disability rights movement addresses the problems of all our
citizens who are different in some respect from what society
considers to be an acceptable American: the 28 year old, 5'10",

ILLUSTRATION 12-4

Committee Report,
from *United States Code Congressional and Administrative News* (paper source)

AMERICANS WITH DISABILITIES ACT OF 1990

P.L. 101–336, see page 104 Stat. 327

DATES OF CONSIDERATION AND PASSAGE

Senate: September 7, 1989; July 11, 13, 1990
House: May 22, July 12, 1990

Senate Report (Labor and Human Resources Committee)
No. 101–116, Aug. 30, 1989
[To accompany S. 933]

House Report (Public Works and Transportation Committee) No.
101–485(I), May 14, 1990
[To accompany H.R. 2273]

House Report (Education and Labor Committee) No. 101–485(II),
May 15, 1990
[To accompany H.R. 2273]

House Report (Judiciary Committee) No. 101–485(III), May 15,
1990
[To accompany H.R. 2273]

House Report (Energy and Commerce Committee) No. 101–
485(IV), May 15, 1990
[To accompany H.R. 2273]

House Conference Report No. 101–558, June 26, 1990
[To accompany S. 933]

House Conference Report No. 101–596, July 12, 1990
[To accompany S. 933]

Cong. Record Vol. 135 (1989)

Cong. Record Vol. 136 (1990)

The Senate bill was passed in lieu of the House bill after amending its language to contain much of the text of the House bill. The House Report (Parts I (this page), II (page 303), III (page 445), IV (page 512)) is set out below and the second House Conference Report (page 565) and the President's Signing Statement (page 601) follow.

HOUSE REPORT NO. 101–485(I)

[page 1]

The Committee on Public Works and Transportation, to whom was referred the bill (H.R. 2273) to establish a clear and comprehensive prohibition of discrimination on the basis of disability, having considered the same, report favorably thereon with an amendment and recommend that the bill as amended do pass.

*   *   *   *   *

267

ILLUSTRATION 12-4   *(continued)*

LEGISLATIVE HISTORY
HOUSE REPORT NO. 101–485(I)
[page 24]

*   *   *   *   *

INTRODUCTION

The Americans With Disabilities Act (ADA) will permit the United States to take a long-delayed but very necessary step to welcome individuals with disabilities fully into the mainstream of American society. The specific provisions of the bill which lie within the jurisdiction of the Committee on Public Works and Transportation are primarily within Titles II and III, dealing with publicly and privately provided transportation services.

With regard to publicly provided transportation services, the bill requires the purchase of new transit vehicles for use on fixed route systems which are readily accessible to, and usable by, individuals with disabilities, including individuals who use wheelchairs. The bill also requires the provision of paratransit services for those individuals whose disabilities preclude their use of the fixed route system.

Transit agencies across the United States have already made some progress in the provision of accessible transit services—35% of America's transit buses are currently accessible. As more and more transit authorities make the commitment to provide fully accessible bus service, the percentage of new bus purchases which are accessible has grown to more than 50% annually. By the mid-1990's many American cities will have completely accessible fixed route systems. Furthermore, many of the transit systems in America already provide some type of paratransit services to the disabled. So, the passage of the ADA will not break sharply with existing transit policy. It will simply extend past successes to even more cities, so that this country can continue to make progress in providing much needed transit services for individuals with disabilities.

With regard to privately provided transportation services, which do not receive the high levels of federal subsidies that publicly provided services do, the requirements of the bill vary according to the size and type of vehicle, as well as according to the type of system on which the vehicle operates.

Nonetheless, in all cases, the Americans with Disabilities Act provides strong guarantees that individuals with disabilities will be

[page 25]

treated with respect and dignity while using transporatation services. After all, the Americans With Disabilities Act is ultimately a civil rights bill. The history of the United States is rich with examples of diversity triumphing over discrimination, but not so rich that this country can ever afford to exclude, or segregate in any way, the significant number of its citizens who have disabilities.

SECTION 1. SHORT TITLE; TABLE OF CONTENTS

Subsection (a) of this section provides that the Act may be cited as the "Americans with Disabilities Act of 1990".

SECTION 2. FINDINGS AND PURPOSES

This section describes the findings and purposes of the Act.

268

ILLUSTRATION 12-5

Floor Debate,
from *Congressional Record* through LexisNexis
Congressional (electronic source)

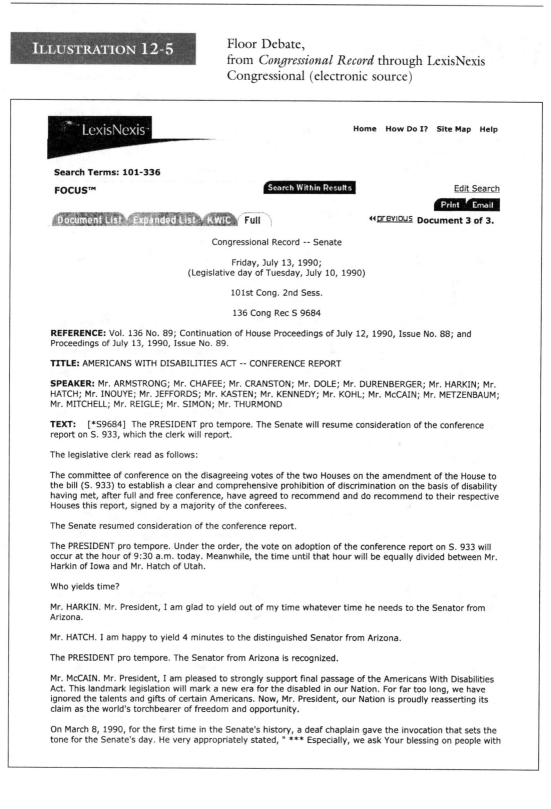

LexisNexis

Home   How Do I?   Site Map   Help

Search Terms: 101-336

FOCUS™   Search Within Results   Edit Search

Print   Email

Document List   Expanded List   KWIC   Full   ◀◀previous Document 3 of 3.

Congressional Record -- Senate

Friday, July 13, 1990;
(Legislative day of Tuesday, July 10, 1990)

101st Cong. 2nd Sess.

136 Cong Rec S 9684

REFERENCE: Vol. 136 No. 89; Continuation of House Proceedings of July 12, 1990, Issue No. 88; and Proceedings of July 13, 1990, Issue No. 89.

TITLE: AMERICANS WITH DISABILITIES ACT -- CONFERENCE REPORT

SPEAKER: Mr. ARMSTRONG; Mr. CHAFEE; Mr. CRANSTON; Mr. DOLE; Mr. DURENBERGER; Mr. HARKIN; Mr. HATCH; Mr. INOUYE; Mr. JEFFORDS; Mr. KASTEN; Mr. KENNEDY; Mr. KOHL; Mr. McCAIN; Mr. METZENBAUM; Mr. MITCHELL; Mr. REIGLE; Mr. SIMON; Mr. THURMOND

TEXT: [*S9684] The PRESIDENT pro tempore. The Senate will resume consideration of the conference report on S. 933, which the clerk will report.

The legislative clerk read as follows:

The committee of conference on the disagreeing votes of the two Houses on the amendment of the House to the bill (S. 933) to establish a clear and comprehensive prohibition of discrimination on the basis of disability having met, after full and free conference, have agreed to recommend and do recommend to their respective Houses this report, signed by a majority of the conferees.

The Senate resumed consideration of the conference report.

The PRESIDENT pro tempore. Under the order, the vote on adoption of the conference report on S. 933 will occur at the hour of 9:30 a.m. today. Meanwhile, the time until that hour will be equally divided between Mr. Harkin of Iowa and Mr. Hatch of Utah.

Who yields time?

Mr. HARKIN. Mr. President, I am glad to yield out of my time whatever time he needs to the Senator from Arizona.

Mr. HATCH. I am happy to yield 4 minutes to the distinguished Senator from Arizona.

The PRESIDENT pro tempore. The Senator from Arizona is recognized.

Mr. McCAIN. Mr. President, I am pleased to strongly support final passage of the Americans With Disabilities Act. This landmark legislation will mark a new era for the disabled in our Nation. For far too long, we have ignored the talents and gifts of certain Americans. Now, Mr. President, our Nation is proudly reasserting its claim as the world's torchbearer of freedom and opportunity.

On March 8, 1990, for the first time in the Senate's history, a deaf chaplain gave the invocation that sets the tone for the Senate's day. He very appropriately stated, " *** Especially, we ask Your blessing on people with

ILLUSTRATION 12-5   *(continued)*

disabling conditions. We pray that they receive not pity but respect; not shame but dignity; not neglect but inclusion."

Mr. President, it is time we took these words to heart. The ADA is a final proclamation that the disabled will never again be excluded, never again treated by law as second-class citizens. Each and every American has something unique and special to offer, and our Nation is a better place because of them.

I am particularly pleased to have played a part in the passage of this legislation. Over 2 years ago, I sought to ensure that our Nation's telecommunication's network was accessible to the 24 million hearing and speech impaired Americans. At that time, the Congress rightly moved to make the Federal Government's telecommunication's network fully accessible.

The telephone has become an essential part of our daily lives. For most people, it is impossible to imagine being without one. Yet for more than 100 years, deaf and hearing impaired individuals have been denied full access to the telephone. We are obligated to correct that situation. Title IV of the ADA will move us closer than ever toward granting the hearing and speech impaired the independence and greater opportunities sought in the other sections of the Americans With Disabilities Act. I am enormously gratified to see its final passage.

Mr. President, this bill is an important step in making the American dream available to all. But I urge the real champions of this legislation, the 43 million disabled Americans, to never allow their vigil to wane. The power of law is great, but it cannot change opinion or overcome prejudice. The freedom to be respected for your abilities is a tenuous concept, and the heroes of this legislation have proved that every person has value and deserve our respect and admiration.

The freedom to pursue the American dream is at the heart of what makes our Nation great. That freedom that encourages diversity makes us a stronger nation. We must never loose sight of it. I want to thank my colleagues, Senators Harkin, Hatch, Dole, and Kennedy for all they have done to make sure that those who are disabled are never again denied what is rightfully theirs, the opportunity to pursue their dreams. But most importantly, Mr. President, I thank the 43 million disabled individuals who never stopped believing in themselves, and never gave up the battle for their equal rights. Our Nation is better for their struggle.

Mr. President, I yield back the remainder of my time.

The PRESIDENT pro tempore. Who yields time?

Mr. HARKIN. Mr. President, I yield myself such time as I may consume.

The PRESIDENT pro tempore. The Senator from Iowa is recognized.

Mr. HARKIN. Mr. President, I am only going to take a minute now and reserve the balance of time toward the end of the period of time that we have before the vote.

I shall take a minute to say how proud I am of the actions the Senate and all of our friends who worked so hard on this legislation have taken. As I said, I will have more to say later, but as the chief sponsor of this bill I just could not be more proud of my fellow Senators, Members of the House, and especially people with disabilities, who have worked so hard for this day. It may be raining outside, but this is truly a day of sunshine for all Americans with disabilities.

Before I go any further, I wish to thank Senator McCain for his work on the section of the bill dealing with the relay system for deaf and hard of hearing people. That means a great [*S9685] deal to me personally and a great deal to my brother, who is deaf. I personally thank Senator McCain for all of his work, effort, and diligence.

Mr. President, I reserve about 5 or 6 minutes for myself later on, so I will yield the floor at this time.

The PRESIDENT pro tempore. The Senator from Utah [Mr. Hatch] is recognized.

Mr. HATCH. Mr. President, I am very proud to be here this morning. I believe this legislation is going to be good for America. For too long the valuable resources available to this Nation from individuals with disabilities have been wasted needlessly. Why? Because of senseless discrimination, intended or not, which subjected persons with disabilities to isolation and robbed America of the minds, the spirit, and the dedication we need

| ILLUSTRATION 12-6 | Presidential Signing Statement, from *United States Code Congressional and Administrative News* (paper source) |

SIGNING STATEMENT
P.L. 101-336

STATEMENT BY PRESIDENT OF THE UNITED STATES

STATEMENT BY PRESIDENT GEORGE BUSH UPON
SIGNING S. 933

26 Weekly Compilation of Presidential Documents 1165,
July 30, 1990

Today, I am signing S. 933, the "Americans with Disabilities Act of 1990."
In this extraordinary year, we have seen our own Declaration of Independence inspire the march of freedom throughout Eastern Europe. It is
altogether fitting that the American people have once again given clear
expression to our most basic ideals of freedom and equality. The Americans
with Disabilities Act represents the full flowering of our democratic principles, and it gives me great pleasure to sign it into law today.

In 1986, on behalf of President Reagan, I personally accepted a report
from the National Council on Disability entitled "Toward Independence." In
that report, the National Council recommended the enactment of comprehensive legislation to ban discrimination against persons with disabilities. The
Americans with Disabilities Act (ADA) is such legislation. It promises to
open up all aspects of American life to individuals with disabilities—employment opportunities, government services, public accommodations, transportation, and telecommunications.

This legislation is comprehensive because the barriers faced by individuals
with disabilities are wide-ranging. Existing laws and regulations under the
Rehabilitation Act of 1973 have been effective with respect to the Federal
Government, its contractors, and the recipients of Federal funds. However,
they have left broad areas of American life untouched or inadequately
addressed. Many of our young people, who have benefited from the equal
educational opportunity guaranteed under the Rehabilitation Act and the
Education of the Handicapped Act, have found themselves on graduation day
still shut out of the mainstream of American life. They have faced persistent discrimination in the workplace and barriers posed by inaccessible public
transportation, public accommodations, and telecommunications.

Fears that the ADA is too vague or too costly and will lead to an explosion
of litigation are misplaced. The Administration worked closely with the
Congress to ensure that, wherever possible, existing language and standards
from the Rehabilitation Act were incorporated into the ADA. The Rehabilitation Act standards are already familiar to large segments of the private
sector that are either Federal contractors or recipients of Federal funds.
Because the Rehabilitation Act was enacted 17 years ago, there is already an
extensive body of law interpreting the requirements of that Act. Employers
can turn to these interpretations for guidance on how to meet their obligations under the ADA.

The Administration and the Congress have carefully crafted the ADA to
give the business community the flexibility to meet the requirements of the
Act without incurring undue costs. Cost may be taken into account in
determining how an employee is "reasonably accommodated," whether the
removal of a barrier is "readily achievable," or whether the provision of a
particular auxiliary aid would result in an "undue burden." The ADA's
most rigorous access requirements are reserved for new construction where

601

2.   Why Would You Research Legislative History Materials?

Legislative history is a unique form of legal authority. The materials created during the legislative process are generated by a government body while creating primary authority—a statute; but they are subordinate to the statute itself. Thus, you will research in legislative history materials when the meaning of a statute is difficult to discern and there is no authoritative case on point. The premise is that the statute should be interpreted so as to effectuate legislative intent, which may be revealed in legislative history materials.

Legislative history research is not without controversy. At the state level, some courts and legislatures disfavor the use of legislative history as a source of the legislature's intent, so you should determine a jurisdiction's stance toward these materials before researching in them. In addition, although a state legislature may produce the materials described above, those materials generally are not readily available; for example, you may have to listen to tapes at a state law library. Thus, researching the legislative history of a state statute is an unusual step.

It is far more common to research the legislative history of a federal statute, at least when a significant issue arises as to its meaning and the client can afford the expense. As you will see in Part B3 below, researching the legislative history of a federal statute is quite possible, although often time-consuming and sometimes tedious. In the right circumstances, the federal courts fairly readily accept legislative history as indicating Congress' intent. This part thus focuses on federal legislative history.

As you work with legislative history materials, keep in mind that the legislature may not have had any intent as to your client's situation. Legislators may not have thought of your client's situation, or circumstances may have changed since the statute's enactment. Even if you find a legislative statement on point, that statement may itself be ambiguous or inconclusive. Or you may find conflicting statements. Also keep in mind that some legislative history materials are weightier than others, the key factors being who generated the materials, how the materials were generated, and how closely they relate to the law as enacted (rather than earlier versions). The hierarchy of legislative documents is as follows:

- ☐ The various versions of a bill as well as rejected and adopted amendments generally are very persuasive evidence of legislative intent.
- ☐ Committee reports are usually considered key documents because they are formally adopted by the committee that has expertise on the topic and the responsibility of making a recommendation on the bill. Conference committee reports are especially important because they arise late in the legislative process and explain the resolution of differences between the House and Senate.
- ☐ Hearing records typically carry less weight. While they may contain useful information, most of the testimony is not given by those who vote on the bill and may reflect the bias of those testifying.

- [ ] Floor debates are controversial because legislators sometimes seek to use them to establish a reading of the legislation that they were unable to incorporate into the statute itself. Nevertheless, courts do rely on floor debates, particularly points made by the bill's sponsors.
- [ ] Committee prints are less commonly used but may contain useful factual background and information from which you can infer the concerns of the legislature.
- [ ] Reports of executive branch agencies also are less commonly used but may discuss the problems that a law was designed to remedy.
- [ ] The executive's action in approving or vetoing a bill may provide indirect evidence of legislative intent, particularly for legislation passed after a veto.

A final word to the wise: To use legislative history materials properly, you must acquaint yourself thoroughly with your law's full legislative history. Otherwise, you will be at risk of relying on unrepresentative fragments.

3. How Do You Research Legislative History?

As you no doubt have surmised, the legislative process and the materials it produces can be lengthy and complicated. Your research in these materials entails four tasks:

(1) identifying the public law;
(2) identifying the legislative steps leading to that law's enactment and the materials generated at each step;
(3) identifying a source for those materials; and
(4) locating, reading, and analyzing the materials.

The following text discusses five practices in federal legislative history research, summarized in Exhibit 12.2. Although other options exist, the five presented here are widely used and involve very credible sources. In brief, they are:

- [ ] Derive information from the statutory code, which serves as the transition from researching the statute to researching its history.
- [ ] Read a key document or two in *United States Code Congressional and Administrative News*, which is a quick and sometimes sufficient option.
- [ ] Work through a compiled legislative history, a more exhaustive and exhausting option available only for major statutes.
- [ ] Explore the materials available through LexisNexis Congressional, an electronic commercial service, and the related paper source, Congressional Information Service.
- [ ] Explore the materials available through THOMAS, an electronic service provided by the Library of Congress.

| EXHIBIT 12.2 | Overview of Legislative History Research |
| | |

Practice	Legislative History Material	Strengths and Weaknesses
Statutory Code	Citations: public law, *Statutes at Large*, U.S.C.C.A.N. (U.S.C.A. only). Text: perhaps textual explanation of amendments.	Good starting point. Only basic citations. No text of documents.
United States Code Congressional and Administrative News	Citations: *Congressional Record*, committee and conference committee reports. Text: reprints or excerpts of one or more committee reports and perhaps a signing statement.	Easiest paper source to use. Includes key documents. Content is limited.
Compiled Legislative History	Citations: varies—may be comprehensive. Text: varies—may be complete for a major law.	May be comprehensive. Manageable because focused on one law. Electronic sources permit key-word and natural-language searching. Available only for fairly major laws.
LexisNexis Congressional & Congressional Information Service	Citations: bills, committee hearings, committee prints, House and Senate documents, committee and conference committee reports, *Congressional Record* debate, presidential signing statements, and public law (depending on how major the law is). Text: wide range of documents (some electronically, some in microfiche).	L.N.C. offers comprehensive citations, links from some citations to documents, full-text searching. C.I.S. offers strong indexing, abstracts, and several points of access. Full-text coverage of documents on L.N.C. begins with 1985 and is quite limited until 1995.
THOMAS	Citations: bills, committee and conference committee reports, floor actions, public law. Text: bills and amendments, *Congressional Record*, committee reports, limited coverage of House hearings.	Provides free access to current information. Affords links to text of amendments and *Congressional Record*. Citation coverage begins in 1973; full-text coverage in 1989 and limited before 1995. Coverage of hearings is limited. Does not contain committee prints or House or Senate documents.

Information technology has had a major impact on legislative history research. Lawyers used to have to visit a federal depository library, use paper indexes, read documents in microfilm or microfiche, and for some materials obtain documents from the Government Printing Office. Now legislative history research involves very current statements of legislative history, searches run in extensive and easily accessible databases, and links from source to source. Unfortunately, electronic sources do not extend backward in time much beyond the last two decades, so for older statutes, you still will engage in a much more cumbersome process. This chapter focuses on the options available for fairly recent statutes, because lawyers generally research the legislative history of recent statutes. Should you need to research the legislative history of an older statute, you would do well to consult with a reference librarian at a federal depository library.

Legislative history in statutory codes:

▶ record all information about the bill and its enactment process

---

Before you set aside the code in which you have researched the statute itself, examine the historical notes following the statute. The amount and type of information will vary depending on the code you are using. For example, the three federal codes all provide the following information:

☐ the public law number and section,
☐ the date of approval,
☐ and the *Statutes at Large* (session laws) citation for the original and amending legislation as well as information about the changes made through the various amendments.

United States Code Annotated also refers to one or more documents printed in *United States Code Congressional and Administrative News*, a basic legislative history source described below. See Illustration 12-7 at page 242.

Researching the Canoga case, we focused on § 12102 of the ADA, which defines "disability." From U.S.C.A., we learned that this provision derives from § 3 of Public Law 101-336, approved July 26, 1990, and found in session law form at page 329 of volume 104 of *Statutes at Large*. We also learned that U.S.C.C.A.N. provides three documents: a House report, a House conference report, and the President's statement.

ILLUSTRATION 12-7   Legislative History References in Statutory Code,
                                           from *United States Code Annotated* (paper source)

---

42 § 12101   OPPORTUNITY FOR THE DISABLED   Ch. 126
Note 7

7. Schools and universities

University's blanket policy prohibiting assignment of roommates to students with disabilities who require personal attendant care unnecessarily separated students with disabilities from those without disabilities and, thus, struck at essence of Americans with Disabilities Act (ADA) and specifically violated statute's stated purpose to provide clear and comprehensive national mandate for elimination of discrimination against individuals with disabilities.   Coleman v. Zatechka, D.Neb. 1993, 824 F.Supp. 1360.

§ 12102. Definitions

As used in this chapter:

(1) **Auxiliary aids and services**

The term "auxiliary aids and services" includes—

(A) qualified interpreters or other effective methods of making aurally delivered materials available to individuals with hearing impairments;

(B) qualified readers, taped texts, or other effective methods of making visually delivered materials available to individuals with visual impairments;

(C) acquisition or modification of equipment or devices; and

(D) other similar services and actions.

(2) **Disability**

The term "disability" means, with respect to an individual—

(A) a physical or mental impairment that substantially limits one or more of the major life activities of such individual;

(B) a record of such an impairment; or

(C) being regarded as having such an impairment.

(3) **State**

The term "State" means each of the several States, the District of Columbia, the Commonwealth of Puerto Rico, Guam, American Samoa, the Virgin Islands, the Trust Territory of the Pacific Islands, and the Commonwealth of the Northern Mariana Islands.

Pub.L. 101–336, § 3, July 26, 1990, 104 Stat. 329.)

HISTORICAL AND STATUTORY NOTES

Revision Notes and Legislative Reports
1990 Acts. House Report No. 101–485(Parts I–IV), House Conference Report No. 101–596, and Statement by President, see 1990 U.S. Code Cong. and Adm. News, p. 267.

CROSS REFERENCES

Auxiliary aids and services as defined in this section for purposes of national service trust fund program, see 42 USCA § 12581.

> **Legislative history in *United States Code Congressional and Administrative News* (U.S.C.C.A.N.):**
>
> ▶ locate pertinent materials through a U.S.C.A. reference, public law number, *Statutes at Large* cite, or the subject index
> ▶ read the opening material to obtain references to additional materials and proceedings
> ▶ read the materials reprinted in U.S.C.C.A.N.

U.S.C.C.A.N., published by West, is a convenient source of session laws and up to several legislative history documents for major laws. It does not, however, contain all or even most of the documents for a law. It is an accessible source often used early in legislative history research.

Each set of bound volumes covers a particular session of Congress and contains two sections: reprints of the *Statutes at Large* session laws and the legislative history documents. The two sections typically appear in separate volumes, and both are organized by public law number.

You can locate the legislative history material for your law by using the reference in U.S.C.A., locating the materials by public law number, finding the reference in the *Statutes at Large* section of U.S.C.C.A.N., or looking up your research terms in the subject index. Once you locate the pertinent material, note the information on the opening page. The legislative history section of U.S.C.C.A.N. typically provides the following for a public law:

- ☐ its public law number and its *Statutes at Large* citation,
- ☐ the dates of consideration and passage of the legislation by both chambers,
- ☐ the numbers of the House and Senate bills,
- ☐ the committees to which the bills were assigned,
- ☐ the numbers and dates of committee reports,
- ☐ the numbers and dates of conference committee reports, and
- ☐ the volumes and years of the *Congressional Record* in which the debates appear.

U.S.C.C.A.N. typically provides one or more committee reports and perhaps also a presidential signing statement. The committee reports are edited to remove duplicative or less helpful information; omissions are shown by asterisks, and the official page numbers are in brackets.

Westlaw's U.S.C.C.A.N. database contains portions of U.S.C.C.A.N. with coverage varying by type of document, for example, public laws since 1973, House and Senate reports since 1948, presidential signing statements since 1986. U.S.C.C.A.N. on Westlaw affords terms-and-connectors and natural-language searching, which can be useful when your research topic is a narrow one captured in distinctive search terms.

When you read a legislative history document, proceed carefully:

- [ ] Read all or most of the document. At least scan parts that may seem off-point; you may find helpful information in a surprising location.
- [ ] Keep an open mind about what you will find. You may indeed find a statement directly and specifically addressing your research topic, or you may find only broad statements about the law's purpose, or you may need to rely on the facts known to and emphasized by legislators.
- [ ] Also, look for both favorable and unfavorable statements, as you would in any other legal authority.
- [ ] Guard against placing too much weight on a sentence or two; be sure to note the context of each pertinent statement.
- [ ] Finally, be sure to examine how influential the pertinent statements were. For example, you should not rely on a statement by a proponent of an amendment that was soundly defeated.

Researching the Canoga case, we found a fairly typical U.S.C.C.A.N. legislative history for the ADA. The opening material, shown in Illustration 12-4 at page 233, reveals that the House and Senate considered separate bills, the Senate bill was enacted, the legislation generated two committee reports (one of which was written by four House committees) as well as two conference committee reports, and debate on the law spanned two years. U.S.C.C.A.N. provides citations and dates for the materials listed.

U.S.C.C.A.N. has reprints of the House committee report, the second conference committee report, and President Bush's signing statement, each fairly typical in the type of information provided:

- [ ] Shown in part in Illustration 12-4 at page 234, the House committee report includes each committee's recommendation on the bill; the text of the bill as recommended by each committee; section-by-section summaries of the bill; concurring and dissenting views of individual committee members; reports from the Congressional Budget Office, estimating the cost of the ADA as proposed by each committee; and analysis of changes that the bill as recommended would make in existing law.
- [ ] The House conference committee report catalogs the differences between the House and Senate bills and notes which version prevailed.
- [ ] Shown in Illustration 12-6 at page 237, the presidential signing statement explains the origins of the bill, counters arguments against the ADA, and highlights the need for public education on the ADA.

Unfortunately, none of the documents address the issue of whether nicotine addiction is a disability under the ADA.

We also ran the search `nicotine /p addiction` in Westlaw's U.S.C.C.A.N. database. We obtained forty documents, many related to appropriations for the Departments of Labor, Health and Human Services, and Education or to the National Great American Smokeout Day, none pertaining to the ADA. Another approach is to restrict the search to the reports on the law you are researching by adding a citation restriction, for example, `CI (101-485 & 101-596)`.

> **Compiled legislative histories:**
>
> ▶ consult a bibliography of compiled legislative histories, and procure and peruse the compilation
> ▶ or identify and search a LexisNexis or Westlaw database for your statute

If your research project merits further consideration of the law's legislative history, you should determine whether there exists a compiled legislative history, that is, a collection of pertinent legislative materials or citations to those materials. As a general rule, compiled legislative histories exist for legislation of widespread importance.

To find out whether a compiled legislative history exists for your law, consult a source such as Nancy P. Johnson, *Sources of Compiled Legislative Histories: A Bibliography of Government Documents, Periodical Articles, and Books*, or Bernard D. Reams, *Federal Legislative Histories: An Annotated Bibliography and Index to Officially Published Sources*. Illustration 12-8 at page 246 is a page from the Johnson bibliography. For each law, the table lists its compiled legislative histories, stating for each compiled history the standard bibliographic information; some means by which to find it, such as its Library of Congress classification number; and the citations and documents provided.

Your next task is, of course, to obtain the compiled history and peruse its contents. Some legislative histories are voluminous, others smaller and less complete. Some have an index, others only a table of contents.

For some major statutes, LexisNexis and Westlaw offer legislative history databases. The chief advantages of an electronic compilation are the availability of key-word and natural-language searching and the ability to search all documents simultaneously.

Researching the Canoga case, we learned from the Johnson bibliography that several publications about the ADA's legislative history exist, in various types of sources. The most extensive is the next-to-last entry, Reams' six-volume set, which provides reports, hearings, and debates. See Illustration 12-8 at page 246.

Both LexisNexis and Westlaw have legislative history databases for the Americans with Disabilities Act. We searched Westlaw's ADA database, which was compiled by the law firm of Arnold & Porter. The database includes the public law, committee reports, the bill and amendments, the hearing record, excerpts of congressional debate, and other miscellaneous transcripts. Our full-text search `employee /s smok!` yielded no documents.

ILLUSTRATION 12-8	Bibliography of Compiled Legislative Histories, from *Sources of Compiled Legislative Histories* (paper source)

PUBLIC LAW BILL NUMBER	STATUTE	ACT ENTRY	CONTENTS — ACTUAL DOCS.			CONTENTS — CITES TO DOCS.		
			REPORTS	HEARINGS	DEBATES	DISCUSSION	LISTS	CITES
101-280 H.J.Res.553	104 Stat. 149	ETHICS REFORM ACT OF 1989: TECHNICAL AMENDMENTS **Tax Management Primary Sources**, 101st Congress, Wash., D.C.: Bureau of National Affairs, 1989.	X					
101-311 H.R. 4612	104 Stat. 267	BANKRUPTCY: SWAP AGREEMENTS & FORWARD CONTRACTS **Collier on Bankruptcy**, 15th ed., N.Y.: Matthew Bender, 1993, Legislative History: App. vols.			X			
101-336 S. 933	104 Stat. 327	AMERICANS WITH DISABILITIES ACT OF 1990 **Americans with Disabilities Act of 1990: Law & Explanation**, Chicago, IL: Commerce Clearing House, 1990. L.C.: KF480.A958 1990					X	X
		The Americans with Disabilities Act: A Practical and Legal Guide to Impact, Enforcement, and Compliance, Wash., D.C.: Bureau of National Affairs, 1990. L.C.: KF480.A957 1990					X	X
		Americans with Disabilities Act: A Survey of the Law, Regulations and Legislative History, New York, N.Y.: Practising Law Institute, 1992.					X	X
		BNA's Americans with Disabilities Act Manual, Wash., D.C.: Bureau of National Affairs, 1992. L.C.: KF480.A6B7	X					X
		The Disabled in the Workplace: Analysis of the Americans with Disabilities Act, N.Y.: Research Institute of America, 1990.					X	X
		Arlene Mayerson, The Americans with Disabilities Act— An Historic Overview, 7 Labor Lawyer 1 (1991).					X	X
		Henry H. Perritt, Jr., **Americans with Disabilities Act Handbook**, 2d ed., New York: Wiley, 1991. L.C.: KF3469.P47 1991					X	X
		Bernard D. Reams, Jr. et al., **Disability Law in the United States: A Legislative History of the Americans with Disabilities Act of 1990, P.L. 101-336**, 6 vols., Buffalo, N.Y.: Hein, 1992. L.C.: KF480.A32A15 1992	X	X	X			
		John G. Tysse & Edward E. Potter, **The Legislative History of the Americans with Disabilities Act**, Horsham, PA: LRP Publications, 1991. L.C.: KF480.A32A15	X	X				

> **Legislative history materials through LexisNexis Congressional and Congressional Information Service:**
>
> ▶ search for and review the law's legislative history statement
> ▶ link to and read potentially pertinent documents
> ▶ obtain additional documents from the related paper collection, Congressional Information Service
> ▶ conduct a key-word search

LexisNexis Congressional (L.N.C.) is a commercial electronic service, provided by although separate from LexisNexis, that is based on an extensive paper and microfiche source, Congressional Information Service (C.I.S.). For relatively recent legislation, from 1970 to date, L.N.C. provides a statement of the main events in a statute's enactment process. In addition, L.N.C. provides some documents, although the coverage varies somewhat; for example, coverage of the *Congressional Record* dates to 1985, bills to 1989, and committee reports to 1989. Finally, L.N.C. is easy to navigate, so it is a leading source even though it is a fairly recent service.

To research a specific law, you would search in the CIS Legislative Histories component by entering the public law number, bill number, or *Statutes at Large* citation. The statement thus obtained includes the following information:

☐ the law's title and a summary of the law;
☐ the bill numbers;
☐ descriptions of debates as reported in the *Congressional Record*;
☐ the titles, dates, and numbers of committee reports;
☐ the same information for committee hearings;
☐ the same information for committee prints; and
☐ a reference to presidential remarks.

See Illustration 12-9 at pages 249–53. Note that the Legislative History statement covers not only the session in which the law was enacted but also previous sessions, if any, in which Congress considered related legislation.

The Legislative History statement includes a link to a bill tracking report for the bill that passed. This report provides the statute's legislative chronology, step by step, including referrals to committees, additions of sponsors, and proposals and actions on amendments.

In addition to noting the law's legislative events, you should pursue the links in the Legislative History statement to the various listed documents. Some links lead to the text of the document. See Illustration 12-5 at pages 235–36, a *Congressional Record* excerpt obtained through L.N.C. Other links lead not to the document itself but to a detailed abstract. See Illustration 12-10 at pages 254–55. Should you be interested in reading a document based on the information in the abstract, you could obtain it in microfiche from the Congressional Information Service, which is organized by accession numbers provided in the L.N.C. abstract, for example, 90-H341-4. See Illustration 12-3 at page 232, hearing testimony obtained from the C.I.S. microfiche collection.

L.N.C. affords other means of access as well. For example, you can search the documents database by entering key words or a subject from the list prepared by L.C.N. or both. You might use this approach when you are not focusing on a particular law or when your research topic is a narrow one captured in distinctive search terms.

More cumbersome than the electronic version, the Congressional Information Service in paper and microfiche covering statutes from 1970 to date has the following major components:

- ☐ *CIS Annual/Abstracts*, which provides descriptions of various legislative history documents and is organized by a system of accession numbers;
- ☐ *CIS Annual Index*, which contains detailed indexes, e.g., by subject or bill number, listing the CIS accession numbers of pertinent documents;
- ☐ *Legislative Histories of U.S. Public Laws*, which is a collection of the Legislative History statements discussed above in regard to LexisNexis Congressional; and
- ☐ the microfiche collection, which encompasses hearing records, committee reports and prints, and other documents.

The first two components are updated on a monthly basis.

Researching the Canoga case, we used LexisNexis Congressional. We first obtained the legislative history statement for Public Law 101-336. See Illustration 12-9 at pages 249–53. We linked to the last item listed in the debates entry, when the Senate agreed to the conference report. We found there Illustration 12-5 at pages 235–36. Of interest is Senator McCain's reference to "43 million disabled Americans"; this number would seem to be too low to include all smokers who could claim addiction to nicotine. We also linked to the hearing abstracts and found the September 13, 1989, hearing before the House Subcommittee on Employment Opportunities of particular interest because it included testimony from a member of the federal Equal Employment Opportunity Commission. See Illustration 12-10 at pages 254–55, the hearing abstract, and Illustration 12-3 at page 232, a page from that testimony obtained from the C.I.S. microfiche collection. We also ran key-word searches for employee smoking and nicotine addiction but obtained no documents.

ILLUSTRATION 12-9   Legislative History Statement,
                          from LexisNexis Congressional (electronic source)

LexisNexis

Home   How Do I?   Site Map   Help

Search Terms: 101-336

FOCUS™   Search Within Results   Edit Search
                                                                      Print   Email

Document List   Expanded List   KWIC   Full   **Document 1 of 1.**

CIS Legislative Histories
Copyright © 1990, Congressional Information Service, Inc.

90 CIS PL 101336; 101 CIS Legis. Hist. P.L. 336

LEGISLATIVE HISTORY OF: P.L. **101-336**

TITLE: Americans with Disabilities Act of 1990

CIS-NO: 90-PL101-336
CIS-DATE: December, 1990
DOC-TYPE: **Legislative History**
DATE: July 26, 1990
LENGTH: 52 p.
ENACTED-BILL: 101 S. 933 Retrieve Bill Tracking report
STAT: 104 Stat. 327
CONG-SESS: 101-2
ITEM-NO: 575

SUMMARY:
"To establish a clear and comprehensive prohibition of discrimination on the basis of disability."

Prohibits discrimination against disabled individuals in employment and public transportation, accommodations, and services.

Establishes a general definition of disability.

TITLE I, EMPLOYMENT.

Restricts use of pre-employment medical examinations and inquiries by employers, labor organizations, and employment agencies. Requires employers to make reasonable accommodations to the limitations of otherwise qualified job applicants or employees with disabilities.

Requires HHS to disseminate a list of infectious and communicable diseases transmissible by handling food.

Provides that the powers and civil and administrative remedies of the EEOC and Department of Justice under the Civil Rights Act of 1964 shall apply to employment discrimination against the disabled.

TITLE II, PUBLIC SERVICES.

Prohibits State and local governments and Amtrak from excluding from programs or services disabled individuals who meet specified eligibility requirements if reasonable modifications of policies or removal of barriers would enable them to participate.

Provides that enforcement for discrimination against the disabled by public entities shall be the remedies in the Rehabilitation Act of 1973.

Requires new vehicles purchased by public entities operating fixed route transportation systems to be readily accessible to and usable by the disabled.

ILLUSTRATION 12-9   *(continued)*

Requires public entities operating fixed route transportation systems to provide paratransit services for individuals whose disabilities preclude the use of the fixed route system.

Requires Amtrak and all commuter rail systems to have at least one car per train readily accessible to and usable by disabled individuals within five years.

Requires Amtrak and key commuter stations to be made readily accessible to disabled individuals within specified time frames.

TITLE III, PUBLIC ACCOMMODATIONS AND SERVICES OPERATED BY PRIVATE ENTITIES.

Prohibits discrimination on the basis of disability by private businesses and other providers of goods, services, or accommodations. Requires businesses to remove barriers and make reasonable modifications of policies in order to provide equal benefits to the disabled, unless such changes are not readily achievable or would result in undue hardship.

Requires OTA to conduct a study to determine transportation access needs of the disabled, and the most cost-effective method of providing disabled individuals with access to buses and bus services.

Requires the Department of Justice to issue regulations regarding prohibition of discrimination in privately owned accommodations and services and DOT to issue regulations on land-based public transportation services.

TITLE IV, TELECOMMUNICATIONS.

Amends the Communications Act of 1934 to require that all telephone common carriers provide relay services for the hearing-impaired and speech-impaired so that they can communicate with persons who are not impaired. Extends FCC regulatory authority to intrastate common carriers for purposes of implementing the relay services requirement.

Requires closed-captioning of all TV public service announcements produced using Federal funds.

TITLE V, MISCELLANEOUS PROVISIONS.

Includes a provision to require the Architectural and Transportation Barriers Compliance Board to issue guidelines for removal of barriers that make goods and services inaccessible to the disabled.

Provides that nothing in the Wilderness Act shall be construed as prohibiting use of wheelchairs in wilderness areas.

Prohibits discrimination on the basis of disability by members of Congress and legislative branch employees.

Amends the Rehabilitation Act of 1973 to revise definitions and make conforming amendments.

CONTENT-NOTATION: Discrimination against the handicapped, prohibition

BILLS: 100 H.R. 192; 100 H.R. 1546; 100 H.R. 4498; 100 S. 2345; 101 H.R. 2273; 101 H.R. 3171; 101 H.R. 4807; 101 S. 1452

DESCRIPTORS:
    AMERICANS WITH DISABILITIES ACT; DISCRIMINATION AGAINST THE HANDICAPPED; DISCRIMINATION IN EMPLOYMENT; TRANSPORTATION OF THE HANDICAPPED; MEDICAL EXAMINATIONS AND TESTS; LABOR UNIONS; EMPLOYMENT SERVICES; DEPARTMENT OF HEALTH AND HUMAN SERVICES; GOVERNMENT INFORMATION AND INFORMATION SERVICES; COMMUNICABLE DISEASES; FOOD POISONING; EQUAL EMPLOYMENT OPPORTUNITY COMMISSION; DEPARTMENT OF JUSTICE; CIVIL RIGHTS ACT; ADMINISTRATIVE LAW AND PROCEDURE; CIVIL PROCEDURE; FEDERAL-STATE RELATIONS; FEDERAL-LOCAL RELATIONS; NATIONAL RAILROAD PASSENGER CORP.; ARCHITECTURAL BARRIERS; RAILROAD ROLLING STOCK; MOTOR BUS LINES; TRANSPORTATION REGULATION; GOVERNMENT AND BUSINESS; OFFICE OF TECHNOLOGY ASSESSMENT; DEPARTMENT OF TRANSPORTATION; TELECOMMUNICATION REGULATION; COMMUNICATIONS ACT; TELEPHONE AND TELEPHONE INDUSTRY; HEARING AND HEARING DISORDERS; SPEECH DISORDERS; TELEVISION; FEDERAL COMMUNICATIONS COMMISSION; REHABILITATION ACT; ARCHITECTURAL AND TRANSPORTATION BARRIERS COMPLIANCE BOARD; WILDERNESS ACT; WILDERNESS

ILLUSTRATION 12-9   *(continued)*

AREAS; CONGRESSIONAL EMPLOYEES

REFERENCES:

DEBATE:

135 Congressional Record, 101st Congress, 1st Session - 1989
  Sept. 7, Senate consideration and passage of S. 933, p. S10701.

136 Congressional Record, 101st Congress, 2nd Session - 1990
  May 17, House consideration of H.R. 2273, p. H2410.
  May 22, House consideration of H.R. 2273, consideration and passage of S. 933 with an amendment, and tabling of H.R. 2273, p. H2599.
  May 24, House insistence on its amendments to S. 933, request for a conference, and appointment of conferees, p. H3070.
  June 6, Senate disagreement to the House amendments to S. 933, agreement to a conference, and appointment of conferees, p. S7422.
  June 26, Submission in the House of the conference report on S. 933, p. H4169.
  July 11, Senate passage of motion to recommit the conference report on S. 933, p. S9527.
  July 12, Submission in the House of the second conference report on S. 933, and House agreement to the conference report, p. H4582.
  July 13, Senate agreement to the conference report on S. 933, p. S9684.

REPORTS:

101st Congress

S. Rpt. 101-116 on S. 933, "Americans with Disabilities Act of 1989," Aug. 30, 1989.
  CIS NO: 89-S543-11
  LENGTH: 107 p.
  SUDOC: Y1.1/5:101-116

H. Rpt. 101-485, pt. 1 on H.R. 2273, "Americans with Disabilities Act of 1990," May 14, 1990.
  CIS NO: 90-H643-1
  LENGTH: 65 p.
  SUDOC: Y1.1/8:101-485/pt.1

H. Rpt. 101-485, pt. 2 on H.R. 2273, "Americans with Disabilities Act of 1990," May 15, 1990.
  CIS NO: 90-H343-6
  LENGTH: 167 p.
  SUDOC: Y1.1/8:101-485/pt.2

H. Rpt. 101-485, pt. 3 on H.R. 2273, "Americans with Disabilities Act of 1990," May 15, 1990.
  CIS NO: 90-H523-8
  LENGTH: 94 p.
  SUDOC: Y1.1/8:101-485/pt.3

H. Rpt. 101-485, pt. 4 on H.R. 2273, "Americans with Disabilities Act of 1990," May 15, 1990.
  CIS NO: 90-H363-9
  LENGTH: 83 p.
  SUDOC: Y1.1/8:101-485/pt.4

H. Rpt. 101-558, conference report on S. 933, "Americans with Disabilities Act of 1990," June 26, 1990.
  CIS NO: 90-H343-12
  LENGTH: 87 p.
  SUDOC: Y1.1/8:101-558

H. Rpt. 101-596, conference report on S. 933, "Americans with Disabilities Act of 1990," July 12, 1990.
  CIS NO: 90-H343-20
  LENGTH: 91 p.
  SUDOC: Y1.1/8:101-596

ILLUSTRATION 12-9   *(continued)*

HEARINGS:

100th Congress

"Hearing on Discrimination Against Cancer Victims and the Handicapped," hearings before the Subcommittee on Employment Opportunities, Committee on Education and Labor. House, June 17, 1987.
   CIS NO: 88-H341-4
   LENGTH: iii+115 p.
   SUDOC: Y4.Ed8/1:100-31

"Americans with Disabilities Act of 1988," hearings before the Subcommittee on the Handicapped, Senate Labor and Human Resources Committee, and the Subcommittee on Select Education, House Education and Labor Committee, Sept. 27, 1988.
   CIS NO: 89-S541-17
   LENGTH: v+96 p.
   SUDOC: Y4.L11/4:S.hrg.100-926

"Oversight Hearing on H.R. 4498, Americans with Disabilities Act of 1988," hearings before the Subcommittee on Select Education, Committee on Education and Labor. House, Oct. 24, 1988.
   CIS NO: 89-H341-36
   LENGTH: v+235 p.
   SUDOC: Y4.Ed8/1:100-109

101st Congress

"Americans with Disabilities Act of 1989," hearings before the Subcommittee on the Handicapped, Committee on Labor and Human Resources. Senate, May 9, 10, 16, June 22, 1989.
   CIS NO: 89-S541-37
   LENGTH: v+849 p.
   SUDOC: Y4.L11/4:S.hrg.101-156

"Joint Hearing on H.R. 2273, the Americans with Disabilities Act of 1989," hearings before the Subcommittee on Select Education and the Subcommittee on Employment Opportunities, Committee on Education and Labor. House, July 18, 1989.
   CIS NO: 89-H341-81
   LENGTH: iii+146 p.
   SUDOC: Y4.Ed8/1:101-37

"Americans with Disabilities Act of 1989," hearings before the Subcommittee on Civil and Constitutional Rights, Committee on the Judiciary. House, Aug. 3, Oct. 11, 12, 1989.
   CIS NO: 90-H521-37
   LENGTH: iv+446 p. il.
   SUDOC: Y4.J89/1:101/58

"Field Hearing on Americans with Disabilities Act," hearings before the Subcommittee on Select Education, Committee on Education and Labor. House, Aug. 28, 1989.
   CIS NO: 90-H341-2
   LENGTH: iii+112 p.
   SUDOC: Y4.Ed8/1:101-56

"Hearing on H.R. 2273, the Americans with Disabilities Act of 1989," hearings before the Subcommittee on Employment Opportunities and the Subcommittee on Select Education, Committee on Education and Labor. House, Sept. 13, 1989.
   CIS NO: 90-H341-4
   LENGTH: iii+168 p.
   SUDOC: Y4.Ed8/1:101-51

"Americans with Disabilities Act," hearings before the Subcommittee on Surface Transportation, Committee on Public Works and Transportation. House, Sept. 20, 26, 1989.
   CIS NO: 90-H641-25

ILLUSTRATION 12-9   *(continued)*

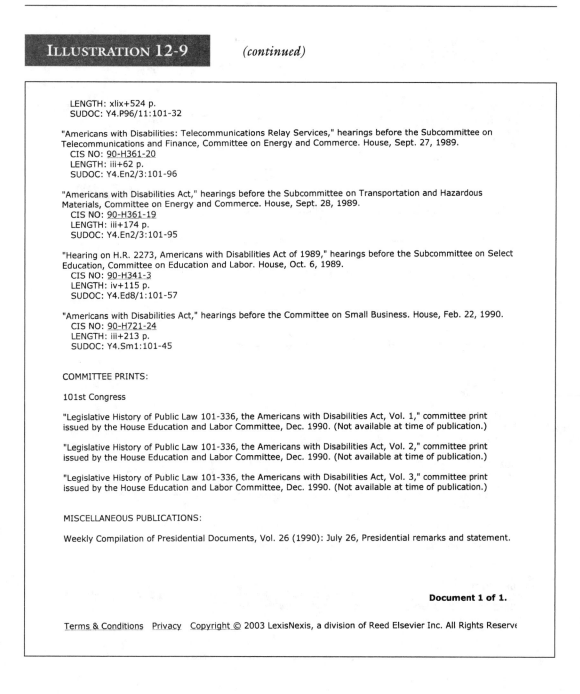

LENGTH: xlix+524 p.
SUDOC: Y4.P96/11:101-32

"Americans with Disabilities: Telecommunications Relay Services," hearings before the Subcommittee on Telecommunications and Finance, Committee on Energy and Commerce. House, Sept. 27, 1989.
    CIS NO: 90-H361-20
    LENGTH: iii+62 p.
    SUDOC: Y4.En2/3:101-96

"Americans with Disabilities Act," hearings before the Subcommittee on Transportation and Hazardous Materials, Committee on Energy and Commerce. House, Sept. 28, 1989.
    CIS NO: 90-H361-19
    LENGTH: iii+174 p.
    SUDOC: Y4.En2/3:101-95

"Hearing on H.R. 2273, Americans with Disabilities Act of 1989," hearings before the Subcommittee on Select Education, Committee on Education and Labor. House, Oct. 6, 1989.
    CIS NO: 90-H341-3
    LENGTH: iv+115 p.
    SUDOC: Y4.Ed8/1:101-57

"Americans with Disabilities Act," hearings before the Committee on Small Business. House, Feb. 22, 1990.
    CIS NO: 90-H721-24
    LENGTH: iii+213 p.
    SUDOC: Y4.Sm1:101-45

COMMITTEE PRINTS:

101st Congress

"Legislative History of Public Law 101-336, the Americans with Disabilities Act, Vol. 1," committee print issued by the House Education and Labor Committee, Dec. 1990. (Not available at time of publication.)

"Legislative History of Public Law 101-336, the Americans with Disabilities Act, Vol. 2," committee print issued by the House Education and Labor Committee, Dec. 1990. (Not available at time of publication.)

"Legislative History of Public Law 101-336, the Americans with Disabilities Act, Vol. 3," committee print issued by the House Education and Labor Committee, Dec. 1990. (Not available at time of publication.)

MISCELLANEOUS PUBLICATIONS:

Weekly Compilation of Presidential Documents, Vol. 26 (1990): July 26, Presidential remarks and statement.

Document 1 of 1.

ILLUSTRATION 12-10

Abstract of Hearing Record,
from LexisNexis Congressional (electronic source)

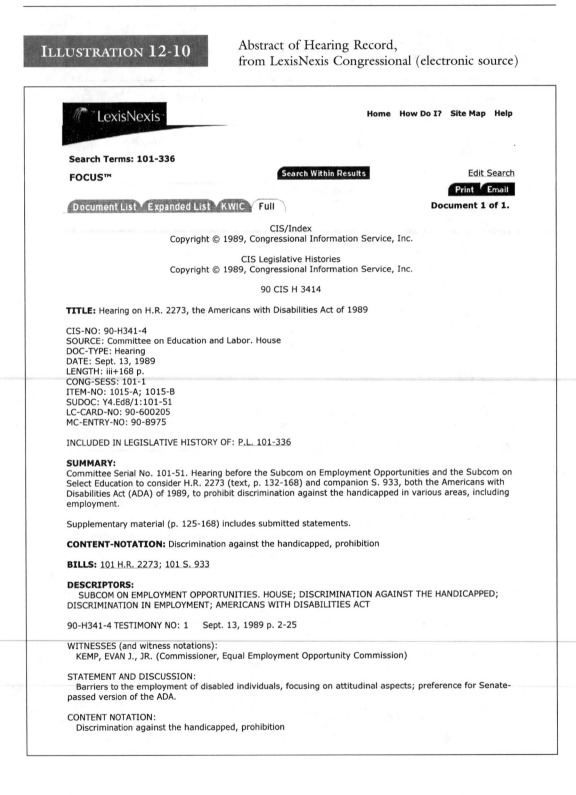

LexisNexis

Home   How Do I?   Site Map   Help

Search Terms: 101-336

FOCUS™

Search Within Results

Edit Search
Print   Email

Document List   Expanded List   KWIC   Full   Document 1 of 1.

CIS/Index
Copyright © 1989, Congressional Information Service, Inc.

CIS Legislative Histories
Copyright © 1989, Congressional Information Service, Inc.

90 CIS H 3414

TITLE: Hearing on H.R. 2273, the Americans with Disabilities Act of 1989

CIS-NO: 90-H341-4
SOURCE: Committee on Education and Labor. House
DOC-TYPE: Hearing
DATE: Sept. 13, 1989
LENGTH: iii+168 p.
CONG-SESS: 101-1
ITEM-NO: 1015-A; 1015-B
SUDOC: Y4.Ed8/1:101-51
LC-CARD-NO: 90-600205
MC-ENTRY-NO: 90-8975

INCLUDED IN LEGISLATIVE HISTORY OF: P.L. 101-336

SUMMARY:
Committee Serial No. 101-51. Hearing before the Subcom on Employment Opportunities and the Subcom on
Select Education to consider H.R. 2273 (text, p. 132-168) and companion S. 933, both the Americans with
Disabilities Act (ADA) of 1989, to prohibit discrimination against the handicapped in various areas, including
employment.

Supplementary material (p. 125-168) includes submitted statements.

CONTENT-NOTATION: Discrimination against the handicapped, prohibition

BILLS: 101 H.R. 2273; 101 S. 933

DESCRIPTORS:
   SUBCOM ON EMPLOYMENT OPPORTUNITIES. HOUSE; DISCRIMINATION AGAINST THE HANDICAPPED;
DISCRIMINATION IN EMPLOYMENT; AMERICANS WITH DISABILITIES ACT

90-H341-4 TESTIMONY NO: 1   Sept. 13, 1989 p. 2-25

WITNESSES (and witness notations):
   KEMP, EVAN J., JR. (Commissioner, Equal Employment Opportunity Commission)

STATEMENT AND DISCUSSION:
   Barriers to the employment of disabled individuals, focusing on attitudinal aspects; preference for Senate-
passed version of the ADA.

CONTENT NOTATION:
   Discrimination against the handicapped, prohibition

ILLUSTRATION 12-10   *(continued)*

TESTIMONY DESCRIPTORS:
  PUBLIC OPINION; EQUAL EMPLOYMENT OPPORTUNITY COMMISSION

90-H341-4 TESTIMONY NO: 2   Sept. 13, 1989 p. 26-124

WITNESSES (and witness notations):
  ROCHLIN, JAY F. (Executive Director, President's Committee on Employment of People with Disabilities)
  DONOVAN, MARK R. (Manager, Community Employment and Training Programs, Marriott Corp)
  RASMUSSEN, DUANE A. (President and Chief Executive Officer, Sell Publishing Co.; representing National Federation of Independent Business, Minnesota Newspaper Association, and Independent Business Association of Minnesota)
  WHAREN, PAUL D. (Project Manager, Thomas P. Harkins, Inc.; representing Associated Builders and Contractors)
  MAYERSON, ARLENE B. (Directing Attorney, Disability Rights Education and Defense Fund)

STATEMENTS AND DISCUSSION:
  Experiences in the development and implementation of programs to facilitate employment of disabled individuals; differing perspectives on H.R. 2273 and companion S. 933, including business concerns regarding employment-related provisions.
  Aspects of prejudice against disabled persons; review of studies on nature and extent of disability-based employment discrimination; analysis of employment-related provisions of the ADA; review of case law stemming from employment discrimination prohibitions under the Rehabilitation Act of 1973; need for the ADA.

CONTENT NOTATION:
  Discrimination against the handicapped, prohibition

TESTIMONY DESCRIPTORS:
  SOCIAL SCIENCE RESEARCH; PRESIDENT'S COMMITTEE ON EMPLOYMENT OF PEOPLE WITH DISABILITIES; BUSINESS; CASE LAW; REHABILITATION ACT; MARRIOTT CORP.; NATIONAL FEDERATION OF INDEPENDENT BUSINESS; MINNESOTA NEWSPAPER ASSOCIATION; INDEPENDENT BUSINESS ASSOCIATION OF MINNESOTA; ASSOCIATED BUILDERS AND CONTRACTORS; DISABILITY RIGHTS EDUCATION AND DEFENSE FUND

Document 1 of 1.

Legislative history through THOMAS:

▶ pull up the entry for your law in the Bill Summary & Status service
▶ review the All Bill Summary & Status Info report
▶ link to and read potentially pertinent documents
▶ conduct a key-word search

In 1995, the Library of Congress introduced THOMAS, a free web-based legislative information service located at thomas.loc.gov. THOMAS tracks the history of bills, beginning with bills introduced in 1973. Its full-text coverage begins later: bills from 1989, the *Congressional Record* from 1989, committee reports from 1995, and selected hearing transcripts from 1997.

THOMAS provides several means of access. Most of the time, the best option is to search by public law number in the Bill Summary & Status service for the session that passed your law. Then link to and peruse the All Bill Summary & Status Info for your law, which lists the events in the law's legislative process in great detail as well as summarizes what is available through the other links. From these two starting points, link to and read potentially pertinent information or documents from the following categories:

☐ bill titles;
☐ bill status with amendments, which lists in great detail the legislative actions on the bill from introduction to presidential action;
☐ committee reports;
☐ related bill details;
☐ amendments;
☐ co-sponsors;
☐ summary of the law; and
☐ text of legislation, which includes various versions, e.g., introduced, reported, engrossed, enrolled.

A particular strength of THOMAS is its extensive coverage of amendments. See Illustration 12-2 at page 231, an amendment, and Illustration 12-11, at page 257, information on the voting on that amendment.

Another option is to conduct a key-word search in one of the document databases, such as committee reports or the *Congressional Record*. This approach entails selecting a session and then keying in your search terms for a full-text search or a search of the index.

Researching the Canoga case, we started with the All Bill Summary & Status Info. We noted with particular interest Senate amendment No. 722, seeking to exclude users of certain drugs, which passed the Senate on September 7, 1989. See Illustration 12-2 at page 231. Congress apparently focused on addiction to other drugs, but this amendment does not clearly address nicotine addiction.

ILLUSTRATION 12-11 Amendment Information,
from THOMAS (electronic source)

Bill Summary & Status for the 101st Congress

Item 18 of 22

PREVIOUS | NEXT
NEW SEARCH | HOME | HELP

S.AMDT.722
Amends: S.933
Sponsor: Sen Armstrong, William L. [CO] (submitted 9/7/1989) (proposed 9/7/1989)

AMENDMENT PURPOSE:
To more clearly define the term "disability".

TEXT OF AMENDMENT AS SUBMITTED: CR S10833

STATUS:

> **9/7/1989:**
> > Proposed by Senator Armstrong.
> **9/7/1989:**
> > Amendment SP 722 agreed to in Senate by Voice Vote.

COSPONSORS(1):

> Sen Hatch, Orrin G. - 9/7/1989 [UT]

We would have run a search in the committee reports database, but its coverage did not extend back far enough to include the 101st Congress. We did run a search for `nicotine addiction` in the *Congressional Record* for the 101st Congress. This yielded twenty-seven documents, including a statement by Senator Armstrong, the proponent of amendment No. 722. In explaining "impulse control . . . and drug-related disorders," he noted the very wide scope of the concept of mental impairment and appended a well-known manual of mental disorders, which includes nicotine withdrawal.[1]

4.   What Else?

More about Congressional Information Service. For older statutes, CIS provides an index, in paper and through LexisNexis Congressional, to the Serial Set (see below) covering 1789 to 1969 as well as the documents themselves in microfiche. CIS also provides paper and electronic indexes and microfiche sets of hearing records, committee prints, and executive documents and reports for pre-1970 legislation.

Congressional Masterfile 1 and *Congressional Masterfile 2* are CD-ROM products providing CIS materials for pre-1970 and 1970-1998 legislation.

The United States Congressional Serial Set. The Serial Set has been published in one form or another, under one title or another, since 1789 by the Government Printing Office. It includes committee reports, House and Senate documents (including presidential statements), and some committee prints.

Congressional Record. The *Congressional Record*, the primary source for debates and votes, is issued on a daily basis and re-issued in annual volumes. The daily version has four separately paginated parts: Senate; House; extensions of remarks; and the daily digest, which summarizes a day's proceedings. The annual *Congressional Record* includes a History of Bills and Resolutions, which provides a brief description of a bill and its key events.

Weekly Compilation of Presidential Documents. This publication is the primary source of presidential signing and veto statements. It is issued weekly and is accompanied by weekly, quarterly, and annual indexes.

GPO Access. The Government Printing Office has long provided copies of federal government documents. Recently, it has made many documents available through the website gpoaccess.gov. At present, the following documents are available from the year listed to date: history of bills from 1983, published bills from 1993, the *Congressional Record* from 1994, hearings from 1997, and committee prints from 1997. You may search the documents from the current session or search the archives.

1. 135 Cong. Rec. S11,173 (1989).

LexisNexis and Westlaw Databases.   In addition to the databases featured above, LexisNexis and Westlaw both provide databases composed of categories of legislative history documents, for example, bill texts from a recent session, the *Congressional Record.*

State Legislative History.   Researching state legislative history generally is not easy. Before embarking on state legislative history research, consult your state legislative website; consult with your state's legislative reference librarian; or consult a text on state legislative history, such as *State Legislative Sourcebook: A Resource Guide to Legislative Information in the Fifty States.*

5.   How Do You Cite Legislative Materials?

Each type of legislative history document has its own citation requirements.

Enacted bills are cited as statutes unless they are used to document legislative history, in which case they are cited as unenacted bills. Unenacted bills are cited with the chamber's abbreviation, the bill number, the number of the Congress, the section number (if any), and the year or date. The name of the bill may be included; if the unenacted bill can be found in a published hearing record or report, that information may be added. Here are two examples:

- ☐ *Bluebook* Rule 13.2: S. 933, 101st Cong. § 1 (1989).
- ☐ *ALWD* Rule 15.1: Sen. 933, 101st Cong. § 1 (May 9, 1989).

The form for a hearing transcript includes the subject matter title, the bill number, the names of the subcommittee (if any) and the committee, the number of the Congress, the page number, the year (or date, for *ALWD*), and identifying information about the witness. Here are two examples:

- ☐ *Bluebook* Rule 13.3: *Americans with Disabilities Act of 1989: Hearing on H.R. 2273 Before the Subcomm. on Employment Opportunities and the Subcomm. on Select Education of the House Comm. on Education and Labor*, 101st Cong. 5 (1989) (statement of Evan J. Kemp, Commissioner, EEOC).
- ☐ *ALWD* Rule 15.7: H.R. Subcomm. on Empl. Opportunities & Subcomm. on Select Educ. of the Comm. on Educ. & Lab., *Americans with Disabilities Act: Hearing on H.R 2273*, 101st Cong. 5 (Sept. 13, 1989).

For committee reports, the form includes the name of the chamber, the numbers of the Congress and the report, page number (if you are citing a particular page), and year or date. If the report is published in U.S.C.C.A.N., a U.S.C.C.A.N. citation should be added. Here are two examples:

- ☐ *Bluebook* Rule 13.4: H.R. Rep. No. 101-485(I) (1990), *reprinted in* 1990 U.S.C.C.A.N. 267.

☐   *ALWD* Rule 15.9: H.R. Rpt. 101-485(I) (May 14, 1990) (reprinted in 1990 U.S.C.C.A.N. 267).

Congressional debates are cited to the *Congressional Record*; the permanent version must be cited if available. The speaker should be identified. Here are two examples:

☐   *Bluebook* Rule 13.5: 136 Cong. Rec. S9,684 (daily ed. July 13, 1990) (statement of Sen. McCain).
☐   *ALWD* Rule 15.12: 136 Cong. Rec. S9,684 (daily ed. July 13, 1990) (statement of Sen. McCain).

C.   PENDING LEGISLATION

Legislative process sources can be used not only to research the legislative history of enacted statutes but also to track the status of pending legislation. Although statutes generally operate prospectively, some clients wisely seek to know about probable future laws so that they can plan ahead. Also, some clients may want to engage in the lobbying process in the hopes of influencing future legislation.

As for federal legislation, two of the sources described in Part B operate in much the same way for pending legislation as they do for enacted laws. THOMAS provides All Bill & Summary Info and legislative documents for pending legislation. LexisNexis Congressional provides a bill-tracking report on pending legislation that parallels its Legislative History statements for enacted laws; it also provides similar links to legislative documents. In both sources, you can search for key words in the database of bill texts. Or if you know the number of the bill, you can use it as your search term.

Westlaw offers a bill-tracking service in its US-BILLTRK database, although the information is less complete and the links are not available. LexisNexis also offers federal bill-tracking. Westlaw also offers Billcast, which predicts a bill's chances of proceeding through each legislative step.

Unlike research into the legislative history of enacted state laws, tracking pending state legislation is fairly easily accomplished. Many state legislatures have websites providing information about activity during the current session. In addition, LexisNexis and Westlaw both provide state bill-tracking databases.

If you were an employment lawyer at the time this text was written, to keep the employers you served up to date, you would be following a federal bill seeking to expand the scope of federal anti-discrimination statutes to prohibit discrimination on the basis of sexual orientation. That bill, S. 1705, sponsored by Senator Edward Kennedy with forty-two co-sponsors, was introduced on October 2, 2003, and referred to the Senate Committee on Health, Education, Labor, and Pensions. Billcast gave it little chance of becoming law.

The New Mexico Legislature's website, legis.state.nm.us, provides a bill-finder function for the current session and several years back, which permits searching by bill number, key words in full text, or a list of bills by broad subjects. Interestingly, we found a bill on the same topic as the federal bill referred to above: prohibiting discrimination in employment based on sexual orientation or gender identity. We sought the report on that bill; could link to basic information, for example, the results of a committee's deliberation, the amendment in the House; and learned that it did indeed pass and was signed by the governor. See Illustration 12-12 at page 262, the initial screen for that bill on the New Mexico Legislature's website, and Illustration 12-13 at page 263, the bill-tracking report from Westlaw.

D.   CONCLUDING POINTS

Legislative process materials are researched for two purposes:

- ☐ legislative history: to gain insight into the legislature's intent in enacting a law and
- ☐ bill tracking: to track progress on pending legislation.

Most legislative history research involves federal statutes. For any law, there may be many documents, including various bills and amendments, hearing records, committee reports, floor debates, and presidential statements; some documents are more authoritative than others. Many legislative history sources exist, so there are many approaches. In addition to gleaning information from a statutory code, you may

- ☐ consult *United States Code Congressional and Administrative News*, which provides key documents in a highly accessible paper source as well as a Westlaw database;
- ☐ if your statute is of widespread significance, peruse a compiled legislative history in paper or through LexisNexis or Westlaw;
- ☐ explore LexisNexis Congressional along with Congressional Information Service, which provide not only information about a law's legislative process but also many of the documents generated in Congress;
- ☐ or use THOMAS, a free web-based legislative information service of the Library of Congress.

In legislative history research more than in any other area of legal research, technology has made information and documents more readily available and easier to research.

To track the status of pending legislation, which is fairly easily accomplished at both the state and federal levels, you may use some of the sources listed above, bill-tracking services on LexisNexis and Westlaw, and the legislature's own website.

ILLUSTRATION 12-12   Bill Finder,
                        from New Mexico Legislature Website (electronic source)

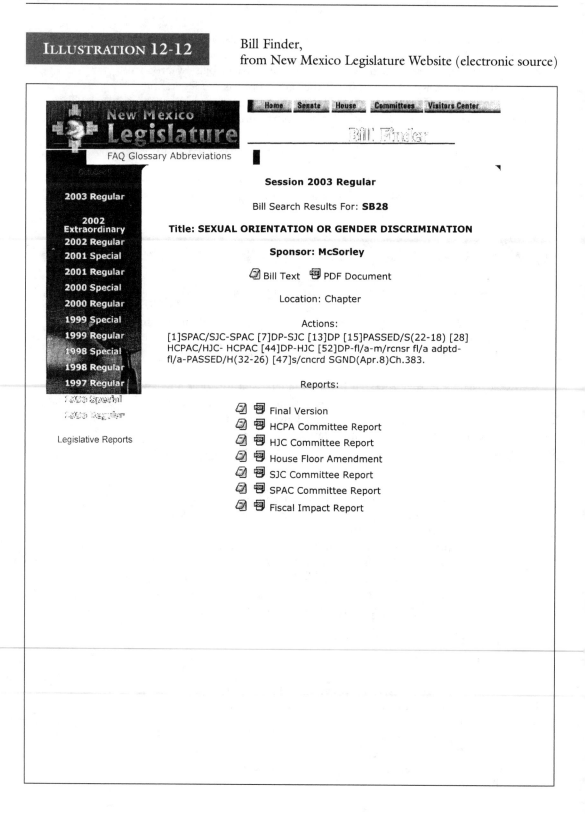

New Mexico Legislature

Home   Senate   House   Committees   Visitors Center

Bill Finder

FAQ Glossary Abbreviations

2003 Regular
2002 Extraordinary
2002 Regular
2001 Special
2001 Regular
2000 Special
2000 Regular
1999 Special
1999 Regular
1998 Special
1998 Regular
1997 Regular
1996 Special
1996 Regular

Legislative Reports

Session 2003 Regular

Bill Search Results For: **SB28**

Title: SEXUAL ORIENTATION OR GENDER DISCRIMINATION

Sponsor: McSorley

Bill Text   PDF Document

Location: Chapter

Actions:
[1]SPAC/SJC-SPAC [7]DP-SJC [13]DP [15]PASSED/S(22-18) [28]
HCPAC/HJC- HCPAC [44]DP-HJC [52]DP-fl/a-m/rcnsr fl/a adptd-
fl/a-PASSED/H(32-26) [47]s/cncrd SGND(Apr.8)Ch.383.

Reports:

Final Version
HCPA Committee Report
HJC Committee Report
House Floor Amendment
SJC Committee Report
SPAC Committee Report
Fiscal Impact Report

| ILLUSTRATION 12-13 | Bill-Tracking Report,
from Westlaw (electronic source) |

2003 NM S.B. 28 (SN)   Page 1
2003 New Mexico Senate Bill No. 28 46th Legislature - First Regular Session
(SUMMARY - STATE NET)

                          NEW MEXICO BILL TRACKING

AUTHOR: McSorley

TOPIC: LAW AND JUSTICE

SUBTOPIC: CIVIL LAW- OTHER

TITLE: Gender and Sexual Orientation Discrimination

LAST AMEND: 03/21/2003

SUMMARY: Makes it unlawful to discriminate based on sexual orientation or gender
identity; prohibits quotas based on sexual orientation or gender identity; relates
to discrimination in employment, public services and facilities, the selling or
leasing of real property, and applications for financial assistance; provides
certain exemptions to the Human Rights Act.

STATUS:
01/21/2003   INTRODUCED.
01/23/2003   To SENATE Committee on PUBLIC AFFAIRS.
01/23/2003   To SENATE Committee on JUDICIARY.
02/07/2003   From SENATE Committee on PUBLIC AFFAIRS: Do pass.
02/26/2003   From SENATE Committee on JUDICIARY: Do pass.
02/26/2003   Passed SENATE. *****To HOUSE.
02/27/2003   To HOUSE Committee on CONSUMER AND PUBLIC AFFAIRS.
02/27/2003   To HOUSE Committee on JUDICIARY.
03/15/2003   From HOUSE Committee on CONSUMER AND PUBLIC AFFAIRS: Do pass.
03/21/2003   From HOUSE Committee on JUDICIARY: Do pass.
03/21/2003   In HOUSE. Amended on HOUSE floor.
03/21/2003   Passed HOUSE. *****To SENATE for concurrence.
03/21/2003   SENATE concurred in HOUSE amendments.
03/21/2003   Eligible for GOVERNOR'S desk.
04/08/2003   Signed by GOVERNOR.
04/08/2003   Chaptered. Chapter No.

TOPIC LIST:
LABOR AND EMPLOYMENT
FAIR EMPLOYMENT PRACTICES [PRIVATE SECTOR]
Employment Discrim & Harassment [Private Sector]
Fair Employment Practices [Private Sector]- Misc
PUBLIC EMPLOYEES
Public Employees- Employment Practices- Misc
Public Employee Discrimination and Harassment
LAW AND JUSTICE
CIVIL LAW- OTHER
Civil Rights, Discrimination, Harassment- Other
CRIMINAL LAW

ADMINISTRATIVE MATERIALS

UNIT

V

In the United States, law is made not only by the judiciary and the legislature but also by administrative agencies. Administrative agencies are involved in almost every aspect of American life. They operate at the federal, state, and local levels. For some matters, a single agency may operate alone; in other fields, there may be an overlap.

Many agencies regulate an industry (such as nuclear energy); others regulate certain practices (such as employment relations) of various industries. An agency may have the power to promulgate regulations, adjudicate cases, prosecute violations of the law, inspect operations, issue licenses, or conduct studies. Some gather data (such as the Census Bureau), and some provide scientific or other expertise in a specialized field.

Agencies have two lawmaking functions: rule-making and case adjudication. Rule-making resembles legislative activity, and case adjudication resembles judicial activity. In this unit, we will use "regulation" to refer to the product of agency rule-making and "agency decision" to refer to the product of case adjudication. As to both, the agency acts in concert with and under the supervision of the legislature, executive, and courts.

☐ The legislature creates the agency through an enabling statute, which establishes the scope of the agency's authority, the goals the agency is to pursue, and the lawmaking functions it may engage in. Legislatures also oversee and fund agencies.

☐ The links between agencies and the executive vary. Typically agency commissioners are appointed by the executive, and the agency may be highly influenced by the executive on matters of policy and budget.

☐ The courts review agency actions. If a court finds the agency's action to be unconstitutional, unauthorized by the enabling statute, inadequately supported by the factual record, or insufficiently explained, it will invalidate or void the action.

Agencies generally are bound to follow not only their particular enabling statutes, but also a jurisdiction's administrative procedure act. These statutes specify how regulations may be promulgated and cases may be adjudicated.

This unit has three chapters:

☐ Chapter 13 covers regulations, with a focus on official sources.
☐ Similarly, Chapter 14 covers agency decisions, with a focus on official sources.
☐ Chapter 15 covers commercial sources that pull together a wide range of legal authorities in a specific practice area, what we have labeled "mini-libraries." Mini-libraries are especially useful in areas involving administrative agencies, so they are covered in this unit.

This unit explores a new issue in the Canoga case. Recall that Ms. Canoga's concern over the no-smoking policy was shared to some extent by her co-workers. See the Canoga case on pages 3–4. Hence, she might claim that the orchestra violated her right to act in concert with her co-workers. A federal statute, the National Labor Relations Act (NLRA), safeguards this right and enables the operations of a major federal agency, the National Labor Relations Board (Board). The Board protects employees who engage in concerted activity, whether through a union or without a union on the scene. The Board has the authority to promulgate regulations and prosecute and adjudicate cases involving violations of the NLRA, called "unfair labor practices."

This unit focuses throughout on federal law. There are analogous authorities, sources, and research methods at the state level.

REGULATIONS

A. WHAT IS A REGULATION?

Federal and state agencies promulgate various types of regulations:

- Legislative, or substantive, regulations are based on a specific statutory delegation of power from the legislature. The statute typically sets forth, in general terms, what conduct is to be regulated and what penalties may be assessed; the legislature delegates authority to the agency to provide the specific regulatory scheme, consistent with the statute.
- Interpretative regulations have substantially less force than legislative regulations; they are an agency's statement of its interpretation of its enabling statute.
- Procedural regulations address how the agency operates.

In general, when an agency promulgates a legislative regulation, it functions as a quasi-legislative body. The agency may act because its enabling statute compels it to act, because the public pressures or petitions it to do so, or because its own studies have identified an area of concern. To create the regulation, the agency may follow one of several processes, as specified in the jurisdiction's administrative procedure act or the agency's enabling statute.

☐ The dominant model is notice-and-comment rule-making, which begins when the agency gives notice to the public of the topic it is about to consider. The public may provide pertinent information to the agency through written submissions or, at the agency's discretion, through written or oral testimony at agency hearings. The agency considers these comments as it develops the final regulation and then promulgates the regulation with a statement of its basis and purpose.

☐ A less common approach is formal rule-making, which entails a trial-type hearing, in which participants may cross-examine witnesses and provide evidence. In formal rule-making, the agency must issue findings and conclusions to support its regulation.

☐ Some agencies engage in hybrid rule-making processes.

By contrast, when an agency promulgates interpretative or procedural regulations it need not engage in such a participatory process. The agency may simply issue a final regulation based on its own internal deliberations, although it may provide for public participation, in its discretion.

In form, an agency regulation resembles a statute. See Illustration 13-1 at page 269. A regulation consists of general rules applicable to a range of persons engaging in certain conduct. Regulations use fairly specific terms because they are intended to give precision to vague statutory language and are to be applied to specific situations. Many employ numerical tests or use technical concepts.

Illustration 13-1 at page 269 is one of the few regulations promulgated by the National Labor Relations Board. It pertains to the Board's exercise of jurisdiction over orchestras.

B.   WHY WOULD YOU RESEARCH REGULATIONS?

All regulations provide insight into what the law is. Indeed, a legislative regulation constitutes the law so long as the regulation meets constitutional requirements, conforms to all applicable statutes, was properly promulgated, and is not arbitrary or capricious. Somewhat in contrast, an interpretative regulation is a significant statement of the agency's interpretation of the pertinent statute, but it may be disregarded by a court that interprets the statute differently. In general, courts do defer to agencies, in recognition of their expertise. Regulations pertaining to agency procedures are important for obvious reasons: They set out the steps, timelines, and details of how to handle a case before the agency.

Agencies exist at various levels of government. Which level of agency governs a particular subject is fixed by statute. Typically, if a federal statute governs, there is a federal agency, and federal regulations will govern too.

ILLUSTRATION 13-1	Agency Regulations, from *Code of Federal Regulations* (paper source)

National Labor Relations Board §103.30

Las Vegas	8:30 a.m.–5 p.m.
29—Brooklyn	9 a.m.–5:30 p.m.
30—Milwaukee	8 a.m.–4:30 p.m.
31—Los Angeles	8:30 a.m.–5 p.m.
32—Oakland	8:30 a.m.–5 p.m.
33—Peoria	8:30 a.m.–5 p.m.
34—Hartford	8:30 a.m.–5 p.m.

[57 FR 4158, Feb. 4, 1992]

PART 103—OTHER RULES

Subpart A—Jurisdictional Standards

Sec.
103.1 Colleges and universities.
103.2 Symphony orchestras.
103.3 Horseracing and dogracing industries.

Subpart B—Election Procedures

103.20 Posting of election notices.

Subpart C—Appropriate Bargaining Units

103.30 Appropriate bargaining units in the health care industry.

Subpart E [Reserved]

Subpart F—Remedial Orders

103.100 Offers of reinstatement to employees in Armed Forces.

AUTHORITY: 29 U.S.C. 156, in accordance with the procedure set forth in 5 U.S.C. 553.

Subpart A—Jurisdictional Standards

§103.1 Colleges and universities.

The Board will assert its jurisdiction in any proceeding arising under sections 8, 9, and 10 of the Act involving any private nonprofit college or university which has a gross annual revenue from all sources (excluding only contributions which, because of limitation by the grantor, are not available for use for operating expenses) of not less than $1 million.

[35 FR 18370, Dec. 3, 1970]

§103.2 Symphony orchestras.

The Board will assert its jurisdiction in any proceeding arising under sections 8, 9, and 10 of the Act involving any symphony orchestra which has a gross annual revenue from all sources (excluding only contributions which are because of limitation by the grant-

or not available for use for operating expenses) of not less than $1 million.

[38 FR 6177, Mar. 7, 1973]

§103.3 Horseracing and dogracing industries.

The Board will not assert its jurisdiction in any proceeding under sections 8, 9, and 10 of the Act involving the horseracing and dogracing industries.

[38 FR 9507, Apr. 17, 1973]

Subpart B—Election Procedures

§103.20 Posting of election notices.

(a) Employers shall post copies of the Board's official Notice of Election in conspicuous places at least 3 full working days prior to 12:01 a.m. of the day of the election. In elections involving mail ballots, the election shall be deemed to have commenced the day the ballots are deposited by the Regional Office in the mail. In all cases, the notices shall remain posted until the end of the election.

(b) The term *working day* shall mean an entire 24-hour period excluding Saturdays, Sundays, and holidays.

(c) A party shall be estopped from objecting to nonposting of notices if it is responsible for the nonposting. An employer shall be conclusively deemed to have received copies of the election notice for posting unless it notifies the Regional Office at least 5 working days prior to the commencement of the election that it has not received copies of the election notice.

(d) Failure to post the election notices as required herein shall be grounds for setting aside the election whenever proper and timely objections are filed under the provisions of §102.69(a).

[52 FR 25215, July 6, 1987]

Subpart C—Appropriate Bargaining Units

§103.30 Appropriate bargaining units in the health care industry.

(a) This portion of the rule shall be applicable to acute care hospitals, as defined in paragraph (f) of this section: Except in extraordinary circumstances and in circumstances in which there

Similarly, if a state statute governs, you will be concerned with a state agency and its regulations. In some areas, more than one statute governs, that is, federal and state statutes overlap, and more than one regulation may apply.

To locate the correct law, you must identify the regulation in effect as of the time of your client's fact situation. A regulation is presumed to be prospective, applying to events arising after its promulgation. Hence, as you research regulations, you must attend to their currency.

As for the Canoga case, the statute on concerted activity is a federal statute, so the regulations of interest are federal regulations. Section 103.2 in Illustration 13-1 at page 269 was promulgated in 1973 and is still in force.

C. HOW DO YOU RESEARCH REGULATIONS?

Regulations currently in force appear in a code of regulations. Like a statutory code, a code of regulations is organized topically and employs a structure that may include titles, chapters, parts, and sections. Indeed, the organization of the code of regulations may parallel the organization of the statutory code, which is not surprising given that regulations derive from enabling statutes. Your regulations research will focus on the code of regulations.

Regulations also appear in a publication reporting the activities of the jurisdiction's various agencies on a frequent basis, for example, daily or weekly; a common name for this publication is "register." In addition to newly promulgated regulations, registers contain explanations of new regulations, proposed regulations, and notices of various sorts. You will research in a register for four reasons:

☐   to update your code research,
☐   to learn about the agency's thinking in promulgating the regulation,
☐   to find a regulation that has been removed,
☐   and to track proposed regulations of interest to your client.

Codes and registers typically are available in paper and electronically, in official and commercial sources. *Bluebook* Table 1 and *ALWD* Appendix 1 list the administrative codes and registers for the federal and state governments. This chapter focuses on official sources; Chapter 15 discusses commercial sources.

Only rarely will you research only the regulations. Most of the time, you also will research the enabling statute as well as agency decisions and judicial cases evaluating, interpreting, and applying the regulation. Thus this part starts with a few words about research in statutes and concludes with a few words about research in agency decisions and judicial case law. See Exhibit 13.1 for a schematic of regulations research. This part focuses on federal regulations; you will use similar sources and practices at the state level.

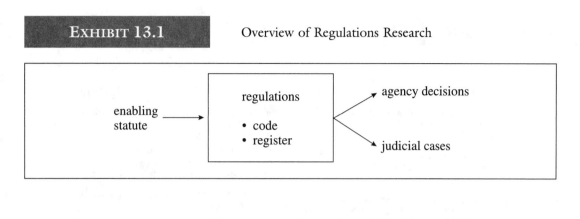

EXHIBIT 13.1   Overview of Regulations Research

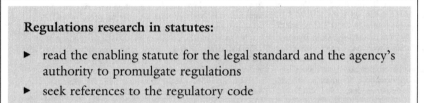

Regulations research in statutes:

▶ read the enabling statute for the legal standard and the agency's authority to promulgate regulations

▶ seek references to the regulatory code

Because an agency is created by statute and its actions must conform to that statute, an important step in regulations research is locating and reading the enabling statute. Chapter 11 covers statutory research. More specifically, as you read the statute, look for the legal standard that the legislature has set for the conduct you are concerned with as well as indications of the agency's authority to promulgate regulations. Furthermore, you should look in the annotation for references to relevant regulations. See Illustration 13-2 at pages 272–74.

Researching the Canoga case, we learned that the enabling statute states that the Board's jurisdiction extends to "employers" whose businesses "affect commerce." These terms are defined broadly, and no exclusions apply on these facts.[1] In § 164(c)(1), Congress gave the Board the authority to decline to assert jurisdiction over categories of employers when the impact on commerce is not sufficient to warrant federal involvement. The annotation in *United States Code Service* for § 164, shown in Illustration 13-2 at pages 272–74, includes general references to 29 C.F.R. parts 101 and 102 as well as a specific reference to § 103.2 of title 29; the references are to the *Code of Federal Regulations*, described below.

---

1. *See* 29 U.S.C. § 152(2), (6), (7) (2000).

| ILLUSTRATION 13-2 | Enabling Statute and Annotation, from *United States Code Service* (paper source) |

---

29 USCS § 163, n 16   LABOR

which protects against interferring with, impeding or diminishing in any way right to strike. Quaker State Oil Refining Corp. v NLRB (1959, CA3) 270 F2d 40, 44 BNA LRRM 2297, 37 CCH LC ¶ 65535, cert den (1959) 361 US 917, 4 L Ed 2d 185, 80 S Ct 261, 45 BNA LRRM 2249.

17. Miscellaneous

Strike, in which employees distribute handbills defaming quality of employer's product as concerted activity, is not protected by 29 USCS § 163. NLRB v International Brotherhood of Electrical Workers (1953) 346 US 464, 98 L Ed 195, 74 S Ct 172, 33 BNA LRRM 2183, 24 CCH LC ¶ 68000.

Union is clearly outside its legitimate function when it demands employer discharge foreman for reason that he or she is "crabby" or too-strict disciplinarian, so that strike called following employer's refusal to discharge foreman is illegal. NLRB v Aladdin Industries, Inc. (1942, CA7) 125

F2d 377, 9 BNA LRRM 548, 5 CCH LC ¶ 60879, cert den (1942) 316 US 706, 86 L Ed 1773, 62 S Ct 1310, 10 BNA LRRM 939.

Wildcat strike in which discharged employees were engaged and for which they were discharged is not such concerted action as falls within protection of 29 USCS § 157. NLRB v Draper Corp. (1944, CA4) 145 F2d 199, 15 BNA LRRM 580, 8 CCH LC ¶ 62368, 156 ALR 989.

Where employer is given notice by two unions that each of them represents his employees, and one union calls strike without offering proof of its majority representation or giving employer opportunity to request such proof or to talk to union's officials, strike is illegal; thus, company is within its rights in discharging strikers, and they are not entitled to reinstatement. Ohio Ferro-Alloys Corp. v NLRB (1954, CA6) 213 F2d 646, 34 BNA LRRM 2327, 26 CCH LC ¶ 68496.

§ 164. Supervisory employees' rights to organize—Membership as condition of employment—Local law applicable—Declination of jurisdiction by board

(a) Supervisors as union members. Nothing herein shall prohibit any individual employed as a supervisor from becoming or remaining a member of a labor organization, but no employer subject to this Act [29 USCS §§ 151–158, 159–169] shall be compelled to deem individuals defined herein as supervisors as employees for the purpose of any law, either national or local, relating to collective bargaining.

(b) Agreements requiring union membership in violation of State law. Nothing in this Act [29 USCS §§ 151–158, 159–169] shall be construed as authorizing the execution or application of agreements requiring membership in a labor organization as a condition of employment in any State or Territory in which such execution or application is prohibited by State or Territorial law.

(c) Power of Board to decline jurisdiction of labor disputes; assertion of jurisdiction by State and Territorial courts. (1) The Board, in its discretion, may, by rule of decision or by published rules adopted pursuant to the Administrative Procedure Act, decline to assert jurisdiction over any labor dispute involving any class or category of employers, where, in the opinion of the Board, the effect of such labor dispute on commerce is not sufficiently substantial to warrant the exercise of its jurisdiction: Provided, That the Board shall not decline to assert jurisdiction over any labor dispute over which it would assert jurisdiction under the standards prevailing upon August 1, 1959.

(2) Nothing in this Act [29 USCS §§ 151–158, 159–169] shall be deemed to prevent or bar any agency or the courts of any State or Territory (including the Commonwealth of Puerto Rico, Guam, and the Virgin Islands), from assuming and asserting jurisdiction over labor disputes over

30

ILLUSTRATION 13-2   *(continued)*

LABOR-MANAGEMENT RELATIONS   **29 USCS § 164**

which the Board declines, pursuant to paragraph (1) of this subsection, to assert jurisdiction.

(July 5, 1935, ch 372, § 14, 49 Stat. 457; June 23, 1947, ch 120, Title I, § 101 in part, 61 Stat. 151; Sept. 14, 1959, P. L. 86-257, Title VII, § 701(a), 73 Stat. 541.)

HISTORY; ANCILLARY LAWS AND DIRECTIVES

References in text:

"The Administrative Procedure Act," referred to in subsec. (c)(1), is Act June 11, 1946, ch 324, 60 Stat. 237, which was repealed by Act Sept. 6, 1966, P. L. 89-554, § 8, 80 Stat. 653, which re-enacted similar provisions as 5 USCS §§ 551–559, 701–706, 1305, 3105, 3344, 5362, and 7521.

Amendments:

1947. Act June 23, 1947 (effective 60 days after enactment, as provided by § 104 of such Act, which appears as 29 USCS § 151 note), amended this section generally. The section formerly related to resolution of conflicts of this Act with other laws; see 29 USCS § 165.

1959. Act Sept. 14, 1959, added subsec. (c).

CODE OF FEDERAL REGULATIONS

National Labor Relations Board–Statements of procedures, 29 CFR Part 101.

National Labor Relations Board–Rules and regulations, Series 8, 29 CFR Part 102.

CROSS REFERENCES

This section is referred to in 18 USCS § 1951.

RESEARCH GUIDE

Federal Procedure L Ed:

22 Fed Proc L Ed, Labor and Labor Relations §§ 52:878, 903, 904, 911, 934, 938.

Am Jur:

48 Am Jur 2d, Labor and Labor Relations §§ 13, 15, 16, 20, 164, 183, 271, 359, 432, 546, 628, 629, 631, 639, 649, 685, 970, 1190.

48A Am Jur 2d, Labor and Labor Relations §§ 1729, 1730, 1797, 2004, 2014.

Am Jur Proof of Facts:

Union's Breach of Duty of Fair Representation, 15 POF2d 65.

Forms:

12 Fed Procedural Forms L Ed, Labor and Labor Relations § 46:677.

WGL Coordinators:

10 Employment Coord, Coverage ¶ ¶ LR-10,702; 11,901.1; 11,904; 11,907.

11 Employment Coord, Prohibited Labor Practices ¶ ¶ LR-21,402; 22,505; 26,055; 26,677.

12 Employment Coord, Prohibited Labor Practices ¶ LR-35,005.

31

ILLUSTRATION 13-2   *(continued; pages 32–67 omitted)*

29 USCS § 164, n 94   LABOR

outside state and also purchased materials in excess of that amount, despite employer's denial of substantially identical commerce allegations in complaint without asserted reason, where, having stipulated to jurisdiction, employer is estopped from denying it in absence of valid ground. Capitan Drilling Co. (1967) 167 NLRB 144, 66 BNA LRRM 1015, 1967 CCH NLRB ¶ 21706, enforced (1969, CA5) 408 F2d 676, 70 BNA LRRM 3258, 59 CCH LC ¶ 13360.

95. Orchestras

NLRB's retail jurisdictional standard applies to orchestras performing "club dates," defined as single engagements, such as at wedding, commencement, bar mitzvah, debutante party, fashion show, or other social event; however, bands selling music to commercial enterprises are governed by the prevailing nonretail standard. Levitt (1968) 171 NLRB 739, 68 BNA LRRM 1161, 1968-1 CCH NLRB ¶ 22512.

NLRB will assert jurisdiction over symphony orchestras having gross annual revenue from all sources of not less than $1 million, excluding only contributions unavailable for use for operating expenses because of limitation by grantor. 29 CFR § 103. 2.

96. Pharmacies

Pharmacy is retail enterprise governed by monetary requirements of NLRB's retail standard. Booker Family Medical Care Center (1975) 219 NLRB 220, 89 BNA LRRM 1702, 1974-75 CCH NLRB ¶ 16041.

97. Private clubs

NLRB has jurisdiction over nonprofit corporation operating private athletic club of 2,300 members, which, in addition to health and recreation facilities, also operates restaurant and furnishes hotel-type accommodations, where during prior fiscal year club derived over $500,000 from sale of food and beverages and made direct and indirect purchases of goods in interstate commerce exceeding $50,000. Denver Athletic Club (1967) 164 NLRB 677, 65 BNA LRRM 1136, 1967 CCH NLRB ¶ 21356.

NLRB will not assert jurisdiction over employer-membership corporation, operating nonprofit singing and eating club, where employer is basically retail enterprise with annual gross income of business, not including membership dues, of less than NLRB's discretionary standard of $500,000 for assertion of jurisdiction over retail enterprise. Syracuse Liederkranz, Inc. (1967) 166 NLRB 782, 65 BNA LRRM 1645, 1967 CCH NLRB ¶ 21651.

In determining NLRB's discretionary standard for retail businesses, membership dues will not be included in calculating volume of business of membership corporation, operating nonprofit singing and eating club. Syracuse Liederkranz, Inc. (1967) 166 NLRB 782, 65 BNA LRRM 1645, 1967 CCH NLRB ¶ 21651.

98. Public transportation systems

Where interstate commerce is unquestionably involved to extent not inconsequential, question of whether NLRB will require showing by bus company of dollar-amount of interstate traffic as predicate to jurisdiction is matter of Board's policy with which court will not interfere in absence of abuse of Board's discretion. NLRB v Parran (1956, CA4) 237 F2d 373, 38 BNA LRRM 2774, 31 CCH LC ¶ 70266.

Jurisdiction will be asserted over bus company, licensed by state and federal authorities, which supplies exclusive chartered and scheduled passenger transportation to nearby United States Air Force base and serves as interstate link with large bus company and numerous commercial airlines to and from such base, where bus company is not only required to maintain adequate transportation service but also to maintain employment conditions in accordance with Air Force regulations, and where labor dispute disrupting bus service would have serious and adverse impact on national defense, in that base served by bus company is vital link in air service between North American continent and Far East, and bus service is only public mass transportation available. Simmons (1968) 171 NLRB 1469, 69 BNA LRRM 1064, 1968-1 CCH NLRB ¶ 22588, supp op (1969) 179 NLRB 641, 72 BNA LRRM 1425, 1969 CCH NLRB ¶ 21362.

NLRB would assert jurisdiction over surface transportation company having tour business and operating buses in Honolulu, where company met standard for public utility or transit system, and for nonretail enterprises. Transportation Associates of Hawaii, Ltd. (1975) 216 NLRB 357, 88 BNA LRRM 1216, 1974-75 CCH NLRB ¶ 15452.

Privately-owned toll bridge connecting mainland to island met Board's discretionary standards for jurisdiction as transit system. Margate Bridge Co. (1980) 247 NLRB 1437, 103 BNA LRRM 1335, 1980 CCH NLRB ¶ 16787.

Privately-owned toll bridge connecting mainland to island met Board's discretionary standards for jurisdiction as transit system. Margate Bridge Co. (1980) 247 NLRB 1437, 103 BNA LRRM 1335, 1980 cch NLRB ¶ 16787.

99. Public utilities

NLRB does not abuse its discretion in asserting jurisdiction over public utility by retroactively applying $250,000 "volume of business" jurisdictional standard, where, at time alleged unfair labor practice occurred, jurisdictional standard was $3,000,000 annual gross volume of business, which

---

Regulations in a regulatory code (*Code of Federal Regulations*):

▶ identify the pertinent regulation by a reference from another source, by use of the finding aids volume in paper, or by a search in the website's database
▶ read the pertinent regulation and related regulations
▶ note the administrative history information
▶ determine the currency of the code

The *Code of Federal Regulations* (C.F.R.) is a codification of the regulations promulgated by the various federal agencies that are currently in force. C.F.R. is published by the United States Government Printing Office (GPO) and is thus the official compilation of federal regulations. C.F.R. is organized topically, and the organization roughly parallels the organization of the federal statutory code. For example, labor statutes appear in title 29 of U.S.C., and labor regulations appear in title 29 of C.F.R. C.F.R. is divided into titles, chapters, parts, sections, and subunits, such as subchapters. C.F.R. is republished annually in four pieces: titles 1-16 as of January 1, titles 17-27 as of April 1, titles 28-41 as of July 1, and titles 42-50 as of October 1.

C.F.R. in paper is a large, multivolume set of softcover books. The color of the cover changes each year, so you can easily see the updating pattern. There are several ways to locate pertinent regulations in the paper C.F.R.:

☐ You may already have a reference from your research in secondary authorities and statutes.
☐ If you do not already have a reference, you may look up your research terms in the subject index in *CFR Index and Finding Aids*, a separate volume accompanying C.F.R.
☐ In the same volume, you may skim the List of CFR Titles, Chapters, Subchapters, and Parts, which outlines C.F.R. See Illustration 13-3 at page 277. Due to the organizational similarity between C.F.R. and the federal statutes, this process is quite easy if you have a statutory citation.
☐ You may use the Parallel Table of Authorities and Rules in *CFR Index and Finding Aids*. If you look up the enabling statute, you will find a reference to the corresponding regulation. See Illustration 13-4 at page 278.

One of these methods may be more effective than the others, so you should be flexible. In general, you will be able to identify a pertinent title and part, but probably not a specific section, through these methods.

The GPO also provides C.F.R. through GPO Access, its website located at gpoaccess.gov, which can be an efficient and low-cost alternative to the paper C.F.R. The content of the website version is the same as the content of the paper C.F.R. To obtain a pertinent regulation through the website version, you may:

☐   search for the regulation by its citation, if you already have a reference from your other research;

☐   browse the Parallel Table of Authorities and Rules;

☐   select a title, then browse the chapters, parts, and sections within that title;

☐   run a key-word search in the entire database, using Boolean commands, truncation, and phrases, such as the agency's name; or

☐   use the search-and-browse function, in which you limit your key-word search to one or several titles or parts of titles. See Illustration 13-5 at page 279.

Once you have identified and obtained a potentially pertinent section or part, you should, of course, examine the material carefully. Examine the table of contents for the chapter containing the pertinent material, and identify all pertinent parts. Be sure to look for definition sections, which may appear at the beginning of and apply throughout a chapter. Read through all sections within the pertinent part, because they are likely to be interconnected. Then take note of the administrative history material in small print at the end of a section or the outline for a part. You may find there a reference to the enabling statute as well as the regulation's date of final promulgation and citation to the *Federal Register* (discussed below). See Illustration 13-1 at page 269.

Timing is important in regulations research. The regulation you find in the current C.F.R. probably is the correct one to use, but there are two situations in which you would not rely on the current C.F.R. regulation. First, if the key events in your client's situation occurred some time ago and the regulation was promulgated more recently, you will need to research historic regulations. There are several official sources of historic regulations: GPO Access provides C.F.R.s from 1997 to date; you may be able to find an old C.F.R. paper or microform set; or you may use the *Federal Register*, described below.

Second, if your client's events are very recent or have yet to happen, you will need to check for very recent regulatory activity. To ascertain how current your C.F.R. research is, look at the first page of the C.F.R. paper volume you are using or consult the list of available titles on GPO Access. To bring your research up to date, you will use the *Federal Register*, discussed below.

Researching the Canoga case, we knew from our research in secondary authority and U.S.C.S. that the pertinent regulation was § 103.2 of title 29. Had we not already found a reference, we could have used the methods described above, including the List of CFR Titles in paper, the Parallel Table of Authorities in paper, and a key-word search within the pertinent title. See Illustrations 13-3 through 13-5 at pages 277–79.

Section 103.2 is presented in Illustration 13-1 at page 269. For the Board to take jurisdiction of Ms. Canoga's case, the orchestra must have revenues (excluding certain grants) of at least $1 million. The regulation was promulgated on March 7, 1973, as reported in volume 38 of the *Federal Register* at page 6177. Our research in C.F.R. title 29 in the fall of 2003 was current through July 1, 2003.

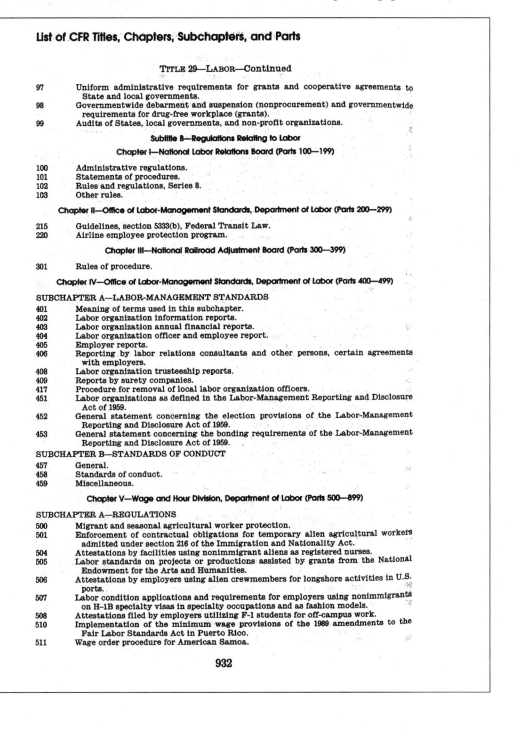

ILLUSTRATION 13-3   List of CFR Titles, Chapters, Subchapters, and Parts, from *CFR Index and Finding Aids* (paper source)

List of CFR Titles, Chapters, Subchapters, and Parts

TITLE 29—LABOR—Continued

97   Uniform administrative requirements for grants and cooperative agreements to State and local governments.

98   Governmentwide debarment and suspension (nonprocurement) and governmentwide requirements for drug-free workplace (grants).

99   Audits of States, local governments, and non-profit organizations.

Subtitle B—Regulations Relating to Labor

Chapter I—National Labor Relations Board (Parts 100—199)

100   Administrative regulations.
101   Statements of procedures.
102   Rules and regulations, Series 8.
103   Other rules.

Chapter II—Office of Labor-Management Standards, Department of Labor (Parts 200—299)

215   Guidelines, section 5333(b), Federal Transit Law.
220   Airline employee protection program.

Chapter III—National Railroad Adjustment Board (Parts 300—399)

301   Rules of procedure.

Chapter IV—Office of Labor-Management Standards, Department of Labor (Parts 400—499)

SUBCHAPTER A—LABOR-MANAGEMENT STANDARDS

401   Meaning of terms used in this subchapter.
402   Labor organization information reports.
403   Labor organization annual financial reports.
404   Labor organization officer and employee report.
405   Employer reports.
406   Reporting by labor relations consultants and other persons, certain agreements with employers.
408   Labor organization trusteeship reports.
409   Reports by surety companies.
417   Procedure for removal of local labor organization officers.
451   Labor organizations as defined in the Labor-Management Reporting and Disclosure Act of 1959.
452   General statement concerning the election provisions of the Labor-Management Reporting and Disclosure Act of 1959.
453   General statement concerning the bonding requirements of the Labor-Management Reporting and Disclosure Act of 1959.

SUBCHAPTER B—STANDARDS OF CONDUCT

457   General.
458   Standards of conduct.
459   Miscellaneous.

Chapter V—Wage and Hour Division, Department of Labor (Parts 500—899)

SUBCHAPTER A—REGULATIONS

500   Migrant and seasonal agricultural worker protection.
501   Enforcement of contractual obligations for temporary alien agricultural workers admitted under section 216 of the Immigration and Nationality Act.
504   Attestations by facilities using nonimmigrant aliens as registered nurses.
505   Labor standards on projects or productions assisted by grants from the National Endowment for the Arts and Humanities.
506   Attestations by employers using alien crewmembers for longshore activities in U.S. ports.
507   Labor condition applications and requirements for employers using nonimmigrants on H-1B specialty visas in specialty occupations and as fashion models.
508   Attestations filed by employers utilizing F-1 students for off-campus work.
510   Implementation of the minimum wage provisions of the 1989 amendments to the Fair Labor Standards Act in Puerto Rico.
511   Wage order procedure for American Samoa.

932

| ILLUSTRATION 13-4 | Parallel Table of Authorities and Rules, from *CFR Index and Finding Aids* (paper source) |

CFR Index

28 U.S.C.—Continued	CFR
	32 Part 516
515—518	28 Part 9
524	28 Parts 9
528	28 Part 45
530B	28 Part 77
534	28 Parts 16, 20
543	28 Parts 600, 603
	32 Part 516
586	28 Part 58
1346	28 Part 543
	32 Parts 536, 842
1498	10 Part 782
1608	22 Part 93
1733	22 Part 131
1746	8 Part 3
	30 Part 870
	34 Part 690
1784	22 Part 92
1821—1825	28 Part 21
1821	22 Part 713
1823	32 Part 534
2112	5 Part 2429
	21 Parts 10, 12—16
	29 Parts 101, 2200
	39 Part 224
	40 Part 23
	46 Part 502
2343—2344	40 Part 23
2401—2402	32 Part 536
2402	32 Part 842
2412	34 Part 21
2461	14 Part 13
	18 Part 385
	20 Parts 356, 702
	30 Parts 723, 845
	32 Part 269
	46 Part 506
	49 Part 213
2461 note	5 Parts 2634, 2636
	10 Parts 2, 13, 207, 218, 430, 501, 601,
	820, 1013, 1017, 1050
	11 Part 111
	12 Parts 19, 263, 308, 509, 1411, 1773,
	1780
	14 Part 383
	15 Parts 6, 25, 28
	16 Part 1
	17 Part 143
	24 Parts 28, 30, 81, 3282, 3500
	27 Part 16
	29 Parts 578—579, 2575, 4071, 4302
	31 Parts 356, 500, 505, 515, 535, 536,
	540, 545, 550, 560, 575, 585, 590—591,
	595, 598
	34 Part 36
	40 Parts 19, 27
	45 Part 672
	49 Parts 215—216, 220, 238, 239, 241,
	244, 1503
2671—2680	14 Part 1261
	22 Part 511
	28 Part 543
	32 Part 536
	38 Part 14
	39 Part 912
	43 Part 22

28 U.S.C.—Continued	CFR
2671—2672	32 Part 842
2672	5 Part 177
	10 Parts 14, 1014
	13 Part 114
	14 Part 15
	15 Part 2
	20 Part 429
	22 Part 304
	24 Part 17
	28 Part 14
	29 Parts 15, 100
	31 Part 3
	32 Part 1280
	33 Part 25
	34 Part 35
	45 Part 35
	46 Part 204
	49 Part 1
2674—2680	32 Part 842
2675	14 Part 15
2679	10 Part 14
	28 Part 15
29 U.S.C.	
9a	29 Part 580
37	45 Parts 95, 204
41a—41b	29 Part 1924
49 et seq	20 Parts 621, 651, 652—656, 658
	29 Parts 42, 507, 508
49k	20 Parts 601, 652, 654
	29 Part 31
49l—2	29 Part 44
50	29 Parts 29, 30
141	5 Part 7101
	29 Part 100
151	29 Parts 101—103
156	5 Part 7101
	29 Parts 100—103
158	29 Part 1420
171	29 Part 1420
172—173	29 Parts 1402—1403
172	29 Parts 1401, 1404
173—174	29 Part 1420
173 et seq	29 Part 1404
175a	29 Parts 1470, 1471
183	29 Part 1420
201 et seq	29 Parts 42, 510, 516, 536, 548,
	775, 782, 790, 1620, 1621
201—219	29 Parts 525, 553, 570, 776, 778—780,
	783—786, 788, 789, 791, 793, 794
203	29 Parts 531, 579, 580
204	5 Part 551
204f	5 Part 551
205—206	29 Parts 511, 616, 617, 619, 697, 699,
	700, 701, 720, 721, 723—730
206	24 Part 7
	29 Parts 552, 1614
207	29 Parts 536, 547—550
208	29 Parts 511, 616, 617, 619, 697, 699, 700,
	701, 720, 721, 723—730
211—212	29 Parts 575, 579, 580
211	29 Parts 515, 516, 519, 525, 530, 1627
213	29 Parts 536, 541, 551, 552
214	29 Parts 519, 520, 528
216	29 Parts 578—580
218	29 Part 575
251 et seq	29 Part 775

ILLUSTRATION 13-5	Boolean Citation List, from Search in GPO Access C.F.R. Database (electronic source)

code of federal regulations

CFR Search Results

Search Database:

Title 29 All Volumes (2003)

For: "ORCHESTRA"

Total Hits: 5

[1]
((LIST OF AVAILABLE CFRs ONLINE))
      Size: 65489 , Score: 1000

[2]
[2003] 29CFR103.2-- Sec. 103.2 Symphony orchestras.
      Size: 787 , Score: 1000

[3]
[2003] 29CFR103-- Subpart A--Jurisdictional Standards
      Size: 1445 , Score: 880

[4]
[2003] 29CFR103-- PART 103--OTHER RULES
      Size: 8221 , Score: 652

[5]
Query Report for this Search
      Size: 654 , Score: 1

> **Regulations in an administrative register (*Federal Register*):**
>
> ▶ use *List of CFR Sections Affected* (L.S.A.) to identify pertinent pages in fairly recent issues of the *Federal Register*
>
> ▶ use tools updating L.S.A. to identify pertinent pages in very recent issues of the *Federal Register*
>
> ▶ read the material in the *Federal Register*, including the regulation itself and the explanatory material

The *Federal Register* is an almost daily publication covering the activities of federal agencies. It focuses on proposed and promulgated regulations, and it serves four research purposes:

☐ C.F.R. is generally within a few months to a year of being current. New regulations are proposed and promulgated daily, so you must update your research beyond C.F.R. in the *Federal Register*, especially if your client is seeking advice about future conduct.

☐ If the regulation as applied to your client's situation is not clear, you may want to learn the agency's thinking behind the regulation. This information appears in the *Federal Register* when a regulation is finally promulgated. See Illustration 13-6 at pages 282–83. You may find pertinent information as well in the agency's notice proposing the regulation, also found in the *Federal Register*.

☐ A regulation that has been removed will no longer appear in C.F.R. You can find it in the *Federal Register* for its date of promulgation.

☐ You can learn about proposed regulations of interest to a client, on which your client may want to comment.

The following discussion focuses on the first purpose.

The *Federal Register* is voluminous; a daily issue in paper may contain more than a hundred pages. Although the material within each issue is arranged alphabetically by agency and there are indexes and tables, it would be burdensome to look through all the daily issues published since the cutoff date for C.F.R. Several tools assist you in identifying pertinent material within the *Federal Register*.

The main tool is *List of CFR Sections Affected*, or L.S.A. L.S.A. is available in paper in a set of softcover books typically shelved at the end of C.F.R. In addition, the GPO provides L.S.A. through its GPO Access website. L.S.A. is published monthly, with later issues cumulating material from earlier issues. Because C.F.R. is re-published on a rolling basis, L.S.A.'s coverage varies by C.F.R. title; you can find coverage information on the first page of the paper version and the introductory screen on the website.

The entries in L.S.A. are organized by title, subtitle, etc., so the standard means of access is to look up the title, subtitle, and chapter pertinent to your research situation. You also may use a key-word search for your regulation in the website L.S.A., for example, `"title 29" AND 103 ADJ 2` (ADJ, connoting adjacent, is a substitute for the decimal point). In each entry, L.S.A. identifies the nature of the recent regulatory activity, for example, addition of a new regulation, revision or removal of an existing regulation, and the page numbers in the *Federal Register* reporting that activity. Note that proposed rules appear at the end of a chapter's listing. See Illustration 13-7 at page 284.

Most of the time, you will need to update L.S.A. as well. Each issue of the *Federal Register* contains a Reader Aids Table of Parts Affected, organized by C.F.R. titles and parts, with entries guiding you to pages in that issue pertaining to the title and part you have selected. This table is cumulative within a month, so you would check the last issue for every month since the current L.S.A. and then the most recent issue for the current month.

If you are researching in GPO Access, you will use two tables: Last Month's List of CFR Parts Affected and Current List of CFR Parts Affected, covering changes since the date of the most recent Last Month's List. GPO Access also provides List of CFR Parts Affected Today. The information from Parts Affected Today is incorporated into the Current List, so Parts Affected Today is most useful when you are closely tracking a proposed regulation. See Illustration 13-8 at page 285, a print-out from the List of CFR Parts Affected Today.

The final step is, of course, to read the material you have identified in the *Federal Register*. You may read it in paper, of course, or retrieve it from the GPO Access *Federal Register* database. Either way, you will find not only the language of the regulation, but also explanatory material, for example, a summary of the regulation, its legal background, information considered by the agency, the evolution of the regulation. In addition, you generally will find the regulation's effective date and an agency contact. See Illustration 13-6 at pages 282–83.

As noted above, you may use the *Federal Register* for purposes other than updating your C.F.R. research. You will use the same sources, albeit in different ways. For example, if you need to read an old *Federal Register* for background information on a current regulation, you could use GPO Access for 1994 to date, or you could turn to a paper or microform copy. If you are checking for recent regulatory activity on a topic of interest to one of your clients, you could conduct a key-word search in the GPO Access database or look in the *Federal Register* subject index, which is organized by agency and topic.

Researching the Canoga case in the fall of 2003, we found that C.F.R. was current through July 1, 2003. So we perused the L.S.A. covering July and August of 2003 and then the website supplements. As you can see from Illustrations 13-7 at page 284 and 13-8 at page 285, although § 102.19(a) was revised, there was no change in the regulation pertinent to the Canoga case, § 103.2.

To learn more about § 103.2, we read the material accompanying it in the 1973 *Federal Register*, using the reference in C.F.R. to find the pages in microfiche. Not surprisingly, the Board's regulation attempts to draw a line between major orchestras whose activities have a pronounced impact on interstate commerce and other orchestras. The Board noted that the $1 million standard could be revised in the future.

ILLUSTRATION 13-6

Final Rule,
from *Federal Register* (paper source)

6176   **RULES AND REGULATIONS**

written statements of exceptions and allegations as to applicable fact and law. Upon request of any party made within such 20-day period, a reasonable extension of time for filing such briefs or statements may be granted and upon a showing of good cause such period may be extended, as appropriate.

(b) *By a court.* Where a case has been remanded by a court, the Board may proceed in accordance with the court's mandate to issue a decision or it may in turn remand the case to a deputy commissioner or judge with instructions to take such action as is ordered by the court and any additional necessary action and upon completion thereof to return the case with a recommended decision to the Board for its action.

§ 802.406   Finality of Board decisions.

A decision rendered by the Board pursuant to this subpart shall become final 60 days after the issuance of such decision unless an appeal pursuant to section 21(c) of the LHWCA is filed prior to the expiration of the 60-day period herein described, or unless a timely request for reconsideration by the Board has been filed as provided in § 802.407.

RECONSIDERATION

§ 802.407   Reconsideration of Board decisions—generally.

(a) Any party in interest may, within no more than 10 days from the filing of a decision pursuant to § 802.403(b) request a reconsideration of such decision.

(b) Failure to file a request for reconsideration shall not be deemed a failure to exhaust administrative remedies.

§ 802.408   Notice of request for reconsideration.

(a) In the event that a party in interest requests reconsideration of a final decision and order, he shall do so in writing, stating the supporting rationale for the request and include any material pertinent to the request.

(b) The request shall be sent or delivered in person to the Clerk of the Board, and copies shall be served upon the parties.

§ 802.409   Grant or denial of request.

All requests for reconsideration shall be reviewed by the Board and shall be granted or denied in the discretion of the Board.

JUDICIAL REVIEW

§ 802.410   Judicial review of Board decisions.

Within 60 days after a decision by the Board has been filed pursuant to § 802.403(b), any party adversely affected or aggrieved by such decision may take an appeal pursuant to section 21(c) of the LHWCA.

§ 802.411   Certification of record for judicial review.

The record of a case including the record of proceedings before the Board shall be transmitted to the appropriate court pursuant to the rules of such court.

Signed at Washington, D.C., this 1st day of March 1973.

PETER J. BRENNAN,
Secretary of Labor.

[FR Doc.73-4262 Filed 3-6-73;8:45 am]

Title 29—Labor

CHAPTER I—NATIONAL LABOR RELATIONS BOARD

PART 103—OTHER RULES

Jurisdictional Standards Applicable to Symphony Orchestras

By virtue of the authority vested in it by the National Labor Relations Act, approved July 5, 1935,[1] the National Labor Relations Board hereby issues the following rule which it finds necessary to carry out the provisions of said Act. This rule is issued following proceedings conforming to the requirements of 5 U.S.C. 553 in which notice was given that any rule adopted would be immediately applicable. On August 19, 1972, the Board published notice of proposed rule making requesting responses from interested parties with respect to the assertion of jurisdiction over symphony orchestras and the establishment of jurisdictional standards therefor. The Board having considered the responses and its discretion under sections 9 and 10 of the Act has decided to adopt a rule asserting jurisdiction over any symphony orchestra having a gross annual revenue of not less than $1 million. The National Labor Relations Board finds for good cause that this rule shall be effective on March 7, 1973, and shall apply to all proceedings affected thereby which are pending at the time of such publication or which may arise thereafter.

Dated at Washington, D.C., March 2, 1973.

By direction of the Board.

[SEAL]   JOHN C. TRUESDALE,
Executive Secretary.

On August 19, 1972, the Board published in the FEDERAL REGISTER, a notice of proposed rule making which invited interested parties to submit to it (1) data relevant to defining the extent to which symphony orchestras are in commerce, as defined in section 2(6) of the National Labor Relations Act, and to assessing the effect upon commerce of a labor dispute in those enterprises, (2) statements of views or arguments as to the desirability of the Board exercising jurisdiction, and (3) data and views concerning the appropriate jurisdictional standards which should be established in the event the Board decides to promulgate a rule exercising jurisdiction over those enterprises. The Board received 26 responses to the notice. After careful

[1] 49 Stat. 449; 29 U.S.C. 151-168, as amended by act of June 23, 1947 (61 Stat. 136; 29 U.S.C. Supp. 151-167), act of Oct. 22, 1951 (65 Stat. 601; 29 U.S.C. 158, 159, 168), and act of Sept. 14, 1959 (73 Stat. 519; 29 U.S.C. 141-168).

consideration of all the responses, the Board has concluded that it will best effectuate the purposes of the Act to assert jurisdiction over symphony orchestras and apply a $1 million annual gross revenue standard, in addition to statutory jurisdiction. A rule establishing that standard has been issued concurrently with the publication of this notice.

It is well settled that the National Labor Relations Act gives to the Board a jurisdictional authority coextensive with the full reach of the commerce clause.[1] It is equally well settled that the Board in its discretion may set boundaries on the exercise of that authority.[2] In exercising that discretion, the Board has consistently taken the position that it would better effectuate the purposes of the Act, and promote the prompt handling of major cases, not to exercise its jurisdiction to the fullest extent possible under the authority delegated to it by Congress, but to limit that exercise to enterprises whose operations have, or at which labor disputes would have, a pronounced impact upon the flow of interstate commerce.[3] The standard announced above, in our opinion, accommodates this position.

The Board, in arriving at a $1 million gross figure,[4] has considered, inter alia, the impact of symphony orchestras on commerce and the aspects of orchestra operations as criteria for the exercise of jurisdiction. Symphony orchestras in the United States are classified in four categories: college, community, metropolitan, and major.[5] Community orchestras constitute the largest group with over 1,000 in number and, for the most part, are composed of amateur players. The metropolitan orchestras are almost exclusively professional and it is estimated that there are between 75 and 80 orchestras classified as metropolitan. The annual budget for this category ranges approximately from $250,000 to $1 million. The major orchestras are the largest and usually the oldest established musical organizations. All of them are completely professional, and a substantial number

[1] See N.L.R.B. v. Fainblatt, 306 U.S. 601.
[2] Office Employees International Union, Local No. 11 [Oregon Teamsters] v. N.L.R.B. 353 U.S. 313; sec. 14(c)(1) of the Act.
[3] Siemons Mailing Service, 122 NLRB 81; Hollow Tree Lumber Company, 91 NLRB 635, 635. See also, e.g., Floridan Hotel of Tampa, Inc., 124 NLRB 261, 264; Butte Medical Properties, d.b.a. Medical Center Hospital, 168 NLRB 266, 268.
[4] As reflected in the rule, this figure includes revenues from all sources, excepting only contributions which, because of limitations placed thereon by the grantor, are not available for operating expenses. These contributions encompassing, for example, contributions to an endowment fund or building fund, are excluded because of their generally nonrecurring nature. (Cf. Magic Mountain, Inc., 123 NLRB 1170.) Income derived from investment of such funds will, however, be counted in determining whether the standard has been satisfied.
[5] The latter three categories are defined by the American Symphony Orchestra League principally on the basis of their annual budgets.

ILLUSTRATION 13-6 *(continued)*

RULES AND REGULATIONS 6177

operates on a year-round basis. For this category the minimum annual budget is approximately $1 million. Presently, there are approximately 28 major symphony orchestras in the United States. Thus, statistical projections based on data submitted by responding parties, as well as data compiled by the Board, disclose that adoption of such a standard would bring approximately 2 percent of all symphony orchestras, except college, or approximately 28 percent of the professional metropolitan and major orchestras, within reach of the Act. The Board is satisfied that symphony orchestras with gross revenues of $1 million have a substantial impact on commerce and that the figure selected will not result in an unmanageable increase on the Board's workload. The adoption of a $1 million standard, however, does not foreclose the Board from reevaluating and revising that standard should future circumstances deem it appropriate.

In view of the foregoing, the Board is satisfied that the $1 million annual gross revenue standard announced today will result in attaining uniform and effective regulation of labor disputes involving employees in the symphony orchestra industry whose operations have a substantial impact on interstate commerce.

§ 103.2 Symphony Orchestras.

The Board will assert its jurisdiction in any proceeding arising under sections 8, 9, and 10 of the Act involving any symphony orchestra which has a gross annual revenue from all sources (excluding only contributions which are because of limitation by the grantor not available for use for operating expenses) of not less than $1 million.

[FR Doc.73–4374 Filed 3–6–73; 8:45 am]

CHAPTER XVII—OCCUPATIONAL SAFETY AND HEALTH ADMINISTRATION, DEPARTMENT OF LABOR

PART 1952—APPROVED STATE PLANS FOR ENFORCEMENT OF STATE STANDARDS

New Jersey Plan; Plan Description; Amendment

In a document issued by this office on January 22, 1973, and published in the FEDERAL REGISTER on January 26, 1973 (37 FR 2426), the New Jersey developmental plan to assume responsibility for the development and enforcement of State occupational safety and health standards in accordance with Part 1902 of Title 29 of the Code of Federal Regulations and section 18 of the Occupational Safety and Health Act of 1970 (29 U.S.C. 667) was approved.

Provisions of that plan require that owners of any structures to be erected and used as places of employment submit plans for approval and comply with specific provisions of special State building codes. However, the decision did not indicate that the pertinent safety and health codes (N.J.A.C. 12:115—Building Code and N.J.A.C. 12:116—Plan Filing) have as their stated and clear purpose

the protection of employees even though the codes may afford some incidental protection to others. Codes that more directly concern other matters such as the protection of the environment and the public at large are properly not incorporated in the plan, and are dealt with elsewhere by the State of New Jersey and its political subdivisions.

The description of the plan in § 1952.-140(b) is accordingly amended to indicate these features of the codes involved by adding a new subparagraph (3) to read as follows:

§ 1952.140   Description of the plan.

*   *   *   *   *

(b) * * *

(3) Safety and health codes which are established by the State of New Jersey to protect employees and which incidentally protect others are considered occupational safety and health standards for the purposes of this subpart.

*   *   *   *   *

(Sec. 18, Pub. L. 91–596, 84 Stat. 1608 (29 U.S.C. 667))

Signed at Washington, D.C., this 1st day of March 1973.

CHAIN ROBBINS,
Acting Assistant Secretary of Labor.

[FR Doc.73–4355 Filed 3–6–73; 8:45 am]

Title 32—National Defense

CHAPTER XVII—OFFICE OF EMERGENCY PREPAREDNESS

PART 1709—REIMBURSEMENT OF OTHER FEDERAL AGENCIES UNDER PUBLIC LAW 91–606.

Eligibility of Certain Expenditures for Reimbursement

1. Section 1709.2 is amended by deleting paragraphs (d), (e), and (f).

Effective date. This amendment shall be effective as of March 1, 1973.

Dated: March 1, 1973.

DARRELL M. TRENT,
Acting Director,
Office of Emergency Preparedness.

[FR Doc.73–4380 Filed 3–6–73; 8:45 am]

Title 41—Public Contracts and Property Management

CHAPTER 3—DEPARTMENT OF HEALTH, EDUCATION, AND WELFARE

PART 3–16—PROCUREMENT FORMS

Subpart 3–16.8—Miscellaneous Forms

Chapter 3, Title 41, Code of Federal Regulations is amended as set forth below. The purpose of this amendment is to inform the public of HEW's use of miscellaneous procurement forms.

It is the general policy of the Department of Health, Education, and Welfare to allow time for interested parties to take part in the rule making process. However, since the amendment herein involves minor technical matters, the public rule making process is deemed unnecessary in this instance.

1. The table of contents of Part 3–16 is amended to add Subpart 3–16.8 as follows:

Subpart 3–16.8—Miscellaneous Forms

3–16.804   Report on procurement.
3–16.804–2   Agencies required to report.
3–16.804–3   Standard Form 37, Report on Procurement by Civilian Executive Agencies.
3–16.852   Equal Opportunity Clause (HEW–386).
3–16.853   Request for Equal Opportunity Clearance of Contract Award (HEW–511).
3–16.854   Notice to Prospective Bidders (HEW–512).
3–16.855   Transmittal Letter (HEW–513).
3–16.856   Procurement Activity Report.

AUTHORITY: 5 U.S.C. 301; 40 U.S.C. 486(c).

Subpart 3–16.8—Miscellaneous Forms

2. Subpart 3–16.8 is added to read as follows:

§ 3–16.804   Report on procurement.

§ 3–16.804–2   Agencies required to report.

Each operating agency, the Office of Regional and Community Development, and the Office of Administrative Services, OS–OASAM, shall report its procurement to the Office of Procurement and Materiel Management, OS–OASAM, for the organization as a whole.

§ 3–16.804–3   Standard Form 37, Report on Procurement by Civilian Agencies.

(a)–(e) [Reserved]

(f) *Frequency and due date for submission of Standard Form 37.* Each report shall be submitted in the original and three copies to arrive at OPMM not later than 30 calendar days after the close of each reporting period.

§ 3–16.852   Equal Opportunity Clause (HEW–386).

Use Form HEW–386, Equal Opportunity Clause, if it is prescribed.

§ 3–16.853   Request for Equal Opportunity Clearance of Contract Award.

Form HEW–511, Request for Equal Opportunity Clearance of Contract Award, is prescribed for use in communicating and transmitting information between the contracting officer and the Office of Civil Rights.

§ 3–16.854   Notice to Prospective Bidders (HEW–512).

Form HEW–512, Notice to Prospective Bidders, is prescribed for use with invitation for bids when bids are estimated to exceed $10,000.

§ 3–16.855   Transmittal Letter (HEW–513).

Form HEW–513, Transmittal Letter, is prescribed for transmitting awards which are subject to the Equal Opportunity clause.

§ 3–16.856   Procurement Activity Report.

(a) *General.* The Procurement Activity Report is designed to provide the Department with essential procurement records and statistics necessary for procurement management purposes and to

ILLUSTRATION 13-7

List of Recent Agency Activity,
from *List of CFR Sections Affected* (paper source)

CHANGES JULY 1, 2003 THROUGH AUGUST 29, 2003

TITLE 28

Chapter V—Bureau of Prisons, Department of Justice (Parts 500—599)

549 Authority citation revised........47849
549.30—549.31 (Subpart B) Added
.... 47849

Proposed Rules:

16...47519
522...46138

TITLE 29—LABOR

Chapter I—National Labor Relations Board (Parts 100—199)

31.2 (g) revised 51366
  (f) and (h) amended 51367
31.3 (d)(1) heading revised...............51366
  (b)(1) introductory text and (d)
  introductory text amended
.... 51367
31.5 (b) and (d) amended.................51367
31.6 (a)(1), (2) and (b) introductory text amended; (b) heading revised...............................51367
31.9 (e) amended.............................51367
31.10 (e) amended 51367
31.12 (a) amended 51367
32 Heading revised...........................51367
32.1 Amended..................................51368
32.2 (a) revised 51367
32.3 Amended 51367, 51368
32.4 (c) heading revised..................51367
  (a), (b)(1)(v), (2), (3), (4)(ii), (5)(i), (6), (7)(i), (c) and (d) amended 51368
32.5 (d) revised 51367
  (a) and (b)(3) amended 51368
32.6 (a)(3)(i) and (ii) amended..........51368
32.8 (a) amended 51368
32.10 (a) amended 51368
32.12—32.17 (Subpart B) Heading revised...............................51368
32.12 (a)(1), (3) and (b)(8) amended...51368
32.13 (a), (b) introductory text, (1), (2) and (d) amended 51368
32.15 (c)(1) amended 51368
32.17 (a) amended 51368
32.26—32.28 (Subpart C) Heading revised...............................51368
32.27 Heading revised; (a), (b)(1), (2), (c) and (e)(3) amended.........51368
32.44 (b) amended 51368

32.46 (c)(2) amended 51368
32.47 (c) amended 51368
102.19 (a) revised 39837

Chapter V—Wage and Hour Division, Department of Labor (Parts 500—899)

697.2 Revised...................................46950
697.4 Revised...................................46951

Chapter XVII—Occupational Safety and Health Administration, Department of Labor (Parts 1900—1999)

1952 Authority citation revised
.... 43460
1952.250—1952.256 (Subpart S) Removed...43460
1956 Authority citation revised
.... 43460
1956.70—1956.74 (Subpart H) Added 43460

Chapter XL—Pension Benefit Guaranty Corporation (Parts 4000—4999)

4022 Appendices B and C amended...41715
  Appendix B amended; Appendix C table amended 48788
4044 Appendix B amended......41715, 48788

Proposed Rules:

35 41512
917...41980
1200—1299 (Ch. X) 46983
1625 41542
1627 41542
1926 ....39877, 39880, 48843

TITLE 30—MINERAL RESOURCES

Chapter I—Mine Safety and Health Administration, Department of Labor (Parts 1—199)

75.362 (d)(2) amended; (d)(3) added..40138

Chapter II—Minerals Management Service, Department of the Interior (Parts 200—299)

250.114 (c) revised...........................43298

ILLUSTRATION 13-8	List of CFR Parts Affected Today, from GPO Access (electronic source)

OFFICE OF THE
FEDERAL REGISTER

LSA SERVICES
- About LSA
- Browse LSA
- Search the LSA

SUPPLEMENTAL
SERVICES
- Current List of CFR
  Parts Affected
- Last Month's
  List of CFR
  Parts Affected
- List of CFR Parts
  Affected Today
- Retrieve a
  Federal Register
  Page (PDF)
- Resource Links

List of CFR Parts Affected Today

This page lists only the CFR parts affected by change(s) appearing in today's *Federal Register*. This listing has been incorporated in the cumulative Current List of CFR Parts Affected.

CFR Parts Affected in the November 20, 2003, issue of the *Federal Register*:

```
                            3 CFR
Administrative Orders:
Presidential Determinations:
No. 2004-8 of November 7, 2003.....................65383

                            7 CFR
1464..............................................65385
Proposed Rules:
1423..............................................65412

                           10 CFR
50................................................65386
Proposed Rules:
50................................................65415

                           12 CFR
Proposed Rules:
614...............................................65417
620...............................................65417
630...............................................65417

                           14 CFR
71................................................65389
95................................................65390
Proposed Rules:
71................................................65417

                           21 CFR
20................................................65392

                           23 CFR
655...............................................65496

                           26 CFR
Proposed Rules:
1.................................................65419

                           30 CFR
707...............................................65622
Proposed Rules:
906...............................................65422
917...............................................65424

                           31 CFR
103...............................................65392

                           33 CFR
```

> **Regulations in agency websites:**
>
> ▶ identify and read the regulation
> ▶ update as needed

Many agencies have websites through which they provide a range of information to the public. If the agency involved in your research topic has such a website, check for a regulations database. That database may be easier to work with than the broader and hence larger C.F.R. database. Identify and use the means of access the agency's website affords, and be sure to check its currency. See Illustration 13-9 at page 287.

Researching the Canoga case, we visited the NLRB's website and easily found the NLRB Rules and Regulations database. We could locate pertinent regulations several ways: by key-word searching, by selecting a part and then reading the outline at the beginning of that part, and by using the topical index. The opening screen indicates that the database is updated as needed. See Illustration 13-9 at page 287. The NLRB's database is particularly valuable because it provides not only the regulation but also the notice of final promulgation with the Board's explanation, that is, the material in the *Federal Register* in Illustration 13-6 at pages 282–83.

> **Regulations research in case law:**
>
> • judicial cases
> • agency decisions

As noted above, the courts evaluate, interpret, and apply regulations, just as they do with statutes. To research these judicial cases, you can use the sources discussed in Chapters 9 and 10, for example, digests, reporters, commercial databases. Other options are similar to approaches used to find cases interpreting a statute as discussed in Chapter 11, for example, reading the case descriptions in an annotated code, KeyCiting or Shepardizing the regulation. See Illustration 13-10 at page 288. In addition, if the agency has adjudicatory powers, you should seek agency decisions interpreting and applying the regulation. Chapter 14 covers researching agency decisions. Judicial cases and agency decisions also may be researched through mini-libraries, as discussed in Chapter 15.

Researching the Canoga case through various methods, including a key-word search in LexisNexis and KeyCiting the C.F.R. section, we learned of a Second Circuit case from 1975 upholding the Board's assertion of jurisdiction under § 103.2.[2] See Illustration 13-10 at page 288.

___

2. *NLRB v. Rochester Musicians Ass'n,* 514 F.2d 988 (2d Cir. 1975).

| ILLUSTRATION 13-9 | Opening Screen of Agency's Regulations Database, from National Labor Relations Board Website (electronic source) |

NLRB Rules and Regulations

The online version of the Rules and Regulations is kept updated as changes are approved by the Board. Revised sections have been inserted to replace old sections. View revisions.

To view PDF files: ▲ Get Acrobat Reader

Search NLRB Rules and Regulations: | | [   ] [Help]

- Preliminary Pages [HTML] [PDF]

- Part 101--Statements of Procedure [HTML] [PDF]

- Part 102--Rules and Regulations [HTML] [PDF]

- Part 103--Other Rules [HTML] [PDF]

- Topical Index [HTML] [PDF]

- NLRB Organization and Functions [HTML] [PDF]

- The Act [HTML] [PDF]

NLRB
Home

July 10, 2003

ILLUSTRATION 13-10   KeyCite Report for Agency Regulation,
                                       from Westlaw (electronic source)

Date of Printing: DEC 17,2003

KEYCITE

CITATION:**29 CFR s 103.2**

Citing References

▷   1   N.L.R.B. v. Rochester Musicians Ass'n Local 66, 514 F.2d 988, 990, 89 L.R.R.M. (BNA)
         2193, 2193, 76 Lab.Cas. P 10,850, 10850 (2nd Cir. Apr 28, 1975) (NO. 471, 74-1940)

Administrative Decisions (U.S.A.)

C   2   Spring Library and Museums Ass'n, 221 NLRB 1209, 1210, 221 NLRB No. 194, 1975 WL
         6564, *3, 91 L.R.R.M. (BNA) 1043 (N.L.R.B. Dec 18, 1975) (NO. AO-173)

▶   3   Rochester Musicians Assn. Local 66, 207 NLRB 647, 648, 207 NLRB No. 110, 1973 WL
         4660, *4, 85 L.R.R.M. (BNA) 1345 (N.L.R.B. Nov 29, 1973) (NO. 3-CB-1939)

Secondary Sources (U.S.A.)

     4   Employment Coordinator P LR-11,942, NONPROFIT INSTITUTIONS. (2002)
     5   Federal Procedure, Lawyers Edition s 52:342, MONETARY THRESHOLDS AND
         OTHER JURISDICTIONAL STANDARDS (2002)
     6   Am. Jur. 2d Labor and Labor Relations s 826, NONPROFIT INSTITUTIONS (2003)
     7   THE BIRTH OF A RULE: THE NATIONAL LABOR RELATIONS BOARD'S USE OF
         INFORMAL RULEMAKING TO PROMULGATE A RULE FOR HEALTH CARE
         BARGAINING UNIT DETERMINATIONS, 1989 Det. C.L. Rev. 1105, 1132+ (1989)

C   8   AGENCY RULES WITH THE FORCE OF LAW: THE ORIGINAL CONVENTION, 116
         Harv. L. Rev. 467, 592 (2002)

     9   NLRB RULEMAKING ON HEALTH CARE COLLECTIVE BARGAINING UNITS:
         PREDICTABILITY, BUT AT WHAT COST, 9 Hofstra Lab. L.J. 483, 513 (1992)

C   10   RULEMAKING: THE NATIONAL LABOR RELATIONS BOARD'S PRESCRIPTION
         FOR THE RECURRING PAINS OF THE HEALTH CARE INDUSTRY, 9 J. Contemp.
         Health L. & Pol'y 377, 418 (1993)

C   11   QUESTIONING THE PREEMPTION DOCTRINE: OPPORTUNITIES FOR
         STATE-LEVEL LABOR LAW INITIATIVES, 5 Widener J. Pub. L. 35, 86 (1995)

D.   WHAT ELSE?

Westlaw, LexisNexis, and Loislaw.   All three services provide databases with the *Code of Federal Regulations* and the *Federal Register*. The content of these databases is the same as in the official sources; there is no annotation (unlike unofficial annotated statutory codes). Thus, you most likely will use the official sources featured in this chapter. Commercial sources may be helpful in some situations, for example, for searching in a subject-specific C.F.R. database, or when seeking a historic regulation in a historic C.F.R. database.

CIS Products.   Congressional Information Service's *Index to the Code of Federal Regulations* features frequent updating and detailed indexing. CIS also provides the text of federal regulations and the *Federal Register* in the *Congressional Universe* service. CIS is a commercial publisher.

Policy and Guidance Statements.   Some agencies issue not only regulations but also less authoritative statements of the agency's approach to common situations. For example, an agency may issue a memo to employees who conduct inspections or prosecute cases. These statements can be very valuable and may be available from the agency or in a mini-library, described in Chapter 15.

Guides to Federal Agencies.   To learn what federal agencies do, how to contact them, and what resources they provide, consult a source such as *The United States Government Manual* (available on the Internet via gpoaccess .gov) and the *Federal Regulatory Directory*.

Presidential Documents.   Two major types of presidential documents are executive orders (typically directed to government officials) and proclamations (general announcements and policy statements). These appear in various publications, including the *Federal Register*, Title 3 of C.F.R., and *U.S. Code Congressional and Administrative News*; some also appear in the federal statutory codes. LexisNexis and Westlaw provide some presidential documents. The *Weekly Compilation of Presidential Documents* and the annual *Public Papers of the President* compile not only executive orders and proclamations, but also other documents, such as announcements and nominations.

State Regulations.   Many state agencies issue regulations. You may find them in an official paper code, through a public website, or in a LexisNexis or Westlaw or Loislaw database. Many states have manuals similar to *The United States Government Manual*. BNA's *Directory of State Administrative Codes and Registers* provides background on the publications of administrative material at the state level.

E. HOW DO YOU CITE REGULATIONS?

Regulations generally are cited to the regulatory code. Provide the regulation's name, if it is commonly known by a name; the code's abbreviation; the numbers needed to identify the regulation; and the date of the code. Here are two examples:

☐ *Bluebook* Rule 14.2(a): 29 C.F.R. § 103.2 (2003).
☐ *ALWD* Rule 19.1: 29 C.F.R. § 103.2 (2003).

Regulations not appearing in a regulatory code are cited to the register. Provide the register's name, the volume and the page number on which the discussion of the regulation or the regulation itself begins, the page number where the portion you are citing appears, and the date. *The Bluebook* also calls for the regulation's commonly used name and eventual codification. Here are two examples:

☐ *Bluebook* Rule 14.2(b): 38 Fed. Reg. 6176, 6177 (Mar. 7, 1973) (to be codified at 29 C.F.R. § 103.2).
☐ *ALWD* Rule 19.3: 38 Fed. Reg. 6176, 6177 (Mar. 7, 1973).

AGENCY DECISIONS

A. What Is an Agency Decision?
B. Why Would You Research Agency Decisions?
C. How Do You Research Agency Decisions?
D. What Else?
E. How Do You Cite Agency Decisions?

A. WHAT IS AN AGENCY DECISION?

Federal and state agencies make many decisions. Agency officials decide how to conduct an investigation, which issues to study, whether to prosecute an alleged offender, etc. This chapter focuses on decisions that are the output of case adjudication. In adjudicating cases, agencies follow the procedures set out in their enabling statutes and the jurisdiction's administrative procedure act.

In formal adjudication, the parties typically are the government, acting as a quasi-prosecutor or claims administrator, and the private party. The case begins with some form of notice, typically in pleadings. There may be discovery (or development of the facts by the lawyers) before the hearing, and preliminary issues may be handled by motion (i.e., by written and oral argument rather than presentation of evidence). The typical hearing resembles a trial with counsel, direct testimony and cross-examination, and exhibits; some evidence may be submitted in writing. The judge, known as an "administrative law judge" (ALJ) or "hearing officer," then renders a recommended decision. That recommendation is reviewed by the commissioners or members of the agency, who may adopt the ALJ's decision or develop their own decision in response to the arguments of counsel.

A formal agency decision more or less resembles a case decided by a court. It includes a statement of the facts as found by the agency, the agency's decision based on those facts, and the reasoning behind the decision. That reasoning typically includes discussion of the statute, any pertinent regulations, judicial cases, and previous decisions of the agency. See Illustration 14-1 at pages 293–96.

Agency decisions, like agency regulations, are subject to judicial review. The decision generally is reviewed first by an intermediate appellate court, not a trial court, because the agency's hearing serves as the trial of the case. The appellate court's ruling may then be appealed to the highest court. The issues before a reviewing court typically are whether there is substantial evidence in the record to support the agency's decision, whether the agency has exceeded its statutory jurisdiction or failed to follow required procedures, and whether the agency has abused its discretion.

Agencies also render opinions through less formal processes. An agency staff member may render an informal opinion based on information provided by the party seeking advice, an independent investigation undertaken by the agency itself, or perhaps a written response provided by a charged party. If the informal opinion constitutes final agency action, it has some precedential force, in that the agency would have to explain a later change of course.

If litigation were pursued in the Canoga case under the federal labor statute, it would begin with Ms. Canoga filing a charge against the employer, which the National Labor Relations Board's staff would investigate. If the investigation indicated that the labor statute had been violated, a Board lawyer would file a complaint against the employer and litigate the case before an ALJ. The Board would review the ALJ's recommendation and either adopt the recommendation or write its own decision. The Board's decision would be subject to review by the courts of appeals for the Tenth Circuit (which encompasses New Mexico) or the District of Columbia (where the Board's offices are) and thereafter by the United States Supreme Court.

Illustration 14-1 at pages 293–96 is an excerpt from a Board decision in a case with some parallel to the Canoga case; the issue is protection from discipline or discharge based on nonunion activities that involve concerted action by employees. In *Morton International*, when two employees handwrote comments on a memo posted by the employer addressing the employer's no-smoking policy, they engaged in protected concerted activity, because they acted together to protest a change in the terms and conditions of their employment.

ILLUSTRATION 14-1   Agency Decision,
from *Decisions and Orders of the National Labor Relations Board* (paper source)

Morton International, Inc. *and* **Martin D. Howell.**
Case 9–CA–30898

November 10, 1994

DECISION AND ORDER

By Members Devaney, Browning, and Cohen

On July 20, 1994, Administrative Law Judge Claude R. Wolfe issued the attached decision. The Respondent filed exceptions and a supporting brief.

The National Labor Relations Board has delegated its authority in this proceeding to a three-member panel.

The Board has considered the record in light of the exceptions and brief and has decided to affirm the judge's rulings, findings,[1] and conclusions and to adopt the recommended Order.

ORDER

The National Labor Relations Board adopts the recommended Order of the administrative law judge and orders that the Respondent, Morton International, Inc., West Alexandria, Ohio, its officers, agents, successors, and assigns, shall take the action set forth in the Order.

[1] The Respondent has excepted to some of the judge's credibility findings. The Board's established policy is not to overrule an administrative law judge's credibility resolutions unless the clear preponderance of all the relevant evidence convinces us that they are incorrect. *Standard Dry Wall Products*, 91 NLRB 544 (1950), enfd. 188 F.2d 362 (3d Cir. 1951). We have carefully examined the record and find no basis for reversing the findings.

Joseph C. Devine, Esq., for the General Counsel.
David J. Millstone and *William A. Nolan, Esqs.*, for the Respondent.

DECISION

STATEMENT OF THE CASE

Claude R. Wolfe, Administrative Law Judge. This proceeding was litigated before me at Dayton, Ohio, on May 17, 1994, pursuant to charges filed on July 15, 1993, and amended on August 24 and October 22, 1993,[1] and complaint issued October 25 alleging Martin D. Howell and Robert Boerner were unlawfully suspended and discharged for engaging in protected concerted activity. Morton International, Inc. (the Respondent) contends the suspensions and discharges were for cause and did not violate Section 8(a)(1) of the National Labor Relations Act (the Act) as alleged.

Upon the entire record, and after considering the demeanor of the witnesses and the posttrial briefs of the parties, I make the following

[1] All dates are 1993 unless otherwise stated.

315 NLRB No. 71

FINDINGS AND CONCLUSIONS

I. THE RESPONDENT'S BUSINESS

The Respondent is a corporation engaged in the manufacture and nonretail sale of adhesives at West Alexandria, Ohio, and during the 12 months preceding the issuance of the complaint, sold and shipped its products valued in excess of $50,000 from its West Alexandria facility to points located outside the State of Ohio. The Respondent is an employer engaged in commerce within the meaning of Section 2(2), (6), and (7) of the Act.

II. SUPERVISORS AND AGENT

At all times material to this proceeding, the individuals named below held the positions set forth opposite their names and have been supervisors and agents of the Respondent within the meaning of Section 2(11) and (13) of the Act.

Randall Bittner—Plant Manager
Jane Paxton—Manager for Human Resources
Leigh Walling—Polyester Supervisor
Bob Napier—Maintenance Supervisor

III. THE ALLEGED UNFAIR LABOR PRACTICES

A. *Chronology*

The facts are not in dispute with respect to the conduct of Boerner and Howell which led to their discharge, and all these facts were known to the Respondent at the time the two were discharged.

On the morning of June 14, at about 2 or 2:30 a.m., Boerner was lunching with a custodian named Snider "Butch" Neusock, and another employee. All were smokers. Snider had placed a memo on the table.[2] The memo was addressed to the Respondent's safety committee and signed, "Morton employee." The memo, in substance complained that the Respondent was not rigidly enforcing its no-smoking policy. The last sentence in the lengthy memo reading, "Also, what about the employees who do not use tobacco products—when will we be able to have a 'non-smoke' break of ten minutes or more every hour?" was composed by Brenda Holfinger, an assistant to the health and safety administrator. Holfinger is a regular hourly paid employee.

Indignant at the content of this memo, Boerner wrote comments on it in bold letters reading in one instance, "Chicken Shit" after the anonymous "Morton employee" appearing as the originator of the memo, and at another point made the observation, without an aquerbian mark "could this be racist" in reference to a sentence reading, "I hate to see them [the Respondent] back down because of pressure from a minority of the employee [i.e., smokers]" warning to his task, Boerner enlarged his commentary by noting at the bottom of the purloined memo. Again in very large letters, "I think the non-smokers should quit their damm [sic] crying and put their thoughts to a more useful purpose for the company!" In the course of his composition of this broadside, Boerner sought assistance in the spelling of a word from Neusock

[2] The custodian was later discharged on the ground he had removed the document from company records in a locked office.

ILLUSTRATION 14-1   *(continued)*

MORTON INTERNATIONAL, INC.   565

who obliged. What word he assisted with is not specified, but I seriously doubt it was, "Damm."

Apart from the minuscule assistance included by Neusock, who made no other contribution to Boerner's effort, none of the three men lunching with Boerner, whom he states shared his views, were in any way party to the writing on or posting of the memo by Boerner, nor is there any evidence they designated him as their representative for any purpose. Boerner left the area after posting the memo with his comments on it.

Enter Howell. At about 4 a.m. he entered the empty lunchroom. Noticing the posted memo with Boerner's amendments, he took it to a table and read it. A smoker himself, Howell was then inspired to add further commentary on the memo. At the very top of the memo he wrote, "Gee, Brenda this isn't you is it? Get a real job you glorified secretary." In response to a statement in the memo referring to "the old days" he penned, "What do you know about the 'old days.'" Directing his attention to the memo claim the company was retreating from a policy, he noted, "what policy? be specific Brenda." Concerning a statement in the memo to the effect that forcing smokers to do so outside in all weather would deter smoking, Howell wrote, "then more of us would miss work for being sick." To this point none of the memo was composed by Brenda Holfinger who typed the memo. Now, however, her sentence quoted above closed the memo and moved Howell to expound, "has production suffered, no, so shut up and stay the hell out of the trailer."[3] Finally, at the bottom of the page, Howell commented on Boerner's adjuration to nonsmokers that they should put their thoughts to a more useful purpose, stating this would be quite difficult for this nonsmoker cause *she* has no "useful thoughts!" Finished with his commentary, Howell made copies and posted them in the breakroom, the smoke trailer, and on a bulletin board by the health and safety office.

Discovering the altered and posted memo, Respondent launched an investigation. As a result the custodian who admitted taking the document from company files as a joke was fired. Boerner and Howell each candidly advised the Respondent of their conduct with reference to the memo. They were suspended pending the results of the Respondent's investigation. Each received a letter from Jane Paxton dated June 15 and reading as follows:

Subject: Suspension Notification Without Pay

As we discussed, the Company is investigating concerns that you may have violated our policies. In particular, we are reviewing policies including but not limited to:

a. Harassment or intimidating language or conduct, . . .

b. Conduct that reflects unfavorably upon the Corporation.

c. Making malicious, false or derogatory statements that may damage the integrity or reputation of the Corporation, its products and performance, or its employees.

d. Destruction, damage, improper disposition, or unauthorized possession or removal from Company

premises of property that does not belong to the employee.

e. Posting, distributing, or circulating any written materials in work areas deemed inappropriate or disruptive.

Pending the outcome of this investigation, you have been suspended. I will be the person investigating these concerns.

What you can expect was discussed as the investigation is conducted. I will review the information and documentation you provided. As appropriate, I will consult with other employees and managers to assist in addressing and resolving the issues, and I will strive to keep you informed of the progress of this investigation.

I want to emphasize some of our expectations of you during this investigation. If you have any questions or concerns about any of these expectations, or about any part of this investigation, please contact me immediately. The expectations for you include the following:

You are expected to cooperate fully throughout the investigation, and be completely honest in answering questions and providing information to the Company.

You are expected to provide us with all of the information and documentation that you believe may help us in conducting this investigation. If you have any information or documentation that may be relevant to this matter and which you have not already provided, please provide immediately.

While this investigation is being conducted, you will be suspended without pay. During this time you must devote your full efforts to help bring this matter to closure. You must remain available during normal working hours to meet and/or provide information to Company representatives.

This is a confidential investigation. You must not discuss this investigation with any person who does not have a legitimate business need to know this information. If you have any questions or concerns about this requirement at any time, please feel free to discuss it further with me.

If you have any questions or concerns about any of these expectations, or about any part of this investigation, you will contact me immediately. I will contact you within the next three days to let you know of the progress of the investigation.

Please let me know if you have any questions, additional information, or want to discuss any of this. As you know, you can reach me at 839–4612.

Completing its investigation, the Respondent gave Boerner and Howell identical dismissal letters dated June 18 and reading as follows:

Subject: Investigation—Termination

We have completed the investigation of the alleged violation of policy listed in your suspension letter of June 15, 1993.

Our conclusions, based on interview with employees and your statement are:

---

[3] Respondent has a trailer to which employees may repair to smoke on their breaks.

ILLUSTRATION 14-1   *(continued)*

While working third shift on Sunday night, June 13th, an employee removed a confidential memo from the locked office of Health & Safety, made a copy and gave it to the Polyester third shift employees. You and one other Polyester employee co-authored derogatory, inflammatory and false comments on the memo, made additional copies and distributed it.

WAL cannot tolerate such actions and multiple violations of company policy. Therefore, your termination is effective immediately due to misconduct. Your final paycheck will include 32 hours of vacation payoff.

B. *Discussion and Conclusions*

The facts are clear and undisputed, but do they show the discharges were unlawful or legitimate? As I have previously stated in *Gatliff Coal*,[4] the answer to such questions depend on whether concerted action is present, whether that action is protected if it is in fact concerted, whether the General Counsel has set forth a prima facie case, the terminations were precipitated by protected concerted activity, and, if General Counsel has such a prima facie case, would Respondent have taken the same action in the absence of the protected activity? The first step in the process of determining these issues is measuring the facts found against the guide set forth in *Meyers Industries*, 268 NLRB 493, 497 (1984) (*Meyers I*), in the following terms:

> In general, to find an employee's activity to be "concerted," we shall require that it be engaged in with or on the authority of other employees, and not solely by and on behalf of the employee himself. Once the activity is found to be concerted, an 8(a)(1) violation will be found if, in addition, the employer knew of the concerted nature of the employee's activity, the concerted activity was protected by the Act, and the adverse employment action at issue (e.g., discharge) was motivated by the he employee's protected concerted activity. [Footnotes deleted.]

and as recited in *Meyers Industries*, 281 NLRB 882, 887 (1986) (*Meyers II*):

> We reiterate, our definition of concerted activity in *Meyers I* encompasses those circumstances where individual employees seek to initiate or to induce or to prepare for group action, as well as individual employees bringing truly group complaints tot he attention of management.

General Counsel, relying on *Meyers I*; *Amelio's*, 301 NLRB 182 fn. 4 (1991); and *Dayton Typographical Service*, 273 NLRB 1205 (1984), contends Boerner's conduct was concerted because other employees were opposed to the suggestions in the memo, Neusock assisted Boerner in the drafting of his comments on the memo, and Boerner's posting of the memo was a solicitation of employee actions and a logical outgrowth of the employees' joint complaint about the memo's stance on smoking.

I do not believe Boerner's conduct was concerted merely because others were opposed to the memo's suggestions inasmuch as there is no persuasive evidence the other three

memo readers, or any one else, authorized him to act on their behalf, or, with respect to the reference to the footnote in *Amelio's*, that Boerner's writings on the memo were necessarily a logical outgrowth of the concerns expressed by the group at the lunchroom table. Moreover, I do not agree that mere assistance in the spelling of a word threw Neusock into concert with Boerner. I do, however, conclude in accord with *Meyers II*, supra, that Boerner was engaged in concerted activity because his uncontroverted and credible testimony that he posted the memo, with his comments thereon. "To let the other people in the plant know—the other smokers know that this had been written and to see if—maybe if they had any comments or any hard feelings, maybe they would express their feelings" warrants a fair conclusion that he was seeking "to initiate or to induce or to prepare for group action" by fellow smokers in opposition to the sentiments expressed in the memo which were contrary to the interest of employees who smoked and in support of his writings on the memo.[5]

When Howell added his words to the memo, he endorsed and joined Boerner's effort in protest of the memo's attack on the existing smoking policy. That he did not then know Howell was the one who added the commentary to the memo is of no consequence. Here two employees reacted adversely to the memo and took complementary action to oppose it because they were smokers concerned in a common goal of preserving the status quo as it related to the policy on smoking. Howell's conduct in copying the notice, with his comments added thereon and posting it in several additional areas was an enlistment in and enlargement of Boerner's effort to inform other smokers of the threat the memo posed to existing smoking policy which was acceptable to employees who smoked.

The Respondent's smoking policy is a term or condition of employment, *Allied Signal*, 307 NLRB 752, 754 (1992), and the concerted activity of Boerner and Howell directed at protesting any change in policy thus concerns a term or condition of employment and is protected. The dismissal letters given to Howell and Boerner flatly stated the reason for their discharge to be "You and one other Polyester employee co-authored derogatory, inflammatory and false comments on the memo, made additional copies and distributed it." This evidences that the Respondent believed they were acting concertedly in writing on and posting the altered memo, and terminated them for engaging in such activity. It is well settled that discharges based on suspected concerted activities violate Section 8(a)(1) of the Act even if the suspected concert did not exist. See, e.g., *American Poly Therm Co.*, 298 NLRB 1057, 1065 (1990); *Gulf-Wandes Corp.*, 233 NLRB 772, 778 (1977).

I conclude the evidence warrants an inference the known or suspected participation of Boerner and Howell in protected concerted activities was a motivating factor in the Respondent's decision to discharge them. The burden rests on the Respondent to show the discharges would have taken place in the absence of protected concerted activity. *Wright Line*, 251 NLRB 1083 (1980); *NLRB v. Transportation Management Corp.*, 462 U.S. 393 (1983).

---

[4] *Gatliff Coal Co.*, 301 NLRB 793 (1991).

[5] The testimony of Jane Paxton that her investigation received a report that the comments at issue were designed to start up trouble evidences that the Respondent recognized the comments were of interest to other employees and would tend to inspire debate.

ILLUSTRATION 14-1   *(continued; page 567 omitted)*

therefore not shown the rule was violated,[6] and I find it was not because no postings were made in work areas. The use of the rule by Respondent as a defense therefore can not prevail. Here again, I conclude Respondent has consciously manufactured a reason that does not exist in order to disguise its true motivation.

The evidence shows Howell and Boerner were engaged in protected concerted activity when they placed their comments on and posted the memo, those activities were a motivating factor in Respondent's decision to discharge them, and General Counsel has made out a prima facie case the Act has been violated. The burden on the Respondent to prove the discharges would have taken place in the absence of any protected activity has not been met. Accordingly, I find General Counsel has proved by a preponderance of the credible evidence that Howell and Boerner were discharged in violation of Section 8(a)(1) of the Act.

To the extent the complaint alleges their suspension during investigation violated the Act, I do not so find. It was not unreasonable for the Respondent to suspend the employees involved in the handling of a document wrongfully extracted from its files while it conducted an appropriate investigation. It is its conduct after it ascertained the facts which runs afoul of the Act.

Conclusions of Law

1. Respondent is an employer within the meaning of Section 2(2), (6), and (7) of the Act.

2. Respondent violated Section 8(a)(1) of the Act by discharging Martin Howell and Robert Boerner on June 18, 1993, because they engaged in protected concerted activity.

3. The unfair labor practices found affect commerce within the meaning of Section 2(6) and (7) of the Act.

The Remedy

In addition to the usual notice posting and cease-and-desist requirements, my recommended Order will require Respondent to offer Howell and Boerner immediate and full reinstatement to their former jobs or, if those jobs no longer exist, to substantially equivalent positions without prejudice to their seniority, or other rights and privileges previously enjoyed, and make them whole for any loss of earnings suffered as a result of the discrimination against them. Backpay shall be calculated and interest thereon computed in the manner prescribed in *F. W. Woolworth Co.*, 90 NLRB 289 (1950), and *New Horizons for the Retarded*, 283 NLRB 1173 (1987). I shall further recommend that Respondent be required to remove from its files any reference to their discharges and notify them in writing that this has been done and that the discharges will not be used against them in any way.

On these findings of fact and conclusions of law and on the entire record, I issue the following recommended[7]

---

[6] Whether the posting rule is valid or not is not before me.

[7] If no exceptions are filed as provided by Sec. 102.46 of the Board's Rules and Regulations, the findings, conclusions, and recommended Order shall, as provided in Sec. 102.48 of the Rules, be adopted by the Board and all objections to them shall be deemed waived for all purposes.

ORDER

The Respondent, Morton International, Inc., West Alexandria, Ohio, its officers, agents, successors, and assigns, shall
1. Cease and desist from
(a) Discharging or otherwise discriminating against employees because they engage in protected concerted activity.
(b) In any like or related manner interfering with, restraining, or coercing employees in the exercise of the rights guaranteed them by Section 7 of the Act.
2. Take the following affirmative action necessary to effectuate the policies of the Act.
(a) Offer Martin D. Howell and Robert Boerner immediate and full reinstatement to their former jobs or, if those jobs no longer exist, to substantially equivalent positions, without prejudice to their seniority or any other rights or privileges previously enjoyed, and make them whole for any loss of earnings or benefits suffered as a result of the discrimination against them, in the manner set forth in the remedy section of this decision.
(b) Remove from its files any reference to the discharges of Howell and Boerner on June 18, 1993, and notify them in writing that this has been done and that the discharges will not be used against them in any way.
(c) Preserve and, on request, make available to the Board or its agents for examination and copying, all payroll records, social security payment records, timecards, personnel records and reports, and all other records necessary to analyze the amount of backpay due under the terms of this Order.
(d) Post at its place of business in West Alexandria, Ohio, copies of the attached notice marked "Appendix."[8] Copies of the notice, on forms provided by the Regional Director for Region 9, after being signed by the Respondent's authorized representative, shall be posted by the Respondent immediately upon receipt and maintained for 60 consecutive days in conspicuous places including all places where notices to employees are customarily posted. Reasonable steps shall be taken by the Respondent to ensure that the notices are not altered, defaced, or covered by any other material.
(e) Notify the Regional Director in writing within 20 days from the date of this Order what steps the Respondent has taken to comply.

---

[8] If this Order is enforced by a judgment of a United States court of appeals, the words in the notice reading "Posted by Order of the National Labor Relations Board" shall read "Posted Pursuant to a Judgment of the United States Court of Appeals Enforcing an Order of the National Labor Relations Board."

APPENDIX

NOTICE TO EMPLOYEES
POSTED BY ORDER OF THE
NATIONAL LABOR RELATIONS BOARD
An Agency of the United States Government

The National Labor Relations Board has found that we violated the National Labor Relations Act and has ordered us to post and abide by this notice.

Section 7 of the Act gives employees these rights.

To organize
To form, join, or assist any union

B.   WHY WOULD YOU RESEARCH AGENCY DECISIONS?

As with agency regulations, the reason for researching agency decisions is that they constitute the the law. The agency is subordinate to the legislature and courts: Its decisions must comport with the constitution, applicable statutes, and the judicial standards described above. A decision meeting these requirements is law and functions as precedent for other similar situations coming within the agency's jurisdiction. Although stare decisis does not operate as forcefully with agencies as with courts, an agency must explain any deviations from earlier decisions.

Once you have located the pertinent statute enabling an agency to act, you will know which agency's decisions to research. Federal statutes give rise to federal agency decisions, and state statutes creating state agencies give rise to state agency decisions.

As for the Canoga case, the statute protecting concerted activity by employees is a federal statute; it creates a federal agency, the National Labor Relations Board, with the authority to adjudicate unfair labor practice cases. So the decisions of interest are Board decisions. The *Morton International* decision in Illustration 14-1 at pages 293–96 is a 1994 Board decision.

C.   HOW DO YOU RESEARCH AGENCY DECISIONS?

As with judicial cases, the agency issues a decision in slip form, typically without editorial enhancements. Decisions traditionally are compiled periodically into paper reporters, and many decisions are posted quite promptly in various databases. Each such reporter and database contains the decisions of a particular agency. Some of these sources are commercial, others are official government sources. This chapter focuses on official sources; Chapter 15 discusses commercial sources.

Only rarely will you research only agency decisions. Most of the time, you also will research the enabling statute and judicial cases reviewing the agency's decisions; in some situations, you also will research the agency's regulations. Thus, this part starts with a few words about research in statutes and regulations and concludes with a few words about research in judicial cases. See Exhibit 14.1 for a schematic of agency decisions research.

This part focuses on the National Labor Relations Board, whose decisional law is extensive and easily researched. For other federal agencies and for state agencies, the official sources may be fewer and more difficult to use. When you first research a particular agency's decision, a good first step is to contact the agency or visit its website; another good option is to consult with a reference librarian in an academic law library.

EXHIBIT 14.1	Overview of Agency Decisions Research

enabling
statute ⟶ (regulations) ⟶ [agency
decisions] ⟶ judicial cases

Agency decisions research in statutes and regulations:

▶ read the enabling statute for the legal standard and the agency's
  adjudicative authority; seek references to agency decisions

▶ as needed, research applicable regulations

When an agency decides cases, it implements the language of its enabling
statute. Hence you should read the enabling statute carefully before turning
to the agency's decisions. Chapter 11 covers statutory research. More specifically, as you read the statute, look for the legal standard governing the case
and also for a description of the agency's authority to adjudicate cases and
the process it must follow. Once you learn that the agency can indeed adjudicate cases, you should look in the annotation for references to agency decisions
(as well as judicial cases). See Illustration 14-2 at page 299.

Furthermore, as you read the pertinent provisions of the enabling statute,
look for indications of the agency's authority to promulgate regulations on
your research topic as well as references to those regulations in the *Code of
Federal Regulations*. Chapter 13 covers regulations research.

Researching the Canoga case, we learned that § 7 of the federal labor
statute protects not only union activity but also other "concerted activities
for the purpose of . . . mutual aid or protection."[1] We did not locate a
regulation on the topic of concerted activity. In the extensive annotations in
United States Code Service, we did find references to various agency decisions
(as well as many judicial cases) under the headings of Activities as Concerted
Activities, Generally and Activity of Single Employee, Generally. See Illustration 14-2 on page 299.

---

1. 29 U.S.C. § 157 (2000).

ILLUSTRATION 14-2

Agency Decision Descriptions in Annotated Code, from *United States Code Service* (paper source)

29 USCS § 157, n 45

LABOR

A conversation may constitute a concerted activity although it involves only a speaker and listener, but to qualify as such it must appear at the very least that it was engaged in with the object of initiating or introducing or preparing for group action or that it had some relation to group action in the interest of the employees. Mushroom Transp. Co. v NLRB (1964, CA3) 330 F2d 683, 56 BNA LRRM 2034, 49 CCH LC ¶ 18921.

In order to protect concerted activities in full bloom, protection must be extended to "intended, contemplated or even referred to" group action lest employer retaliation destroy incipient employee initiative aimed at bettering terms of employment and working conditions. Hugh H. Wilson Corp. v NLRB (1969, CA3) 414 F2d 1345, 71 BNA LRRM 2827, 60 CCH LC ¶ 10205, cert den (1970) 397 US 935, 25 L Ed 2d 115, 90 S Ct 943, 73 BNA LRRM 2600, 62 CCH LC ¶ 10724.

Activities of employees engaged in, with, or on behalf of, other employees, and not solely by or on behalf of particular employees themselves, are concerted activities for purpose of mutual aid or protection within meaning of 29 USCS § 157. Top of Waikiki, Inc. v NLRB (1970, CA9) 429 F2d 419, 74 BNA LRRM 2678, 63 CCH LC ¶ 10999.

"Concerted activity" means the employee must be acting with or on behalf of other employees, and not solely by and on behalf of the discharged employee himself. NLRB v C &I Air Conditioning, Inc. (1973, CA9) 486 F2d 977, 84 BNA LRRM 2625, 72 CCH LC ¶ 14048.

For individual claim or complaint to amount to concerted action, it must not be made solely on behalf of individual employee, but must be made on behalf of other employees or at least be made with object of inducing or preparing for group action and have some arguable basis in collective bargaining agreement. ARO, Inc. v NLRB (1979, CA6) 596 F2d 713, 101 BNA LRRM 2153, 86 CCH LC ¶ 11250, 56 ALR Fed 728.

Concerted activity includes activity of individual employee when that employee is acting on behalf of only one other employee. Wilson Trophy Co. v NLRB (1993, CA8) 989 F2d 1502, 143 BNA LRRM 2008, 124 CCH LC ¶ 10622, reh, en banc, den (1993, CA8) 125 CCH LC ¶ 10740.

Two employees as well as a dozen or a thousand can act in concert for their mutual aid and protection. Tex-Togs, Inc. (1955) 112 NLRB 968, 36 BNA LRRM 1129, enforced (1956, CA5) 231 F2d 310, 37 BNA LRRM 2768, 30 CCH LC ¶ 69849.

It is not necessary for employees to band together and overtly manifest by physical action discontent before NLRB will find that concerted activity, for even individual protests which resound to groups' benefit are protected concerted activity. Aro, Inc. (1976) 227 NLRB 243, 94 BNA LRRM 1010, 1976-77 CCH NLRB ¶ 17662, enforcement

den (1979, CA6) 596 F2d 713, 101 BNA LRRM 2153, 86 CCH LC ¶ 11250, 56 ALR Fed 728.

Contrary to prior decision in Alleluia Cushion Co. (1975) 221 NLRB 999, Board will not find protected concerted activity unless employee engages in or with or own authority of other employees, and not solely on behalf of employee himself. Meyers Industries, Inc. (1984) 268 NLRB 493, 115 BNA LRRM 1025, 1983-84 CCH NLRB ¶ 16019, remanded (1985) 244 US App DC 42, 755 F2d 941, 118 BNA LRRM 2649, 102 CCH LC ¶ 11346, cert den (1985) 474 US 948, 88 L Ed 2d 294, 106 S Ct 313, 120 BNA LRRM 3392 and cert den (1985) 474 US 971, 88 L Ed 2d 320, 106 S Ct 352, 120 BNA LRRM 3392, 103 CCH LC ¶ 11585, on remand (1986) 281 NLRB 882, 123 BNA LRRM 1137, 1986-87 CCH NLRB ¶ 18184, affd (1987) 266 US App DC 385, 835 F2d 1481, 127 BNA LRRM 2415, 107 CCH LC ¶ 10226, cert den (1988) 487 US 1205, 101 L Ed 2d 884, 108 S Ct 2847, 128 BNA LRRM 2664, 129 BNA LRRM 3016, 109 CCH LC ¶ 10534.

46. Activity of single employee, generally

Employee who was discharged after acting alone in complaining to employer about violation would have been protected from discharge under 29 USCS § 157 by simply getting together with co-workers to complain. Prill v NLRB (1987) 266 US App DC 385, 835 F2d 1481, 127 BNA LRRM 2415, 107 CCH LC ¶ 10226, cert den (1988) 487 US 1205, 101 L Ed 2d 884, 108 S Ct 2847, 128 BNA LRRM 2664, 129 BNA LRRM 3016, 109 CCH LC ¶ 10534.

Activity of single employee in enlisting support of fellow employees for their mutual aid and protection is as much concerted activity as is ordinary group activity. Owens-Corning Fiberglas Corp. v NLRB (1969, CA4) 407 F2d 1357, 70 BNA LRRM 3065, 59 CCH LC ¶ 13356.

Truckdriver engaged in concerted activity by refusing to drive truck which he felt unsafe where he obtained instructions to do so from union official, sought to involve other union members and have them present during dispute with employer, and employer was aware of union involvement. McLean Trucking Co. v NLRB (1982, CA6) 689 F2d 605, 111 BNA LRRM 3185, 97 CCH LC ¶ 10166.

Single employee's filing of worker's compensation claim is not protected concerted activity, notwithstanding employee is member of collective bargaining group. Flick v General Host Corp. (1983, ND Ill) 573 F Supp 1086, 114 BNA LRRM 3576.

Employee who, in good faith, refuses to drive tractor-trailor truck on ground that condition of truck constitutes abnormally dangerous working condition is engaged in concerted activity under 29

> **Agency decisions in the agency's own compilation—reporter or database:**
>
> ▶ discern the scope, coverage, and means of access of the compilation
> ▶ locate potentially pertinent decisions
> ▶ carefully read the pertinent decisions

Some agencies publish decisions in paper reporters, others in databases made available through public websites, others a combination of the two. *Bluebook* Table 1 and an *ALWD* appendix (available through the website alwd.org) list official reporters of federal agency decisions. Each such compilation has its own particular features. The following discussion focuses on the Board's compilations; you probably will find other compilations similar in general design if not identical in detail.

For many decades, the Board has published its decisions in paper reporters, called *Decisions and Orders of the National Labor Relations Board*. As with reporters of judicial cases, decisions are published in the order issued. Thus, a digest is needed to identify pertinent decisions within the various volumes. The Board employs a highly structured and detailed outline of the issues it considers, the Classification Outline. See Illustration 14-3 at page 302. Its staff write brief descriptions of each decision and assign the descriptions to a topic within the classification outline. (The classification outline and the decision descriptions function like the West key-number system and headnotes, discussed in Chapter 9.)

For most recent Board decisions, dating from 1992 to the present, you will use the Board's classification system through NLRB CITENET, a feature of the NLRB website. A standard approach is to scan the list of chapters and select a potentially pertinent one, then scan the topics within that chapter and select a potentially pertinent topic, then run a key-word search of the descriptions assigned to that chapter and topic. You will thereby obtain the descriptions of pertinent decisions, but not the decisions themselves. See Illustration 14-4 at page 303.

For older cases, you will use the *Classified Index of National Labor Relations Board Decisions and Related Court Decisions*, a set of hardcover volumes, each covering several years of NLRB decisions. Despite its title, this publication is really a digest, in which the decision descriptions are presented within the classification outline.

Once you identify potentially pertinent decisions by use of the classification outline, you will obtain the decisions in either the paper *Decisions and Orders* or through the NLRB Decisions database made available at the Board's website. Note that the two compilations cover different time periods. *Decisions and Orders* in paper dates to 1935; the NLRB Decisions database dates back to 1984 and is updated very promptly as the Board issues new decisions.

When you use the classification outline to identify potentially pertinent decisions, you learn about the range of issues addressed by the Board and how the various issues relate to each other. If you do not need this information and believe that you can state your research topic well in a Boolean search, keeping in mind that NLRB Decisions dates only to 1984, you could run a search in that database. See Illustration 14-5 at page 304, which is a partial citation list from such a search. Although the citation list you thus obtain does not tell you much about the decisions, you can readily link to the decisions themselves.

Of course, you should carefully read the decisions you have found. As with judicial cases, you should learn the outcome of the case, discern the rule used by the agency to decide the case, understand the facts of the case and the court's reasoning about those facts, identify the leading authorities referred to, and examine any dissenting and concurring opinions. Be sure you fully understand how the decision is structured. Many agency commissioners incorporate the recommended findings and conclusions of the ALJ.

Researching the Canoga case, we arrived at chapter 506 topic 2001–5000, Employee Rights Protected by Section 7, Concerted Activity Defined in the classification index. See Illustration 14-3 at page 302. A search for that topic and the term `smoke` in NLRB CITENET yielded the *Morton International* decision. See Illustration 14-4 at page 303. We also ran the search `"concerted activity" AND smok*` in the NLRB Decisions database; *Morton International* was the second case listed. See Illustration 14-5 at page 304.

Updating and citing agency decisions:

▶ judicial cases
▶ Shepard's through LexisNexis or KeyCite through Westlaw

As with judicial cases, the law made through agency decisions evolves over time. Later agency decisions may affect the validity of an earlier agency decision in various ways, for example, overruling, modifying, distinguishing, citing with approval. By researching agency decisions thoroughly, you should obtain more recent agency decisions on your research topic and should thereby learn of any changes in the law at the agency level.

In addition, you should research in judicial cases, with several purposes in mind:

☐ You should, of course, learn whether the agency decision on which you plan to rely has been reviewed by a court and what the outcome was.
☐ You should learn whether the agency decision has been cited in other judicial cases involving different parties but addressing your research topic.

ILLUSTRATION 14-3

Classification Outline, from *Classification Outline with Topical Index for Decisions of the National Labor Relations Board and Related Court Decisions* (paper source)

506 EMPLOYEE RIGHTS PROTECTED BY SECTION 7	2017-6700 Activities prohibited by statute
	2017-8300 Conduct violating valid provisions of contract
0100 **GENERALLY**	2017-9100 Conduct in derogation of bargaining representation
0114 RIGHT OF SELF-ORGANIZATION	2033 BOARD HAS FUNCTION OF BALANCING CONFLICTING EMPLOYEE AND EMPLOYER INTERESTS
0128 RIGHT TO FORM, JOIN, OR ASSIST LABOR ORGANIZATIONS	2033-5000 Exercise of economic pressure not unlawful per se
0142 RIGHT TO BARGAIN COLLECTIVELY THROUGH REPRESENTATIVE OF OWN CHOOSING	2050 EMPLOYER'S MISTAKEN BELIEF AS TO ACTIVITY'S PROTECTED STATUS IMMATERIAL
0156 RIGHT TO ENGAGE IN OTHER CONCERTED ACTIVITIES FOR PURPOSE OF COLLECTIVE BARGAINING	2060 EMPLOYEES' MISTAKEN BELIEF AS TO VALIDITY OF GRIEVANCE IMMATERIAL
0170 RIGHT TO ENGAGE IN OTHER CONCERTED ACTIVITIES FOR MUTUAL AID OR PROTECTION	2067 UNION MEMBERSHIP IMMATERIAL
	2083 UNION ACTIVITY NEED NOT BE INVOLVED OR COLLECTIVE BARGAINING CONTEMPLATED
0180 ATTITUDE TOWARD MANAGEMENT REFLECTING DISSATISFACTION WITH WORKING CONDITIONS AND/OR LACK OF SUCCESS OF UNION CAMPAIGN, ETC.	3000 **REFUSAL TO CROSS PICKET LINE**
	3001 GENERALLY
0184 RIGHT TO REFRAIN FROM EXERCISE OF SECTION 7 RIGHTS	3001-5000 Employer may replace non-striking employee refusing to cross line if business reasons so require
0184-0100 Generally	3033 AT PREMISES OF ANOTHER EMPLOYER
0184-5000 Subject to membership requirement of valid agreement	3033-0100 Generally
	3033-2500 Right protected by 8(b)(4) proviso
0188 RIGHT TO BE FREE FROM UNFAIR, IRRELEVANT, OR INVIDIOUS TREATMENT BY REPRESENTATIVE	3033-5000 Primary picket line
	3033-7500 Secondary picket line
0188-5000 Differentiation on basis of sex	3033-8700 Picket line at state subdivision
0192 RIGHTS DERIVED FROM OTHER FEDERAL LABOR STATUTES	3067 AT OWN EMPLOYER'S PREMISES
	3067-0100 Generally
2000 **NATURE OF ACTIVITIES PROTECTED**	3067-1700 Primary line of another union at employee's place of work
2001 GENERALLY	
2001-5000 Concerted activity defined	3067-3300 Primary line of union representing unit of which employee is not member
2017 NOT ALL CONCERTED ACTIVITIES PROTECTED	3067-5000 As result of sympathy strike
2017-0800 Activity of such character as to render employee unfit for further service	3067-6700 Secondary picket line which is primary line of another union
2017-1700 Activities tending to disrupt employer's or union's operations	4000 **OBJECTIVE AS DETERMINANT OF PROTECTED STATUS OF ACTIVITY**
2017-2500 Activities relating to intra-union affairs	4001 GENERALLY
2017-3300 Cessation of work for personal reasons	4001-5000 Racial discrimination
2017-4000 No impact upon terms and conditions of employment	4033 OBJECTIVES WARRANTING PROTECTION OF ACTIVITY
2017-5000 Resort to prohibited means	4033-0100 Generally

82

ILLUSTRATION 14-4   Results of Search for Agency Decisions,
                        from NLRB CITENET (electronic source)

NLRB CITENET
Classified Index
The Electronic Network

Skip Navigation   Comments

NLRB Home   Banner   Search Heading   Search Digest   Search Case Name   User Guide

Classification Digest Search Results
Total Found: 2   **Criteria:**: 50620015000: Decision Type B: smoke

Do Search Within Search	**View CiteNet Abbreviations**

List All Results in new window (this will allow you to view and/or print the entire list)

	Next	Last

506-2001-5000-0000 Concerted or protected activity defined

Digest: [E's suspension and discharge of 2 Ees for writing on and posting memo dealing with enforcement of E's no-smoking policy, unlawful, since Ees were engaged in protected concerted activity; Ees' action of altering memo was taken to initiate or induce other fellow **smoker**s in opposition to sentiments of memo; Ees took action to oppose memo in attempt to preserve status quo as it related to smoking policy; E's smoking policy is term and condition of employment and Ees' concerted action directed at protesting change in policy thus concerns a term and condition of employment and is protected activity; E's dismissal letters, stating "You and one other ... Ee," indicates E believed Ees were acting concertedly in writing on and posting altered memo]

Case Name: Morton International, Inc.

Case Number:9-CA-30898 **Decision Date:**November 10, 1994

Type: Board   **Citation Number:**315 NLRB No. 71

Members:DBC   **Tracking ID:**1994-784

	Next	Last

NLRB Home | Banner | Search Heading | Search Digest | Search Case Name | User Guide | CiteNet Abbr. | Comments

Today's date: November 6, 2003

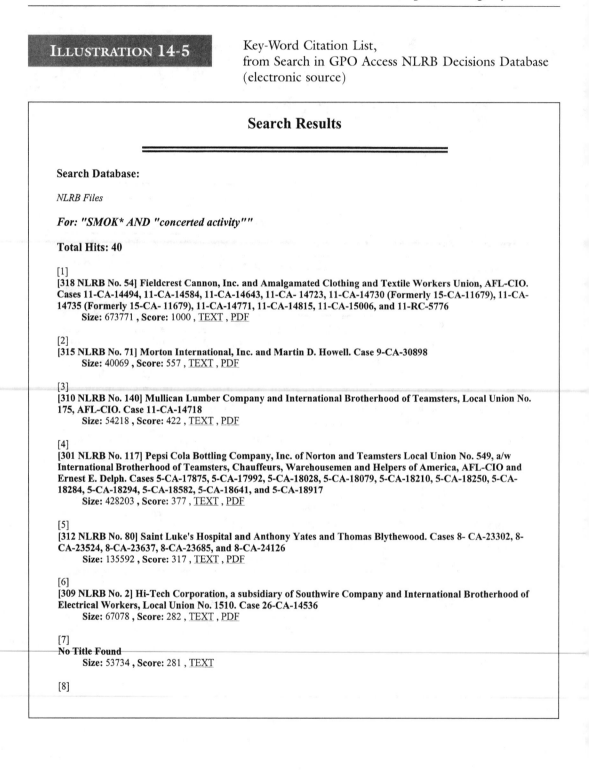

ILLUSTRATION 14-5   Key-Word Citation List,
                          from Search in GPO Access NLRB Decisions Database
                          (electronic source)

Search Results

Search Database:

NLRB Files

For: "SMOK AND "concerted activity""*

Total Hits: 40

[1]
**[318 NLRB No. 54] Fieldcrest Cannon, Inc. and Amalgamated Clothing and Textile Workers Union, AFL-CIO.
Cases 11-CA-14494, 11-CA-14584, 11-CA-14643, 11-CA- 14723, 11-CA-14730 (Formerly 15-CA-11679), 11-CA-
14735 (Formerly 15-CA- 11679), 11-CA-14771, 11-CA-14815, 11-CA-15006, and 11-RC-5776**
    Size: 673771 , Score: 1000 , TEXT **,** PDF

[2]
[315 NLRB No. 71] Morton International, Inc. and Martin D. Howell. Case 9-CA-30898
    Size: 40069 , Score: 557 , TEXT **,** PDF

[3]
**[310 NLRB No. 140] Mullican Lumber Company and International Brotherhood of Teamsters, Local Union No.
175, AFL-CIO. Case 11-CA-14718**
    Size: 54218 , Score: 422 , TEXT **,** PDF

[4]
**[301 NLRB No. 117] Pepsi Cola Bottling Company, Inc. of Norton and Teamsters Local Union No. 549, a/w
International Brotherhood of Teamsters, Chauffeurs, Warehousemen and Helpers of America, AFL-CIO and
Ernest E. Delph. Cases 5-CA-17875, 5-CA-17992, 5-CA-18028, 5-CA-18079, 5-CA-18210, 5-CA-18250, 5-CA-
18284, 5-CA-18294, 5-CA-18582, 5-CA-18641, and 5-CA-18917**
    Size: 428203 , Score: 377 , TEXT **,** PDF

[5]
**[312 NLRB No. 80] Saint Luke's Hospital and Anthony Yates and Thomas Blythewood. Cases 8- CA-23302, 8-
CA-23524, 8-CA-23637, 8-CA-23685, and 8-CA-24126**
    Size: 135592 , Score: 317 , TEXT **,** PDF

[6]
**[309 NLRB No. 2] Hi-Tech Corporation, a subsidiary of Southwire Company and International Brotherhood of
Electrical Workers, Local Union No. 1510. Case 26-CA-14536**
    Size: 67078 , Score: 282 , TEXT **,** PDF

[7]
No Title Found
    Size: 53734 , Score: 281 , TEXT

[8]

☐ You should discern whether judicial cases addressing your research topic but not referring to the agency decision use the rule articulated in the agency decision or some other rule.

As you research judicial cases, keep in mind the precedential structure in the area of law you are researching, that is, be sure you know which courts review agency decisions from your geographic region. Under the federal labor statute, for example, the parties may appeal an agency decision to either of two federal appeals courts: the circuit in which the events arose and the D.C. Circuit (where the Board is located). Therefore, the agency decision, if appealed, would be reviewed by one or the other of these courts, so you should research the law of both circuits as well as the Supreme Court.

To research judicial cases, you can use the sources described in Chapters 9 and 10, for example, digests, reporters, commercial databases. Because the agency decision and related judicial cases involve a statute and possibly also a regulation, you can use the sources described in Chapter 11 to locate cases involving a statute, such as the case descriptions in an annotated code, and the sources described in Chapter 13 to locate cases involving a regulation, for example, citing the regulation.

A key step in researching judicial cases is citing; the same is true of researching agency decisions. You may Shepardize agency decisions through LexisNexis and KeyCite them through Westlaw. Both services provide the history of the agency decision and a list of authorities referring to the agency decision, including other agency decisions, judicial cases, and secondary authorities. And both services supplement the list in various ways, for example, symbols indicating the status of the cited agency decision, words or symbols indicating how the citing authority treated the agency decisions. See Illustration 14-6 at page 306, a Shepard's report for the *Morton International* decision.

Also keep in mind that the legislature may amend the statute or the agency may amend the regulation on which an agency decision relies and thereby change the law. You should discover this through your research in statutes and regulations, as discussed in Chapter 11 (statutes) and Chapter 13 (agency regulations).

Researching the Canoga case, we updated our research various ways. We Shepardized *Morton International* and learned that it has no subsequent history and has been cited in six Board decisions and no judicial cases. Through Illustration 14-2 at page 299, the U.S.C.S. statutory annotation, we learned of a leading judicial case on the topic of concerted activity, *Prill v. NLRB*,[2] a 1987 decision of the highly influential D.C. Circuit. The rule applied in *Morton International* accords with *Prill*.[3]

2. 835 F.2d 1481 (D.C. Cir. 1987), *cert. denied,* 487 U.S. 1205 (1988).
3. The Board's decisions in *Prill* are the *Meyer's Industries* decisions cited in the upper-right-hand corner of Illustration 14-2 at page 299; they are cited in *Morton International,* in Illustration 14-1 at page 295.

| ILLUSTRATION 14-6 | Shepard's Report for Agency Decision, from LexisNexis (electronic source) |

Signal: **A** Citing Refs. With Analysis Available
Trail: **Unrestricted**

Morton Int'l, 315 N.L.R.B. 564, 1994 N.L.R.B. LEXIS 910, 147 L.R.R.M. (BNA) 1280, 1993-94 NLRB Dec. (CCH) P15540, 315 N.L.R.B. No. 71 (1994)

SHEPARD'S SUMMARY ♦ Hide Summary

Shepard's **FULL Summary:A** - Citing Refs. With Analysis Available
No subsequent appellate history. Prior history available.
Citing References:
  Neutral Analyses: **Interim Decision (2)**
  Other Sources: Statutes (1)

PRIOR HISTORY (1 citing reference) ♦ Hide Prior History

1. Morton Int'l, 1994 N.L.R.B. LEXIS 534 (N.L.R.B. July 20, 1994)

▸   **Affirmed by, Adopted by (CITATION YOU ENTERED):**
     Morton Int'l, 315 N.L.R.B. 564, 1994 N.L.R.B. LEXIS 910, 147 L.R.R.M. (BNA) 1280, 1993-94
     NLRB Dec. (CCH) P15540, 315 N.L.R.B. No. 71 (1994)

CITING DECISIONS (6 citing decisions)

NATIONAL LABOR RELATIONS BOARD

2. **Cited by:**
   BTNH, Inc., 1998 N.L.R.B. LEXIS 514 (N.L.R.B. July 29, 1998)

3. **Cited by:**
   Vets Int'l Armored Car, 1998 N.L.R.B. LEXIS 38 (N.L.R.B. Jan. 29, 1998)

4. **Interim decision at:**
   Timekeeping Sys., 323 N.L.R.B. 244, 1997 N.L.R.B. LEXIS 177, 154 L.R.R.M. (BNA) 1233, 323
   N.L.R.B. No. 30 (1997)

        323 N.L.R.B. 244 p.248

5. **Cited by:**
   Timekeeping Sys., 1996 N.L.R.B. LEXIS 740 (N.L.R.B. Nov. 12, 1996)

6. **Interim decision at:**
   World Fashion, 320 N.L.R.B. 922, 1996 N.L.R.B. LEXIS 125, 153 L.R.R.M. (BNA) 1120, 320 N.L.R.B.
   No. 90 (1996)

        320 N.L.R.B. 922 p.925

7. **Cited by:**
   Securitites Indus. Automation Corp., 1996 N.L.R.B. LEXIS 28 (N.L.R.B. Jan. 30, 1996)

D.   WHAT ELSE?

LexisNexis and Westlaw.   Both services provide databases of agency decisions, which are kept current, generally extend back in time farther than agency website databases, and provide additional search options. For example, Westlaw's database of NRLB decisions dates to 1935, the date the Board was established.

State Agency Decisions.   Potential sources of state agency decisions are Westlaw and LexisNexis databases as well as agency websites. If these fail, a good next step is to contact the agency itself.

Informal Opinions.   Some agencies issue opinion letters about specific situations on which advice is sought, so as to avoid litigation. An example is the private letter ruling of the Internal Revenue Service. To learn how to research such informal decisions, contact the agency, check its website, or check a library catalogue.

E.   HOW DO YOU CITE AGENCY DECISIONS?

To properly cite an agency decision, you would provide the decision's name, official reporter citation, and date. The *ALWD* rule also requires the agency's abbreviation in the parenthetical.

- ☐   *Bluebook* Rule 14.3: *Morton Int'l, Inc.,* 315 N.L.R.B. 564 (1994).
- ☐   *ALWD* Rule 19.5: *Morton Intl., Inc.,* 315 N.L.R.B. 564 (Natl. Lab. Rel. Bd. 1994).

Mini-Libraries

CHAPTER

15

A. What Are Mini-Libraries, and Why Are They Useful?
B. How Do You Research in Mini-Libraries?
C. What Else?
D. How Do You Cite to Mini-Libraries?

A. WHAT ARE MINI-LIBRARIES, AND WHY ARE THEY USEFUL?

For some areas of the law, commercial publishers compile what we are calling "mini-libraries," comprehensive and current collections of primary and secondary authorities. The traditional term for this type of source is "looseleaf service," because mini-libraries do indeed appear in multivolume paper looseleaf binders. An increasingly common alternative is a subscription electronic service. We are discussing these sources in this unit because they are particularly useful for locating administrative materials. Although they vary considerably, mini-libraries share three important characteristics.

First, they bring together, into one source, a wide range of primary and secondary authority. Comprehensive mini-libraries include judicial case law, statutes, administrative regulations, and agency decisions, some at the federal and state levels. Many mini-libraries also contain commentary, and the most comprehensive include practice materials (such as forms), reports of pending cases or bills, and summaries of interesting conferences or studies.

Second, mini-libraries are updated frequently and thereby provide fairly current material. They are published in formats that facilitate updating.

Third, the best mini-libraries provide significant assistance to the researcher through refined finding tools, such as indexes, topic outlines, and case digests. Because a mini-library covers only one area of law, these tools can be very detailed, and one set of tools covers various types of legal authority.

B. How Do You Research in Mini-Libraries?

Because each mini-library is unique, research practices vary from source to source. The following discussion first sets out steps you might take in a paper looseleaf service, then describes options available in electronic media. The discussion features *Labor Relations Reporter*, a looseleaf service published by the Bureau of National Affairs, and its electronic counterpart. The federal concerted activity issue featured in this unit serves as the example.

Administrative materials in paper looseleaf services:

- ▶ locate an appropriate looseleaf service
- ▶ examine it and its instructional material
- ▶ consult the general index
- ▶ read the commentary for background and references
- ▶ locate and read the statutes and administrative regulations
- ▶ use the case digest to locate pertinent cases
- ▶ read judicial case law and agency decisions
- ▶ cite the primary authority

A paper looseleaf service uses binders that can be easily opened for insertion and deletion of pages; as new material arrives, it is slipped into the binder, adding to or replacing older material. The set of materials usually includes several binders, each with one or more sections set off by tabs. Extensive looseleaf services also include separate volumes for older material, such as cases or agency decisions.

Locate and examine the looseleaf. To determine whether an appropriate looseleaf service exists, consult a library catalog; examine *Legal Looseleafs in Print*, by Arlene L. Eis; or check Table 16 in *The Bluebook* (abbreviations for services).

Once you have identified a pertinent looseleaf, look over the entire set:

- ☐ Examine the various binders, and gain some understanding of the materials each contains.
- ☐ Look for a section describing how to use the looseleaf, typically located in the first binder, and read it.
- ☐ Also look for a statement indicating the currency of the various components. See Illustration 15-1 at page 312. Pages are re-issued as needed, and most pages bear a date of issuance. If you find a page that was issued some years ago, you will want to know when it was last considered for updating.
- ☐ Also locate the general index and any updates, as well as tables of authorities, such as statutes or regulations.

☐   Figure out where the commentary material, statutes, regulations, cases, and decisions appear.

☐   Locate the most recent information, typically in a separate binder or section of a binder; also locate any hardbound or other volumes containing more dated information, such as cases or agency decisions.

Consult the index(es). Many looseleafs are divided into several parts by types of authority (for example, commentary, statutes) or by jurisdiction (federal, individual states). Thus, there may be more than one index: a general index for the entire looseleaf and subsidiary indexes for the various parts. Furthermore, these indexes may have one or more updates, so you should be sure to note the currency of each index. As a general rule, consult the general index first and then any pertinent subsidiary indexes. See Illustration 15-2 at page 313.

As you move from the index to the text, take special care to discern the looseleaf's numbering scheme. The looseleaf may be organized and numbered by unit, chapter, section, paragraph, or page, or, most likely, a combination of these.

Read the commentary. Ordinarily you will move from the index to the commentary portion of the looseleaf. The commentary is likely to be fairly current, present a detailed discussion, and contain references to primary authority. See Illustration 15-3 at pages 314–15.

Research statutes and regulations. If you are using a looseleaf service to research an area of law governed by an administrative agency, you will want to read the pertinent statute and any regulations the agency has promulgated on your research topic. Most looseleafs afford several means of locating statutes and regulations: through the general index, through references in the commentary section, through a subsidiary index to the statutes and regulations sections, through a table of contents at the beginning of a set of statutes or regulations, and through tables of statutes or regulations. Federal and state materials typically appear in separate sections or binders.

Research cases and decisions. A looseleaf service covering an area of law governed by an administrative agency may also contain judicial case law and agency decisions. Indeed, a looseleaf service may well include judicial cases not reported in general case reporters, informal agency decisions that are difficult to locate in government sources, and very new decisions.

Looseleafs also typically contain detailed, topically arranged digests of the cases. The general index, commentary, or subsidiary index for the cases or decisions sections may point you to pertinent topics within the digest; you also may find it useful to skim the digest outline. See Illustration 15-4 at page 316. The digest may appear in multiple volumes, for example, the newest digest material in the looseleaf binders, older materials in softcover or hardbound books. Thus, you typically must work through recent material and then back in time. As you examine the digest, seek potentially pertinent judicial cases, agency decisions, or both. See Illustration 15-5 at page 317.

Once you have identified potentially pertinent cases, you would, of course, read them in the looseleaf service. They may appear in hardbound volumes or looseleaf volumes. The looseleaf may or may not give the official citation to material published in official reporters.

Citate primary authority. To update and expand your research, use the looseleaf's citator, if one exists. If there is none, use Shepard's or KeyCite, especially for judicial cases and agency decisions.

Researching the Canoga case. *Labor Relations Reporter* (L.R.R.) is a comprehensive looseleaf service covering employment law published by the Bureau of National Affairs (BNA). The general index and other finding aids appear in the *Master Index* binders. The *Labor Relations Expediter* binders contain commentary, statutes, and regulations, while *State Laws* binders contain state statutes and regulations. L.R.R. presents case material in digests and reporters, with the most recent material appearing in binders and the dated material in the hardbound volumes. There is no citator.

In the General Index, we located the heading Termination of Employment and focused on the subheading Protected Activities, Bias, LMRA. ("LMRA" is the abbreviation for the Labor Management Relations Act, the private sector labor statute.) See Illustration 15-2 at page 313. The two references are to the Labor Relations Outline (LR) and to the Labor Relations Expediter (LRX). The small print at the bottom explains the abbreviations and tells you how current this index is (December 2002, when this research was conducted in the fall of 2003).

We pursued the reference to LRX 510:207 and located a portion of the Labor Relations Expediter that discusses concerted activities. See Illustration 15-3 at pages 314–15. The commentary mentions several agency decisions, including the landmark decision, *Meyers Industries.*

We could locate both the federal statute and the Board's regulations in the Text of Laws and Regulations section in the *Labor Relations Expediter* binder. As to the latter, L.R.R. provides references to the enabling statute and the citation to the *Federal Register* where the regulation was promulgated in final form. We checked for a parallel New Mexico statute but found none.

To research case law backwards from the present in L.R.R. entails reviewing the very recent materials filed under the Cumulative Digest and Index (CDI) tab in the *Master Index* binder, then older softcover volumes, and then even older hardbound volumes. The most recent cases appear in the *Labor Management Relations: Decisions of Boards and Courts* binder, while older ones appear in hardbound volumes called *Labor Relations Reference Manual* (L.R.R.M.).

We turned to our case law research with a good lead: Both the General Index and the Labor Relations Expediter pointed to LR 52.2532 et seq. See Illustrations 15-2 at page 313 and 15-3 at page 314. The Labor Relations Outline of Classifications is a very refined topical outline that appears in the *Master Index* binder. Topic 52 is Employer Discrimination in Regard to Employment, and subtopic .2532 is one of a series of subtopics related to concerted activities. See Illustration 15-4 at page 316. We then read the case descriptions in the L.R.R. digest. The L.R.R. digest covers court cases as well as Board decisions. Illustration 15-5 at page 317 is from the hardbound digest volumes covering 1991-1995; it describes the Board decision in *Morton International.* That case appears in volume 147 of the L.R.R.M. reporter.

L.R.R. does not itself include a citator; it is possible, however, to KeyCite or Shepardize L.R.R.M. cases and decisions.

ILLUSTRATION 15-1   Looseleaf Service Updating Material,
                              from BNA's *Labor Relations Reporter* (paper source)

BNA, INC.

LABOR RELATIONS REPORTER®
FAIR EMPLOYMENT PRACTICES

Manual

No. 982   November 24, 2003

HIGHLIGHTS ...

The U.S. Supreme Court refuses to review a Seventh Circuit ruling that a shareholder in an Illinois medical practice was not an "employee" for purposes of coverage under the Age Discrimination in Employment Act. See 411:306.

Subscriber Alert: The general index for BNA's Labor Relations Reporter is updated regularly at http://www.bna.com/lrr/lrrindx.htm. There is no charge for accessing this on-line service.

FILING INSTRUCTIONS

> **Note:** Section headings on the left of the page correspond to section tabs in the reference service. Remove pages listed in the column headed "Take Out Pages." Insert pages listed in the column headed "Put In Pages." A series of dots in either column indicates there are no pages to be removed or inserted. Retain only the most current filing instructions sheet in front of Binder 8.
>
> **Customer Assistance:** If you have any problems with missing pages or other questions regarding the filing of these binders, call toll-free: 1-800-372-1033.
>
> *Discarded pages can be recycled.*

	Take Out Pages	Put In Pages
BINDER 8		
403 — FEDERAL LAW: TEXT OF RULES, REGULATIONS, GUIDELINES		
EEOC: Records and Reports (reprinted) ...	403:55-403:67	403:55-403:66
Uniform Guidelines on Employee Selection Procedures (reprinted)	403:349-403:388	403:349-403:374

COPYRIGHT INFORMATION

ILLUSTRATION 15-2   Looseleaf Service General Index,
from BNA's *Labor Relations Reporter* (paper source)

TER

GENERAL INDEX   A 977

TERMINATION OF EMPLOYMENT—Contd.
Obscenity
    LR ▶ 118.640
    LA ▶ 118.640
    LRX 510:227
—Discrimination, LMRA, LR ▶ 52.2728
—Management, employee use toward, LA ▶ 118.6523
—Public employees, LA ▶ 100.552510
OFCCP equal opportunity survey, defined, FEPM 441:504
Off-duty or off-premises misconduct, LA ▶ 118.634
—Public employees, LA ▶ 100.552505
Overtime, refusal to work
    LR ▶ 118.658
    LA ▶ 118.658
    LRX 510:235
—Discrimination, LMRA, LR ▶ 52.2731
—Public employees, LA ▶ 100.552570
Past practice, LA ▶ 24.355
Performance. *See* Incompetence and inefficiency, *this heading*
Personal appearance, LA ▶ 118.639
—Public employees, LA ▶ 100.552529
Personnel files, remedies for bias
    FEP ▶ 228.251
    AD ▶ 228.251
Physical disabilities. *See* Disabled employees, *this heading*
Physical tests, failure to submit, LA ▶ 118.655
—Public employees, LA ▶ 100.552565
Picketing
    LR ▶ 118.660
    LA ▶ 118.6601
—Discrimination, LMRA, LR ▶ 52.341
—Employees' failure to repudiate illegal strike or violent picketing, LMRA, LRX 670:310
Political affiliation. *See* POLITICAL ACTIVITIES, *subheading:* Affiliation
Polygraph tests. *See* Lie detectors, *this heading*
Poor performance, LRX 510:233
Post leaving, LA ▶ 118.654
—Public employees, LA ▶ 100.552555
Pregnancy, FEPM 421:508
—Federal employees, FEP ▶ 110.4018
—Weight requirements, "too fat" case, FEPM 421:502
Procedure
    LR ▶ 118.301 et seq.
    LA ▶ 118.301 et seq.
    LRX 510:224
—Public employees, LA ▶ 100.5523
Productivity. *See* Incompetence and inefficiency, *this heading;* Loafing, *this heading*
Promotion before, LRX 650:107
Protected activities, bias, LMRA
    LR ▶ 52.2532 et seq.
    LRX 510:207
Protest against, picketing objects, LR ▶ 81.257
Psychological evaluations, LA ▶ 118.655
—Public employees, LA ▶ 100.552565

Public employees
    LR ▶ 100.641, ▶ 100.647
    LA ▶ 100.5501 et seq.
—Mitigation of damages, LA ▶ 100.559525
Quitting jobs distinguished
    LR ▶ 118.07
    LA ▶ 118.07
—Discrimination, LMRA, LR ▶ 52.257
Racial bias, FEP ▶ 108.30251
—Abolition of job, FEP ▶ 108.30263
—Absenteeism, FEP ▶ 108.30257
—Availability of work, FEP ▶ 108.30263
—Dishonesty of employees, FEP ▶ 108.30259
—Falsification of job applications, FEP ▶ 108.30259
—Federal employees, FEP ▶ 110.3515
—Incompetence, FEP ▶ 108.30255
—Insubordination, FEP ▶ 108.30253
—Job qualifications, FEP ▶ 108.30255
—Misconduct of employees, FEP ▶ 108.30253
—Performance on job, FEP ▶ 108.30255
—Tardiness, FEP ▶ 108.30257
—Theft, FEP ▶ 108.30259
Reasons
    LR ▶ 118.632 et seq.
    LA ▶ 118.632 et seq.
See also specific reasons for discharge
—Discrimination, LMRA, LR ▶ 52.2672
—Just cause. *See* Just cause, *this heading*
—Public employees, LA ▶ 100.552501 et seq.
Reemployment, union-security contracts, LRX 730:316
—Illegally discharged employees, LRX 730:316
—Legally discharged employees, LRX 730:316
—Maintenance of membership, LRX 730:316
Refusal to give doctor's certificate, LA ▶ 118.655
—Public employees, LA ▶ 100.552565
Reinstatement. *See* REINSTATEMENT
Religious bias, FEP ▶ 108.1118
—Federal employees, FEP ▶ 110.5015
Remedies
    LR ▶ 118.801 et seq.
    LA ▶ 118.801 et seq.
—Discrimination, LMRA, LRX 510:221
—Public employees, LA ▶ 100.559501 et seq.
Resignation, FMLA benefits. *See* FMLA, *this heading*
Restitution by public employees, LA ▶ 100.5512
Retaliatory discharge. *See* RETALIATION
Safety, LA ▶ 118.659
—Public employees, LA ▶ 100.552575
Scope of employers' rights, bias, LMRA, LRX 510:204
Section 8(a)(1) of LMRA, 8(a)(3) distinguished, bias, LMRA, LRX 510:204
Section 8(a)(3) of LMRA, 8(a)(1) distinguished, bias, LMRA, LRX 510:204
—Limits, LRX 510:201
Section 8(a)(4) of LMRA, limits, LRX 510:201
Severance pay. *See* SEVERANCE PAY
Sex bias, FEP ▶ 108.4112
—Federal employees, FEP ▶ 110.4016

*Consult individual Manual indexes for more recent information.
LA▶ = Labor Arbitration Outline; LR▶ = Labor Relations Outline;
*LRX = Labor Relations Expediter; *SLL = State Labor Laws;
WH▶ = Wages and Hours Outline; *WHM = Wages and Hours Manual

| ILLUSTRATION 15-3 | Looseleaf Service Commentary, from BNA's *Labor Relations Reporter* (paper source) |

No. 660   DISCHARGE   LRX 510:207

42 LRRM 2620 (CA 2 1958); *NLRB v. Coal Creek Co.*, 204 F2d 579, 32 LRRM 2089 (CA 10 1953); *NLRB v. Mallick & Schwalm Co.*, 198 F2d 477, 30 LRRM 2529 (CA 3 1952).

However, the NLRB's view is that the facts in each case determine whether employees are protected by the act when they take concerted action to protest the selection or termination of a supervisor. Where the identity and capability of a supervisor has a direct impact on employees' own job interests, the board has found that they are legitimately concerned with his identity and have a protected right to protest his termination. *Puerto Rico Foods Products Corp.*, 242 NLRB 899, 101 LRRM 1307 (1979).

Strikes to protest the discharge of supervisors have been found unprotected because the means of protest were not reasonably related to the ends sought. *Dobbs Houses v. NLRB*, 325 F2d 531, 54 LRRM 2726 (CA 5 1963); *Abilities & Goodwill v. NLRB*, 612 F2d 6, 103 LRRM 2029 (CA 1 1979). The NLRB has disagreed, saying that reasonableness is not a test for determining whether a strike is protected. The test, the board says, is whether the discharge of the supervisor had an impact on the strikers in the performance of their jobs. *Plastilite Corp.*, 153 NLRB 180, 59 LRRM 1401 (1965). "The application of Section 7 does not depend on the manner or method by which employees choose to press their dispute, but rather on the matter they are protesting," the court said. *Puerto Rico Food Products*, 242 NLRB 899, 101 LRRM 1307 at 1309 (1979).

The NLRB's order in *Puerto Rico Food Products* was denied enforcement. It was not shown that the work stoppage in fact was a protest over the actual conditions of the strikers' own employment, the court said, adding that the means of protest must also be "reasonable." *Puerto Rico Food Products v. NLRB*, 619 F2d 153, 104 LRRM 2304 (CA 1 1980).

The same court held that an employer lawfully fired 11 supervisors and employ-

ees for sending its president a letter requesting the discharge of the general manager at one of the employer's hotels. Reversing the NLRB, the court said the case involved "simply a dispute among managerial employees into which several non-supervisory employees were drawn." *NLRB v. Sheraton Puerto Rico Corp.*, 651 F2d 49, 107 LRRM 2735 (CA 1 1981).

One court has held that a strike seeking the reinstatement of supervisors may be protected if the individuals involved are not employer representatives for the purpose of adjusting grievances or collective bargaining. *NLRB v. Puerto Rico Rayon Mills*, 293 F2d 941, 48 LRRM 2947 (CA 1 1961).

Discharge of 'managerial' employee (LR ▶ 52.041, 52.05) — Reversing the NLRB, the Eighth Circuit upheld the discharge of a managerial employee for failing to remain neutral during an organizing campaign. The purpose of the act, the court said, is to protect "workers," not individuals who are not members of any bargaining unit and who are more closely aligned with management than with the bargaining unit. *NLRB v. North Arkansas Electric Co-op*, 446 F2d 602, 77 LRRM 3114 (CA 8 1971)

§ 7. Concerted employee activities under LMRA. (LR ▶ 52.2532 et seq.) LMRA Sec. 7. declares the employees' right "to engage in other concerted activities for the purpose of collective bargaining or other mutual aid or protection." The obvious forms of concerted activities are joining a union, soliciting other employees to join, attending union meetings, going on strike, etc. But the area of "concerted activities" protected by the LMRA is broader.

To be "concerted," an employee's activity must be engaged in with or on the authority of others, not solely by and on behalf of the employee himself. To establish the illegality of discipline based on such activity, the NLRB's general counsel must show not only that the activity was "concerted," but that the employer knew of its concerted nature, that it was

ILLUSTRATION 15-3   *(continued)*

LRX 510:208 DISCHARGE No. 660

"protected" by the LMRA, and that the discipline in fact was motivated by this protected concerted activity. *Meyers Industries*, 268 NLRB 493, 115 LRRM 1025 (1984), overruling *Alleluia Cushion Co.*, 221 NLRB 999, 91 LRRM 1131 (1975); see also *Walls Mfg. Co.*, 128 NLRB 487, 46 LRRM 1329 (1960) and *Myers Products Corp.*, 84 NLRB 32, 24 LRRM 1216 (1949).

The District of Columbia Circuit ordered the board to reconsider its *Meyers* ruling. *Prill v. NLRB* (Meyers Industries), 755 F2d 941, 118 LRRM 2649 (1985).

On reconsideration, the board adhered to its definition of concerted activities. It also stressed that its *Meyers I* definition encompasses those circumstances where individual employees seek to initiate, induce, or prepare for group action, as well as individual employees bringing truly group complaints to the attention of management. *Meyers Industries*, 281 NLRB No. 118, 123 LRRM 1137 (1986).

The District of Columbia Circuit affirmed. The board's definition under which an employee's conduct is not "concerted" unless it is engaged in with or on the authority of other employees, is a reasonable interpretation of Section 7 of the act, the court said. *Prill v. NLRB* (Meyers Industries), 835 F2d 1481, 127 LRRM 2415 (1987).

An individual employee who reasonably and honestly invokes a right set forth in his collective-bargaining contract is engaged in concerted activity, the U.S. Supreme Court held, approving the NLRB's *Interboro* doctrine. An employee's refusal to drive a truck he claimed had bad brakes was concerted even though he did not refer explicitly to the contract's safety provision, the court concluded. *NLRB v. City Disposal Systems*, 465 US 822, 115 LRRM 3193 (1984); *Interboro Contractors*, 157 NLRB 1295, 61 LRRM 1537 (1965), enforced, 388 F2d 495, 67 LRRM 2083 (CA 2 1967).

In *Prill II*, the District of Columbia Circuit ruled that the board's *Meyers I* definition of concerted activities was not inconsistent with the *Interboro* doctrine.

Concerted activity may take place where only "one person is seeking to induce action from a group." *Salt River Valley Assn. v. NLRB*, 206 F2d 325, 32 LRRM 2598 (CA 9 1953). Thus, it is illegal to discharge one employee for seeking overtime for company workers. *NLRB v. Lion Brand Mfg. Co.*, 146 F2d 773, 15 LRRM 870 (CA 5 1945). Where "one employee discusses with another the need for union organization, their action is 'concerted' . . . for it involves more than one employee, even though one be in the role of speaker and the other of listener." *Root-Carlin*, 92 NLRB 1313, 27 LRRM 1235 (1951). Two employees' informal protest against the elimination of overtime work was held protected although the employees had no authorization from other employees. *Ohio Oil Co.*, 92 NLRB 1597, 27 LRRM 1288 (1951).

Employees have the right to engage in concerted activities "even though no union activity be involved," and even though no collective bargaining is "contemplated" by the employees involved. *NLRB v. Phoenix Mutual Life Insurance Co.*, 167 F2d 983, 22 LRRM 2089 (CA 7 1948), cert. denied, 335 US 845, 22 LRRM 2590 (1948). A meeting of dissident union members to seek a change in the union's bargaining policy is protected. *NLRB v. NuCar Carriers*, 189 F2d 756, 28 LRRM 2160 (CA 3 1951), cert. denied, 342 US 919, 29 LRRM 2384 (1952).

Employees who quit work about five minutes early to hold a grievance meeting in a nonunion plant were engaged in protected activity, NLRB has held. *Quaker Alloy Casting Co.*, 135 NLRB 805, 49 LRRM 1578 (1962), enforced, 320 F2d 260, 53 LRRM 2532 (CA 3 2963).

Processing a grievance is concerted activity. *NLRB v. City Disposal Systems*, supra; *Farmers Union Coop. Marketing Assn.*, 145 NLRB 1, 54 LRRM 1298 (1963).

Refusing to remove pro-boycott signs from a car in an employer's parking lot is concerted activity. *Firestone Tire &*

ILLUSTRATION 15-4	Looseleaf Service Outline of Case Digest, from BNA's *Labor Relations Reporter* (paper source)

C-I 112   MASTER INDEX BINDER

▶ 52.—Contd.

.229 —Strikers, refusal to hire

Discharge and layoffs

.241 —Discharge generally

.242 —What constitutes a discharge; layoff distinguished; forced retirement

.243 —Layoffs in general; permanent or temporary layoffs; disciplinary layoff

.247 —Successive layoffs or discharges; discharge following reinstatement

.251 —Contracts with unions, violation of; termination of contract

—Concerted activities; protected activities

.2532 ——In general

.2533 ——Abstention from concerted activity

.2534 ——Activities in advance of or apart from organization; individual activities

.2535 ——Boycotts; "disloyalty" to employer

.2536 ——Grievances generally; bypassing contract procedure; union officers and agents, protection in performance of union duties

.2537 ——Meetings, conferences, and hearings

.2538 ——Wage demands

.2539 ——Strikes, picketing, and slowdowns as protected

.2541 ——Minority demands; dissident groups; intraunion disputes

.2542 ——False or abusive statements or threats

.2543 ——Racial, national origin, or sex discrimination, protest against

.2544 ——Work jurisdiction disputes

.257 —Quit or discharge; constructive discharge; retraction of resignation

.259 —Discharge following transfer or refusal to accept transfer; attempt to discredit employee; entrapment

—Reasons for discharge, discipline, layoff or refusal to reinstate

.2672 ——In general

.2678 ——Demand by union or fellow employees; intraunion disputes and rival unions

.2682 ——Absence or tardiness; leave of absence; overstaying leave; leaving plant or work place

.2683 ——Accident record, driving rules, law violations, criminal record

.2684 ——Altercations with others; fighting; violence

▶ 52.—Contd.

.2690 ——Communist activities; refusal to testify

.2692 ——Damage to or loss of machines, materials, etc.

.2695 ——Discourtesy toward or complaints by customers

.2696 ——Dishonesty, false statements, theft, or disloyalty to employer; lie-detector tests

.2697 ——Dissatisfaction, or criticism of management

.2698 ——Garnishment of wages

.2700 ——Horseplay

.2704 ——Insubordination

.2708 ——Intoxication; use or possession of liquor, drugs

.2716 ——Loafing, sleeping, or talking

.2718 ——Low production or impeding production

.2722 ——Negligence, inefficiency, or incompetence

.2724 ——Offensive personal characteristics; quarrelsomeness; "troublemakers"; bad attitude

.2725 ——Outside work; competing business; "moonlighting"

.2726 ——Physical or mental disability; failure to submit to physical examination or give doctor's certificate; age of employee; contagious diseases

.2728 ——Profanity, name calling, obscene language or conduct

.2729 ——Plant rules generally; successive violations

.2730 ——Reduction or redistribution of work; elimination of jobs; availability of work after discharge or layoff; automation

.2731 ——Refusal to work overtime or accept job assignment

.2738 ——Solicitation or other union activity on company time or property

.2740 ——Threats by employees

.2744 ——Wearing union buttons or other display of insignia

—Background circumstances indicating or rebutting discrimination in discharge, discipline, layoff, or refusal to reinstate

.2751 ——In general

.2752 ——Anti-union background of employer, proof of; union animus

.2756 ——Comparative treatment

.2758 ——Timing of dismissal; extent of union activity

.2764 ——Grievances or bargaining demands, presentation of; suits against employers

| ILLUSTRATION 15-5 | Looseleaf Service Case Digest, from BNA's *Labor Relations Reporter* (paper source) |

▶ **52.2536** (Contd.)

that her selection for termination was "aggravated" by "maternity thing."—*Id.*

Employer lawfully discharged *EEO* officer, where employer made business decision to discharge relatively highly paid, skilled employee, and to redistribute her duties among remaining, less skilled but lower paid employees, in order to reduce its significant operating losses.—*Id.*

Employee's conduct in opposing, together with co-workers, property management company's selection of leasing agent as its property manager constitutes protected concerted activity within meaning of LMRA, despite claim that employee's opposition was based on personal antipathy which existed between him and agent. —*Atlantic-Pacific Construction Co. d/b/a Atlantic-Pacific Management* (312 NLRB 242, 9/20/93) 145 LRRM 1176

Employer that manages apartment complex unlawfully terminated employee, since termination was motivated by employee's protected concerted activity of opposing, together with co-workers, employer's selection of leasing agent as property manager.—*Id.*

Employer unlawfully discharged employee who it believed was acting with co-workers in complaining about work assignments and other working conditions; it failed to demonstrate that discharge would have occurred even in absence of employee's protected concerted activity. —*U.S. Service Industries Inc.* (314 NLRB 30, 6/13/94) 146 LRRM 1203

Employer unlawfully discharged employee who discussed recently announced "advanced training class" with co-workers, since employee's conduct constitutes protected concerted activity; class was mandatory condition of employment, where workers who failed to attend it were subject to disciplinary action. —*Goemon America Inc.* (314 NLRB 504, 7/22/94) 146 LRRM 1282

Employer unlawfully appraised adversely employee's performance and then reprimanded him, since these actions were motivated by his protected concerted activity of participating in discussion and presentation of complaints concerning pay and other working conditions. —*FPC Holdings Inc. d/b/a Fiber Products* (314 NLRB 1169, 9/16/94) 147 LRRM 1127

Employer unlawfully designated two employees for layoff at future date; designation occurred after employer unlawfully had reprimanded employees because of their protected concerted activity of participating in discussion and presentation of complaints concerning pay and other working conditions.—*Id.*

Employer unlawfully issued written reprimands to three employees and discharged six others, since these actions were motivated by employees' protected concerted activity of walking off their jobs after painting contractor left their work area in chaotic condition. —*Vemco Inc.* (314 NLRB 1235, 9/21/94) 147 LRRM 1139

Employer unlawfully suspended and then discharged employee who, after conferring with co-workers, drafted and then solicited signatures on letter which was presented to employer's president and which complained about working conditions, particularly personnel director's alleged "favoritism" and "unfairness." —*Brother Industries (U.S.A.) Inc.* (314 NLRB 1218, 9/20/94) 147 LRRM 1230

Two employees were engaged in protected concerted activity when, after seeing co-worker's memorandum claiming that safety committee has failed to rigidly enforce no-smoking policy, they wrote on memo their opposition to its message and posted copies; one employee testified that posting was intended to elicit comments or opinions of fellow smokers. —*Morton International Inc.* (315 NLRB 564, 11/10/94) 147 LRRM 1280

Employer unlawfully discharged two employees who, after seeing co-worker's memorandum criticizing safety committee for allegedly failing to rigidly enforce no-smoking policy, wrote on memo their opposition to its message and then posted copies of memo.—*Id.*

Employer unlawfully declared lawfully laid-off employee ineligible for rehire, since reason was employee's protected concerted activity of being "loudest complainer" in group of workers who protested allegedly low wages and lack of benefits; employee never was intoxicated on the job and his drinking never interfered with production or caused safety problem. —*Cardinal Industries Inc. International Grooving & Grinding Div.* (315 NLRB 1303, 1/13/95) 148 LRRM 1187

Employer whose bargaining agreement provides for payment for certain amount of time spent by stewards in handling of grievances unlawfully refused union steward's re-

Options for administrative materials research in electronic mini-libraries:

- search the table of contents or indexes
- run a search in one or more components
- peruse the case digest
- use the embedded links
- employ the citator

Commercial publishers increasingly are offering mini-libraries through subscription electronic services. Like paper looseleaf services, electronic mini-libraries offer a wide range of frequently updated material, including primary authority and commentary, organized into components and accessible through finding tools such as indexes and digests. An electronic mini-library also offers options not available in a paper looseleaf service:

☐ You can perform a Boolean search, typically by use of truncated words, phrases, and proximity connectors, and possibly also a natural-language search.

☐ You can elect to search one or several of the components simultaneously.

☐ You may be able to move quickly from one component to another through embedded links.

☐ The online materials are completely cumulated so you need not look in several places for current materials.

However, the retrospective coverage of the electronic service may vary from the paper service, especially as to cases and decisions, so it is important to determine its beginning date of coverage.

Before you use an electronic mini-library, you should explore a bit; a good strategy is to read the orienting materials, which may be found in the opening screens, a tutorial, or descriptions of the various components. In particular, seek to discern:

☐ what types of authorities are included in which components;

☐ what the coverage of each component is, e.g., how far back the case collection goes, how up to date the statutory materials are;

☐ whether you can browse or search a table of contents or index;

☐ what the key-word search protocols are, e.g., the available connectors, handling of phrases; and

☐ how readily you can link from one component to another.

See Illustration 15-6 at pages 319–21, the content overview for a portion of the BNA Labor & Employment Law Library.

ILLUSTRATION 15-6	Electronic Service Overview, from BNA's Labor & Employment Law Library (electronic source)

Labor & Employment Law Library   **ISSN 1527-7356**

CONTENT OVERVIEW

LRRM - Decisions of NLRB

Decisions of NLRB
volumes 117 through current
(cases published beginning September 1984)

The **Decisions of NLRB** collection reports decisions by the National Labor Relations Board and advice memoranda of the NLRB General Counsel.

Within this collection, you can search for any word or phrase in the text of opinions and/or in the editorial materials prepared by BNA. You also can combine words and phrases with any "field" searches, for example, with date, jurisdiction, NLRB member (judge), or case name. Cases included in your search results are arranged in reverse chronological order (latest cases first), with NLRB decisions first.

In addition to powerful search capabilities, you can move quickly to related information by clicking on link zones. You can:

• link from "LRRM" citations to the NLRB parallel cites
• link from case references directly to the text of the cited case
• link from footnote references to footnote text
• link to the Outline of Classification to browse related numbers

LRRM - Decisions of Court

Decisions of Courts
volumes 117 through current
(cases published beginning September 1984)

The **Decisions of Court** collection reports decisions by:
• The U.S. Supreme Court
• U.S. Courts of Appeals, including the U.S. Court of Appeals for the Federal Circuit
• U.S. District Courts
• U.S. Court of Federal Claims and its predecessor, the U.S. Claims Court
• U.S. Tax Court
• State Courts of various levels
• Arbitrators
• Administrative Agencies

Within this collection, you can search for any word or phrase in the text of opinions and/or in the editorial materials prepared by BNA. You also can combine words and phrases with any "field" searches, for example, with date, jurisdiction, judge, or case name. Cases included in your search results are arranged in tribunal order, highest to lowest, and in reverse chronological order (latest cases first) within each tribunal
In addition to powerful search capabilities, you can move quickly to related information by clicking on link zones. You can:

ILLUSTRATION 15-6   *(continued)*

Labor & Employment Law Library   ISSN 1527-7356

- link from "LRRM" citations to parallel citations
- link from headnote numbers to corresponding numbers in text where the referenced point of law is discussed
- link from case references directly to the text of the cited case
- link to lower court cases
- link from footnote references to footnote text
- link to the Outline of Classification to browse related numbers

LRRM - Outline of Classification

This collection classifies all headnotes written to accompany cases published in *LRRM Decisions of NLRB and Courts,* volumes 66 through current (cases published beginning September 1967), and the descriptors which delineate the subject matter covered by each classification number. Clicking on any classification number in the outline takes you to all headnotes in cases classified under that number. After double-clicking on an underlined class number, clicking on "Contents" produces a list of the cases retrieved, arranged in tribunal order, highest to lowest, and in reverse chronological order within each tribunal.

LRRM - Parallel Cites

The Parallel Citations table is a list of all cases published in *LRRM Decisions of NLRB and Courts,* that have parallel citations by reason of their publication in other reporting services. The table is arranged in citation number order, with NLRB decisions first. Each entry includes the following information:
- case name
- citation and its parallel citation(s)
- tribunal
- docket number or decision number
- date of decision

Clicking on the BNA or parallel citation in any entry takes you to the heading of the corresponding case in the full text of decisions.

LRRM - Statute Coordination List

The Statute Coordination List provides cross-references from each section of the major federal laws on labor and employment to the numbers listed in the *LRRM Outline of Classification* that represent the issues found in sections of the U.S. Code. This collection breaks down the principal acts section-by-section and provides a brief statement of the subjects covered by sections for which classification numbers exist. You can jump to full text of the statutes by clicking on the page cite of the manual where the statute is located. You can also link to the Outline of Classification and to the headnotes of cases classified under the number referenced.

ILLUSTRATION 15-6   *(continued)*

Labor & Employment Law Library   ISSN 1527-7356

LRRM Topic Finder

The Topic Finder is an alphabetical arrangement by major subjects and subheadings of all topics covered in *LRRM Decisions of NLRB and Courts*. References are to classification numbers under which cases construing the subject are classified. Clicking on any underlined classification number in the Topic Finder takes you to that number in the Outline of Classifications. Clicking on any classification number in the outline takes you to all headnotes in cases classified under that number.

Finding List of Unions

Unions are often referred to by a popular name, rather than by the official title. The Finding List of Unions, limited to national and international unions (or subordinate branches thereof), designates the union's popular name first. This is followed by the official name of the national and international union and then by acronym.

Labor Relations Expediter

The *Labor Relations Expediter* provides overview discussions of labor and employment law. More detailed coverage of selected topics is provided in the other manuals of this product. In addition, the Expediter includes federal labor and employment primary source material.

Researching the Canoga case in that mini-library, we first ran a simple search for concerted activity in the Labor Relations Expediter and obtained the same text as Illustration 15-3 at pages 314–15. We then focused on finding judicial cases and agency decisions in the Decisions of NLRB and Decisions of Court components. We could accomplish this task various ways. For example, we could identify a pertinent classification number by browsing or searching in the Topic Finder (an index) or the Outline of Classification (a table of contents); we could then link to the descriptions of cases pertaining to that number. Or we could run a key-word search in the two decisions components. We did the latter; our search was `"concerted activity"` and `smok*`. Note that both decisions components date only to 1984. No judicial cases fit the search; eleven Board decisions did, including *Morton International* (third on the list).

C.   WHAT ELSE?

Mixed Media.   While this chapter presents two distinct versions of a mini-library, one a paper looseleaf, the other an electronic service, you may well use a combination of the two. A publisher may offer or a library may have some parts in paper, others electronically.

Current Awareness Publications.   Comprehensive looseleafs have current awareness publications, which are frequently published pamphlets that permit a regular reader to keep abreast of recent developments. The pamphlet may contain synopses of recent legal authorities, analyze significant new laws, recount the results of recent studies, report on important conferences, and list upcoming events. In addition, some legal authorities, especially new statutes and regulations, often are first available in paper media in pamphlets issued by looseleaf publishers. Current awareness publications may be filed in their own binder and covered by a periodic index.

Westlaw and LexisNexis.   Westlaw and LexisNexis offer databases containing some looseleaf materials. The offering may be selective, that is they may provide only portions of a paper looseleaf service.

D.   HOW DO YOU CITE TO MINI-LIBRARIES?

Most authorities located in a mini-library appear elsewhere in preferred sources, such as a code of regulations or official reporter of agency decisions. Nonetheless, you may cite to a looseleaf on occasion. The most common situation is when you are citing to a very recent agency decision not yet available in the agency's official reporter. When citing to a looseleaf, you must provide information about the authority as well as its location in the looseleaf. Here are two examples, on the assumption the decision is not yet published:

- ☐ *Bluebook* Rules 14.3 and 19: *Morton Intl., Inc.*, 315 N.L.R.B. No. 71, 147 L.R.R.M. (BNA) 1280 (Nov. 10, 1994).
- ☐ *ALWD* Rules 19.5 and 28.1: *Morton Intl., Inc.*, 147 Lab. Rel. Ref. Man. (BNA) 1280 (Natl. Lab. Rel. Bd. Nov. 10, 1994).

RULES OF PROCEDURE AND LEGAL ETHICS

UNIT

VI

PRELIMINARY POINTS

This unit explores the methods and materials used to research rules that govern litigation and the practice of law. These rules are primary authority because they are created by various government bodies acting in their official capacities. This unit has two chapters.

Chapter 16 discusses rules governing the procedural aspects of litigation in the courts. Each jurisdiction has its own rules of procedure, and most have several sets for different phases and types of litigation. These overarching rules for a jurisdiction may be supplemented by rules developed by a single court or district. Rules governing other legal proceedings, such as international disputes and commercial arbitration, bear some similarity to the rules of procedure discussed here; those rules are beyond the scope of this book.

Chapter 17 discusses the law governing the ethical conduct of lawyers, that is, rules of professional responsibility. The chapter focuses on state rules of professional responsibility and the model rules and codes prepared by the American Bar Association.

For examples, this unit turns again to the Canoga case, stated on pages 3–4. Assume that, as Ms. Canoga's lawyer, you have identified viable claims and unsuccessfully sought a settlement from the orchestra. With reluctance, Ms. Canoga has decided to pursue litigation. The two specific issues to be researched are stated within the two chapters.

RULES OF PROCEDURE

A. WHAT ARE RULES OF PROCEDURE?

Although the distinction is not always clear, most lawyers distinguish substantive law from procedural law. Substantive law governs the rights, duties, and powers of people and entities as they carry out their personal and business affairs. By contrast, procedural law regulates how a case is brought before a particular tribunal and how the case proceeds from its inception until a final outcome is reached. Lawyers and litigants must observe procedural law throughout the litigation, and procedural law assists the court and lawyers in administering justice fairly and efficiently.

In most jurisdictions, some procedural law appears not in the rules of procedure, as this chapter uses that term, but in the statutes of the jurisdiction. For example, statutes typically govern how quickly you must bring a claim (statutes of limitation) and which court has the power to adjudicate a claim (jurisdiction). This chapter focuses on rules of procedure; Chapter 11 covers statutory research.

Most jurisdictions have several sets of rules of procedure, each addressing certain phases and types of litigation. Exhibit 16.1 sets out the typical arrangement. Furthermore, a particular court (such as family or small claims court) or judicial district may have additional local or court rules outlining the details of its practice. In essence, rules of procedure cover major topics; local or court rules cover minor points.

EXHIBIT 16.1	Rules of Procedure	
	Civil Cases	*Criminal Cases*
Pre-trial pleadings discovery motions	civil procedure	criminal procedure
Trial	evidence civil procedure	evidence criminal procedure
Post-trial	civil procedure	criminal procedure
Appeals	appellate procedure	appellate or criminal appellate procedure

Rules of procedure are created either by the legislature, by the court, or through interaction of both branches of government. At the federal level, the United States Constitution is not clear whether primary authority for procedural rules belongs to Congress or the federal courts. Most commentators believe that Congress has the right to prescribe rules of procedure for the federal courts, while the individual federal courts may issue local rules on matters not covered by Congress' rules. As a practical matter, Congress has delegated a great deal of authority to the United States Supreme Court.

The enactment of the Federal Rules of Civil Procedure (FRCP) is an example of this delegation. In 1934, Congress gave the Supreme Court the power to prescribe rules of procedure for the federal district courts and the District of Columbia, as well as the obligation to report to Congress.[1] In 1935, the Supreme Court appointed an Advisory Committee on Civil Rules to prepare a draft. After making some changes, the Supreme Court adopted the rules in 1937 and submitted them to Congress via the Attorney General. Although these rules were never formally adopted by both houses of Congress, the rules became effective in 1938. The FRCP have been amended by the Supreme Court from time to time since then.

Most states have delegated authority to make procedural rules to the highest state court or a special governmental body; some state legislatures then review and adopt the rules. In other states, the legislature or other advisory body drafts a bill containing the needed procedural rules, and the legislature enacts the bill according to its usual process of statutory enactment. Many states' procedural rules are modeled after the federal rules.

---

1. The Rules Enabling Act of 1934, ch. 651, 48 Stat. 1064 (1934).

Each set of rules is organized topically, generally chronologically. The Federal Rules of Civil Procedure, for example, are arranged roughly in the sequence in which litigation usually proceeds in the trial court:

☐ introductory rules;
☐ commencement of a lawsuit, including service of process, filing of pleadings, the form of pleadings and motions, and designation of parties to the suit;
☐ discovery, such as depositions and interrogatories;
☐ the trial itself and post-trial motions;
☐ judgments and remedies; and
☐ specialized and miscellaneous matters.

Each rule describes the litigation practice it covers, stating what is or is not permissible. Each rule is separately numbered, often with subdivisions. Accompanying the rule may be notes or comments prepared by the advisory committee, which typically discuss the purpose of the rule, previous rules that have been superseded or amended, and perhaps proposed amendments that were rejected. Although the notes of the advisory committee are not mandatory authority, they are highly persuasive.

The illustrations in this chapter pertain to the following variation on the Canoga case: Assume, as Ms. Canoga's lawyer, that you have decided to file suit on her behalf. The complaint concludes with a signature block, which is a blank for your signature, your name typed below the blank, and information about your firm typed below that. Somehow the complaint was filed with the clerk of court without your signature. Instead, it carries the signature of Ms. Canoga, who came into your office the day the complaint was filed to review it and sign some other papers. So, you need to learn whether the complaint is valid as filed, and, if not, how to correct it, if possible.

Federal Rule of Civil Procedure 11 governs the signing of documents submitted to the courts in a civil case and the significance of the signature. See Illustration 16-1 (at pages 330–32). Note that Rule 11 has been amended several times in recent decades; each amendment is explained in the advisory committee's notes. Local Civil Rule 10 of the United States District Court for the District of New Mexico addresses various details of papers filed with that court, including defects in the signature. See Illustration 16-2 (at page 333). The New Mexico state rule of procedure on the same topic is Rule 1-011, Illustration 16-3 (at pages 334–35).

ILLUSTRATION 16-1

Federal Rule of Civil Procedure,
from *Federal Civil Judicial Procedure and Rules* Deskbook
(paper source)

Rule 9   RULES OF CIVIL PROCEDURE

liability was "integrally linked with the determination of non-liability" of the admiralty defendant, and that "section 1292(a)(3) is not limited to admiralty claims; instead, it refers to admiralty cases." 899 F.2d at 1297. The advantages of permitting appeal by the nonadmiralty defendant would be particularly clear if the plaintiff had appealed the summary judgment in favor of the admiralty defendant.

It must be emphasized that this amendment does not rest on any particular assumptions as to the meaning of the § 1292(a)(3) provision that limits interlocutory appeal to orders that determine the rights and liabilities of the parties. It simply reflects the conclusion that so long as the case involves an admiralty claim and an order otherwise meets statutory requirements, the opportunity to appeal should not turn on the circumstance that the order does—or does not—dispose of an admiralty claim. No attempt is made to invoke the authority conferred by 28 U.S.C. § 1292(e) to provide by rule for appeal of an interlocutory decision that is not otherwise provided for by other subsections of § 1292.

GAP Report on Rule 9(h). No changes have been made in the published proposal.

Rule 10.   Form of Pleadings

(a) **Caption; Names of Parties.** Every pleading shall contain a caption setting forth the name of the court, the title of the action, the file number, and a designation as in Rule 7(a). In the complaint the title of the action shall include the names of all the parties, but in other pleadings it is sufficient to state the name of the first party on each side with an appropriate indication of other parties.

(b) **Paragraphs; Separate Statements.** All averments of claim or defense shall be made in numbered paragraphs, the contents of each of which shall be limited as far as practicable to a statement of a single set of circumstances; and a paragraph may be referred to by number in all succeeding pleadings. Each claim founded upon a separate transaction or occurrence and each defense other than denials shall be stated in a separate count or defense whenever a separation facilitates the clear presentation of the matters set forth.

(c) **Adoption by Reference; Exhibits.** Statements in a pleading may be adopted by reference in a different part of the same pleading or in another pleading or in any motion. A copy of any written instrument which is an exhibit to a pleading is a part thereof for all purposes.

ADVISORY COMMITTEE NOTES

1937 Adoption

The first sentence is derived in part from the opening statement of former Equity Rule 25 (Bill of Complaint—Contents). The remainder of the rule is an expansion in conformity with usual state provisions. For numbered paragraphs and separate statements, see Conn.Gen.Stat., 1930, § 5513; Smith-Hurd Ill.Stats. ch. 110, § 157(2); N.Y.R.C.P., (1937) Rule 90. For incorporation by reference, see

N.Y.R.C.P., (1937) Rule 90. For written instruments as exhibits, see Smith-Hurd Ill.Stats. ch. 110, § 160.

Rule 11.   Signing of Pleadings, Motions, and Other Papers; Representations to Court; Sanctions

(a) **Signature.** Every pleading, written motion, and other paper shall be signed by at least one attorney of record in the attorney's individual name, or, if the party is not represented by an attorney, shall be signed by the party. Each paper shall state the signer's address and telephone number, if any. Except when otherwise specifically provided by rule or statute, pleadings need not be verified or accompanied by affidavit. An unsigned paper shall be stricken unless omission of the signature is corrected promptly after being called to the attention of the attorney or party.

(b) **Representations to Court.** By presenting to the court (whether by signing, filing, submitting, or later advocating) a pleading, written motion, or other paper, an attorney or unrepresented party is certifying that to the best of the person's knowledge, information, and belief, formed after an inquiry reasonable under the circumstances,—

(1) it is not being presented for any improper purpose, such as to harass or to cause unnecessary delay or needless increase in the cost of litigation;

(2) the claims, defenses, and other legal contentions therein are warranted by existing law or by a nonfrivolous argument for the extension, modification, or reversal of existing law or the establishment of new law;

(3) the allegations and other factual contentions have evidentiary support or, if specifically so identified, are likely to have evidentiary support after a reasonable opportunity for further investigation or discovery; and

(4) the denials of factual contentions are warranted on the evidence or, if specifically so identified, are reasonably based on a lack of information or belief.

(c) **Sanctions.** If, after notice and a reasonable opportunity to respond, the court determines that subdivision (b) has been violated, the court may, subject to the conditions stated below, impose an appropriate sanction upon the attorneys, law firms, or parties that have violated subdivision (b) or are responsible for the violation.

(1) **How Initiated.**

(A) **By Motion.** A motion for sanctions under this rule shall be made separately from other motions or requests and shall describe the specific conduct alleged to violate subdivision (b). It shall be served as provided in Rule 5, but shall

---

Complete Annotation Materials, see Title 28 U.S.C.A.

ILLUSTRATION 16-1   *(continued)*

PLEADINGS AND MOTIONS   **Rule 11**

not be filed with or presented to the court unless, within 21 days after service of the motion (or such other period as the court may prescribe), the challenged paper, claim, defense, contention, allegation, or denial is not withdrawn or appropriately corrected. If warranted, the court may award to the party prevailing on the motion the reasonable expenses and attorney's fees incurred in presenting or opposing the motion. Absent exceptional circumstances, a law firm shall be held jointly responsible for violations committed by its partners, associates, and employees.

(B) On Court's Initiative. On its own initiative, the court may enter an order describing the specific conduct that appears to violate subdivision (b) and directing an attorney, law firm, or party to show cause why it has not violated subdivision (b) with respect thereto.

(2) Nature of Sanction; Limitations. A sanction imposed for violation of this rule shall be limited to what is sufficient to deter repetition of such conduct or comparable conduct by others similarly situated. Subject to the limitations in subparagraphs (A) and (B), the sanction may consist of, or include, directives of a nonmonetary nature, an order to pay a penalty into court, or, if imposed on motion and warranted for effective deterrence, an order directing payment to the movant of some or all of the reasonable attorneys' fees and other expenses incurred as a direct result of the violation.

(A) Monetary sanctions may not be awarded against a represented party for a violation of subdivision (b)(2).

(B) Monetary sanctions may not be awarded on the court's initiative unless the court issues its order to show cause before a voluntary dismissal or settlement of the claims made by or against the party which is, or whose attorneys are, to be sanctioned.

(3) Order. When imposing sanctions, the court shall describe the conduct determined to constitute a violation of this rule and explain the basis for the sanction imposed.

(d) Inapplicability to Discovery. Subdivisions (a) through (c) of this rule do not apply to disclosures and discovery requests, responses, objections, and motions that are subject to the provisions of Rules 26 through 37.

(As amended Apr. 28, 1983, eff. Aug. 1, 1983; Mar. 2, 1987, eff. Aug. 1, 1987; Apr. 22, 1993, eff. Dec. 1, 1993.)

ADVISORY COMMITTEE NOTES

1937 Adoption

This is substantially the content of [former] Equity Rules 24 (Signature of Counsel) and 21 (Scandal and Impertinence) consolidated and unified. Compare former Equity Rule 36 (Officers Before Whom Pleadings Verified). Compare to

similar purposes, *English Rules Under the Judicature Act* (The Annual Practice, 1937) O. 19, r. 4, and *Great Australian Gold Mining Co. v. Martin*, L.R. 5 Ch.Div. 1, 10 (1877). Subscription of pleadings is required in many codes. 2 Minn.Stat. (Mason, 1927) § 9265; N.Y.R.C.P. (1937) Rule 91; 2 N.D.Comp.Laws Ann. (1913) § 7455.

This rule expressly continues any statute which requires a pleading to be verified or accompanied by an affidavit, such as: U.S.C., Title 28:

§ 381 [former] (Preliminary injunctions and temporary restraining orders)

§ 762 [now 1402] (Suit against the United States)

U.S.C., Title 28, § 829 [now 1927] (Costs; attorney liable for, when) is unaffected by this rule.

For complaints which must be verified under these rules, see Rules 23(b) (Secondary Action by Shareholders) and 65 (Injunctions).

For abolition of former rule in equity that the averments of an answer under oath must be overcome by the testimony of two witnesses or of one witness sustained by corroborating circumstances, see 12 P.S.Pa. § 1222; for the rule in equity itself, see *Greenfield v. Blumenthal*, C.C.A.3, 1934, 69 F.2d 294.

1983 Amendment

Since its original promulgation, Rule 11 has provided for the striking of pleadings and the imposition of disciplinary sanctions to check abuses in the signing of pleadings. Its provisions have always applied to motions and other papers by virtue of incorporation by reference in Rule 7(b)(2). The amendment and the addition of Rule 7(b)(3) expressly confirms this applicability.

Experience shows that in practice Rule 11 has not been effective in deterring abuses. See 6 Wright & Miller, *Federal Practice and Procedure: Civil* § 1334 (1971). There has been considerable confusion as to (1) the circumstances that should trigger striking a pleading or motion or taking disciplinary action, (2) the standard of conduct expected of attorneys who sign pleadings and motions, and (3) the range of available and appropriate sanctions. See Rodes, Ripple & Mooney, *Sanctions Imposable for Violations of the Federal Rules of Civil Procedure* 64–65, Federal Judicial Center (1981). The new language is intended to reduce the reluctance of courts to impose sanctions, see Moore, **Federal Practice** ¶ 7.05, at 1547, by emphasizing the responsibilities of the attorney and reenforcing those obligations by the imposition of sanctions.

The amended rule attempts to deal with the problem by building upon and expanding the equitable doctrine permitting the court to award expenses, including attorney's fees, to a litigant whose opponent acts in bad faith in instituting or conducting litigation. See, e.g., *Roadway Express, Inc. v. Piper*, 447 U.S. 752 (1980); *Hall v. Cole*, 412 U.S. 1, 5 (1973). Greater attention by the district courts to pleading and motion abuses and the imposition of sanctions when appropriate, should discourage dilatory or abusive tactics and help to streamline the litigation process by lessening frivolous claims or defenses.

The expanded nature of the lawyer's certification in the fifth sentence of amended Rule 11 recognizes that the litigation process may be abused for purposes other than delay.

Complete Annotation Materials, see Title 28 U.S.C.A.

ILLUSTRATION 16-1   *(continued; page 90 omitted)*

PLEADINGS AND MOTIONS   Rule 11

under consideration. In many situations the judge's participation in the proceedings provides him with full knowledge of the relevant facts and little further inquiry will be necessary.

To assure that the efficiencies achieved through more effective operation of the pleading regimen will not be offset by the cost of satellite litigation over the imposition of sanctions, the court must to the extent possible limit the scope of sanction proceedings to the record. Thus, discovery should be conducted only by leave of the court, and then only in extraordinary circumstances.

Although the encompassing reference to "other papers" in new Rule 11 literally includes discovery papers, the certification requirement in that context is governed by proposed new Rule 26(g). Discovery motions, however, fall within the ambit of Rule 11.

1987 Amendment

The amendments are technical. No substantive change is intended.

1993 Amendments

Purpose of revision. This revision is intended to remedy problems that have arisen in the interpretation and application of the 1983 revision of the rule. For empirical examination of experience under the 1983 rule, see, *e.g.,* New York State Bar Committee on Federal Courts, *Sanctions and Attorneys' Fees* (1987); T. Willging, *The Rule 11 Sanctioning Process* (1989); American Judicature Society, *Report of the Third Circuit Task Force on Federal Rule of Civil Procedure 11* (S. Burbank ed., 1989); E. Wiggins, T. Willging, and D. Stienstra, *Report on Rule 11* (Federal Judicial Center 1991). For book-length analyses of the case law, see G. Joseph, *Sanctions: The Federal Law of Litigation Abuse* (1989); J. Solovy, *The Federal Law of Sanctions* (1991); G. Vairo, *Rule 11 Sanctions: Case Law Perspectives and Preventive Measures* (1991).

The rule retains the principle that attorneys and pro se litigants have an obligation to the court to refrain from conduct that frustrates the aims of Rule 1. The revision broadens the scope of this obligation, but places greater constraints on the imposition of sanctions and should reduce the number of motions for sanctions presented to the court. New subdivision (d) removes from the ambit of this rule all discovery requests, responses, objections, and motions subject to the provisions of Rule 26 through 37.

Subdivision (a). Retained in this subdivision are the provisions requiring signatures on pleadings, written motions, and other papers. Unsigned papers are to be received by the Clerk, but then are to be stricken if the omission of the signature is not corrected promptly after being called to the attention of the attorney or pro se litigant. Correction can be made by signing the paper on file or by submitting a duplicate that contains the signature. A court may require by local rule that papers contain additional identifying information regarding the parties or attorneys, such as telephone numbers to facilitate facsimile transmissions, though, as for omission of a signature, the paper should not be rejected for failure to provide such information.

The sentence in the former rule relating to the effect of answers under oath is no longer needed and has been eliminated. The provision in the former rule that signing a

paper constitutes a certificate that it has been read by the signer also has been eliminated as unnecessary. The obligations imposed under subdivision (b) obviously require that a pleading, written motion, or other paper be read before it is filed or submitted to the court.

Subdivisions (b) and (c). These subdivisions restate the provisions requiring attorneys and pro se litigants to conduct a reasonable inquiry into the law and facts before signing pleadings, written motions, and other documents, and prescribing sanctions for violation of these obligations. The revision in part expands the responsibilities of litigants to the court, while providing greater constraints and flexibility in dealing with infractions of the rule. The rule continues to require litigants to "stop-and-think" before initially making legal or factual contentions. It also, however, emphasizes the duty of candor by subjecting litigants to potential sanctions for insisting upon a position after it is no longer tenable and by generally providing protection against sanctions if they withdraw or correct contentions after a potential violation is called to their attention.

The rule applies only to assertions contained in papers filed with or submitted to the court. It does not cover matters arising for the first time during oral presentations to the court, when counsel may make statements that would not have been made if there had been more time for study and reflection. However, a litigant's obligations with respect to the contents of these papers are not measured solely as of the time they are filed with or submitted to the court, but include reaffirming to the court and advocating positions contained in those pleadings and motions after learning that they cease to have any merit. For example, an attorney who during a pretrial conference insists on a claim or defense should be viewed as "presenting to the court" that contention and would be subject to the obligations of subdivision (b) measured as of that time. Similarly, if after a notice of removal is filed, a party urges in federal court the allegations of a pleading filed in state court (whether as claims, defenses, or in disputes regarding removal or remand), it would be viewed as "presenting"—and hence certifying to the district court under Rule 11—those allegations.

The certification with respect to allegations and other factual contentions is revised in recognition that sometimes a litigant may have good reason to believe that a fact is true or false but may need discovery, formal or informal, from opposing parties or third persons to gather and confirm the evidentiary basis for the allegation. Tolerance of factual contentions in initial pleadings by plaintiffs or defendants when specifically identified as made on information and belief does not relieve litigants from the obligation to conduct an appropriate investigation into the facts that is reasonable under the circumstances; it is not a license to join parties, make claims, or present defenses without any factual basis or justification. Moreover, if evidentiary support is not obtained after a reasonable opportunity for further investigation or discovery, the party has a duty under the rule not to persist with that contention. Subdivision (b) does not require a formal amendment to pleadings for which evidentiary support is not obtained, but rather calls upon a litigant not thereafter to advocate such claims or defenses.

The certification is that there is (or likely will be) "evidentiary support" for the allegation, not that the party will prevail with respect to its contention regarding the fact. That summary judgment is rendered against a party does

---

Complete Annotation Materials, see Title 28 U.S.C.A.

91

ILLUSTRATION 16-2

Local Civil Rule,
from nmcourt.fed.us (electronic source)

10.2 Titles of Papers.
   (a)   Identification of Substance. The title of a paper must clearly identify its substance.
   (b)   Responses or Replies. The title of a response or a reply must identify by title and approximate date of filing the paper to which it responds.
   (c)   Affidavit. The title of an affidavit must identify by title and approximate date of filing the paper it supports.

10.3 Filing of Non-Conforming Papers.
   (a)   Acceptance of Papers. The Clerk will not refuse to file any paper because it is not in proper form.
   (b)   Signature. Any paper filed without signature will be stricken unless it is signed within fourteen (14) calendar days after the omission is called to the party's attention.
   (c)   Non-Conforming Papers. The Clerk will give to the submitting party written notice of a deficiency and deadline for correcting the deficiency. The Clerk will also provide any applicable forms and instruction sheets. Failure to remedy a deficiency or to show good cause for non-compliance within forty-five (45) calendar days from the date of notice may result in dismissal of the action without prejudice in accordance with D.N.M.LR-Civ. 41.2.

10.4 Attachments to Pleadings. Exhibits are not attached to a pleading unless the documents attached form the basis for the action or defense.

10.5 Page Limit for Exhibits. Exhibits to a motion, response or reply, including excerpts from a deposition, must not exceed fifty (50) pages unless all parties agree otherwise. If agreement cannot be reached, then the party seeking to exceed the page limit must file a motion in accordance with D.N.M.LR-Civ. 7. A party may file only those pages of an exhibit which are to be brought to the Court's attention.

10.6 Highlighting of Exhibits. The portions of an exhibit the party wishes to bring to the Court's attention must be highlighted in the original, the copy for the Court and the copy for each party. Highlighting must be apparent on exhibits that are scanned and filed and/or served electronically.

10.7 Non-duplication of Exhibits. An exhibit should be submitted only once and may later be referred to by document title and filing date. An exhibit may be submitted more than once, however, if the submitting party wishes to bring to the Court's attention portions of the exhibit different from those previously highlighted under D.N.M.LR-Civ. 10.6.

RULE 11.   Signing of Documents.

11.1 Signatures. The Court will treat a duplicate signature as an original signature, and a document filed or served by electronic transmission is considered signed in accordance with FED. R. CIV. P. ll(a).

-- 7 --

| ILLUSTRATION 16-3 | State Rule of Civil Procedure, from *New Mexico Rules Annotated* (paper source) |

II. CAPTION.

All parties on one side not one party. — The New Mexico Rules of Civil Procedure, as well as the common understanding of what is meant by a party to a lawsuit, are inconsistent with the position that all parties on one side of a lawsuit are but one party. Romero v. Felter, 83 N.M. 736, 497 P.2d 738 (1972).

III. PARAGRAPHS.

The objective of the paragraph is clarity in pleading. At the same time dilatory motions for separate paragraphing or separate statements are discouraged, since rigid requirements are not laid down. Jernigan v. New Amsterdam Cas. Co., 69 N.M. 336, 367 P.2d 519 (1961).

Multiple counts arising from one transaction considered alternative pleadings. — Where a complaint is in separate counts, and all counts arise from the same transaction or occurrence, such a complaint will be considered as a whole with the counts to be viewed as alternative pleadings of one cause of action even though against more than one defendant; each count need not be sufficient in itself nor state a claim upon which relief can be granted. Jernigan v. New Amsterdam Cas. Co., 69 N.M. 336, 367 P.2d 519 (1961).

Even flagrant violators have right to amend. — It was an abuse of discretion by the trial court to dismiss complaint without leave to amend although it disclosed flagrant disregard of this rule. Hambaugh v. Peoples, 75 N.M. 144, 401 P.2d 777 (1965); Peoples v. Peoples, 72 N.M. 64, 380 P.2d 513 (1963).

Complete statement of specific facts for contest necessary. — Allegation in notice of election contest that "by reason of the erroneous receiving, counting, tallying, and return of the votes . . . the correct result thereof was not certified to the county canvassing board" was not a sufficiently complete statement of the specific facts on which the grounds for contest were based. Ferran v. Trujillo, 50 N.M. 266, 175 P.2d 998 (1946) (decided under former law).

Request for specific money damages. — Where filing of original complaint initiating civil action preceded the effective date of this rule, a subsequent amended complaint was not subject to Subsection B's prohibition of requests for specific money damages. R.A. Peck, Inc. v. Liberty Fed. Sav. Bank, 108 N.M. 84, 766 P.2d 928 (Ct. App. 1988) (decided under former law).

IV. ADOPTION BY REFERENCE.

Pleadings from a separate case. — Subdivision C of this rule does not authorize a party to incorporate by reference pleadings from a separate case into the pleadings in the case at bar. Bronstein v. Biava, 114 N.M. 351, 838 P.2d 968 (1992).

Not necessary to attach notice of default to complaint. — While the giving of written notice of default as provided for in a lease is a condition precedent, in pleading performance it is sufficient to aver generally that all such conditions have been performed and it is not necessary to attach the notice or copy thereof to the complaint. City of Hot Springs v. Hot Springs Fair & Racing Ass'n, 56 N.M. 317, 243 P.2d 619 (1952).

1-011. Signing of pleadings, motions and other papers; sanctions.

Every pleading, motion and other paper of a party represented by an attorney, shall be signed by at least one attorney of record in the attorney's individual name, whose address and telephone number shall be stated. A party who is not represented by an attorney shall sign the party's pleading, motion or other paper and state the party's address and telephone number. Except when otherwise specifically provided by rule or statute, pleadings need not be verified or accompanied by affidavit. The rule in equity that the averments of an answer under oath must be overcome by the testimony of two witnesses or of one witness sustained by corroborating circumstances is abolished. The signature of an attorney or party constitutes a certificate by the signer that the signer has read the pleading, motion or other paper; that to the best of the signer's knowledge, information and belief there is good ground to support it; and that it is not interposed for delay. If a pleading, motion or other paper is signed with intent to defeat the purpose of this rule, it may be stricken as sham and false and the action may proceed as though the pleading or other paper had not been served. If a pleading, motion or other paper is not signed, it shall be stricken unless it is signed promptly after the omission is called to the attention of the pleader or movant. For a willful violation of this rule an attorney or party may be subjected to appropriate disciplinary or other action. Similar action may be taken if scandalous or indecent matter is inserted. A "signature" means an original signature, a copy of an original signature, a computer generated signature or any other signature otherwise authorized by law.

[As amended, effective January 1, 1987; August 1, 1989; January 1, 1997.]

Committee commentary. — New Mexico has enacted an Electronic Authentication Documentation Act which provides for the Secretary of State to register electronic signatures using the public key technology. See Section 14-15-4 NMSA 1978.

Cross references. — For verification of petition in divorce actions, see 40-4-6 NMSA 1978. For verification of pleadings in action for seizure of illegal oil, see 70-2-32 NMSA 1978.

The 1997 amendment, effective January 1, 1997, added the last sentence defining "signature".

Compiler's notes. — This rule, in conjunction with Rule 1-005, is deemed to have superseded 105-510 and 105-705, C.S. 1929. It is further deemed to partially

ILLUSTRATION 16-3   *(continued)*

1-011   RULES OF CIVIL PROCEDURE FOR THE DISTRICT COURTS   46

supersede 105-415, C.S. 1929, and to supersede 105-424, 105-425, 105-821, C.S. 1929.

Purpose. — The primary goal of this rule is to deter baseless filings in district court by testing the conduct of counsel. Rivera v. Brazos Lodge Corp., 111 N.M. 670, 808 P.2d 955 (1991).

The objectives sought by this rule and the wording of the rule primarily place a moral obligation upon the lawyer to satisfy himself that there are good grounds for the action or defense. This requires honesty and good faith in pleading. Rivera v. Brazos Lodge Corp., 111 N.M. 670, 808 P.2d 955 (1991).

The "good ground" provision in this rule is to be measured by subjective standards at the time of the signing of the pleading. Any violation depends on what the attorney or litigant knew and believed at the relevant time and involves the question of whether the litigant or attorney was aware that a particular pleading should not have been brought. Rivera v. Brazos Lodge Corp., 111 N.M. 670, 808 P.2d 955 (1991).

The "good ground" provision of this rule is measured by a subjective standard: Any violation depends on what the attorney or litigant knew and believed at the relevant time (the signing of the pleading) and involves the question of whether the litigant or attorney was aware that a particular pleading should not have been brought. Lowe v. Bloom, 112 N.M. 203, 813 P.2d 480 (1991).

Husband signing pleading as attorney-in-fact equivalent to wife signing. — Where defendant did not personally sign the answer in the prior suit, in which appeared the admission of the debt later sued upon, but in her answer in the later suit she admitted her deceased husband signed the answer in the prior suit as attorney for her and himself, and no question had been raised as to his authority to sign the answer as her attorney or to make the admission on her behalf, then his signature on her behalf to the answer in the prior suit had the same effect as if she had personally signed. Smith v. Walcott, 85 N.M. 351, 512 P.2d 679 (1973).

Where an appellant is obviously present before the court and vigorously pursuing his case — although his name is missing from the caption of the case and he has erroneously designated someone else as the appellant — the court and all those concerned may yet have sufficient knowledge of the parties and their positions to hear the merits of the case. Mitchell v. Dona Ana Sav. & Loan Ass'n, 111 N.M. 257, 804 P.2d 1076 (1991).

Pleading stricken when required verification omitted. — Where a verification is required and is omitted, the pleading may be stricken out or judgment may be had on the pleadings. Hyde v. Bryan, 24 N.M. 457, 174 P. 419 (1918) (decided under former law).

Where the attorney objected to the judgment which included sanction, and the court also gave him notice through the order to show cause, this afforded the attorney not only the essential facts but also the notice and an opportunity to be heard; the attorney was afforded all the process he was due. Dona Ana Sav. & Loan Ass'n v. Mitchell, 113 N.M. 576, 829 P.2d 655 (Ct. App. 1991).

Sworn statement not required. — Service of a sworn statement before imposing sanctions is not required. Dona Ana Sav. & Loan Ass'n v. Mitchell, 113 N.M. 576, 829 P.2d 655 (Ct. App. 1991).

Motion to vacate a judgment need not be verified. Sheppard v. Sandfer, 44 N.M. 357, 102 P.2d 668 (1940) (decided under former law).

District court improperly imposed sanctions against an attorney for willfully failing to disclose the pendency of an action in another state involving the same issue, where the sanction awarded was based on what the attorney failed to disclose to the court, as opposed to a defect in his pleading. Cherryhomes v. Vogel, 111 N.M. 229, 804 P.2d 420 (Ct. App. 1990).

Sanctions should be entered against an attorney rather than a party for violation of the "good ground" requirement of this rule only when a pleading or other paper is unsupported by existing law rather than unsupported by facts. Rivera v. Brazos Lodge Corp., 111 N.M. 670, 808 P.2d 955 (1991).

Procedural due process. — Rule 11 sanctions should be imposed rarely, they should be levied only if the mandates of procedural due process are obeyed. Rivera v. Brazos Lodge Corp., 111 N.M. 670, 808 P.2d 955 (1991).

Determining whether process is due in a Rule 11 case requires an application of familiar principles of due process. The timing and content of the notice and the nature of the hearing will depend upon an evaluation of all the circumstances and an appropriate accommodation of the competing interests involved. Rivera v. Brazos Lodge Corp., 111 N.M. 670, 808 P.2d 955 (1991).

Appellate review of Rule 11 determination. — An appellate court should apply an abuse-of-discretion standard in reviewing all aspects of a trial court's Rule 11 determination. An abuse of discretion will be found when the trial court's decision is clearly untenable or contrary to logic and reason. Rivera v. Brazos Lodge Corp., 111 N.M. 670, 808 P.2d 955 (1991).

Case was remanded to the district court for the entry of findings and conclusions on the imposition of Rule 11 sanctions, where the supreme court was unable to review whether an abuse of discretion occurred in the imposition of sanctions for the filing of plaintiff's complaint without speculation about the subjective knowledge of the relevant facts and applicable law held by plaintiff and his attorney at the time of filing. Rivera v. Brazos Lodge Corp., 111 N.M. 670, 808 P.2d 955 (1991).

Evidence of willful violation lacking. — An earlier action for attorney fees was disposed of through a voluntary dismissal without prejudice and with no answer having been filed. The later filing of a malpractice claim against the plaintiffs in the earlier action was not a violation of this rule. Whether the claim for malpractice was a compulsory counterclaim in the earlier action was a question on which reasonable lawyers and judges could have differed. Lowe v. Bloom, 112 N.M. 203, 813 P.2d 480 (1991).

Am. Jur. 2d, A.L.R. and C.J.S. references. — 61B Am. Jur. 2d Pleading §§ 881 to 898.

Sufficiency of verification of pleading by person other than party to action, 7 A.L.R. 4.

Perjury in verifying pleadings, 7 A.L.R. 1283.

Civil liability of attorney for abuse of process, 97 A.L.R.3d 688.

Comment Note—General principles regarding imposition of sanctions under Rule 11, Federal Rules of Civil Procedure, 95 A.L.R. Fed. 107.

Imposition of sanctions under Rule 11, Federal Rules of Civil Procedure, pertaining to signing and verification of pleadings, in actions for defamation, 95 A.L.R. Fed. 181.

Imposition of sanctions under Rule 11, Federal Rules of Civil Procedure, pertaining to signing and verification of pleadings, in action for wrongful discharge from employment, 96 A.L.R. Fed. 13.

Imposition of sanctions under Rule 11, Federal Rules of Civil Procedure, pertaining to signing and verification of pleadings, in actions for securities fraud, 97 A.L.R. Fed. 107.

B.   WHY WOULD YOU RESEARCH RULES OF PROCEDURE?

If your client's case is being or likely will be litigated, you would research procedural rules to learn the proper steps for carrying out the litigation. Procedural rules are binding, of course, on the litigants and their lawyers. Failure to follow the applicable procedural rules impedes the efficient resolution of the case and may be grounds for dismissal of the suit or for sanctions against the party or the lawyer.

As already noted, reflecting our federalist system, rules of procedure exist at both the federal and state levels. To ascertain which set of rules applies, determine whether your claim will be pursued in federal or state court. A federal court applies federal rules, and a state court applies its state's rules. Federal procedural rules apply even when a federal court is adjudicating a claim based on the substantive law of a state, as occurs in diversity jurisdiction cases, for example. Furthermore, you should figure out which specific state or federal court is involved and research that court's local rules.

Even when you are in state court and your issue is governed by a state rule, you may research federal law, because many state rules parallel federal rules. There are far more published cases regarding federal rules than state rules, in part because some federal trial court opinions are published. Hence, when researching state rules, lawyers often look to federal cases as persuasive precedent.

C.   HOW DO YOU RESEARCH RULES OF PROCEDURE?

The focus of research in procedural rules is, of course, the text of the rule, but the rule is rarely the end point of your research. You often will look to the following authorities as well, listed from most to least weighty:

- ☐ judicial cases interpreting and applying the rule,
- ☐ advisory notes or comments, and
- ☐ secondary authority.

As with any type of research, jurisdiction matters. For example, if you are researching a state rule of procedure, you would focus on cases from that state's courts, read the advisory committee notes from that state, and seek secondary authority regarding that state's rules. Before you seriously consider authority pertaining to a rule from a sister jurisdiction, such as a federal case or treatise when you are researching state rules, you must determine whether the two rules are identical or very similar.

EXHIBIT 16.2	Sequence and Sources of Research in Rules of Procedure

Source	*Materials*
secondary authorities, e.g., treatises	discussions of and citations to leading primary authorities; may include rules, committee notes, and forms
deskbook	rules, and advisory committee notes; may include forms
statutory codes, including paper, commercial service's rules database	rules and advisory committee notes; also case descriptions and citations to secondary authorities if code is annotated
digests and reporters, case law databases, case citators	judicial cases
court websites	rules, including local rules; forms

To obtain this range of authorities, you will use paper and electronic sources also used in researching substantive law. You very likely also will use a deskbook, so called because they are used so often that most lawyers keep a copy close at hand. See Exhibit 16.2. The following discussion suggests a standard sequence and focuses primarily on research in federal rules; you will use comparable sources and methods when you research state rules.

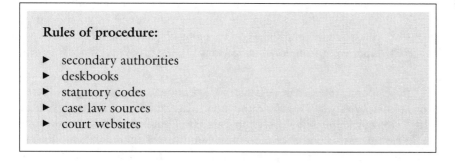

Rules of procedure:

▶ secondary authorities
▶ deskbooks
▶ statutory codes
▶ case law sources
▶ court websites

Secondary authorities. Especially if your research topic is new to you, you should consider beginning your research in secondary authority. The standard choice is a well-regarded treatise, many of which provide the rules and committee notes as well as the author's analysis. On the federal side, many lawyers turn to either *Federal Practice and Procedure* by Charles Alan Wright, Arthur R. Miller, and others, or *Moore's Federal Practice*. Both are multivolume treatises covering civil, criminal, and appellate procedure; Wright and Miller also covers evidence. In many states, there is a comparable treatise on state law.

Once you become fairly well versed in procedural law, you probably will begin your research in the rules themselves and consult secondary authorities at a later point in your research, to obtain an expert's discussion of the law or find citations to leading cases.

Deskbooks. Procedural rules are published in their most compact form in deskbooks. A deskbook is a one- or two-volume publication that usually contains the text of a jurisdiction's various sets of rules of procedure, notes or comments of the advisory committee on those rules, and some model forms. See Illustration 16-4 (at page 341), the table of contents for a representative federal rules deskbook. However, deskbooks do not contain case annotations or extensive commentary. Because most deskbooks are published annually and not updated until the next edition is published, they are fairly current but not necessarily completely up to date. Researching in deskbooks generally entails four steps:

(1)   To locate a pertinent rule within a deskbook, use a general index for the deskbook, the index to the pertinent set of rules, or the table of contents at the beginning of a set of rules.

(2)   Read the rule much as you would read a statute. You should read the entire rule, not just a subdivision that seems to be on point; skim nearby rules; and closely read any other rules to which your rule refers.

(3)   Next read the advisory committee notes to learn about the drafters' intent and any amendments to the rule. If the rule has been amended, you will need to seek cases arising under the current language and avoid relying on cases arising under the old language.

(4)   Finally, check for forms that accompany your rule. Forms in a deskbook are intended only to illustrate an appropriate format of pleadings. Forms generally appear in an appendix to the set of rules. See Illustration 16-5 (at page 342), a federal form for various types of jurisdictional allegations.

Researching the signature issue in the Canoga case, we selected West's *Federal Civil Judicial Procedure and Rules.* In the table of contents for the FRCP, we quickly found Rule 11 in Part III, Pleadings and Motions. Rule 11's title refers to signing of pleadings. Subdivision (a) requires a pleading to be signed by the attorney (or the party, but only where the party is not represented by an attorney); an unsigned pleading is stricken unless promptly corrected after being called to the attorney's attention. See Illustration 16-1 (at page 330). The Advisory Committee Notes to the 1993 Amendments explain how to correct the omission: by signing the filed pleading or submitting a signed duplicate. See Illustration 16-1 (at page 332).

Statutory codes. Although rules of procedure are not enacted in the same way as statutes are, they generally appear somewhere in or along with the jurisdiction's statutory code (see Chapter 11). For example, *United States Code Annotated* presents the FRCP after Title 28, the judiciary title; *United*

States Code Service presents rules of procedure in rules volumes at the end of the set. For a few states, procedural rules appear with the administrative code rather than the statutory code.

Just as with statutory research, you should use an annotated code when available. Annotated codes provide the rules and advisory committee notes, as do deskbooks. Annotated codes also permit you to expand your research beyond the material provided in a deskbook:

- ☐ You will find descriptions of cases interpreting the rule.
- ☐ You will find references to secondary authorities.
- ☐ Annotated codes are updated more frequently than deskbooks, so you may find recent amendments to the rule that do not yet appear in the deskbook.

See Illustration 16-3 (at pages 334–35), drawn from the rules volume of the annotated New Mexico code.

As with statutory codes, LexisNexis and Westlaw, as well as Loislaw, provide rules of procedure in various configurations, within a full statutory code database or in a rules database, with or without annotations. For example, LexisNexis provides the U.S.C.S. version of the Federal Rules of Civil Procedure in the FRCP database. For the most part, you will want to search in this type of database; it is narrower than a full statutory code database yet also includes case descriptions that may contain your research terms.

Case law sources. Judicial decisions discussing rules of procedure abound; indeed nearly every case has at least a brief mention of the point in the litigation at which the court has been asked to rule, which lawyers call the case's "procedural posture." Some cases discuss the procedural rule only briefly, others extensively. To research cases regarding a procedural rule, you would use the same sources and methods you would use to research an issue of substantive law, including the West digest and reporter system, commercial electronic services, public websites, and case citators (see Chapters 9 and 10). If you are researching federal law, you may use, in addition to the other West reporters, *Federal Rules Decisions*, which contains federal district court cases discussing the Federal Rules of Civil Procedure and the Federal Rules of Criminal Procedure (as well as proposals for rule changes and articles on procedural topics by judges, lawyers, and professors).

Researching the signature issue in the Canoga case, we researched in LexisNexis' Federal Court Cases Combined database and ran the search `unsigned /s pleading /s attorney or lawyer`. We found several cases, including *Operating Engineers Local 139 Health Benefit Fund v. Rawson Plumbing, Inc,*[2] in which a company's officer who was not an attorney signed the company's answer; the court declined to treat this as a default but rather ordered the company to file an answer signed by an attorney within twenty days.

---

2. 130 F. Supp. 2d 1022 (E.D. Wis. 2001).

Court websites. In recent years, to improve accessibility and efficiency, many courts have developed websites that offer a wide array of information. For example, you may find the court's local rules and standard forms used by that court.

Researching the signature issue in the Canoga case, we found Illustration 16-2 (at page 333) through nmcourt.fed.us, the website of the United States District Court for the District of New Mexico. Local Rule 10.3(b) adds some detail to Rule 11 by indicating that a pleading filed without a signature will be stricken unless signed within fourteen days following the notice to the party of the omitted signature.

D.   WHAT ELSE?

Specialized Reporters of Procedural Law.   *Federal Rules Service* and *Federal Rules of Evidence Service* digest and report cases regarding federal civil procedure and evidence respectively. They contain some cases not published in the West reporters discussed in Chapter 10.

Notice of Rules Amendments.   Various publications provide prompt notice of amendments to rules of procedure. For example, advance sheets of West's federal reporters do so for federal rules. State legal newspapers and bar publications typically do so for state rules, and some states have advance rules services similar to advance legislative services. Many lawyers, especially litigators, monitor such developments regularly. Other good options may be court or bar association websites.

Form Books.   Many practitioners rely on form books, which contain sample forms and pleadings. These sample forms can be useful, but they must be used with care. Major difficulties can result from selecting the wrong form, an outdated form, or a standard form that does not precisely fit the needs of a particular case. Sources of forms for use in federal courts include *Bender's Federal Practice Forms* and *West's Federal Forms*. State forms may be available in state practice treatises and continuing legal education materials.

Specialized Courts.   Some specialized courts, such as the federal bankruptcy courts, have their own rules of procedure. You can research these rules through the sources described in this chapter or in a mini-library for the practice area (see Chapter 15).

Citing Rules of Procedure.   As with statutes, rules of procedure and some local court rules may be cited through Shepard's on LexisNexis, KeyCite on Westlaw, or GlobalCite on Loislaw. You would cite a rule for the same reasons you would cite a statute: to learn of amendments, cases declaring the rule void or unconstitutional, cases interpreting and applying the rule, and secondary authorities discussing the rule. The availability of the citator service and the extensiveness of the results varies from service to service.

ILLUSTRATION 16-4

Deskbook Table of Contents,
from *Federal Civil Judicial Procedure and Rules*
(paper source)

TABLE OF CONTENTS

VIII

ILLUSTRATION 16-5   Form from Deskbook,
from *Federal Civil Judicial Procedure and Rules*
(paper source)

Form 1B   **RULES OF CIVIL PROCEDURE**

pursuant to section 2074 of this title, which was to take effect Dec. 1, 1991, was nullified by Congress, see section 11 of Pub.L. 102–198, set out as a note under section 2074 of this title.

Form 2. Allegation of Jurisdiction

(a) Jurisdiction founded on diversity of citizenship and amount.

Plaintiff is a [citizen of the State of Connecticut][1] [corporation incorporated under the laws of the State of Connecticut having its principal place of business in the State of Connecticut] and defendant is a corporation incorporated under the laws of the State of New York having its principal place of business in a State other than the State of Connecticut. The matter in controversy exceeds, exclusive of interest and costs, the sum specified by 28 U.S.C. § 1332.

(b) Jurisdiction founded on the existence of a Federal question.

The action arises under [the Constitution of the United States, Article ___, Section ___]; [the ___ Amendment to the Constitution of the United States, Section ___]; [the Act of ___, ___ Stat. ___; U.S.C., Title ___, § ___]; [the Treaty of the United States (here describe the treaty)][2] as hereinafter more fully appears.

(c) Jurisdiction founded on the existence of a question arising under particular statutes.

The action arises under the Act of ___, ___ Stat. ___; U.S.C., Title ___, § ___, as hereinafter more fully appears.

(d) Jurisdiction founded on the admiralty or maritime character of the claim.

This is a case of admiralty and maritime jurisdiction, as hereinafter more fully appears. [If the pleader wishes to invoke the distinctively maritime procedures referred to in Rule 9(h), add the following or its substantial equivalent: This is an admiralty or maritime claim within the meaning of Rule 9(h).]

[1] Form for natural person.

[2] Use the appropriate phrase or phrases. The general allegation of the existence of a Federal question is ineffective unless the matters constituting the claim for relief as set forth in the complaint raise a Federal question.

NOTES

1. Diversity of citizenship. U.S.C., Title 28, § 1332 (Diversity of citizenship; amount in controversy; costs), as amended by PL 85–554, 72 Stat. 415, July 25, 1958, states in subsection (c) that "For the purposes of this section and section 1441 of this title [removable actions], a corporation shall be deemed a citizen of any State by which it has been incorporated and of the State where it has its principal place of business." Thus if the defendant corporation in Form 2(a) had its principal place of business in Connecticut, diversity of citizenship would not exist. An allegation regarding the

principal place of business of each corporate party must be made in addition to an allegation regarding its place of incorporation.

2. Jurisdictional amount. U.S.C., Title 28, § 1331 (Federal question; amount in controversy; costs) and § 1332 (Diversity of citizenship; amount in controversy; costs), as amended by PL 85–554, 72 Stat. 415, July 25, 1958, require that the amount in controversy, exclusive of interest and costs, be in excess of $10,000. The allegation as to the amount in controversy may be omitted in any case where by law no jurisdictional amount is required. See, for example, U.S.C., Title 28, § 1338 (Patents, copyrights, trade-marks, and unfair competition), § 1343 (Civil rights and elective franchise).

3. Pleading venue. Since improper venue is a matter of defense, it is not necessary for plaintiff to include allegations showing the venue to be proper. See 1 *Moore's Federal Practice*, par. 0.140[1–4] (2d ed. 1959).

(As amended Apr. 17, 1961, eff. July 19, 1961; Feb. 28, 1966, eff. July 1, 1966; Apr. 22, 1993, eff. Dec. 1, 1993; Apr. 29, 1999, eff. Dec. 1, 1999.)

ADVISORY COMMITTEE NOTES

1966 Amendment

Since the Civil Rules have not heretofore been applicable to proceedings in Admiralty (Rule 81(a)(1)), Form 2 naturally has not contained a provision for invoking the admiralty jurisdiction. The form has never purported to be comprehensive, as making provision for all possible grounds of jurisdiction; but a provision for invoking the admiralty jurisdiction is particularly appropriate as an incident of unification.

Certain distinctive features of the admiralty practice must be preserved in unification, just as certain distinctive characteristics of equity were preserved in the merger of law and equity in 1938. Rule 9(h) provides the device whereby, after unification, with its abolition of the distinction between civil actions and suits in admiralty, the pleader may indicate his choice of the distinctively maritime procedures, and designates those features that are preserved. This form illustrates an appropriate way in which the pleader may invoke those procedures. Use of this device is not necessary if the claim is cognizable only by virtue of the admiralty and maritime jurisdiction, nor if the claim is within the exclusive admiralty jurisdiction of the district court.

Omission of a statement such as this from the pleading indicates the pleader's choice that the action proceed as a conventional civil action, if this is jurisdictionally possible, without the distinctive maritime remedies and procedures. It should be remembered, however, that Rule 9(h) provides that a pleading may be amended to add or withdraw such an identifying statement subject to the principles stated in Rule 15.

1993 Amendments

This form is revised to reflect amendments to 28 U.S.C. §§ 1331 and 1332 providing jurisdiction for federal questions without regard to the amount in controversy and raising the amount required to be in controversy in diversity cases to fifty thousand dollars.

Complete Annotation Materials, see Title 28 U.S.C.A.

280

E. HOW DO YOU CITE RULES OF PROCEDURE?

A citation to a rule of procedure consists of the abbreviation for the set of rules and the rule number. Here are two examples:

- ☐ *Bluebook* Rule 12.8.3: Fed. R. Civ. P. 11.
- ☐ *ALWD* Rule 17.1: Fed. R. Civ. P. 11.

You may, on occasion, cite the notes of an advisory committee. Here are two examples:

- ☐ *Bluebook* Rule 3.5: Fed. R. Civ. P. 11 advisory committee's notes.
- ☐ *ALWD* Rule 17.1: Fed. R. Civ. P. 11 advisory comm. nn.

If there is more than one set of advisory committee notes, you may want to add a date for clarification.

RULES OF PROFESSIONAL RESPONSIBILITY

CHAPTER 17

A. WHAT ARE RULES OF PROFESSIONAL RESPONSIBILITY?

Lawyers have a unique role in our society. Lawyers affect the decisions of their clients and the outcomes of matters that often are confidential and difficult. Because of their expertise and training, lawyers often serve as judges, legislators, executive officers, or administrators. Lawyers also are major participants in law reform efforts. Thus, lawyers often are in positions to exert enormous power over the affairs of their clients and over the public at large.

With power comes the obligation to assure that lawyers act responsibly and are held accountable for irresponsible actions. Early on, the legal profession policed itself. Over time, that approach has given way to modified self-regulation.

Regulation of the legal profession now is a matter primarily of state law. In each state, either the the supreme court or the legislature promulgates rules of professional responsibility. Typically, an advisory committee recommends and drafts new rules and changes to existing rules, which are then published for review and comment by the legal community and the public before adoption.

The American Bar Association (ABA) has played a major role in the development of rules of professional responsibility. The ABA adopted its first rules in the 1908 Canons of Professional Ethics. These canons were not mandatory, but bar associations and courts did look to them for guidance in establishing standards of conduct and in disciplining lawyers.

The ABA later adopted a more comprehensive set of rules, the 1969 Model Code of Professional Responsibility (Model Code), which was widely adopted. It had a three-part structure: the Canons serving as broad principles; Ethical Considerations (ECs) providing aspirational and explanatory provisions; and Disciplinary Rules (DRs) setting minimum, mandatory standards.

In response to criticism of the 1969 Model Code, the ABA appointed a special Commission on Evaluation of Professional Standards (the Kutak Commission) to study and revise the Model Code. After wide debate, the ABA adopted the Model Rules of Professional Conduct (Model Rules) in 1983. The Model Rules, which have a simpler structure than the Model Code, have been adopted by many states, often with some modifications. The Model Rules have been revised from time to time, including a major revision known as Ethics 2000, completed in 2002.

The overall organization of a set of professional responsibility rules is, of course, topical. See Exhibit 17.1, which lists the topics of the current ABA Model Rules. The format of an individual rule varies from state to state, depending on whether the state follows the three-part structure of the Model Code, the unitary rule structure of the Model Rules, or a variation on these models. Most publications of state rules include some type of commentary, whether the ABA commentary or commentary from the state's drafting committee. Illustration 17-1 (at pages 347–49) is a New Mexico rule that follows the format of the Model Rules.

As important as rules of professional responsibility are, they are not the only laws governing lawyers. For example, egregious professional misconduct can result in criminal penalties. Failure to provide competent representation to a client may constitute legal malpractice, for which the client may recover monetary damages from the lawyer.

The illustrations in this chapter pertain to the following variation on the Canoga case: After researching the legal claims Ms. Canoga could pursue, you have tentatively decided to represent her in New Mexico state court as to her New Mexico breach of contract and Employee Privacy Act claims but not to pursue a claim under the federal Americans with Disabilities Act (ADA). You have various reasons for this decision, including doubts about the validity of the claim, concerns about the time and expense needed to litigate that claim, an already heavy caseload, and significant family obligations in the coming months.

Limiting the scope of representation is a topic governed by rules of professional responsibility, in New Mexico by Rule 16-102 part c. See Illustration 17-1 (at page 347).

| EXHIBIT 17.1 | List of ABA Model Rules of Professional Conduct |

1.0   Terminology

Client-Lawyer Relationship

1.1   Competence
1.2   Scope of Representation and Allocation of
       Authority
1.3   Diligence
1.4   Communication
1.5   Fees
1.6   Confidentiality of Information
1.7   Conflict of Interest: Current Clients
1.8   Conflict of Interest: Current Clients: Specific
       Rules
1.9   Duties to Former Clients
1.10   Imputation of Conflicts of Interest: General
       Rule
1.11   Special Conflicts of Interest for Former and
       Current Government Officers and
       Employees
1.12   Former Judge, Arbitrator, Mediator or Other
       Third-Party Neutral
1.13   Organization as Client
1.14   Client with Diminished Capacity
1.15   Safekeeping Property
1.16   Declining or Terminating Representation
1.17   Sale of Law Practice
1.18   Duties to Prospective Client

Counselor

2.1   Advisor
2.2   (Deleted)
2.3   Evaluation for Use by Third Persons
2.4   Lawyer Serving as Third-Party Neutral

Advocate

3.1   Meritorious Claims and Contentions
3.2   Expediting Litigation
3.3   Candor toward the Tribunal
3.4   Fairness to Opposing Party and Counsel
3.5   Impartiality and Decorum of the Tribunal
3.6   Trial Publicity
3.7   Lawyer as Witness
3.8   Special Responsibilities of a Prosecutor
3.9   Advocate in Nonadjudicative Proceedings

Transactions with Persons Other Than Clients

4.1   Truthfulness in Statements to Others
4.2   Communication with Person Represented by
       Counsel

4.3   Dealing with Unrepresented Person
4.4   Respect for Rights of Third Persons

Law Firms and Associations

5.1   Responsibilities of Partners, Managers, and
       Supervisory Lawyers
5.2   Responsibilities of a Subordinate Lawyer
5.3   Responsibilities Regarding Nonlawyer
       Assistants
5.4   Professional Independence of a Lawyer
5.5   Unauthorized Practice of Law;
       Multijurisdictional Practice of Law
5.6   Restrictions on Right to Practice
5.7   Responsibilities Regarding Law-related
       Services

Public Service

6.1   Voluntary Pro Bono Publico Service
6.2   Accepting Appointments
6.3   Membership in Legal Services Organization
6.4   Law Reform Activities Affecting Client
       Interests
6.5   Nonprofit and Court-Annexed Limited Legal
       Services Programs

Information About Legal Services

7.1   Communications Concerning a Lawyer's
       Services
7.2   Advertising
7.3   Direct Contact with Prospective Clients
7.4   Communication of Fields of Practice and
       Specialization
7.5   Firm Names and Letterheads
7.6   Political Contributions to Obtain
       Government Legal Engagements or
       Appointments by Judges

Maintaining the Integrity of the Profession

8.1   Bar Admission and Disciplinary Matters
8.2   Judicial and Legal Officials
8.3   Reporting Professional Misconduct
8.4   Misconduct
8.5   Disciplinary Authority; Choice of Law

ILLUSTRATION 17-1	State Rule of Professional Conduct and Annotation, from *New Mexico Rules Annotated* (paper source)

pline attorneys. It was not intended to provide a foundation for civil liability. Garcia v. Rodey, Dickason, Sloan, Akin & Robb, 106 N.M. 757, 750 P.2d 118 (1988).

Failure to comply with the Rules of Appellate Procedure constituted a violation of this rule. In re Dawson, 2000-NMSC-024, 129 N.M. 369, 8 P.3d 856.

Attorney's failure to docket an appeal and lying to his client for seven years about the status of the appeal violated numerous rules and warranted indefinite suspension from practice. In re Roberts, 119 N.M. 769, 895 P.2d 669 (1995).

Bankruptcy practice. — An attorney's failure to address a potential secured claim against his client in a bankruptcy proceeding was a violation of Rules 16-101 and 16-804. In re Elmore, 1997-NMSC-020, 123 N.M. 79, 934 P.2d 273.

Rule violated. — See In re Cutter, 118 N.M. 152, 879 P.2d 784 (1994).

Law reviews. — For note, "Legal Malpractice — Liability for Failure to Warn: First National Bank of Clovis v. Diane, Inc.", see 16 N.M.L. Rev. 395 (1986).

For article, "Attorney as Interpreter: A Return to Babble," 20 N.M.L. Rev. 1 (1990).

For note, "Professional Responsibility — Attorneys Are Not Liable to Their Clients' Adversaries: Garcia v. Rodey, Dickason, Sloan, Akin & Robb, P.A.," see 20 N.M.L. Rev. 737 (1990).

Am. Jur. 2d, A.L.R. and C.J.S. references. — 7 Am. Jur. 2d Attorneys at Law §§ 67 to 73.

Legal malpractice by permitting statutory time limitation to run against client's claim, 90 A.L.R.3d 293.

What statute of limitations governs damage action against attorney for malpractice, 2 A.L.R.4th 284.

Adequacy of defense counsel's representation of criminal client regarding argument, 6 A.L.R.4th 16.

Adequacy of defense counsel's representation of criminal client regarding speedy trial and related matters, 6 A.L.R.4th 1208.

Adequacy of defense counsel's representation of criminal client regarding hypnosis and truth tests, 9 A.L.R.4th 354.

Adequacy of defense counsel's representation of criminal client regarding guilty pleas, 10 A.L.R.4th 8.

Adequacy of defense counsel's representation of criminal client regarding post-plea remedies, 13 A.L.R.4th 533.

Adequacy of defense counsel's representation of criminal client regarding appellate and postconviction remedies, 15 A.L.R.4th 582.

Adequacy of defense counsel's representation of crim-

inal client regarding incompetency, insanity and related issues, 17 A.L.R.4th 575.

Incompetence of counsel as ground for relief from state court civil judgment, 64 A.L.R.4th 323.

Negligence, inattention, or professional incompetence of attorney in handling client's affairs in matters involving real estate transactions as ground for disciplinary action — modern cases, 65 A.L.R.4th 24.

Negligence, inattention, or professional incompetence of attorney in handling client's affairs in tax matters as ground for disciplinary action—modern cases, 66 A.L.R.4th 314.

Negligence, inattention, or professional incompetence of attorney in handling client's affairs in estate or probate matters as ground for disciplinary action—modern cases, 66 A.L.R.4th 342.

Negligence, inattention, or professional incompetence of attorney in handling client's affairs in family law matters as ground for disciplinary action—modern cases, 67 A.L.R.4th 415.

Negligence, inattention, or professional incompetence of attorney in handling client's affairs in personal injury or property damage actions as ground for disciplinary action—modern cases, 68 A.L.R.4th 694.

Negligence, inattention, or professional incompetence of attorney in handling client's affairs in criminal matters as ground for disciplinary action—modern cases, 69 A.L.R.4th 410.

Negligence, inattention, or professional incompetence of attorney in handling client's affairs in bankruptcy matters as ground for disciplinary action — modern cases, 70 A.L.R.4th 786.

Legal malpractice in handling or defending medical malpractice claim, 78 A.L.R.4th 725.

Misconduct involving intoxication as ground for disciplinary action against attorney, 1 A.L.R.5th 874.

Legal malpractice in defense of criminal prosecution, 4 A.L.R.5th 273.

Ineffective assistance of counsel: compulsion, duress, necessity, or "hostage syndrome" defense, 8 A.L.R.5th 713.

Legal malpractice: negligence or fault of client as defense, 10 A.L.R.5th 828.

Ineffective assistance of counsel: Right of attorney to withdraw, as appointed defense counsel, due to self-avowed incompetence, 16 A.L.R.5th 118.

Admissibility and effect of evidence of professional ethics rules in legal malpractice action, 50 A.L.R.5th 301.

7 C.J.S. Attorney and Client §§ 77 to 87; 7A C.J.S. Attorney and Client §§ 254 to 262.

16-102. Scope of representation.

A. **Client's decisions.** A lawyer shall abide by a client's decisions concerning the objectives of representation, subject to Paragraphs C, D and E, and shall consult with the client as to the means by which they are to be pursued. A lawyer shall abide by a client's decision whether to accept an offer of settlement of a matter. In a criminal case, the lawyer shall abide by the client's decision, after consultation with the lawyer, as to a plea to be entered, whether to waive jury trial and whether the client will testify.

B. **Representation not endorsement of client's views.** A lawyer's representation of a client, including representation by appointment, does not constitute an endorsement of the client's political, economic, social or moral views or activities.

C. **Limitation of representation.** A lawyer may limit the scope of the representation if the limitation is reasonable under the circumstances and the client gives informed consent.

ILLUSTRATION 17-1   *(continued)*

16-102   RULES OF PROFESSIONAL CONDUCT   552

D. **Course of conduct.** A lawyer shall not engage, or counsel a client to engage, or assist a client, in conduct that the lawyer knows is criminal or fraudulent or which misleads the court, but a lawyer may discuss the legal consequences of any proposed course of conduct with a client and may counsel or assist a client to make a good faith effort to determine the validity, scope, meaning or application of the law.

E. **Consultation on limitations of assistance.** When a lawyer knows that a client expects assistance not permitted by the Rules of Professional Conduct or other law, the lawyer shall consult with the client regarding the relevant limitations on the lawyer's conduct.

[As amended, effective March 15, 2001.]

COMMENT TO MODEL RULES

Compiler's notes. — The Comment to Model Rule 1.2 published after Rule 16-102 includes proposed revisions to the ABA Comment that were included in the ABA Ethics 2000 Committee report.

The New Mexico rule differs from the ABA model rule in that the New Mexico version inserts "engage, or" and "or which misleads the court" in Paragraph D.

ABA COMMENT TO MODEL RULES AS PROPOSED TO BE MODIFIED:

Scope of Representation

Both lawyer and client have authority and responsibility in the objectives and means of representation. The client has ultimate authority to determine the purposes to be served by legal representation, within the limits imposed by law and the lawyer's professional obligations. Within those limits, a client also has a right to consult with the lawyer about the means to be used in pursuing those objectives. At the same time, a lawyer is not required to pursue objectives or employ means simply because a client may wish that the lawyer do so. A clear distinction between objectives and means sometimes cannot be drawn, and in many cases the client-lawyer relationship partakes of a joint undertaking. In questions of means, the lawyer should assume responsibility for technical and legal tactical issues, but should defer to the client regarding such questions as the expense to be incurred and concern for third persons who might be adversely affected. Law defining the lawyer's scope of authority in litigation varies among jurisdictions.

In a case in which the client appears to be suffering mental disability, the lawyer's duty to abide by the client's decisions is to be guided by reference to Rule 1.14 [Rule 16-114 NMRA].

Independence from Client's Views or Activities

Legal representation should not be denied to people who are unable to afford legal services, or whose cause is controversial or the subject of popular disapproval. By the same token, representing a client does not constitute approval of the client's views or activities.

Services Limited in Objectives or Means

The scope of services to be provided by a lawyer may be limited by agreement with the client or by the terms under which the lawyer's services are made available to the client. When a lawyer has been retained by an insurer to represent an insured, for example, the representation may be limited to matters related to the insurance coverage. A limited representation may be appropriate because the client has limited objectives for the representation. In addition, the terms upon which representation is undertaken may exclude specific means that might otherwise be used to accomplish the client's objectives. Such limitations may exclude actions that the client thinks are too costly or that the lawyer regards as repugnant or imprudent.

Although this rule affords the lawyer and client substantial latitude to limit the representation, the limitation must be reasonable under the circumstances. If for example, a client's objective is limited to securing general information about the law the client needs in order to handle a common and typically uncomplicated legal problem, the lawyer and client may agree that the lawyer's services will be limited to a brief telephone consultation. Such a limitation, however, would not be reasonable if the time allotted was not sufficient to yield advice upon which the client could rely. Although an agreement for a limited representation does not exempt a lawyer from the duty to provide competent representation, the limitation is a factor to be considered when determining the legal knowledge, skill, thoroughness and preparation reasonably necessary for the representation. *See* Rule 16-101 NMRA.

Although Paragraph C does not require that the client's informed consent to a limited representation be in writing, a specification of the scope of representation will normally be a necessary part of the lawyer's written communication of the rate or basis of the lawyer's fee as required by Rule 16-105(B) NMRA.

All agreements concerning the scope of representation must accord with the Rules of Professional Conduct and other law. *See e.g.*, Rules 16-101, 16-108 and 16-506 NMRA.

Criminal, Fraudulent and Prohibited Transactions

A lawyer is required to give an honest opinion about the actual consequences that appear likely to result from a client's conduct. The fact that a client uses advice in a course of action that is criminal or fraudulent does not, of itself, make a lawyer a party to the course of action. However, a lawyer may not knowingly assist a client in criminal or fraudulent conduct. There is a critical distinction between presenting an analysis of legal aspects of questionable conduct and recommending the means by which a crime or fraud might be committed with impunity.

When the client's course of action has already begun and is continuing, the lawyer's responsibility is especially delicate. The lawyer is not permitted to reveal the client's wrongdoing, except where permitted by Rule 1.6 [Rule 16-106 NMRA]. However, the lawyer is required to avoid furthering the purpose, for example, by suggesting how it might be concealed. A lawyer may not continue assisting a client in conduct that the lawyer originally supposes is legally proper but then discovers

ILLUSTRATION 17-1   *(continued)*

---

is criminal or fraudulent. Withdrawal from the representation, therefore, may be required.

Where the client is a fiduciary, the lawyer may be charged with special obligations in dealings with a beneficiary.

Paragraph (d) [D] applies whether or not the defrauded party is a party to the transaction. Hence, a lawyer should not participate in a sham transaction; for example, a transaction to effectuate criminal or fraudulent escape of tax liability. Paragraph (d) [D] does not preclude undertaking a criminal defense incident to a general retainer for legal services to a lawful enterprise. The last clause of paragraph (d) [D] recognizes that determining the validity or interpretation of a statute or regulation may require a course of action involving disobedience of the statute or regulation or of the interpretation placed upon it by governmental authorities.

[Revised effective March 15, 2001.]

COMPILER'S ANNOTATIONS

The 2001 amendment, effective March 15, 2001, rewrote Paragraph C which read "A lawyer may limit the objectives of the representation if the client consents after consultation".

Duty to take essential steps and consult with client. — When one contracts with an attorney for legal services, it is not the client's responsibility to initiate all inquiries to the attorney in order to insure that essential steps are being taken. Furthermore, it is within the scope of an attorney's obligations to a client to provide the information, advice, and reassurances necessary to allay unnecessary concerns that the client may have. Where attorney does none of these things, he violates this and other rules. In re Carrasco, 106 N.M. 294, 742 P.2d 506 (1987).

Attorney's failure to consult with his clients concerning the objectives of the representation and the means by which the objectives were to be pursued violated Paragraph A of this rule. In re Houston, 1999-NMSC-032, 127 N.M. 582, 985 P.2d 752.

Dual role of guardian ad litem. — The dual role of a guardian ad litem to represent the best interests of a child while also presenting the child's wishes to the court even if they conflict with the position of the guardian ad litem conforms to the requirements of the Rules of Professional Conduct. State ex rel. Children, Youth & Families Dep't v. Esperanza M., 1998-NMCA-039, 124 N.M. 735, 955 P.2d 204.

Lawyers are officers of court and are always under obligation to be truthful to the court. Woodson v. Phillips Petroleum Co., 102 N.M. 333, 695 P.2d 483 (1985).

Public defenders are not excused from compliance with the Code of Professional Responsibility (now the Rules of Professional Conduct) even though they are paid with public funds. State v. Martinez, 97 N.M. 540, 641 P.2d 1087 (Ct. App. 1982).

Attorney's duty upon appeal. — An attorney representing a client on appeal should first seek to convince the client of the wisdom of the attorney's professional judgment, but, failing such persuasion, the client's contention should be presented. The manner of such presentation is solely for the attorney, subject, however, to Rule 7-102(A) (now Rules 16-102, 16-303 and 16-304 NMRA) which prohibits an attorney from knowingly advancing unwarranted claims and from knowingly making false statements of law or fact. State v. Boyer, 103 N.M. 655, 712 P.2d 1 (Ct. App. 1985).

Abandonment of issues on appeal. — The strict language of this rule and Rule 7-102 (now Rules 16-102, 16-303 and 16-304 NMRA) allows attorneys to abandon frivolous issues, or even non-frivolous issues, once the attorney has found one non-frivolous issue to argue with vigor on appeal. State v. Boyer, 103 N.M. 655, 712 P.2d 1 (Ct. App. 1985).

Abandonment of client warrants suspension. — Where an attorney abandons his client and the case, despite his having been paid a substantial fee, he violates this rule and warrants suspension. In re Chowning, 100 N.M. 375, 671 P.2d 36 (1983).

Six-month suspension and other penalties warranted since attorney accepted one-half of fee and failed to represent client, allowing default to be entered against client. In re Trujillo, 110 N.M. 180, 793 P.2d 862 (1990).

Suspension warranted where conflicting interests impair independent judgment. — If a lawyer allows his independent professional judgment on his client's behalf to be impaired by his representation of conflicting interests and, through negligence and acceptance of undue influence and instructions from others, he unintentionally aids an embezzlement scheme in which his client is the victim, such conduct warrants suspension from practice of law for a 30-day period and thereafter until reinstated as provided by the rules of the supreme court. In re Dilts, 93 N.M. 131, 597 P.2d 316 (1979).

Censure and fine for false and misleading brief. — An attorney was publicly censured and fined $1,000 for knowingly making false, misleading and inaccurate statements in a brief to the court of appeals in violation of this rule (former Rule 7-102). In re Chakeres, 101 N.M. 684, 687 P.2d 741 (1984).

Restitution made only under pressure is entitled to no weight as a mitigating factor. In re Stewart, 104 N.M. 337, 721 P.2d 405 (1986).

Misappropriation of funds. — Attorney's conversion to his own use of money received from a client to have a liquor license transferred to her name violated Rules 1-102, 6-101, 7-101 and 9-102 of the Code of Professional Responsibility (now see Rules 16-102, 16-104, 16-115 and 16-804 of the Rules of Professional Conduct). In re Gallegos, 104 N.M. 496, 723 P.2d 967 (1986).

One-year suspension warranted. — Attorney's actions warranted a one-year suspension since he made misrepresentations to a court, failed to return unearned fees, failed to render an accounting to a client and acted otherwise to prejudice the administration of justice. In re Arrieta, 104 N.M. 389, 722 P.2d 640 (1986).

Indefinite suspension warranted. — Sixteen violations of nine rules governing professional responsibility, involving misrepresentation, neglect, improper fee-splitting, disrespect to various tribunals, and other conduct prejudicial to the administration of justice resulted in defendant's being suspended indefinitely from the practice of law. In re Quintana, 104 N.M. 511, 724 P.2d 220 (1986).

Indefinite suspension was warranted because an attorney violated Paragraph A by failing to abide by a client's decisions concerning the objectives of the representation. The attorney also violated the following rules: Rule 16-101 NMRA, by failing to provide competent representation; Rule 16-103 NMRA, by failing to

B.   WHY WOULD YOU RESEARCH RULES OF PROFESSIONAL RESPONSIBILITY?

The rules of professional responsibility adopted by a state supreme court or legislature govern the conduct of most lawyers in that state. Most rules set mandatory standards of conduct; for example, a lawyer shall not commingle client funds. A few set aspirational guidelines; for example, a lawyer should aspire to provide fifty hours of pro bono service annually.

Professional responsibility rules are enforced through various mechanisms. In a typical model, a state disciplinary committee hears complaints regarding allegations of professional misconduct, issues decisions, and disciplines noncomplying lawyers. Professional sanctions include private or public censure, suspension of one's license to practice law, and disbarment. In addition to the state regulatory entity, some local bar associations have ethics committees that hear complaints about attorney misconduct and make findings and recommendations to the state authorities.

A violation of an ethical standard also may expose an attorney to liability to the client for malpractice or, in very serious cases, to criminal penalties. In short, failure to meet ethical standards not only harms the client and the profession but can also carry grave personal consequences for the attorney.

C.   HOW DO YOU RESEARCH RULES OF PROFESSIONAL RESPONSIBILITY?

Researching an issue of legal ethics centers on the state's rules of professional responsibility but rarely stops there. A rule is rarely so specific that its application is self-evident; many situations involve complex facts and competing interests. Thus, you very often will consider the following authorities, in addition to the rule, listed from most to least weighty:

- ☐ judicial cases interpreting and applying the rule;
- ☐ the state agency's ethics opinions;
- ☐ comments to the rule;
- ☐ bar association advisory opinions;
- ☐ ethics opinions from the ABA Standing Committee on Ethics and Professional Responsibility, both formal (statements intended to clarify a rule or address a topic of general interest) and informal (responding to a specific inquiry and involving less common concerns); and
- ☐ secondary authority.

As with any other type of research, jurisdiction matters. That is, a mandatory precedent is weightier than a persuasive precedent, and an ethics opinion from your state is weightier than one from a sister state. Note that before you rely on authority from a sister state or the ABA, you should ascertain whether your state's rule is identical or very similar to that of the sister state or the ABA model; there are variations from state to state.

To obtain this range of authorities, you will use a variety of sources, both paper and electronic. See Exhibit 17.2. While some sources, such as treatises and case digests, are not unique to ethics research, others are. The discussion below suggests a standard sequence, from sources one nearly always uses, to sources used mostly for complex or difficult research topics.

EXHIBIT 17.2	Sequence and Sources of Legal Ethics Research

Source	*Materials*
secondary authorities, e.g., treatise, Restatement	discussion of and citations to leading primary authorities
deskbook	rules, comments of advisory committee or adopting authority
unannotated code	rules, possibly comments
annotated code	rules, comments of advisory committee or adopting authority, historical notes, case descriptions, references to secondary authorities
commercial electronic service's rules database	same as deskbook or unannotated or annotated codes
public website	rules, possibly comments
digests and reporters, case law databases, case citators	judicial cases
specialized reporters, commercial service's ethics opinions database, public website, ethics agency	ethics opinions from state agencies and bar committees
ABA publications	
• *Compendium of Professional Responsibility Rules and Standards*	current rules, predecessors, other rules and standards, selected ABA ethics opinions
• *Annotated Model Rules of Professional Conduct*	rules, comments, discussion of leading judicial decisions and ethics opinions
• *Recent Ethics Opinions* and older compilations	ABA formal and informal opinions
• abanet.org/cpr	wide range of ABA materials (and links to state websites)

> **Legal ethics:**
>
> ▶ secondary authorities
>
> ▶ your state's rule and comments
>
> ▶ your state's judicial cases
>
> ▶ your state's ethics opinions
>
> ▶ persuasive authorities, especially ABA materials

Secondary authorities.   Especially if your research topic is new to you, you should consider beginning your research in secondary authorities. A good first choice is a well-regarded treatise; one example is *The Law of Lawyering* by Geoffrey C. Hazard, Jr., and W. William Hodes, which includes analysis of illustrative scenarios. Another good option is *ABA/BNA Lawyers' Manual on Professional Conduct.* See Illustration 17-2 (at pages 355–56).

A fairly new secondary authority in the area of legal ethics is the Restatement (Third) of the Law Governing Lawyers, promulgated in 2000. The Restatement draws not only on rules of professional responsibility but also on case law, including legal malpractice cases. In some areas, the Restatement position departs from the Model Rules as they read before Ethics 2000. The format of this new Restatement parallels that of other Restatements.

Once you become fairly well versed in legal ethics, you probably will begin your research in the rules themselves and consult these secondary authorities at a later point in your research.

Researching the Canoga case, we read the discussion in the *ABA/BNA Lawyers' Manual,* which refers to Rule 1.2(c), a Louisiana case permitting a lawyer to handle some claims but not others, other judicial cases, state ethics opinions, and an ABA formal opinion. See Illustration 17-2 (at pages 355–56).

Your state's rules and comments.   For most states, the text of professional responsibility rules is published in the same deskbook that contains the state's rules of procedure (see Chapter 16). A state deskbook typically contains the rules of professional responsibility and some explanatory material as well, such as the comments of the advisory committee or adopting authority, but not references to cases or other authorities. Deskbooks are issued annually; thus, very recent amendments and new rules will not be included.

Most state codes include professional responsibility rules (see Chapter 11). In an annotated code, the rules are annotated in a manner similar to statutory provisions, including any comments of the state advisory committee, historical notes regarding previous rules, case descriptions, and references to secondary sources. See Illustration 17-1 (at pages 347–49).

Professional responsibility rules are available in electronic media as well. Westlaw and LexisNexis both provide professional responsibility rules in their state rules databases. In addition, you may find the rules through a public website, such as the supreme court's website or a bar association website.

Researching the Canoga case, we used *New Mexico Rules Annotated.* New Mexico Rule 16-102(c) permits a limited scope of representation that is reasonable under the circumstances, when the client gives informed consent. The annotation includes the ABA Ethics 2000 committee report and notes a New Mexico 2001 amendment to paragraph C, which introduces the requirement of reasonableness under the circumstances.

Your state's judicial cases.   Once you have explored the sources discussed above, you will be ready to read cases interpreting and applying the pertinent rule. In addition to the case descriptions in an annotated code, you can use case digests, searches in a case law database (probably a commercial service, possibly a public website), and case citators to identify pertinent cases, which you can read in a reporter or database. As with all case law research, be sure to cite each case (see Chapters 9 and 10).

Researching the Canoga case, we read the case descriptions in the New Mexico annotated rules volume, but none were pertinent. See Illustration 17-1 (at page 349).

Your state's ethics opinions.   If your state ethics agency or bar association issue ethics opinions, you should research these next. See Illustration 17-3 (at page 357).[1] You may find them or descriptions of them in one or more of the following sources:

☐   a specialized reporter, such as *ABA/BNA Lawyers' Manual on Professional Conduct* and *National Reporter on Legal Ethics and Professional Responsibility;*
☐   a Westlaw or LexisNexis ethics opinions database covering your state;
☐   the website for your state's ethics agency or bar association; and
☐   the office of the ethics agency or bar association.

See Illustration 17-4 (at page 358), from the *ABA/BNA Lawyers' Manual* and Illustration 17-5 (at page 359) from the New Mexico State Bar Association website. The latter provides the opinions as well as the synopses (located, interestingly, under Risk Management). Be sure that you know whether any opinion you find is binding or merely advisory. Keep in mind that it is, in any event, less authoritative than a judicial case.

Researching the Canoga case, we did not find an opinion on our research topic from New Mexico.

Persuasive authorities.   If, after exploring the sources listed above, you still need further guidance, you should turn to persuasive materials. Good options are to consult a treatise, the Restatement, or a periodical article (several journals focus on legal ethics), or other secondary authority.

Very likely, your research at this stage will come to focus on the ABA rules because of their influence on state rules around the country. As a first

---

1. We selected a Pennsylvania opinion on the Canoga topic, for lack of an available pertinent New Mexico opinion.

critical step, be sure to compare the language of your state's rule to that of the ABA's rule. The commentary to your state's rule in the deskbook or annotated code may provide this information; if not, you will need to do the comparison yourself. If your state's rule is identical to the ABA rule, you can adopt what you learn about the ABA rule; if your state's rule differs from the ABA rule, you will need to adapt what you learn about the ABA rule. Not surprisingly, several ABA publications provide a wide range of useful information:

☐ *ABA Compendium of Professional Responsibility Rules and Standards*, excerpted in Illustration 17-6 (at pages 360–62), which is a deskbook containing the current Model Rules; its predecessors, with conversion tables to the current Model Rules; other ABA standards, such as the Standards for Imposing Lawyer Sanctions; and selected ethics opinions from the ABA Standing Committee on Ethics and Professional Responsibility;

☐ *Annotated Model Rules of Professional Conduct*, which provides a concise discussion of and references to leading judicial cases and ethics opinions along with the rules;

☐ compilations of the ABA Standing Committee's formal and informal opinions, e.g., *Formal and Informal Opinions 1983-1998*, *Recent Ethics Opinions*, available in paper as well as through Westlaw and LexisNexis; and

☐ the ABA Center for Professional Responsibility website, abanet.org/cpr, where you will find not only ABA materials, such as background on Ethics 2000 and synopses of significant ABA Standing Committee Opinions, but also links to state websites.

In addition, you may find it helpful to read judicial cases and ethics opinions from other states. You will find references to these in most of the sources discussed above. In particular, two good paper options are the *ABA/BNA Lawyers' Manual* and the *National Reporter*. Strong electronic options are Westlaw's METH-CS and METH-EO, multistate judicial decisions and ethics opinions databases respectively (the latter is the source of Illustration 17-3 at page 357); LexisNexis' ETHCAS, which combines state case law and ethics opinions; and LexisNexis' ETHOP, the electronic version of the *National Reporter*.

Researching the Canoga case, we consulted the *ABA Compendium* and found the same comments provided in the annotation to the New Mexico rule. Through Westlaw, we found a nonbinding opinion from the Pennsylvania Bar Association supporting a decision to represent a client at trial but not on appeal. See Illustration 17-3 (at page 357).

ILLUSTRATION 17-2

Treatise Discussion,
from *ABA/BNA Lawyers' Manual on Professional Conduct*
(paper source)

No. 240   SCOPE OF THE RELATIONSHIP   31:309

Tactics

On the other hand, decisions that involve tactics and trial strategy are reserved for the professional judgment of the criminal defense lawyer after consultation with the client. See, e.g., *People v. McKenzie*, 668 P.2d 769 (Cal. 1983) (lawyer makes tactical and strategic decisions such as what witnesses to call, how to conduct cross-examination, choice of jurors, and motions); *State v. Davis*, 506 A.2d 86 (Conn. 1986) (general rule is still that witness selection is tactical decision for lawyer, notwithstanding state constitutional provision that gives defendant right "to be heard by himself and by counsel . . . and to have compulsory process to obtain witnesses in his behalf"); see also *Strickland v. Washington*, 466 U.S. 668 (1984) (judicial scrutiny of counsel must be deferential and indulge strong presumption that counsel's ·conduct involved reasonable professional assistance and was sound trial strategy); see generally ABA Standards for Criminal Justice, ch. 4, Defense Function 4-3.1(b), 4-5.2(b) (3d ed. 1993).

Although the line between substantive and tactical issues may at times be difficult to draw, courts have deferred to the lawyer's judgment in a wide variety of matters. See, e.g., *New York v. Hill*, 528 U.S. 110 (2000) (lawyer may make scheduling decisions; lawyer agreed to trial delay outside time limits of Interstate Agreement on Detainers); *Darden v. Wainwright*, 477 U.S. 168 (1986) (defense lawyers in capital murder case did not render ineffective assistance by not introducing mitigating evidence at sentencing, as such approach would have opened door to evidence in rebuttal); *Sexton v. French*, 163 F.3d 874 (4th Cir. 1998) (whether to file pretrial motion to suppress confession is tactical decision for lawyer to make); *Poole v. United States*, 832 F.2d 561 (11th Cir. 1987) (defense lawyer's decision to stipulate to easily provable matter—that institutions defendant allegedly robbed were federally insured—was tactical; therefore, client consent was not needed); *United States v.*

Clayborne, 509 F.2d 473 (D.C. Cir. 1974) (lawyer may decide to decline cross-examination); *State v. Gibbs*, 758 A.2d 327 (Conn. 2000) (lawyer may decide whether to file motion to dismiss for lack of speedy trial); *People v. Segoviano*, 725 N.E.2d 1275 (Ill. 2000) ("The only trial-related decisions over which a defendant ultimately must have control are: whether to plead guilty; whether to waive a jury trial; whether to testify in his own behalf; whether to appeal; and whether to submit a lesser-included offense instruction"); *State v. Mecham*, 9 P.3d 777 (Utah 2000) (lawyer retains responsibility for making tactical decisions, including whether to pursue motion to suppress evidence); *State v. Oswald*, 606 N.W.2d 207 (Wis. Ct. App. 1999) (change of venue request is tactical decision for lawyer to make); *State v. Burnette*, 583 N.W.2d 174 (Wis. Ct. App. 1998) (lawyer may decide whether to strike potential juror for cause).

Limiting Scope of Representation

A lawyer may limit the scope of the representation provided that "the limitation is reasonable under the circumstances and the client gives informed consent." Rule 1.2(c). Such limitations have long been recognized. For example, a lawyer and a client can agree that:

● the lawyer will handle only certain types of claims and not others, see, e.g., *Delta Equipment & Construction Co. v. Royal Indemnity Co.*, 186 So. 2d 454 (La. Ct. App. 1966);

● the lawyer will represent the client on a specific transaction without assuming any general duties to the client beyond the sufficiency of the relevant documents, see, e.g., *Grand Isle Campsites v. Cheek*, 249 So. 2d 268 (La. Ct. App. 1971), modified, 262 So. 2d 350 (La. 1972); or

● litigation will be conducted only at the trial level, see, e.g., *Young v. Bridwell*, 437 P.2d 686 (Utah 1968).

The requirement of reasonableness generally means that the limitation may not impair a client's rights or the lawyer's legal or ethical obligations. *Hartford Ac-*

ILLUSTRATION 17-2   *(continued)*

31:310   LAWYER-CLIENT RELATIONSHIP   No. 240

cident & Indemnity Co. v. Foster, 528 So. 2d 255 (Miss. 1988) (insurance policy may not contain provisions limiting ethical duties owed by insurance company lawyers to insured clients); *Greenwich v. Markhoff*, 650 N.Y.S.2d 704 (App. Div. 1996) (law firm may be liable for malpractice for failure to file personal injury action on behalf of client even though retainer agreement purported to limit scope of representation to workers' compensation claim; agreement did not obviate firm's duty to apprise client that personal injury action might lie); *Parents Against Drunk Drivers v. Graystone Pines Homeowners' Ass'n*, 789 P.2d 52 (Utah Ct. App. 1990) (retainer agreement may not grant lawyer control over settlement of case, in contravention of ethics rules).

The lawyer must clearly explain any limitations. See, e.g., *Johnson v. Freemont County Board of Comm'rs*, 85 F.3d 489 (10th Cir. 1996) (although separate representation is permissible for government official sued in both official and individual capacity, for lawyer to limit representation to official capacity, lawyer must consult with client about exposure in individual capacity and client must consent to limitation); *In re Bancroft*, 204 B.R. 548 (Bankr. C.D. Ill. 1997) (in context of bankruptcy proceedings, Rule 1.2(c) requires lawyer to explain to debtor "the nature of the bankruptcy process, what problems could or will be encountered, how those problems should be addressed, and the risks or hazards, if any, associated with those problems. Consent involves a clear understanding on the part of the debtor as to these factors and the possible results of a debtor proceeding without an attorney being present"); *Indianapolis Podiatry PC v. Efroymson*, 720 N.E.2d 376 (Ind. Ct. App. 1999) (when limiting scope of representation, extent of required disclosure to client is "similar, if not identical, to that required in the context of a conflict of interest"); Colorado Ethics Op. 101 (1998) (lawyer providing unbundled legal services must explain limitations of representation, including types of services not being pro-

vided, risks associated with limitations, and warning that client may face legal issues he may not understand); New York City Ethics Op. 2001-3 (2001) (lawyer may limit scope of representation to avoid conflict with current or former client, provided that client whose representation is limited consents after full disclosure and limitation does not so restrict representation as to render it inadequate); see also ABA Formal Ethics Op. 96-403 (1996) (lawyer hired by insurer to represent insured must advise insured that lawyer plans to proceed at direction of insurer in accordance with insurance contract).

'Unbundling'

Representation that is limited in scope, often referred to as "unbundled" legal services, is a means of giving clients a choice of something between obtaining full representation with respect to an entire legal matter and no representation at all. These types of services may be particularly useful for those who cannot afford to hire a lawyer to represent them but who may desire limited legal advice or may want assistance in drafting a document. See Colorado Ethics Op. 101 (1998) (approving provision by lawyers of unbundled legal services in litigation and nonlitigation contexts); see generally Hyman & Silver, *And Such Small Portions: Limited Performance Agreements and Cost/Quality/Access Trade-Off*, 11 Geo. J. Legal Ethics 959 (1998); McNeal, *Redefining Attorney-Client Roles: Unbundling and Moderate-Income Elderly Clients*, 32 Wake Forest L. Rev. 295 (1997); Zacharias, *Limited Performance Agreements: Should Clients Get What They Pay For?*, 11 Geo. J. Legal Ethics 915 (1998).

Ghostwriting

Lawyers who are asked to provide limited, behind-the-scenes legal services to pro se litigants should be cautious, particularly if asked to "ghostwrite" documents to be filed with a court. Some courts have found such conduct to be improper because it misleads the court and may violate civil procedure rules (e.g.,

ILLUSTRATION 17-3	Advisory Opinion from State Bar Association Committee, from Westlaw Ethics Opinions Database (electronic source)

PA Eth. Op. 94-172   Page 1
(Cite as: 1994 WL 928104 (Pa.Bar.Assn.Comm.Leg.Eth.Prof.Resp.))

```
            Pennsylvania Bar Association Committee on Legal Ethics and Professional
                                      Responsibility


                              Informal Opinion Number 94-172
                                    November 9, 1994
```

You were retained by Client to represent her in a criminal matter. As part of your initial negotiations, you agreed to represent Client up through and including a jury trial, for a certain fee. After the jury trial, you agreed with Client to represent her at the sentencing for an additional fee. You explicitly discussed with Client that this fee did not include representing her at any appeal. On October 14, 1994, following the sentencing, you sent Client a letter advising her of the November 14, 1994 deadline for filing an appeal, summarizing the possible issue on which she might want to appeal, indicating that your "representation of [Client] has terminated with the sentencing hearing", setting forth your rates for handling the appeal, and advising her that she most likely would be eligible for the Public Defender and should make an application as soon as possible.

Yesterday you received a telephone call from Client's sister. She related that Client had made an application to the public defender's office, which said that it would not process the application, that you were obligated to file the appeal, and that if you did not, you would be brought before the Ethics Committee [Disciplinary Board.] You telephoned the Public Defender's office to determine whether sister had accurately communicated its position. A lawyer at the PD's office confirmed that the PD's office will not process Client's application for assistance until after you have filed the Notice of Appeal and the Docketing Statement (which includes a Statement of Matters Complained of, and will list you as attorney of record.) The Public Defender representative did not assert that Client believed she had retained you for the appeal. Rather, this representative said that it was the office practice to require the private attorney to file these items.

You inquired whether you are ethically obligated to represent Client in the appeal. In particular, you asked whether you are ethically able to limit the scope of your representation to the trial representation only.

It is my opinion that ethically, a lawyer may limit the scope of the lawyer's representation of a client. I know of no ethics rule which would require a lawyer who has handled a criminal trial to always handle the criminal appeal. (And, indeed, I can think of strong reasons against a rule that required the criminal trial lawyer to always handle the appeal. This kind of obligation might serve to discourage lawyers from handling certain criminal trial.)

The basis for my opinion is Rule 1.2(c) of the Rules of Professional Conduct. This provision, entitled "Scope of Representation", says: "A lawyer may limit the objectives of the representation if the client consents after a full disclosure of the circumstances and consultation." I believe that my interpretation is supported by the leading commentators and treatises in the area. See, e.g., G. Hazard & W. Hodes, The Law of Lawyering §1.2:401 (2d ed. 1994) ("Rule 1.2 recognizes that the client-lawyer relationship is based on contract. In the normal course of events,

ILLUSTRATION 17-4

Synopses of Ethics Opinions,
from *ABA/BNA Lawyers' Manual on Professional Conduct*
(paper source)

No. 227

1101:6001

ETHICS OPINIONS

New Mexico

STATE BAR OF NEW MEXICO

Opinions are issued by the Advisory Opinions Committee of the State Bar of New Mexico. The bar may be contacted at 121 Tijeras St., N.E., P.O. Box 25883, Albuquerque, NM 87125, (505) 842-6132, fax (505) 843-8765.

Opinion 1996-1 (6/8/96) **Limited liability companies; Partnerships.** A lawyer may join with other lawyers as partners in a Registered Limited Liability Partnership for the practice of law. The lawyer must order the partnership's affairs to provide accountability under the ethics rules, and should explain to clients the ramifications of this form of practice. N.M. Stat. Ann. 53-6-1 to 53-6-14, 53-19-1 to 53-19-74, 54-1-1 et seq., 54-144 to 54-148, 56-6-3; Rules 16-101, 16-108, 16-201, 16-501 to 16-504; ABA 865, 91-360.

Opinion 1996-2 (9/14/96) **Recorded conversations; Evidence; Witnesses; Communication with witnesses.** A lawyer is not prohibited from secretly tape recording an interview with a potential witness in a civil or criminal matter. Considerations include: Is the recording likely to make the lawyer a witness? Did the lawyer make any false or misleading statements to the witness? Did the lawyer trick or coerce the witness? Did the lawyer fail to disclose something or to clarify his role? Is the witness represented or likely to be represented? If the lawyer determines that a secret recording is otherwise justified, he must disclose it whenever failing to do so would be untruthful or misleading. Opinion 1988-6 is modified. Opinion 1988-6; Fed.R.Civ.P. 26(a); SCRAs 16-306, 16-401, 16-403; ABA 337; ABA i1320, 1407.

Opinion 2000-1 (undated) **Credit cards; Trust accounts; Retainer agreements.** A lawyer may not accept a retainer deposit against future fees paid by credit card where the credit card company deducts its processing fee before depositing the fees into the lawyer's credit card account, and the lawyer makes up the deduction out of his own funds before depositing the entire amount into his client trust account. This would create the possibility of a failure to maintain the required separation of lawyer and client funds. Rules 16-108(E), 16-115(A), 17-204(A)(1)(2).

Opinion 2000-2 (6/20/00) **Insurance representation; Billing; Confidentiality; Conflicts of interest.** A lawyer retained by an insurance company to defend insureds may not submit client bills to third-party auditors without the informed consent of the client. Ordinarily, a lawyer in this position may not even seek consent from the client because inherent conflicts of interest may compromise the lawyer's independent professional judgment. An attempt by the lawyer to obtain the client's consent could be interpreted as favoring the insurer's and lawyer's interests to the detriment of the client's interest and should therefore be avoided. Rules 16-102, 16-104, 16-106, 16-107(B), 16-108(F), 16-201, 16-504(C).

ILLUSTRATION 17-5   Ethics Opinions Summaries,
from New Mexico State Bar Website (electronic source)

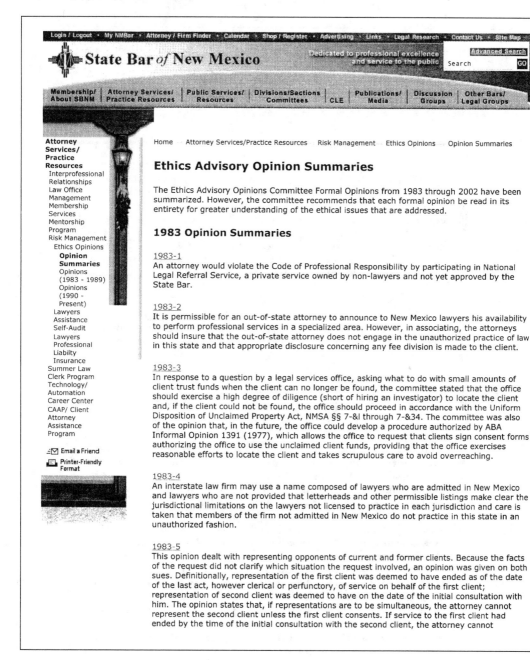

Ethics Advisory Opinion Summaries

The Ethics Advisory Opinions Committee Formal Opinions from 1983 through 2002 have been summarized. However, the committee recommends that each formal opinion be read in its entirety for greater understanding of the ethical issues that are addressed.

1983 Opinion Summaries

1983-1
An attorney would violate the Code of Professional Responsibility by participating in National Legal Referral Service, a private service owned by non-lawyers and not yet approved by the State Bar.

1983-2
It is permissible for an out-of-state attorney to announce to New Mexico lawyers his availability to perform professional services in a specialized area. However, in associating, the attorneys should insure that the out-of-state attorney does not engage in the unauthorized practice of law in this state and that appropriate disclosure concerning any fee division is made to the client.

1983-3
In response to a question by a legal services office, asking what to do with small amounts of client trust funds when the client can no longer be found, the committee stated that the office should exercise a high degree of diligence (short of hiring an investigator) to locate the client and, if the client could not be found, the office should proceed in accordance with the Uniform Disposition of Unclaimed Property Act, NMSA §§ 7-8l through 7-&34. The committee was also of the opinion that, in the future, the office could develop a procedure authorized by ABA Informal Opinion 1391 (1977), which allows the office to request that clients sign consent forms authorizing the office to use the unclaimed client funds, providing that the office exercises reasonable efforts to locate the client and takes scrupulous care to avoid overreaching.

1983-4
An interstate law firm may use a name composed of lawyers who are admitted in New Mexico and lawyers who are not provided that letterheads and other permissible listings make clear the jurisdictional limitations on the lawyers not licensed to practice in each jurisdiction and care is taken that members of the firm not admitted in New Mexico do not practice in this state in an unauthorized fashion.

1983-5
This opinion dealt with representing opponents of current and former clients. Because the facts of the request did not clarify which situation the request involved, an opinion was given on both sues. Definitionally, representation of the first client was deemed to have ended as of the date of the last act, however clerical or perfunctory, of service on behalf of the first client; representation of second client was deemed to have on the date of the initial consultation with him. The opinion states that, if representations are to be simultaneous, the attorney cannot represent the second client unless the first client consents. If service to the first client had ended by the time of the initial consultation with the second client, the attorney cannot

| ILLUSTRATION 17-6 | ABA Model Rule of Professional Conduct and Comments, from *ABA Compendium of Professional Responsibility Rules and Standards* (paper source) |

COMPENDIUM OF PROFESSIONAL RESPONSIBILITY RULES AND STANDARDS

[4] A lawyer may accept representation where the requisite level of competence can be achieved by reasonable preparation. This applies as well to a lawyer who is appointed as counsel for an unrepresented person. See also Rule 6.2.

Thoroughness and Preparation

[5] Competent handling of a particular matter includes inquiry into and analysis of the factual and legal elements of the problem, and use of methods and procedures meeting the standards of competent practitioners. It also includes adequate preparation. The required attention and preparation are determined in part by what is at stake; major litigation and complex transactions ordinarily require more extensive treatment than matters of lesser complexity and consequence. An agreement between the lawyer and the client regarding the scope of the representation may limit the matters for which the lawyer is responsible. See Rule 1.2(c).

Maintaining Competence

[6] To maintain the requisite knowledge and skill, a lawyer should keep abreast of changes in the law and its practice, engage in continuing study and education and comply with all continuing legal education requirements to which the lawyer is subject.

RULE 1.2: SCOPE OF REPRESENTATION AND ALLOCATION OF AUTHORITY BETWEEN CLIENT AND LAWYER

(a) Subject to paragraphs (c) and (d), a lawyer shall abide by a client's decisions concerning the objectives of representation and, as required by Rule 1.4, shall consult with the client as to the means by which they are to be pursued. A lawyer may take such action on behalf of the client as is impliedly authorized to carry out the representation. A lawyer shall abide by a client's decision whether to settle a matter. In a criminal case, the lawyer shall abide by the client's decision, after consultation with the lawyer, as to a plea to be entered, whether to waive jury trial and whether the client will testify.

(b) A lawyer's representation of a client, including representation by appointment, does not constitute an endorsement of the client's political, economic, social or moral views or activities.

(c) A lawyer may limit the scope of the representation if the limitation is reasonable under the circumstances and the client gives informed consent.

(d) A lawyer shall not counsel a client to engage, or assist a client, in conduct that the lawyer knows is criminal or fraudulent, but a lawyer may dis-

28

ILLUSTRATION 17-6   (continued)

ABA MODEL RULES OF PROFESSIONAL CONDUCT   **Rule 1.2**

cuss the legal consequences of any proposed course of conduct with a client and may counsel or assist a client to make a good faith effort to determine the validity, scope, meaning or application of the law.

Comment

Allocation of Authority between Client and Lawyer

[1] Paragraph (a) confers upon the client the ultimate authority to determine the purposes to be served by legal representation, within the limits imposed by law and the lawyer's professional obligations. The decisions specified in paragraph (a), such as whether to settle a civil matter, must also be made by the client. See Rule 1.4(a)(1) for the lawyer's duty to communicate with the client about such decisions. With respect to the means by which the client's objectives are to be pursued, the lawyer shall consult with the client as required by Rule 1.4(a)(2) and may take such action as is impliedly authorized to carry out the representation.

[2] On occasion, however, a lawyer and a client may disagree about the means to be used to accomplish the client's objectives. Clients normally defer to the special knowledge and skill of their lawyer with respect to the means to be used to accomplish their objectives, particularly with respect to technical, legal and tactical matters. Conversely, lawyers usually defer to the client regarding such questions as the expense to be incurred and concern for third persons who might be adversely affected. Because of the varied nature of the matters about which a lawyer and client might disagree and because the actions in question may implicate the interests of a tribunal or other persons, this Rule does not prescribe how such disagreements are to be resolved. Other law, however, may be applicable and should be consulted by the lawyer. The lawyer should also consult with the client and seek a mutually acceptable resolution of the disagreement. If such efforts are unavailing and the lawyer has a fundamental disagreement with the client, the lawyer may withdraw from the representation. See Rule 1.16(b)(4). Conversely, the client may resolve the disagreement by discharging the lawyer. See Rule 1.16(a)(3).

[3] At the outset of a representation, the client may authorize the lawyer to take specific action on the client's behalf without further consultation. Absent a material change in circumstances and subject to Rule 1.4, a lawyer may rely on such an advance authorization. The client may, however, revoke such authority at any time.

[4] In a case in which the client appears to be suffering diminished capacity, the lawyer's duty to abide by the client's decisions is to be guided by reference to Rule 1.14.

Independence from Client's Views or Activities

[5] Legal representation should not be denied to people who are unable to afford legal services, or whose cause is controversial or the subject of pop-

29

ILLUSTRATION 17-6   *(continued)*

COMPENDIUM OF PROFESSIONAL RESPONSIBILITY RULES AND STANDARDS

ular disapproval. By the same token, representing a client does not constitute approval of the client's views or activities.

Agreements Limiting Scope of Representation

[6] The scope of services to be provided by a lawyer may be limited by agreement with the client or by the terms under which the lawyer's services are made available to the client. When a lawyer has been retained by an insurer to represent an insured, for example, the representation may be limited to matters related to the insurance coverage. A limited representation may be appropriate because the client has limited objectives for the representation. In addition, the terms upon which representation is undertaken may exclude specific means that might otherwise be used to accomplish the client's objectives. Such limitations may exclude actions that the client thinks are too costly or that the lawyer regards as repugnant or imprudent.

[7] Although this Rule affords the lawyer and client substantial latitude to limit the representation, the limitation must be reasonable under the circumstances. If, for example, a client's objective is limited to securing general information about the law the client needs in order to handle a common and typically uncomplicated legal problem, the lawyer and client may agree that the lawyer's services will be limited to a brief telephone consultation. Such a limitation, however, would not be reasonable if the time allotted was not sufficient to yield advice upon which the client could rely. Although an agreement for a limited representation does not exempt a lawyer from the duty to provide competent representation, the limitation is a factor to be considered when determining the legal knowledge, skill, thoroughness and preparation reasonably necessary for the representation. See Rule 1.1.

[8] All agreements concerning a lawyer's representation of a client must accord with the Rules of Professional Conduct and other law. See, e.g., Rules 1.1, 1.8 and 5.6.

Criminal, Fraudulent and Prohibited Transactions

[9] Paragraph (d) prohibits a lawyer from knowingly counseling or assisting a client to commit a crime or fraud. This prohibition, however, does not preclude the lawyer from giving an honest opinion about the actual consequences that appear likely to result from a client's conduct. Nor does the fact that a client uses advice in a course of action that is criminal or fraudulent of itself make a lawyer a party to the course of action. There is a critical distinction between presenting an analysis of legal aspects of questionable conduct and recommending the means by which a crime or fraud might be committed with impunity.

[10] When the client's course of action has already begun and is continuing, the lawyer's responsibility is especially delicate. The lawyer is required to avoid assisting the client, for example, by drafting or delivering documents

30

D. WHAT ELSE?

Proposed State Rules. Proposed amendments to a state's rules generally appear in a state bar journal or legal newspaper, as do newly adopted rules.

Proposed ABA Rules. Drafts of new rules and the reports of studies that the ABA undertakes concerning new rules often are published as separate publications to permit the ABA membership to make comments. Furthermore, proposed amendments as well as recently adopted rules and comments are published in the *ABA Journal* and on the ABA website.

Specialized Rules of Professional Conduct. In addition to the Model Rules, the ABA has promulgated several specialized sets of standards, such as the Model Code of Judicial Conduct and the Model Rule for Temporary Practice by Foreign Lawyers.

Citing Ethics Materials. You may KeyCite state rules on Westlaw and Shepardize state rules and ABA materials on LexisNexis.

E. HOW DO YOU CITE RULES OF PROFESSIONAL RESPONSIBILITY?[2]

A citation to a state rule of professional responsibility consists of the abbreviation for the set of rules and the rule number. Here are two examples:

- ☐ *Bluebook* Rules 12.8.3 and 12.8.5 (by analogy): N.M. R. Prof'l Conduct 16-102.
- ☐ *ALWD* Rule 17.1: N.M. R. Prof. Conduct 16-102.

Citation to a state ethics opinion includes the issuing organization; type of opinion; number; and date, if the date is not part of the number. Here are two examples:

- ☐ *Bluebook* Rule 12.8.6: Pa. Bar Ass'n Comm. on Legal Ethics and Prof'l Responsibility, Informal Op. 94-172.
- ☐ *ALWD* Rule 17.4: Pa. B. Assn. Informal Ethics Op. 94-172.

Citation to ABA ethics materials is fairly similar to the forms stated above and covered by the same rules.

---

2. It is interesting that, in both citation manuals, citation to ethics materials is not covered as thoroughly or as clearly as citation to other authorities.

CONCLUSION

UNIT

VII

DEVELOPING AN INTEGRATED RESEARCH STRATEGY

A. Introduction: The ap*ART*ment Problem
B. Four Research Journals
C. Our Observations

A. INTRODUCTION: THE ap*ART*MENT PROBLEM

Now that you have worked with a range of legal research sources, you should realize that there is no one "right" or "best" way to research any particular situation. You have options as to which commentary to explore, which media to use for case law research, which publication of court rules to employ, etc. At the same time, you must somehow accomplish the necessary task—locating the law that governs your situation.

To help you see how varied legal research can be, we asked four law students to research the following situation, which we invented for this purpose:

A nonprofit organization, ap*ART*ment, is negotiating for a loan from a large commercial bank in Baltimore, Maryland. The loan would fund ap*ART*ment's renovation of an abandoned building near downtown Baltimore. The site is now known as the Rainbow Building, and ap*ART*ment believes it would convert easily to mixed-use space. The lower level would consist of shops, galleries, and other small businesses clustered around an open gathering space. The upper levels would consist of studio spaces and residential apartments for artists with limited financial resources. The hope is that the project would help to rejuvenate an area that once was a thriving light-industrial area but now is largely abandoned.

One concern is the potential for crime committed against tenants. Property crimes are common in the vicinity of the Rainbow Building (indeed, the Rainbow Building has been heavily vandalized), and the incidence of assault in the area is well above the city's average. City officials hope that projects such as the one under discussion will lead to improvements in safety in the area as the number of abandoned buildings drops. Nonetheless, the area now is, and probably will continue to be, a somewhat risky location. In light of this, ap*ART*ment proposes to use various safety measures, such as lighting, security systems, and surveillance cameras.

During the last meeting between the bank's lending officer and ap*ART*ment's executive director, the twin issues of safety and liability arose. The bank expressed concern that ap*ART*ment could be exposed to significant liability should a serious crime against a tenant occur. (Given ap*ART*ment's thin capitalization, a large recovery against the organization could threaten the financial viability of the project.) Furthermore, should a lawsuit be brought and not resolved promptly, the adverse publicity could scare away tenants and undermine the financial stability of the project.

In response, the executive director of ap*ART*ment expressed doubt that ap*ART*ment would be liable for crimes committed by other people against its tenants, suggested that perhaps the tenants could agree in the lease not to seek recovery against ap*ART*ment should such a situation occur, and noted that the court probably would promptly dismiss any lawsuit brought against ap*ART*ment in such a situation.

Both representatives agreed that their concerns merit assessment by a lawyer.

In 1999, for the fifth edition of this text, we assigned two students—Jennifer Henderson and Richard Soderberg—to research the situation for the bank. Two students—Steve Brunn and Vickie Loher—researched the situation for ap*ART*ment. Their journals and their conclusions follow. Following the journals are our observations. As you read this chapter, you should think how you would approach this research project and how you would update their research.

B.　FOUR RESEARCH JOURNALS

As you read the following journals, keep these points in mind: The journals chronicle research processes; they are not complete analyses of the legal issues and facts. We have presented the main steps each researcher took and have omitted detail for purposes of brevity. Full citations appear only for the major authorities and then only for the first reference to an authority. The research was conducted for purposes of providing the lay of the land to the respective clients; had we presented the four researchers with a specific case in litigation, they probably would have researched further.

Between each journal and the researcher's conclusion is a simplified statement of the research process. Regular typeface connotes paper research; italics connotes online research.

1.   Researching for the Bank

a.   Jennifer Henderson

I vaguely recalled discussing in torts a building owner's liability for crimes of third parties, as well as discussing in contracts clauses similar to that proposed here. Because torts and contracts generally are state law issues, I decided I would be researching Maryland law. I generated a list of key words. The list included: landlord, tenant, contracts, leases, apartment.

Because I did not have a state encyclopedia for Maryland, I consulted *Corpus Juris Secundum* and *American Jurisprudence 2d*. I found general information in C.J.S. about a landlord's liability to tenants for injuries from dangerous and defective conditions and a discussion of exculpatory contracts in Am. Jur. 2d. In particular, the Am. Jur. 2d discussion provided the term *exculpatory clause* that I had not remembered before. I also read the Am. Jur. 2d discussion of assault and battery, which provided a cross-reference to A.L.R. Annotations.

Taking that clue, I moved to A.L.R. In the A.L.R. Index, I found references to two pertinent annotations: *Validity of Exculpatory Clause in Lease Exempting Lessor from Liability*, 49 A.L.R.3d 321, and *Landlord's Obligation to Protect Tenant against Criminal Activities of Third Persons*, 43 A.L.R.3d 331.

I moved to Westlaw and did a find search for the first annotation. I found three Maryland cases listed in the jurisdictional table, including *Eastern Avenue Corp. v. Hughes*, 180 A.2d 486 (Md. Ct. App. 1962), a case which was also mentioned in C.J.S. for the proposition that a landlord may absolve itself from liability for a tenant's injury, absent a statutory prohibition.

I jumped into the *Eastern Avenue* case, my first primary authority. I saw a red flag, indicating that the case is no longer good law. So I jumped into KeyCite and learned that *Eastern Avenue* has been noted in a later case as being superseded by a Maryland statute, Maryland Code Annotated, Real Property section 8-105 (1996 & Supp. 1998). That statute provides that exculpatory clauses encompassing a landlord's negligence "on or about the leased premises" in areas "not within the exclusive control of the tenant" are void as against public policy.

To obtain cases interpreting the statute, I examined the annotation to section 8-105 and reviewed the list of cases from the A.L.R. annotation; I also KeyCited the first cases I found and followed up on the list of citing cases. I found several cases interpreting the statute, from both the Maryland state courts and the federal courts sitting in diversity, including *White v. Walker-Turner Division*, 841 F. Supp. 704 (D. Md. 1993), and *Prince Phillip Partnership v. Cutlip*, 582 A.2d 992 (Md. Ct. App. 1990). KeyCiting the *Prince Phillip* case, I discovered a 1998 law review article on exculpatory clauses in Maryland, published in volume 27 of the *University of Baltimore Law Review*. According to KeyCite, the cases interpreting the statute are good law.

Shifting to the liability issue, I did a find search on Westlaw for the A.L.R. annotation at 43 A.L.R.3d 331. A red flag appeared, signaling that there is a new annotation on the topic, at 43 A.L.R.5th 207, *Landlord's Liability for Failure to Protect Tenant from Criminal Acts of Third Person.* The opening material of that annotation states that the previous rule favoring landlords is giving way to a rule favoring tenants.

Through the newer annotation, I found two important state court cases, *E.G. Rock v. Danly*, 633 A.2d 485 (Md. Ct. App. 1993), and *Scott v. Watson*, 359 A.2d 548 (Md. Ct. App. 1976); the latter appears to be the leading case. *Scott* holds that a landlord may be liable in certain instances for crimes committed against tenants by third parties in the premises' common areas; key factors include the landlord's actual or constructive knowledge of earlier criminal activity on the premises, the landlord's voluntary assumption of a duty to protect the tenant, and the reasonableness of the protective measures at issue.

When I KeyCited my cases, I found they are good law. I also found additional cases, including unpublished federal appellate cases, a published federal district court case, and some state court cases involving attacks by dogs. KeyCite again directed me to a potentially pertinent periodical article, this time regarding the liability issue, published in the summer 1998 issue of *Real Estate Law Journal*.

I then wondered whether ap*ART*ment might be protected from suit on the grounds that it is a nonprofit organization. I ran a search or two in Maryland state case law databases, but found nothing to support this premise.

My client also is concerned about obtaining a speedy resolution of any litigation. I paged through the Maryland Rules books that are part of Michie's *Annotated Code of Maryland*. I looked for the two rules that are familiar to me from the federal rules, Rule 12 on motions to dismiss and Rule 56 on summary judgment. This did not work, so I consulted the index. There I found references to Circuit Court Rules 2-322 (motions to dismiss) and 2-501 (summary judgment). I reviewed these rules in the Maryland Rules book, perused the case descriptions in the annotations, and KeyCited the rules and the main cases.

I learned from the rules and cases that ap*ART*ment could move for dismissal even before answering, by asserting that the complaint on its face is deficient. On such a motion, the court must accept the facts as pleaded. The court may grant the motion, deny it, grant the tenant the opportunity to correct the deficiencies by filing an amended complaint, or defer ruling on the motion until trial. A second alternative is a motion for summary judgment later in the proceedings. To prevail, ap*ART*ment would have to show there is no genuine issue of material fact and that it is entitled to judgment as a matter of law. Again the court favors the non-movant, and the court may grant the non-movant additional time to develop the case through discovery.

Jennifer Henderson	
exculpatory clause	encyclopedias → A.L.R. Index → A.L.R. → *cases* → *statute* → *cases* → *KeyCite* → *periodical article*
liability	A.L.R. Index → A.L.R. → *cases* → *KeyCite* → *periodical article*
dismissal	rules book → *cases* → *KeyCite*

Conclusion.   I would advise the bank that it should proceed with caution on the loan. If ap*ART*ment gets sued for a crime against a tenant, it may very well be held liable, depending on the circumstances. Moreover, a clause extinguishing liability would probably be unenforceable, and there is no guarantee that the suit could be disposed of quickly. Nevertheless, the bank may want to proceed. The benefits to the community from the project and the bank's image as a good citizen contributing to those benefits may outweigh the risks involved.

b.   Richard Soderberg

I started by brainstorming terms for the following categories:

- [ ] who: tenant, landlord, artist, professional
- [ ] what: living quarters, apartment, lease, rental space, business space, professional building, crime, liability, waiver, release
- [ ] where: Baltimore, Maryland, apartment building, residential area
- [ ] why: recover damages, avoid liability, attract tenants, promote artistic development, improve the area
- [ ] legal: landlord liability, premises liability, waiver, release
- [ ] relief: damages

I began by looking, in paper sources, for secondary authority. I found a Landlord and Tenant volume of Am. Jur. 2d and reviewed the table of contents until I identified section 551. That section indicates that there is no liability for landlords with regard to crimes against tenants. It provided a reference to 43 A.L.R.3d 331. (I neglected, however, to check the encyclopedia's pocket part.)

I moved to that A.L.R. annotation. The scope note warned that the annotation does not cover statutes. The general rule stated in the annotation was consistent with that stated above, although the annotation also mentioned a provision in the Restatement (Second) of Torts that imposes liability for failure to protect another from crime when the plaintiff and defendant stand in a special relationship. There were no Maryland cases covered in the annotation. Then I learned from the pocket part that there is a newer, superseding annotation at 43 A.L.R.5th 207. (Had I checked the Am. Jur. 2d pocket part, I would have been directed to the newer annotation.)

The annotation at 43 A.L.R.5th 207 was more detailed than the older annotation and included descriptions of three Maryland cases, including *E.G. Rock* and *Scott*. [See the first journal for a brief statement of the *Scott* rule.] I looked in the annotation for key words related to the other issue, such as release, waiver, disclaimer, and exculpatory, but found nothing. The pocket part did not discuss Maryland cases.

I then decided to research Maryland statutory law. In the *Annotated Code of Maryland*, I looked for my key terms under the subject heading Landlord and Tenant in the index. I learned of a statute regarding exculpatory clauses in the landlord-tenant setting, section 8-105 of the Real Property article. [See the first journal for a brief statement of that statutory rule.] I also found some less pertinent statutes, one (section 2-120) providing that the occurrence of crimes does not constitute a latent defect in the premises.

I wanted to strengthen my case law research, so I looked in the *Maryland Digest 2d* in the Landlord and Tenant materials, in particular under key numbers 162 and following, regarding injuries from dangerous conditions. I looked in the pocket part and the pamphlet supplementing the pocket part. I found the *E.G. Rock* and *Scott* cases, as well as some others.

I decided to verify that my leading cases were still good law. I used Westlaw's KeyCite program. *E.G. Rock* had no negative history; *Scott* had been distinguished by a Massachusetts case, which would not affect its status in Maryland.

I also wanted to find case law interpreting the exculpatory clause statute, section 8-105, so I proceeded to the MD-ST-ANN database on Westlaw and entered the search `exculpat! /s landlord`. I learned of seven cases and six secondary authorities referring to the statute. The list included *White*, *Prince Phillip*, and *Shell Oil Co. v. Ryckman*, 403 A.2d 379 (Md. Ct. App. 1979). The latter explains that the statute does not apply if the premises are exclusively within the control of the tenant.

I looked in the cases I had already located for indications of the likelihood of a prompt dismissal of any lawsuit that might arise. In *White*, the defendant obtained summary judgment on the basis of a valid exculpatory clause. On the other hand, the *Prince Phillip* court held the clause invalid, and the case went on to fairly prolonged litigation.

Richard Soderberg

liability	encyclopedia → A.L.R. → (Restatement) → cases → *KeyCite*
exculpatory clause	annotated code → statute
liability	digest → cases → *KeyCite*
exculpatory clause	*statutory database → cases*
dismissal	cases → procedural rule

Conclusion. I would counsel the bank to consider giving ap*ART*ment the loan. There is reliable authority that ap*ART*ment would not be held liable to its tenants if it takes reasonable precautionary measures. Should crimes occur on the premises, ap*ART*ment must act reasonably to prevent future crimes, and it appears prepared to do so, since it is already willing to take precautionary measures. A landlord also must act properly in carrying out any safety measures it takes on, and I see no reason to fear that ap*ART*ment would act improperly. We should, however, forget the idea of ap*ART*ment seeking to exculpate itself. Any attempt to do so will not be upheld by the courts if the clause violates the statutory prohibition.

2.   Researching for ap*ART*ment

a.   Steve Brunn

I started with a short list of research terms: landlord, tenant, crime, third person, lease, liability, vicarious liability, negligence, and exculpatory clause.

As for the issue of liability, I read the Am. Jur. 2d discussion of land-lord's liability for disturbances. The most useful reference I found there was to an A.L.R. annotation regarding crimes by third persons, found at 43 A.L.R.3d 331. I looked over that annotation and read the accompanying case, *Kline v. 1500 Massachusetts Avenue Apartment Corp.*, 439 F.2d 477 (D.C. Cir. 1970). That case holds that a landlord does owe a duty to take reasonable steps to protect a tenant from foreseeable criminal acts by intruders. Although it is a leading case, it is not mandatory precedent in Maryland.

To locate primary mandatory authority on this issue, I turned first to the *Annotated Code of Maryland.* I explored various subheadings of Landlord and Tenant in the index, but I found nothing on the liability issue. Nor did I find anything pertinent in the session law service.

I then turned to the *Maryland Digest 2d* and skimmed the table of contents for the Landlord and Tenant topic. I identified *Doe v. Montgomery Mall Ltd. Partnership*, 962 F. Supp. 58 (D. Md. 1997), as a pertinent case. I read it in the reporter and found that Maryland law does recognize landlord liability for criminal acts by third persons under some circumstances. *Doe* led me to several Maryland state court cases and identified one, *Scott,* as the seminal case. [See the first journal for a brief statement of the *Scott* rule.]

As for the issue of exculpatory clauses, I learned from Am. Jur. 2d that the law on such clauses differs from state to state. I did not find any useful citations to Maryland cases in the encyclopedia. So I read a discussion in the Williston treatise on contracts, which was not easy to locate, and another in the Friedman treatise on leases, which was much easier to locate. I learned from my treatise research that courts do not look favorably on exculpatory clauses for public policy reasons and strictly construe such clauses in leases. Furthermore, the Williston treatise provided a reference to a Maryland case, *Adloo v. H.T. Brown Real Estate, Inc.*, 686 A.2d 298 (Md. Ct. App. 1996). That case sets out general principles limiting the enforceability of exculpatory clauses and identifies the fairness of the transaction and the public interest as pertinent factors.

Seeking additional mandatory primary authority, I searched the index to the *Annotated Code of Maryland.* Nothing stood out among the many subheadings under Landlord and Tenant.

I turned to the *Maryland Digest 2d* and looked under various headings, such as contracts, leases, limitations on liability, and bailments. The most useful find was a description of *White*, a 1993 federal court case, digested in the pocket part. The *White* court relied on a state statute, section 8-105. I turned to that statute (which I had not found earlier for some reason). I read it in the annotated code and noted additional cases from the annotation. [See the first journal for a brief statement of that statutory rule.] I checked for updates in the session law service but found nothing.

Before I shifted to computer-based sources, I researched in the Maryland Rules volumes. The index directed me to Rule 2-501 regarding summary judgment. I read that rule and the annotation material and checked a few of the listed cases. I learned that the Maryland rule resembles the federal summary judgment rule. [See the first journal for a brief discussion of summary judgment.]

At this point, I turned to online research, which, for cost reasons, I use primarily to doublecheck and update my paper research. I KeyCited *Doe*, which had only two citing sources, one a 1999 law review article in volume 33 of the *University of San Francisco Law Review*. I looked at that article and learned about a California case in which a key factor was whether a neighborhood is inherently dangerous. I KeyCited *Scott*, which has been cited by nearly seventy cases, none undermining its status as good law; I looked at the cases examining *Scott*, but found nothing new. I KeyCited *Adloo*, which led me to a federal case, *Cornell v. Council of Unit Owners Hawaiian Village Condominiums, Inc.*, 983 F. Supp. 640 (D. Md. 1997). I KeyCited *White* and section 8-105 along with the other cases listed in the annotated code as interpreting that statute; these authorities all checked out, and I came across no new authorities.

As one last step, I ran Westlaw searches in the Maryland state court cases (MD-CS) database. The first two natural-language searches addressed the two main issues I had been researching; I found nothing new. The third search `rejuvenation or revitalization` was aimed at deriving discussion by the courts of a policy concern in ap*ART*ment's project—the public's interest in revitalizing the city. I found one useful case in the dozen I retrieved, *Donnelly Advertising Corp. v. City of Baltimore*, 370 A.2d 1127 (Md. 1977), in which the court discussed this policy, although the legal issue was not the same as in our case.

Steve Brunn	
liability	encyclopedia → A.L.R. → annotated code → digest → cases
exculpatory clause	encyclopedia → treatises → cases → annotated code → digest → cases → statute → cases
dismissal	rules book → rule → cases
liability	*KeyCite → periodical article → persuasive precedent*
exculpatory clause	*KeyCite case and statute*
liability	*natural-language search*
exculpatory clause	*natural-language search*
policy issue	*Boolean search → case*

Conclusion.   I believe there is some risk of liability for crimes committed against tenants. The dangerousness of the neighborhood contributes to the foreseeability of harm. As for breach of duty, ap*ART*ment's current plans may meet the standard of reasonableness, but it may need to increase its protective measures if criminal activity does occur. As for an exculpatory clause, Maryland law has shifted, from favoring them to restricting their use. Ap*ART*ment should include a clear clause in its lease, but not expect it to be enforced in court unless it conforms to the statute, there was no unfairness in the parties' transaction, and the public policy favoring revitalization of the city benefits ap*ART*ment. The exculpatory clause issue could well be decided on summary judgment, but the liability issue may not be amenable to summary judgment.

b.   Vickie Loher

I discerned three issues: (1) whether ap*ART*ment could be liable for crimes committed against tenants by third parties, (2) whether ap*ART*ment could limit that liability by a term in its lease, and (3) what standards the court would follow in dismissing a lawsuit by a tenant on summary judgment. Because I was fairly confident of my background understanding of the issues, I proceeded directly to primary authority.

I started in the *Annotated Code of Maryland,* more specifically the index. I read the entries under the subject heading Landlord and Tenant. I identified nine potentially pertinent sections, including such topics as homicide, implied covenant of quiet enjoyment, and disclosures about property. The sections all appeared in the Real Property volume. I reviewed each section in the main volume and the pocket part. The only actually pertinent section is section 8-105. [See the first journal for a brief statement of that statutory rule.]

I then perused the annotation to that section. I identified three cases as fitting the research problem the best: *Prince Phillip*, *White*, and *Cornell.*

I turned to the *Maryland Digest 2d* to look for cases on the first issue in particular. I reviewed the outline of the Landlord and Tenant topic and decided to focus on cases under the heading Premises and Enjoyment and Use Thereof and subheading Injuries from Dangerous or Defective Condition, that is, key numbers 162 through 170. I reviewed the case descriptions to identify the most useful cases. I selected fourteen cases, including *Scott*, *E.G. Rock*, *Adloo*, and *Doe.* [See the first journal for a brief statement of the *Scott* rule.]

I updated my cases through KeyCite. The cases are still good law. I did discover additional cases through KeyCite, including a recent federal appellate decision.

To locate the information I needed about the procedural issue, I searched in Westlaw's MD-RULES database; my search was `"summary judgment"`. This search retrieved Maryland's summary judgment rule. The rule itself states the two-part standard: absence of a genuine issue of material fact and entitlement to judgment as a matter of law. The cases appearing in the annotation further develop the rule's standard. Furthermore, I reviewed a case I had encountered earlier, *Pittman v. Atlantic Realty Co.*, 732 A.2d 912 (Md. Ct. App. 1999), which does not address my substantive issues but does discuss summary judgment; I KeyCited the case as well. As persuasive precedent, in a federal case, the appeals court upheld summary judgment on the grounds the landlord had no duty to protect against armed robbery when there had been only a single robbery, not involving a gun or actual harm to the victim. *Nails v. Community Realty Co.*, 166 F.3d 333 (4th Cir. 1998) (per curiam).

Vickie Loher	
exculpatory clause	annotated code → statute → cases
liability	digest → cases
liability/ exculpatory clause	*KeyCite → additional cases*
dismissal	*rules database → cases → KeyCite*

Conclusion. Should ap*ART*ment take over the building, it would have a duty to exercise reasonable care to keep the common areas safe. It is already aware of break-ins and must take reasonable measures to eliminate conditions contributing to break-ins. If it becomes aware of assaults, it must similarly act to prevent assaults. If ap*ART*ment voluntarily undertakes to provide security for tenants, it must be sure it does so properly. By statute, ap*ART*ment cannot enforce a lease provision regarding liability for losses that occur in areas not within the exclusive control of the tenant. However, the statute would not void a provision covering injuries in an area within the exclusive control of the tenant. Hence, it would be advisable for ap*ART*ment to place a clause of the latter sort within the leases. As for the likelihood of a prompt resolution of any lawsuit, ap*ART*ment might prevail if it can argue that its duty had not yet arisen, due to low crime levels within the building; otherwise a lawsuit is likely to raise fact issues for a jury's determination.

C.   OUR OBSERVATIONS

Ultimately, all four researchers came to focus on the same few leading authorities: the *Scott* case, section 8-105, Rule 2-501, and related cases. There are, of course, both similarities and differences among the four research processes described above. The differences tend to be matters of detail, while the similarities reveal matters of importance.

All four researchers began with an analysis of the facts, so as to generate research terms or issues. For all of them, as to the two main issues, two concepts proved to be key: landlord-tenant and exculpatory clause. The former was apparent at the outset; for some, the latter term took some research to identify. All four also zeroed in quickly on Maryland state law as the law to research.

Most of the four researchers began in secondary sources. They used encyclopedias, treatises, and A.L.R.s for background and references to primary authority.

Most of the researchers used a state digest to identify pertinent cases. All used the state's annotated code and drew from that source not only the statutory language but also descriptions of pertinent cases. Most took a similar approach to the procedural issue.

All of the researchers took care to update their research and verify the status of their leading authorities as good law, through such tools as pocket parts, supplementary pamphlets, session law services, KeyCite, and computer searches.

All researchers mixed paper and electronic research. All four used Key-Cite. Beyond that, they differed as to how much they used Westlaw. Two notes: Due perhaps to William Mitchell's proximity to the headquarters of the West Group, Westlaw tends to be more popular than LexisNexis in our region. It did not surprise us that no one used Internet research tools; we have not emphasized them as much in our research course as Westlaw, and the journals were written in 1999, when Internet research was not well developed.

Each of the four journals shows the truth of the saying "one thing led to another." For example, one researcher found pertinent law review articles while KeyCiting leading cases. As another example, one researcher found the statute through a leading federal court case. Even so, there is a clear sense of direction in each research journal; each researcher pursued each of the three issues as distinct, but related, tasks.

The four journals also show the truth of the saying "nobody's perfect." For example, one researcher did not initially realize that there was a new annotation because he did not check an encyclopedia pocket part. Another did not initially identify the statute in the index to the annotated code. Nonetheless, they both corrected their missteps; their research processes were thorough enough to provide safeguards against missteps.

When we designed the problem, we wondered whether the lawyers for the bank would approach the task any differently than the lawyers for ap*ART*ment. As you can see, all four researchers came to the same set of authorities. This is as it should be, for the role of a lawyer in a counseling setting is to find and apply the law pertinent to the client's situation, as a neutral looking at the problem would, and build a legal strategy for the client on that objective assessment.

We hope that the four research journals, and indeed the rest of this book, have shown you how to accomplish legal research. We also hope that you will use your research skills to benefit your clients and those affected by their actions.

RESEARCH SITUATIONS
AND
PRACTICE SETS

The following materials constitute research exercises, each consisting of two parts.

☐ First, we have provided realistic research situations to be researched. Most of the time, you will have a choice of situation or state in which to research.

☐ Second, we have provided sets of questions—the practice sets. Each set of questions guides you through a research process, such as development of research terms and issues, encyclopedia research, electronic research in cases.

Some practice sets have their own research situations; other practice sets share research situations, so you can see how various sources work together. There are practice sets for all chapters but Chapters 1, 8, and 18; some chapters have one practice set, others more than one.

Please note: All practice sets ask for a proper citation to the source you have been using. Follow *The Bluebook* or *ALWD Citation Manual* as instructed by your professor.

All pages in this part of the book are perforated. Thus, you can tear out the practice sets for submission to your professor. Take care not to tear out the research situations that are used for multiple practice sets.

EIGHT COGNITIVE TASKS

SECONDARY AUTHORITIES

You will be selecting one of the research situations stated below for the following practice sets for Units I and II:

Chapter 2.   Eight Cognitive Tasks
Chapter 3.   Encyclopedias
Chapter 4.   Treatises
Chapter 5.   Legal Periodicals
Chapter 6.   A.L.R. Annotations
Chapter 7.   Restatements

Unless otherwise instructed by your professor, you should select one research situation to work for all of these practice sets. We suggest that you leave pages 381–85 in your book (or at least do not turn them in to your professor), so you will have ready access to the texts of the research situations as you work through each practice set.

Each situation is set in a specified state; focus on that state when a question asks about primary authority from the jurisdiction in the research situation.

Research Situation A:

Your clients, a group of tenants, live in a six-story apartment building located in Redwood City, California. The building is owned and managed by Cost Mor Company. Several weeks ago, Cost Mor's maintenance staff, protesting poor working conditions and low wages, went on strike. The garbage hauler has refused to cross the picket line to empty the apartment's garbage receptacle. As a consequence, rotting garbage has accumulated in the basement of the building, causing offensive odors and an influx of rodents and cockroaches that have since infested the entire apartment building. Apparently, the lease says nothing about this problem. The tenants who have contacted you each have several months remaining on their leases, yet they would like to terminate their leases and vacate.

Must the tenants continue to live in these uninhabitable conditions, or may they consider themselves in effect constructively evicted and now legally abandon the premises?

Research Situation B:

Mr. Jeff Chain contacted you for assistance in resolving a dispute over personal property. The following events took place in Columbus, Ohio: Just prior to serious and difficult surgery, Mr. Joshua Rex (Mr. Chain's employer) handed his pocket watch, a valuable family heirloom, to the attending nurse and instructed her: "If I do not recover from this surgery, give the watch to my gardener, Mr. Chain, as a gift of gratitude for his many years of friendship." Sadly, Mr. Rex died during the surgery. The nurse handed over the watch to Mr. Chain a few days later and told him that it was a gift from Mr. Rex.

A dispute has now arisen over the pocket watch. Mr. Rex's only child, Lucille, claims the watch as heir of her father's entire estate—all personal and real property remaining in the estate passed to her upon the death of her father. Mr. Chain asserts that the watch was delivered to the nurse, on his behalf, as an inter vivos gift from his employer and friend, and thus it does not pass through the estate.

Did Mr. Rex give away his pocket watch as a valid gift causa mortis, effective while he was still alive, or does the watch pass through the estate to Ms. Rex?

Research Situation C:

Ms. Karen Selleck is an artist who specializes in realistic paintings of cats, often used on greeting cards and calendars. Although her artwork is well known, especially among cat lovers, she is not well known. Of course, she has pedigree cats herself, which she shows in cat shows near her home in Little Rock, Arkansas. Apparently, she and one of her cats were photographed at a show there, without her permission. The picture, which is lovely, now appears in advertising circulars for a popular cat food company. Ms. Selleck wants to maintain her privacy and is incensed that her picture is being used for a commercial purpose without her consent.

Is the cat food company liable to Ms. Selleck for invading her privacy by using her likeness without her permission?

Research Situation D:

Mr. Edi Hasan has long owned a hilly parcel of land on Hidden Lake, New York. Because of the rough terrain, he had no access to the lake. In 1975, in order to gain easy access by foot to the beach, he bought an easement, or private servitude, from his neighbor to the west, Ms. Colleen Therrien. Over the years, Mr. Hasan and his guests wore a footpath into the sand as they used the easement for beach access. In 1993, Mr. Hasan bought the entire adjacent parcel of land east of his home and built a driveway on this parcel, which provided direct access to a boat dock that he constructed on the lake. Since this driveway was completed, Mr. Hasan has not used the easement located on Ms. Therrien's property, and it has grown over by grasses and weeds. Ms. Therrien assumed that Mr. Hasan had abandoned the footpath located on her land and started construction for a new boathouse, which will make use of the easement impossible.

Was the easement terminated when Mr. Hasan discontinued its regular use?

Research Situation E:

Your client, Mr. Jian Lo, owns land in Rivercity, Missouri. Several years ago, the adjoining landowner, Creekside Condos, Inc., built several new apartment buildings. While preparing the land for the new buildings, Creekside raised the height of its land and constructed several large levees and retaining walls of stone and concrete. In past years, surface water created by melting snow in higher elevations and springtime rainfall has run across the land owned by Creekside and drained into nearby Ripple Creek. However, since Creekside constructed the levee and retaining walls on its property, the surface water has been unable to drain naturally and now floods onto Mr. Lo's land every year, causing damage to the basement of his home.

Mr. Lo claims that Creekside's levees and retaining walls constitute a private nuisance in that they interfere with the natural flow of the surface water and cause flooding that damages his land. Is Creekside liable for diverting the surface water onto his land?

Research Situation F:

While a graduate student in Atlanta, Georgia, Ms. Sharl Suddarth offered her used stereo system for sale by placing an ad on the bulletin board in her college dorm. A few days later, Mr. Andrew Tjia contacted her about the stereo. During their discussions, Mr. Tjia told Ms. Suddarth that he had seen the notice on the dorm bulletin board. After chatting about college life (Mr. Tjia said that he was pursuing graduate studies in business), they agreed to the following terms: Mr. Tjia would pay $500 immediately and an additional $1500 before the end of the semester. The terms were put into writing, and both signed the agreement.

Mr. Tjia took possession of the stereo equipment but never paid the remaining debt. When Ms. Suddarth attempted to contact Mr. Tjia so that she could enforce the contract, she called the phone number she had been given. Mr. Tjia's mother answered the phone and told Ms. Suddarth, "I have no information about any stereo or any contract. Andrew is a boy, only sixteen years of age, and had no capacity to agree to such a deal. It was unwise for you to deal with a minor." Mr. Tjia appears to be much older than sixteen. He was not a student at the college and had seen Ms. Suddarth's advertisement while visiting his sister at the dorm.

Is Mr. Tjia estopped from denying the validity of the contract, despite the fact that he is a minor (or, in legal jargon, an infant), because he lied about his age?

Research Situation G:

SodaPop, LLC often advertised its products to the public by offering prizes or rewards as part of a contest. One of the more recent TV ads introducing yet another contest involved a young actor wearing head-to-toe sportswear—jacket, shorts, cap, and sneakers—each plastered with the SodaPop logo. In this ad, the actor paraglided onto a moving yacht, also painted with the SodaPop logo and jam-packed with other young people wearing SodaPop logo sportswear. As he landed on a tub of ice and SodaPop bottles, the young actor yelled, "Sail on in—it only takes a million SodaPop bottle labels to get on board!"

Ms. Francesca Latham and several of her colleagues who worked in a recycling center in upstate New York collected 1,000,000 SodaPop labels and delivered them to the SodaPop corporate office in New York City.

When Ms. Latham demanded her prize—a yacht—the SodaPop executive officer refused her demand and told her that there was no binding contract. He argued that "no one could reasonably believe the prize we offered for gathering bottle labels was a yacht! It was a joke!" Instead, SodaPop delivered head-to-toe SodaPop sportswear outfits to Ms. Latham and each of her friends.

This matter raises several contract law issues; other law clerks are researching the statute of frauds, promise or performance as a means of acceptance, and interpretation of the offer. You have been asked to focus specifically on the lightheartedness of the contest. Specifically, was this lighthearted advertisement an offer for a contract—1,000,000 labels for a yacht— that is binding if someone complied with the terms of the contest?

Research Situation H:

Ms. Mary Dobette accepted a new job in Metropolis, Illinois. Because she was not at all familiar with Metropolis, she engaged Mr. Valdik Andre, a real estate broker who had many years of experience, to serve as her agent and to assist her in finding a home to purchase. During a house-hunting trip in Metropolis, Mr. Andre showed Ms. Dobette a lovely home listed at below market price, located immediately across the street from a small park. Ms. Dobette was particularly attracted to the home because of its proximity to the park. When she asked Mr. Andre why the home was selling for a low price, he informed her that the seller had retired and was eager to sell. In fact, Mr. Andre knew that the park had been a landfill and that toxic waste had been found recently on the land. It was only after the home purchase was completed that Ms. Dobette learned about the toxic conditions on the park land.

Can Ms. Dobette hold her real estate broker liable for breach of his fiduciary duties as her agent because he failed to disclose the information he knew about the nearby park land?

Research Situation I:

About eighteen months ago, Mr. Rhek Subozc underwent invasive surgery at a hospital in his hometown, Jackson, Mississippi. Although the surgery was long and difficult, he has recovered fully. After his most recent complete physical examination, his doctors told him that he was in excellent health and should go about his normal life activities. Then, last week, Mr. Subocz received a letter from the head surgeon at the hospital, informing him that one of the surgeons who had participated in his surgery has just learned that she is HIV positive. Whether the surgeon carried the AIDS virus at the time of the surgery, the letter explained, was unknown. The letter did explain in detail why it was highly unlikely that Mr. Subocz had been exposed to the AIDS virus during the surgery and offered free HIV testing and counseling. Mr. Subocz was shocked by this news and now fears that he may have been exposed to the AIDS virus during the surgery. He has been extraordinarily nervous and has been unable to sleep at night.

Mr. Subocz wants to know whether he can sue his surgeon for negligent infliction of emotional distress based on his fear of contracting AIDS.

Research Situation J:

A process server served Mr. Tam Stefan Loretan at his home in San Antonio, Texas, with a summons and complaint in a lawsuit stemming from an unresolved legal matter pending in state court. Mr. Loretan accepted service and read the legal documents carefully but then realized that there was a misnomer—the summons referred to "T. Steve Loretan" as the named party defendant. Mr. Loretan, who goes by the name Tam, discarded the documents. Recently, Mr. Loretan learned that a default judgment in the case had been entered against him by the court.

Given that there was a mistake with regard to his name on the summons he received, can Mr. Loretan now set aside the default judgment?

Practice Set for Chapter 2. From Curiosity to Closure: Eight Cognitive Tasks

Your Name   Professor

_____   _____

Circle the letter of the research situation you selected (see pages 381–85):

A   B   C   D   E   F   G   H   I   J

1. Weigh the equities of your client's situation, and jot down your answers to the following questions:

(a) What are the *appealing* aspects of your client's situation?

_____

_____

_____

_____

(b) What are the *unappealing* aspects of your client's situation?

_____

_____

_____

_____

(c) If you were the lawmaker, what rule would you devise to govern this situation?

_____

_____

_____

_____

2. Read through the research situation carefully. List the main concepts for each of the eight categories on the next page. If you are not able to identify concepts for a category, leave it blank.

factual who

_____

_____

factual what

_____

_____

factual when

_____

_____

factual where

_____

_____

factual why

_____

_____

legal theory

_____

_____

relief

_____

_____

procedure

_____

_____

3. Look up one of your legal terms from the last three categories above in a legal thesaurus. List your initial term and up to five related terms that could be pertinent to your research situation.

_____

_____

_____

4. Look up one of your legal terms in a legal dictionary.

(a) Write out or paraphrase the definition; you need not include references to other sources.

_____

_____

_____

_____

_____

(b) Provide the proper citation for the above definition.

_____

_____

5. Select three factual or legal concepts you have listed. For each, think of related terms, such as synonyms, antonyms, broader terms, and narrower terms. Present them here, whether in ladder, wheel, or list form, or a combination of these.

6. Based on your work in questions 2 through 5, formulate a potential research issue for your research situation. The issue should link factual concepts with related legal concepts.

_____

_____

_____

_____

_____

7. Draft a search you might run in an electronic source. Follow the LexisNexis or Westlaw Boolean protocols described in Chapter 2.

(a) Check which set of protocols you followed:

_____ LexisNexis   _____ Westlaw

(b) Write out your draft search.

_____

_____

_____

(c) What does this search ask the computer to do?

_____

_____

_____

Practice Set for Chapter 3. Encyclopedias

Your Name

Professor

_____   _____

Circle the letter of the research situation you selected (see pages 381–85):

A   B   C   D   E   F   G   H   I   J

Note: If you have not yet developed research terms for the research situation you selected, do so before you begin this practice set. See the practice set for Chapter 2.

1. Circle the encyclopedia you will be using:

Am. Jur. 2d   C.J.S.   state encyclopedia identified by your professor

2. Locate pertinent section(s) in your chosen encyclopedia. Describe your research process. Example: I looked up the following terms in the index: . . . .

_____

_____

_____

3. From the pertinent section(s), note here the law that pertains to your research situation.

_____

_____

_____

_____

_____

_____

_____

_____

_____

4. Examine the footnotes to those section(s) for references to primary authority. List two or three authorities that could be pertinent to your research situation. If possible, find primary authority from the jurisdiction in your research situation. (You need not use proper citation form.)

_____

_____

_____

_____

_____

5. If you are researching in paper, to update and expand your research, consult updating material, such as a pocket part or pamphlet supplement. Did you find any additional information that is pertinent to your research situation? If so, record it here. If not, write "none."

_____

_____

_____

_____

6. Provide the proper citation to the material you read in the encyclopedia, including the updating material as appropriate.

_____

_____

7. Has your research in the encyclopedia brought forth any legal or factual concepts that you had not yet identified? If so, state them here.

_____

_____

_____

_____

Practice Set for Chapter 4. Treatises

Your Name   Professor

_____   _____

Circle the letter of the research situation you selected (see pages 381–85):

A   B   C   D   E   F   G   H   I   J

Note: If you have not yet developed research terms for the research situation you selected, do so before you begin this practice set. See the practice set for Chapter 2.
Your research situation involves the following area(s) of law:

Research Situation A:	property, real property, landlord and tenant
Research Situation B:	property, personal property, gifts, donative transfers
Research Situation C:	torts, privacy
Research Situation D:	property, real property, servitudes, easements
Research Situation E:	torts, nuisance, real property, water law
Research Situation F:	contracts
Research Situation G:	contracts
Research Situation H:	agency, real estate transactions
Research Situation I:	torts, damages
Research Situation J:	judgments, civil procedure

1. Use the library catalog and the research terms that you have developed to locate a treatise covering the area of law in your research situation.

(a) Which subject heading(s) and subheading(s), if any, did you use in the catalog?

_____

_____

(b) List the title and call number of a treatise on your research topic.

_____

_____

2. By browsing the shelves containing that call number, locate another treatise on your subject. State its title.

_____

_____

3. Select one of the treatises you have located. By use of its index or table of contents, locate the pertinent part(s) of the treatise. Note here the law that pertains to your research situation, as explained in the treatise.

_____

_____

_____

_____

_____

_____

_____

_____

_____

4. Examine the footnotes to the part(s) you read for references to primary authority. List two or three authorities that could be pertinent to your research situation. If possible, find primary authority from the jurisdiction in your research situation. (You need not use proper citation form.)

_____

_____

_____

_____

_____

5. To update and expand your research, check for the following updating materials.

(a) Check those that you do find, and state the date of the most recent update.

_____ pocket part
_____ supplemental softcover pamphlet
_____ supplemental hardbound volume
_____ looseleaf supplement
_____ looseleaf page replacement

_____ date of most recent update

(b) Did you find any additional information that is pertinent to your research situation? If so, record it here. If not, write "none."

_____

_____

_____

_____

6. By looking at the treatise itself, what can you tell about the treatise's credibility and usefulness based on the factors discussed in Chapter 4?

_____

_____

_____

_____

_____

7. Provide the proper citation to the material you read in the treatise, including the updating material as appropriate.

_____

_____

_____

8. Has your research in treatises brought forth any legal or factual concepts that you had not yet identified? If so, state them here.

_____

_____

_____

_____

PRACTICE SET FOR CHAPTER 5. LEGAL PERIODICALS

Your Name   Professor

_____   _____

Circle the letter of the research situation you selected (see pages 381–85):

A   B   C   D   E   F   G   H   I   J

Note: If you have not yet developed research terms for the research situation you selected, do so before you begin this practice set. See the practice set for Chapter 2.

1. Select a legal periodical index, and search for one or two articles pertinent to your research situation.

(a) Which index did you select?

_____

(b) Describe your research process. Example: I ran a search for . . . in the subject index.

_____

_____

_____

(c) List the titles of up to three potentially pertinent articles. (You need not use proper citation.)

_____

_____

_____

_____

_____

_____

_____

2. Run a search in Westlaw's Journals and Law Reviews database or the LexisNexis US Law Reviews and Journals, Combined database.

(a) Check the service you used.

_____ Westlaw   _____ LexisNexis

(b) Write out your search.

_____

_____

(c) List the titles of up to three potentially pertinent articles. (You need not use proper citation.)

_____

_____

_____

_____

_____

_____

3. Select one or the other of the articles listed below, identified by journal, author, and year of publication, for your research situation. We are directing you to a few pages of a specific article to facilitate your professor's evaluation of your work on the following questions. Obtain the article in paper or through Westlaw or LexisNexis. Circle your choice:

A.   Thomas Jefferson Law Review, Zucker, 1998, III A-C
       Washington University Law Quarterly, Smith, 1994, I-III
B.   Columbia Law Review, Kreitner, 2001, II
       Washington Law Review, Andrews, 1990, IV
C.   South Carolina Law Review, Smith, 2002, III-IV
       Tennessee Law Review, Bratman, 2002, II-IV
D.   Nebraska Law Review, Sterk, 1998, IV
       Southwestern University Law Review, Bloch and Parton, 2001, IV
E.   Missouri Environmental Law and Policy Review, Davis, 1995, all parts
       University of Arkansas at Little Rock Law Journal, Looney, 1996, II-III
F.   Hastings Law Journal, Hartman, 2000, II C
       Ohio Northern University Law Review, DiMatteo, 1994, II A
G.   Missouri Law Review, Cohen, 2000, all parts
       Nevada Law Journal, Rowley, 2003, I A-B
H.   Boston College Environmental Affairs Law Review, Waldstein, 1988, II
       Loyola University of Chicago Law Journal, Meyer, 1992, I A 1-2
I.   Thurgood Marshall Law Review, Cole, 1994, III
       Villanova Law Review, Rees, 1994, all parts
J.   Baylor Law Review, Miller, 1994, II-IV
       John Marshall Law Review, Kaplan and Craft, 1993, I A-B

What type of article does it appear to be—a student comment or note, a lead article, an essay, or something else? (Note that some student-written articles show the author's name only at the end of the article, not on the title page or in the table of contents.)

_____

4. Skim the opening and concluding portions of your article, if any, to get a sense of the article. Then read the part(s) of the article listed in question 3.

(a) Note here the law that pertains to your research situation, as explained in the article.

_____

_____

_____

_____

_____

_____

_____

_____

(b) Does the article critique current law or propose changes in the law? If so, summarize the author's position.

_____

_____

_____

_____

5. Examine the footnotes for the part(s) listed above for references to primary authority. List two or three authorities that could be pertinent to your research situation. If possible, find primary authority from the jurisdiction in your research situation. (You need not use proper citation form.)

_____

_____

_____

_____

6. By looking at the journal and article, what can you tell about the article's credibility and usefulness based on the factors discussed in Chapter 5?

_____

_____

_____

_____

_____

7. Provide the proper citation to the article you have reviewed.

_____

_____

_____

8. Has your research in legal periodicals brought forth any legal or factual concepts that you had not yet identified? If so, state them here.

_____

_____

_____

_____

9. **Optional Question:** Use Westlaw's KeyCite or LexisNexis' Shepard's service to citate the article.

(a) Check the service you used.

_____ Westlaw's KeyCite   _____ LexisNexis' Shepard's

(b) Is your journal covered by the citator you used?

_____

(c) If so, what did you learn about the article from using the citator?

_____

_____

_____

_____

PRACTICE SET FOR CHAPTER 6. A.L.R. ANNOTATIONS

Your Name   Professor

_____   _____

Circle the letter of the research situation you selected (see pages 381–85):

A   B   C   D   E   F   G   H   I   J

Note: If you have not yet developed research terms for the research situation you selected, do so before you begin this practice set. See the practice set for Chapter 2.

1. Locate one or more annotations pertinent to your research situation.

(a) Describe your research process. Example: I ran the following search in LexisNexis/ Westlaw: . . . ; I looked up the following terms in the index: . . . .

_____

_____

_____

(b) State the title(s) of one or two pertinent annotation(s).

_____

_____

_____

_____

_____

_____

2. Locate one of the annotations you listed in your answer to question 1. Examine the editorial aids at the outset of the annotation, to locate pertinent sections of the annotation. Which sections appear to be most pertinent? How did you identify those sections?

_____

_____

_____

_____

3. Read the pertinent sections of the annotation. Note here the law that pertains to your research situation, as explained in the annotation, as well as any guidance the annotation provides as to patterns in the case law.

_____

_____

_____

_____

_____

_____

_____

_____

4. List the name(s) of one or two case(s) from the jurisdiction in your research situation. If there are none, list the names of two cases from other jurisdictions, and note their jurisdictions. Be sure to check the supplement, if you are researching in paper. (You need not use proper citation form.)

_____

_____

_____

_____

_____

5. List up to three secondary authorities cited in the annotation that you would consider pursuing. (You need not use proper citation form.)

_____

_____

_____

_____

_____

6. If you are researching in paper, to update and expand your research, consult the pocket part. Did you find any additional information that is pertinent to your research situation? If so, record it here. If not, write "none."

_____

_____

_____

7. Provide the proper citation to the annotation, including any additional material in the pocket part.

_____

_____

_____

8. Has your research in A.L.R.s brought forth any legal or factual concepts that you had not yet identified? If so, state them here.

_____

_____

_____

Practice Set for Chapter 7. Restatements

Your Name   Professor

_____   _____

Circle the letter of the research situation you selected (see pages 381–85):

A   B   C   D   E   F   G   H   I   J

Note: If you have not yet developed research terms for the research situation you selected, do so before you begin this practice set. See the practice set for Chapter 2.

Although you sometimes would do a comprehensive search of more than one Restatement topic and series, for this assignment, use the following Restatement topic and series for your research situation:

Research Situation A:	Property 2d (Landlord and Tenant)
Research Situation B:	Property 2d (Donative Transfers)
Research Situation C:	Torts 2d
Research Situation D:	Property 3d (Servitudes)
Research Situation E:	Torts 2d
Research Situation F:	Contracts 2d
Research Situation G:	Contracts 2d
Research Situation H:	Agency 2d
Research Situation I:	Torts 2d
Research Situation J:	Judgments 2d

1. Locate one or more Restatement sections pertinent to your research situation.

(a) Describe your research process. Example: I looked up the following terms in the index: . . . .

_____

_____

_____

(b) List the section number(s) and topic(s).

_____

_____

_____

2. Read the rule(s) in the section(s) you listed above, and determine which rule is most pertinent to your research situation. Write out that rule, or paraphrase it if it is lengthy.

_____

_____

_____

_____

_____

_____

_____

_____

3. Read the material following that rule (comments, illustrations, and reporter's notes). Also skim any cross-referenced section(s) and the section(s) in the vicinity of the section you used for question 2. Note here additional legal concepts or refinements of the rule that pertain to your research situation.

_____

_____

_____

_____

_____

_____

4. Provide the proper citation to the Restatement:

(a) rule

_____

(b) most pertinent comment or illustration

_____

_____

5. Locate and review the case summaries for the Restatement section you cited above. List the name(s) of one or two cases from the jurisdiction in your research situation. If there are none, list the names of two cases from other jurisdictions, and note their jurisdictions. (You need not use proper citation form.)

_____

_____

_____

_____

_____

6. Has your research in Restatements brought forth any legal or factual concepts that you had not yet identified? If so, state them here.

_____

_____

_____

_____

RESEARCH
SITUATION
AND
BACKGROUND
READING FOR
UNIT III AND
UNIT IV

CASE LAW

ENACTED LAW

(STATE STATUTES)

You will be researching the research situation stated below for the following practice sets for Units III and IV:

Chapter 9 First Practice Set.	Paper Reporters and Digests
Chapter 9 Second Practice Set.	Electronic Research in Case Law
Chapter 10 Practice Set.	Case Citators
Chapter 11 First Practice Set.	State Paper Codes and Session Laws
Chapter 11 Second Practice Set.	Electronic Research in State Statutes

You will have a choice of states for the Paper Reporters and Digests, State Paper Codes and Session Laws, and Electronic Research in State Statutes practice sets. Unless otherwise instructed by your professor, you should select the same state for those three practice sets. For the other practice sets, you will be assigned a state.

We suggest that you leave pages 409–13 in your book (or at least do not turn them in to your professor), so you will have ready access to the research situation and background material as you work through each practice set.

Your Research Situation:

Your client, Lauren Gray, is a physical therapist who recently inherited a farm with stables from her favorite aunt. The farm has ten acres and adjoins a state park, which permits horseback riding on designated trails. Although the stables could hold ten horses, there currently are only two, both owned and maintained by Ms. Gray's cousins, who ride them on the weekends and are accomplished equestrians.

Ms. Gray would like to open a riding stable with a special mission: to provide horseback riding experiences for adult riders with fair to moderate physical disabilities, such as cerebral palsy. She has visited therapeutic stables elsewhere in the state and has been impressed with the results. Her cousins are very enthused about the idea and would assist her in selecting appropriate horses, equipment, and employees and volunteers who would offer the lessons and lead the trail rides. Ms. Gray has discussed the idea with medical providers in the area and determined that there is significant interest.

Ms. Gray has contracted with a small business consultant, who urged her to seek legal advice on the topic of a stable's liability to riders who may be injured during a lesson, while on a trail ride, or before or after the sessions. Ms. Gray would undertake to provide the safest situation possible, but accidents do happen. While Ms. Gray seeks legal advice, the consultant will be looking into the availability and cost of insurance for riding stables.

The consultant also suggested that she ask a lawyer to determine whether the stable would need a state or local license.

Below are excerpts from several secondary authorities. We have omitted the citations so that you will need to use the means of access afforded by the primary sources.

Equine activities are a popular form of recreation for an estimated thirty million people. Organizations and businesses have responded to the demand by hosting shows, clinics, and competitions in addition to providing rental animals and lessons to the general public. Given the nature of equine activities, accidents may result in serious injuries and even death of participants. In some cases, accidents arise from the negligence of the equine owner or sponsor; others arise from the negligence or unfortunate mishaps of the injured participant. Litigation and insurance costs related to accidents constitute a major expense for some equine professionals, individuals, businesses, and groups.

A major reason for these high costs is the serious nature of the injuries. Riding horses may involve greater risk of fatal injury than most other sports, such as football and hockey. A study of hospital emergency room data during 1989-90 disclosed that approximately twenty percent of the total reported 121,274 horseback-related injuries were head or neck injuries. The infrequent use of protective helmets among equestrian riders was a contributing factor to these injuries.

Terence J. Centner, *The New Equine Liability Statutes*, 62 Tenn. L. Rev. 997, 997-98 (1995).

Where horses are involved there is virtually unbounded potential for injuries that can happen unpredictably and without a moment's warning. The gentlest horse could spook during a riding lesson and its rider could fall off; a guest could slip and fall down a stairway leading to the hayloft; someone might get kicked by a horse stabled in the barn.

. . .

[C]onduct, to be negligent, must fall below a legal standard designed to protect others.

Someone can be negligent, as a matter of law, without ever intending to inflict harm on another. . . . "Gross negligence" (sometimes compared with "willful and wanton misconduct"), by comparison, is understood in many states to involve an act or omission in reckless disregard of the consequences affecting the life or property of another.

The law recognizes differences between negligence and gross negligence, which can be illustrated by the following examples. A public riding facility that has carelessly forgotten to adjust a horse's cinch before sending him out on the first ride of the day will probably be found negligent if the saddle slips and the rider is injured. The facility that saddles its horses with broken cinches or girth straps, knowing that the equipment could break at any time, will likely be found to have committed acts of gross negligence (or in some states, willful and wanton misconduct) when the equipment breaks and injures the rider.

In evaluating whether negligence exists, courts often consider the foreseeability of harm that may occur when the defendant engaged in the complained-of act or the defendant's failure to act which causes injury to another.

. . .

In many states, damages in negligence lawsuits can include *but are not limited to* compensation for: the injury suffered; damaged or destroyed personal property; medical and hospital bills; harm to marital relations (called "loss of consortium"); lost past and future earnings; and physical and emotional "pain and suffering." By comparison, if a defendant is found to have acted intentionally or maliciously, courts in several states might order him, her, or a legal entity, to pay the plaintiff "punitive damages." These types of damages are designed to punish the defendant and to discourage similar wrongful conduct by others.

Below are a few examples of some settings in which injured people have, over the years, sued individual horse owners, professionals, and stables for negligence in connection with equine activities:

- *"Vicious or Dangerous" Propensities.* Courts in many states have found people negligent if they knew or had reason to know that a horse had particular dangerous propensities to injure others (through biting, kicking, bolting, or bucking) but failed to take protective action such as post appropriate warning signs, properly restrain or confine the horse, or do other things. . . .
- *Failing to Properly Supervise.* Negligence lawsuits have asserted that the defendant failed to properly supervise the plaintiff, which caused the injury. These types of lawsuits have historically been directed against riding instructors and riding academies.
- *Equipment Defects.* In some cases, negligence may be predicated on the manner in which a horse is equipped to be ridden or used. These cases usually involve defective or improperly-adjusted saddles or harnesses.
- *Unsuitability.* Some negligence cases assert that the defendant (usually a riding stable or professional), failed to properly match the horse and rider, based on the plaintiff/rider's actual or stated level of ability and experience. Plaintiffs, in these cases, often need to prove that the defendant had a duty to properly match the horse and rider and should have known of the unsuitability. . . .

Depending on the facts involved in a particular case and the law that applies in a given state, a defendant can present several possible defenses in response to negligence claims involving personal injuries. These defenses may include *but are not limited to*: the plaintiff's own negligence contributed to the injuries . . . ; the defendant's alleged negligence, even if it occurred, did not directly cause the plaintiff's injuries; the danger was "open and obvious" to the plaintiff so no warning was needed; assumption of risk (the plaintiff knew the activity involved was dangerous but proceeded anyway); and/or the plaintiff signed a legally enforceable release of liability.

Julie I. Fershtman, *Equine Law & Horse Sense* 90-93 (1996).

To be binding and enforceable, the law requires that the person who signs the release fully know the actual facts, including the risks, and knowing these risks and facts, voluntarily elects to assume the risks in return for being allowed to participate in the activity. In the usual case where a potential rider is asked to sign a release before riding the horse, for the release to be effective, the prospective rider must either know or be advised of all the potential risks and misfortunes that he could encounter in riding the horse. Knowing all of these facts and risks, that rider goes ahead and, after fully reading the language of the release, signs it. It is easy to see how difficult relying on releases can be in the horse industry where releases are often thrown in front of the riders immediately before the group mounts for the ride. . . . [R]outine, wholesale releases can be ineffective.

While some releases are useless, well-drafted releases that are properly used and executed may protect horse businesses from negligence liability. The courts of a number of states have considered the effect of various releases. The decisions have universally examined the language of the particular release, the age of the signer, and the circumstances of the signing.

. . .

In all of the cases . . . where releases were upheld, they had been signed by competent adults and were drafted by or with the assistance of attorneys. Too often releases are just common forms that are readily available and are too broad or vague to be enforceable. Horse businesses that are properly run should be aware that a matter as important as the avoidance of liability claims, should not be left to amateurs.

George G. Johnson, Jr., *In the Balance: The Horseman's Guide to Legal Issues* 72-73 (1993).

While mishaps may inherently accompany equine activities, interest groups are advancing a new group of statutory provisions to limit the liability of persons sponsoring or operating equine activities. Washington was the first state to enact statutory provisions in 1989, and subsequently thirty-two states have adopted statutes that provide qualifying defendants immunity from liability for injuries and death to participants of selected equine activities. Moreover, bills on similar legislation have been or are being considered in fourteen other states. The body of enacted legislation may be termed the equine liability statutes. The original purpose for the adoption of the statutes was to provide qualified immunity for equine professionals and sponsors of equine activities; however, this purpose has been broadened to expand the group of persons that may qualify for statutory relief. The statutory provisions vary considerably in terms of persons qualifying for immunity and the causes of action that may be defeated by the statutory grant of immunity.

Terence J. Centner, *The New Equine Liability Statutes*, 62 Tenn. L. Rev. 997, 999-1001 (1995).

§ 9. Generally

A state has the power—which the legislature may exercise directly or may delegate to one of its subdivisions, such as a municipal corporation, or to a commission—to require licenses of those who operate public amusements and places of public amusement and entertainment. The legislature may also validly delegate the power of revocation to a municipality or other political subdivision.

§ 10. Licensing power as to particular amusements and places of amusement

The licensing power of the state and its authorized municipal subdivisions, or administrative commissions, has been exercised as to theaters, motion-picture theaters and motion-picture operators or projectionists; traveling shows; circuses and carnivals; adult-oriented establishments; amusement parks; baseball and baseball parks; boxing and wrestling contests, and persons connected therewith; horse or animal racing, and persons connected with racing, such as owners, trainers, and jockeys; pool and billiard halls and tables, and bowling alleys; miniature golf courses; public dances and dance halls; video games; live entertainment; and jukeboxes.

27A Am. Jur. 2d *Entertainment and Sports Law* §§ 9-10 (1996).

FIRST PRACTICE SET FOR CHAPTER 9. PAPER REPORTERS AND DIGESTS

Your Name   Professor

_____   _____

Your research situation is stated at pages 409–10, followed by some useful excerpts from secondary authorities. For this practice set, research the following issue:

What is the common law rule governing a stable's liability to an injured rider?

Do not research statutes, which will be covered in later practice sets. Circle the state in which you will perform your research:

Arizona	Georgia	Texas
Colorado	Illinois	Washington
Florida	Ohio	Wisconsin

1. List at least five research terms suggested by the research situation, the secondary authorities we have provided, and the issue stated above.

_____

_____

2. Name the appellate courts in your selected state and the reporters in which their decisions appear. (Remember that Table T.1 in *The Bluebook* and Appendix I in *ALWD Citation Manual* provide this information.)

_____

_____

_____

3. (a) Which West digests cover cases decided by the appellate court(s) in the state you selected?

_____

_____

(b) Select one of those digests. Identify at least two potentially useful topics and, within each topic, two or more pertinent key numbers. List them, and explain how you found them. Example: I looked up the following terms in the Descriptive Word Index: . . . .

_____

_____

_____

_____

(c) Assemble the main volumes and supplements, such as pocket parts and supplement pamphlets, needed to research the topic of Animals back to 1940. Identify the digest and series, types of volumes you gathered, and their dates. Example: state digest, second series, main volume 1984, pocket part 2003.

_____

_____

(d) Skim the outline of the Animals topic, and identify at least four potentially useful key numbers. List them.

_____

(e) Skim the digest paragraphs until you locate a digest paragraph for the case fitting the description below. We are directing you to a single case to facilitate your professor's evaluation of your work on the following questions.

Arizona Court of Appeals 1989
Colorado Court of Appeals 1974
Florida District Court of Appeal (Judge Stevenson) 1997
Georgia Court of Appeals 1950
Illinois Court of Appeals 1961
Ohio Court of Appeals First District 1949
Texas Court of Civil Appeals (Houston) 1972
Washington Court of Appeals 1978[1]
Wisconsin Supreme Court 1972

(f) Record the case name and citation information as it appears in the digest.

_____

_____

1. The Washington Supreme Court decision is also published. It affirms the court of appeals but provides less insight into the legal rules.

(g) Under which key number did you find the digest paragraph, and what specific point does that key number cover?

_____

4. Locate that case in a West reporter, read it, and provide the following information about the case:

(a) the facts of the case and the outcome

_____

_____

_____

_____

_____

_____

_____

_____

(b) the rule of law governing a stable's liability to an injured rider

_____

_____

_____

_____

_____

(c) the number(s) of the headnote(s) (not the topic and key number) corresponding to the rule you stated above

_____

(d) whether there is a concurrence or dissent or both and, if so, the main point(s)

_____

_____

_____

_____

5. Provide a proper citation for the case; assume that you need not provide a parallel citation or public-domain citation.

_____

_____

6. What would your next research step be, as to the case you just read and cited?

_____

7. Locate a recent advance sheet for the West reporter you have been using.

(a) Record the reporter volume(s) and page numbers contained in that advance sheet.

_____

(b) Locate the digest material in that advance sheet. Does it contain any digest paragraphs under the Animal topic and key numbers you listed for question 3(d)? If so, note the name(s) of the case(s). If not, write "none."

_____

_____

8. Based on your reading for this practice set, should Ms. Gray be concerned about the stable's liability to injured riders? Why, or why not?

_____

_____

_____

_____

_____

_____

_____

SECOND PRACTICE SET FOR CHAPTER 9. ELECTRONIC RESEARCH IN CASE LAW

Your Name   Professor

_____   _____

Your research situation is stated at pages 409–10, followed by some useful excerpts from secondary authorities. For this practice set, research the following issue in **Minnesota** case law:

Is a contract releasing a stable from liability to an injured rider enforceable?

Do not research statutes, which will be covered in later practice sets.

1. List at least five research terms suggested by the research situation, the secondary authorities we have provided, and the issue stated above.

_____

_____

2. Log on to Westlaw or LexisNexis. Indicate which service you selected.

_____ Westlaw   _____ LexisNexis

Select the database containing only decisions of the Minnesota state courts. State the name of the database. Which courts' decisions are included, and, as to each court, what year did coverage begin?

_____

_____

_____

3. Run one or more natural-language searches until you obtain at least one pertinent case. Write out your successful search.

_____

_____

_____

_____

Print the list of citations from that search, that is, only the case names and citations, not editorial material. Also print the first page of up to three pertinent cases. Attach your print-outs to this practice set, and mark them Q3.

4. Now run one or more terms-and-connectors searches until you obtain a reasonable number of cases, including at least one pertinent case.

(a) Write out your successful search.

_____

_____

(b) By running that search, what did you ask the computer to do?

_____

_____

_____

_____

Print the list of citations from that search, as well as the first page of up to three pertinent cases. Attach your print-outs to this practice set, and mark them Q4. If one or more cases for this question are the same as for question 3, you need not make additional first-page print-outs; rather mark the print-out Q4 as well as Q3.

5. If you are using Westlaw, now research with KeySearch. If you are using LexisNexis, now research with Search Advisor. Describe your research process.

_____

_____

_____

_____

Print the list of citations from that search. Attach it to this practice set, and mark it Q5.

6. Compare and contrast the results of the three searches.

_____

_____

_____

_____

_____

_____

7. Select the most useful case you have found through your research in Westlaw or LexisNexis. Read that case; you may want to read the case in a reporter or download or print it, rather than read it online.

(a) State the name of the case.

_____

_____

(b) State the facts of the case and the outcome.

_____

_____

_____

_____

_____

_____

_____

_____

(c) State the rule of law governing a contract term seeking to release a stable from liability to an injured rider.

_____

_____

_____

_____

_____

(d) Based on that case, should Ms. Gray pursue using a contract to reduce or eliminate the stable's liability to injured riders? Why, or why not?

_____

_____

_____

_____

_____

_____

8. Assume that a colleague recalls reading, at least a decade ago, a federal appellate decision written by a long-time family friend, Judge Don Lay, in which the jury returned a verdict of $1 million or more against a stable or perhaps a rodeo sponsor. Your colleague recalls that the events occurred in one of the plains states, probably North or South Dakota or Nebraska.

(a) Select an appropriate database. State the name of the database.

_____

(b) Run one or more searches to locate the case. Write out your successful search.

_____

_____

(c) By running that search, what did you ask the computer to do?

_____

_____

_____

Print out the first page of the case you obtained, attach your print-out to this practice set, and mark it Q8.

9. Explore researching in public websites by answering the following questions about the courts in the area where you live:

(a) Does the supreme court of your state post its decisions? If so, state the website's URL; the years of coverage; and search options, e.g., Boolean searching, docket number.

_____

_____

_____

(b) Does the United States court of appeals for your federal circuit post its decisions? If so, state the website's URL; the years of coverage; and search options, e.g., Boolean searching, docket number.

_____

_____

_____

PRACTICE SET FOR CHAPTER 10. CASE CITATORS

Your Name   Professor

_____   _____

     Your research situation is stated at pages 409–10. Assume that you are researching in **Louisiana.** You have located *Alfonso v. Market Facilities of Houston.* Below is the first page of that case.

Defendant proved that it would cost him $12,000.00 to have someone else do the job. We therefore agree with the award of $6500.00 damages given by the trial judge. *See Scheppegrell v. Barth,* 239 La. 42, 117 So.2d 903 (1960). Plaintiff argues that defendant has failed to show damages because the barge was never resandblasted. However, an injured party is not required to repair his damages prior to instituting suit. *Scheppegrell,* above; *Wooten v. Central Mutual Insurance Co.,* 182 So.2d 146 (La. App. 3rd Cir. 1966).

For the reasons assigned, the judgment is affirmed at appellant's costs.

AFFIRMED.

KEY NUMBER SYSTEM

Janis Phelps Alfonso, wife of and Vernon ALFONSO, and Sandra Serigne Alfonso, wife of and Ralph Alfonso

v.

MARKET FACILITIES OF HOUSTON, INCORPORATED and Money Hill Plantation, Incorporated.

No. 11753.

Court of Appeal of Louisiana,
First Circuit.

Feb. 13, 1978.

Rehearing Denied March 20, 1978.

Writ Refused May 5, 1978.

Suit was brought against recreational facility and its insurer for personal injuries sustained when plaintiffs were thrown from horses they were riding at the facility. The 22nd Judicial District Court, Parish of St. Tammany, Stephen A. Duczer, J., dismissed plaintiff's suit and they appealed. The Court of Appeal, Ellis, J., held that: (1) since plaintiffs were active participants in a trail ride and could not be considered as innocent third parties and were also in con-

trol of the two horses at the time of the accident, they were not entitled to recover under the strict liability provisions of the code, and (2) no negligence on the part of the defendants was shown.

Affirmed.

1. Animals ⬅67

In order to hold the owner of an animal strictly liable for damages to another done by the animal, there must be a domestic animal, which is actually or constructively under the control of the owner, or of which he has an obligation to restrain, the presence of which causes an unreasonable risk of harm to others and which injures an innocent third party. LSA–C.C. arts. 2317, 2321.

2. Livery Stable Keepers ⬅11

Where plaintiffs were active participants in trail ride and could not be considered as innocent third parties and were also in control of two horses at the time the horses threw them, they were not entitled to recover under the strict liability provisions of the code governing damage to another done by a domestic animal. LSA–C.C. arts. 2317, 2321.

3. Theaters and Shows ⬅6(1)

Operators of recreational facilities are not the insurers of the safety of their patrons, but must conduct their operations in such a way as to not expose the patron to an unreasonable risk of harm, considering the nature of the facilities provided.

4. Theaters and Shows ⬅6(17)

One who voluntarily utilizes recreational facilities assumes the reasonably foreseeable risks which are inherent in the use thereof.

5. Livery Stable Keepers ⬅11

In suit brought against recreational facility for personal injuries sustained when plaintiffs were thrown from horses they were riding at the facility, no negligence on the part of the defendants was shown or that they exposed plaintiffs to an unreasonable risk of harm which was not inherent in horseback riding.

---

1. Select an electronic citator, and indicate your choice below:

Shepard's on LexisNexis _____   KeyCite on Westlaw _____

Obtain and print out the complete report on *Alfonso*. Attach the print-out to this practice set.

2. Does *Alfonso* have prior or subsequent history? Explain.

_____

_____

_____

3. Does the report list Louisiana cases citing *Alfonso* favorably or adversely? Explain.

_____

_____

_____

_____

_____

_____

_____

4. Has *Alfonso* been cited in cases outside Louisiana? Explain.

_____

_____

_____

5. List the first three cases you would read, in order of priority, and explain your choices.

first _____

_____

_____

_____

second _____

_____

_____

_____

third _____

_____

_____

_____

6. From what you can tell from the report, is *Alfonso* still good law? Explain.

_____

_____

_____

_____

7. List up to three potentially useful secondary authorities (by volume, abbreviation of the source, and page number) citing *Alfonso*, in the order you would choose to read them.

_____

_____

_____

8. Does *Alfonso* have a parallel citation? Explain.

_____

_____

FIRST PRACTICE SET FOR CHAPTER 11. STATE PAPER CODES AND SESSION LAWS

Your Name   Professor

_____   _____

Your research situation is stated at pages 409–10, followed by some useful excerpts from secondary authorities. For this practice set, research the following issue:

Is the liability of a stable owner to an injured rider governed by state statute? If so, what is the statutory rule?

Circle the state in which you will perform your research:

Arizona	Georgia	Texas
Colorado	Illinois	Washington
Florida	Ohio	Wisconsin

1. List at least five research terms suggested by the research situation, the secondary authorities we have provided, and the issue stated above.

_____

_____

2. Name the statutory code(s) for your jurisdiction. (Remember that Table T.1 in *The Bluebook* and Appendix I in *ALWD Citation Manual* provide this information.)

_____

_____

3. Identify the pertinent statute in the annotated code, in paper, for your state. Describe your research process. Example: I looked up the following terms in the index: . . . .

_____

_____

_____

4. Assemble the volumes you need to locate the current language of the pertinent statute: generally a bound volume, pocket part or supplement pamphlet for the bound volume, and softcover updates covering the entire code (typically shelved at the end of the code). Give the types of volumes, including their dates of coverage, that you must use to be sure your statutory research is current.

_____

_____

_____

5. Read the statute carefully. State the statute's rule governing a stable's liability to an injured rider.

_____

_____

_____

_____

_____

_____

_____

_____

_____

_____

_____

_____

_____

6. Provide the proper citation for the section(s) you used to answer question 5.

_____

7. Does the statute refer to other statutes? If so, note the section number(s).

_____

8. Examine the statutory history notes following the section you used to answer question 5 (or the definitions section if you used more than one section).

(a) State the year that statutory section was originally enacted, and give the session law reference for the original law. You need not use proper citation form.

_____

(b) If the section has been amended since it was first enacted, note the reference to the most recent amendment by its session law citation. You need not use proper citation form.

_____

(c) If you were researching a situation that occurred on April 1, 1997, would the language of the current statute have been in effect then? Explain your answer.

_____

_____

_____

_____

(d) Assume now that a different, earlier version of the statute was indeed in effect on April 1, 1997. What source would you examine to find the statutory language that was in effect then?

_____

9. Examine the annotation for the section(s) you used to answer question 5.

(a) List the names of one or two cases that discuss the statute. You need not use proper citation form. **Note:** If you were doing actual research, you would, of course, read the cases, but you need not do so for this practice set. You need not use proper citation form.

_____

_____

_____

_____

(b) List the citations of one or two secondary authorities, if any, that could be pertinent to your research situation. You need not use proper citation form.

_____

_____

_____

_____

_____

10. Based on your reading for this practice set, should Ms. Gray be concerned about the stable's liability to injured riders? Why, or why not?

_____

_____

_____

_____

_____

_____

_____

_____

SECOND PRACTICE SET FOR CHAPTER 11. ELECTRONIC RESEARCH IN STATE STATUTES

Your Name   Professor

_____   _____

Your research situation is stated at pages 409–10, followed by some useful excerpts from secondary authorities. For this practice set, research the following issue:

Does state law provide for licensing of stables for recreational horseback riding, whether by a state agency or local government?

Note: If your state does not appear to have a statute governing riding stables, locate and proceed with a licensing statute pertaining to breeding and selling or racing horses.

Assume that this topic is governed by a state statute. Circle the state in which you will perform your research:

Arizona	Georgia	Texas
Colorado	Illinois	Washington
Florida	Ohio	Wisconsin

1. List several research terms suggested by the research situation, the secondary authorities we have provided, and the issue stated above.

_____

_____

2. Select a commercial electronic service and a database providing the statute and annotations. Indicate your choice of service:

Westlaw _____   LexisNexis _____

State the name of the database. How recent is the information in that database?

_____

_____

3. First run one or more terms-and-connectors searches, in the full text of the statutes and annotations, until you obtain a pertinent statute.

(a) Write out your successful search.

_____

_____

(b) By running that search, what did you ask the computer to do?

_____

_____

_____

Print the list of citations from that search, that is, only the statutory names and code number(s). Attach your print-out to this practice set, and mark it Q3.

4. Read the pertinent statute carefully.

(a) Are stables licensed in your assigned state? If not, are the breeding and sale or racing of horses licensed? Explain.

_____

_____

_____

_____

_____

_____

_____

(b) Provide a citation to the statute, citing to the version you have read in Westlaw or LexisNexis (which may not be the preferred source to cite).

_____

5. Focus on the most important or first section of the statute. Does the service you are using provide any indication that that section has recently been or may soon be amended? If so, explain what you have learned.

_____

_____

_____

6. Peruse the annotation. List one to three authorities, of whatever type, that you would read to understand the statute. You need not use proper citation form.

_____

_____

_____

7. Now search for the statute by a different method. Describe your research process and its results. Example: I ran the following natural-language search: . . . .

_____

_____

_____

_____

_____

8. Shift to a session law database that contains the newest laws of your assigned state.

(a) What is the name of the database?

_____

(b) Write a search that you could enter in that database to locate new legislation on the topic addressed by the statute you used to answer question 4.

_____

(c) Run that search. What did you learn?

_____

_____

9. Now select a cases database that permits terms-and-connectors searching.

(a) State the name of the database and its dates of coverage.

_____

(b) What search would you enter to locate cases, within the past year, that cite the statute you used for your answer to question 4?

_____

(c) Run that search. What did you learn?

_____

_____

10. Based on your reading for this practice set, should Ms. Gray plan to seek a license for the stable? Explain.

_____

_____

_____

_____

_____

_____

_____

11. **Optional Question:** Return to the annotated code database. Identify and read a statute or constitutional provision that sets the default effective date for new laws in your assigned state.

(a) Describe your research process.

_____

_____

_____

(b) What does the statute or constitutional provision say about the default effective date?

_____

_____

(c) Provide the proper citation to the statute or constitutional provision.

_____

12. Explore researching in public websites by answering the following questions about statutes in the state where you live:

(a) Is there a public website for your state's laws and statutes? If so, list its URL.

_____

(b) Which years and sessions does the website cover?

_____

(c) How may you search the website?

_____

_____

RESEARCH
SITUATIONS
AND PRACTICE
SETS
FOR UNIT IV,
CHAPTERS 11
AND 12

ENACTED LAW
(FEDERAL STATUTES)

You will be selecting one of the research situations stated below for the following practice sets for Unit IV:

Chapter 11 Third Practice Set. Federal Codes and Session Laws
Chapter 12 Practice Set. Legislative Process Materials

Unless otherwise instructed by your professor, you should select one research situation to work for both practice sets.

We suggest that you leave pages 435–38 in your book (or at least do not turn them in to your professor), so you will have ready access to the texts of the research situations as you work through both practice sets.

Research Situation A:

Your client, thirteen-year-old Daryl Sweeny, was arrested for allegedly robbing a federal savings and loan. After spending six days in jail, he was released on bond. One condition of the bond was that he remain at home after school unless accompanied by one of his parents. Seventy days passed between the time of your client's arrest and the time of his trial.

The partner who gave you this assignment has suggested the following issue to research in federal statutes: *Does the speedy trial statute requiring a delinquent to be brought to trial within thirty days if he is in detention apply when a juvenile is released from custody to his parents on restrictive bail conditions?*

Research Situation B:

Your client, Perfecto Marine Services, delivers cargo along Florida's Intracoastal Waterway. Recently one of your client's boats and her tow were moored at an unloading site in the intracoastal waters, and the crew was unloading cargo. (A mooring is a permanent location; anchorage is a temporary location.) Although the day was clear when unloading began, a dense fog developed, and a tugboat pushed an empty oil barge into your client's boat, effectively destroying it. At the time of the accident, your client's boat did not have on its all-round lights.

The partner who gave you this assignment has suggested the following issue to research in federal statutes: *Does the federal inland navigation statute requiring a vessel at anchor to display all-round lights apply to a moored vessel?*

Research Situation C:

Your client, Joseph Kanne, was found mentally incompetent to stand trial by a federal district court. The court concluded, furthermore, that as he was mentally retarded, he always would be incompetent to stand trial.

The partner who gave you this assignment has suggested the following issue to research in federal statutes: *Does a federal insanity defense statute require the court to commit your client to the custody of the Attorney General if there is no possibility that the client will regain sanity, or may it dismiss the charges against him?*

Research Situation D:

Your client, a South Dakota Indian tribe, opened a blackjack gaming enterprise on its South Dakota reservation on April 15, 1988. At the time the enterprise began, it was classified as a class II, rather than a class III, gaming enterprise, under a grandfather provision in federal Indian gaming law. (A grandfather provision permits an organization to retain the status it enjoyed before a new law was enacted.) The tribe wants to increase the number of blackjack tables and expand the number of hours the game may be played.

The partner who gave you this assignment has suggested the following issue to research in federal statutes: *If a tribe operates a class II blackjack operation under a grandfather clause in Indian gaming law, is it likely to lose that classification if it increases the number of its blackjack tables and the hours the game may be played but does not increase its wager limits or prize pots?*

Research Situation E:

Your client, the Army Corps of Engineers, gave Whitmore Construction a contract to build a dam. The construction company encountered unexpected site conditions and government testing requirements in building the dam, so eighteen months before completion of the project, it filed a claim with the contracting officer for an equitable adjustment of the contract price. When the adjustment was denied, the company sued to obtain the price adjustment. The Claims Court found the federal government liable for some increased costs and awarded the contractor those costs plus interest on the costs from the date the contractor notified the contracting officer of its claim.

The partner who gave you this assignment has suggested the following issue to research in federal statutes: *Does the interest to be paid on a public contractor's damages accrue from the date it files its claim with the contracting officer if on that date the contractor had not yet incurred the total costs that it later recovered?*

Research Situation F:

Your client, Mr. Luke Grant, operates a precious metals reclamation facility. This facility takes old computer parts, shreds them, and then through various processes extracts the valuable metals. A dangerous toxic substance, polychlorinated biphenyl (PCB), is used in this process. Recently the Environmental Protection Agency (EPA) obtained an ex parte administrative warrant to inspect the facility. During the inspection, the EPA administrator photocopied records and photographed the premises. Now he has subpoenaed several employees' testimony.

The partner who gave you this assignment has suggested the following issue to research in federal statutes: *Does the EPA have the authority under the Toxic Substances Control Act to obtain an ex parte warrant to inspect a facility that produces toxic substances and to photocopy records and photograph the facility?*

Research Situation G:

Your client, Mr. Andrew Unger, paid $10,500 cash to a local bank so it could wire $10,000 to his daughter, Lillian, in California. The bank asserts that it wired the money, but Lillian claims that she never received it.

The partner who gave you this assignment has suggested the following issue to research in federal statutes: *Is Mr. Unger's cash payment and the subsequent transfer of the money an "electronic fund transfer" that is protected by federal statute?*

Research Situation H:

Your client, Julia Davidson, has been charged with being "about to transport" more than $10,000 outside the United States without filing the customs report required of those who import or export large amounts of currency. She was arrested at a hotel in Manhattan about ten hours before she was to leave Kennedy Airport for Madrid.

The partner who gave you this assignment has suggested the following issue to research in federal statutes: *Is it a federal crime to attempt not to file the customs report required of those who import or export large amounts of currency?*

Research Situation I:

Attorney Jack Chisholm represents a bank that sued Shirley DeMars to recover the balance due on her defaulted car loan. In an attempt to settle the suit, Mr. Chisholm wrote Ms. DeMars a letter listing the amount she owned under the loan agreement plus an amount owed for insurance purchased by the bank when Ms. DeMars did not keep the car insured as she had promised. Ms. DeMars claims that the attorney's representation of the amount of her debt was false and constituted an attempt to collect an amount not authorized by the loan agreement. She wants to sue him.

The partner who gave you this assignment has suggested the following issue to research in federal statutes: *Is an attorney who regularly, through litigation, tries to collect consumer debts a "debt collector" within the meaning of federal statutes that regulate fair debt collection practices for consumer debts?*

Research Situation J:

Your client, attorney Andrea Newby, handled a bankruptcy proceeding for a corporate client. Because corporations seeking bankruptcy protection lack the funds to pay all their debts, the court must authorize payment for any legal work on the case. Your client submitted her bill to the court, but the court refused to authorize payment for some of the work done by her paralegal.

The partner who gave you this assignment has suggested the following issue to research in federal statutes: *Is an attorney entitled to separate compensation for all the work done by a paralegal on a bankruptcy case, and if so, what is the standard for the compensation?*

Third Practice Set for Chapter 11. Federal Codes and Session Laws

Your Name _____   Professor _____

Circle the letter of the research situation you selected (see pages 435–38):

A   B   C   D   E   F   G   H   I   J

1. List several research terms suggested by your research situation and the issue we stated.

_____

_____

2. Select one of the two annotated federal codes, *United States Code Annotated* or *United States Code Service*; you may research in paper or electronic media. Identify the pertinent statute. Describe your research process. Example: I looked up the following terms in the index . . . ; I ran the following search in Westlaw: . . . .

_____

_____

_____

_____

3. Obtain the current language of the pertinent statute. Indicate how you assured that your research is current. Example: I checked the following volumes of U.S.C.S.: . . . ; the Westlaw database was current to . . . .

_____

_____

_____

_____

4. Review the statute carefully. State the statutory language that governs your research situation.

_____

_____

_____

_____

_____

_____

_____

_____

_____

5. Does the statute refer to other statutes? If so, note the title(s) and section number(s).

_____

6. Provide the proper citation for the section(s) you used to answer question 4.

_____

7. Examine the statutory history notes following the section you used to answer question 4 (or the definitions section, if you used more than one section).

(a) State the year that statutory section was originally enacted, and give the session law reference for the original act. You need not use proper citation form.

_____

(b) If the statutory section has been amended since it was first enacted, note the reference to the most recent amendment by its session law citation. You need not use proper citation form.

_____

8. Examine the annotations for the section(s) you used to answer question 4. Identify a case that appears pertinent to your research situation and fits the description below. We are directing you to a single case to facilitate your professor's evaluation of your work on this question. If you were doing actual research, you would, of course, consider other pertinent cases.

Research Situation A:	a 1976 Fifth Circuit case
Research Situation B:	a 1988 Eleventh Circuit case
Research Situation C:	a 1989 Seventh Circuit case
Research Situation D:	a 1990 Eighth Circuit case
Research Situation E:	a 1991 or 1998 Federal Circuit case

Research Situation F: a 1988 District of Rhode Island case
Research Situation G: a 1990 District of Colorado case
Research Situation H: a 1988 Southern District of New York case
Research Situation I: a 1995 United States Supreme Court case
Research Situation J: a 1994 Third Circuit case

(a) Provide the name of the case as given in the case description.

_____

_____

(b) What, according to the case description, does that case say that is pertinent to your research situation? If you were doing actual research, you would, of course, read the case itself.

_____

_____

_____

_____

_____

_____

(c) List the references, from the annotation, to one or two secondary sources, if any, that could be pertinent to your research situation.

_____

_____

_____

_____

9. **Optional Question:** Use Westlaw's KeyCite or LexisNexis' Shepard's service to citate the section(s) you cited in your answer to question 6.

(a) Check the service you used.

Westlaw's KeyCite _____   LexisNexis' Shepard's _____

(b) Determine whether your section(s) has or have been adjudicated constitutional or unconstitutional. Record the name and citation of one such case, if any.

_____

_____

10. Based on the materials you have read, what is the probable answer to your research issue?

_____

_____

_____

_____

_____

_____

_____

_____

_____

Practice Set for Chapter 12. Legislative Process Materials

Your Name   Professor

_____   _____

Circle the letter of the research situation you selected (see pages 435–38):

A   B   C   D   E   F   G   H   I   J

Legislative History

1. If you have not already done so, locate and read in *United States Code Annotated* or *United States Code Service* the statute that pertains to your research situation. Note the title and section number of the statutory section containing the language that most directly addresses your research situation.

_____

2. Locate the statutory history notes for the statutory section you identified in question 1. Record the following legislative history information for the public law enacted in the year stated below. Your answers need not be in proper citation form.

Research Situation A:	1974
Research Situation B:	1980
Research Situation C:	1984
Research Situation D:	1988
Research Situation E:	1978
Research Situation F:	1976
Research Situation G:	1978
Research Situation H:	1984
Research Situation I:	1986
Research Situation J:	1978

(a) public law number

_____

(b) date of bill's approval by the President

_____

(c) *Statutes at Large* citation

_____

3. Check at least one source to see if a compiled legislative history exists for your law. Good sources for this task include *Sources of Compiled Legislative History, Federal Legislative History*, LexisNexis, and Westlaw.

(a) Note here the source you checked.

_____

(b) Identify the reference to one compiled legislative history, if you found one.

_____

_____

4. Using the source of your choice, identify the following information, if available, for your public law. Good sources for this task include *United States Code Congressional and Administrative News*, LexisNexis Congressional, and THOMAS. If there is no available information for an item listed below, write in NA.

Source used: _____

(a) the bill number of the enacted law

_____

(b) the bill number of any companion bill

_____

(c) a hearing from the Congress that enacted the bill

_____

_____

_____

_____

(d) a committee print from the Congress that enacted the bill

_____

_____

_____

(e) a House report number for the bill from the Congress that enacted the bill

_____

(f) a Senate report number for the bill from the Congress that enacted the bill

_____

(g) the conference committee report number

_____

(h) two to three citations to the *Congressional Record* for a discussion of the bill that was enacted (volume and date, or volume and page, and a description of the action taken)

_____

_____

_____

_____

_____

_____

(i) one legislative history document for the law from a Congress prior to the Congress that enacted the law

_____

_____

5. Obtain the legislative history document(s) listed below. Scan the opening pages and passages listed below.

Research Situation A:	S. Rep. No. 93-1011, page 7
Research Situation B:	S. Rep. No. 96-979, page 11
Research Situation C:	S. Rep. No. 98-225, page 236
Research Situation D:	S. Rep. No. 100-446, pages 8-11
Research Situation E:	*Congressional Record* for October 12, 1978, pages S36266-67 (Sen. Byrd's statement)
Research Situation F:	H.R. Conf. Rep. No. 94-1679, pages 87-88
Research Situation G:	S. Rep. No. 95-915, pages 3-4
Research Situation H:	S. Rep. No. 98-225, pages 301-03 (related to H.R. Rep. No. 98-1030)
Research Situation I:	H.R. Rep. No. 99-405, pages 1-7
Research Situation J:	H.R. Rep. No. 95-595, pages 329-30

(a) Note any pertinent guidance.

_____

_____

_____

_____

_____

_____

_____

_____

(b) Provide the proper citation for the material you read.

_____

_____

6. Before you relied on that document, what would you do?

_____

_____

_____

Pending Legislation

7. Select a source to assist you in locating pending legislation that could be pertinent to your research situation. Good options include LexisNexis Congressional, THOMAS, and a bill tracking database on LexisNexis or Westlaw.

Source used: _____

(a) Describe your search method in that source.

_____

_____

_____

(b) Note here the bill name and number for a pending bill pertinent to your research situation, if any.

_____

_____

(c) Note the most recent action taken on the bill.

_____

_____

RESEARCH
SITUATIONS
AND
PRACTICE SET
FOR UNIT V,
CHAPTERS
13, 14, 15

ADMINISTRATIVE MATERIALS

You will be selecting one of the research situations stated below for the practice set covering the following chapters in Unit V:

Chapter 13.   Regulations
Chapter 14.   Agency Decisions
Chapter 15.   Mini-Libraries

Research Situation A:

Your client is the professional basketball team, the Midtown Marvels. The general manager of the team would like to hire a few teenagers to serve as ball boys and ball girls at home games. Research the federal law on employing fourteen- and fifteen-year-olds in these positions.

Agency: Wage and Hour Division of the Department of Labor

Research Situation B:

Matt Adams and Bert Shaw recently bought a house. They financed the mortgage through Rainbow Bank. Mr. Adams and Mr. Shaw are concerned because the bank failed to include in the finance charge the cost of mortgage insurance (also known as credit life and disability insurance) required by the bank. Research whether Rainbow Bank has violated federal law on truth in lending regarding computation of finance charges.

Agency: Federal Trade Commission

Research Situation C:

Mike Johnson owns a factory that processes corrosive chemicals (which do not qualify as toxic or hazardous chemicals). All employees are required to follow strict safety procedures; however, accidents still may occur with chemicals coming into contact with an employee's skin or eyes. Mr. Johnson is concerned about the adequacy of the on-site medical services and first aid facilities. Research the federal safeguards, including quick-drenching facilities, for employees working with corrosive chemicals.

Agency: Occupational Safety and Health Commission (within the Labor Department)

Research Situation D:

You work in the Department of Agriculture's general counsel's office. Nearly five years ago, several food scientists employed by the DA were transferred from the DA to an international organization working on food distribution systems in Africa. The letters of consent by the DA to the transfers state that the term is five years. The international organization has requested that the employees be permitted to stay another five years. The employees have indicated that they believe that several additional years would prove very beneficial, and they are willing to stay so long as they do not lose their rights to reemployment at the DA upon their return to the United States. Research the reemployment rights of an federal employee transferred to an international organization.
    Agency: Office of Personnel Management

Research Situation E:

Your client, George Stevens, owns a clothing manufacturing company. Mr. Stevens is concerned that some foreign companies are exporting large quantities of sweaters to the United States at less than fair value. Mr. Stevens' company manufactures sweaters that are very similar to the imported sweaters and he believes that his business may be adversely affected by the imports. Research federal law on whether an industry has been materially injured by the dumping of foreign merchandise.
    Agency: International Trade Commission (in the Commerce Department)

Research Situation F:

Your client, Shari Jenkins, is a registered broker-dealer who does not belong to a securities association. Ms. Jenkins deals in unexempted securities and would like to know if she is required to join a securities association. Research federal law on exemptions from registration of brokers and dealers.
    Agency: Securities and Exchange Commission

Research Situation G:

Richard Boydon is opening a small retail electronics store. He would like to know what rules he must adhere to regarding the display and availability of warranties on his products as to customers. Research federal law governing availability and display of warranties of consumer products.
    Agency: Federal Trade Commission

Research Situation H:

Stephanie Cairn is the president of Willow Valley Bank, which is a member of the Federal Reserve System. Ms. Cairn is a passive investor in Gotti, Inc., a corporation managed by Mr. Gotti. Gotti, Inc., has received loans from Willow Valley Bank. Mr. Gotti recently asked Ms. Cairns to submit a request to the bank board to extend the credit on the loans to Gotti, Inc. Research federal law on extending credit; ignore issues relating to dollar-amount limits.

   Agency: Federal Reserve System

Research Situation I:

Lynn Traynor heads the human resources department at a juvenile correction facility that employs forty persons. The facility houses both male and female juveniles; however, the living areas are strictly segregated by sex. Recently, a female employee requested a transfer from being a female group leader to a male group leader. Ms. Traynor denied the request. She is concerned about privacy considerations for the young male juveniles. The position of group leader requires the employee to conduct body searches and supervise bathroom areas. Research exceptions to the federal prohibition against sex discrimination in employment.

   Agency: Equal Employment Opportunity Commission

Research Situation J:

Your client, Waste Recyclers, Inc., laid off Mary Collins in March of last year. The federal National Labor Relations Board ruled that Ms. Collins' lay-off was an unfair labor practice and has ordered Waste Recyclers to pay Ms. Collins backpay. The parties have not been able to come to any agreement about backpay, so the NLRB has issued and served on Waste Recyclers a notice of hearing without backpay specification. Research whether Waste Recyclers must file an answer to the NLRB prior to the hearing.

   Agency: National Labor Relations Board

PRACTICE SET FOR UNIT V. ADMINISTRATIVE MATERIALS

Your Name   Professor

_____   _____

Circle the letter of the research situation you selected (see pages 447–49):

A   B   C   D   E   F   G   H   I   J

The following questions ask for five types of authority:

- commentary;
- the enabling statute;
- the agency regulation;
- an agency decision, if available; and
- a judicial case, if available.

For every research situation, you should find at least the first three. You may or may not be able to find an agency decision and judicial case. The questions stated below are less directive than the questions for the other practice sets because there are so many options for research in administrative materials and various good research approaches.

1. Locate and read secondary authority discussing your research topic.

(a) Explain how you located the secondary authority.

_____

_____

_____

_____

(b) Indicate how up-to-date the secondary authority is.

_____

(c) State the legal rule presented in the secondary authority.

_____

_____

_____

_____

_____

(d) List two or three primary authorities referred to in the secondary authority.

_____

_____

_____

(e) Provide a proper citation to the secondary authority.

_____

_____

2. Locate and read the enabling statute governing your research topic and agency.

(a) Explain how you located the statute.

_____

_____

(b) Indicate how you made sure that you have the current statutory language.

_____

_____

(c) State the statutory rule governing your research situation.

_____

_____

_____

_____

_____

(d) Provide a proper citation to the section(s) stating that rule.

_____

(e) Indicate whether the statute grants the agency the power to promulgate regulations and adjudicate cases, and cite the section(s) of the statute that so provide.

_____

_____

_____

_____

3. Locate and read the regulation governing your research situation.

(a) Explain how you located the regulation.

_____

_____

_____

(b) Indicate how you made sure that you have the current regulation.

_____

_____

(c) State the language of the regulation that governs your research situation.

_____

_____

_____

_____

_____

(d) State when the regulation was adopted and where in the Federal Register you could find notice of the final regulation.

_____

(e) Provide the proper citation to the regulation.

_____

(f) Check whether the agency is currently considering any changes to the regulation. State what you found, and explain how you researched current agency activity.

_____

_____

4. Locate and read, if available, an agency decision on your research topic, and verify that it is still good law. If your agency does not adjudicate cases, write NA below. If your agency does adjudicate cases, but you did not find a pertinent agency decision, answer only question (a) below. If your agency does adjudicate cases, and you did find a pertinent agency decision, append a copy of the decision, and answer all of the following questions.

(a) Explain how you researched agency decisions.

_____

_____

_____

(b) Briefly state the facts of the decision and its holding.

_____

_____

_____

_____

_____

_____

_____

_____

(c) Explain how you verified that the decision is good law.

_____

(d) Provide a proper citation to the agency decision.

_____

_____

5. Locate and read, if available, a judicial case on your research topic, and verify that it is still good law. If you did not find a pertinent judicial case, answer only question (a) below. If you did find a pertinent judicial case, append a copy of the case, and answer all of the following questions.

(a) Explain how you researched judicial cases.

_____

_____

_____

(b) Briefly state the facts of the case and its holding.

_____

_____

_____

_____

_____

_____

_____

(c) Explain how you verified that the case is good law.

_____

(d) Provide a proper citation to the case.

_____

_____

6. In light of your answers to the first five questions, what advice would you give your client?

_____

_____

_____

_____

_____

_____

RESEARCH
SITUATION
AND
PRACTICE SET
FOR UNIT VI,
CHAPTER 16

RULES OF PROCEDURE

Here is your research situation for the practice set for Unit VI, Chapter 16, Rules of Procedure:

You clerk for a state trial court judge, and your judge has asked you to research a procedural matter now before the court.

The Plaintiff, Ms. Andrea Rupp, had worked in the marketing department for Tjia Audio, LLC, a high-end audio-visual company, for several years. Tjia Audio dismissed Ms. Rupp a year ago, shortly after she celebrated her fiftieth birthday.

Following her dismissal, Ms. Rupp filed an age discrimination lawsuit against Tjia Audio. Her complaint alleges that she was qualified for and properly performed her job, that she was dismissed due to age, and that Tjia Audio now has a significantly younger employee performing the job. Ms. Rupp has asserted that the marketing supervisor often made derogatory comments publicly about Ms. Rupp's age; specifically, she alleges that her supervisor commented in a belittling manner that Ms. Rupp was a full decade older than any other employee and frequently called her "Grandma" in front of co-workers.

In her prayer for relief in the discrimination suit, Ms. Rupp seeks damages for "humiliation and emotional distress" because of these and other comments. As part of its defense in the pre-trial discovery stage of the lawsuit, Tjia Audio seeks to compel Ms. Rupp to undergo a medical examination into her mental state. Ms. Rupp refused, and now the matter is before your judge.

If Ms. Rupp's mental condition is not directly in controversy in the age discrimination suit, should the state trial court compel her to undergo the mental examination?

Below is an excerpt from the Wright and Miller treatise. We have omitted the citations so that you will need to use the means of access afforded by the primary sources.

An order for the physical or mental examination of a party is not granted as of right. When the matter is contested it is addressed to the sound discretion of the trial court. Moreover, the requirements in the rule that the moving party show "good cause" and that the condition to be examined is "in controversy," the Supreme Court said in Schlagenhauf v. Holder, are plainly expressed limitations on the use of the rule rather than "a mere formality."

These limitations, the Court said,

---

are not met by mere conclusory allegations of the pleadings—not by mere relevance to the case—but require an affirmative showing by the movant that each condition as to which the examination is sought is really and genuinely in controversy and that good cause exists for ordering each particular examination. Obviously, what may be good cause for one type of examination may not be so for another. The availability of the movant to obtain the desired information by other means is also relevant.

. . .

Applying these principles to the case before it, the Court in Schlagenhauf found that the trial court's order requiring that defendant submit to a battery of examinations was not justified. That litigation grew out of a collision in which a Greyhound bus driven by Schlagenhauf ran into the rear of a truck, and the owner of the truck asserted a claim against Greyhound and Schlagenhauf. Greyhound asserted that the truck had not used proper rear lights. The truck owner alleged that Schlagenhauf was "not mentally or physically capable" of driving the bus safely and that Greyhound "knew that the eyes and vision of said Robert L. Schlagenhauf [were] impaired and deficient." It also submitted its attorney's affidavit stating that Schlagenhauf had admitted in his deposition that he had seen red lights on the rear of the truck ten to fifteen seconds before the accident and that he had been in another similar accident, and that another witness had seen these lights from a distance of one-half to three-quarters of a mile. The district court ordered Schlagenhauf to submit to examinations in internal medicine, ophthalmology, neurology and psychiatry.

The Supreme Court granted a writ of mandamus, reasoning that [the rule] requires more than mere relevancy. Since Schlagenhauf had not put his condition in issue, the Court found that the necessary showing "plainly" had not been made. . . .

Obviously the [issue] is intensely fact-specific, and cases since Schlagenhauf have made individual decisions, both allowing and refusing examination.

8A Charles Alan Wright et al., *Federal Practice and Procedure* § 2234.1 (2d ed. 1994).

Practice Set for Chapter 16. Rules of Procedure

Your Name   Professor

_____   _____

Circle the state in which you will perform your research:

California	Michigan	Nebraska
Colorado	Minnesota	North Dakota
Florida	Montana	Texas
Georgia		

1. List several research terms suggested by the research situation and the treatise excerpt.

_____

_____

2. Locate the pertinent state rule and accompanying comments, if any. Good sources for this task include a deskbook; the state's annotated code or rules volume; and LexisNexis, Westlaw, or Loislaw databases.

(a) Identify the source you selected.

_____

(b) Explain how you located the pertinent rule. For example: I scanned the table of contents; I used the following terms in the index: . . . ; I ran the following search: . . . .

_____

_____

_____

(c) State the language of the rule that governs your situation.

_____

_____

_____

_____

_____

_____

(d) Provide a proper citation to that rule.

_____

(e) Read the accompanying comments following the rule, if any. If they provide any insight into the rule that is pertinent to the situation, note it here.

_____

_____

_____

_____

_____

3. Locate a state court case interpreting the rule. Good sources for this task include the state's annotated code or rules volume, along with case reporters; digests and reporters; and LexisNexis or Westlaw databases.

(a) Identify the source(s) you selected.

_____

_____

(b) Explain how you located the case. Examples: I scanned the case descriptions under the topic . . . in the annotation to the rule; I ran the following search: . . . .

_____

_____

_____

(c) State the facts and the outcome of the case.

_____

_____

_____

_____

_____

_____

_____

(d) State what the case adds, if anything, to your understanding of the rule.

_____

_____

_____

_____

_____

(e) What must you do before you rely upon that case?

_____

(f) With the information you have from your research to this point, provide the proper citation to that case; assume that you need not provide a parallel citation or public-domain citation.

_____

_____

4. Assume that you deem it useful to examine federal law on the same issue. Select one or more sources that provide the federal rules of civil procedure, their advisory committee notes, and federal cases. For lists of good types of sources, see questions 2 and 3 above.

(a) Locate the pertinent federal rule and the advisory committee notes. Describe your research process; identify the source you used and the means of access you used.

_____

_____

_____

_____

_____

(b) How closely does the federal rule's language parallel the language of the state rule you have examined? Explain.

_____

_____

_____

_____

_____

(c) If the advisory committee notes provide any insight into the federal rule that is pertinent to the situation, note it here.

_____

_____

_____

_____

_____

(d) Provide a proper citation for the federal rule.

_____

(e) Locate a case interpreting the rule, decided by any federal district court or federal circuit court of appeals. Describe your research process; identify the source(s) you used and the means of access you used.

_____

_____

_____

_____

(f) Attach a copy or print-out of the first page of the pertinent case and the page(s) containing the pertinent discussion to this practice set, and mark it Q4.

5. Based on the materials you have read, should the court compel the plaintiff to undergo the exam? Why, or why not?

_____

_____

_____

_____

_____

_____

_____

_____

RESEARCH
SITUATION
AND
PRACTICE SET
FOR UNIT VI,
CHAPTER 17

RULES OF PROFESSIONAL RESPONSIBILITY

Here is your research situation for the practice set for Unit VI, Chapter 17, Rules of Professional Responsibility:

You are an associate in the law firm of Sutheera, Miller, & Anderson, LLP, which was retained by Apex World Co. to provide legal services in creating a joint venture with a European company. Apex distributes climbing and trekking equipment to retail shops throughout the United States. Recently, Apex entered into negotiations to establish a joint venture with Euro Peak Touring, a European company that markets off-road mountain bikes. Creating the joint venture would involve U.S. law and the law of several European countries.

Because your firm has extensive experience with similar transactions, Apex hired your firm. Apex had a tight deadline and specified that the work be done within a month; this schedule posed significant challenges given the work commitments already made to other clients. Accordingly the retainer agreement set a $10,000 commitment fee as well as a $40,000 flat fee for the legal work, for example, research, negotiations, drafting of documents. The retainer agreement called for payment of $30,000 upon signing, specified as the $10,000 commitment fee and half of the flat fee; the remaining $20,000 was due upon completion of the transaction.

Apex paid the first $30,000 upon signing the agreement, and the firm promptly deposited this payment in the Apex trust account. Two days later, the deal between Apex and Euro Peak fell apart, and Apex so informed the firm. To that point, firm lawyers had put in only ten hours (worth about $2,000, if Apex had agreed to hourly billing).

The senior partner in charge of the Apex matter wants to know what the firm's ethical obligation is vis-à-vis the $30,000 the firm has been paid. Only the $10,000 commitment fee is designated "non-refundable" in the retainer agreement. Is the fee unreasonable or excessive? Is the firm obligated to refund it, now that the representation is terminated?

Below is an excerpt from the Restatement of Lawyers on the topic.

> A fee payment that does not cover services already rendered and that is not otherwise identified is presumed to be a deposit against future services. The lawyer's fee for these services will be calculated according to any valid fee contract or, if there is none, under the fair-value standard. . . . If that fee is less than

the deposit, the lawyer must refund the surplus. . . . If the fee exceeds the deposit, the client owes the lawyer the difference. The deposit serves as security for the payment of the fee. . . .

A client and lawyer might agree that a payment is an engagement-retainer fee . . . rather than a deposit. Clients who pay a fee without receiving an explanation ordinarily will assume that they are paying for services, not readiness. . . . A client and lawyer might also agree that an advance payment is neither a deposit nor an engagement retainer, but a lump-sum fee constituting complete payment for the lawyer's services. Again, the lawyer must adequately explain this to the client. In any event, an engagement-retainer or lump-sum fee must be reasonable. . . . If the lawyer withdraws or is discharged prematurely or for other misconduct, the contractual fee might be subject to reduction. . . .

Restatement (Third) of Law Governing Lawyers § 38 cmt. g (2000).

PRACTICE SET FOR CHAPTER 17. RULES OF PROFESSIONAL RESPONSIBILITY

Your Name   Professor

_____   _____

Circle the state in which you will perform your research:

Arizona	Kansas	Ohio
Colorado	Minnesota	Oregon
Indiana	New York	Washington
Iowa		

1. List several research terms suggested by the research situation and the Restatement excerpt.

_____

_____

2. Locate the state rule governing lawyers' fees and accompanying comments, if any. Good sources for this task include a deskbook; the state's annotated code or rules volume; and LexisNexis, Westlaw, or Loislaw databases.

(a) Identify the source you selected.

_____

(b) Explain how you located the pertinent rule. For example: I scanned the table of contents; I used the following terms in the index: . . . ; I ran the following search: . . . .

_____

_____

_____

(c) State the language of the rule that governs this situation.

_____

_____

_____

_____

_____

(d) Provide a proper citation to that rule.

_____

(e) Read the accompanying comments following the rule, if any. If they provide any insight into the rule that is pertinent to the situation, note it here.

_____

_____

_____

_____

_____

(f) Follow up on any rules referred to in the rule or comments, and note what else, if anything, you learned.

_____

_____

_____

_____

_____

3. Locate a state court case interpreting the rule in a disciplinary context (rather than a fee dispute or award of attorney fees). Note that many disciplinary cases have only one party (the lawyer) in the case name; others include the name of the disciplinary agency as well as the lawyer's name. Good sources for this task include the state's annotated code or rules volume, along with case reporters; digests and reporters; and LexisNexis or Westlaw databases.

(a) Identify the source(s) you selected.

_____

_____

(b) Explain how you located the case. Examples: I scanned the case descriptions under the topic . . . . in the annotation to the rule; I ran the following search: . . . .

_____

_____

_____

(c) State the facts and the outcome of the case.

_____

_____

_____

_____

_____

_____

_____

_____

(d) State what the case adds, if anything, to your understanding of the rule.

_____

_____

_____

_____

(e) What must you do before you rely upon that case?

_____

(f) With the information you have from your research to this point, provide the proper citation to that case; assume that you need not provide a parallel citation or public-domain citation.

_____

_____

4. Assume that you deem it useful to examine the ABA Model Rules on this topic. Select a source that provides the Model Rules along with the ABA comments. Good sources for this task include ABA publications (such as _Annotated Model Rules of Professional Conduct_ and _ABA Compendium_) and treatises.

(a) How closely does the model rule's language parallel the language of the state rule you have examined? Explain.

_____

_____

_____

_____

_____

(b) If the advisory committee notes provide any insight into the model rule that is pertinent to the situation, note it here.

_____

_____

_____

_____

5. Assume that you deem it useful to examine ethics opinions on this topic. Select a source that provides ethics opinions from the state you selected or, if that state's ethics opinions are not reasonably available, ABA ethics opinions. Good sources for this task include *ABA/BNA Lawyers' Manual on Professional Conduct*, Westlaw and LexisNexis databases, and the ethics agency's web site.

(a) Identify the source you selected, and explain how you located a pertinent ethics opinion.

_____

_____

_____

(b) What guidance does the opinion provide?

_____

_____

_____

_____

_____

_____

(c) Provide a proper citation to that ethics opinion.

_____

6. Based on the materials you have read, should the firm refund any or all of the $30,000? Explain.

_____

_____

_____

_____

_____

_____

_____

_____

INDEX

Page numbers in italics denote illustrations.